Paradigms in Public Policy

Marcus Carson
Tom R. Burns
Dolores Calvo
(eds.)

Paradigms in Public Policy

Theory and Practice of Paradigm Shifts in the EU

PETER LANG
Frankfurt am Main · Berlin · Bern · Bruxelles · New York · Oxford · Wien

Bibliographic Information published by the Deutsche Nationalbibliothek
The Deutsche Nationalbibliothek lists this publication in the Deutsche Nationalbibliografie; detailed bibliographic data is available in the internet at http://dnb.d-nb.de.

Cover design:
Olaf Glöckler, Atelier Platen, Friedberg

The chapter of Peter A. Hall first appeared in Comparative Politics and is reprinted with permission of the author as well as the Journal:
Peter A. Hall, "Policy Paradigms, Social Learning, and the State: The Case of Economic Policymaking in Britain," Comparative Politics, 25 (April 1993), 275-96

ISBN 978-3-631-57905-3

www.peterlang.de

Preface

Understanding continuity and change in society constitutes one of the fundamental challenges to social scientists, policymakers, and everyday citizens. Such an understanding is particularly important in the realm of democratic policymaking, where agents driven by divergent principles and alternative goals struggle to preserve or reform policy, law, and institutions. The works collected in this volume offer an approach to systematic and deeper understanding of stability and change in public policy.

One of the key elements in this collected work is that its investigations and theoretical analyses contribute to the understanding of how "ideas matter" in policy and institutional change. Policy action is driven, shaped and regulated by the ways in which cognitive perspectives frame problem situations and analyses – and also call for and legitimize the involvement of particular authorities, experts, problem – definitions and solutions.

Over the past twenty years a constellation of concepts, principles, and models has emerged which entail a promising new approach to capturing the interactions between ideas, organized actors, and institutions in political, administrative and related social processes. This work investigates and theorizes *public policy paradigms,* within which policy ideas are embedded and on the basis of which policies are framed, articulated, and implemented. To our knowledge, this book is the first comprehensive theoretical and empirical treatment of public policy paradigms. It considers theoretically the architecture of paradigms, their role in framing and organizing action, and the ways in which paradigm transformations are brought about. The theory construction draws upon three major developments in the social sciences: institutional theory, cognitive sociology, and social movements theory.

This book presents key early works that introduced and applied the concept of public policy paradigm, then seeks also to extend those efforts by specifying and analyzing processes of paradigm formation and development based on the "sociology" and "politics" of paradigms (innovation, competition, alliance formation, proselytizing, power and control processes, etc.). The paradigm concept itself is of course most often associated with Thomas Kuhn's work. Kuhn's paradigm was inherently political in nature, making it suitable for the examination of conceptual models that apply to the political sphere, as in this book. The broader conception of what may be referred to as "the socio-politics of paradigms" is therefore particularly applicable to public policy processes such as those investigated in this book.

The general goal of this book is to develop and apply public policy paradigm theory in investigations and analyses of policy dynamics and developments. The theory might be characterized as "cultural-institutional", in that it emphasizes the importance of socially transmitted cognitive-normative models, institutional rule-based structures that organize human activity, and ways in which organized actors mobilize and struggle to realize their ideals as well as to pursue more mundane interests. This approach is illustrated through a selection of a few classic studies relating back to the earliest applications of the paradigm concept to issues of public policy: Jane Jenson in 1989, Peter Hall in 1992, and William Coleman et al. in 1996. We include these together with Yves Surel's systematic comparative overview of paradigm theory and other cognitive approaches to policymaking. We are very fortunate to be able to reproduce all of these key articles here and also provide additional case studies and analyses from our own EU research on policymaking. These cases cover policy territory ranging from food security and chemicals to energy, climate change, and gender.

The individual case studies identify the mechanisms linking ideas and cognitive frameworks to institutional arrangements and to policy outcomes and developments. The cases focus on the actors who formulate or bear ideas trying to exercise influence over policymaking; they also identify and analyze the conditions under which actors manage to exercise their influence – or fail to do so. Policy paradigms serve, among other things, as a conceptual structure within which public issues and problems can be framed and provide a type of modern totem around which supporters of the paradigm may collect and coordinate. But paradigms also constrain and bias policies that policymakers are likely to consider and select.

In sum, we see the emergence of a systematic theory and body of empirical knowledge of what are referred to as *public policy paradigms*. The theory combines cognitive-normative models, institutional analysis, and strategic interactions in which organized actors seek both to realize their ideals and pursue their interests. An important goal of this book has been to set out the foundations of the theory and provide a range of applications. The book also identifies several of the methodological principles and rules of method that characterize public policy paradigm research. Finally, in a more general sense, the book illustrates the usefulness and potentialities of public policy paradigm research program(s).

Marcus Carson, Tom R. Burns, and Dolores Calvo
Stockholm, Stanford/Uppsala, and Gothenburg
Summer, 2009

Contents

Preface ... 5
Contents ... 7
Abbreviations ... 9

Part One: Introduction

Chapter 1. Introduction ... 11
Chapter 2. Yves Surel:
The Role of Cognitive and Normative Frames in Policymaking ... 29

Part Two: Selected Classic Studies of Public Policy Paradigm Shifts

Chapter 3. Jane Jenson:
Paradigms and Political Discourse: Protective Legislation in France and the United States before 1914 ... 45
Chapter 4. Peter A. Hall:
Policy Paradigms, Social Learning, and the State. The Case of Economic Policymaking in Britain ... 67
Chapter 5. William D. Coleman, Grace D. Skogstad, and Michael M. Atkinson:
Paradigm Shifts and Policy Networks: Cumulative Change in Agriculture ... 93

Part Three: EU Policy Paradigms, Their Applications, and Shifts

Chapter 6. EU Institutions and Policymaking: A Brief Overview ... 117
Chapter 7. Theoretical Framework and Methods for Conducting the EU Research on Paradigms and Paradigm Transformations ... 141
Chapter 8. Marcus Carson:
Mad Cows, Pollutted Poultry, and the Transformation of EU Food Policy ... 171
Chapter 9. Marcus Carson:
From Freely Traded to Product-non-grata: Banning Asbestos in the European Union ... 201
Chapter 10. Tom R. Burns, Dolores Calvo, and Marcus Carson:
The "REACH" Saga: A Revolution in Regulating Chemicals ... 225

Chapter 11. Svein S. Andersen:
The Emergence of an EU Energy Policy Paradigm 261
Chapter 12. Tom R. Burns:
The Irony of the EU Climate Policy:
A Crooked Path to a Paradigm Shift 285
Chapter 13. Dolores Calvo, Tom R. Burns and Marcus Carson:
Toward a New Social Order? Mainstreaming Gender Equality
in EU Policymaking 311
Chapter 14. Paradigm Shift and Regime Change:
Case Comparisons and Analysis 359

Part Four: Extensions and Conclusions

Chapter 15. Elaborating Public Policy Paradigm Theory 377
Chapter 16. Conclusions 409

Bibliography 413
Index 441

Abbreviations

ACC	American Chemical Council
AI	Asbestos Institute
AmCham	American Chamber of Commerce
ANDEVA	Association Nationale De Défense Des Victimes De L'amiante (Nat'l Assoc. of Asbestos Victims)
AOSIS	Association of Small Island States
BEUC	European Consumers' Organization
BSE	Bovine Spongiform Encephalopathy, A.K.A. Mad Cow Disease
CAP	Common Agricultural Policy
CC	Competitivity Council
CDM	Clean Development Mechanism (Kyoto)
CEDAW	Convention on the Elimination of All Forms of Discrimination against Women
CEEP	European Centre of Enterprises with Public Participation
CEFIC	European Chemical Industry Council
CJD	Creutzfeld-Jacobs Disease
CMR	carcinogenic, mutagenic or toxic for reproduction
COP	Conference of the Parties under the UN Framework Convention on Climate-Change
COPA	Comité Des Organisations Professionnelles Agricoles
CSC	Catholic Confédération Des Syndicats Chrétiens
CSTEE	Scientific Committee on Toxicity, Ecotoxicity, and the Environment
DAC	Development Assistance Committee in the EU
DG	Directorate General of the EU Commission
EAGGF	European Agricultural Guidance and Guarantee Fund
ECHA	European Chemicals Agency
ECJ	European Court of Justice
ECSC	European Coal and Steel Community
EDC	European Defense Community
EEA	European Environmental Agency
EEB	European Environmental Bureau
EFSA	European Food Safety Authority
EFTA	European Free Trade Area
EINECS	European Inventory of Existing Commercial Chemical Substances
ELINCS	European List of Notified Chemical Substances
EP	European Parliament
EPA	Environmental Protection Agency
EPC	European Political Community
EPHA	European Public Health Alliance
ERT	European Round Table of Industrialists

ETS	Emission Trading Scheme
ETUC	European Trade Union Confederation
EWL	European Women's Lobby
FGTB	Fédération Générale Du Travail De Belgique
GATT	General Agreement on Tariffs and Trade
GHG	Green house gases
GM/GMO	Genetically Modified/Genetically Modified Organism
Group 77	In the UN context a coalition of developing countries
IBAS	International Ban Asbestos Secretariat
ICCA	International Council of Chemical Associations
IG	Intergovernmental Conference
ILO	International Labor Organization
IPCS	International Program on Chemical Safety
JI	Joint Implementation (Kyoto)
LRI	Long-range Research Initiative of the Chemical Associations (CEFIC, ACC, ICCA)
MEP	Member, European Parliament
NAP	National Allocation Plan for ETS and Kyoto mechanism
NGO	Non-government organization
NRC	Natural Resources Canada
OECD	Organization for Economic Cooperation and Development
OPEC	The Organization of the Petroleum Exporting Countries
OSHA	Occupational Safety and Health Administration, US Dept. Of Labor
PAM	Policies and Measures
PBT	persistent, bioaccumulative and toxic properties
POP	persistent organic pollutants
REACH	Registration, evaluation, authorization, and restriction of chemicals
SCORE	Stockholm Center for Organizational Research
SEA	Single European Act
TEU	Treaty on European Union
TPA	Third Party Access in the EU gas regulation
TUTB	Trade Union Technical Bureau
UN	United Nations
UNCED	UN Conference on Environment and Development ("Earth Summit", "Rio Summit")
UNCHE	UN Convention on the Human Environment
UNEP	United Nations Environmental Program
UNICE	Union of Industrial and Employers' Confederations of Europe
V-CJD	Variant Creutzfeld-Jakobs Disease
vPvB	very persistent and very bioaccumulative
WAVE	Women Against Violence Europe
WEU	Western European Union
WHO	World Health Organization
WTO	World Trade Organization
WWF	World Wildlife Fund

CHAPTER 1

Introduction

The policy paradigm concept has emerged over the past decade and a half as a useful tool for analyzing and comprehending the interactions between ideas, institutions, and organized actors engaged in political and administrative processes.[1] It has proven to be a particularly interesting and useful approach with which to investigate and theorize about public policy paradigms within which policy ideas are located and the basis upon which policies are formulated. The paradigm concept is of course most often associated with Thomas Kuhn's work.[2] Much of Kuhn's analysis using his paradigm concept was inherently political in nature, making it potentially suitable for the investigation of conceptual models that apply to the political sphere, as demonstrated in this book. The broader conception of what might be referred to as a "socio-cognitive" model of politics of paradigms is therefore par-

[1] The concept continues to be used in a manner closer to Thomas Kuhn's original usage: see Ritzer (1975), Dunlap et al (2002), and Dunlap (2008), among others (see footnote 2).

[2] *A Note on Thomas Kuhn*: One cannot take up the notion of paradigm without also acknowledging the scholar who introduced the concept into the humanities and social sciences. This is all the more important given that policy paradigm shares some characteristics with Thomas Kuhn's scientific paradigm (Hall, 1993), although there are fundamental differences also. We (and others who use the concept) draw on the familiarity of Kuhn's concept, and refer specifically to his work in the process of elaborating it as a concept for use in the public policy context. Like the Kuhnian paradigm (Kuhn, 1962), a policy paradigm is a cognitive model shared by a particular community of actors and which facilitates problem solving. It provides a conceptual framework that helps actors interpret events and their causes, aides in their identification and definition of relevant problems and solutions, and suggests what kinds of criteria might provide useful measures of success or failure. Kuhn's concept of scientific paradigm shares these characteristics.
Kuhn's central concept for describing the process of theory replacement in science was fundamentally political; he emphasized the persuasive aspects of scientific discourse, including the use of power and inherent path dependencies, and even employed political metaphors such as "revolution" to describe a certain type of innovative period in science (Restivo 1983). But whereas conflicts over norms and values are intrinsic to disputes in relation to politics and policymaking, science is generally seen as operating in much more settled territory. Kuhn's characterization of science as a largely interest and values-driven enterprise is part of what generated such intense controversy about his work (Stephens 1973; Kuhn & Conant et al. 2000; Ohlsson 2000). How well suited the concept is to conceptual developments in either the natural or social sciences has remained a subject of controversy, but that is a separate matter and not a debate to be taken up here. Our claim is that the paradigm concept is very suitable to the analysis of politics and public policy.

ticularly applicable to public policy processes. We see the need for a more comprehensive theoretical framework making use of the concept of *public policy paradigm*, which has already proven quite useful in investigating and explaining such matters as:

- complex ideas as political objects and political forces;
- effect of such ideas on the real world, that is in the formulation of public policies and programs with real consequences;
- the components of public policy paradigms, their characteristic dimensions, their complexity.[3] This consideration may be extended to deconstruct or decode deep assumptions or ideological underpinnings, for instance concerning the role of public authority, principles of institutional arrangements, and the nature of certain types or groups of human beings (or humanity in general).
- the key mechanisms of paradigm formation and development;
- the conditions of paradigm politics and paradigm shifts. Paradigm politics may be analytically distinguished from other forms of politics, for instance, politics as usual, the politics of (re)distribution, where, for instance, an established paradigm defining fairness or justice is not at issue.
- the institutionalization (and de-institutionalization) of a public policy paradigm.

1. Theoretical and Methodological Points of Departure

The work presented in this book lies at in the intersection of three expansive bodies of literature: the literature on policymaking and policy processes, socio-cognitive analyses, and the "new" institutionalism. These are briefly discussed in this and section 2.

1.1 Theories of Public Policy and Policymaking Processes

The voluminous literature on public policy dates back more than fifty years. The multitude of strategies and approaches can be roughly categorized based on whether they place their emphasis on the influence of a) structural characteristics of society or policymaking institutions (Lasswell 1951; Easton 1965; Kitschelt 1986; Steinmo & Thelen et al. 1992); b) on the role of cognitive factors such ideas, norms, ideology, culture and attention in policy change (Gamson 1992; Hall 1993; Kingdon 1995; van Dijk 1998; Bacchi 1999; Baumgartner and Jones 2002; Jones and Baumgartner 2005); c) or on the characteristics and configurations of actors (typically collective) in preserving or challenging existing policies or pressing for new ones (Lasswell 1951; Olson 1971; Dalton and Kuechler 1990; Sabatier and Jenkins-Smith 1993; Knoke, Pappi et al. 1996; Sabatier 1999).

These categories do not provide clean distinctions, especially given that the increasing tendency over time has been to straddle categories, typically with one pro-

[3] Thomas Kuhn notoriously left the paradigm concept underspecified.

viding a dependent, the other an independent variable. For example, while the cases presented in Steinmo et al. (1992) emphasize the structural factors that generate powerful path dependencies, they also examine the role of competing ideas or changing power relationships that contribute to divergence from established patterns. Hall's 1989 anthology is approached from a similar historical institutionalist perspective, but with a shift of emphasis to analyzing the role of Keynesian ideas in driving institutional changes in economic policy. Sabatier's advocacy coalition framework can be characterized as a theory of coalition politics, yet it focuses on shared elements of sometimes divergent belief systems as the glue that binds groups of actors that coalesce to press for particular policy remedies. In contrast, Haas's (1992) epistemic communities constitute a very different type of actor configuration, bound more by shared core values than particular policy goals.

The clear tendency in the scholarly work noted above is a realization that the categories are interconnected by feedback loops that make them simultaneously dependent and independent variables. This generates serious problems for theoretical or methodological frameworks that approach characteristics such as policymaking institutions, societal cleavages and alliances, interests, or belief systems as more or less fixed. And while we would identify the contents of this book as emphasizing and elaborating the role of ideas in policymaking processes, our more general ambition is to specify important linkages between the three broad categories of ideas/culture, institutions, and actors and show how they interrelate. We will return to these shortly. First, however, we briefly take up two broad research traditions in which our efforts are rooted.

Neo-institutional theories recognize that these compromises are not merely the result of packages of bargains made by state actors pursuing their economic self-interest. Rather, they are the result of bargains and compromises made by changing configurations of influential actors who are guided by their own cognitive models of how the world is constructed, and from within which they pursue their perceived ideal and material interests. This research is therefore guided by the view that rationality is context bound, operating within the parameters of these cognitive models (Nee 1998). This theoretical orientation broadly challenges perspectives in which the role of rationality dominates in the policy process (Andersen 2001). Indeed, Majone has gone so far as to argue that "policymaking can hardly be considered a rational enterprise" (Majone 1992). Although the role of rationality in policy making may be circumscribed, rationally constructed explanations are important in the process of giving accounts for decisions made.

1.2 The Importance of Policy Ideas and Cognitive Models

As scholars, we may see the world not only through our individual perspectives, but through the collective scientific frameworks with which we take in, evaluate, sort, and in other ways manage the information available to us (Sabatier 1999; cf. Kuhn 1962). This is no less true for actors engaged in activities such as political debate and policy processes. In each case, such models are social constructed and transmitted and may have real material consequences.

Efforts to map out the architecture of socio-cognitive models are plentiful in the public policy and social movements literature, some of which is addressed to the question of how particular ideas become policy or formal rules, and how claims are framed and anchored to make them relevant to the intended audience. The common theme among these diverse approaches is the attempt to systematically relate policy ideas to one another, to interested actors, and to change processes. This broad body of work characterizes conceptual systems in terms of *culture* (Geertz 1973; Johnston 1995; Lane and Ersson, 2002), *ideology* (Tilton, 1990:248-280; Thompson, 1990; Cormack, 1992; Denzau and North, 1993; van Dijk, 1995), *belief systems* (Gelb, 1989; Sabatier and Jenkins-Smith, 1993; Sabatier, 1999b), *policy paradigms* (Burns and Carson, 2005, 2002; Carson, 2001, 2004; Andersen, 1999; Coleman et al., 1997; Hall, 1993; Hall, 1992), *frames or master frames* (Snow et al., 1986; Snow and Benford, 1992; Benford and Snow, 2000; Fligstein, 2001a; Hobson, 2003b), and *discourses* (Dryzek, 1996a; Hobson et al., 2002; Jakobsson, 2002). These concepts address themselves to many of the same general phenomena, although with varying emphases and at different levels. As a consequence of the proliferation of concepts that has taken place, often largely in isolation from one another, there are important areas in which these diverse concepts overlap and tend to shade into one another in general use. However, as both Oliver and Johnston (2000) and Surel (2000) note, these various conceptual categories differ in scope, function, and focus. Because they do different kinds of work, they are not interchangeable.

Pamela Oliver and Hank Johnston (2000) provide a telling example of this general phenomenon in their critical analysis of developments in framing theory, a particularly important theoretical and research agenda in the social movements research of the past two decades. Both recognized social movement scholars themselves, Oliver and Johnston highlight the ways in which the concepts of frame or master frame have often come to be used in place of ideology. They argue "the power of frame theory is lost if 'frame' is made to do the work of other concepts" and moreover, that "frame concepts are most powerful precisely if they are sharply distinguished from ideology (Oliver and Johnston 2000:37-38). The core distinction is that a "frame" is a "schemata of interpretation" (Goffman 1972) that enables actors to make sense of an occurrence or event by placing it in context. For Oliver and Johnston, that context is captured in the concept of ideology. The "framing" activities that social movements or other actors engage in refer to the frequently conscious processes by which a claim or phenomenon is contextualized and anchored in a particular system of ideas or beliefs. Framing theory benefits from pairing with ideology or a similar concept that provides the necessary tools for analyzing the interrelated system of assumptions, values, norms, and beliefs *within which issues are framed.* They acknowledge, however, that ideology also comes with certain complications.

We shall return to ideology in a moment, but given the plethora of overlapping concepts, we share Oliver and Johnston's sense of need for a bit of organizing and specification of concepts to improve clarity. Our primary goal is to locate the policy paradigm concept among the numerous complementary and somewhat overlapping concepts. The sketch we offer here has limited ambitions, therefore, and should not be taken as an effort to produce any kind of full-fledged typology.

"Culture" is likely the most all-encompassing concept of those we list. As Johnston and Klandermans (1995:4) note, cultural "codes, frames, institutions, and values have evolved over long periods of time and, for the most part, function as the broadest and most fundamental context for social action". Yet they also acknowledge culture as "broad and often imprecise...difficult to operationalize". Margaret Archer (1996) has observed that culture and structure are often juxtaposed as opposites, and more or less mutually exclusive. Taking issue what that characterization, she makes the case that culture contains its own characteristic structure and logic which can be specified in terms of its many sub-elements. The phenomenon characterized by concepts such as ideology, paradigms, and frames constitute some of those sub-elements of culture. Overall, we understand culture in Blumer's (1969) sense of the term to mean the characteristic ways in which members of a society or social group tend to conceptualize, attribute meaning, and interact in relation to the various spheres of social activity. In Blumer's usage, culture need not be internally consistent or coherent; it is rather the sum total of characteristics that he identifies.

In contrast to culture, "ideology" is conceptualized by most social theorists as a system of beliefs (Thompson, 1990; Eyerman and Jamison 1991; van Dijk 1998). As such, it possesses structure as well as a need for some measure of internal consistency and coherence. Ideology as it is generally employed entails some set of causal explanations derived from a collection or complex of basic underlying assumptions (which may remain hidden or taken for granted). The question of whether these assumptions and explanations represent some kind of Marxian "false consciousness" or are an accurate depiction of real conditions is one of the significant points of debate around the concept of ideology (Thompson, 1990). An important byproduct of the long and rich history of ideology is that the concept has accumulated a good deal of baggage, including competing conceptions and pejorative uses that create significant problems. This history and diversity has been summarized quite well elsewhere (see for example, Thomson, 1990; van Dijk, 1998) and we shall not dwell on it here. However, two of the issues are particularly relevant. First, the level of generality at which ideology is often used contributes to its being perceived as only loosely coupled to empirical reality. Adams (1989), for example, argues "there is no division between theory and understanding: the two are conflated so that the theory is the understanding [...] these theories are self-validating.

Such a view of ideology describes a belief system that is largely impervious to empirical reality. A somewhat more sympathetic view would argue that ideology must be tempered with reality if it is to be in any way implemented. This is the general direction advocated by scholars such as Thompson, van Dijk, and Oliver and Johnston. We are sympathetic to these goals, but it does leave three important questions on the table. First, can the long and complex history of ideology as a concept be meaningfully settled so that it does not remain a distraction and a deterrent for its use? Second, given the impossibility of answering the first question, is taming ideology by making it a middle-range theoretical and analytical concept the best way to address the gap identified by Oliver and Johnston (2000) and others. Third, would successfully taming ideology and bringing it down to earth deprive us of a useful meta-level concept?

These are not merely rhetorical questions. Because it is understood by many as a type of belief system that lacks any day-to-day rootedness in reality, we see ideology as well suited to describing a very general level of belief system. Other concepts are available to fill the middle level space in which policy-related ideas and belief systems must be much more closely bound to actual social conditions – especially those defined as problems. It is here we see concepts such as belief systems and policy paradigm to be especially important. A systematic examination of specific formulations of these two concepts is taken up by Yves Surel in the next chapter, so rather than dwell on it here we note that like Surel, we understand Hall's adaptation of paradigm concept to be quite similar to belief system as described by Sabatier and Jenkins-Smith. However, belief system is also a more general concept.

The overriding reasons for preferring the concept of policy paradigm can be summarized in terms of 1) its operation at the analytical level at which policymaking takes place (see chapters of Coleman and Hall); 2) the specific conceptual elements and problem-solving notions it entails, and which are linked to or become embodied in institutional arrangements (Burns and Carson, 2004; Carson, 2001; Andersen, 1999); and 3) its emphasis on contradiction and incommensurability as generating conditions conducive to change (Hall, 1993). This includes the emergence of anomalies that an institutionalized paradigm has difficulty explaining and coping with – and that may in fact be a byproduct of the successes and failures of policies guided by that paradigm (Burns and Carson, 2002).

In addition to being used to characterize oral and written communication and symbolic action, the term "discourse" is sometimes used to describe a conceptual model that we would refer to as a policy paradigm, ideology, or belief system. The multiple traditions that make use of the concept of discourse or discourse analysis (Chilton, 2005), suggest, as did Oliver and Johnston earlier, that it is best not to overextend the conceptual tools that are available. We therefore employ the concept of discourse to describe the various kinds of communication that constitute a paradigm, express the details of its institutionalized form, and which may be used to challenge an established paradigm. As already noted, all or part of a policy paradigm may constitute a "frame", but they are not the same thing. Framing is carried out by referencing a particular paradigmatic element or the paradigm as a whole.

2. Investigating Public Policy Paradigms

2.1 Defining Policy Paradigm

Policy paradigm is a powerful cognitive-normative concept that permits the analysis of distinctly different, sometimes incommensurable ways of conceptualizing the issues, problems, interests, goals, and remedies involved in policymaking. It can be characterized as containing a generally coherent complex of assumptions and principles, simplifying metaphors, and interpretive and explanatory discourses. It represents a shared conceptual framework through which adherents envision "how things should be" and "how the world works", and with which they define the kinds of issues that should be considered social problems. This conceptual framework helps impose order on a chaotic environment in which actors engaged in making or influencing public policy are frequently required to make decisions with limited expertise, inadequate or contradictory information, and often on a comparatively short time frame.

Within this context, the policy paradigm conditions choices and frames potential opportunities by shaping the conceptual parameters – the boundaries of what is thinkable, possible, or acceptable, and it endows certain courses of action with meaning. It defines the kinds of actions and institutional structures considered to be good or bad, the boundaries between right and wrong, appropriate and inappropriate, and the sense of what does or does not constitute a problem. A policy paradigm enables actors to interpret events and their causes, invests certain actors with credibility and authority, suggests what the various rights and responsibilities of actors should be, and guides action (Burns and Carson, 2002; Hall, 1993). A given paradigm is therefore realized in three types of processes: cognition and meaning, expression and action, and in its institutionalization.[4]

[4] Other research dating from the 1980s using the paradigm concept in the sense of the work presented here more than in the Kuhnian "scientific paradigm conception" has been carried on by an international group including Giovanni Dosi, Leda Gitahy, and Carlota Perez, and Hubert Schmitz (Dosi, 1982, 1984; Gitahy, 2000; Perez, 1983, 1985; Schmitz, 1989). They developed the concept of the techno-economic paradigm to conceptualize the technical, managerial, and organizational ideas and practices applied in administering and regulating industrial production. They were interested in describing and analyzing, among other things, the diffusion and establishment of the new paradigm of Neo-fordism of industrial organization, one differing significantly from the old Fordist/Taylorist paradigm. The paradigm structure, methods, and management techniques and related practices were largely drawn from, or adapted from the Japanese model – but adapted and conceptualized in, for instance, the Brazilian context. They observed and analyzed how norms, models of behavior, and practices were revised, if not transformed in some instances.

The central theoretical concept of our work, public policy paradigm, is essentially a shared model of reality that guides policymakers' problem-solving activities. The various interested groups and individuals in society may share this model, or may challenge it. The policy paradigm concept has been employed in several settings to analyze the effects of systematic conceptual changes on public policy (Jenson 1989; Hall 1992; Hall 1993; Coleman 1998; Carson 2001; Burns and Carson 2002; Carson 2004; Burns and Carson 2005; Carson 2008). Jane Jenson (1989) for example, employs "societal paradigm" as a conceptual model for analyzing changes in the ideas guiding labor market and social in pre-World War I France and the United States. Peter Hall (1993; 1992), outlines a concept of policy paradigm shift generated by policy anomalies and failures leading to a broader, partisan policy debate. Coleman et al. (1997) describe an alternative path to paradigm change that is more negotiated and corporatist in nature. Andersen (1999), Carson (2001, 2004), and Burns (2008) employ it to understand unanticipated policy developments in European Union policy.

The policy paradigm concept fits within a wider theoretical framework emphasizing the role of social institutions in conditioning policymaking processes and other forms of social interaction. With only a few exceptions, however, relatively little has been done to elaborate the paradigm concept beyond Hall's adaptation. Several factors argue that such elaboration is likely to produce additional insights regarding the process of policy change in general, as well as developments specific to the European Union. An important theoretical goal of this anthology, therefore, is to further elaborate the concept of policy paradigm, its internal logical architecture, and its relationships with institutions, actors, and their discourses.

Our particular development of the paradigm concept builds on Jenson (1989), Hall (1993), Coleman, (1998), Andersen (1999), Surel (2000), Campbell (2002), Burns and Carson (2002, 2005), and Carson (2001, 2004, 2008), who have conceptualized the paradigm as a socio-cognitive model employed in solving public issues or problems. Andersen (1999:2) characterizes policy paradigms as a category of "cultural frame", a concept also employed by Fligstein (2001a). Surel (see Chapter 2 in this book) considers both Hall's policy paradigm and Sabatier and Jenkins-Smith's (1993) belief system in similar terms, as a specific type of "cognitive and normative frame" applied to policymaking, and within which individual issues or policy questions can be contextualized and "framed". These usages are consistent with the definition of paradigm used in this work.

Significant changes in policy – such as the rise and fall of Keynesian economic policies, the emergence of strong environmental policies, or the unfolding of programs aimed at improving equality between women and men – often unfold over periods of time that extend to a decade or more (Pierson, 2001; Sabatier, 1999c, 1999b; Sabatier and Jenkins-Smith, 1993). Even in situations of urgent crisis, the seeds of that crisis often can be traced back to earlier developments, including the results of actions or inaction guided by earlier policies. In contrast to many sociological approaches, historical institutionalism (Steinmo, et al., 1992; Hall, 1989) employs the historical timeline to provide analytical structure, identifying "historical preconditions", tracing changes in values, normative beliefs, and policy models over time as they are formalized and institutionalized. This constitutes the socio-historical and cognitive environment within which institutions are created and function; events and developments are embedded in this broader context. This approach shares some of the character of the historian's particularistic reading of social change, while embracing the capacity of a sociological analysis to understand overall patterns of social interaction and change. This strategy informs important efforts within the welfare state literature, for example, to trace the conditions that have contributed to the evolution of welfare state arrangements (Korpi, 1994; Esping-Andersen, 1992; Steinmo, 1989; Baldwin, 1990). A strength of this approach is that it generates a great deal of rich detail. An important weakness is that its explanations sometimes tend toward functionalism or simple path dependency, explaining historical preconditions with earlier preconditions; change that represents divergence from that path is more difficult to explain (Thelen and Steinmo, 1992:14-15). Although this tendency is common, it is not universal, however, as illustrated by Peter Hall's (1989) efforts to tackle it directly. Hall and his collaborators present a compelling picture of the emergence and development of Keynesian ideas in guiding economic policy in the US and Europe, and how they were institutionalized in unique ways in specific institutional environments.

The historical institutionalism demonstrates that while discrete preferences are shaped by institutional context, broader goals and what constitutes self-interest are as well (Thelen and Steinmo, 1992). It also illustrates especially well the powerful tendencies toward path dependencies and stability (Immergut, 1992). Taking important cues from sociology, Hall's approach (1993, 1992, 1989) significantly expands this picture, giving systematic expression to the role of a coherent complex of policy ideas by tracing their adoption and institutionalization in formal policy over a period spanning two decades.

2.2 Core Tenets

Ideas Matter – It should already be clear that our basic starting point is a core assumption that "ideas matter". This is no longer a controversial assertion, as evidenced by the expanding academic emphasis on the power of ideas in politics and policy during the past two decades. Denzau and North (1993:1) argue, for example: "it is simply not possible to make sense out of the diverse performance of economies and polities both historically and contemporaneously if individuals really knew their self interest and acted accordingly. Instead, people act in part upon the basis of myths, dogmas, ideologies, and 'half-baked' theories". More recently, Campbell (2002) argues that still more effort needs to be devoted to understanding "how ideas, that is, theories, conceptual models, norms, world views, frames, principled beliefs, and the like, rather than self-interest, affect policy making".[5]

The ideas we are most concerned with here are interconnected and interdependent – particularly in the form of structured complexes of ideas that constitute the conceptual models through which actors perceive and understand the world. The conceptualizations of an issue or the kinds of issues that are to be handled in a policy area are therefore considered fundamentally important. At the same time, the feedback effects of new or existing policies may have a profound effect on the conceptual models. Conceptual models structure and constrain where and how policy alternatives are developed, what kinds of rules and actions are seen as appropriate and legitimate, and which kinds of actors are considered to be the appropriate and legitimate authorities for dealing with the issue. The work presented in this anthology therefore emphasizes the role of ideas and ideals in the processes by which actors seek to initiate new policies and restructure policymaking institutions or defend those already established.

An acknowledgement that perceptions of interests are inherently subjective and model dependent has important consequences for assumptions about policy decisions and the notion that preferences are guided by rationality and the self-interest of powerful actors. Clear cut policy preferences based on self-interest may be difficult to straightforwardly determine. It is well-understood that policy preferences and the perception of self-interest are likely to be guided by perceived opportunities for material gains, by cognitive models that define what is "right and appropriate", and by the nature and quality of relationships with other actors. These separate kinds of considerations often collide and conflict with one another because they can be difficult to measure, weigh against one another, and evaluate in comparable terms. There is also great variation in the way in which "interests" or "self-interest" are defined[6]. They are frequently used in largely economic terms to mean material interest (see, for example, Moravcsik, 1998). This stands in contrast to motivations guided by "a logic of appropriateness" (March and Olsen, 1989), which are driven by more altruistic-like values and norms. In short, rationality is dependent on the cognitive model being used, "bounded rationality" limits the ability to

---

[5] Campbell (2002:21) points out the undue stress on "interests" to the neglect of ideas: Political sociology and political science have focused on how the pursuit of self-interest affects politics and policy making in advanced capitalist societies. This has been true for pluralist, elite, neo-Marxist, historical institutionalist, and rational choice theories. Scholars have paid far less attention to how ideas, that is, theories, conceptual models, norms, world views, frames, principled beliefs, and the like, rather than self-interests, affect policy making. This is surprising given Max Weber's famous dictum that ideas have profound effects on the course of events, serving like switchmen who direct interest-based action down one track or another.

[6] Our use of the term "interest" distinguishes between "ideal" and "material" interests, although where not specified, "interests" can be taken to mean material interests.

weigh alternatives, and the information available for making decisions is often either insufficient or incorrect (Denzau and North 1993).

In general, the analytical strategy is to trace the process of fundamental policy change as it evolves from ideas and through action to become institutionalized. The basic elements of this change process include: a) the emergence of new phenomena that are defined as problems or the redefinition of existing phenomena as pressing problems, then impelled by new claims and demands for structural change made by organized interests and policy entrepreneurs, b) the replacement of an established complex of policy ideas with a new one that is not comparable in the same terms, and c) the institutionalization of the new set of ideas in the form of new norms, policy competencies, revised or new organizational structures and goals, and new types or groups of actors defined as having a legitimate role to play. This brings us to our next core assumption.

Institutions Matter Also – A second core tenet, which also has become a cliché within academic discourse, is that "institutions matter". At the heart of the "new" institutionalism (Burns and Flam, 1987; Powell and DiMaggio, 1991; Thelen and Steinmo, 1992; Brinton and Nee, 1998; Hollingsworth et al., 2002) lies a common recognition and understanding that both "socio-cognitive" and "structural" factors provide the context, the impetus, and the tools for political struggle and other forms of social interaction, although there are diverse strategies for applying this shared core[7] (Hall and Taylor, 1996). The core tenets enumerated here are part and parcel of the new institutionalism – particularly the sociological institutionalism that provides much of the theoretical grounding for this work

The "new" institutionalism, and the sociological neo-institutionalism in particular, seeks to integrate the reciprocal influences of socio-cognitive phenomena and

---

[7] Of Hall and Taylor's three major categories of neo-institutional approaches, the new institutional economics is less useful in this context because it continues to relegate conceptual models largely to the background. In general, it can be said that the new institutional economics breaks from mainstream rational choice theory with the concession that there are both cognitive and structural constraints that underlie preference formation and "rational" choices. If rational choices are context bound, then institutions can be seen as part of the context that creates constraints. But seen from the individual level of "rationality within constraints", or "context-bound rationality" (Brinton and Nee, 1998; Nee, 1998; Bourdon, 1996), one can distinguish as "context" not only structural/institutional constraints, but also cultural/cognitive constraints. Such cognitive constraints are pushed into the background largely through the assumption of rational actors seeking to maximize their material self-interest, although important concessions have been made to the problems of the limits of rationality and to incomplete and unevenly distributed information. Diverging still further from the strict rationality assumption is economic historian Douglass North. North (1981) points to the importance of belief systems, in this case in terms of ideology, in explaining individual and group preferences and action that cannot be accounted for by rational choice models. He points out that preferences and beliefs are shaped not only by institutional arrangements, but also by lived experience, and goes as far as calling for a new theory of ideology to more systematically account for the ways in which cognitive models both structure constraints and serve as enabling tools.

structural forces on human interaction and agency. Socio-cognitive factors are generally grouped under concepts such as "ideas" "norms" and "frames", as well as complexes of these individual elements under concepts such as "paradigms", ideology and "mental models", and even "culture". This provides the broad cognitive context for the public policy paradigm, which is the concept used to map the relationships between public policy and changing complexes of ideas. Structuring is conceptualized in terms of institutions, which can be characterized as complexes of rules and procedures that shape human interactions in a given sphere of activity (Burns and Flam, 1987). Agency, typically collective, is seen as embodied in a broad range of actors. This encompasses organizations at multiple levels, including states, transnational and supranational organizations, NGOs, corporations, policy networks, etc. It also includes individual actors – typically in specialized roles such as "policy entrepreneurs" or "skilled individuals" (Fligstein, 2001b). Also considered part of the neo-institutional family is historical institutionalism, which emphasizes the importance of historical context and the ways in which it influences the development of public policy over time.

The sociological neo-institutionalism includes a variety of approaches that emphasize cognitive and ideational factors (Burns and Carson, 2002; Campbell, 2002; Fligstein, 2001b; Hobson, 2000a; Ahrne, 1994; Arditi, 1994; DiMaggio and Powell, 1991). These often draw implicitly or explicitly on Berger and Luckmann's (1969) classic work, which among other things emphasizes the socio-cognitive processes by which practices become institutionalized (Scott, 1987:493). "Institutionalization involves the processes by which social processes, obligations, or actualities come to take on a rule-like status in social thought or action" (Meyer and Rowan, 1977:341). This suggests an important link between socio-cognitive models and institutions, which Scott (1987:497-498) summarizes in his insight that "institutionalized belief systems constitute a distinctive class of elements that can account for the existence and/or the elaboration of organizational structure". Attention to these "classes of elements" permits the construction and analysis of the belief systems to which he refers.

Ideas do not float freely and conceptualizations are often contested. Some conceptual models of issues and policy sectors are better established than others, and they may be supported and reinforced by established rules-of-the-game (both formal and informal) that guide how and by whom such questions are to be dealt with, and how rules are to be made or altered. Institutions are conceptualized here as systems of rules that govern social interaction and may be normative (shared understandings) or formalized (i.e. laws, procedures, etc.) (North, 1991; Burns and Flam, 1987). Institutionalized systems of rules condition power relationships (Burns and Flam, 1987). They also generate inertia, or path dependencies, based on how similar issues have been handled in the past, especially the recent past, and based on the power relationships defined in those rules and the underlying assumptions embedded in them (Thelen and Steinmo, 1992). There may be substantial inconsistencies, incompatibilities, or incommensurability, between what is considered the most compelling way of thinking about a set of policy issues or problems, and the way in which existing institutionalized rules dictate that it should be dealt with. This can result in obstacles to effective problem solving, undermined legitimacy, and political tensions that destabilize the existing social order (Burns and Carson, 2002).

Two established strategies for integrating cultural/cognitive factors within the new institutionalism entail relating them to social organization or the institutionalized structures of discrete spheres of societal activity that they inspire (Ahrne, 1994; Powell and DiMaggio, 1991; Burns and Flam, 1987), or to the historical timeline (Pierson, 1998; Thelen and Steinmo, 1992; Hall, 1989). Each of these is relevant to the case studies taken up in this research. For example, there has long been an awareness of "organizational culture" as a distinct phenomenon embedded in "organizational structure" (Perrow, 1979). The European Commission, for example, is a "multi-organization" (Cram, 1994), with the various Directorates General (DGs) guided by distinctly different organizational missions and cultures. The sociological and historical institutionalisms use in varying degrees existing institutional/organizational structure and time frames to impose order on the flow of ideas. At the institutional level where the Treaties help define EU competence in the various policy sectors, there are different logics reflected in the procedures, voting rules, capacity to act, etc. These have developed over time, so that it is possible to trace the evolution of paradigmatic ideas as new ones become institutionalized (Pierson, 1998), replacing earlier guiding logics.

Actors, Networks, and Alliances – A third tenet in our approach is that "actors, networks, and alliances matter". Where constellations of individual and organized actors emerge in competition with one another, they may take a variety of different forms. They are characterized in the literature as policy networks (Coleman et al., 1997; Knoke et al., 1998), policy advocacy coalitions (Sabatier and Jenkins-Smith, 1993), epistemic communities (Haas, 1992), social movements (McCarthy and Zald, 1967), peak organizations, and the variety of terms describes the different logics that define them.

Organized actors may choose to engage or not to engage on a particular set of policy proposals based on a number of different rationales. Such rationales may be relational (helping allies or seeking to block opponents), interest-based (such as engaging as an opportunity to gain public attention or to protect financial or power interests), values or ideals-based (engaging in pursuit of ideal interests), or more typically, some combination of these. For example, choices to engage may be conditioned by the quality and nature of relationships with other organized or individual actors (Bordieu, 1996). For example, an organization may lend its support as a favor to an ally or repay a debt – or in an effort to punish an organization seen as unfriendly. It is considered natural that organizations that share common overall goals and values would join forces to support specific policy proposals. However, it is also quite common for groups sharing common goals to take different sides in particular policy struggles. An interesting current example is the way in which environmental organizations were divided in their support of the climate change legislation in the US House of Representatives (known as the Waxman-Markey Bill). That split was based on very different ideas about how to achieve shared goals. A contrasting picture is found in the kind of "strange bedfellows" coalitions that form to support specific proposals, yet are composed of organizations whose long-term goals are values are in at odds with one another. Such an example can be found in Hajer's (1995) analysis of ecological modernization, in which business and environmental groups came together in spite of their pursuit of very different long-term agendas. A third variation on this theme is the case in which an organized actor lends support not because of support for a particular policy proposal, but because a secondary or side effect of the proposal serves other goals in which the organization is interested. This is also a common phenomena and often part of weaving together alliances that are sufficiently powerful to prevail on a given policy proposal. In the EU context, there are frequently overlaps between actors pursuing substantive policy goals and those who wish to move authority to the European level – or block such developments.

The important point with these differing examples is that the diverse array of types of alliances is possible based a combination of relational factors, material interests, and shared conceptual models, and the ways in which particular elements are held to be more central and important than others and thereby prioritized.

2.3 Key Features of Public Policy Paradigm Theory

The public policy paradigm is a shared conceptual model used for political problem solving. However, it is more encompassing than a simple problem solving model, since it is the model used to construct the very problems it is used to address (see Bacchi, 1999; Sabatier and Jenkins-Smith, 1993). It does so, starting from core assumptions, by defining priority among competing policy principles and goals. Within that context, the paradigm delineates the suitable means for achieving goals, and identifies what kinds of expertise should be considered legitimate and relevant, and who should be considered competent authorities responsible for decision making and for implementing corrective measures. The actors who advance the model are themselves are likely to be defined in it, giving it a self-referential aspect. When institutionalized, a policy paradigm shapes the production and distribution of societal resources, forms guidelines for how benefits and related costs are distributed, structures power relationships, and defines "logics of appropriateness".

Overall, this book presents three key results about public policy paradigms:
(I) **The functions/uses of public policy paradigms** in interpreting social reality, identifying problems and solutions, and guiding judgment and policymaking and its implementation;

(II) **The structure of policy paradigms**. "Paradigm" may be investigated in terms of its particular properties as well as in terms of its function – and the relationship between its internal structure and its functions. A public policy paradigm defines problems or types of problems and their sources which are to be publicly addressed, and identifies the available strategies and resources to deal with these problems (or categories of problems). It defines also actors (and their roles in what take place), for instance, those who should have public authority in relation to the application and development of public policy and, in particular, this policy paradigm. Included in this are also "other agents" ("the other") including scapegoats (Jews, immigrants, Muslims, etc.) or conditions of fate/"destiny". Furthermore, a paradigm usually identifies agents capable (knowledgeable, authoritative experts) of dealing with the problems ("experts", "good fairies", magicians). Note that experts, for instance, do not usually control material resources or have great economic or political power (but, nevertheless, may play influential roles).

(III) **The socio-political process of transforming or constructing and establishing a paradigm** (related to the social construction of "problems" to be solved, designs, strategies, decisions). Here, of course, one is alerted to the mechanisms (rational, non-rational, or irrational, or even self-destructive) that drive paradigm developments. The work presented here identifies five basic social mechanisms of public policy paradigm shifts: (i) *Change in perspective of a dominant agent.* For instance, an authoritarian leader or dictator changes her perspective, adopts a new paradigm, and puts it into operation. (ii) *A power shift* brings a new agent with another paradigm to leadership (those involved may include outside actors or possibly an alliance of some insiders and outsiders). Replacing an earlier elite to institutionalize the new paradigm may occur through force, as in a coup d'etat or a violent revolution, through democratic process, such as elections or nominations, or through societal negotiation. Demographic mechanisms are also important bringing about generational/cohort shifts. (iii) *Negotiation among multiple agents* producing a new order – with compromises – is a common mechanism. One can distinguish between co-operative "negotiation" (because of convergent of interests ("solidarity of interests") or because of solidarity of sentiments ("solidarity coordination"), on the one hand, or competitive or antagonistic "negotiation", on the other hand. (iv) *Diffusion and mimicry* of a New Institutional Paradigm (mimetic function) (for example, Campbell refers to the diffusion of world environmental culture through NGOs and UN agencies). (2002:25). Autonomous agents are inter-connnected in communication networks which spread "new practices" and "ideas". (v) *Unintended agentic development of a new institutional paradigm* The actors who introduce and develop the changes leading to a new paradigm often do not intend to do so, but instead *drift* into what turns into an unexpected and unintended paradigm shift.[8] A new tech-

[8] Cultural change, associated with an eventual paradigm shift, may occur in the most subtle and incremental ways. An institutional order may erode as a result of actors introducing in an ad hoc manner alien rules into the domain. For example, market concepts and conduct rules such as

nology or technique, new institutional positions or member competencies and commitments which, to all appearances, only lead to relatively minor changes in the institutional procedures and rules may in the long run actually cause problems which cannot be effectively analyzed and dealt with within the framework of the established paradigm – and give rise to consideration of radically new approaches and principles.

The policy paradigm concept offers a number of advantages. Its components can be identified, and as we show, there is a logical structure to a public policy paradigm. At the same time, the theory allows for – and seeks out – gaps and contradictions, both within a paradigm and between a paradigm and the institution(s) in which it is embedded. A policy paradigm also is recognized as incomplete – which may result in unanticipated problems. These offer "cracks" in which claims can be made successfully.

Other advantages of the paradigm concept lie in its relation to other important concepts related to ideas and cognitive processes. For example, a paradigm is the basis of framing processes and the production of frames. It is free of the intellectual and political baggage often associated with ideology. It explains path dependencies and change processes in the complex relationships between actors, institutional arrangements, culturally-rooted understandings.

Finally, the policy paradigm speaks to different kinds of collectivities. Policy advocacy coalitions (Sabatier and Jenkins-Smith, 1993) may be composed of groups that advocate radically different paradigms, but which coalesce around agreement on a specific paradigmatic element shared in common: a shared problem definition, a preferred set of remedies, trust in a particular type of expertise. In contrast and epistemic community is formed by those who develop and adhere to a public policy paradigm. That is, "paradigm-epistemic communities" consist of networks of professionals and experts with an authoritative claim to policy-relevant knowledge, who share a set of normative beliefs, causal models, notions of empirical validity, and a common policy enterprise (Campbell, 2002:30; Haas, 1992).

3. Overview of the Book

We have divided this book into four parts. Part I consists of this chapter and that of Yves Surel in the following chapter; Part II, a section with previously published articles that may be considered early classics in the application of the policy paradigm concept; Part III contains our own case studies of paradigm shifts in specific policy sectors in European Union policy and Part IV offers analysis and some concluding reflections.

---

profit seeking may be applied to such domains as the family, community, or health care system, and result in the attenuation of the earlier organizing principles such as solidarity and justice – in turn leading to the disappearance of the entire old patterns of activity and their replacement by new ones.

In the next chapter Yves Sorel gives an insightful analysis and overview of three important cognitive-normative approaches in policymaking research. This defines the larger context of the work presented in this book.

Part Two of the book provides a selection of a few studies of public policy paradigm shifts, which have become classic exemplars. Jane Jenson is one of the first, if not the first, to apply the paradigm concept to public policy. In Chapter 3, Jenson's 1989 article considers historical shifts in France and the USA before 1914, focusing on the introduction of legislation "protecting" the conditions under which women participated in certain occupations as well as providing infant and maternal protection. In Chapter 4, Peter Hall analyzes the shift in England from Keynesian economic policy to monetarism with a 1993 article that quite rightly received widespread attention.[9] Coleman (1998) and Coleman et al. (1997) responded to Hall, challenging the generality of his model of abrupt shifts. Coleman argued rather that shifts in paradigms could be negotiated in a more or less gradual way and accomplished substantial change through a piecemeal transition.

Part Three presents a selection of cases from our EU comparative policy research (1997-2008), in which we investigated a number of paradigm shifts in diverse sectors. We found the EU was a crucible of public policy initiatives and major policy shifts. The case studies included here concern food (Chapter 8), chemicals including the special case of asbestos (Chapters 9 and 10), climate change (Chapter 12), and gender (Chapter 13). Svein Andersen, in adddition to his own EU research program has also collaborated with us on our EU research program, and contributes a chapter here (Chapter 11) on the EU policy paradigm shift relating to natural gas in Europe. Chapter 14 concludes Part Three, identifying the different patterns of shifts and de-

---

[9] In Hall's perspective, Keynesianism and monetarism were quintessential examples of public policy paradigm differences: (1) policy prescriptions or strategies diverged; (2) their models of the situation (causal factors) also differed – they were based on a fundamentally different conception of how the economy itself worked. While Keynes viewed the private economy as unstable and in need of intermittent fiscal adjustments, monetarists saw the private economy as stable and that discretionary policy was an impediment to efficient economic performance. This was an argument against fiscal activism.

On the other hand, Keynesians attributed fluctuations in economic output and inflation to the cycle of the "real economy" or excessive wage and price pressure; on the other hand, monetarists took the position that fluctuations in output and inflation were primarily caused by excessive changes in the rate of growth of the money supply. Keynesians believed also that they could reduce the rate of unemployment by altering the fiscal levels, while monetarists contended that the jobless were not the responsibility of the state because unemployment would converge on a "natural rate" fixed by conditions in the labor market rather than by the macroeconomic stance." The paradigm change entailed a radical shift in the hierarchy of goals guiding policy, the instruments relied on to effect policy, and the setting of those instruments.

The policy regime shifts entailed also changes in the discourses employed by policymakers and in the analyses employed by policymakers and in the analysis of the economy on which policy was based. And the locus of power/authority shifted away from administrators (and economists) to mass media people and the leadership of the government.

velopments in the case studies. The chapter also draws conclusions about what the results show concerning EU policymaking and the integration process.

Part Four concludes the book. We synthesize PPP theory based on the research of others as well as our own. It is argued that a PP paradigm is an idealized rule regime with a particular structure (diverse components or complexes); it takes ideal (or purely conceptual forms) as well as operative or practical forms. Also, the chapter identifies the processes whereby regime shifts take place.

CHAPTER 2

The Role of Cognitive and Normative Frames in Policymaking

Yves Surel

There has been an increasingly important shift in the analysis of public policy in recent years, with the development of an approach which emphasises the influence of ideas, general precepts and representations, over and above social evolution and state action. This approach is based on the belief that cognitive and normative elements play an important role in how actors understand and explain the world, and has stimulated a variety of works from various approaches. However, what these have in common, be it more or less explicit, is the goal of establishing the importance of the dynamics of the social construction of reality in the shaping of historically-specific and socially legitimate frames and practices (Berger and Luckmann 1969).

This new research orientation, emphasising the importance of cognitive and/or normative elements, has been the object of attempts at modelling, with a view to systematising and conceptually constructing the role of these logics of the social construction of knowledge and meaning in State action. Amongst numerous works, three approaches can be identified, informed by a recognition of the importance of values, ideas and representations in the study of public policy. Developed separately in the course of the 1980s, albeit informed by quite different perspectives, these conceptual models are primarily based on notions of paradigm (Hall 1993), of *advocacy coalition* (Sabatier and Jenkins-Smith 1993, Sabatier 1998), or on the notion of the *référentiel*, as defined by Bruno Jobert and Pierre Muller (Jobert and Muller 1987; Faure et al. 1995). According to Peter Hall, recourse to such conceptualisations is especially well-suited to the analysis of political phenomena, and in particular to public policy insofar as "politicians, officials, the spokesmen for social interests, and policy experts all operate within the terms of political discourse that are current in the nation at a given time, and the terms of political discourse generally have a specific configuration that lends representative legitimacy to some social interests more than others, delineates the accepted boundaries of state action, associates contemporary political developments with particular interpretations of national history, and defines the context in which many issues will be understood" (Hall 1993, 289).

In spite of what are at times important differences, these conceptualisations all share a macro-level questioning which aims to shed light on the influence of global social norms on social behaviour and public policy, and to integrate into the analysis at times previously neglected normative variables (cf in particular the voluminous literature which focuses exclusively on cognition and expertise, Radaelli 1995). Cognitive and normative frames, which as a general expression brings together paradigms (Hall), belief systems (Sabatier) and *référentiels* (Jobert and Muller), are intended to refer to coherent systems of normative and cognitive elements which define, in a given field, "world views", mechanisms of identity formation, principles of action, as well as methodological prescriptions and practices for actors subscribing to the same frame. Generally speaking, these frames constitute conceptual instruments, available for the analysis of changes in public policy and for the explanation of developments between public and private actors which come into play in a given field.

The main purpose of this article is therefore to offer a critical review of these different models, by isolating their internal characteristics, and to see what type of research orientation they give rise to, explicitly or implicitly, for the analysis of public policy.

Elements of Cognitive and Normative Frames

The three notions discussed below include very similar elements, albeit grouped differently. Within each grouping we can make an analytical distinction between three or four elements which may be located on a hierarchical scale (Table 2.1) established with reference to the original definition of the notion of paradigm (Kuhn 1970; Chalmers 1987; Surel 1995). These different elements which combine to produce a coherent paradigmatic frame, include: (a) metaphysical principles, (b) specific principles, (c) forms of action, and (d) instruments.

Table 2.1. Elements of cognitive and normative frames

	Paradigm	**Advocacy Coalition Framework**	**Référentiel**
Metaphysical principles	Policy paradigm	Deep core	Values Images
Specific principles		Policy core	Norms
Forms of action	Choice of instruments		Algorithms
Instruments	Specifications of instruments	Secondary aspects	

(a) Metaphysical principles

The different models evoked here are first built on the belief that values and metaphysical principles define what is sometimes called a "world view", abstract precepts circumscribing what is possible in a given society, identifying and justifying the existence of differences between individuals and/or groups, and locating various social processes on a hierarchical scale. For Sabatier, for example, the *deep core* includes "basic ontological and normative beliefs, such as the relative valuation of individual freedom versus social equity, which operates across virtually all policy domains" (Sabatier 1998, 103). This first grouping of elements can therefore be located in the normative stratum where we also find elements which condense values specific to a given frame, in the form of representations, beliefs etc.

For example, in his study of the macro-economic policies pursued in Great Britain in the 1970s and 1980s (Hall 1992), Peter Hall identifies a shift from Keynesian-inspired principles to neo-liberal or monetarist ones. Underlying each of these models was a different world view. In the neo-liberal model, the rational and responsible individual was placed to the fore, the model thereby allying itself to a simplistic form of social Darwinism ("the beneficial effect of the market will ensure that the best come out on top, who will thus enhance the prosperity of all"). On the other hand, the Keynesian paradigm recognised the existence of collective duty to cure the ills of modern society, starting from a vision of economic processes which challenge the necessary and beneficial nature of the free hand of the market.

(b) Specific principles

In second place, these cognitive frames comprise specific principles, which in various ways follow from the most general and abstract principles. Drawing on Kuhn, this second layer includes elements, notably hypothetical-deductive statements, which allow the operationalisation of values in one domain and/or particular policy and/or subsystem of public policy. It is undoubtedly at this level that the differences between the models are the greatest. Whilst the work of Peter Hall implicitly rests on a hierarchy of degrees of abstraction (even if the normative and cognitive elements are both covered by the general notion of policy paradigm) Sabatier argues that the principles which allow us to make distinctions are very closely connected to differences in diffusion and social embeddedness. For Sabatier, there is a difference between the *deep core* and the *policy core* which is not only linked to their position in the hierarchy (the deepest and most general beliefs appearing in the *deep core*) but also concerns their scope: the *deep core* affects the whole of society (or at least a sizeable community) whereas the *policy core* refers only to a subsystem of public policy.

To put it more generally, taking the original conceptualisation of Kuhn, we have, above all, a cognitive component which defines legitimate strategies with respect to objectives more or less explicitly prescribed by general principles. Peter Hall thus shows that the differences between Keynesian and monetarist paradigms hinge on distinct macro-economic policy objectives (the fight against unemployment in the first case, against inflation in the second). And these specific principles are closely related to the normative stratum, insofar as they aim to define clear prescriptions for public-policy making. For example, the European Monetary Union was inspired by a monetarist "world view", that helped to define suitable precepts for the formulation of macro-economic policies (McNamara 1998).

(c) Forms of action

The above-mentioned grouping of cognitive and normative elements is linked to practical considerations of the most appropriate methods and means to achieve the defined values and objectives. Again, by analogy with Kuhn's work, for scientific methods to be inextricably linked to metaphysical principles and hypothetical-deductive models specific to a particular paradigm, it is necessary to identify forms of action appropriate for the trajectories sought, with respect to the values which characterise a frame. In other words, cognitive and normative frames not only construct "mental maps" but also determine practices and behaviours. In the case of the State, they delimit the choice of instruments to implement a particular strategy.

Peter Hall, using the same example as before of macro-economic policy, shows that the techniques employed vary considerably according to the paradigm adopted. The mechanisms used to boost consumption through an expansive budgetary policy characteristic of Keynesian approaches, contrast, for example, with the monetarist's emphasis on control of the money supply and the more systematic use of monetary policy instruments. The mobilisation of instruments is therefore by no means a neutral decision; rather it matches certain normative and practical imperatives laid out by the previous elements.

(d) Instruments

Finally, the last level is concerned with the specification of instruments which is shaped by the whole of the frame, to ensure their congruence with the other elements. In Paul Sabatier's analysis of the role of secondary aspects within belief systems characteristic of an "advocacy coalition", he includes for example minor decisions which may, within a particular program, be concerned with budgetary allocations, administrative regulations and so on. The cognitive and normative frame therefore delimits the scope of the necessary and potential instruments and the relative importance of each of them (legislative or regulatory mechanisms, interest rate level etc.).

Overall, it is the combination of these elements, which gives rise to particular mental maps. The definition of a "societal paradigm" offered by Jane Jenson sums up well what underpins the specificity of these cognitive and normative frames, that is to say, "a shared set of interconnected premises which make sense of many social relations. Every paradigm contains a view of human nature, a definition of basic and proper forms of social relations among equals and among those in relationships of hierarchy, and specification of relations among institutions as well as a stipulation of the role of such institutions. Thus, a societal paradigm is a meaning system as well as a set of practices" (Jenson 1989, 239). Beyond their differences, these distinct conceptualisations all in fact posit the existence of an ensemble of general principles and values defining the relations and identities of actors, in particular through forms of thought which delimit, hierarchically rank and legitimate social distinctions, all the while setting priorities for action in a given community. In addition, the consequences of these different cognitive and normative societal frames are to legitimate some groups rather than others, mark out the terrain for public action, as well as to define the possibilities for change in a particular subsystem. They thereby determine as much the world views themselves as the practices that follow from them.

However, such models raise problems linked to the different allocation of the elements making up a cognitive and normative frame. Thus, the articulation between the different layers is at times ambiguous, at others, deterministic. Far from always clarifying the relations between metaphysical principles, forms of action and practical elements, in fact these models most often posit an internal coherence and a hierarchical ordering which enhance the normative elements. Furthermore, the links between these cognitive and normative variables and the institutional context are rarely made explicit, the problem made all the worse by the semantic imprecision in the terms at times introduced by the various tendencies of neo-institutionalism (ideas forming an explanatory variable of institutions in one case are themselves institutions in others, cf. Hall and Taylor 1996; for the sociological institutionalism, cf. Powell, Di Maggio, 1991).

The Fundamental Dynamics of Cognitive Frames

Certain authors (cf. notably Mériaux 1995) have underlined the more or less explicit functionalist perspective present in these different approaches. Beyond the particular inspirations and origins of each model, it is in fact possible to see that cognitive frames all sustain several fundamental processes which act as the social functions of integration in a given community. In setting up a view of the world and determining legitimate practices, they seem in particular to be shaped by the production of identity mechanisms and the distribution of power (1), as well as by their capacity to manage social tensions (2).

(1) The production of identity and the allocation of power

As in the cultural conception of ideology put forward by Geertz (Geertz 1964), one of the principal "functions" of a cognitive and normative frame shared by a certain number of actors, is effectively to develop a "collective consciousness" in them, in other words, a subjective sense of belonging, producing a specific identity. Cognitive and normative frames allow actors to make sense of their worlds, and to locate themselves and develop in a given community, by defining the field for exchange, by allowing meaning to be conferred on social dynamics, and by determining the possibilities for action. They thereby contribute to the construction of individuals or groups as social actors in a particular field.

The management of the connection between values, representations, global norms etc and their "counterparts" at the level of the subsystem always underlies a paradigm or a *référentiel* (the global/sectoral relationship, in Jobert and Muller's terms), this articulation resulting in identity production. The existence of a cognitive and normative frame is therefore both a source of boundaries, which constitute a group and/or an organisation and/or a subsystem in itself, and a source of forms of articulation and the overlapping of these boundaries, allowing the adherents of a particular matrix to view themselves in relation to a wider whole. The configuration of the medical profession is a good example of this, in the way it has established the norms and principles of its constitution which in turn define the legitimate boundaries of the profession itself, as well as the nature of its relations with other actors; patients, the State, social security agencies (Hassenteufel 1997).

Similarly, cognitive and normative frames are fundamentally constituted and modified by the interplay of actors. Far from being simple "revelations", paradigms are, on the contrary, the product as well as the determinant, of exchanges between individuals, groups and the State in a given society. From this point of view, Sabatier, as well as Jobert and Muller, underline the privileged role of certain actors in public policymaking, both in producing and diffusing cognitive and normative frames. As such, the notion of the *policy broker* in Sabatier's work refers to a category of actors characterised by their capacity to make the link between one subsystem and another, and to facilitate the integration of subsystems of public policy in the global public sphere. For Jobert and Muller, these mediators, genuine organic intellectuals in the Gramscian sense, "hold a strategic decision-making position insofar as they construct the intellectual context in which negotiations and conflicts take place, and alliances are created, which lead to the taking of decisions" (Muller 1994, 50).

What the modification of such a paradigm or global *référentiel* leads to is thus a decentring of sites of power, more than the substitution of one elite for another (Hall 1993). As a paradigm shift occurs, it is the nature and stability of social exchanges which are transformed through the reallocation of power. In the case of the macro-economic policies analysed by Hall, the shift to a monetarist paradigm, whilst being based on a change in the political elite with the return of the Conservatives to power under the leadership of Margaret Thatcher, above all brought about a transformation of the relationships between the Treasury and other government departments (in a particularly long-lasting and significant way for the conduct of policymaking).

Still, such approaches leave to one side or marginalize other basic variables which focus primarily on the interests of actors, partially because of the conditions under which such forms of understanding public policy came into being. As Radaelli (1995) reminds us, the placing to the fore of cognitive and normative variables dates primarily from the work of Lindblom which, since the 1960s, has tended to question traditional approaches focused on the nature of interests and power relations in the shaping of decision-making and public policy. Consequently, even if the logics of power relations are present in most of these works, they are subordinate to the focus on the identification of actors sharing the same cognitive and normative frame.

The relationship between interests and cognitive and normative variables has recently been made clearer in a response by Paul Sabatier to certain critiques of his *advocacy coalition framework*. More or less "summoned" to locate himself in relation to supporters of rational choice models, Sabatier clarified that from his point of view, actors are only rational at the instrumental level, maximising exclusively at this "lower" level the resources available to them, according to defined objectives. Yet the determination of these objectives is fundamentally linked to cognitive and normative frames specific to a given subsystem. Sabatier therefore considers that "actors always perceive the world through a lens consisting of their preexisting beliefs" (Sabatier 1998, 109).

If we accept this position on the relationship between values and interests (which many do not, at least *a priori*), this last variable can nevertheless serve to clarify certain important processes. How can the structure of interests, for example, influence the production of cognitive and normative frames? Is there not an asymmetry in resources and positions which explains why a particular category of actors succeeds in playing the role of mediator or *policy broker*? Furthermore, what is the degree of internal homogeneity of a subsystem identified by the sharing of the same cognitive and normative frame?

(2) The management of tension and conflict

To answer these questions we need to explore the second basic dynamic isolated above to describe the "functioning" of cognitive and normative frames: how a frame is able to manage social tensions and to contain conflict. The coherence of cognitive and normative factors in the same frame is in fact successively characterised by the setting up of a causal explanation of the ongoing processes (Stone 1988), then by defining principles and particular practices for action. It is usually necessary to manage the tensions inherent in "anomalies" in the social organism in seeking not so much the means to resolve them (political activity is not interested in solutions to enigmas, cf Schon and Rein 1994), as a way to deal with their effects and consequences. Each subsystem thus succeeds, through the cognitive and normative frame which characterises it, in managing the conflicts and tensions arising from its location in global society.

The management of social tensions does not, however, mean the disappearance of all forms of conflict, given the multiplicity of paradigms in each subsystem. Most of the models evoked here recognise the existence of competing paradigms in any context, each sustained by distinct configurations of actors. Such dynamics appear in Sabatier's model, which shows clearly that "within the subsystem, [...] actors can be aggregated into a number (usually one to four) of 'advocacy coalitions', each composed of actors from various governmental and private organizations who both (a) share a set of normative and causal beliefs and (b) engage in a non-trivial degree of co-ordinated activity over time" (Sabatier 1998, 103).

Instead of unifying and homogenising the social sphere where it "functions", the paradigm consequently acts more as a bounded space for conflict, between the subsystem and the global community, as inside the subsystem itself (Jobert makes a distinction here between "debates which take place within the same *référentiel* and controversy about the *référentiel* itself", Jobert 1992, 221). A cognitive and normative frame thus marks out the terrain for social exchanges and disagreements, rather than simply supporting an unlikely consensus. A dominant paradigm is thus by no means an exclusive one.

Table 2.2. The dynamics of cognitive and normative frames

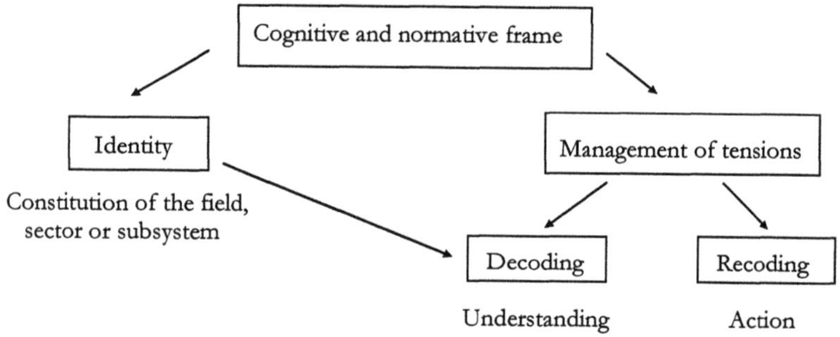

The appropriateness of these cognitive and normative frames, notably for understanding transitional phases where social tensions are revealed which require new adjustments based on new principles, is best represented visually in a simplified form (see Table 2.2). General changes such as in the social division of labour generate tensions in structures and entrenched social values, which in turn lead to new definitions of basic assumptions and to certain behavioural changes. These also imply a new conception of the individual defined as a producer, and the adaptation of different social spaces. Such approaches are located in a developmental, indeed an evolutionary, perspective, which explains why the notion of change is one of their fundamental attributes.

Paradigm Change

The processes discussed above beg a level of questioning, beyond that concerning their components and their dynamics, as to the elements which provoke a break and thereby characterise a shift from one frame to another. If we consider this more closely, what these different models primarily aim to explain are the ways in which change comes about in public policy, and alongside this, the evolution of power relations in a given subsystem of public policymaking. By so doing, they have helped 'relativise' classical approaches to understanding policymaking based on individual rationality, both theoretically and in terms of their explanatory power. Indeed, recognition of the importance of cognitive and normative logics has led to a reconsideration of the traditional conclusions of incrementalist theories (Lindblom 1959). Centred on the idea of a paradigm shift as the bearer of "extraordinary" changes in public policy, these approaches are therefore interested in a complex host of social processes, which oblige most social actors to make radical normative and cognitive adaptations, going beyond the simple and marginal adjustments required by incrementalism. Two tendencies dominate here: that which looks for causes or bearers of change, and the analysis of the various forms of these changes.

Bearers of Change

In the identification of 'elements of rupture' which can instigate a paradigm change, different approaches highlight particular dynamics capable of modifying felt cognitive and normative stability. Two general elements seem able, separately or together, to prompt the development of new global norms, namely, transformations of economic conditions, and/or a serious crisis affecting the subsystem under consideration.

A more or less substantial modification of economic dynamics and structures seems to be one of the principal triggers of crisis, adjustment or production of cognitive or normative frames. Sabatier's model, in part presented in terms of 'systems', thus considers socio-economic variation as one of the possible elements of these "exogenous shocks" which comprise "changes in socio-economic conditions, public opinion, system-wide governing coalition, or policy outputs from other subsystems" and which are "a *necessary, but not sufficient*, cause of change in the *policy core* attributes of a governmental program" (Sabatier 1998, 118, emphasis in original).

To take an example, neo-liberalism may be conceived as a form of response to the economic oil crises of the 1970s, and to more recent economic transformations. At the end of the 19th century, Emile Durkheim identified the phenomenon of anomie, resulting from transformations caused by ruptures to traditional socio-economic structures, in his analysis of the consequences of the social division of labour (Durkheim 1964). Similarly, we can hypothesise that the industrial revolution was gradually able to modify the underlying assumptions and contexts of social exchanges and public policy. However, beyond its detrimental effects, the consequences of the industrial revolution also obliged social actors to rethink the contexts and assumptions of their actions in order to confer meaning and legitimacy on a set of processes which would otherwise have been perceived as problematic.

Another event or series of events which may spark a particularly serious political crisis is war; either with a foreign power or a civil war. This kind of a shock can provoke a trauma leading most political actors to more or less consciously try to make a clean slate of the past, in order to solve the problems perceived as provoking the crisis, and to argue for different institutional frameworks and principles for action. Accordingly, this kind of trauma tends to destroy the prevalent paradigm and can help individuals and organisations to define alternative way of thinking. Thus the wars experienced by France in the 19th century can be understood as catalysts, if not the direct triggers, of important re-evaluations of the fundamental principles upon which socio-political stability was built at the time. In particular, the shock of the defeat of 1940 was a genuine trauma for the French, signalling a change in the way France was viewed in the world, in the guiding principles of state action and in the perception of social hierarchies and legitimate social exchanges.

Elements of the above theories may be used in conjunction with those developed in the work of John Kingdon and John Keeler on "political windows" (Kingdon 1984; Keeler 1993). Analysing the different processes which traditionally characterise public policy, John Kingdon was able to show that the culmination of favourable dynamics may allow the opening of a political window, that is "an opportunity for advocates of proposals to push their pet solutions, or to push attention to their special problems" (Kingdon 1984, 173). Whilst suspending the ordinary conditions of politics, such situations not only permit greater input into agenda-setting but also offer the actors concerned a wider scope for action, which effectively allows them to modify public policy in a non-incremental way. As a result, changes in public policy paradigms are achieved.

Different Ways of Achieving Change

Whilst the analysis of different ways of achieving policy change is at the heart of Peter Hall and Paul Sabatier's work, it is a more marginal consideration for Jobert and Muller. Peter Hall (1993) clearly articulates the main orientations of this shift in the analysis in policymaking which seeks to challenge the conclusions traditionally drawn by public policy analysis. Following Lindblom's work on the contexts of decision-making, which are revealed to be complex to the point of allowing only marginal (incremental) changes in public policy, most research in this area has concluded that the state is relatively unchanging. In practice, political and administrative actors can only advance public policy through what they learn from the environments they are located in, or from their own capacity for action (for a review of the literature on learning, see Bennett and Howlett 1992).

All the approaches to public policy discussed here acknowledge the relevance of these ways of achieving change. This is particularly so for the *advocacy coalition framework* model which, whilst accepting a priori the possibility of change in the *deep core* of belief systems, nonetheless considers this to be extremely rare, Sabatier going as far as to coin it a "religious conversion". The notion of learning appears in the recent works of Bruno Jobert (1994) as a means of modifying the coherence and the degree of generality which formerly characterised the notion of the *référentiel*. More systematically, the theme of learning is also found in two of the ways of achieving a change in public policy isolated by Peter Hall. Here, learning remains a pertinent notion to describe occasional adjustments which affect the "lower" levels of cognitive and normative frames. Speaking of first and second order changes, Hall shows that it is learning which explains instrumental changes in the first order, second order changes mainly concerning "the development of new policy instruments" (Hall 1993, 280).

However, Peter Hall adds the possibility of third-order changes to these traditional mechanisms, which he describes as processes through which "not only were the settings of policy changed but the hierarchy of goals and set of instruments employed to guide policy shifted radically as well" (Hall 1993, 283-4). This is analogous to Kuhn's conceptualisation of a paradigm crisis, such processes thus primarily referring to the growing incapacity felt by actors to view changing social relations according to previous frames.

Concerning public policy programs, a political crisis can consequently come about, characterised by "a phase of public policymaking during which dominant representations no longer succeed in interpreting the development of a social field in a way that satisfies the actors concerned, and can therefore no longer successfully structure and legitimate the action of the State. It is in this sense that a 'political crisis' produces problems [...]" (Muller and Surel 1996, 93). This last notion is close to that of "anomaly" used by Hall with reference to Kuhn's work, which describes the growing incapacity of a given paradigm to manage social tensions or to offer satisfying and/or legitimate public policy solutions, thus reaching a "critical juncture" (Collier and Collier 1991) which itself creates favourable conditions for the more or less substantial re-evaluation of the general or specific principles of the subsystem under consideration. Taking the example of macro-economic policies pursued by the British government in the 1970s in response to the oil crises, Hall shows that the Keynesian strategies employed for counter-cyclical economic revival (primarily boosting demand) produced unintended consequences, due to the combination of inflation and unemployment. The resulting loss of confidence in the Keynesian paradigm as the dominant reference point of macro-economic policy opened the way for the neo-liberal paradigm to take hold (Hall 1992, 1993).

The Multiplicity of Cognitive and Normative Frames

These different elements, relating to the components, the "functions" as well as to the forms of a change of cognitive and normative frames, constitute the principal features of these different conceptualisations. An increasing number of empirical studies informed by these models testifies to their success, which can undoubtedly be explained by their capacity to integrate certain long-standing questions in political science into the field of public policy analysis. In particular they seek an articulation within the antagonistic pairing of conflict and cooperation, which, according to Jean Leca (1997), is the Janus' face of political science. Similarly, such modelling has attempted, more or less explicitly, to construct certain dynamics associated with the dialectical oppositions between thought and action, past and present, continuity and change, order and disorder, unity and division, and so on. Lastly, from the viewpoint of public policy analysis, it has been possible to develop models, separate from those informed by a rationalist position, which are capable of explaining the processes of "extraordinary" change in public policy.

A number of critiques have nonetheless emerged recently, pointing to the problematic implications of these approaches for both empirical and theoretical research. The excessive emphasis on cognitive and cognitive variables as well as the methodological problems they pose (How are cognitive and normative frames to be identified? To what extent are they appropriate to describe the practices of actors and the development of public policy?) have sometimes led to the purely rhetorical use of these notions, underestimating the forms of mobilisation, of diffusion, indeed of instrumentalisation, that these frames have at times been subject to. Isolating the role of cognitive and normative macro-frames effectively poses a problem of identification and explanation of the multiplicity of these principles, values and global representations within different units of analysis, as well as of the hierarchical co-existence of societal paradigms, both old and new. Rather than going no further than the falsely naive statement that the same frame produces varied social usages, it may be more useful to question these differences through the construction of spatial, temporal and even intersectoral comparisons, whilst also seeking to integrate certain variables which have hitherto been neglected or marginalized: the interests of actors, and the role of institutions (Hall 1997).

Constructing a Comparative Analytical Grid

If, for example, we suppose that a nation is a subsystem, each country being subjected to a similar meta-norm (neo-liberalism in the recent past), it may effectively be possible to isolate discrepancies in the diffusion of these societal paradigms. The particular reception of the same societal paradigm in each country allows us to identify and compare the dynamics of the operationalisation of these norms, in part linked to the specific structure of interests and institutional configuration in each national context.

In the course of the 1980s, the same meaning has not been accorded to neo-liberal ideology in France, Britain, the United States and Germany for instance. The particular instrumentalisation of very similar normative inputs has not produced the same cognitive and normative frame in each country. To put this very simply, we could say that the neo-liberal norm was taken on board with relative ease and in full, in the United States and Britain, while it was more strongly contested in France and Germany (Jobert 1994). Likewise, representations of Europe vary from one country to another, beyond the presumed unity of the ideas promoted by EU agencies. The usage of the concept of "Europe", notably in government speeches which seek to legitimate current reforms in monetary policy, varies strongly from one Member State to another, in some in an attempt to justify the status-quo (Britain), others building on it to push forward significant public policy changes (Italy).

The same kind of hypotheses can equally be applied to research based on temporal comparisons (Bartolini 1993). Taking the nation state as the basic unit of analysis, we can seek to construct relatively simple indicators (number of privatisations, financial market reforms etc.) where variations reveal the mechanisms of time-lag between the different countries. Alongside the different modes of adaptation in each country, we find different rhythms, first in the uptake of a new frame, with some countries ahead and others behind, as well as in their diffusion and development. Equipped with such an array of hypotheses, we can for example, draw attention to the relatively early embracing of neo-liberal ideas in the United States, and attempt to isolate the pertinent variables which explain these different forms and sequences of adoption. The turning points, during which a shift seems to occur more quickly, could equally be correlated with certain trigger factors such as a change of government, an "objective" and/or "subjective" worsening of a crisis, or external pressures.

This analytical grid can finally be used to explore intersectoral comparisons, showing how the same global dynamics produce a variety of outcomes according to the sector. Within the same country, certain socio-economic fields are found to be more or less in sync with new cognitive and normative frames. The different processes which result from this may be associated as much with a strategy of closure and/or resistance as with a partial adaptation to global logics, or even a total conversion of the sector to the new precepts, modes of action and instruments implied by the new global *référentiel*.

Such examples show that the spread of new ideas, principles of action and forms of action does not come about in a "revolutionary" way from scientific development, but rather from a more or less radical re-evaluation of ways of legitimising groups and social exchanges, as well as through more or less substantial modifications to legitimate frameworks and forms of public policy. In practice, the penetration of neo-liberal ideas has provoked strong resistance from mechanisms intrinsic to national policy styles, in particular due to the mobilisation of interest groups. Furthermore, such an analysis also reveals the existence of institutional and normative grids specific to each country, which play a part in modifying the substantial content of dominant cognitive and normative frames to ensure their compatibility with the previous structures of exchange and action characteristic of that country.

In seeking to understand the factors which explain these specificities and the various forms of resistance to the same general principles in different countries, Pierson (1997) shows the importance of the influence of the past in the structuring of institutional and normative configurations in each country. He makes use of the notion of "historical causality" developed by Stinchcombe (1968) to shed light on the existence of a logic of "path dependency". This logic includes the processes of the progressive sedimentation of normative and institutional frames of social exchange and public policymaking, a sedimentation which is then able to determine mechanisms of resistance and/or "translation". The implanting of customs within bureaucracies and the enmeshing of interests and values between the groups concerned and administrative departments therefore appear amongst the constitutive factors of institutional, relational and cognitive grids which have a bearing on the penetration of new global cognitive and normative frames.

Factors Underpinning the Variation in Frames

We can attempt to isolate certain elements which account for spatial and/or temporal and/or sectoral differences, arising from the mechanisms of variation of a similar global cognitive and normative frame. Several factors are relevant here, namely (1) the extent and the nature of the previous paradigm, and (2) the institutional configurations specific to each country which act as filters to the dominant paradigm.

(1) The importance of the previous societal paradigm

The emergence of a new frame is not a case of the substitution of one paradigm for another, as Kuhn posits for the natural sciences, but rather occurs through associations and new hierarchical rankings of elements that may already exist. Far from making a clean slate of the past, a new societal paradigm must in effect be composed of previous cognitive and normative structures, which explains possible retranslations of the elements of the frame, possible "delays" from one subsystem to another in the adoption of these new elements, and above all, the mechanisms of resistance a new frame gives rise to. Neither does a dominant paradigm "destroy" previously legitimate frames, rather it comes to constitute the reference point in relation to which these older structures must adapt.

Consequently, the diffusion of a new paradigm gives rise to complex and at times contradictory mechanisms of adaptation. For example, the European Monetary Union was not just an application of a "pure" neo-liberal policy paradigm. On the contrary, Kathleen McNamara was able to show that "the governments of Europe followed a pragmatic, not ideologically purist, type of monetarism" (McNamara, 1998: 67), which was the outcome of the previous policy paradigms and the product of European political leader's bargaining.

(2) Specific institutional configurations

In this general expression, which seeks to integrate interests and institutions in the analysis of cognitive and normative frames, we can bring together the particular political and administrative structures of a country or a sector, the forms of organisation of social exchanges in a particular field, or the judicial framework determining the rules of the game and the hierarchies between actors, the instruments etc. The modes of structuring social exchanges, sometimes institutionalised even within political or administrative departments, comprise a host of factors able to explain both variations in the translation of a particular cognitive and normative frame, and its diverse rhythms of diffusion. Indeed, several authors have underlined the importance of coalitions, arenas and forums, constituted around precise public policies, and formed around a particular paradigm, which are thus able to act as centres of resistance and/or grids modifying the content as well as the progress of a new set of cognitive and normative models (Baumgartner and Jones 1993; Sabatier 1993; Jobert 1994; Radaelli 1998).

Defining the arena as a group of actors sharing particular "orders of comprehension" (taking up this idea from Dunsire 1978), Dudley and Richardson (1996) were able to show how this was so in policies on the development of trunkroads in Britain. The structuring of policies around a number of mechanisms mastered and legitimated by the transport department, engineers, and lorry-drivers' union representatives, allowed the establishment of a kind of protective shield against any outside influence for many years. The enmeshing of the dominant normative and cognitive structures, the institutionalisation of social exchanges in a specific context, and a number of public programs operated as screens to new paradigms, if the "institutions" themselves were not challenged. In the precise case of British trunkroads, it seemed that a transformation of dominant values (increased value placed on the protection of the environment) in conjunction with economic crisis (increase in the cost of fuel, decrease in public investment) contributed to the undoing of the existing coalition and at the same time the displacement of the logics of exchange (integration of new actors, notably environmental groups) and the legitimate cognitive and normative models. Such an example shows the possible succession of forms of change: an incremental logic, when the entrenched institutional and normative grids continue to function; a change of paradigm, associated with internal and/or external destabilisation of these same legitimate grids.

Generally speaking, these notions arise out of the hope to isolate the sites of mobilisation of cognitive and normative frames and to see how the interests of actors and the variable institutionalisation of their relationships tends to modify the content and the scope of a societal paradigm. However, it is not only a question of occasional adjustments to original theorisations, essentially centred on the dynamics of diffusion, as these still leave to one side the question of the modes of production of cognitive and normative frames. How do they emerge in a given field? According to what power relations and what balance of power? Do cognitive and normative frames not sometimes constitute the post-hoc rationalisations for institutional transformations or changes in power relations (cf. on this point, Majone, 1992)?

These sets of problems are undoubtedly less a basis for the rejection of the analytical models discussed here than a starting point for complementary research, as well as a warning against the sometimes excessive use of cognitive approaches. In certain cases, such notions have tended to fuel an invasion of erudite discourse (similar to that concerning the "social construction of reality", cf de Lara 1997). This undoubtedly relates once again to their aptitude for questioning the processes which underpin the dialectics of structure/agency, micro/macro, continuity/change and so on. However, it is perhaps time to make use of the plethora of case studies already conducted to achieve a certain conceptual precision and greater methodological rigour, whilst seeking to integrate previously neglected variables; a step which some authors have already undertaken, modifying and clarifying the content and the scope of their own conceptualisations (cf. Sabatier 1998, 1999; and especially, Hall 1997, 1998).

Acknowledgments

I would like to thank Yves Mény, Patrick Le Galès, Pierre Muller, Bruno Palier and the anonymous reviewers for their comments on earlier versions of this article. I would like to address special thanks to Dawn Lyon for what was much more than a translation.

CHAPTER 3

Paradigms and Political Discourse: Protective Legislation in France and the United States Before 1914[1]

Jane Jenson

Introduction

Social theory has struggled recently to cast off legacies of structuralist analyses that tend towards functionalism. Political economy and political sociology now provide an array of approaches exploring the role of agency. As part of this process they have also turned towards a new type of analysis and approach to history. The first change considers discourses, broadly conceptualized as interpretative frameworks, critical to the process by which social relations are constituted. The second change derives from the assumption that within the constraints of structures, people do make their own history; this alteration shifts the focus to the specificities of patterns of social relations and power among actors in different times and space.

By examining state policies regulating women's behaviour in France and the United States before 1914, defined as laws "protecting" the conditions under which women participated in certain occupations and those providing maternal and infant protection, this article addresses the dialectic between structure and agency. It proposes a conceptualization of the contribution of the politics of both representation and state policy to systems of ongoing social relations and the circumstances of their change. Central to the method is the notion that meaning systems, around which actors constitute collective identities, are a crucial analytic focus. For this reason the article explores the ways in which particular identities were embedded in the societal paradigms that followed from the institutionalization of new social relations in the French and American regimes of accumulation in the late nineteenth century. As welfare programmes began to take shape, stabilization brought new roles for the state. The specifics of such programmes depended in part upon the visions of social relations carried by major actors both inside and outside the state. However, the contribution which actors could make depended not only on the

[1] This is a revised version of a paper presented to the "Seminar on State and Capitalism Since 1800" at the Center for European Studies, Harvard University. Thanks for thoughtful comments on earlier drafts to Greg Albo, Linda Gordon, Peter Hall, Rianne Mahon, Sonya Michel, Mark Neufeld, Sid Tarrow, Sandra Whitworth and the reviewers. Support for this research came from the Social Sciences and Humanities Research Council of Canada, grant 410-86-0238.

strategies adopted but also on the characteristics of the structures within which they lived. Not everything was possible.

The Societal Paradigm and Regulation

Thinking about social relations must begin from analytic scepticism about systemic reproduction. It must ask *how* social relations take on stabilized forms—that is, how regulation occurs—even though these relations are contradictory.[2] The idea that social relations balance between stability and change reflects the fragility of societal reproduction. Yet lengthy periods of economic and social stability do occur, during which a set of institutional forms, procedures and habits reproduce social relations. As such, to the observer's eye they constitute structures. But since social relations are not experienced by actors as structures, we might well ask how it happens that structures of social relations continue across time.

One answer to this query asserts that what the observer apprehends as a structure of social relations is both a structure *and* a terrain in which actors, under constraint to be sure, constantly make their own history. This perspective posits that actors are simultaneously *subjects of structures* and *acting subjects* carrying in their practices and meaning systems the possibilities of both social stability and change.[3] With a notion of the *simultaneity* of subjectivity, the world of experience becomes as "real" as that of structures.[4] While the long-term analytic task is to comprehend the link between the two realities, a first step is to appreciate the "reality" of the realm of action and meaning.

A social relation depends on *both* practices and their meanings. Despite their contradictions, social relations can sometimes be stabilized—that is, be in regulation—because of the set of practices and meanings of actors in that time and place. Understanding social relations in this way makes history open-ended because politi-

---

[2] This theoretical argument comes in part from my elaboration of notions developed within the French regulation approach. For sociological versions, see Alain Lipietz, *Mirages and Miracles* (London: Verso, 1987); Alain Lipietz, "Rebel Sons: The Regulation Approach," *French Politics and Society* 5 (1987), 3-17; and Alain Lipietz, "Building an Alternative Movement in France," *Rethinking Marxism* 1 (1988), 2-17.

[3] Three fallacies which derive from not acknowledging this simultaneity have plagued social theory. The first fallacy is the denial of any dilemma by arguing that structures create subjects or subjects create structures. Advocates of both positions have been hegemonic at different points in time. A second fallacy involves admitting both structural effects and agency, but then seeking actors capable of recognizing the effects of structures and "escaping" to become the agents of historical change. From this perspective, only some actors are capable of imagining change while others are destined to be no more than unconscious, albeit perhaps unwilling, supporters of existing structures. Accepting that all actors are capable of being acting subjects—but only sometimes—is the third fallacy. The argument of this article rejects all three positions.

[4] This distinction can be called one between two worlds, the esoteric world of structures and the exoteric realm of everyday life, or Marx's "enchanted world." See Alain Lipietz, *The Enchanted World: Inflation, Credit and the World Crisis* (London: Verso, 1985), especially chap. 1.

cal action contributes to social relations being in regulation or in crisis. A search for understanding social relations might begin, then, in the realm of politics.

Politics in capitalist democracy involves representation, which is in part the social construction of collective identities. Actors bearing collective identities attempt to carve out a constituency for themselves. Out of this process comes the mobilization of interests, which are also social constructions. The politics of representation necessarily entails conflict because it involves disputes over which collective identities will achieve represention. Resolution of basic questions about who the main protagonists are to be, in turn, places broad limits on the definition of interests. Politics therefore involves the formation of collective identities as much as it entails conflict among groups and organizations over disputed claims about who gets what, when and how.

The terrain on which actors struggle for representation is the *universe of political discourse,* a space in which socially-constructed identities emerge in discursive struggle. As actors with a variety of collective identities co-exist in the universe of political discourse, their practices and meaning systems jostle with each other for social attention and legitimacy. At issue are conflicts over the represention and reproduction of power relations based on difference. In any social formation a multitude of relationships of difference exist. Age, sex, race, property ownership, workplace activities and language are but a few of the differences which might take on social meaning. In many cases, inequality of power accompanies recognition of difference. For example, the recognition of childhood is usually accompanied by the subordination of children to adults. The recognition of racial difference has led to the evils of racism. Nevertheless, it is also obvious that the mere existence—or even recognition—of difference does not automatically lead to congealment of a system of unequal power. Such a system is socially constructed. Thus, progressive social forces have struggled against the divisive effects of racism and property ownership in the name of equality, positing a universality of human dignity against inequities of power structured around these differences. Similarly, sexual difference may cross all other relations, such that things female are subordinated to things male, or such a process of differentiation may be effaced through the political actions of resistance in the name of equality in difference. Therefore, we must always ask which specific differences are politicized and how they are politicized.

Answering this question demonstrates that not all collective identities can gain attention because actors are not equally powerful in their own social contexts. Indeed, actors frequently depend for their influence on their ability to contribute to the institutionalization of meaning systems, through a *societal paradigm.*[5] A societal pa-

---

[5] The term derives from grammar, where a paradigm links different forms of the same root, thereby ordering difference and demonstrating connections across forms which might not otherwise appear linked. The best-known use of the concept in social science is by T. S. Kuhn who suggests that paradigms are historical constructs, whose selection from a range of possible paradigms is based on struggle for allegiances. Paradigms illuminate the world until the contradictions which

radigm is a shared set of interconnected premises which make sense of many social relations. Every paradigm contains a view of human nature, a definition of basic and proper forms of social relations among equals and among those in relationships of hierarchy, and specification of relations among institutions as well as a stipulation of the role of such institutions. Thus, a societal paradigm is a meaning system as well as a set of practices. If a paradigm's set of interconnected premises comes to be widely shared as the result of a social *compromise*, such a paradigm is hegemonic.

Societal paradigms are not always hegemonic, however. Indeed, the constitution of a hegemonic paradigm is one factor which establishes whether social relations are in regulation or in crisis. If a hegemonic societal paradigm exists, competing identities will make little headway. As contradictions intensify, however, the previously hegemonic societal paradigm will no longer provide an account of emerging conditions; actors may adopt competing collective identities because they make better sense of the new situation. Periods of crisis are likely to be moments of efflorescence in the universe of political discourse, since competing actors who bear a variety of collective identities may successfully struggle to extend the reach of their representational systems. If the crisis evolves into a set of social relations in regulation, a new societal paradigm is likely to accompany it and to contain some contribution from actors who gained new representational strength in the universe of political discourse during the crisis.

Since a hegemonic societal paradigm incorporates contenders for representational power in any social formation through a process of inclusion and exclusion, only some identities can be constituted within a societal paradigm. Yet, competing meanings for the same power relation may continue to exist in the universe of political discourse, perpetuated by the practices of actors who are excluded from the societal compromise and whose influence is marginal. This marginality exists because, once constituted, the effect of a hegemonic social paradigm is like a shadow cast back into the universe of political discourse, leaving in darkness and invisibility any identities not included within its terms and blurring into invisibility power relations whose meanings can not be seized. Those contenders for political and ideological influence included in the hegemonic paradigm can recognize themselves because they have an identity *and* can be recognized by others.

The constitution of a hegemonic societal paradigm, within which only some collective identities are represented, is the product of politics in its broadest sense. Any number of institutions—ranging from political parties, trade unions and other social movements to the varied apparatus of the state, churches and scientific establishments—may be identified as the multiple sites of its constitution. Therefore, as a

they can no longer absorb permit other scientists to imagine an alternative and gain support for that vision. See T. S. Kuhn, *The Structure of Scientific Revolutions* (Chicago: University of Chicago Press, 1970).

hegemonic paradigm enters into crisis, political expression of its crisis will differ across social formations as will competition among identities.[6]

This section has focussed on the world of lived relations, of subjectivities experienced in representations both to oneself and to others. The emphasis was chosen to underline the place of this kind of subjectivity, rather than to deny the real importance of ongoing structures which provide the constraints within which agents make history. Since the latter are also part of the story, this essay should be read more as one of retrieval than as complete in itself. Nevertheless, it should be clear that accepting the argument as proposed involves rejecting the proposition that identities are imposed by structures, whether these structures are labelled capitalism or patriarchy.

Representations of Gender: Workplace and Infant Protection

At the end of the nineteenth century both France and the United States underwent a fundamental restructuring of economic relations. France was finally industrializing, while the US was becoming the industrial model for the world. As a result, both countries experienced a moment of profound uncertainty. Much jostling over representation characterized the universe of political discourse because a hegemonic societal paradigm, making sense of new conditions and ordering the relationships of social actors, did not exist but was, as we can see in hindsight, under construction.

French and American politicians and social activists spoke in apocalyptic terms of social instabilities while reformers campaigned for state regulation of the effects of urbanization, immigrant labour forces, declining birth rates, restructuring industry and economic uncertainty. A consequence of this ferment was that the universe of political discourse in both countries was rich in competing representations of identities. By the first years of the twentieth century, however, social relations had become more stabilized and identities combined in paradigmatic forms which endured for much of this century.

Out of these two situations of economic restructuring came state policies which contained quite dissimilar representations of social relations. In particular, there were variations in the gendering effects of the two hegemonic paradigms which eventually took form. In France, prevalent gender identities included the assumption that economic activity of both single and married women was valid. French state policies reflected this assumption and facilitated the dual roles of worker and mother. Legislation protecting working women and their infants developed within the labour code, mirroring a certain consensus that even if women workers were not exactly the same as men, women *were* nonetheless workers. In the US, by way of contrast, state policies did not reflect the same assumption about the possibility

[6] Jane Jenson, "'Different' but not 'Exceptional': Canada's Permeable Fordism," *Canadian Review of Sociology and Anthropology* 26 (1989), 69-94, explores such variations for Canadian politics.

of combining two roles; "two-channel" programmes took form, addressing men as workers and women as mothers.[7] The remainder of this article explicates this difference through an examination of the history of workplace and infant protection in the two countries: it focusses on actors' strategies which culminated in hegemonic societal paradigms after a moment of economic restructuring.

In both countries, infant mortality and public health were major social problems connected not only to labour force needs and national honour but to more general fears about social instability. By the late nineteenth century French demographers had announced a dramatic decrease in the birth rate. Many concerned groups considered depopulation a threat to the nation, particularly in the event of another war with Germany. The American birth rate also declined throughout the nineteenth century so that by the 1890s, only France had a lower rate.

In 1913 France legislated prenatal and compulsory postnatal leave for women working in industrial and commercial establishments. Most importantly, the bill mandated a daily allowance to compensate for lost wages during eight weeks before and after childbirth to women of French nationality who habitually worked for wages outside the home as workers, employees or domestics, if their personal means were limited.[8]

The explanation for infant mortality preferred by French demographers and policy experts was an overly hasty return to work by new mothers because of their poverty rather than the maternal occupation per se.[9] The decision to provide paid leaves reflected a widely held assumption that women's paid labour, even after marriage and during childbearing years, was widespread, inevitable and even desirable. Yet, something had to be done so that women could combine productive and reproductive activities. Representatives of capital, revolutionary and reformist workers' organizations, nationalists, social Catholics and feminists all united around a discourse which emphasized the nation's needs and demanded state policy.[10]

Other programmes for infant health also reflected efforts to reconcile work and childbearing. For example, municipalities trying to reduce child abandonment and thus raise the birth rate (since so many children left to asylums died quickly), aided poor mothers whether they were single or married, but always intended that women

[7] Barbara Nelson, "The Gender, Race, and Class Origins of Early Welfare Policy and the Welfare State: A Comparison of Workmen's Compensation and Mothers' Aid," paper presented to the Colloquium on Gender and the Origins of the Welfare State, Center for European Studies, Harvard University, November 1987.

[8] Mary Lynn McDougall, "Protecting Infants: The French Campaign for Maternity Leaves, 1890s-1913," *French Historical Studies* 13 (1983), 79-105; and Françoise Thébaud, "Donner la vie: Histoire de la maternité en France entre les deux guerres" (unpublished Thèse de Troisième cycle, Paris VII, 1982).

[9] For details of this analysis see Jane Jenson, "Gender and Reproduction: Or, Babies and the State," *Studies in Political Economy* 20 (1986), 17-18.

[10] McDougall, "Protecting Infants," 92.

would continue to earn their own living.[11] Moreover, reformers attending the first International Congress of *Gouttes de Lait* in Paris in 1905 clearly understood that poor women in the paid labour force were primarily in need of pure milk for their babies.[12]

Infant health also concerned reformers who advocated regulation of the hours of women's work. In 1892 the French legislature limited women's work to 11 hours per day, including an hour of rest, and prohibited night work. An extension in 1900 covered men working in the same unit of production.[13] Reducing women's hours was part of the strategy of the labour movement to win reductions for everyone, in a campaign that was a direct response to the effects of economic restructuring and social problems. According to the unions, an eight-hour day would alleviate structural unemployment, reduce the psychological and physical stress of labour processes for unskilled workers, eliminate overproduction, increase time for family life (in particular by giving the father more time with his family) and result in healthier workers.[14] But it was not only the labour movement which advocated reduced hours. Social Catholics and radical republicans, including employers, also argued that a general reduction of working time would increase efficiency and productivity while helping families.[15]

Embedded in the discussion was the notion that shorter hours would enable women to do housework and look after their children better. Giving families more time together provided a core theme for the labour movement and for business, which saw social peace and national well-being as hostage to long hours which left children unsupervised, homes disrupted (thus encouraging men to seek solace in the café), and infants without proper food.[16] The goal was always to gain this

---

[11] In the Department of the Seine (Paris) by the late 1880s, municipal officials were willing to pay a poor mother the entire cost of a wet nurse (the same amount as the average weekly wage of an unskilled working woman) in order to discourage unmarried mothers from giving up their babies. The remainder of the costs of maintaining the mother and child were to be paid for by the earned income of the mother, however. See Rachel Fuchs, "Morality and Poverty: Public Welfare for Mothers in Paris, 1870-1900," *French History 2* (1988), 290-94, 304.

[12] John B. Blake, "Origins of Maternal and Child Health Programs," in Barbara G. Rosencrantz (ed.). *The Health of Women and Children* (New York: Arno, 1977), 21.

[13] For a detailed description of these regulations, see Marilyn Boxer, "Protective Legislation and Home Industry: The Marginalization of Women Workers in Late Nineteenth- and Early Twentieth-Century France," *Journal of Social History* 20 (1986), 46-47.

[14] Gary S. Cross, "The Quest for Leisure: Reassessing the Eight-Hour Day in France," *Journal of Social History* 18(1984), 198-99.

[15] Mary Lynn McDougall, "Paternalism, Patriarchy and Protection: The Rhetoric of Labor Reform, 1880s and 1890s," paper presented to the Annual Meeting of French Historical Studies, Columbia, South Carolina, March 1988, 4-5.

[16] This citation from a subsequent union campaign to protect the eight-hour day captures the theme of the movement: "... if the eight-hour day was lost, not only would wages decrease but the worker would 'lose dignity,' would not be able to educate himself or his family and women would

reform for all workers, and gaining it for women was celebrated as a breach which would necessarily widen.

The development of "protective" legislation in the US took a quite different course, since trade unions did not lead a movement for legislating reduced hours. The craft-dominated American Federation of Labor preferred a collective bargaining strategy, winning employer by employer; indeed, by the late nineteenth century many unionized male workers had negotiated reduced hours. It was therefore left to those parts of the reform movement which were concerned with the social conditions of women, among whom feminists were a most prominent segment, to advocate legislative restriction of women's hours and occupations.

Protection of women had an uneven history until the landmark case of *Muller* v. *Oregon,* which was decided by the Supreme Court in 1908 and provided justification for differential treatment of women and men workers.[17] This view of protection emerged in a period when liberalism was at it height in American legal doctrine. Freedom of contract, set out in the similarly landmark case of *Lochner* v. *New York* in 1905, dominated the Court's position on labour relations.[18] Since *Lochner* had found it "unreasonable" to limit the hours of work of male bakers, the National Consumers' League and Louis Brandeis (who prepared the arguments in the *Muller* case) were forced to argue within the Court's discourse, demonstrating that limitation of women's hours was, by contrast, "reasonable." They marshalled statistical and anecdotal material from around the world to demonstrate that long hours and night work harmed women's long-term health. This strategy of argument, which was labelled the Brandeis Brief, made two arguments: first, drawing from the emerging scientific literature on work, it claimed there was a link between fatigue, overwork and low productivity so that shorter hours were simply more efficient. A second claim was that long hours and night work threatened the "mothers of future generations."[19] The Supreme Court adopted the second view, writing into the *Muller* decision the notion that there were innate differences between women and men, thus permitting women's protection even if it infringed on freedom of contract.[20] However, the *Lochner* decision held for men, with their different biology and social responsibilities.

Maternal and infant protection also entered into debates about limiting women's hours and occupations. The Brandeis Brief prominently discussed the effects of

---

have 'to return to the slavery of housework after a longer workday.'" See Cross, "The Quest for Leisure," 202.

[17] *Muller* v. *Oregon,* 208 U.S. 412.

[18] Lochner v. New York, 198 U.S. 45.

[19] Susan Lehrer, *Origins of Protective Labor Legislation for Women, 1905-1925* (Albany: State University of New York Press, 1987), 20, 34.

[20] Ann Corinne Hill, "Protection of Women Workers and the Courts: A Legal Case History," *Feminist Studies* 5 (1979), 253.

long hours and night work on infant mortality rates.[21] Nevertheless, the US did not develop leaves, paid or unpaid, for either pregnant women or new mothers despite the concern for the birth rate expressed during the First World War:

> *The belief that motherhood was woman's primary mission could have been used as an argument in support of federal maternity benefits. The same belief, however, was a rationale for ignoring the plight of women who could not take time off from work to recuperate or to nurse, or who feared they would lose their jobs if they did so. Women who were both mothers and workers were not supposed to exist. They were invisible.*[22]

As maternity leaves fell by the wayside, American attention turned to infant protection and reformers directed their efforts towards infant care through two kinds of initiatives. One provided pure or sterilized milk through a system of milk stations. The other involved programmes to purify the milk supply as a whole. Both philanthropists and state officials promoted these efforts.[23] Such programmes clearly reflect the invisibility of working mothers. Using philanthropic or municipal milk stations as the primary mechanism for reaching new mothers assumed that women were free in the daytime to visit the station and to pass time following its programmes. Just as in other programmes such as Mother's Aid, then, policies of infant and maternal protection contributed to the institutionalization of two channels of state welfare, one for working men and one for mothers.[24] Women who crossed the boundaries—working mothers—found no programmes to meet their needs.

In France, the process of gendering involved an assumption that women worked. In addition to paid maternity leaves, reformers agitated for nursing rooms in factories, as well as creches and organized instructional programmes in factories during the daytime and in neighbourhoods during the evenings. In the US, however, assumptions about gender made working mothers invisible and encouraged state policies that separated the channels shaping women and men's social roles. How can we understand this cross-national difference in the representation of gender relations and the gendering effects of state policies? Why did two states in similar

---

[21] Judith A. Baer, The Chains of Protection: The Judicial Response to Women's Labor Legislation (Westport: Greenwood Press, 1978), 61.

[22] Richard W. Wertz and Dorothy C. Wertz, *Lying-in: A History of Childbirth in America* (New York: Free Press, 1977), 224. In 1916, the American Association for Labor Legislation proposed federal maternity benefits modelled on northern European examples. Any woman earning less than $100 a month (that is, most women working for wages) would have received two-thirds of her wages plus free medical care for two weeks before and six weeks after delivery, on the condition that she did not work in that period. The law did not pass.

[23] Blake, "Origins of Maternal and Child Health Programs," 13-18; and Wertz and Wertz, *Lying-in*, 202.

[24] Mothers' Aid pensions, which some states began by 1911, marked a shift in anti-poverty policy away from day nurseries and other programmes which permitted mothers to work and toward programmes which foreclosed the category of working mother. See Sonya Michel, "From Civic Usefulness to Federal Maternalism," paper presented to the Berkshire Conference of Women's Historians, Wellesley College, June 1987.

periods of social uncertainty develop quite different policies directed towards working women and mothers?

Gendering Effects in the Politics of the Third Republic

The nineteenth century in France brought economic upheaval. Agricultural and craft production remained economically and politically central but industrialization did proceed, although slowly and under the control of paternalistic capitalists who were unwilling to countenance workers' organizations. Industrial production, export growth and the expansion of wage labour initially occurred under a system of competitive regulation in a context of economic and political liberalism.[25] But competitive regulation could not endure. By the end of the century political parties, trade unions and social movements, including a feminist movement, shifted political discourse towards the identity of *citizen-producer,* a shift anchored in new forms of political organization as well as economic modernization and an expanded role for the state.

The consolidation of a common discourse into a hegemonic paradigm followed from diagnoses of the social and economic instability and misery which the French labelled the "social question." Numerous politicians, trade unionists, feminists, social theorists and state experts who explored social conditions in Paris and other cities discovered misery, squalor, immorality, starvation, prostitution and infant mortality, all considered to be symptoms of a severe social problem. Competitive regulation seemed to be digging its own grave.[26]

Social observers pointed to the failure of the wage system to pay women enough to support even themselves; women with children were in substantially worse straits. Thus, poverty itself became gendered; women's poverty represented everyone's poverty and feminized misery loomed as a crucible of social instability.[27] Concern about saving the children of the poverty-stricken, which had prompted state facilities for abandoned children as well as childcare for working women in state nursery schools *(écoles maternelles),* fed into hysteria about national decline after the loss to Germany. A sense that the social changes of the nineteenth century and

---

[25] For half a century the 1791 *Loi de Chapelier* by codifying an "atomistic" labour market prevented wage-earners from defending their interests. By the end of the century it was replaced by a set of institutions and actors representing a more collectively-determined wage relation. See Robert Boyer, "Wage Formation in Historical Perspective: The French Experience," *Cambridge Journal of Economics* 3 (1979), 106.

[26] In the debates about pauperism and pauperization in the nineteenth century, three issues were intertwined: the inevitable growth of wage labour, the inadequacy of workers' wages and their aleatory character which maintained workers in a situation of uncertainty. See Henri Hatzfeld, *Du Paupérisme à la sécurité sociale: Essai sur les origines de la sécurité sociale en France, 1850-1940* (Paris: Armand Colin, 1971), 25.

[27] Joan Scott, "'L'Ouvrière! Mot impie, sordide...' Women workers in the Discourse of French Political Economy, 1840-1860," in Patrick Joyce (ed.), *The Historical Meaning of Work* (Cambridge: Cambridge University Press, 1987), 119-42.

the liberal ideology which had given meaning to it were at the root of the problem informed popular and expert perceptions of the real decline in population size. Therefore, within the concern about depopulation was an analytic link to competitive regulation of the economy and lack of social services.

As industrialization reshaped France's geography and economic relations and as changing imperial relations altered its international position, national identity needed redefinition. For some *la France* was a country of native-born Frenchmen and their loyal wives but this vision trembled before an industrializing France in which land was less legitimate as a source of wealth, in which factory employment brought all sorts of "foreign influence" and in which workers demanded more power. For others, the national identity could only embrace and control such restructuring. The resolution of the competition came with a specific social compromise which recognized the terrifying and destructive aspects of urbanization and industrialization and tried to ameliorate them; it broadened the notion of citizenship and politics to incorporate immigrants and new social strata and fostered a new political form, the political party based on mass mobilization. This compromise brought some consolidation of democratic politics and the defeat of conservative nationalism by the combined forces of radicals, radical-socialists and socialists, whose different names were only "des prénoms: le nom de famille est républicain."[28] French statism also acquired new meaning.

The Dreyfus Affair was symbolically important because at that moment a large segment of the French petite bourgeoisie, the linchpin of the new politics, detached itself from the clerically-based nationalism which had so influenced the first decades of the Third Republic.[29] The resolution of that conflict announced the political compromise that made a paradigm containing the universalizing identity of citizen-producer hegemonic. Unions, co-operatives, professional societies and single-issue movements contributed to it, granting support to important social and labour policies which gave some stability to relations both in the workplace and in the broader society.[30] While the consensus remained fragile, it did exist. Third Republic politics could deal with workers' political mobilization in ways that earlier regimes could not, although the dominance of the petite bourgeoisie and paternalistic capital meant that workers' organizations remained on the margins of politics.

---

[28] Madeleine Rebérioux, Christiane Dufrancatel and Béatrice Slama, "Hubertine Auclert et la question des femmes à 'l'immortel congrès' (1879)," *Romantisme: Revue du dix-neuvième siècle* 13-14 (1976), 48.

[29] At this time traditional Catholicism was ejected from the social compromise, although social Catholicism which was willing to accept the Republic did join the consensus. See Madeleine Rebérioux, *La République radicale? 1898-1914* (Paris: Seuil, 1975), 83-87.

[30] One testimony to economic stabilization is the synchronization of wage levels and cost of living which developed by the end of the nineteenth century. See Boyer, "Wage Formation in Historical Perspective," 107. On the stabilizing effects of social policies see John Weiss, "Origins of the French Welfare System: Poor Relief in the Third Republic, 1871-1914," *French Historical Studies* 13 (1983), 47-78.

One important consequence of the social construction of these practices and meanings was that they carried within them mechanisms of gendering which shaped and limited women's identities. Seeking their own political and social emancipation—their own access to citizenship in particular—French women could adopt these identities. Prior to the consolidation of the paradigm, the universe of political discourse contained a range of feminist positions which jostled each other to shape meaning systems and feminist politics for the next century. The feminist movement, reconstituted after the defeat of the Paris Commune in 1871, was very pluralistic. Nevertheless, feminists who were comfortable with the identity of citizen-producer and who could manipulate its discourse were most influential within the movements for social reform; it was those elements of feminism which contributed to the total reform package. For example, one strand of feminism, led by Leon Richer and Maria Deraismes insisted that feminism was reasonable, realistic and centred on the reform of civil rights. It demanded equality in order to allow women to fulfil their obligations as wives and mothers, as well as to receive a better education and to exercise an "interesting" profession.[31] Political rights were not central to this feminism, which focussed more on extending women's civil rights in a society that, under the terms of the Civil Code, made the husband the patriarchal head of the family unit. Other strands of feminism which were closer to the workers' movement demanded education, better working conditions and higher wages for women. But the partisan left feared that female suffrage would help the right and the Church; hence parties of the left adopted very convoluted positions on the suffrage issue.

It was in large part the ability of feminists to speak to or in the discourse of their allies which determined the influence of feminism in the universe of political discourse. Those strands of feminism which fit the vision of republican men (demanding, for example, secular education for girls, expanded civil rights for married women or protection of infants for the nation) or of socialist men (demanding, for example, unionization, higher wages and protection of all workers) fared best. Those feminists for whom political rights were a central goal found few allies and were marginal to the societal paradigm in which political rights remained unabashedly male.[32] One effect of this balance of power within the women's movement was that pre-1914 feminists paid a good deal of attention to the conditions of women's work but relatively less attention to their right to vote.

As a movement of resistance, however, the fate of feminism rested not only on the actions of women but also on the practices of the movement's political allies and their understanding of gender relations. Indeed, French feminists were on the margin of contemporary debates; they depended on these allies to carry their voices

[31] Rebérioux et al., "Hubertine Auclert et la question des femmes," 133.

[32] Hubertine Auclert represented this strand. Her socialist feminism advocating complete equality including suffrage failed because republicans feared female suffrage would reinforce the church and thus bring about the political defeat of republican forces. See ibid.

and demands into policy arenas. One of these allies was the labour movement, which was an active promoter of both protection for working mothers and of reduced hours for all workers.

By the beginning of the twentieth century, the French labour movement had moved beyond a simple protectionist position and towards revolutionary syndicalism, which contained a broader and more egalitarian discourse on women's role. Committed to a class revolutionary stance and confronted with rising rates of female employment and with the frequent preference of capitalists for female rather than male workers, the Confederation Generale du Travail (CGT) moved to organize women in the paid labour force. The Couriau Affair was a crucial turning point for the labour movement. In this 1913 controversy, the upper levels of the CGT disciplined the Lyon Printers' Federation for denying union membership to a female printer, Emma Couriau, and for expelling her husband because he refused to forbid her to seek work and union membership. The dispute was resolved only after the intervention of feminists and the national labour movement in what had been a local controversy.

The resolution of the Couriau Affair in the direction of equality and acceptance of working women's rights was tremendously influential within the labour movement.[33] No longer did unions or their political allies systematically promote policies based on an assumption that women's employment was "unnatural." As debates on infant protection and legislation concerning hours of work revealed to French unions and the social reformers close to them, the world which people imagined was one in which women were not necessarily confined to the home. Instead, the imagined ideal was one in which there was sufficient time for both work and family, for leisure and home life. As political struggle shaped a hegemonic societal paradigm that was being institutionalized out of the conflict *between* organizing labour and other economic actors over the social place to be granted workers, and out of the conflict *within* the labour movement over the form its organization would take, there occurred a process of gendering. Struggle within the labour movement resulted in consequential choices about gender relations and these choices had implications for the identity which working women might adopt.

But it was not only unions and left-wing parties which contributed gendering effects. Politics in the Third Republic was very much an expression of the economic position of the petite bourgeoisie which was engaged in craft and agricultural production as well as shopkeeping. One key petit bourgeois philosophy was Solidarism, which united the political organizations of that class with the growing corps of state experts, university-based social theorists and reforming Catholics influenced

[33] Charles Sowerwine, "Workers and Women in France before 1914: The Debate over the Couriau Affair," *Journal of Modern History* 55 (1983), 411-41; and Marie-Hélène Zylberberg-Hocquard, *Féminisme et syndicalisme en France* (Paris: Anthropos, 1978).

by *Rerum Novarum.*[34] In brief, Solidarism stressed the reciprocal rights and duties of citizens and the state. Citizens owed loyalty to each other and ultimately to the state because of their interdependence (solidarity) and society, composed of these links of rights and duties, resembled a contract. In this way, the philosophy of Solidarism provided reformers with a rationale for early social programmes and laid the foundation of state welfare.

The society envisaged by this social theory was very different from that of either pure liberalism or class society.[35] Solidarism described a society of collectivities rather than individuals, of families rather than classes. Associative action in mutualism, syndicalism and co-operatives was central to Solidarism, as was the idea of the family as the basic social unit. Moreover, given the family practices of the social groups to which Solidarism appealed, the notion of working women was quite natural. In agriculture, small shops and artisans' workshops, production depended on wives' and daughters' contributions. Such a family-centred philosophy did not promote assumptions that women should be economically inactive.

A direct consequence of the social compromise of the late nineteenth century was the shaping of bourgeois feminism. The "solution" of Solidarism and the left-centre alliance which came out of the Dreyfus Affair gave life to women's identity as citizen-producer. Bourgeois feminists acted in a political situation in which philosophies of individualism were overwhelmed by fears of excessive liberalism and the social costs of a laissez-faire state. The Solidarist solution to the social problem of nineteenth-century France effectively undermined any feminism which would have pushed for the simple equality of women; such an idea was not legitimate within the hegemonic paradigm. Thus, although organizations did exist which advocated such a reform and although the identity of independent women therefore did exist within the universe of political discourse, the position had little representational power to make its identity visible and its organization viable.

Instead, the only viable French feminism in this period was that which joined the alliance of radical republicans out of its support for freemasonry, anticlericalism or the Rights of Man (which continued to exclude women). In that alliance, however, the position of women was contradictory. On the one hand, their male colleagues did support emancipatory reforms and instituted some important changes. On the other hand, the social doctrine which provided the glue for the elements of the paradigm assigned a separate and not necessarily equal role to women as it elevated the family to the status of fundamental social unit.

Therefore, feminists were caught in a dilemma. If they wished to improve women's situation, which was after all their primary goal, they were required to operate within a paradigm which recognized them and had to use the prevailing discourse. But using the discourse of the paradigmatic identity of citizen-producer helped to

---

[34] J. E. S. Hayward, "The Official Social Philosophy of the French Third Republic: Léon Bourgeois and Solidarism," *International Review of Social History,* 6 (1961), 19-48.
[35] Weiss, "Origins of the French Welfare System," 57.

reproduce this identity, thereby confirming that women's duty was to produce children for the *patrie*.[36] It was never the case that children were to be the only product of women, however; women would and should be economically productive. The identity of citizen-producer could be adopted by women who saw themselves as both workers and mothers; such state policies as infant protection and limitations on hours of work sustained this identity, reproducing gender relations in which women's place was in the family although not necessarily in the home. In the terms of the paradigm, working women like working men owed their first loyalty to the family and through it to the state. Other more individualistic collective identities disappeared from view. Present as alternatives in the past, these identities continued to live in the shadow world of the universe of political discourse as did more critical class identities, to be activated later as the contradictions of the new mode of regulation intensified.

Gendering Effects in the United States Before 1914

The lack of workplace recognition of unions made party politics and legislative reforms crucial routes to reform in France, where a highly centralized state left little space for regional variation. In the US federalism and a political ideology of liberalism encouraged a "state of courts and parties" in which legislatures were less important as organizers of politics than were the courts, especially the Supreme Court.[37] By the last decade of the nineteenth century the United States was the world's first industrial power; manufacturing was generating more national income than agriculture. Such industrialization brought immigration, urbanization and the development of a huge mass market. Political and economic uncertainty accompanied these developments and a hegemonic societal paradigm did not exist. Instead, the universe of political discourse contained a wide variety of potential responses to these unsettled conditions by actors jostling for attention and power.

The American courts played a substantial role in this process. Although they recognized that the continent-wide scale of economic order might require new governing authority, the courts did not lay aside the mantle of rational policymaker. Therefore, any efforts at reform would engage the courts which had appropriated for themselves the right to act as economic arbiters. All efforts to make the state more subject to legislative or bureaucratic control had to pass through the courts and were therefore subject to its definition of proper state involvement.[38]

---

[36] Feminists did insist that women's rights had to be expanded if women were to perform their duties; as well, they demanded improvements in the conditions of maternity, women's education and working conditions. See Karen Offen, "Depopulation, Nationalism and Feminism in Fin-de-Siècle France," *American Historical Review* 89 (1984), 652.

[37] Stephen Skowronek, Building a New American State: The Expansion of National Administrative Capacities, 1877-1920 (Cambridge: Cambridge University Press, 1982), 39-46.

[38] Ibid, 166.

The impact of this requirement to work within the terms of the courts is very clear in the case of legislation regulating women's hours and occupations. As described above, the *Muller* decision was grounded in a discourse of difference, specifically biological difference between women and men. Only with that argumentation was the Supreme Court willing to by-pass its standard of "freedom of contract." Efforts by the National Consumers' League or other reform groups to introduce workplace regulation foundered on the Court's insistence on upholding its definition of laissez-faire liberalism.

Nevertheless, this was a moment of political change out of which eventually emerged a newly strengthened central government. In the process, a large number of actors jockeyed for position to define the future of American politics and state/society relations. Out of that jostling in a moment of economic and social restructuring came a hegemonic societal paradigm which was doubly bifurcated around an identity of *specialized citizens*. The first dichotomy was between workplace and political identities, as the realms of work and politics were separated.[39] This was in many ways a classic paradigm of liberal democracy, dividing the world functionally so that the economy and politics appeared to be separate entities. Economic relations were to follow "market principles" while distributive politics was rationalized to be an improvement of the market at the margin when distortions occurred. Thus, the state was to function as an inspector, limit monopolies and provide help for those who could not compete. In addition, this paradigm incorporated much optimism about technological progress and the mutability of economic and social conditions through the application of science and technology.

A second dichotomy divided the political realm, driving a gender cleavage deep into notions of citizenship. Whereas in France in these years the fundamental social unit was the family, headed by men in whom exclusive political rights resided, emerging concepts of American women's citizenship were individualist but founded on "difference." They transferred into politics and especially into new social programmes notions of female qualities of nurture and maternity which had earlier sustained a strict gender divide between "private" and "public" realms. In this way, the two channels for state welfare which addressed men as workers and women as unremunerated mothers were established as feminist reformers and their allies pressed for new state action. Once the societal paradigm of specialized citizenship was in place, it became very difficult for other identities for women or for a more egalitarian feminism to gain representational legitimacy, living as they did at the margins of the universe of political discourse.

The feminist movement as a whole contributed important terms to the doubly-bifurcated paradigm of specialized citizenship. Feminism in the early twentieth cen-

[39] Martin Shefter, "Trade Unions and Political Machines: The Organization and Disorganization of the American Working Class in the Late Nineteenth Century," in Ira Katznelson and Aristide Zolberg (eds.), *Working-Class Formation: Nineteenth-Century Patterns in Western Europe and the United States* (Princeton: Princeton University Press, 1986), 197-276.

tury extended the emphasis of the nineteenth-century women's movement on equal rights by stressing programmes and practices to increase women's individuality.[40] Feminists made use of a complicated discourse. They argued for a common human condition as the legacy of and the founding rock of their liberalism; out of that argument came the claim for citizenship rights, especially suffrage. Simultaneously, however, feminists employed a discourse of difference which described and even defined women as more nurturing, more maternal, more caring than men.[41] The injection of this female perspective into the political world would improve it immensely, they insisted, and therefore women needed the vote. By making group claims to citizenship, feminists were identifying women as an important segment of the American political process, one which had hitherto been excluded but which deserved a place.

The gendering effects of the doubly-bifurcated paradigm made women's identity depend on their position within the nation as mothers of the future generation and as citizens with a different responsibility to the collectivity than men. Citizenship was gendered, in other words, along biological lines. Women were highly visible, both as the proponents of state welfare reform and as objects of reform but their identity was overdetermined by their potential for maternal nurturing, in both the private and the public realms.

The birth control movement was an important source of this discourse which identified motherhood as women's vocation. Women reformers had long sought control over reproduction; this goal was more widely shared than even the vote.[42] Yet, by the first decades of the twentieth century voluntary motherhood was attacked as contributing to race suicide.[43] Middle-class women who tried to control their reproduction were accused of contributing to the decline of Yankee stock and the values on which "the nation had been built," as fears increased about immigration. The possibilities of "motherhood as a career," was a discourse intended to confront such assaults but a discourse which made even more invisible those women who were not full-time mothers. As well, this response reinforced the notion that women's duty to the nation passed exclusively through their maternal roles.

An important location for feminist politics was the Progressive movement whose politics was not only deeply influenced by the claims and actions of women but also vilified as effeminate.[44] At first the very notion of such reform, in which the state rather than market forces or political parties took responsibility for relieving

---

[40] Nancy F. Cott, *The Grounding of Modern Feminism* (New Haven: Yale University Press, 1987), 6-7 and chap. 1.

[41] Linda Gordon, Women's Body, Women's Right: A Social History of Birth Control in America (New York: Viking, 1976), 99-100.

[42] Ibid., xv.

[43] Ibid., chap. 6.

[44] Paula Baker, "The Domestication of Politics: Women and American Political Society, 1780-1920," *American Historical Review* 89 (1984), 628, 640.

poverty and other forms of misery, was defined as the equivalent of "unmanly" politics. In the end, "feminized" policies did develop, coming from a privatized sector of philanthropic organizations led by women and providing models for early social programmes for mothers.

Progressive reformers were important actors in the consolidation of a compromise around the hegemonic societal paradigm at the end of the nineteenth century. They were optimistic about "progress" and technological improvement. Because Progressives believed that a simplistic acceptance of market-driven outcomes would lead to a series of unfortunate (albeit unintended) effects, they demanded greater state regulation ranging from the control of corporate concentration and new regulatory agencies to governmental inspection of food-processing. Embedded in this political position was an abiding faith in technical achievement and the work of policy experts acting on behalf of the state. Infant protection, in this way, developed a programmatic identity which maximized the role of science and medicine in producing healthy babies. The widely-distributed sterilized bottle became the symbol of the diffusion of "scientific" childcare from doctors to middle-class mothers to working-class mothers.

The National Consumers' League (NCL) was a central actor in the Progressive movement. It sought out the weaknesses in the system, the places where the exceptionally needy were ignored. Originally the NCL identified all workers as needing protection from long hours and bad working conditions, but the opposition of trade unions and courts soon turned its focus towards women and children. Making claims on behalf of such groups through the Brandeis Brief and other similar strategies, the NCL reinforced rather than challenged the link between women and maternity, and the notion of biological difference from men.[45]

Disputes over the length of the working day rocked the American economy. However, with the growth of the American Federation of Labor (AFL) in the last decades of the nineteenth century workers sought redress almost exclusively through collective bargaining.[46] Such a privatized regulation of the wage relation involved primarily skilled workers or workers whose industrial production could be considered skilled. Because other workers' wage relation was less institutionalized, they suffered the effects of uncertainty and lack of a living wage. Many such workers were women; only in the first decades of the twentieth century did their situation begin to stabilize, after state regulation of hours and conditions of work was established through the political struggles of reform movements, often led by women.

The union movement, dominated by men, feared the effects of female employment on male wages. The solution chosen by unions was to seek some "protective" legislation which would limit women's labour force participation and simultaneous-

[45] Nancy Cott argues that the link between Progressive politics and the woman's movement was around the discourse of difference. See Cott, *The Grounding of Modern Feminism,* 21.

[46] Schefter, "Trade Unions and Political Machines."

ly to bargain hard for the family wage.[47] This support for legislative action was one of the few times the AFL departed from its preferred strategy of eschewing political action for workplace bargaining. The low levels of organization of women workers provided the rationale. Given organized labour's focus on workplace struggles, it is hardly surprising that labour leaders did not play a role in the demand for infant protection. For them the family remained a "private" realm, regulated by women and men without union or state guidance. At the same time, any actions which might encourage more women to seek paid work were to be avoided because, according to the AFL, unorganized women would only drive down men's wages and make it more difficult for men to support their wives and children. The logic was tight and it clearly excluded the notion that women's wage work was a desirable state of affairs.

Much of the organization of working women which did occur before the First World War was the result of efforts by the Women's Trade Union League (WTUL), composed of middle-class and working-class women. After numerous efforts to set up union locals and affiliate with the AFL, the WTUL met a series of obstacles.[48] One was a difficulty in fitting women's work into skill categories which the AFL was willing to recognize; therefore, male-dominated unions sometimes rejected WTUL applications for affiliation. At the same time a long-standing commitment to the AFL made it impossible for the WTUL to advocate any other form of unionism. In addition, the League encountered the same difficulties establishing permanent unions among a diverse and transient labour force that other organizers had described. Eventually, therefore, the WTUL decreased its emphasis upon organization and increased its calls for protective legislation. Its discourse shifted from one which stressed the commonalities of female and male workers, expressed through their desired affiliation with the same unions, towards one which emphasized gender difference.

In the US, then, organizations like the AFL and WTUL as well as the dominant strands of feminism contributed to different identities for working women versus men within the societal paradigm. Women, according to male unionists, were temporary workers whose marriages removed them from the labour force. Women's extraordinary weakness in the workplace derived from their lack of unionization, which in turn permitted an exception to the usual union practice of insisting on making gains in the workplace rather than through legislation. For the WTUL women workers were also different from men in that the former were caught up in family and work situations that led to their unusual exploitation. The way to deal with the

---

[47] Lehrer, *Origins of Protective Labor Legislation for Women,* 126, 142. The labour movement led demands for protective legislation for women until 1890, after which middle-class reformers directed the campaign. See Baer, *The Chains of Protection,* 33.

[48] This analysis of the WTUL is primarily from Nancy Schrom Dye, "Feminism or Unionism? The New York Women's Trade Union League and the Labor Movement," *Signs* 3 (1975), 111-25; and Lehrer, *The Origins of Protective Labor Legislation for Women,* chap. 6.

problem, for the WTUL, was to stress these differences and make demands for protective legislation.

In the paradigm of specialized citizenship, women's needs and contributions followed from their supposed potential for maternal nurturing, translated into political action. Unmarried working girls were the "mothers of the future" and as such they required protective legislation to safeguard their futures. Yet, this resort to the state transgressed the very rules of separation of work and politics which characterized the American paradigm at the time. "Real" workers bargained privately in non-partisan unions. Workers who made claims on the state did no more than reconfirm their "otherness" in the terms of the societal paradigm. Moreover, because the paradigm contained no space for their identity as workers, working "girls" appeared exceptions (because they were temporary workers) while married working women became invisible. Thrust into the political realm in this way, women's identity became overdetermined by biology and prey to discursive construction by actors, such as the courts, which saw women simply as mothers.

The feminist movement which had grown out of the nineteenth century woman's movement, confounded by the societal paradigm and its identity of specialized citizenship, became entangled in a contradiction within the paradigm. Because work and politics were separated, there was little legitimacy for demands by trade unions or reformers for the state to regulate the conditions of work; when feminists agitated for protective legislation for women at work or in maternity, they solidified popular notions of women as mothers, as "other" than workers, as minors. This classification of women as "wards of the state" put them in the same category as children, native peoples and other groups which were considered to lack the capacity to care for themselves. Within the terms of the hegemonic societal paradigm, as long as women remained in need of state protection they could never participate in the polity as men did. If the feminist movement stressed the special nature of "femaleness," the result was to contribute to the embedding of gender differences in the heart of welfare programmes, a difference according to which men were fully adult workers and citizens while women were mothers for the nation but not workers. But if feminists argued strictly for equality in the real world of a segmented labour force, hostile unions and bosses, and courts driven by an ideology of "freedom of contract," women's lives would continue to be difficult.

The practical effect of stressing an identity of difference is seen in the ways that protective legislation, women's work and suffrage intertwined discursively before 1914. The belief that political power would follow from the vote encouraged many women reformers to combine demands for protective legislation with demands for suffrage.[49] In the US the vote emerged as a primary goal, a tool for reform, whereas in France the left feared female suffrage as a buttress for the church while Solidar-

[49] Robin Miller Jacoby, "The Women's Trade Union League and American Feminism," *Signs,* 3 (1975), 126-40.

ists saw it as unnecessary in a society of families whose male head could represent the whole. Many French feminists dared not pursue enfranchisement. Eventually the American suffrage movement succeeded in gaining political rights for women earlier than in France and American women could participate, even before gaining the vote, in the design of social welfare programmes. But the cost of this early victory in the US was the creation of a two-channel welfare system, with women's lives limited by the state's willingness to recognize their "special qualities" and confine them to a single social role.

Conclusion

This article has explored the ways in which hegemonic societal paradigms constructed out of the processes of institutionalization of new social relations in France and the US at the end of the nineteenth century came to promote particular representations of gender relations. In neither country did the hegemonic paradigm emerge magically or simply out of political debates. Each developed as a solution to real problems faced by economic, social and political institutions which, in pursuing their strategies, made use of representations of gender within their own world views. One result was that dominant groups embedded their representations of gender in emerging state welfare policies; these representations continued as the gendering effects of policies once the latter were in place. In France those concerned about demographic catastrophe as well as Solidarists, the left and bourgeois feminists provided an impetus for state policies which reconciled paid work and maternity. In the US by way of contrast, middle-class Progressivism, a feminist movement which emphasized women's "nurturing" qualities and a union movement fearful of paid work and legislative regulation developed no policies for working mothers.

Throughout this story all actions for social programmes have taken place within a context in which representations of gender—and the identities which contained these representations—were crucial organizers of the political terrain. French working women, both single and married, were commonplace and state programmes to protect women and children reflected a widely-shared acceptance of this social fact. The new universalizing identity of citizen-producer incorporated the idea that citizens produced both in the workplace and in the home. The duality of women's citizenship roles was crucial for the way in which welfare policy took form; programmes to meet women's needs as workers and as mothers were inscribed in labour legislation. Yet notions of citizenship in this paradigm were not individualized, so that forces for reform could advocate greater workplace rights for women at the same time as they opposed female suffrage. Women as individual actors remained enclosed and invisible within the family. It was always the family which needed both healthy and rested parents in order to produce the nation's babies.[50]

In the US a doubly-bifurcated identity emerged, based on the liberal democratic assumption of a separation between politics and work as well as between public and private. American women were invisible as workers for everyone but those who argued for their "exceptional" needs. Women's political rights were claimed almost exclusively because of their supposed maternal qualities. A consequence of the collective identity of specialized citizen for women was a "two-channel" social policy which addressed women as mothers and men as workers and constituted state welfare as a feminized realm, responding to the politics of women and their allies.

At this time of the pre-history of the welfare state in these two countries, then, the collective identities available to women differed. Each provided points of strength and points of weakness. Operating within the interstices of two distinct universes of political discourse which provided different limitations on the space in which they could manoeuvre, French and American women continued after 1914 to search for the route towards emancipation, liberation and equality in difference.

[50] For a consideration of how these notions affected interwar politics, see Jane Jenson, "Both Friend and Foe: Women and State Welfare," in Claudia Koontz, Renate Bridenthal and Susan Mosher Stuard (eds.), *Becoming Visible: Women in European History* (2nd ed.; Boston: Houghton Mifflin, 1987), 535-56.

CHAPTER 4

Policy Paradigms, Social Learning, and the State. The Case of Economic Policymaking in Britain

Peter A. Hall

The study of comparative politics has been heavily influenced over the past decade by theories of the state. Initially developed by neo-Marxists in response to the persistence of capitalism, such theories now take a variety of forms.[1] Their central contention is that the state, broadly understood as the executive, legislative, and judicial apparatus of the nation, has an important impact of its own on the nature of public policy and considerable independence from organized social interests and the electoral coalitions that might otherwise be said to drive policy. In the words of one state theorist, policy should not be seen as "a vector diagram in which a series of pressures are brought to bear on the state, which then moves in the direction it is pushed by the strongest societal forces."[2] In this respect, theories of the state offer a useful, if occasionally overstated, corrective to pluralist emphases on the societal sources of policy.[3]

However, all research programs leave some questions unanswered, and this one poses particularly difficult ones. What motivates the actions of the state, if it is not the factors previously identified by pluralist analysis? How are we to conceive of the policy process if not as a response to societal pressure? In this regard, the negative force of the state theorists' case against more traditional lines of thought has not been matched by their positive attempts to construct an alternative conception of policymaking. To suggest that policymakers respond instead to the "national interest" leaves us wondering how this national interest comes to be defined.[4] Similarly, to argue that policy reflects a "parallelogram of preferences" among public officials themselves or the outcome of a "bureaucratic politics" in which "where you stand

[1] For reviews see Stephen Krasner, "Approaches to the State," *Comparative Politics*, 16 (January 1984), 223-46; Martin Carnoy, The State and Political Theory (Princeton: Princeton University Press, 1984); and Peter Evans et al., eds., Bringing the State Back In (New York: Cambridge University Press, 1985).

[2] Stephen Krasner, *Defending the National Interest* (Princeton: Princeton University Press, 1978), p. 26.

[3] For dissenting views, see Gabriel Almond, "The Return to the State," *American Political Science Review*, 82 (1988), 853-74, and the several responses that follow his article.

[4] Cf. Krasner, ibid.

depends on where you sit" imports a rather underspecified model of pluralism back into the state itself.[5] Even the argument that "policy legacies" determine the course of subsequent policy raises questions about why some legacies are more influential than others.[6] The recent work that focuses our attention on the state has been of great value, but the state at which we are now looking largely remains a black box.[7]

In the face of this dilemma, theorists of the state have been casting about for an alternative conception of the policy process with which to complete their account of policy. Out of these endeavors, one concept has begun to appear with particular frequency. That is the concept of policymaking as social learning. The notion of politics as learning has origins in work on cybernetics and organization theory, and psychologically oriented versions of it have been applied with some success to the process of foreign policymaking.[8] However, the formulation that has had the most influence on theories of the state is the one presented in Hugh Heclo's distinguished study of social policymaking in Britain and Sweden. In Heclo's words: "Politics finds its sources not only in power but also in uncertainty—men collectively wondering what to do. ... Governments not only 'power' ... they also puzzle. Policymaking is a form of collective puzzlement on society's behalf. ... Much political interaction has constituted a process of social learning expressed through policy."[9]

There is a profound insight here, and it has been taken up with enthusiasm by theorists of the state. In an influential review essay, Theda Skocpol observes that Heclo's work "suggests how to locate and analyze autonomous state contributions to policymaking, even within constitutional polities nominally directed by legisla-

---

[5] Eric Nordlinger, On the Autonomy of the Democratic State (Cambridge, Mass.: Harvard University Press, 1981), p. 15; Graham Allison, The Essence of Decision (Boston: Little Brown, 1971), pp. 162-81.

[6] Margaret Weir and Theda Skocpol, "State Structures and the Possibilities for 'Keynesian' Responses to the Great Depression in Sweden, Britain and the United States," in Evans et al., eds., pp. 107-168.

[7] Cf. Peter Gourevitch, "The Second Image Reversed: The International Sources of Domestic Politics," *International Organization*, 32 (Autumn 1978), 881-912.

[8] See Karl Deutsch, *The Nerves of Government* (New York: Free Press, 1963); Chris Argyris and Donald Schon, Organizational Learning (Reading: Addison-Wesley, 1978); Richard Rose, "Lesson Drawing across Time and Space," Working Paper of the Centre for the Study of Public Policy, University of Strathclyde, February 1989; and for representative works in the area of foreign policy Lloyd Etheredge, "Governmental Learning: An Overview," in S. Long, Handbook of Political Behavior, vol. 2 (New York: Plenum Press, 1981), pp. 73-161; Lloyd Etheredge, *Can Governments Learn?* (New York: Pergamon, 1985); Joseph Nye, "Nuclear Learning and U.S.-Soviet Security Regimes," *International Organization*, 41 (1987), 371-402; John Steinbrunner, *The Cybernetic Theory of Decision* (Princeton: Princeton University Press, 1974); Ernst B. Haas, *When Knowledge Is Power* (Berkeley: University of California Press, 1992); and Emanuel Adler and Beverly Crawford, eds. *Progress in Postwar International Relations* (New York: Columbia University Press, 1991).

[9] Hugh Heclo, *Modern Social Politics in Britain and Sweden* (New Haven: Yale University Press, 1974), pp. 305-6.

tures and electoral parties," and Paul Sacks argues that "the 'politics as learning' approach implies that elements within the state, acting, presumably, in pursuit of the national interest, decide what to do without serious opposition from external actors," thereby confirming a central tenet of state theory.[10] The notion of social learning is on the verge of becoming a key element in contemporary theories of the state and of policymaking more generally.

However, there are two major problems with the concept of social learning as hitherto employed by theorists of the state. First, it has been presented in only the sketchiest of terms. Unlike the psychologically oriented versions of learning theory that have been explored more fully in studies of foreign policy and the procedurally oriented versions presented by organization theorists, the concept of social learning presented by Heclo and taken up by theorists of the state emphasizes the role of ideas in policymaking. But those who use the concept have yet to develop an overarching image of the way in which ideas fit into the policy process or a clear conception of how those ideas might change.

Second, it is not at all clear that the process of social learning actually accords as completely as many think with the notion of an autonomous state. Social learning has generally been treated as a dimension of policymaking that confirms the autonomy of the state, but it may well be a process that is intimately affected by societal developments rather than one that takes place largely inside the state itself.

This point speaks to a central division within current analyses of the state. Recent theories of the state can be divided into two types. On one side is a set of analyses that might be described as state-centric in that they emphasize the autonomy of the state from societal pressure. These works suggest that policy is generally made by public officials operating with considerable independence from organizations like interest groups and political parties that transmit societal demands.[11] On the other side is a range of theories that might be called state-structural. They, too, emphasize the impact on policy of the state's structure and its actions, but they are less inclined to insist on the autonomy of the state vis-a-vis societal pressure. Instead, they accord interest groups, political parties, and other actors outside the state an important role in the policy process. Their main point is that the structure and past activities of the state often affect the nature or force of the demands that these actors articulate.[12] If social learning is a process that takes place largely inside

---

[10] Theda Skocpol, "Bringing the State Back In: Strategies of Analysis in Current Research," in Evans et al., eds., p. 12; Paul Sacks, "State Structure and the Asymmetrical Society," Comparative Politics, 12 (April 1980), 358.

[11] Representative works include Krasner, *Defending the National Interest*; Nordlinger; and Sacks.

[12] For representative works in this vein, see Peter Katzenstein, "Domestic Structures and Strategies of Foreign Economic Policy," in Peter Katzenstein, ed., *Between Power and Plenty* (Madison: University of Wisconsin Press, 1978), ch. 9; Theda Skocpol and John Ikenberry, "The Political Formation of the American Welfare State in Historical and Comparative Perspective," *Comparative Social Research*, 6 (1983); Weir and Skocpol.

the state itself, it will accord well with the arguments of state-centric theorists. However, to the extent that social learning involves much broader participation and conflict within the political system as a whole, it will be more consonant with the state-structuralist approach.

The object of this article is to examine the nature of social learning and the more general process whereby policies change with a view to resolving some of these issues. At the outset, I take up a number of questions about how the learning process proceeds and attempt to specify more fully the roles that ideas play in policymaking. I then test the central propositions of the conventional learning model and my expanded version against a series of cases of different kinds of policy change, with the following questions in mind. How should we understand the relationship between ideas and policymaking? How do the ideas behind policy change course? Is the process of social learning relatively incremental, as organization theory might lead us to expect, or marked by upheaval and the kind of "punctuated equilibrium" that often applies more generally to political change.[13] Are bureaucrats the principal actors in social learning, or do politicians and societal organizations also play a role? Finally, I explore the implications of these cases for state-society relations with particular attention to the relationship between social learning and the autonomy of the state.

The cases that this article examines are all drawn from a specific empirical setting, namely, that of macroeconomic policymaking in Britain between 1970 and 1989. A broad concept such as social learning deserves to be explored in many contexts; no single case can fully resolve these issues. However, the setting of macroeconomic policymaking in Britain is an ideal one against which to test the prevailing conceptions of social learning and their implications for state theory. On the one hand, economic policymaking is a knowledge-intensive process, long associated with concepts of learning. As Heclo observes: "Nowhere is the importance of such learning and alteration of perspective more clearly demonstrated than in the economic doctrines prevalent in any given period."[14] On the other hand, economic policymaking in Britain figures heavily in the most prominent attempts by state theorists to apply the concept of learning.[15] It also provides excellent cases against which to test state-centric arguments that the learning process is dominated by officials and highly placed experts, since the power of official experts should be at its maximum in a highly technical field like macroeconomic policymaking and in nations like Britain that have unusually hierarchical and closed bureaucracies.

---

[13] David Braybrooke and Charles Lindblom, *A Strategy of Decision* (Glencoe: Free Press, 1963), and Stephen Krasner, *Approaches to the State.*

[14] Heclo, p. 312.

[15] Economic policymaking in Britain is one of the cases examined by Weir and Skocpol as well as Sacks, and, of course, Britain provided one of the cases in which Heclo developed his concept of social learning.

The Process of Social Learning

We can begin from what might be termed the prevailing model of social learning as utilized by contemporary theorists of the state. It is heavily based on Heclo's work, but the state theorists take his cautious formulations somewhat farther. The image of learning that they present has three central features.

First, they suggest that one of the principal factors affecting policy at time-1 is policy at time-0. In Sacks' words: "The most important influence in this learning is previous policy itself."[16] Policy responds less directly to social and economic conditions than it does to the consequences of past policy. In Weir and Skocpol's terms, the interests and ideals that policymakers pursue at any moment in time are shaped by "policy legacies" or "meaningful reactions to previous policies."[17]

Second, the key agents pushing forward the learning process are the experts in a given field of policy, either working for the state or advising it from privileged positions at the interface between the bureaucracy and the intellectual enclaves of society. Heclo observes that "[f]orced to choose one group among all the separate political factors as most consistently important... the bureaucracies of Britain and Sweden loom predominant in the policies studied."[18] On the whole, this model tends to downgrade the role of politicians in social learning and to attribute particular importance to the officials or experts who specialize in specific fields of policy.

Finally, this view of social learning emphasizes the capacity of states to act autonomously from societal pressure. Heclo rejects the view that outside factors, such as socioeconomic development, elections, political parties, and organized interests, play a primary role in the development of social policy and concludes, albeit cautiously, that "if one were forced to hold the policy process static and choose between an essentially pluralistic or elitist interpretation, then our tentative conclusions . . . would suggest the greater interpretive power of the latter." Sacks and others go even farther to argue that accounts of social learning "reveal the substantial autonomy of the state from societal pressures in its formulation of policy goals."[19]

---

[16] Sacks, p. 356.

[17] Weir and Skocpol, p. 119; cf. Heclo, p. 315.

[18] Heclo, p. 308 et passim; Weir and Skocpol, pp. 138 et passim.

[19] Heclo, p. 318; Sacks, p. 356. Although I have emphasized the points on which Heclo and theorists of the state seem to agree, there are some issues on which their views diverge. For instance, is policy learning driven primarily by past failures or successes? Heclo (p. 303) notes that policy "has most frequently evolved as a corrective less to social conditions as such and more to the perceived failings of past policy," while Weir and Skocpol (p. 120) put more emphasis on the way in which policy builds on its past successes. Similarly, is the nature of policy learning seriously affected by the institutional structure of the state or not? Weir and Skocpol (p. 126) argue that it is, while Heclo (p. 308) tends to stress the role of individuals in the learning process. On this see also Hugh Heclo, "Policy Dynamics," in Richard Rose, ed., *The Dynamics of Public Policy* (Beverly Hills: Sage, 1976), p. 76.

It should be apparent that this is a relatively schematic model that needs to be fleshed out in several respects. To begin with, the concept of social learning itself should be defined more clearly. Learning is conventionally said to occur when individuals assimilate new information, including that based on past experience, and apply it to their subsequent actions. Therefore, we can define social learning as a deliberate attempt to adjust the goals or techniques of policy in response to past experience and new information. Learning is indicated when policy changes as the result of such a process.[20]

In addition, we should allow for the possibility that the learning process may take different forms, depending on the kinds of changes in policy that are involved. That is to say, the concept of social learning should be disaggregated. In order to do so, we can think of policymaking as a process that usually involves three central variables: the overarching goals that guide policy in a particular field, the techniques or policy instruments used to attain those goals, and the precise settings of these instruments. For instance, if the goal of the policy is to alleviate the financial problems of the elderly, the chosen instrument might be an old age pension, and its setting would be the level at which benefits were set. We want to distinguish the learning process associated with a simple change in the level of benefits from that associated with potentially more radical transformations in the basic instruments of policy or its overarching goals.

Building on these distinctions, we can identify three distinct kinds of changes in policy and illustrate each from cases of macroeconomic policymaking in Britain over the 1970-89 period.

First, the levels (or settings) of the basic instruments of British policy, such as the minimum lending rate or the fiscal stance, were altered at frequent intervals during the 1970-89 period, even when the overall goals and instruments of policy remained the same. Most of the adjustments made in the annual budget took this form: the settings of the government's policy instruments were modified in the light of past experience and projections for the future performance of the economy. We can call the process whereby instrument settings are changed in the light of experience and new knowledge, while the overall goals and instruments of policy remain the same, a process of first order change in policy.

Second, there were several instances in the 1970-89 period when the hierarchy of goals behind British macroeconomic policy remained largely the same but the basic techniques used to attain them were altered, as a result of dissatisfaction with past experience. These episodes included the introduction of a new system of mon-

[20] Note that this does not necessarily mean that policy becomes better or more efficient as a result of learning. Just as a child can learn bad habits, governments, too, may learn the "wrong" lessons from a given experience. Although learning usually improves the capacity of a state to attain its policy goals, it need not always do so, and a government's overall goals may also be open to question on other grounds. The main point is that learning reflects a deliberate attempt to adjust policy in the light of past experience and policy-relevant knowledge.

etary control in 1971, the development of a new system of "cash limits" for public spending control in 1976, and the movement away from strict targets for monetary growth in 1981-83. Changes of this sort, when the instruments of policy as well as their settings are altered in response to past experience even though the overall goals of policy remain the same, might be said to reflect a process of second order change.

Finally, the British experience of 1970-89 was also marked by a radical shift from Keynesian to monetarist modes of macroeconomic regulation, which entailed simultaneous changes in all three components of policy: the instrument settings, the instruments themselves, and the hierarchy of goals behind policy. Such wholesale changes in policy occur relatively rarely, but when they do occur as a result of reflection on past experience, we can describe them as instances of third order change.[21]

In order to understand how social learning takes place, we also need a more complete account of the role that ideas play in the policy process. After all, the concept of social learning implies that ideas are central to policymaking, even if it says little more than that about the role they play. To construct a more robust formulation, let us begin from Anderson's fruitful observation that "the deliberation of public policy takes place within a realm of discourse ... policies are made within some system of ideas and standards which is comprehensible and plausible to the actors involved."[22] More precisely, policymakers customarily work within a framework of ideas and standards that specifies not only the goals of policy and the kind of instruments that can be used to attain them, but also the very nature of the problems they are meant to be addressing. Like a *Gestalt,* this framework is embed-

---

[21] It should be apparent that this classification reflects a lexical ordering: first order learning represents a change in the simplest of policy variables; second order learning changes both instruments and their settings; and third order learning entails a change in all three sets of variables. We can also imagine a process of "fourth order learning" similar to the one that Argyris and Schon (pp. 18-26) call "deutero-learning," in which policymakers learn how to learn. However, a full discussion of that topic is beyond the scope of this study.

[22] Charles Anderson, "The Logic of Public Problems: Evaluation in Comparative Policy Research," in Douglas Ashford, ed., Comparing Public Policies (Beverly Hills: Sage, 1978), p. 23. I have benefited from several discussions with Rosemary Taylor on this subject. For related formulations, see Donald Schon, "Generative Metaphor: A Perspective on Problem-Solving in Social Policy," in Andrew Ortony, ed., *Metaphor and Thought* (Cambridge: Cambridge University Press, 1977), pp. 254-83; Jack L. Walker, "The Diffusion of Knowledge, Policy Communities and Agenda Setting: The Relationship of Knowledge and Power," in John E. Tropman et al., eds., *New Strategic Perspectives on Social Policy* (New York: Pergamon, 1981); Peter Marris, *Community Planning and Conceptions of Change* (London: Routledge and Kegan Paul, 1982); Douglas Ashford, *The Emergence of the Welfare States* (Oxford: Basil Blackwell, 1986); Martin Rein, "Frame Reflective Policy Discourse," Leyden Institute for Law and Public Policy Working Paper 3, 1986; Jane Jenson, "Paradigms and Political Discourse: Protective Legislation in France and the United States before 1914," Canadian Journal of Political Science, 22 (June 1989), 235-58; and Frank Dobbin, "The Social Construction of the Great Depression," *Theory and Society* (forthcoming).

ded in the very terminology through which policymakers communicate about their work, and it is influential precisely because so much of it is taken for granted and unamenable to scrutiny as a whole. I am going to call this interpretive framework a policy paradigm.

Macroeconomic policymaking in Britain has clearly revolved around this sort of policy paradigm. For most of the postwar period, British policy was based on a highly coherent system of ideas associated with John Maynard Keynes. Once adapted to the organization of the British financial system, Keynesian ideas were institutionalized into the procedures of the British Treasury and formalized as the "neoclassical synthesis" in many standard texts. They specified what the economic world was like, how it was to be observed, which goals were attainable through policy, and what instruments should be used to attain them. They became the prism through which policymakers saw the economy as well as their own role within it.[23]

These policy paradigms are rather like the scientific paradigms that Thomas Kuhn has identified, and we can take advantage of this analogy to develop some hypotheses about how the learning process in public policymaking might proceed.[24] For instance, reference to Kuhn allows us to locate the different kinds of policy change relative to one another. First and second order change can be seen as cases of "normal policymaking," namely of a process that adjusts policy without challenging the overall terms of a given policy paradigm, much like "normal science." Third order change, by contrast, is likely to reflect a very different process, marked by the radical changes in the overarching terms of policy discourse associated with a "paradigm shift." If first and second order changes preserve the broad continuities usually found in patterns of policy, third order change is often a more disjunctive process associated with periodic discontinuities in policy. One striking implication of this analysis would be that first and second order changes in policy do not automatically lead to third order changes. As in the case of scientific change, normal policymaking can proceed for some time without necessarily precipitating a paradigm shift. The latter is engendered quite differently.

The process of first order change is likely to display the features of incrementalism, satisficing, and routinized decision making that we normally associate with the

---

[23] See Samuel Brittan, Steering the Economy (Harmondsworth: Penguin, 1970); Paul Mosely, The Making of Economic Policy (Brighton: Wheatsheaf, 1984); and F. T. Blackaby, ed., British Economic Policy 1960-74 (Cambridge: Cambridge University Press, 1979), for works that illustrate this point.

[24] Thomas Kuhn, *The Structure of Scientific Revolutions* (Chicago: University of Chicago Press, 1970). Of course, Kuhn's arguments have generated considerable controversy among philosophers of science, but they remain highly suggestive and potentially even more applicable beyond the natural sciences. Cf. Imre Lakatos and Alan Musgrave, eds., *Criticism and the Growth of Knowledge* (Cambridge: Cambridge University Press, 1970), and Joseph Rouse, *Knowledge and Power* (Ithaca: Cornell University Press, 1987).

policy process.[25] Second order change and the development of new policy instruments may move one step beyond in the direction of strategic action. But third order change is more problematic: the literature provides far less guidance for modeling this sort of process. Nevertheless, we can draw on the Kuhnian image of scientific progress to develop some hypotheses about how the process of paradigm shift or third order change in policy might proceed.

Such an account should begin from the observation that paradigms are by definition never fully commensurable in scientific or technical terms. Because each paradigm contains its own account of how the world facing policymakers operates and each account is different, it is often impossible for the advocates of different paradigms to agree on a common body of data against which a technical judgment in favor of one paradigm over another might be made.[26] Three important implications follow.

First, the process whereby one policy paradigm comes to replace another is likely to be more sociological than scientific. That is to say, although the changing views of experts may play a role, their views are likely to be controversial, and the choice between paradigms can rarely be made on scientific grounds alone. The movement from one paradigm to another will ultimately entail a set of judgments that is more political in tone, and the outcome will depend, not only on the arguments of competing factions, but on their positional advantages within a broader institutional framework, on the ancillary resources they can command in the relevant conflicts, and on exogenous factors affecting the power of one set of actors to impose its paradigm over others.

Second, issues of authority are likely to be central to the process of paradigm change. Faced with conflicting opinions from the experts, politicians will have to decide whom to regard as authoritative, especially on matters of technical complexity, and the policy community will engage in a contest for authority over the issues at hand. In other words, the movement from one paradigm to another is likely to be preceded by significant shifts in the locus of authority over policy.

Finally, instances of policy experimentation and policy failure are likely to play a key role in the movement from one paradigm to another. Like scientific paradigms, a policy paradigm can be threatened by the appearance of anomalies, namely by developments that are not fully comprehensible, even as puzzles, within the terms of the paradigm. As these accumulate, ad hoc attempts are generally made to stretch the terms of the paradigm to cover them, but this gradually undermines the

---

[25] Cf. Charles Lindblom, *The Policy-Making Process* (Englewood Cliffs: Prentice Hall, 1968); Aaron Wildavsky, *The New Politics of the Budgetary Process* (Boston: Little Brown, 1968); Richard Rose and Terrence Karran, *Taxation by Inertia* (London: Allen and Unwin, 1987).

[26] In this respect, many policy paradigms resemble those found in natural science. For an argument that elaborates and establishes this point more fully with regard to the Keynesian and monetarist paradigms in economics, see Peter A. Hall, *The Political Dimensions of Economic Management* (Ann Arbor: University Microfilms, 1982), ch. 2.

intellectual coherence and precision of the original paradigm. Efforts to deal with such anomalies may also entail experiments to adjust existing lines of policy, but if the paradigm is genuinely incapable of dealing with anomalous developments, these experiments will result in policy failures that gradually undermine the authority of the existing paradigm and its advocates even further.

Therefore, the movement from one paradigm to another that characterizes third order change is likely to involve the accumulation of anomalies, experimentation with new forms of policy, and policy failures that precipitate a shift in the locus of authority over policy and initiate a wider contest between competing paradigms. This contest may well spill beyond the boundaries of the state itself into the broader political arena. It will end only when the supporters of a new paradigm secure positions of authority over policymaking and are able to rearrange the organization and standard operating procedures of the policy process so as to institutionalize the new paradigm.

How well does this expanded image of social learning fit the course of British macroeconomic policymaking in the 1970-89 period? And what are the implications of this case for contemporary theories of the state? To answer these questions, we need to explore empirical cases representative of each of the three types of policy change. These are drawn from the process of macroeconomic policymaking in Britain since 1970. Because space permits only a brief review of each case, I concentrate on those features most relevant to the model of social learning outlined above.[27]

First-Order Change

As noted above, first order changes in policy took place every year during this period, and often more than once a year, as policymakers adjusted the budget judgment in response to the revealed consequences of past policy and new developments. The broad outlines of the process are well-known. The process was analytical, in the sense that the settings of fiscal and monetary instruments were adjusted to attain a specified set of macroeconomic targets, but also highly foutinized, in that the range of options canvassed in any year was generally restricted by the conventions of the reigning paradigm. For much of the period, such adjustments to policy can be predicted with a "satisficing" model of decision making.[28]

This process of first order change corresponds quite closely to the image of social learning current in state theory. Policy at time-1 was deliberately formulated and justified in terms of the outcomes of policy at time-0, as the annual Financial Statement and Budget reports indicate, and there is ample evidence that experts within the civil service played a dominant role in the process. They controlled both the ad-

[27] Ibid, for a more extended discussion of these cases.

[28] See Paul Mosley, ch. 4 et passim; and Hugo Young and Ann Sloman, *But Chancellor: An Inquiry into the Treasury* (London: British Broadcasting Corporation, 1984), pp. 65-83.

vice going to the chancellor and the forecasts on which that advice was based. The prime minister and chancellor could push policy more in one direction than another, as Edward Heath did by pressing for all-out growth in 1972 and James Callaghan did by insisting on a lower-rate band for taxes in 1978, but they lacked the technical expertise to take the direction of macroeconomic management out of the hands of their officials, and other ministers had virtually no influence over macroeconomic policymaking.[29]

As theorists of the state would predict, the process of first order change also seems to have been relatively insulated from the kind of pluralist pressures we often associate with the broader political system. A variety of groups made representations to the chancellor before each budget, but these were largely discounted at the Treasury. The Confederation of British Industry secured minor concessions in return for a promise to police retail prices in 1971, and the government made some alterations to policy in exchange for the Trades Union Congress' agreement to an incomes policy in 1975-76, but these instances must be balanced against the far more numerous occasions over this period when the demands of outside groups were ignored.[30]

Second-Order Change

At less frequent junctures between 1970 and 1989, British governments also made second order changes to policy. That is to say, they altered the instruments of macroeconomic policy without radically altering the hierarchy of goals behind policy. I will examine three representative cases, one drawn from each of the three administrations in office during this period.

The first case is that of Competition and Credit Control (CCC), the name given to a series of alterations made to the system of monetary control beginning in 1971. There is an ample literature on this episode, and it can be reviewed briefly.[31] The British clearing banks had been arguing for some years that the existing system of quantitative controls on lending was hampering their ability to compete with foreign firms entering the British market, but the new scheme was initiated by senior officials at the Bank of England only after they, too, found that the existing system was becoming unworkable and had concluded, after a long series of studies, that the UK demand for money was stable enough to support a system of monetary control based primarily on interest rate changes. Lacking the expertise to examine the scheme fully, the Treasury gave it only a cursory review and then sold it to the

---

[29] William Keegan and Rupert Pennant-Rae, *Who Runs the Economy?* (London: Temple Smith, 1979); Hall; Peter Browning, *The Treasury and Economic Policy 1964-1985* (London: Longman, 1986), p. 331 et passim.

[30] See Young and Sloman, pp. 75-77; Hall, pp. 657-74.

[31] For detailed accounts of this episode, see K. K. F. Zawadski, *Competition and Credit Control* (Oxford: Blackwell, 1981); Michael Moran, *The Politics of Banking* (London: Macmillan, 1986), ch. 3; David Gowland, *Monetary Policy and Credit Control* (London: Croom Helm, 1978); and Hall, ch. 3.

government as a way of encouraging competition in the banking system. When bank lending rose faster than expected in 1972-73, however, the prime minister balked at the interest rate increases proposed by the Bank, the money supply (M3) rose by 60 percent in 1972-73, and another system of quantitative controls, known colloquially as the "corset," was ultimately imposed in July 1973. The experiment as a whole was something of a minor disaster.

The next case of second order change had a happier outcome but many of the same features as the first. It involved the introduction of a new system for controlling public expenditure, known as a "cash limits" system, that replaced the traditional method of planning public expenditure in volume terms with a set of limits on departmental expenditure formulated in nominal pounds sterling. Once again, the impetus for change came from growing dissatisfaction with the previous system of expenditure control, which peaked in 1974-75 when spending apparently rose by £4.9 billion more than could be accounted for by published spending plans or announced changes to those plans.[32] Initiated by senior civil servants at the Treasury, the new system was tried out on public sector building programs in 1974-76 and introduced more broadly for the fiscal year 1976-77. It was accompanied by several additional measures designed to strengthen the hand of the Treasury against spending ministers, and it facilitated deep cuts in the projected rate of spending in subsequent years.[33]

A third case of second order change in policy occurred in 1981-85, as the Thatcher government gave up its attempt to implement a system of monetary base control (MBC) and gradually moved away from a monetary policy oriented primarily to rigid targets for the rate of growth of M3. The government enshrined targets for M3 in the Medium Term Financial Strategy (MTFS) announced with the March 1980 budget and, shortly thereafter, directed its officials to devise a system for monetary base control, but by 1985 the government had all but abandoned strict targets for M3 and any plan for MBC. Once again, officials played the key role in persuading ministers that a change in their plans was necessary.[34] Officials at the Bank of England resolutely resisted MBC on the grounds that under such a system they would lose control of short-term interest rates, and, as successive attempts to control the rate of growth of M3 failed, both Bank and Treasury officials persuaded the chancellor to turn to other indicators of monetary stringency and eventually to incorporate exchange rate movements into his calculations. By 1985 a multitude of measures was utilized to assess monetary growth, the central targets were largely notional, the practice of "overfunding" the public sector deficit once employed to

---

[32] See Expenditure Committee, House of Commons, The Financing of Public Expenditure, First Report 1975-76, HC-69 (London: HMSO, 1976).

[33] Leo Pliatzky, *Getting and Spending* (Oxford: Blackwell, 1982); Hugh Heclo and Aaron Wildavsky, *The Private Government of Public Money*, 2nd ed. (London: Macmillan, 1981), introduction.

[34] See William Keegan, *Mrs. Thatcher's Economy Experiment* (Harmondsworth: Penguin, 1984), ch. 5.

control M3 had been terminated, and monetary policy was guided for the most part by ad hoc considerations.[35]

Although only a brief review of these cases has been possible here, what is most striking about all of them is that they accord remarkably well with the image of social learning presented by state-centric theorists. In each case, changes were made to policy instruments primarily in response to dissatisfaction with past policy rather than in response to new economic events alone. Competition and Credit Control was inspired by the growing unworkability of existing controls on credit and their distorting effects on banking competition rather than by the underlying course of monetary growth. The inflationary conditions of 1975-76 made some reduction in public expenditure desirable, but the new system of cash limits was a direct response to the apparent failure of existing methods for planning public expenditure. Likewise, modifications made to the system of monetary control in 1981-85 were motivated primarily by dissatisfaction with the unworkability of a system based on rigid targets for the monetary base.

It is also notable that officials, rather than politicians, played the most central role in each instance of social learning. CCC was initiated by Bank officials on the basis of studies begun before the Heath government took office, and its presentation was simply tailored to fit the prevailing Conservative platform. The system of cash limits was also devised by officials before the Labour government came to office and presented to the chancellor as a solution when appropriate problems arose, much as a "garbage can" theory of decision making would suggest.[36] The resistance of the prime minister delayed the move away from monetary targets in the 1980s, but once again those pushing most strongly for a change were the civil servants who had to operate the policy.

All of these are also cases in which the state acted rather autonomously. The system of cash limits was never really the object of pressure from outside actors; what pressure came from the financial press was itself largely engineered by Whitehall.[37] In the case of CCC, the clearing banks had been seeking relief from quantitative controls for some time, but the Bank moved toward a new system only when its own calculations indicated (albeit incorrectly) that a stable demand for money existed. Similarly, there had been vociferous critics of monetary targets since their inception in 1976, but the Thatcher government moved away from them only when its own policy experts concluded they were unworkable.

In light of these cases, we might well conclude that the prevailing image of social learning is correct in all its essentials. However, the most important transforma-

---

[35] See Browning; and David Smith, *The Rise and Fall of Monetarism* (Harmondsworth: Penguin, 1987), ch. 8.

[36] Cf. M. Cohen, J. March, and J. Olsen, "A Garbage Can Model of Organizational Choice," *Administrative Science Quarterly*, 17 (1972), 1-25.

[37] Pliatzky, p. 139.

tion in policy over this period was one characterized by third order change, and before reaching any conclusions, we should examine this process as well.

Third Order Change

In addition to the first and second order changes discussed here, much more dramatic changes in British macroeconomic policy also took place during the 1970-89 period. These changes are commonly associated with the movement from a Keynesian mode of policymaking to one based on monetarist economic theory. Although the movement began around 1976, the most intense break in policy came after a Conservative government led by Margaret Thatcher was elected in 1979. Not only were the settings of policy changed but the hierarchy of goals and set of instruments employed to guide policy shifted radically as well. Inflation replaced unemployment as the preeminent concern of policymakers. Macroeconomic efforts to reduce unemployment were rejected in favor of balanced budgets and direct tax reductions. Monetary policy replaced fiscal policy as the principal macroeconomic instrument, and it was reoriented toward fixed targets for the rate of monetary growth. Many regulatory instruments associated with state intervention, such as incomes policies, exchange controls, and quantitative limits on bank lending, were eliminated. This was a clear case of third order change in policy.[38]

What was the character of this process of third order change? How did policy change so radically? Although the election of Margaret Thatcher as prime minister is a key component of the story, it is not the only component. After all, new governments under determined leaders had been elected before. Similarly, although poor levels of economic performance and rising rates of inflation helped to provoke change, to cite them alone does not tell us more about the process of change. We need a conceptual framework for understanding the process whereby British macroeconomic policy changed during the 1970s and 1980s.

For that purpose, it is useful to return to the concept of a "policy paradigm." Keynesianism and monetarism were quintessential examples of such paradigms. Although something of a new synthesis between them has emerged in recent years, during the period examined here, namely the 1970s and early 1980s, these two economic ideologies were distinct paradigms. Not only did the policy prescriptions of monetarists diverge from those of the Keynesians, they were also based on a fundamentally different conception of how the economy itself worked. Whereas Keynesians viewed the private economy as unstable and in need of intermittent fiscal adjustment, monetarists saw the private economy as stable and discretionary policy as an impediment to efficient economic performance. Whereas Keynesian policy-

38 See James Alt, "Old Wine in New Bottles: Thatcher's Conservative Economic Policies," in Barry Cooper, Alan Kornberg, and William Mishler, eds., *The Resurgence of Conservatism in the Anglo-American Democracies* (Durham: Duke University Press, 1987), pp. 217-57; and Wilhelm Buiter and Marcus Miller, *The Thatcher Experiment: The First Two Years*, Brookings Papers on Economic Activity, 2 (1980), 315-79.

makers attributed fluctuations in economic output and inflation to the cycles of the real economy or excessive wage and price pressure, monetarists took the view that fluctuations in output and inflation were caused primarily by excessive changes in the rate of growth of the money supply. And if Keynesian governments had believed that they could reduce the rate of unemployment by altering the fiscal stance ever since the famous 1944 white paper on that subject, monetarists contended that the jobless were not the responsibility of the state because unemployment would converge on "natural rate" fixed by conditions in the labor market rather than by the macroeconomic stance.[39]

When monetarism replaced Keynesianism as the template guiding policy, there was a radical shift in the hierarchy of goals guiding policy, the instruments relied on to effect policy, and the settings of those instruments. Moreover, these changes were accompanied by substantial changes in the discourse employed by policymakers and in the analysis of the economy on which policy was based. In short, the third order change in British policymaking that occurred during this period was accompanied by a wholesale shift in policy paradigms. This provides us with an important clue in understanding the character of this process of change. It should resemble the process of paradigm change drawn from the Kuhnian model and outlined above. Although the relevant events can be described here in only the briefest of terms, they display many of the features a Kuhnian model would lead us to expect.

The process was initiated early in the 1970s by a series of economic developments, of which the most important was rising rates of inflation, soon to be joined by stagnating levels of growth and employment. These developments were disturbing in themselves, but they were particularly threatening to the Keynesian paradigm because it could neither fully anticipate nor explain them. In other words, they were "anomalies" in the Kuhnian sense, which called into question the adequacy of Keynesian analyses of the economy. The most famous, although by no means only, anomaly was the simultaneous increase in inflation and unemployment that seemed to vitiate the Phillips curve on which Keynesian policy had long been based.

Partly because these events were anomalous in terms of the prevailing policy paradigm, they led to a series of mistaken forecasts and policy failures. Only some of these problems can be enumerated here.[40] On serious underestimates of the rate of inflation, the government fueled an inflationary spiral with cost-of-living agreements in 1973. Unable to interpret the impact of the 1974 oil price increases on

[39] For more extended discussions of the differences between the Keynesian and monetarist paradigms, see Alex Chrystal, *Controversies in Macroeconomics* (London: Philip Allen, 1979); Keith Cuthbertson, *Macroeconomic Policy* (London: Macmillan, 1979); Hall, ch. 1; and Sir Keith Joseph, *Reversing the Trend* (London: Barry Rose, 1975).

[40] For more detailed accounts, see Hall, chs. 2-4; Jock Bruce-Gardyne, *Whatever Happened to the Quiet Revolution?* (London: Charles Knight, 1974); Keegan and Pennant-Rae; Martin *Holmes, Political Pressure and Economic Policy 1970-74* (London: Butterworth, 1982).

British business, the Treasury endorsed corporate tax increases in March of that year, only to have to offset them with emergency relief later that fall. Underestimates of the relative price effect on public sector consumption led to serious miscalculations of public spending and the public sector borrowing requirement in 1974-75. A misjudged attempt to nudge sterling down on the foreign exchanges in the spring of 1976 precipitated a run on the pound that ended with recourse to the IMF and severe spending cuts in 1977. These were widely perceived to be significant policy failures, and such failures did much to discredit the prevailing policy paradigm.

The government reacted with a series of policy experiments that were basically ad hoc attempts to recover control of the economy by adjusting traditional Keynesian practices. However, the effect of these adaptations was to stretch the intellectual coherence of the paradigm that was supposed to be guiding policy to the point of breaking. The most prominent effort was a series of incomes policies implemented in 1972-73 and 1975-77 to cope with inflation. But incomes policies ate away at one of the Keynesian paradigm' greatest sources of appeal, its ability to promise effective economic management without intervening directly in the affairs of individual economic actors.[41] Several years of tortuous negotiations with the unions ate away at the authority of both the government and the Keynesian paradigm.

Similar problems with the financial markets further eroded this authority. As a result of unanticipated shifts in the behavior of the markets for government debt that were linked to the effects of CCC and rising levels of debt, the Labour government found itself held hostage with increasing frequency to demands emanating from the markets for spending cuts or interest rate increases. It experimented with monetary targets in 1976-77 but found that they simply enhanced the leverage of the financial markets over the government.[42] The effect was to impair the capacity of public officials to cope with unemployment in a Keynesian manner. Keynesian doctrine gradually lost coherence and credibility in the eyes of politicians, officials, and the public. The prime minister himself told the 1976 Labour Party conference: "We used to think you could just spend your way out of recession and increase employment by cutting taxes and boosting spending. I tell you in all candour that option no longer exists. . . ."[43]

---

[41] See Robert Skidelsky, "The Decline of Keynesian Politics," in Colin Crouch, ed., *State and Economy in Contemporary Capitalism* (London: Croom Helm, 1979), pp. 55-86; and Anthony Crosland, *The Future of Socialism* (London: Strauss-Farrar, 1956).

[42] For a more detailed discussion, see Peter A. Hall, "The Movement from Keynesianism to Monetarism: Institutional Analysis and British Economic Policy in the 1970s," in Sven Steinmo, Kathleen Thelen, and Frank Longstreth, eds., *Structuring Politics: Historical Institutionalism in Comparative Analysis* (New York: Cambridge University Press, 1992), pp. 90-113.

[43] Cited in Keegan and Pennant-Rae, p. 101; cf. Joel Barnett, *Inside the Treasury* (London: Andre Deutsch, 1982); and David Coates, *Labour in Power?* (London: Longman, 1980), ch. 1. The policy experiments initiated in this period have led some analysts to suggest that monetarist policy really began under the 1974-79 Labour government. But the conception of policy paradigms presented

As a result of these developments, the locus of authority over macroeconomic issues began to shift. Hitherto, the Treasury had enjoyed a virtual monopoly of authority over such matters. By 1976, distrustful MPs forced the government to release details of the secret Treasury model to the general public. The prime minister overruled the Treasury in favor of the Bank of England on several key issues in 1977. And even the Chancellor of the Exchequer lost enough faith in his own officials that an unusual number of them left the Treasury shortly after 1976.[44]

One feature of this shift in the locus of authority was an extraordinary intensification in debate about economic issues in the media and financial circles. As the Treasury lost influence, what we might call the outside "marketplace in economic ideas" expanded dramatically in the 1975-79 period. New research institutes devoted to economic affairs were created; financial institutions expanded their economic research departments; and the already high volume of economic commentary in the press grew larger and even more sophisticated. Macroeconomic management became the subject of an intense public debate.[45]

Economic commentators and public figures alike began to search for alternatives to the Keynesian paradigm. The monetarist paradigm soon became the principal challenger to Keynesian doctrine, in large part because it was the most coherent and highly developed alternative, having achieved substantial support among American economists. Its major rival, propounded by the Cambridge Economic Policy Group, was still closely associated with Keynesianism and suffered a critical loss of credibility when some of its core predictions linking the budget deficit to the balance of payments failed in 1975-76. However, monetarism still had very little support from British economists, who remained overwhelmingly Keynesian. This was not a case in which the bulk of expert opinion shifted, drawing policymakers along in its wake.

Instead, political, as opposed to purely economic, criteria became the key factor behind the success of the monetarist paradigm. By 1975 the debate about policy paradigms spilled over into the political arena and became the object of electoral competition. Seeking a weapon with which to attack the vulnerable leadership of their own party and then the Labour government, Margaret Thatcher and a few others took up a competing economic paradigm based on monetarist doctrine. They were genuinely seeking new solutions to Britain's economic problems, but

---

here allows us to distinguish the situation in 1976-79 from that after 1979. The Labour government's moves toward informal monetary targets and greater emphasis on the PSBR were simply ad hoc adjustments to the Keynesian paradigm. The underlying terms of policy discourse had not yet changed. Labour policymakers still believed in their responsibility for unemployment, the usefulness of incomes policies, and fiscal activism. They were at best "unbelieving monetarists"; the true believers came to power only in 1979 when Thatcher was elected to office.

[44] See especially Keegan and Pennant-Rae.

[45] See Hall, *The Political Dimensions of Economic Management*, ch. 6; and Wayne Parsons, *The Power of the Financial Press* (New Brunswick: Rutgers University Press, 1990).

they embraced the monetarist solution in large measure because it also had substantial political appeal.[46]

Monetarism had political appeal, first, because it provided a coherent challenge to the policies of the Labour government. However, monetarism had a special appeal to Conservatives, and especially those on the right wing of the party, because it provided a new rationale for many measures which they had long supported. The monetarist critique of fiscal activism contained a new set of arguments for the long-standing Conservative position that public spending and the role of the state in the economy should be reduced. The monetarist idea that the "natural rate" of unemployment could be decreased only by reducing the power of the trade unions also fit well with the Conservatives' growing antipathy toward the unions.[47]

Conservative politicians saw that monetarism could be presented in terms that had broader public appeal as well. By the end of the 1970s, a decade of tortuous negotiations over incomes policies had rendered both the trade unions and neocorporatist arrangements increasingly unpopular. The government seemed impotent in the face of continuing economic problems and powerful unions. Monetarism offered a simple but appealing prescription for all of these dilemmas. Its advocates argued that the government could discipline the unions and eliminate inflation, the most serious economic problem of the 1970s, simply by adhering to a strict target for the rate of growth of the money supply. In the face of such a target, the unions would have to reduce their wage demands in order to avoid unemployment. In short, monetarism was presented as a doctrine that could restore the authority of the government as well as resolve Britain's economic problems.[48]

Once the monetarist paradigm was taken up by the Conservatives, its fate came to depend heavily on their electoral fortunes, which were conditioned by a wide range of factors. The policy failures associated with the stretching of the Keynesian paradigm, culminating in the collapse of incomes policy during the winter of 1979, probably contributed more to the Conservative's electoral victory that May than did the positive appeal of monetarism.[49] When policy paradigms become the object of

---

[46] This has often been true of new economic ideas more generally. For an analysis of the acceptance of Keynesian ideas that emphasizes the importance of both their "economic viability" and "political viability," see Peter A. Hall, "Conclusion: The Politics of Keynesian Ideas," in Peter A. Hall, ed., *The Political Power of Economic Ideas: Keynesianism across Nations* (Princeton: Princeton University Press, 1989), pp. 360-91.

[47] For perceptive discussions, see Robert Behrens, *The Conservative Party from Heath to Thatcher* (London: Saxon House, 1980), ch. 5; Hugo Young, *One of Us* (London: Macmillan, 1989); and Peter Jenkins, *Mrs. Thatcher's Revolution* (Cambridge, Mass.: Harvard University Press, 1988).

[48] See especially Joseph, Reversing the Trend; and Andrew Gamble, "The Free Economy and the Strong State," in Ralph Milliband and John Saville, eds., *The Socialist Register 1979* (London: Merlin, 1979), pp. 1-25.

[49] See Ivor Crewe, "Why the Conservatives Won," In H. R. Penniman, ed., *Britain at the Polls, 1979* (Washington, D.C.: American Enterprise Institute, 1981), pp. 263-306.

open political contestation, the outcome depends on the ability of each side to mobilize a sufficient electoral coalition in the political arena.[50]

Once in office, Thatcher played a key role in institutionalizing the new policy paradigm. She packed the influential economic committees of the cabinet with its supporters, appointed an outside monetarist to be chief economic advisor at the Treasury, and in conjunction with a few advisors, virtually dictated the outlines of macroeconomic policy for several years. The locus of authority over policymaking in this period again shifted dramatically towards the prime minister. Over time, an aggressive policy of promoting civil servants who were highly pliable or sympathetic to monetarist views implanted the new paradigm even more firmly. By 1982, the operating routines at the Treasury and the Bank of England as well as the terms of policy discourse had shifted decisively toward monetarism.[51]

How well does this case of third order change in policy fit the image of social learning used by contemporary analysts of the state? It should be apparent that this case deviates from the model in some important respects. First, it was not civil servants or policy experts engaged by the government, but politicians and the media, who played the preeminent role in this process of policy change. The vast majority of government economists were virtually as Keynesian in 1979 as they had been in 1970. The monetarist assault was led by influential journalists, such as William Rees-Mogg and Samuel Brittan, and key politicians like Margaret Thatcher and Sir Keith Joseph, who persuaded others of the advantages of their cause and virtually forced the Whitehall machine to alter its mode of macroeconomic policymaking.

Moreover, this process of policy change did not take place primarily within the confines of the state itself. On the contrary, it began with a shift in the locus of authority away from the Treasury toward a growing marketplace of economic ideas outside the state. The ensuing struggle to replace one policy paradigm with another was a societywide affair, mediated by the press, deeply imbricated with electoral competition, and fought in the public arena.

Conclusion

This analysis has important implications for contemporary theories of the state. By disaggregating the process whereby policy changes into three subtypes according to the magnitude of the changes involved and by invoking the concept of policy paradigms, we can discern more variation in social learning than hitherto recognized. The processes of first and second order change in policy correspond quite well to the image of social learning presented by Heclo and many theorists of the state.

---

[50] For the classic elaboration of this argument, see Peter Gourevitch, *Politics in Hard Times* (Ithaca: Cornell University Press, 1986).

[51] See Keegan, *Mrs. Thatcher's Economic Experiment*; James Alt, "Crude Politics: Oil and the Political Economy of Unemployment in Britain and Norway, 1970-85;" *British Journal of Political Science*, 17 (April 1977), 149-99; and Jock Bruce-Gardyne, *Mrs. Thatcher's First Administration* (London: Macmillan, 1984).

Changes in policy at time-1 were clearly a response to policy at time-0 and its consequences. Experts in the public employ were primarily responsible for policy innovation, and the learning process as a whole took place primarily inside the state itself.

However, the process of third order change which moved Britain from Keynesian to monetarist modes of policymaking was quite different. Policy at time-1 was certainly a response to the consequences of policy at time-0, but politicians rather than experts played a dominant role, and the process spilled well beyond the boundaries of the state to involve the media, outside interests, and contending political parties. Policy changed, not as a result of autonomous action by the state, but in response to an evolving societal debate that soon became bound up with electoral competition.

These findings call into question the tendency of state-centric theories to associate social learning with the autonomy of the state. Only some kinds of social learning seem to take place inside the state itself. The process of learning associated with important third order changes in policy can be a much broader affair subject to powerful influences from society and the political arena. Moreover, this appears to be true even in a technically complex field like macroeconomic policymaking, where the state should be most autonomous from societal pressure.

This analysis sheds light on state-society relations more generally. To begin with, it suggests that the stark dichotomy between state and society often drawn by state-centric theory should be revised in order to allot a significant role to the political system, defined as the complex of political parties and interest intermediaries that stand at the intersection between the state and society in democratic polities. The monetarist paradigm ultimately triumphed over its Keynesian rival by means of partisan electoral competition. Those who seek to "bring the state back in" to political analysis should not simultaneously read the political system out of their analyses.[52]

However, this case indicates that we need an even more expansive concept of state-society relations than such traditional conceptions of the political system provide. Political parties and organized interests groups are not the only "transmission belts" between the state and society. There were three other mechanisms through which significant pressure from society was placed on the British government to shift modes of economic policymaking.

The most obvious of these mechanisms was the media. Although we habitually acknowledge its presence, we rarely incorporate an adequate appreciation of the

[52] This point is also made in Peter A. Hall, *Governing the Economy* (New York: Oxford University Press, 1986), pp. 27 ff. The most sophisticated theorists of the state have already begun to explore the relationship between the institutional structure of the state and the party system. For interesting examples of such analyses, see Ann S. Orloff and Theda Skocpol, "Why Not Equal Protection? Explaining the Politics of Public Social Spending in Britain, 1900-1911, and the United States, 1880s-1920s," *American Sociological Review*, 49 (1984), 726-50; and Martin Shefter, "Party and Patronage: Germany, England, and Italy," *Politics and Society*, 1 (1977), 404-51.

importance of the media into our analyses. In this case, the British press did not simply transmit the range of views to be found among economists about the direction of economic policy; it magnified the prominence given to monetarist doctrine and catapulted monetarist thinking onto the public agenda.[53] The press is both a mirror of public opinion and a magnifying glass for the issues that it takes up.

Little noticed but especially important in the 1975-79 period was the pressure that the financial markets, notably for government debt and foreign exchange, placed on the government. Many of the ad hoc adjustments towards monetarism made by the 1974-79 Labour government were forced on it by the behavior of the financial markets, and the popularity of monetarist doctrine in these markets influenced both the Bank of England and the government. We are accustomed to the view that governments face an electoral constraint, but we should not forget that they also confront significant market constraints in the sphere of finance as well.[54]

Finally, the 1970s saw a vast expansion in the outside marketplace for economic ideas. The media and City brokerage houses were important participants in this marketplace, but they were not the only ones. Fueled by the release of the Treasury's econometric model, new research institutes sprang up, and a host of pamphlets about economic policy began to circulate. In short, where once there was virtually no external commentary on macroeconomic policy, something similar to a "policy network" or "issue network" sprang up to provide outsiders with influence over a formerly closed policy process.[55]

In some respects, these observations pull us back toward traditional models of policymaking as a struggle for power in which competing interests press their views on the government. The contest for electoral power that brought Thatcher to office was certainly central to the triumph of monetarism. Here, as in many instances, it would be an error to see politics exclusively in terms of collective puzzle-solving. To borrow Heclo's unusual verbs, many of the actors involved in changing policy not only "puzzle"; they also "power."

---

[53] For elaboration, see Hall, *The Political Dimensions of Economic Management*, ch. 6, and Parsons, ch. 6.

[54] This point is most often appreciated by those who study the long-term development of the state; cf. Charles Tilly, ed., *The Formation of National States in Western Europe* (Princeton: Princeton University Press, 1975). On British developments in the 1970s, see Hall, *The Political Dimensions of Economic Management*, chs. 5-7; and David Gowland, *Controlling the Money Supply* (London: Croom Helm, 1982).

[55] For representative works on this topic, see R. A. W. Rhodes, "Power Dependence, Policy Communities and Inter-Governmental Networks," Public Administration Bulletin, 49 (1985), 4-31; Hugh Heclo, "Issue Networks and the Executive Establishment," in Anthony King, ed., *The New American Political System* (Washington, D.C.. American Enterprise Institute, 1978), pp. 87-124; Katzenstein, Between Power and Plenty; Jeffrey Berry, "Subgovernments, Issue Networks, and Political Conflict," in Richard Harris and Sidney Milkis, eds., *Remaking American Politics* (Boulder: Westview, 1989), pp. 239-60; and the issue no. 1 of *Governance*, 2 (1989).

Does this mean that it would be inappropriate to describe the process of third order policy change described here as a case of social learning? I think not. The critical actors in this process inside both the state and society were not simply seeking to advance their own interests. They were also seeking solutions to Britain's economic problems. The 1970s were dominated by collective puzzlement and uncertainty about the economy, and the effort to regain control over it was an intensely intellectual quest marked by highly sophisticated debate in the media, the political parties, and the City, as well as among policymakers. The play of ideas was as important to the outcome as was the contest for power. For these reasons, it seems highly appropriate to describe this process as one of social learning.

The important point here is that "powering" and "puzzling" often go together. Both are dimensions of the process whereby policy changes, especially in democratic polities, whose institutions tend to combine the two endeavors. Politicians compete for office precisely by propounding new solutions to collective problems which appeal to the electorate. Officials advance their own fortunes within the bureaucracy partly by devising new approaches to old dilemmas. The institutional arrangements designed to marry the public interest to private interests in a democracy rarely work perfectly, but they do operate so as to militate against a rigid distinction between power-based and ideas-based models of politics. The competition for power can itself be a vehicle of social learning.[56]

The principal contribution of a social learning perspective is to draw our attention to the role of ideas in politics. It reminds us that state-society relations cannot adequately be described entirely in terms of the "pressures" that each exerts on the other, whether through parties, organized interests, administrative organs, or policy networks. The state is also linked to society by a flow of ideas between the two spheres. Politicians, officials, the spokesmen for social interests, and policy experts all operate within the terms of political discourse that are current in the nation at a given time, and the terms of political discourse generally have a specific configuration that lends representative legitimacy to some social interests more than others, delineates the accepted boundaries of state action, associates contemporary political developments with particular interpretations of national history, and defines the context in which many issues will be understood.[57]

In various respects, then, the terms of political discourse privilege some lines of policy over others, and the struggle both for advantage within the prevailing terms

---

[56] This point is one of the themes of Samuel H. Beer's work; see his essay, "In Search of a New Public Philosophy," in King, ed., *The New American Political System*, pp. 217-257, and *Modern British Politics* (New York: Norton, 1982).

[57] Cf. Jenson; Walker; Hall, "Conclusion," pp. 383-6; E. E. Schattschneider, *The Semi-Sovereign People* (New York: Holt, Rinehart and Winston, 1961), p. 68 et passim; William Connolly, *The Terms of Political Discourse* (Princeton: Princeton University Press, 1983); Frank R. Baumgartner, *Conflict and Rhetoric in French Policymaking* (Pittsburgh: University of Pittsburgh Press, 1989); and Rosemary C. R. Taylor, "The Politics of Prevention," *Social Policy*, 13 (Summer 1982), 32-41.

of discourse and for leverage with which to alter the terms of political discourse is a perennial feature of politics. Organized interests, political parties, and policy experts do not simply "exert power"; they acquire power in part by trying to influence the political discourse of their day. To the degree they are able to do so, they may have a major impact on policy without necessarily acquiring the formal trappings of influence.[58] The resultant flow of ideas is an important dimension of the process in which policy is made.

However, this dimension of policymaking has proven especially difficult to model.[59] Like subatomic particles, ideas do not leave much of a trail when they shift. What this article contributes to the analysis of such matters is a specific argument about the way in which ideas condition policymaking and how they change, organized around the concept of "policy paradigms." Policy paradigms can be seen as one feature of the overall terms of political discourse. They suggest that the policymaking process can be structured by a particular set of ideas, just as it can be structured by a set of institutions. The two often reinforce each other since the routines of policymaking are usually designed to reflect a particular set of ideas about what can and should be done in a sphere of policy.[60] But the ideas embodied in a policy paradigm have a status somewhat independent of institutions that can be used, as in the case of monetarism, to bolster or induce changes in institutional routines.

To illustrate this point, we need go no further than to compare the 1970-74 government under Edward Heath and the 1979-83 government of Margaret Thatcher. Both were Conservative governments, elected on promises to lower inflation, cut taxes, and reduce the role of the state in the economy. When rates of unemployment began to rise and recession loomed, however, the Heath government made a famous U-turn back toward reflation and interventionist policies, while the Thatcher government held fast to its deflationary course. What explains the difference? In part, of course, Thatcher learned from Heath's experience, suggesting once again that policy is strongly influenced by past experience. However, the platform on which Heath was elected was a jerrybuilt structure with no underpinning in an alternative economic theory, while Thatcher's was based on a much more fully

[58] The arguments that political parties put forward on the hustings, for instance, may push forward political debate in such a way as to advance particular lines of policy even when those parties lose the election. Ironically, this is one respect in which the implications of the social learning approach that Heclo has done so much to promote call into question his tests for the influence of elections and interest groups on social policy. See Heclo, *Modern Social Politics*, pp. 288-301.

[59] For significant attempts that acknowledge the difficulties, see John W. Kingdon, *Agendas, Alternatives and Public Policies* (Boston: Little, Brown, 1984), and the review of the "community power debate" in Steven Lukes, *Power: A Radical View* (London: Macmillan, 1974).

[60] One of the best illustrations of this can be found in the way in which both the economic model of the Treasury and the procedures for formulating annual budgets long reflected Keynesian assumptions. See Brittan, *Steering the Economy*; Paul Ormerod, *Economic Modelling* (London: Heinemann, 1979); and Heclo and Wildavsky, *The Private Government of Public Money*.

elaborated monetarist paradigm. Thus, when recession loomed and both governments faced intense pressure from producer groups for reflation, Heath had nothing to fall back on, other than a Keynesian paradigm that dictated reflation. Thatcher, by contrast, was able to appeal to the monetarist paradigm for authoritative arguments with which to resist mounting pressure for reflation.[61]

With the concept of policy paradigms, then, we can better understand variations in the autonomy of the state. Many analysts have argued that the capacity of a state to resist societal pressure depends on its institutional structure.[62] However, this observation generates a puzzle: how is it that a state with an unchanging structure often seems to be more autonomous from societal pressure at some times than at others or in some fields of policy than others? The answer suggested here is that the autonomy of the state in a given field of policy may also depend on whether there is a coherent policy paradigm present there. Policymakers are likely to be in a stronger position to resist pressure from societal interests when they are armed with a coherent policy paradigm. If it does not dictate the optimal course for policy, at least it provides a set of criteria for resisting some societal demands while accepting others. Precisely for this reason, the presence of a coherent policy paradigm greatly enhanced the autonomy of the Thatcherite state in the economic sphere. Conversely, when such a paradigm is absent or disintegrating, policymakers may be much more vulnerable to outside pressure, as the 1974-79 Labour government was once the Keynesian paradigm began to collapse. In this context, it becomes important to understand how and why policy paradigms change.

Building on Kuhn's formulation of such idea systems, I have generated a number of hypotheses about the process whereby policies change and tested them against cases of British economic policymaking during the 1970s. Several features of the process were striking. Policy displayed a specific kind of trajectory. The presence of a policy paradigm generated long periods of continuity punctuated occasionally by the disjunctive experience of paradigm shift.[63] The processes whereby different kinds of changes in policy occurred were quite distinctive. First and second

---

[61] Bruce-Gardyne, *Whatever Happened to the Quiet Revolution and Mrs. Thatcher's First Administration.* Conversely, when the monetarist paradigm itself began to lose coherence and credibility, Thatcher had much more difficulty resisting pressure for deviations in policy from both inside and outside the state. In particular, having resisted reflation in 1980-81, she acceded to it in 1986-87 when wealth effects unanticipated by the paradigm obscured the level of demand in the economy.

[62] For perceptive analyses, see Eric Nordlinger, "Taking the State Seriously," in Samuel P. Huntington and Myron Weiner, eds., *Understanding Political Development* (Boston: Little Brown, 1987), pp. 353-90; Katzenstein, ed., *Between Power and Plenty*; and Evans et al., eds., *Bringing the State Back In.* For an alternative argument to the effect that the state is more autonomous during periods of depression, war, and reconstruction, see Fred Block, "The Ruling Class Does Not Rule: Notes on the Marxist Theory of the State," *Socialist Review*, 33 (May-June 1977), 6-28.

[63] In this respect, the presence of policy paradigms may help to explain the process of "punctuated equilibrium" that Krasner identifies; see Krasner, "Approaches to the State."

order change took place within a relatively closed policy network and did not cumulate into third order change. The latter displayed particular features. New economic developments of the sort that occur all the time were not sufficient to generate paradigm change. That process was initiated by a specific kind of event, namely by events that proved anomalous within the terms of the prevailing paradigm. They gave rise to policy failures that discredited the old paradigm and led to a wide-ranging search for alternatives and to a process of experimentation with modifications to policy. Central to this process was a shift in the locus of authority over policy. Shifts in the locus of authority seem to be a critical component of the process whereby paradigms shift. Finally, the process leading to changes of this magnitude could not be confined inside the state itself; it was ultimately effected by means of electoral competition and a broader societal debate.

These observations should help us to understand how policy changes over time in other nations and fields of policy as well. Needless to say, not all fields of policy will possess policy paradigms as elaborate or forceful as the ones associated with macroeconomic policymaking. Such paradigms are most likely to be found in fields where policymaking involves some highly technical issues and a body of specialized knowledge pertaining to them. As the scope of the modern state has expanded, however, governments have found themselves involved in more and more spheres of policymaking of this type. The policy spheres of arms control, environmental regulation, and energy policy, among others, usually have such a character.

Similarly, policy paradigms are likely to have greatest impact in institutional settings where policy is superintended by experts or by administrators with long tenures in office. In such a context, policy paradigms are likely to become intertwined with firmly established operating procedures and departmental routines. The British civil service provides the acme of such settings, and we can expect to see some cross-national variation in the degree to which policy paradigms are embedded in institutional routines.

Only in some cases, then, will it be appropriate to speak of a fully elaborated policy paradigm. In others, the web of ideas affecting the direction of policy will be looser and subject to more frequent variations. Even here, however, we should not discount altogether the impact that an overarching set of ideas can have on policy. The most cynical bureaucrats and politicians must still rationalize their actions in terms that will draw popular support, provide a semblance of consistency, and motivate those who have to carry out the relevant policies. Moreover, their actions are invariably based on a particular understanding of that sphere of the world which policy addresses. The terms of discourse in which that sphere and the policies appropriate to it are discussed constrain and enable often in highly specific ways. Even where the *Leitmotiv* of policy is simply an overarching metaphor, such as the "war on drugs" or the "problem of welfare mothers," the metaphor and its attendant elaborations can structure many aspects of what is to be done. Policymaking in virtually all fields takes place within the context of a particular set of ideas that recognize some social interests as more legitimate than others and privilege some lines of policy over others.[64]

Without denying the impact of material interests on the policy process, we need to know much more than we now do about the role that ideas play in policymaking and in the process whereby policies change. I have suggested a number of hypotheses here with specific applications. The most important step we can take, however, is to note that it is not necessary to deny that politics involves a struggle for power and advantage in order to recognize that the movement of ideas plays a role, with some impact of its own, in the process of policymaking. This analysis cautions us against positing too rigid a distinction between "politics as social learning" and "politics as a struggle for power." It suggests that "powering" and "puzzling" are often intertwined in the formation of public policies. To see this most clearly, we need more studies of the evolution of policy over time, a subject that has often been neglected relative to static, one-shot comparisons of policy across nations.[65]

Similarly, while recognizing the usefulness of "bringing the state back in," this analysis cautions us against positing too rigid a distinction between the state and society and against an insistence on the autonomy of the state. To move forward, we need more nuanced analyses of the multiple ways in which state and society can be linked. Only then will the conditions under which governments act with more rather than less autonomy become clear. The investigation of such issues can be enriched by a more refined appreciation of the role of ideas in politics and by studies of the dynamics whereby policies change over time.

Acknowledgments

I would like to acknowledge the support of the German Marshall Fund during the preparation of this article. For critical comments, I am grateful to James Alt, Daniel Bell, Ernst Haas, Jane Jenson, Peter Katzenstein, Jonah Levy, Paul Pierson, Richard Rose, Jim Shoch, Theda Skocpol, David Soskice, Rosemary Taylor, Carol Weiss, the members of the Harvard CROPSO seminar, and the editors and referees.

---

[64] For representative examples, see Jenson; Marris; Kathryn Sikkink, *Ideas and Institutions: Developmentalism in Brazil and Argentina* (Ithaca: Cornell University Press, 1991); Judith Goldstein, "The Impact of Ideas on Trade Policy," *International Organization*, 42 (Winter 1989), 31-72; Michael Shafer, *Deadly Paradigms* (Princeton: Princeton University Press, 1988); Gilbert Rozman, *The Chinese Debate about Soviet Socialism* (Princeton: Princeton University Press, 1987); Nina Halpern, "Social Scientists as Policy Advisors in Post-Mao China," *Australian Journal of Chinese Affairs*, 19/20 (1988), 215-40; Yuen Foon Khong, *Analogies of War* (Princeton: Princeton University Press, 1992); and Deborah Stone, *Policy Paradox and Political Reason* (Boston: Scott, Foresman, 1988).

[65] The evolution of policy over time has not been studied as fully as it might. For two of the few works addressed to this problem, see Rose, ed., *The Dynamics of Public Policy*; and Brian W. Hogwood and B. Guy Peters, *Policy Dynamics* (Brighton: Wheatsheaf, 1983), as well as some of the literature on the development of the welfare state such as Peter Flora and Arnold Heidenheimer, eds., *The Development of Welfare States in Europe and America* (New Brunswick: Transaction, 1981).

CHAPTER 5

Paradigm Shifts and Policy Networks: Cumulative Change in Agriculture[1]

William D. Coleman, Grace D. Skogstad, and Michael M. Atkinson

Neo-institutionalist theorists have significantly shaped our understanding of the possibilities for radical policy change. In emphasizing the impact of institutions on actors' resources and incentives, both rational choice and historical institutionalists remind us that early institutional choices create locked-in paths of development which in turn inhibit radical policy shifts (North 1990, 16). Political interests learn how the institutional framework operates and mobilize political power according to the incentives it provides. The policies created within this framework provide feedback to these interests, suggesting how to reorganize or create new alliances to maintain and extend favourable policies (Pierson 1996; Weir and Skocpol 1985). This learning process suggests why, in the absence of institutional upheaval, policy change is much more likely to be incremental than radical.

This characterization of the change process raises a serious question for students of public policy: is it possible to change policy significantly without either changing or by-passing existing policymaking institutions? Some neo-institutionalists, like Peter Hall, are pessimistic. Hall (1993) posits three orders of policy change. First order change implies changes in the settings of policy instruments, while second order change entails the replacement of one policy instrument with another. In both cases, state actors proceed rather autonomously and no institutional change is required (Hall 1993, 281). Third order change, however, constitutes a dramatic departure in policy goals, based on a new theoretical and ideological framework or paradigm, and typically involves both state and societal actors. Hall suggests that a paradigm shift occurs when anomalies accumulate, policies fail, and the authority of the original policy paradigm is undermined. Hall draws his conclusions about paradigmatic change from an analysis of the shift from Keynesian to monetarist macroeconomic policy in Great Britain. The rapid rejection of Keynesianism in favour of monetary discipline was based on policy feedback, in

[1] An earlier version of this paper was presented to the Annual Meeting of the American Political Science Association, September 1995. The authors would like to thank fellow panellists at this meeting and Peter A. Hall for comments on the paper. Research supported by the Social Sciences and Humanities Research Council of Canada, Research Grant, 410-92-0260.

this case increasing evidence that fiscal activism was producing unexpected and undesirable consequences. Policy failure in the form of a deterioration in financial markets set the stage for institutional changes, particularly in the composition of the policy community. Politicians became more important than bureaucrats and social forces beyond parties and interest groups expanded the range of policy discourse. This reconfiguration of institutional actors expedited social learning on a broad scale and made third order change possible.

In this article we posit an alternative to Hall's version of sweeping policy change based on institutional realignments. Like Hall's, this alternative route to paradigm shift assumes the accumulation of first and second order changes. However, the transition is much more gradual and there is no requirement that significant institutional change precede policy change. What is required is a distribution of power within institutions that allows actors to understand the consequences of public policies and visualize alternative policy paradigms (Pierson 1993:615). Learning of this kind induces adjustment and planned policy change that eventually constitutes a paradigm shift. We develop this argument for a second, cumulative trajectory to paradigm shift by examining agricultural policy change in three countries: the United States, Canada, and Australia. Agricultural policy is an instructive case study because it has been based on a common and distinctive paradigm in most developed countries in the post Second World War period. What we will call the state-assisted paradigm rests on two fundamental principles: first, the agriculture sector contributes to national policy goals and therefore merits special attention; and, second, the price mechanism is a sub-optimal means of achieving an efficient and productive agricultural sector. Imperfect markets combine with unmanageable natural risks and concern for food security to give governments a large role in subsidizing agricultural production.

In OECD countries these principles have set the stage for the pursuit of three key policy goals. First, agricultural producers should receive an income from farming sufficient to ensure an adequate standard of living. Second, increased efficiency should be achieved by the adoption of new technology to permit intensive agricultural production. Finally, marginal farmers deserve assistance in becoming efficient, commercially viable producers. Different countries have embraced the elements of this state-assisted paradigm to differing degrees, often choosing different policy instruments. But all have subscribed in some measure to these policy goals and in some countries agriculture is organized almost entirely around them.

In the past decade, this state-assisted policy paradigm has come under increasing pressure from neo-liberal critics who fault it for such problems as overproduction, high government costs, and international trade tensions. This pressure has intensified further as agriculture has become more fully integrated into international trade discussions at the regional (EU, NAFTA) and global (GATT) levels. An alternative paradigm, what we will call the market liberal paradigm, while always present in policy discourse, has now emerged to challenge state-assistance. In this paradigm market allocation takes precedence over state intervention, and efficiency over equity. The central tenets are as follows: first, agriculture should be understood as an economic sector like all others and agricultural policy should not be premised on serving other policy goals; second competitive markets, in which only supply and demand determine prices, should be the source of producers' incomes; third, only those producers who can earn an income from the sale of commodities in these free markets should remain active in agriculture; and, finally, individual producers should be responsible, mainly through private insurance markets, for protecting themselves against income losses due to natural conditions.

As we will show below, there are strong intimations that what Hall (1993, 278-9) calls "third-order" change is underway in agricultural policy as countries begin to shift from the state-assisted to the market liberal paradigm. However, the pattern of change does not conform, at least not entirely, to the one that Hall has sketched out. We will argue that political institutions – specifically policy networks – and the character of policy feedback, combine to determine whether paradigm shifts are the products of a politicized process of social learning conducted in partisan forums (the Hall model), or of a slower, but equally decisive, process managed within relatively closed policy communities.

Political Change, Policy Feedback and Policy Networks

In his work on social welfare policy, Pierson (1993, 1994) highlights several ways in which policy feedback varies across policy areas.

(1) Public policies provide incentives or resources that either inhibit or facilitate the organization of groups.
(2) Policies may or may not encourage the creation of networks that "lock in" a particular path of policy development for groups or for mass publics.
(3) The effects of policies are highly visible or practically invisible to mass publics.
(4) Some policies are readily traceable by mass publics to government elites while the sources of other policies are obscure.

An examination of these dimensions suggests that policy feedback processes will differ significantly between macroeconomic policy, the subject of Hall's analysis, and other policy areas, including the area we have chosen, price and income support policies in agriculture (see Table 5.1). The fiscal and monetary policy instruments employed in the service of macroeconomic policy objectives provide diffuse benefits and costs to individuals directly. In this respect, they offer few incentives or resources for the formation of interest groups. If lock-in effects occur with macroeconomic policies, they are with individuals or firms who invest and save based on expectations of how governments will behave in the face of economic growth or recession. However, the effects of macroeconomic policies – higher or lower taxes, higher or lower interest rates, and higher or lower unemployment – are highly visible to mass publics and readily traceable to government leaders. It is not surprising, therefore, that policy failures and "anomalies" will provoke a broad public debate about the role of government, a debate that will spill easily into battles among political parties for the hearts and minds of the electorate.

Table 5.1. Comparison of Policy Feedback in Macroeconomic and Agricultural Policy

Policy Feedback	Macroeconomic Policy	Agricultural Price and Income Support Policies
Incentives and resources for group formation	Low	High
Lock-in effects	High on mass publics, low on groups	Low on mass publics, high on groups
Visibility to mass publics	High	Low
Traceability of policy effects to government elites	High	Low

Government authorities formulate and implement macroeconomic policy in a state-directed policy network that operates in relative isolation from interest groups, but with direct, visible effects on mass publics.[2] As Table 5.1 suggests, policy feedback differs significantly for agricultural price and income support policies. By their very character, these policies deliver obvious benefits to producers of particular commodities while diffusing costs to mass publics. In this respect, they provide incentives and occasionally resources to agricultural interest groups wishing to improve or to preserve these benefits. The systems of interest associations spawned by such policies mobilize farmers as specialized producers of commodities and gradually lock them in to expectations about state assistance and even to certain choices on crop selection. The effects of price and income support policies are highly visible to agricultural producers themselves but ordinarily less so to mass publics who have difficulty in tracing variations in food costs directly to government authorities.

In short, the policy feedback from agricultural programmes invites the formation and institutionalization of policy networks where interest groups feature much more prominently than they do in the state- directed network found in macroeconomic policy. Of course, groups are central actors in several different types of policy networks (van Waarden 1992). The two most important network types in agricultural policy are pressure pluralism and (sectoral) corporatism. Which of these forms

[2] We draw our discussion of network types from Coleman and Skogstad (1990), Atkinson and Coleman (1989) and van Waarden (1992).

emerge will be a function of broader institutional factors and of the policy instruments used to support prices and incomes.[3]

Although the literature on these two network types is large and complex, there is now sufficient consensus to rely on three central properties to distinguish them from each other. First, in pressure pluralist networks, associations compete with one another not only for the ear of the state, but also for members. Rather than interest domains being controlled by groups with representational monopolies as in corporatism (Schmitter 1979; Williamson 1989), pluralist domains are competitive terrains where various groups scramble to represent as many of the potential members as possible.

Second, associational systems in pressure pluralist networks feature low levels of vertical and horizontal integration. Associations with more general domains such as those that attempt to represent all farmers do not take the form of peak associations as in corporatism; more specialized groups representing wheat producers or dairy farmers do not belong to these general farm organizations. In addition, in corporatist networks, associations have long-standing institutionalized relationships with one another. In contrast, in pressure pluralism, associations tend to cooperate on an ad hoc basis, with ties dissolving once the occasion for common political action disappears.

Finally, associations in corporatist networks have a "public status" (Williamson 1989), while those in pluralist networks do not. Public status includes obtaining resources from the state, participating directly in policy formulation, or receiving a delegation of state authority to implement public policies. In pressure pluralism, associations act as policy advocates, seeking to influence policy from the outside.

These two policy networks have rather different capacities to sustain the process of cumulative policy change that results in a paradigm. In order for the cumulative road to be taken, a policy network must provide an environment where communicative action favouring deliberation and discussion over preferences and strategies can take place (Risse-Kappen, 1996). Under such circumstances, decision-making takes on what Scharpf (1989, 261) calls a "problem-solving" style where there develops "an orientation to common interests, values or norms which are distinct from the individual self-interest of participants and which, therefore, may facilitate voluntary agreement even when sacrifices in terms of individual self-interest are necessary..." Clearly, a change from considering self-interest to common interests can lead to new preference orderings and revised or new policy strategies.

Corporatist policy networks are more likely to favour and sustain such communicative action for three reasons. First, Risse-Kappen emphasizes that communicative action requires informal relationships among participants in the policy com-

[3] For some analysis of conditions favouring different types of networks in agriculture, see Keeler (1987), Culpepper (1993), Jobert and Muller (1987), Skogstad (1990), and Coleman and Skogstad (1995).

munity. Bernd Marin (1985, 110-12) notes that corporatism involves a curious dialectic between formality and informality. As we have noted, structures of representation involve highly formal, strongly representative peak associations. These join with state actors in fora that emphasize parity of representation and often consensus decision-making. With these formal structures and rules in place, actual policy discussions and relationships among actors involved tend to be highly informal and flexible. In pressure pluralist networks, contacts among competing groups representing different interests tend to be more formal than informal, if they take place at all.

Second, communicative action is facilitated if relationships among policy actors are non-hierarchical. Parity representation and consensus decision-making in corporatist networks favour dialogue over powerplays and the assertion of authority. In contrast, group-state relations in pressure pluralist networks often follow a typical hierarchical pattern, with the group trying to influence state actors who are not inclined to share their authority.

Finally, Risse-Kappen observes that deliberative decision-making works best when participants possess collectively shared beliefs and understandings. Corporatist networks comprise a rather stable set of organizations that work together over a number of years. Participants tend to develop an appreciation of the problems and points of view of other actors which, in times of stress, facilitates adoption of a problem-solving decision-making style. Conversely, pressure pluralist networks cannot claim the same stability in relationships. The opportunities for developing shared beliefs and understandings among groups, and between groups and state actors, are few if any. Accordingly, we argue in this paper that significant policy change is unlikely to be achieved inside a pluralist policy network where group self-interest will be dominant. In this type of network, policymaking is reactive rather than anticipatory, and premised on preserving, not challenging the dominant policy paradigm. If significant change is to come, then the more likely sources are political and societal actors outside the sectoral policy network. In contrast, a corporatist network is more likely to create an environment conducive to promoting the long term collective interest of the sector rather than the short term interest of specific groups. In this environment, network participants negotiate policy changes which, over time and with hindsight, can constitute a paradigm shift.

We are not suggesting, however, that all corporatist networks will foster the communicative action just described. Lehmbruch (1984) has argued that sectoral corporatism often takes the form of a self-interested robbers coalition that can be even more effective than pressure pluralism in preserving the status quo. Scharpf (1988:273) has hypothesized that corporatist networks featuring an unanimity decision-making rule and a bargaining policy style may suffer from all the pathologies of the "joint decision trap."

We develop our argument by focusing on price and income support policies which are closely associated with the state-assisted paradigm in agriculture. We look first at trajectories of policy change in three pluralist networks: cereal grains in Canada and in the US, and dairy products in the US. We show that to the extent that significant changes take place in these networks, they tend to conform closely to Hall's conception of a paradigm shift. We then examine three examples of policy change in corporatist networks: cereal grains and dairy in Australia, and dairy in Canada. Here too we find evidence of significant policy change, but these changes are negotiated within the policy network and outside the broader partisan arena.

Pressure Pluralist Policy Networks

In the 1990s, significant market liberal reforms to expenditure policy instruments have occurred in the American grains and dairy sectors, and, to a lesser extent, in Canada's grain sector. In the US, the appreciable retrenchment of the state from the agriculture sector, represented by the passage of the 1996 farm bill, followed Hall's proposed trajectory. Instigated by the Republican Congressional victory in 1994, agricultural policy reform was caught up in a broader public and partisan discussion, about the appropriate role of the state in the economy. The hypothesized relationship between pressure pluralism, on the one hand, and Hall's process of externally imposed paradigm change, on the other, is also supported by developments in Canada's cereal grains sector. Market liberal changes to one of the core policy instruments, transportation subsidies for export grain, and the prospect of a paradigmatic shift in another, the Canadian Wheat Board, have both been initiated from outside the pressure pluralist network. These initiatives tend to provoke a broad, often partisan political debate, and one that involves other institutions, including the judiciary.

Policy change related to the third core policy instrument, income support and stabilization, furnishes an even more interesting laboratory for the study of the relationship between policy networks and patterns of change. Although group structures fit the pressure pluralist model, beginning in 1989, the federal government created a corporatist-type forum that initiated a more deliberate, planned shift toward the market liberal paradigm. But in the absence of an associational system with representational monopolies and significant horizontal and vertical integration, this process could not be sustained. The inherent pluralism of the sector, combined with competitive federalism, handicapped policy consensus and made a concerted transition to less costly, neoliberal, policy instruments more protracted. As expected, when discussion occurs in a pressure pluralist network, competing self-interested groups and provincial governments undermined much of the consensus developed in the (temporary) quasi-corporatist network. The further market liberal changes that occurred in 1995 were imposed by actors outside the policy network and were driven by deficit reduction considerations.

Cereal Grains – United States of America

With few exceptions, the associational systems in US agriculture conform well to a pressure pluralist model. General farm organizations like the American Farm Bureau Federation (AFBF), the National Farmers Union (NFU), the National Farmers Organization (NFO) and the National Grange seek to represent the common interests of all agricultural producers. The general farm organizations, however, do not act as peak associations and are not linked to more specialized associations like the National Association of Wheat Growers and the US Wheat Associates, which represent cereal grain growers on a national plane. All these general and specialized farm groups, not to mention those functioning at the state-level, compete to represent cereal producers. Moreover, depending upon the issue, each faces either a potent ally or a formidable opponent in the North American Export Grains Association, the voice of the private grain traders. The resulting fragmentation of farm interests lowers significantly the likelihood of a co-operative and interdependent farm lobby (Browne 1988, 115).

The core instruments that support wheat prices originated in the 1933 Agricultural Adjustment Act. By the early 1980s, these instruments had evolved to include government-fixed loan rates that established a minimum or floor price for each crop, a deficiency payment which covered the gap between a politically determined (above anticipated market levels) target price and the higher of the market price or loan rate, and acreage reduction requirements that entailed setting aside acreage as a condition for receiving government program payments. Budgetary pressures were responsible for a series of changes in the early 1980s and in the 1985 and 1990 farm bills that made these instruments (for example, the lowering of target prices) more responsive to market signals.

These nods in the direction of market liberalism, however, were more than offset by the return in force of a policy instrument used in the 1950s and 1960s (Cochrane and Ryan 1976: ch. 7): export subsidies for wheat and other commodities. These new subsidies led to significant expenditures in the late 1980s and early 1990s. Actual expenditures remained in excess of $20 billion in 1993 (Brooks and Carter 1994:1). In short, prior to the pivotal 1994 Congressional elections, the US retained its traditional policy instruments in cereal grains and revived export subsidies. Consistent with the state-assisted paradigm, farm incomes were more dependent on government payments than at any time in the past.

Two important forces exogenous to the policy network combined to force the beginnings of a systematic move to a more market liberal policy. The first included budget deficits and budget-conscious politicians. By the 1990 Farm Bill, reducing agriculture expenditures had become a fact of life for farm programmes. As preparations began for the 1995-96 Farm Bill, the Congressional Budget Office figures led the Budget Committee to call for a reduction in agricultural expenditures of a startling 13.4 billion dollars by 2002.

The second catalyst to market liberal change was the neo-liberal Republican majority win in Congress in 1994. Pressed by the House of Representatives' leadership, the Chairman of the House of Representatives Agricultural Committee, Pat Roberts, introduced a significant market liberal reform in an August 1995 proposal entitled "Freedom to Farm", reprising the concept popularized by Ezra Taft Benson, Eisenhower's Secretary of Agriculture. The process of constructing this new Farm Bill differed significantly from the traditional pressure pluralist process. Congressional sub-committees were relatively uninvolved in crafting the legislation and hearings played a much smaller role than in the past. Discussions in both the Senate and the House continued throughout the fall, with no final decisions being taken as agriculture was caught in the broader struggle between the President and the Congress over the federal budget. Only after a temporary resolution of the Executive-Congressional conflict did the farm bill move forward. The Federal Agricultural Improvement and Reform (FAIR) Act was signed by President Clinton on 4 April 1996.

The history of US agricultural policy and the characteristics of pressure pluralism both imply that radical change is unlikely to come from within the policy network. At this stage the 1996 FAIR Act represents a giant step toward the neo-liberal paradigm. The fact that it has occurred largely apart from the traditional pluralist process is consistent with our hypothesized relationship between pressure pluralism and Hall's trajectory.

The overall thrust of the 1996 farm bill is clearly market-oriented. It seeks to reorient production decisions, to move them away from incentives offered by government programs and towards market conditions. Whereas previous policy instruments supported farmers' incomes on a product basis, with price support levels a function of market prices, the 1996 Farm Bill decouples payments from both production decisions and market prices. Grain producers have the opportunity to enter a seven-year contract for a support payment that is independent of the market price and largely independent of the commodity produced. Individual payments accruing from these production flexibility contracts are based on historical planting patterns: their aggregate amount is fixed and declines sharply during the seven year duration of the bill. Farmers are no longer obliged to practise production controls in order to receive these "market transition" payments. As well, the acreage consigned to conservation reserve programmes is now capped.

Together these changes and the elimination of many traditional policy instruments suggest the term "radical policy reform" is merited. Moreover, in terms of sheer expenditure reductions, the transformation of the state's role in US agriculture is rather breath-taking: in contrast to the record high $26 billion figure of 1986 (Brooks and Carter 1994, 147, 148), the FAIR Act predicts commodity program payments of $5.6 billion in 1996 and $4.1 billion in 2001. Nonetheless, there is some reason for caution in describing the FAIR Act as constituting a full paradigm shift. The 1996 farm bill retains instruments to pursue some traditional objectives of

American agricultural policy. Export subsidies remain, although allotted expenditure amounts have declined as required by the Uruguay Round Agreement on Agriculture. The US Government also continues to support producers' incomes, albeit at a declining rate. The signing of the death certificate for the state-assisted paradigm must await the termination of government income support in 2002 and the removal of remaining production restrictions.

Dairy – United States of America

In the absence of horizontal and vertical linkages among general and commodity-specific farm groups, representational monopolies are rare in the US dairy sector and competition for members among groups is more the norm. Increasing regional diversity in dairy production added significantly to the obstacles faced by the National Milk Producers Federation in its attempt to represent the sector: "By the late 1970s, the NMPF had more and more difficulty finding common positions with which to govern the industry. By the middle of the 1980s regional cleavages in the industry became so intense that the NMPF was losing its ability as a consensus builder" (Young, Lindberg and Hollingsworth 1989:138). In the largest dairy state, California, separate organizations representing dairy producers and dairy cooperatives remain outside the NMPF umbrella. This pluralism is compounded at the state level. For example, in the dairy-significant state of Wisconsin, distinct organizations represent dairy cooperatives, larger dairy producers (Wisconsin Farm Bureau), and smaller producers (Wisconsin-NFO).

Policy instruments in the US dairy sector have been relatively stable for the past 60 years. The three core policy instruments implementing the state-assisted paradigm in dairy included: price supports normally above world price levels for manufactured dairy products; fixed minimum prices above international market prices for fluid milk; and import quotas on (lower cost) dairy imports. These income stabilization instruments were supplemented by the occasional use of two other instruments to control supply: export subsidies and domestic food programs targeted to needy groups (Cochrane and Ryan 1976: 274-9).

Tentative moves in the direction of the market liberal paradigm throughout the 1980s dropped government price supports for manufacturing milk to a level that failed to cover dairy farmers' cash costs by the mid-1990s. In the 1980s, in an attempt to reduce government costs and revive prices, new voluntary supply programs paid farmers to reduce their dairy herds and milk sales. Notwithstanding these changes, the tenacity of the state-assisted paradigm in dairy was illustrated by retention of fixed minimum prices through the marketing order system and by the introduction of new subsidies for dairy product exports in 1987. In fact, by the mid-1990s, the Dairy Export Incentive Program's removal of excess dairy products made it the most important dairy price support program in the country.

In the mid-1990s, when the US farm bill was being drafted, the dairy programs were caught up in the same two exogenous forces noted earlier for cereal grains:

budgetary pressures and a Republican majority in Congress hostile to the concept of "state assistance." Under the 1996 FAIR Act, support prices for dairy products are scheduled to fall further between 1996 and 1999, when the price supports will disappear in favour of a recourse loan programme. This plan removes the classic instrument of state assistance in place since the Great Depression and replaces it with a minimal, much more market-oriented policy. How important the change was remains debatable because dairy price supports had already declined in significance because of higher market prices in the 1990s (Gardner 1995, 56). The removal of production assessments did leave dairy farmers with one less disincentive to increase production. An additional earlier reform, required by the 1993 Uruguay Round Agreement on Agriculture, eliminated import quotas and replaced them with high tariffs and minimum import access requirements.

But these examples of limited market liberal reforms coexist alongside several remaining state-assistance instruments: a slightly reformed federal marketing order system, renewed domestic food programs, and export subsidies. Moreover, the 1996 farm bill opens the possibility for enhanced regional regulation of dairy marketing and a new dairy export trading agency. In short, as with US grains policy, the changes made to US dairy policy in 1996 are consistent with Hall's model. Pressure pluralist networks favoured the status quo in the 1980s and early 1900s; strong partisan political forces, marshalled outside the sectoral policy community, were the instigators of major policy change in a neo-liberal direction.

Cereal Grains – Canada

Decidedly less pluralistic than the American grains sector, association structures in Canada's cereal grains sector none the less conform to the model of a pressure pluralist network. Both general farm organizations and groups representing exclusively cereal grain producers divide on ideological lines as they compete for members and the ear of governments. There is no exclusive peak grains association as exists in Australia. The Western Canada Wheat Growers Association (WCWG) and the Western Barley Growers Association (WBGA) take a decidedly market liberal orientation that pits them against the traditionally dominant wheat pools in Alberta, Saskatchewan, and Manitoba. Individually, and together under the associational rubric of Prairie Pools, the wheat cooperatives uphold state-assisted principles. At the level of general farm organizations, the organizationally weak National Farmers' Union (NFU) offers a more radical alternative to the better resourced and more influential Canadian Federation of Agriculture (CFA). Both espouse the state assisted paradigm, the CFA being somewhat more pragmatic and flexible in its endorsation. However, neither the CFA nor NFU can speak authoritatively for the grains sector.[4]

[4] The market-oriented commodity groups (the WCWGA and the WBGA) are not members of the CFA. Although Prairie Pools is an affiliated member, the CFA is without general farm associ-

1. Transportation Subsidies and Orderly Marketing

Forces exogenous to the policy network have catalyzed reform of grain transportation subsidies and orderly marketing. The pressure pluralist network has been largely incapable of resisting external pressures and negotiating the change process. Transportation subsidies known as the Crowsnest Rates, introduced in 1897, had become a significant transfer to producers by the 1960s. Following a classical pluralist debate that spilled into the partisan and federal-provincial arenas, a first order change came in 1983 when these transfers to the railways were capped. The magnitude of the export subsidies continued to make them an attractive target for proponents of deficit and debt reduction, and when the GATT Agreement on Agriculture required that they be reduced, these subsidies were eliminated in 1995. Prairie grain transportation costs are now determined by the market, with the government presence remaining only in the form of legislated maximum freight rates (Canada 1995, 44).

A similar inability to contain policy reform debate within the traditional pluralist policy network is also revealed in current discussions of grain marketing. For over half a century, the Canadian government has supported the "orderly marketing" of grain through a state-authorized, monopoly agency for export sales of wheat (since 1943) and barley (since 1949). The Board did lose some of its domestic monopoly in 1973 but retains its crucial status as a single-desk exporter of Canadian wheat and barley. In the mid-1990s, the Board has come under siege, bombarded by the WCWG, the WBGA and individual producers imbued with the market liberal paradigm. US private grain traders and producers have also weighed in heavily, labelling the Board's activities as unfair trading practices. The federal government, with the support of a majority of cereals producers and the wheat pools, resisted these pressures for change. But its efforts to broker a consensus within the farm community in 1995-96, by entrusting a handful of farm leaders to advise it on the future role of the Wheat Board, have not contained the debate. A minority of disgruntled grain growers circumvented the legal authority of the Wheat Board. The debate over the Board's status as a single-desk export seller is now in the legal arena as the Federal Court of Canada hears a claim of a group of 21 individual producers and the Alberta Barley Commission and Western Barley Growers Association that the Board's practices contravene Canada's Charter of Rights and Freedoms. In 1995-96 individual farmers were arrested at the Canadian-US border when they attempted to sell grain without Wheat Board authorization. A broader, increasingly partisan, and inter-governmental debate has followed showing that the policy network is in jeopardy of being displaced. If the Wheat Board is to fall as a state-assisted policy instrument, it will come following a process that resembles increasingly that outlined by Hall.

ation members in two of the three prairie provinces. The NFU is handicapped in its representational claims by its small membership base of farm families.

2. Income Support and Stabilisation Policies

Income stabilisation policies became a permanent state-assisted policy instrument for cereal grains producers in the 1970s. The Western Grains Stabilization Programme was not designed to mask market signals completely, but to stabilize net cash income in the prairie grain-growing region (Skogstad 1987, 58-59). This stabilization program, to which farmers contributed financially, became severely depleted by the mid-1980s. In the wake of globally depressed prices, the Canadian government responded by supporting grain growers' incomes with expensive direct payments to producers. The high cost of these programs could not be sustained over the long term by a national government under increasing domestic and international pressure to restrain its spending and reduce its deficit.

Faced with this crisis, the federal government made a concerted attempt, consistent with corporatist models, to involve the associational system directly in policy formulation by bringing together a broadly representative group of producers and provincial government officials. Known as Grains 2000, this group was an explicit attempt by the Minister of Agriculture to widen the policy network beyond the usual "experts" to include producers themselves.

The corporatist network achieved a consensus on two new income programs that moved in a market liberal direction: one based on gross revenue insurance and the other on income stabilization. Both programs emphasized the producer's responsibility, alongside the state, for stabilizing individual income. The new income stabilization measure, in particular, sought to minimize government interference with producers' production decisions by stabilizing the net income of the whole farm, rather than income earned from sales of a particular commodity.

This widened (and temporary) corporatist network is credited with enabling the consensus on these new programs which were incorporated in the 1991 federal Farm Income Protection Act. Interviews reveal the kind of negotiated change possible in a corporatist network. A federal official observed that the opportunity for producers to discuss programs and policy allowed them "to appreciate that issues are more complex than what most people perceive them to be". Another official noted that the corporatist environment made it possible to achieve a greater degree of consensus by giving everyone "a pretty good idea as to what sort of compromise is going to have to be made" (Interview, Agriculture Canada, February 1993). In contrast to traditional pluralist consultation and decision-making, he explained that "I would much rather have the industry making the trade-offs, and being cognizant of the need for tradeoffs, through a better mutual understanding of the differences that exist-..."

Notwithstanding these positive reviews, this nascent corporatist network began to unravel in the mid-1990s. Flaws in program design, provincial and federal budgetary pressures, and the need to render domestic income safety nets compatible with the terms of the GAiT Agreement on Agriculture, had led to further consideration of income stabilization measures that built on the 1991 consensus. These discussions took place within a neo-corporatist type group that included ten provincial and three federal officials, and nineteen representatives of farm organizations (Tower 1994, 8; Belzile 1994). But the reassertion of provincial interests revealed the weaknesses inherent in the pluralist associational system. Intergovernmental bargaining soon replaced the neo-corporatist consultative committee. Producer groups reverted to lobbying from the outside and a pluralist network once again became the order of the day (Wilson 1995a, 1995b).

The new national farm safety net program agreed to by Canada's provincial and federal officials in April 1996, while building on the 1991 corporatist consensus, bows to producer and provincial self-interest as one would expect in a pressure pluralist network. The programs will differ significantly from one province to another, with some provinces being much more market liberal than others. Similar to transportation subsidies, deficit reduction forces from outside have also intervened, with the result that the net contribution by governments has fallen significantly. The 1995 federal Budget announced a 30 per cent reduction in expenditures in income support programs in the three-year period ending in 1997-98. This diminished government support, the Government noted, requires the industry to move away "from a reliance on government financial programs to an increased reliance on returns from the marketplace" (Agriculture and Agri-Food Canada 1995, i).

In summary, by 1996, cereal grains policy in Canada had moved significantly toward market liberalism. Transportation subsidies for exports had ended, fiscal retrenchment had cut back support for incomes, and orderly marketing was being questioned and attacked in partisan political discussions and before the courts. Similar to the US, pressure pluralist networks are proving themselves unable to manage such strong outside pressures favouring a paradigm shift. Quite a different picture emerges as we turn now to examine corporatist policy networks.

Corporatist Policy Networks

We have hypothesized that the pattern of change will differ in at least two ways when corporatist rather than pressure pluralist or state-directed policy networks are in place. First, the formulation and implementation of change will be negotiated and managed, thus remaining under the control of the corporatist network, rather than being imposed from the outside following a partisan political debate. Second, instead of sudden, rather large, breaks with past policy (as in the 1996 Farm Bill) or no change at all, policy change will follow a cumulative negotiated path, which, over time, can culminate in a paradigm shift.

Developments in three corporatist networks – dairy policy in Australia and Canada, and cereal grains policy in Australia – support our expectations to some degree. In all three cases, policy does move in a negotiated, cumulative fashion away from the state-assisted paradigm. For the most part, policy change is also controlled by the network without broader partisan rumblings or interference. For example, the debate over orderly marketing in cereals in Australia remains much more confined to the policy network than the same debate just described in Canada. But there may be limits on how far change will go. Although corporatist networks are capable of finding policy solutions that move policy in a market liberal direction, they also are effective bulwarks for certain state-assisted policy instruments. Thus orderly marketing remains a core principle in the Australian cereals grain sector and administered production and pricing are retained in Canadian dairy policy. Only in the Australian dairy sector does the policy trajectory appear likely to culminate in policy changes constituting paradigm shift by the turn of the century.

Dairy – Australia

Prior to the late 1960s, the Australian dairy sector benefited from four sets of price and income policy instruments: subsidies on exported products, price support of exported manufactured milk products, underwriting of export prices, and state milk marketing boards with buying and selling monopolies. The rising treasury costs of these measures resulted in export subsidies first being capped, then eliminated in 1973. A second and more important shift in a market liberal direction came in the 1980s when the Minister in charge of the Department of Primary Industries and Energy (DPIE), John Kerin, announced his intention to reduce state assistance for the dairy sector, focusing in particular on price supports.

Although at this time policymaking took place in a pressure pluralist policy network, structural conditions were in place that could support a corporatist policy network, a change favoured by Kerin. Both Australian dairy producers and manufacturers of dairy products were already organized into federated "peak" structures. The Australian Dairy Farmers' Federation (ADFF) groups state dairy or farmers federations representing dairy farmers. The representative of manufacturers of dairy products, the Australian Dairy Products Federation (ADPF), included as members almost all the large and medium-sized dairy manufacturers, and many of the smaller private firms and cooperatives.

The Minister took advantage of these structures to create a new intrasectoral organization equipped to participate in a corporatist policy network, the Australian Dairy Industry Council (ADIC). The ADIC membership included 23 producer (ADFF) representatives, 19 processor/manufacturer (ADPF) representatives, and four members of other bodies. Its mandate was to draw together the major and potentially conflicting interests in the sector for the purpose of advising the DPIE Minister on the implementation of dairy policy reform. Its voting structure ensured that no one sector (manufacturers or producers) could achieve decisions without the support of another sector.

In agreeing to participate in the formulation of policy through the ADIC, both the ADFF and the ADPF had to change their own internal organizations. Dairy producers were pushed to reduce and resolve conflicts between regions and to give more careful consideration to manufacturers' perspectives. As an executive of the ADFF phrased it in a 1993 interview:

... it was recognized that if we were to make the ADIC effective, and farmers were to have a strong voice in that process, the ADFF had to be more effective in its policy development. But it couldn't just purely and simply operate in a very parochial manner. It had to take into account the views of others and try and find some mechanism to ensure those views were taken into account.

The ADPF hired a full-time executive director for the first time, and increased its policy expertise. As one of ADFF's senior executive explained, strategic planning exercises initiated by the ADFF enabled intrasectoral differences to be bridged, an understanding of "each others" perspectives and each others' ideals and goals' to develop, and "a national perspective" to emerge (Interview, July 1993).

From this process came an internal industry consensus that the dismantlement of government support and its restructuring of the dairy industry proceed at a predictable pace, and that the transition not be too disruptive or too rapid (Interview, ADIC, July 1993). Working with the ADIC in this corporatist network, the Minister succeeded with his objective of lowering price supports, while conceding that fiscal retrenchment would proceed over a long period of time.

Consequently, the Labor Government reduced its financial support and protection for the dairy sector in two stages. The first stage (the Dairy Plan, 1986-92) was resisted by producers and processors alike. When state governments and Senate members rallied on their behalf, the government was forced to slow down the pace of change and give the industry more time to adjust. Accordingly, from 1986 to 1992, both domestic and export prices continued to be supported. The second stage reforms (the Crean Plan, 1992-97) were negotiated within the ADIC where, in the words of a senior ADIC official, "exhaustive consensus-making" and concessions on a timetable for their implementation, garnered the dairy industry's support and minimized discord. By the turn of the century, the removal of administered pricing and the end of export underwriting will have produced a virtual paradigm shift, with Australian domestic prices for manufacturing milk being reduced to the international price. As summarized by an executive of the ADIC in an interview in July 1993: "in the dairy industry they've had 30 years of restructuring our industry and in 30 years they've been winding down this administrative pricing system and turning the industry into one competitive on world markets ..." Because the whole economy was moving to become more competitive on world markets, the dairy industry did not feel itself to be "isolated or targeted", the same official added.[5]

Dairy – Canada

Programmatic changes in the late 1960s and early 1970s consolidated a state-assisted paradigm in Canadian dairy policy whose central pillar is national milk supply management. Its key policy instruments are supply quotas on milk production, import controls, and administered milk pricing. Producers are assured a target

[5] The only remaining instruments associated with the state-assisted model are monopoly state marketing boards which purchase and sell fluid milk at regulated prices. But even fluid milk prices will drop with the lower manufacturing milk prices.

price by means of direct government support payments on industrial milk and cream, and an offer-to-purchase program which supports dairy product prices at government-established levels. Additionally, producer levies have financed the export of surplus dairy products.

Since the early 1970s, dairy policy formulation and administration have taken place within a more comprehensive corporatist policy network than in Australia. This network accommodated Canada's federal system wherein provincial governments have responsibility for (fluid) milk marketing within their borders while the federal government has legal authority for extra-provincial and export marketing of industrial or manufacturing milk. At the heart of the network has been the government-appointed state agency, the Canadian Dairy Commission (CDC). Responsible for administering national dairy support policies, the CDC works closely with provincial dairy officials and industry representatives to coordinate supply management policies. Intergovernmental liaison has occurred in the Canadian Milk Supply Management Committee (CMSMC), a decision-making committee composed of provincial representatives and chaired by the CDC that sets the annual national industrial milk production target and oversees its allocation among provinces. Representatives of national consumer, processor and producer organizations have been non-voting members. Other elements of the network have included representative committees (and working groups) which advise the CDC on various matters, including dairy product pricing.

Producer representatives in this corporatist network are accountable to the Dairy Farmers of Canada (DFC) whose members include provincial milk marketing boards, dairy associations and cooperatives. Representatives of the primary processors are likewise responsible to a monopoly association, the National Dairy Council of Canada (NDCC). The CDC is itself designed to balance interests: the chair is normally an experienced career official, while the vice-chair and commissioner represent, respectively, dairy producers and dairy processors/traders.

Beginning in the late 1980s and continuing into the mid-1990s, a combination of domestic and international changes placed considerable pressure for change on the state-assisted paradigm in dairy. The pressure came from processors and further processors (manufacturers that use processed dairy products in other food products) whose competitiveness vis-'a-vis their US counterparts was undermined by various features of Canadian supply management.[6] A GATT Panel ruling in 1989 that Canadian restrictions on the import of yoghurt and ice cream were illegal, reiterated the need to ensure further processors' access to competitively priced dairy products. International trade agreements created further pressures. Effective January 1992, the NAFTA precluded the export of dairy products to the US where the exported product is supported by producer levies. This pressure on the then

[6] The account here draws on a number of government documents as well as interviews with dairy industry officials. See Agriculture Canada (1989:55-59; 1994a; 1994b); Consultation Committee on the Future of the Dairy Industry (1992a, 1992b); Canadian Dairy Commission (1995, 1996).

current method of subsidizing dairy product exports was extended by the GATT/WTO Agreement on Agriculture, signed in December 1993. Effective 1995, new export subsidies are outlawed and existing export subsidies must be reduced in volume and value. The agreement also required import controls to be converted to tariff rate equivalents and a rise in the overall volume of imports.

Although none of the GATT/WTO requirements was life-threatening in the short term to supply management and the state assistance paradigm in dairy, the trade agreement severely undermined the logic of domestic market sharing. It attacked the heart of Canadian supply management by breaking the former Article XI link between production controls and import prohibition. As such, the rationale for cooperative behaviour between producers and processors at the centre of the corporatist network was seriously undermined. Those dairy producers and processors whose geographic location and size afforded them a competitive edge over their domestic counterparts had new incentives to go their own way.

When dairy policymaking is surveyed from 1989 through 1996, two conclusions emerge. First, despite these threats to communicative action, policy continued to be formulated and implemented in a corporatist network, but one where the government added players less committed to the state-assisted paradigm. Second, the policy changes negotiated in the network reflect an attempt to accommodate market liberal pressures into a policy framework that remains centered on the principles of the state-assisted paradigm.

The first changes to the policy network came in 1989 when the federal minister of agriculture struck a Task Force on National Dairy Policy as part of a wholesale review of national agricultural policy. In addition to dairy producers, processors, and the CDC, the task force membership included state officials and further processors and consumers. A number of the recommendations of the Task Force (1989-91) were acted upon, including two that altered permanently decision-making in the policy network. First, the CDC's authority was enlarged as the government transferred responsibility for administered pricing from political officials in the Cabinet to the CDC. Second, the new sectoral interests (consumers, further processors), both more committed to market liberal principles, were accorded a formal advisory role in dairy pricing policy.

Now at the centre of an expanded corporatist network, the CDC capitalized on the likelihood of de-stabilizing changes in international trading rules to urge the producers and processors to build a closer partnership. It also recommended that they extend that partnership to further processors, whose lack of support and trust could only jeopardize supply management. After a report from a "Consultation Committee" (1992a, 1992b) and further discussions in still another joint government-sector forum, the Dairy Industry Strategic Planning Committee (DISPC), a committee established by the Minister of Agriculture in early 1994 to offer recommendations on how to implement GATT provisions. Within the CMSMC, a consensus on policy reforms was found that was subsequently accepted by federal provincial ministers in late 1994.

This protracted seven-year (1989-96) debate within the dairy corporatist network has resulted in some significant market liberal changes in dairy policy instruments. Lower prices for certain classes of milk now give manufacturers access to a portion of their milk supplies and dairy ingredients at US-competitive prices. Changes in the administered pricing system insulate producers less from market pressures. Finally, after first reducing its manufacturing milk subsidy, the Government of Canada announced it would be phased out by the year 2000. The corporatist dairy network was unable to overturn the government's decision, but it was able to have the subsidy phased out over a five year period, rather than terminated more abruptly. However, the core instruments in the state assisted paradigm, production controls and administered pricing, remain intact and a new policy instrument has been found to replace export subsidies.

Canadian dairy policy reform illustrates the capacity of a corporatist network to adjust policies significantly in the face of destabilizing pressures. Such policy adjustment has been possible because of the willingness of sectoral groups and provincial governments to rise above self-interested behaviour to engage in problem-solving for the sector as a whole. Producers in all provinces have made concessions to secure the viability and growth of the Canadian dairy industry. Officials of the DFC and the CDC report that as trust and shared understanding of problems developed over time, so did the resolution to solve problems collectively. The resulting cohesiveness of producers and processors and their consensus on appropriate reforms secured governments' support for policy changes that reformed, but did not dismantle, supply management and the state assisted paradigm in the dairy sector.

Cereal Grains – Australia

The trajectories of policy change in Australian cereals follow two distinctive patterns. Similar to Canada, the state-assisted paradigm in the sector rested on instruments designed to stabilize producer incomes and to regulate domestic and export marketing through a monopoly body, the Australian Wheat Board (AWB). The first attacks on these instruments came in the mid to late 1980s from a Labor government concerned about budgetary costs and committed to a more market driven primary sector. Grain producers fought these attacks, with rather mixed results, in a classical pressure pluralist fashion. After these defeats, the principal producers' organization, the Grains Council of Australia (GCA), sought to work with the government in a corporatist policy network. Successfully implanted, this network now has encouraged a negotiated, managed approach to policy change that retains the state-assisted idea of orderly marketing, all the while introducing a series of complementary market liberal changes.

Grains producers have been organized at the national level since 1930 when the Australian Wheatgrowers Federation was founded. Unlike Canada which lacks such a national group, the AWF was able in the 1960s and 1970s to add as full members affiliate organizations from each state (Trebeck 1990, 130). Reflecting the increased diversity in crop choices by its members, the association changed its name to the Grains Council of Australia in the 1980s. The GCA is fully integrated into the national associational system, serving as the grains commodity council in the National Farmers Federation. With a highly representative position bordering on a monopoly, the GCA was much better prepared for corporatist policymaking than its Canadian counterparts.

Two core elements of the state-assisted paradigm came under attack in the 1980s. Since 1979, producers incomes were to be stabilized by a price underwriting arrangement which guaranteed growers a price based on pooled returns to the AWB over a 3 year period. The scheme was triggered for the first time in 1986-87, resulting in a payout of 200 million dollars. In addition, the domestic grain handling, shipping and marketing system was investigated by a government advisory body with a decidedly market liberal bent, the Industries Assistance Commission, and by a royal commission. Both concluded that the system was inefficient and costly. The IAC proposed the end of price underwriting and of the domestic marketing and selling monopoly of the AWB. Taking pressure pluralist broadsides from growers and state governments, the Commonwealth government moved policy in a decidedly market liberal direction with the passage of the 1989 Wheat Marketing Act.

Price underwriting ended to be replaced by a government guarantee on a portion of the AWB's borrowing to pay the first advance (Piggott 1990, 300), leaving growers to draw their returns virtually exclusively from the market place. The Act also undercut the second pillar in the state-assisted paradigm, regulated marketing, when it removed the Australian Wheat Board's monopoly in the domestic grains market. This move signalled the Labor Government's commitment to domestic market deregulation and greater exposure of the grains sector to competitive forces. The 1989 Act left intact, however, the monopoly over the purchase and sale of export grain that the Wheat Board has enjoyed since 1939. But, it did serve notice of the Government's clear intention to eliminate its remaining financial assistance to the wheat industry. The new legislation also provided for a producer-funded capital pool to finance Wheat Board marketing activities once Government financial underwriting of Board borrowing ended. This Wheat Industry Fund was envisaged as playing a future vital role in funding initial producer payments: a key component of the price pooling system.

Similar to the 1996 US Farm Bill and to the end of transportation subsidies in Canadian grains, this decided shift in a market liberal direction came from outside a pressure pluralist network led by governments concerned with fiscal rectitude or neo-liberal ideas or both. The pattern of change was to shift significantly when the

GCA began to draw on its comparatively higher level of organizational development to work with a government already predisposed toward corporatist policy-making. The grain growers (GCA 1993) concluded that "preservation of the status quo is unacceptable in an economy becoming increasingly internationalized," and recognized the need to devise a strategic plan to ensure the prosperity of the sector in the face of impending changes. After identifying several critical issues, it established corporatist networks, called strategic planning units, to address these issues. These corporatist networks became a forum in which further dismantlement of the state-assisted paradigm was resisted, and grower consensus was sought for a mechanism that would enable the Wheat Board to be replaced with a producer-financed and controlled national grain marketing agency.

A "Working Party", composed of representatives of the GCA, the AWB, and officials from DPIE, sought a quid pro quo with the Commonwealth Government. The Wheat Board's single desk export seller status would be retained, as would Government underwriting of its borrowing, during a transitional period. At the end of the period, a new grower-financed marketing organization, financially and commercially independent of the Commonwealth Government, would replace the Wheat Board and assume its export monopoly (Hooke 1993, 44-5).

In beginning to move in this direction, the first step was the 1992 Wheat Marketing Act. Described by farmers as "a significant victory for grain growers" (NSW Farmers Association 1993: 2), this law arrested further dismantlement of the grain marketing regulatory framework and prolonged the transitional period. The Government extended its guarantee of Wheat Board borrowing until 1999, delayed its decision on whether to de-regulate export grain marketing until the conclusion of the Uruguay GAFT Round, and continued the Wheat Industry Fund.

At this point, the corporatist network was expanded to bring all industry players together to evaluate the competitive position of the Australian grains sector and the appropriateness of continuing state support for regulated export marketing. Joining the original tripartite working party (the Grains Council, the Australian Wheat Board and DPIE officials) were representatives of state grain boards, state grain handling associations, flour millers, private grain marketing bodies, maltsters and brewers. This group commissioned an independent consultants' report which endorsed continuation of the existing institutional arrangements in Australian grain marketing: that is, single desk export selling under the Wheat Board "until GATT produces demonstrable benefits" (Booz-Allen and Hamilton 1995, 13). The recommendation, observed the consultants, was contrary to "the current run of economic doctrine and public policy" and the apparent preference of the Australian government for deregulation (Booz-Allen and Hamilton 1995, 4-5).

By 1996, after prolonged debate, a consensus was found among Australian grain growers on the appropriate restructuring of the Wheat Board to make it a more commercialized operation directly accountable to and owned by growers. The export marketing monopoly of the Wheat Board would be retained and its operations eventually wholly funded by producers (through the Wheat Industry Fund). Within the corporatist network of the Grains Council, the Australian Wheat Board and DPIE, a working body was developing, at the DPIE Minister's request, a comprehensive package of legislative reform for the Wheat Board for the next five years. Such reforms would incorporate both Australian grain growers's resolve to negotiate the retention of the principle of orderly marketing that is central to the state-assisted paradigm, in exchange for some market liberal changes, specifically, the Australian Government's determination to end its financial guarantee of Wheat Board borrowings in 1999.

Conclusion

Since the 1980s, policy communities in agriculture have operated in a decision-making environment significantly different from that which prevailed during the consolidation of the state-assisted paradigm. Domestic budgetary constraints and international trade agreements have limited governments' regulatory and expenditure capacities. Based on the response of governments to these constraints in the agricultural policy area, two more general conclusions can be drawn.

First, the evidence suggests that a fundamental shift in the basic principles governing public policies, to wit a change in the policy "paradigm", may follow two quite distinctive trajectories: the sweeping, third-order change described by Hall, or the more deliberate pattern of change described in this paper. This second trajectory features a more managed, planned, even anticipatory series of changes that are negotiated between state actors and group representatives around a new set of basic principles. Rather than a paradigm shift that follows a society-wide debate in the partisan political arena or a principled confrontation in the judicial system, the paradigm change we have described is gradual and results from negotiations conducted over a number of years within the relatively depoliticized confines of an existing policy network.

Second, we have argued that theories of policy change can build fruitfully on Hall's analysis by using two other concepts in the comparative public policy literature: policy feedback and policy networks. The analysis of policy feedback draws attention to the specific effects of different policy types on the reactions of mass publics and the structures of interest group representation. Macroeconomic policies tend to be more visible to mass publics and more traceable to political authorities than agricultural policies. Macroeconomic policies are also less likely to stimulate interest group efforts to protect programme benefits. We thus found group politics to be a much more prominent feature of paradigm change in agricultural policy than did Hall in the case of macroeconomic policy.

We also found support for the hypothesis that policy networks shape the decision-making rules and decision-making style that govern policy change. Following Risse-Kappen and Scharpf, we demonstrated that corporatist policy networks lend themselves to the cumulative, negotiated, problem-solving trajectory to paradigm change whereas state-directed or pressure pluralist networks are more likely to be associated with crisis-driven change.

Clearly, the policy network in place conditions the characteristics of policy feedback. For example, although similar regulatory policies for grain marketing were in place in Australia and Canada, the politics of changing these policies differed. The corporatist network in Australia helped keep policy change less visible to mass publics than did the pluralist network in Canada. In addition, the corporatist network provided significant incentives to producers to channel their feedback through existing groups. In contrast, in Canada, the pluralist arrangements have left the field more open to the creation of new ad hoc groups and provide fewer disincentives to direct political action by producers. Further exploration of the interrelationships among policy paradigms, policy feedback, and policy networks will be instrumental to building comparative theories of policy change.

Finally, the analysis here suggests that the politics of how paradigm change comes about are significant for political and institutional stability. In Hall's trajectory, paradigm change is convulsive, involving national political conflict, often of a partisan sort, and drawing large parts of the population into the debate. In the second trajectory outlined here, fundamental change comes more slowly, conserves political stability, and comes through the effective functioning of existing institutions. It also engages the whole citizenry less. Future research might explore whether these differences in the politics of paradigm change have an impact on the eventual success of the design and implementation of the policy instruments associated with this change, or to reprise Hall, on the successful return to "normal politics."

CHAPTER 6

EU Institutions and Policymaking: A Brief Overview

1. EU Relevance for Public Policy Paradigm Research

The EU is itself a highly interesting political system and context for policymaking, as suggested earlier. Among other things: (1) there is often great diversity and complexity in many EU policy processes; in part, this is because of the rich variety of actors involved in most EU policy processes arising because of the complex arrangements of the EU supra-system, the EU member states themselves and their various government and quasi-governmental agencies, and the multiple, often highly specialized NGOs; (2) the EU responds to problems not dealt with adequately at the national level; as a result, there is often an obvious EU centralization driver; (3) the Commission is a super-entrepreneur, trying to bring about PP paradigm shifts through creating or adopting new paradigms.

In addition to our own research on EU policymaking in selected sectors for more than 10 years, other substantial research material has been available on this relatively new and developing policymaking system.

The following sections provide a minimum overview of the EU's development and current structure, starting with a briefing on historic background.

2. The Historical Foundations of the European Idea

The evolution of the European Union has edeged forward step by step from idea to reality over the past half century by a spectrum of actors that includes nation-states, national and transnational organizations, and the entrepreneurial individuals that sometimes inspired or led them, or worked within them. They have been guided by blend of idealism and self-interest, the proportions of which have varied by actor and over time. Choices have also been guided and conditioned by the accumulated experience embodied in specific institutional arrangements, by the understandings about how these have either worked or failed, and by the new political opportunities that these have presented. To the extent that such institutional arrangements have been deemed to have worked well, they have been more resistant to change; where they were deemed to have failed in significant ways, new institution-building opportunities have opened up, the stage set with greater opportunities for political innovation.

A virtual alphabet soup of new treaties and organizations (both European and international – see Table 6.1) emerged in the decade following the Second World

War. These agreements were penned by individual European states seeking gains – gains defined in terms of fostering economic development and stability, but to a large extent in terms of securing American aid for post-war reconstruction. But there were also elements of idealism, and not only based on avoidance of new military conflict, but on seeking to construct a new world order based on democratic and humanitarian principles[1]. Many of these treaty based arrangements faltered or simply faded into relative oblivion, others have remained strictly intergovernmental arrangements, while the organization that was to become the EU evolved through several stages, seemingly having taken on a life of its own.

Table 6.1. Major Treaty Revisions of the European Union

Treaty Name	Place Signed	Date Signed	Effective Date
Treaty establishing the European Coal and Steel Community (ECSC)	Paris	18 April 1951	23 July 1952
Treaty establishing the European Community (EEC)	Rome	25 March 1957	1 July 1958
Treaty establishing the European Atomic Energy Community (Euratom)	Rome	25 March 1957	1 July 1958
Single European Act (SEA)	Luxembourg, The Hague	17/28 Feb. 1986	1 July 1987
Treaty on European Union (TEU)	Maastricht	7 Feb. 1992	1 Nov. 93
Treaty of Amsterdam	Amsterdam	2 Oct. 1997	1 July 1999
Treaty of Nice	Nice	26 Feb. 2001	1 Feb. 2003

The evolution of the European Union has by no means followed some inexorable developmental path, but neither can it be characterized as merely the product of self-interested interstate bargains. Important aspects of the rough outlines and directions of the EU are remarkably consistent with ideas being developed by influential intellectuals, and later by the resistance movement, long before the final shots of the Second World War were fired. Entrepreneurial leaders, including familiar names such as Jean Monnet and Altiero Spinelli, worked independently of European states (although often in cooperation with them) and infused the movement with ideals and strategies, and with their own often-considerable personal energies for furthering the process of European integration. They spoke to – and helped shape – the hopes and expectations of European people who hoped not to

[1] The United Nations, founded in 1945, and the Council of Europe, founded in 1949, are examples of international organizations based primarily on the latter principles.

be forced to endure yet another war. Other familiar names – Konrad Adenauer, Guy Mollet, Robert Schuman, Paul Henri Spaak, among numerous others – moved the political levers that brought member states on board. More recently, a diverse range of transnational NGOs, labor, and business organizations have emerged, seeking to help shape EU developments and connect them with the various expectations of the particular groups of people with whom they work.

Below we summarize key elements of the ideational and policy development of the EU, describing some of the historical conditions that form the backdrop against which all EU policy has emerged and evolved over the past half century. In doing so, it highlights some of the lofty ideals, practical concerns, and vested interests that have helped make the EU into far more than a free trade zone or international organization, the practical arrangements seen as suitable for achieving the long-term goals, and the institutional path-dependency that has contributed to the EU remaining something less that a federal state. It emphasizes not so much the string of Treaties from Paris to Amsterdam, but the spaces between that represent the backdrop for negotiating the series of "grand bargains" that define the competence of the Union. The Treaties are seen here as markers or signposts along a path, a sort of taking stock of the issues around which a significant level of consensus has been reached and consolidating the results. These, in turn, serve as a sort of base camp for subsequent excursions. The overall goal of chapter is to sketch out the ideational, institutional, and policy context within which the changes tracked in the individual case studies unfold.

3. Early Steps Toward European Integration

In the still-settling dust of World War II, European leaders participating in the May 1948, Congress of Europe called for the establishment of a democratic structure for cooperation and integration in the form of a European Parliament. In addition to political union, their proposals also envisioned a single European defense force, an integrated economic system, and common citizenship (although without loss of nationality), organized as some form of federation of European states. There was a great sense of need to revive battered economies and rebuild political institutions, and participants hoped for new approaches that could serve to help avoid repeating the mistakes of the past (Holland, 1994). The offer from the U.S. of enormous sums of money for reconstruction via the Marshall plan in exchange for formally cooperating provided added impetus for developing and institutionalizing effective forms of cooperation (Nicoll and Salmon, 1994).

The first concrete steps, however, included neither a European Parliament nor anything resembling European federation. Cooperation arrangements instead followed a model of intergovernmental negotiations protective of national sovereignty, but which could nevertheless facilitate the coordination of U.S. aid. The Organization for European Economic Cooperation (OEEC), formed in 1948, "did nothing to challenge the sovereignty of individual governments... the virtue of cooperation was extolled, not the principle of integration" (Holland, 1994:23). A second intergovernmental organization, the Western European Union (WEU), was launched soon after. It was established by the "Brussels Treaty" (the Treaty on Economic, Social, and Cultural Collaboration and Collective Self-Defence) to help counter the increasing possibility of renewed military aggression in Europe (De Schoutheete, 2000:118), and was in large part a response to Soviet actions in Central Europe. The treaty's key provision was a commitment to mutual defense in the event any of the signatories became the target of armed aggression. It is notable that the treaty establishing the WEU also called for the progressive political integration of Europe. It included no specific provisions for pursuing this integration, however, and was in practice guided by the principle of state sovereignty and independence (Holland, 1994). Many of the important defense-related activities envisioned for the WEU in the Brussels Treaty were soon made redundant by the creation of the North Atlantic Treaty Organization (NATO) in 1950. Nevertheless, the WEU provided the foundation for subsequent negotiations that resulted in the more ambitious proposal to establish a European Defense Community (EDC) in which Belgium, France, Italy, Luxembourg, the Netherlands, and the Federal Republic of Germany were to participate. However, those efforts were left in shambles as the governing coalition in France shifted due to internal political factors, leading to the subsequent refusal of the French National Assembly to ratify the Treaty (Parsons, 2002).

These initial efforts to establish stable European partnerships began with strong agreement about what was to be avoided rather than with a clear consensus on what forms the new European cooperation should take. A sense of "never again" and desire to achieve a lasting peace was reinforced by an increasing perception among political leaders and other influential individuals that nationalism and competition for scarce resources had been the root causes of two European "civil wars" already during the first half of the 20th century (Spinelli and Rossi, 1998 [1944]; Holland, 1994). The all too fresh memories of recent war and the beginnings of new economic and security tensions assured that these concerns remained foremost in leaders' minds. They helped generate a plethora of new treaties and collaborative efforts. For a variety of reasons, however, the great strides called for by the 1948 Congress of Europe were far larger than the steps to which all European national governments were prepared to commit. But although more conventional intergovernmental modes seemed to have prevailed in the initial steps taken toward European reconstruction and future security, calls for some sort of federal model for European cooperation were not without significant support.

3.1 Seeking Peace and Prosperity: The Beginnings of the Modern European Idea

Winston Churchill's 1946 Zurich speech is frequently singled out as marking the beginning of the idea of a European Union. Churchill used the occasion to call for a "kind of United States of Europe" with a reconciled France and Germany at its center, which "if well and truly built, will be such as to make the material strength of a single state less important". His plea included a note of urgency: "I must give you a warning. Time may be short...the cannons have ceased firing. The fighting has stopped; but the dangers have not stopped. If we are to form the United States of Europe, or whatever name it may take, we must begin now". However, while Churchill suggested a path and institutional configuration for pursuing peace, the role he envisioned for Britain in the enterprise remained ambiguous.

Churchill may have been the first head of state to call for a formally united Europe in the post war period, but he built on a perception shared by many other prominent leaders and intellectuals that the only hope of securing a lasting peace was to effectively restrain national rivalries and competition. The League of Nations had failed to accomplish this task; something else was clearly needed. The idea of some form of European federation had deep roots; it was being cultivated by influential intellectuals and by the resistance movement already during the early stages of the War; Churchill was clearly aware both of these sentiments and of some of their history (Bidmead, 1948).

Even as the Axis powers shifted their war machines into full gear, the resistance movement had already begun looking hopefully to its conclusion and the steps that would be necessary to avoid another repetition. Altiero Spinelli, who would later emerge to become an important champion of European integration and an eventual EU Parliamentarian, wrote his federalist paper, the Ventotene Manifesto, in 1941 in collaboration with fellow prisoner Ernesto Rossi. Spinelli, a resolute anti-fascist and active member of the Italian Communist Party, had been a law student at the time of his arrest for his opposition to Mussolini's regime. Rossi, a professor of economics, had been imprisoned for his role as a leader of the social-liberal organization Giustizia e Libertá (Pinder, 1998). By the time the two met in 1939, the then-30 year-old Spinelli had already spent ten years in incarceration.

While imprisoned, Spinelli read insatiably and followed events and developments elsewhere in the world – including Stalin's rise to power. Spinelli's commitment to the social justice-oriented values he found in communism seems to have remained strong, but the totalitarian character of Soviet communism disturbed him; it was perhaps too near his own experience in fascist Italy. He sought explanations in discussion and in books, and "impressed by non-Marxist writers and resenting the straitjacket of communist doctrine, he challenged the party line and was expelled in 1937" (Pinder, 1998:69).

Rossi introduced Spinelli to ideas of the British Federalists, among them Lionel Robbins and William Beveridge[2]. The "mental clarity and precision" and non-

[2] Lionel Robbins, a political and economic liberal, became a professor at the London School of Economics (LSE) in 1929 at the age of 30 and remained there until 1961. William Beveridge was Director of the LSE from 1919 to 1937, and is widely regarded as a father of the modern welfare state.

ideological character of their work were to leave a strong impression on Spinelli. Robbins's distinctive contribution was identifying the "contradiction between an international economy and the insistence on national sovereignty, which allowed international economic forces to escape a proper framework of law" (Pinder, 1998:5). Robbins argued "the characteristic institutions of a liberal society are inconceivable without government...the mere absence of violence is not a sufficient condition for the efficient working of free enterprise...it must be restrained within suitable limits by a framework of institutions. Neither property nor contract are in any sense natural" (Robbins, 1998 [1937]:50-51).

Beveridge, summarizing the important themes of federalist thinking in "Peace and Federation?", addressed himself to the broader political question: "How can justice in place of war be established as the arbiter among nations?" (Beveridge, 1998 [1940]:31).

> *Federation has been proposed above for a limited area. Limitation of area is essential; federalism is a strong remedy for a virulent disorder; it is not a healing lotion that can be sprayed over the world. World federation is for the millennium. The federation projected here is for the next peace treaty: it is a federation of nations which from fresh experience of war will be determined to make as certain as they can that war will never be repeated"... "Federation across national boundaries is a plan so new that it will be rejected by some critics as Utopian...The plan of this paper is Utopian, for it aims at making a world different from the world that we have known for nearly a generation. The plan dares and needs to be Utopian because the choice is no longer between Utopia and the pleasant, ordered world that our fathers knew. The choice is between Utopia and Hell (Beveridge, 1998 [1940]:35).*

These writings clearly identified the abuse of concentrated power as a problem that urgently needed to be addressed – an analysis strongly shared by Spinelli. As Robbins pointed out, abuse of power was not the sole province of national governments; market failures, arising from unregulated or insufficiently regulated international markets, contributed to the instability and conflict that fostered the Nazi and Fascist rise to power. The arguments contained in these and other federalist papers provided Spinelli with a coherent set of ideas and remedies that were consistent with both his values and his experience – and that of many of his fellow prisoners. Eugenio Colorni summarized their conclusions:

> *Thus is was that in the minds of various people the central idea was forged that the basic contradiction which causes crises, wars, poverty, and the exploitation that afflicts society is the existence of sovereign States which exist geographically, economically, and militarily, which consider other States as competitors and potential enemies and which live in a perpetual state of bellum omnium omnes with respect to each other (Colorni, 1944).*

Spinelli and Rossi set about drafting a manifesto to argue that constructing a European federation could preclude a return of totalitarian government and war. Named after the island on which had Mussolini imprisoned them, the Ventotene Manifesto was unequivocal in its description of the specific urgent problem to which federalism would be the solution: it was the combination of nationalism and capitalist imperialism that had fostered conditions favorable to the development of fascism. Nationalism and the totalitarian state were the principal threat to human liberty, and these must be combated. The manifesto was equally clear in its identification of the necessary positive goals of a "united Europe". "As soon as this era ends the historical process of struggle against social inequalities and privileges will be restored in full...In order to respond to our needs, the European revolution must be socialist, i.e. its goal must be the emancipation of the working classes and the creation of more humane conditions for them" (Spinelli, 1941:11). At the same time, it left room for a diversity of actors and beliefs of "countless shades and nuances, stretching from very conservative liberalism to socialism and anarchy...They hope for the end of dictatorships, conceiving this as restoring the people's insuppressible right to self-determination" (Spinelli, 1941:6-7). The Manifesto was circulated widely within the resistance movement, the original scribbled by hand on cigarette papers, and smuggled off the island in the false bottom of a tin box.

Spinelli's substantial contribution, however, was perhaps less in his writings than it was in his subsequent efforts to bring the idea of a united Europe to fruition. Upon his release from confinement in the fall of 1943, he helped found the Movimento Federalista Europeo (MFE-European Federalist Movement), and dedicated his life to organizing, mobilizing, and lobbying for a federal Europe in Italy, and internationally. He would carry out his work from outside the European institutions for the next 27 years[3]. He "made his prime objective the construction of Europe, to be achieved, not through the channels of foreign affairs, but by a democratic struggle based on supranational and constitutional criteria" (Albertini, 2002:1-2).

In fact, Spinelli was by no means alone; he was part of a much larger movement, and one he helped foster. If Churchill helped make the federalist idea widely accessible by popularizing it with a familiar and then-sympathetic metaphor, Spinelli, Rossi, and the British Federalists contributed an intellectual coherency of thought and proposals for action. Their ideas offered an internally consistent complex of remedies for addressing a persistent and serious problem, clearly pointing toward something more than intergovernmental "European cooperation".

It was the strategic sense of French diplomat and businessman Jean Monnet, however, which was to prove pivotal to setting it in motion. As was the case with Spinelli and others, for Monnet, "while Europe was a political and economic concept, it was above all 'a moral idea'" (Holland, 1994). Monnet was in many ways a remarkably unremarkable character; the son of an entrepreneur (his family started a brandy label in competition with the Hennessy & Martell labels), he enjoyed financial success but not great wealth. He worked closely with leading political figures in Europe and the United States, but never held political office. "He was not highly educated, nor an intellectual or political philosopher; he exhibited no special elo-

[3] Spinelli was nominated to serve as a member of the EEC executive commission in 1970. In 1976 he was elected to the European Parliament as an independent on the Communist Party list. He served until his death in May of 1986.

quence as a writer or public speaker; he had too little tolerance for detail to make a model bureaucrat. He possessed, however, extraordinarily shrewd judgment about politics and economics, combined with an uncommon gift for networking and friendship. He had, we would say today, the best Rolodex on three continents" (Schuker, 2000:16-17). That "Rolodex" had been accumulated through the years during a variety of international efforts: working to expand the family's brandy business (prior to WW-I), helping coordinate economic cooperation and efforts to ensure the shipment military supplies during both world wars, and working for the League of Nations during the inter-war years (only to resign in frustration as it began to collapse) (Fransen, 2001). In summarizing his general orientation toward the endeavor he embraced as his life's' mission, Holland (1994:44) characterizes Monnet as "primarily an economic functionalist" and "secondly an incremental federalist". But economic functionalism was a strategy he employed in his efforts to move forward in increments toward the goal of European Union. It was here he most differed with people such as Spinelli, who as a true federalist, believed that the window of opportunity generated by the dislocations of war would be brief, and that rapid movement toward European integration would be required. On the goals of foreclosing the possibilities for future war and a decent chance for a good life for average citizens, the two were of quite the same mind.

Monnet saw the establishment of effective institutions as the long-term key to success on European integration (Holland, 1994:10). It was Monnet who, with a small circle of associates, drafted a proposal for combining French and German steel and coal production under a supranational High Authority – the proposal that became the Schuman Declaration (1950), and eventually became the basis for the Paris Treaty establishing the European Coal and Steel Community (ECSC) in 1952. Its purpose was to remove the raw materials needed to wage any future war from the control of individual governments (Nicoll and Salmon, 1994). The organization of the ECSC reflected this sense of the importance of institution building, and the future-oriented focus of not only Monnet, but also of other key leaders including French Foreign Minister Robert Schumann and German Chancellor Konrad Adenauer. But if Schumann and Adenauer were motivated by the same lofty ideals that drove Monnet, Spinelli and others, they were also constrained by political and practical considerations. The ECSC Treaty proved to be an expression of both.

It was not the formal cooperation of the original six member states (with France and Germany in the lead that distinguished the ECSC Treaty from others; it was the particular form it took. The institutions established under the ECSC included a High Authority as the administrative entity, an Assembly (although the Common Assembly possessed no formal power), and a Court of Justice for adjudicating disputes between states. A Council of Ministers had not been part of Monnet's original proposal, but was incorporated into the Treaty to assuage the concerns of some members that some sort of checks on the ECSC administrative branch might be necessary. The model for this new set of institutions was not drawn up from scratch, but from Monnet's own experience of the structural failures of the League of Nations, and his experience of the organizational structures that contributed to success in his work to facilitate and coordinate economic cooperation and the supply of essential supplies during two World Wars.

No less remarkable than the parties' agreement to pool their coal and steel production was their willingness to vest substantial independent rulemaking authority in the High Authority of the new supranational organization. Parsons (2002) attributes this choice to a combination of the idealism of supporters of federalism (in large part, French), political and economic self-interest (both French and German), and a general political stalemate about the best way to proceed that defied conventional France political alliances and divisions. The French discussion included relatively equal political groupings guided by three different general models of how to proceed. In addition to advocates of European community who supported federalism, a second camp included traditionalists such as de Gaulle who remained strongly committed to preserving national sovereignty, and supporters of a looser confederation of states, who were most inclined toward British-style proposals of a close cooperation European free trade area that required little or no transfer of sovereignty. Since these groupings cut across the normal boundaries of political parties and alliances, the situation was unusually fluid. Once Schumann and Adenauer had struck an agreement, Schumann maneuvered around the division of political elites and absence of a public outpouring of either support or opposition for the Treaty through the skillful use of his political power and agenda setting prerogatives to gain French Parliamentary approval of the ECSC Treaty[4].

Monnet, Schumann, and Adenauer had grander plans in mind – the ECSC was for them only a groundbreaking first step. These larger goals were no secret, as Monnet amply illustrated in his comments on the Schuman proposals: "We can never sufficiently emphasize that the six Community countries are the fore-runners of a broader united Europe, whose bounds are set only by those who have not yet joined. Our Community is not a coal and steel producers' association: it is the beginning of Europe" (Monnet, 1978:216). European "integration" had finally entered its formative early stages of institutionalization, helped over a threshold that had previously represented an insurmountable barrier by a combination of historical and circumstantial factors. These factors had radically altered actor and power relationships – in part by destabilizing existing social institutions – and fostered a greater openness to new ideas and approaches. Thus, the EU as a peace project

[4] There are competing interpretations of these developments. Intergovernmentalists (see Moravcsik, 1998 and others) tend to interpret the individual states' choices as rational and self-interest serving. Neo-functionalists and federalists (see Haas, 1948; Mitrany, 1948) tend to see ideational factors and structural-functional needs as the driving forces. My characterization supports Parsons' (2002) interpretation that all these factors were important, but that the relative balance between them opened the way for political entrepreneurs who were especially skilled and strategically positioned to tip the balance in one direction or another and overcome historical inertia.

began with the economic integration in the strategic commodities of war. Jean Monnet had found the political opening he was hoping for. It was a tentative, but decisive step.

3.2 The Circuitous Path to Rome, 1957

The early years of ECSC were generally judged to be a success, although it is unclear whether this success resulted from the work of the ECSC itself, or from endogenous conditions (Nugent, 1995:42). By the late 1950s, however, the ECSC had failed a crucial test – a crisis generated by overcapacity in coal production. In a general pattern to be often repeated in subsequent decades, member states rejected the Community proposal and reverted to developing their own individual strategies and policies for dealing with the overcapacity, at least partially retreating from the agreed-upon principles of the ECSC. In the longer run, the decline of importance of coal and steel has greatly reduced the importance of the concrete arrangements established in the ECSC. The institutional arrangements initiated with the ECSC, however, exerted a powerful influence on the future European Economic Community and eventual European Union.

For Monnet, Schuman, and many others, the ECSC was intended to be a significant step toward a united Europe, not the end of the line. Efforts to negotiate two important components of further European integration were launched almost before the ink was dry on the ECSC treaty: the European Defense Community (EDC) and the European Political Community (EPC). The EDC negotiations were launched in parallel with the ECSC negotiations by French Prime Minister René Pleven, and based on his belief in the need to more comprehensively integrate West Germany (which was not in NATO). The EDC proposal called for creation of a European army for common defense under the authority of common political institutions (Nugent, 1995:53). These envisioned political institutions were patterned after the ECSC institutional forms, with a Joint Defense Commission, a Council of Ministers, an advisory Assembly, and a Court of Justice, and would have ultimately subsumed the ECSC institutions to form the European Political Community. The Treaty was signed in May 1952 by the same six states that had joined to form the ECSC. France, however had come under new leadership based on issues unrelated to foreign policy (Parsons, 2002) and was skittish about German rearmament even in the context of a joint project. In the absence of Schumann's consummate political skill in a position where they gained leverage, ratification problems emerged, and the French National Assembly rejected the proposed Treaty in late 1954 by, thereby killing the effort. The envisioned common political institutions, in the form of the European Political Community, never reached the ratification stage. The EPC was abandoned with the failure of the European Defense Community, there being nothing to place under its authority.

In the wake of this sobering failure, the Six original signatory states regrouped and renegotiated. ECSC foreign ministers took up new proposals from the Benelux countries at a conference in Messina in the summer of 1955. The conference charged Belgium's Socialist Foreign Minister Paul-Henri Spaak with the task of heading up a committee of representatives of the national governments. The committee was to prepare a report that would serve as the basis for another round of negotiations[5]. Here too, French domestic politics unrelated to the question of "Europe" spilled over into the process. Conservative French Foreign Minister Pinay went beyond his mandate at Messina to accept the appointment of the study Committee, proposing the most pro-Community participant (Spaak) to head the committee, then sent his most pro-community deputy to represent France. He subsequently went even further and joined with other delegations to permit Spaak's team to draft the entire report themselves, which contributed to making a coherent plan, but one that bore little resemblance to official French positions (Parsons, 2002:68). The proposal linked the European Economic Community (EEC) proposal with Euratom, which Monnet[6] had been working to promote in France, and explicitly drew on the ECSC as its model for institutional structures.

The reactions to the Spaak proposals in France were unenthusiastic at best, with government bureaucrats, agriculture, and business groups taking a broadly negative view. But yet another political shift took place in 1956 with a Left-Center coalition gaining power by a narrow margin on a social policy platform. The surprise selection of the pro-community Socialist party leader Guy Mollet by conservative Independent French President René Coty placed key governmental positions and institutional leverage in the hands of supporters of European integration. This enabled them to leverage sufficient support and ameliorate enough of the opposition to sign the treaties negotiated on the basis of the Spaak Report and quickly engineer their ratification by the French Parliament four months later, in July 1957.

The result was the Treaties of Rome: the European Atomic Energy Community (Euratom) Treaty and the Treaty on European Economic Community (EEC), which entered into effect January 1, 1958. Cooperation around establishing the Common Market provided the common denominator, which required the development of a common trade policy and the progressive removal of trade barriers between member states and their substitution with joint external tariffs. This proved a still challenging, but critically lower set of hurdles to clear than overt integration of defense capabilities or political authority. This was in part because it followed a wider trend of economic internationalization that was already underway (Griffiths, 1995), and in part because a critical mass of interests within the individual member states perceived a relatively rapid payoff in terms of access to their

[5] Great Britain was also invited to participate, but was pushing its own even looser association of states in a free trade area, and withdrew from the negotiations after failing to gain support. It eventually succeeded in forming the European Free Trade Association.

[6] Monnet had resigned his position with the ECSC to establish the Committee for the United States of Europe, whose membership was composed primarily of Social Democrats and Christian Democrats, and eschewed business leaders (Cowles et al, 2001).

neighbor's markets (Moravcsik, 1998). Even so, its success may have had as much to do with unusually skilled and idealistic political leaders and with timing as with any anticipated material gains. The Treaties of Rome established more than a free trade zone. They expanded what could only be characterized as experimental supranational institutional arrangements beyond coal and steel; they also carried within them language pointing to the loftier social purposes of integration, even if they were given little concrete expression.

3.3 From Grand Goals to Concrete Policies

The Treaties of Rome mark the official beginnings of what would eventually become the European Union. They mark a new period of institution building – of fleshing out the policies of the European Economic Community and the European Atomic Energy Community and of developing the organizational structures that would implement them. In short, the Treaties formalized the policymaking institutions and procedures, enumerated the range of goals and purposes for which the EEC was the intended vehicle, and defined legal authority and intermediate steps for achieving some of those goals. But from the broader vision of political, economic, and social change that inspired many of those who had worked to establish the EEC, only a limited number of elements were concretely realized in the new arrangements. While the overall combination of social and economic goals provided important inspiration, comparatively little concrete competence was invested in the EEC on social issues – the delegated authority and defined work plan from which to proceed was limited largely to the economic sphere.[7] The result was that "in the EEC, the future rules on trade were set out fairly clearly, but only guiding principles were laid down for social policy and for agricultural policy" (Nugent, 1995:44).

This vagueness regarding the social dimension did not stop its development in its tracks, but it did make the process more tentative and exploratory – and politically uncertain. It should be also noted, however, that such vagueness was at least in part a function of the fact that the elaboration of social policy in European welfare states was still in its relatively early stages during the 1950s when the groundwork was being laid for the future EU (Scharpf, 2002; Baldwin, 1990). In addition, there was a sense that social policy differences between member states would be harmonized naturally as a byproduct of market integration.

4. EU Structure: A Brief Sketch

This section summarizes the structural characteristics of the EU institutional arrangements in which policymaking takes place; then it operationalizes the policy paradigm as a conceptual tool. Since the EU is a system of governance still under

---

[7] Notable excepts to this were the European Social Fund, Health and Safety Regulations, and even the CAP was seen as a redistributive welfare arrangement.

construction, it is unusually fluid and flexible. Nonetheless, its general framework has been in place since the 1950s.

Operationalizing the paradigm concept is approached in two steps. The first is to outline the key elements that constitute the EU paradigms that represent the dominant competing visions of the EU. This is approached through identifying how the different paradigms assign priority to market versus social goals, how they define who should participate in the processes related to policymaking and how, and how they define where, or at what level of governance the issues associated with competing goals should be decided.

The second step is to outline the process of paradigm construction with consideration for the categories of actors involved, the kinds of problem solutions that are conceivable, and the concrete goals that are developed from those. These different elements can be identified empirically in the policy discourses: the various arguments, explanations, and giving of accounts. This process entails more than the emergence of a new paradigm, however. Since an existing model already occupies the conceptual and institutional space, the process entails not only constructing a new paradigm, but also pushing out the old one – or more accurately, relegating its guiding principles to secondary or lower priority status. This process can be traced at the level of interaction between the respective discursive complexes identified in Chapter 2, and also within those complexes. Developments on both these levels can be identified in the various policy discourses already outlined.

4.1 EU Governance: Policymaking Bodies Participation, and Policy Instruments

Considerable effort has been devoted over the past decade to charting out just what kind of political creation the EU represents (Jachtenfuchs, 2002; Christiansen et al., 2001; Stone-Sweet et al., 2001; Rosamond, 2000; Sandholtz and Stone-Sweet, 1998; Andersen and Eliassen, 1996b; Marks et al., 1996; Leibfried and Pierson, 1995b). Much of this research and theorizing focuses on EU governance, which Chryssochoou (1999:3) characterizes as "an institutionalized system of rule without the formal/legal attributes of competence embedded in authoritative state structures". This approach marks the EU as embodying a new form of rulemaking system, although there remains an influential body of research efforts that see the EU principally as the accumulated outcomes of member state negotiations, and therefore nothing fundamentally new (Moravcsik, 1998).

Clearly, the EU is not a state in the traditional European or even contemporary international sense; it represents a new form of supra-national authority. In principle, it is still based on strong national systems that are surrendering – or have surrendered – varying degrees and types of national sovereignty across a wide spectrum of policy areas. Although European Community law has priority over the conflicting law of a member state, the rate of implementation and degree of compliance vary a great deal.

The EU is not, in general, a political system in which policymaking elites are held accountable by citizens for their public policies and actions, and where they compete by offering alternative programs and vie for popular support at the European level. In this sense, it is not a typical political democracy (Schmitter 1996a:7).[8] The direct influence of citizens through formal representative democracy plays only a marginal role in EU governance (Andersen and Burns, 1996); individual citizens voting in free, fair, and competitive Euro-elections are able to exercise little or no influence over the composition of Euro-authorities. It is largely this break with normative expectations that has generated discussions of the "democratic deficit". There have been, however, a variety of efforts to address this problem of democratic legitimacy, although the channels available for extracting accountability remain substantially different than in a conventional parliamentary democracy.

Even if it fails to qualify as a conventional state, the EU does make policy, the scope of which has increased substantially over time (Hix, 1999b). With no conventional EU-level "government" making policy, "governance" has emerged as a widely embraced concept for capturing the policymaking processes taking place. Jachtenfuchs and Kohler-Koch (2003:4) characterize governance as "the continuous process of setting explicit goals for society and intervening into it in order to achieve those goals". Recognition of the quasi-federal nature of EU governance has led to the extension of this concept into "multi-level governance" (Hooghe and Marks, 2001; Scharpf, 2001, 1997a). Schmitter (2004) prefers to refer to this as "poly-centric governance" in recognition of the fact that governance extends not only across levels (local, national, supranational, etc.), but that there is also functional specialization over levels that varies with the particular policy sector. Schmitter is clearly correct on this point, which is borne out in the case studies taken up in this work. The term multi-level governance is used here both for the sake of simplicity and because the concept of levels is most relevant to this analysis. However, it should be understood to encompass the poly-centric nature of EU policy making authority.

While the European Union cannot be considered democratic in any conventional sense, neither is it merely a vehicle for dismantling member state level regulation of the market. In practice, it is characterized by a form of sector-specific governance which is highly differentiated and includes multiple forms of representation, and which has been characterized as a type of participatory or organic democracy (Burns, 1999; Andersen and Burns, 1996). A wide spectrum of special interests, organizations, and value-committed groups engage in or are drawn into governance processes. Rather than depending solely upon parliamentary representatives, organized actors in the EU seek to articulate their own positions and participate themselves. They often have both the capacity and opportunity to engage di-

[8] Although parliamentary institutions are considered the core of Western political systems, they are currently undergoing systematic erosion (Andersen and Burns, 1996; Burns, 1999).

rectly and forcefully in policy and administrative processes they consider relevant to their interests. However, these organizations vary a great deal in power and influence, both formally and informally. They include member states, regional and transnational business associations, regional and transnational NGOs, and Brussels-based lobbying efforts, among others.

As a multi-level policymaking system, the EU is highly open and dynamic, with poorly defined boundaries between its functions, jurisdictions, and authorities. These conditions provide significant opportunities for entrepreneurial actors and informal politics (Andersen andBurns, 1996). Entrepreneurial actors – both within the system and outside of it (who have resources and/or are organized and seek to influence policy or restructure the system in practice), may mobilize resources and formulate specific legitimating discourses, framing and shaping particular policies as well as new institutional arrangements. However, such entrepreneurship operates within constraints. These include general constitutional (Treaty-based) and institutional constraints, as well as the opposition of other agents. Nationally-oriented agents who seek to protect national sovereignty, for example, may seek to block the further expansion of EU powers and structures (Burns and Carson, 2003).

4.2 EU Policymaking Institutions

More or less in place since the Treaties of Rome, the core EU institutional arrangements include bureaucratic/administrative (the Commission), democratic representation (European Parliament), legislative with quasi-national representation (Council of Ministers), judicial (the European Court), and inter-governmental negotiative (the European Council) institutions. The boundaries between the functions and roles of the different institutions are in practice unclear and flexible. "Public" authority is dispersed in these arrangements, which integrate public and private actors. A clear center of authority is lacking, as is a clear division of powers; the formal procedures that regulate the various EU level policy networks are weak[13] (Burns et al., 2001). The Commission plays the central role in initiating legislation. The Council and Parliament have the final responsibility for making decisions and passing judgment on Commission proposals. Parliament has earlier been politically weak, with limited initiative or positive influence, although its role and strength have been progressively increased over time. Overall, this set of policymaking institutions embodies many crosscurrents and tensions as a result of contradictory, institutionalized values and rule complexes, as is the case with any large complex of institutions (Burns and Flam, 1997). The concrete ways in which these crosscurrents conflict, coexist, and reinforce one another shape the institutional environment in which policymaking and policy development takes place.

The European Commission (Commission)

Thus far in the history of the EU, the Commission has been the most consistently important entrepreneur. The EU literature often describes the Commission as a strategic actor that has been able to skillfully exploit political openings and policy opportunities as they have opened up (Cram, 2001; Fligstein, 2001a; Bellier, 1997; Cram, 1994). It has the formal role as initiator of policy proposals and the central role in building consensus and orchestrating support behind those proposals. The Commission has the task of balancing and mediating national interests as well as interest group opinions in order to come forward with proposals that will be also accepted by the Council of Ministers and the European Parliament. However, it is also an actor with goals of its own. One core *raison d'être* of the Commission is to promote European integration, and it uses a variety of venues and means for achieving its goals (Wendon, 1998). The Commission has often co-operated with the European Court of Justice (ECJ) to promote European integration, since the ECJ shares with the Commission a preference for deeper integration (Pollack, 1998b:249). The Commission is active in taking initiatives and shaping EU policies, and in the consultation process, engaging lobbyists and experts. Other European policymaking bodies are obviously important, but they primarily come into view as they reinforce, reshape, scale back, and/or legitimize the activities and initiatives of the Commission.

The Commission is by no means a monolithic entity. Not only do the individual Commissioners frequently have different political goals and views, the Directorates General, they oversee have markedly different missions. There is considerable variation in the goals of the respective DGs, and some are clearly more influential than others. During the development of the Single Market, for example, DG Enterprise (the former DG-III – Industry), carried probably the greatest weight. Others, such as DG Employment and Social Affairs (formerly DG-V) were seen as weaker and unsure of their mandate (although this has changed over the past several years) as in the case of DG Employment (Sutton, 1998). Even with clearly defined competence, it takes time to establish networks of experts, develop legitimizing discourses, fine-tune arguments, and gain authority and influence in relation to other DGs, and in relation to other important actors in the EU complex.

Clearly, the Commission is a powerful actor in its own right and a creative and important entrepreneur in EU policymaking and institutional reform. The Commission has further strengthened its position through linkages and coalition building with European lobbyists and interest associations. Indeed, it has been an explicit policy of the Commission to encourage direct contact with specialized affected interests and organizations, as well as those who mobilize expertise. Much of this contact takes place in diverse, specialized policy networks. In a system that lacks conventional democratic legitimacy and accountability, this can be seen as an alternative approach to developing some form of constituency and the legitimacy it entails.

The European Parliament (EP)

Although the early calls for a European Union called for a full-fledged European Parliament, the EP began much more modestly as an Assembly with only advisory powers. It formally became the European Parliament in 1962, and the first direct elections of EU Parliamentarians were held in 1979 and are now held every five years. Each successive Treaty since the Single European Act (1987) has expanded the powers of the Parliament, so that although it lacks the powers of national parliaments, there are opportunities for the EP to exert significant leverage. It has limited powers of initiative in that it can formally adopt its own proposals for legislation, although the Commission is not obligated to act on them. Similarly, its participation in the early stages of policy discussions can influence the nature and direction of eventual proposals. The EP also exercises leverage and influence under any of several formal procedures (these include consultation, cooperation, and co-decision – See Nugent, 1995:174-186). In 1999, the EP precipitated the resignation of the Santer Commission following a series of Commission missteps and scandals.

The Council of Ministers

The Council of Ministers is the principal legislative body of the EU. However, it is limited in that it can generally act only on the basis of proposals from the Commission[9]. The Presidency of the Council rotates every six months, and Council of Ministers meetings are typically convened by the country that holds the Presidency. These meetings are often used to focus an agenda based on the issues a country has decided to prioritize during its presidency. Voting his handled by one of three procedures. Simple majority votes may be taken on non-controversial technical issues, while a qualified majority (QMV) is sufficient for matters pertaining to completion of internal market. Unanimity is required where the Treaties do not provide for lesser majorities, and in practice, the goal is to reach a consensus. In practice, the Council of Ministers is several councils, made up of the relevant ministers in a given policy area (Nylander, 2000).

The European Court of Justice (ECJ)

The ECJ is responsible for adjudicating and applying EU law, and for interpreting the general provisions of the Treaties. Based in Luxembourg, The ECJ is comprised of 15 judges who serve six year staggered terms, one from each member state. Final decisions are taken by a simple majority vote, but unlike the US Supreme Court, there is no provision for dissenting opinions, and the results of votes are kept confidential (Hix, 1999). The ECJ has demonstrated a general bias toward further integration, and has proven itself a skillful and politically savvy policy entrepreneur in its own right. Over the course of EU history, the ECJ has made a crucial contribution to European integration through its success in constitutionalizing the Treaties through establishing two key principles. The first is the supremacy of EU

[9] There are ways around this limitation, through "soft-law" types of informal or non-binding agreements, through the adoption of resolutions and recommendations, or through invoking Article 152 of the EEC Treaty (1958), which permits the Council to submit proposals to take certain actions in the absence of Commission initiatives Nugent, 1995:124).

law over the law of member states; the second is the "direct effect" of EU law, which permits private citizens to bring legal actions against member states based on EU law. These principles have gained increased importance as the scope of EU law has broadened and deepened.

Table 6.2. European Union Policy Instruments

	Instrument	Description
"Hard Law"	**Regulations**	Binding in their entirety on all member states. Regulations are directly applicable as law at member state level, and need not be transposed into national law.
	Directives	Binding on all member states in terms of results to be achieved, but national governments are free to choose the particular means by which those results are to be achieved. Directives must be transposed into national law.
"Soft Law"	**Recommendations**	Non-binding recommendations
	Open Method of Coordination (OMC)	Formalized at the 2000 Lisbon summit, the OMC is a systematic process of setting employment related goals, and monitoring and reporting.
	Action Program	A work plan for the Commission that enumerates specific measures to be taken as well as a timeline.
	White Paper	Policy Paper produced by the Commission in consultation with the Council and Parliament. A White Paper typically includes an enumeration of specific goals and an itemization of specific measures expected to be necessary to meet those goals. A White Paper has no legal force, but is often followed by "hard law" proposals.
	Green Paper	Policy paper produced by the Commission that outlines in a specific policy sector a set of "European" problems, related goals, and the types of approaches that might serve to remedy the identified problems. Broadly speaking, Green Papers are used to shape, identify and build consensus.
	Other modes of consensus building	Identification and definition of common problems, development of bodies of shared knowledge and common measurements, benchmarking, monitoring, research funding, the cultivation of policy networks and constituencies, and other potentially consensus-building activities and procedures.

4.3 "Social Competence" and Policy Instruments

The EU has a number of formal and informal means available for promoting its policies (Table 6.2) – or what Héritier (2001) aptly characterizes as "overt and covert institutionalization". Formal legislation includes Directives and Regulations, which have force of law, and Recommendations, which amount to formal suggestions to member states, but with no obligations attached. In and of themselves, these are comparatively straightforward, follow established procedures, and are registered in the official journals. However, the informal, or "soft law" means are no less important, especially in areas where the legal basis in the Treaties is comparatively weak or unclear. In several instances, the use of soft measures has set the stage for the eventual development of formal, "hard law" measures[10], and arguably, even to Treaty reforms.

Soft law measures include not only the Action Programs developed by the Commission, but also a multitude of consensus facilitating measures and activities carried out within specific policy areas. These include development of Green Papers, White Papers, the development of common knowledge pools and measurements, benchmarking, monitoring, research funding, the cultivation of policy networks and constituencies, and other potentially consensus-building activities and procedures. While such activities are a long-standing part of the Commission's repertoire (Burns and Carson, 2003; Cram, 1997), they have been developed and refined over time. Such means were systematized and formalized with regard to employment policy at the March 2000 Lisbon summit as the Open Method of Coordination (Trubek and Trubek, 2003; Jacobsson, 2002, 2001).

As pointed out earlier, the EU has historically lacked the legal authority to produce much "hard law" – to legislate directly applicable rules – on most social questions. This stands in stark contrast to the clearly defined competence on market making goals that was put in place in the Treaties of Rome, and then expanded in the Single European Act (SEA). It also differs greatly from member states, whose legal competence to take action on social concerns has been well established, though not unchallenged, through long traditions of social regulation and welfare programs. Where the EU does have the authority to take legislative action on the social concerns, the typical requirement of unanimity among member states presents a significant hurdle. In some areas, such as health services, it is explicitly barred from playing more than a coordination and facilitation role[11], although such limitations do not apply to the market aspects of health services. Organizational capacity to pursue the development of European-level social issues is also limited. This is partially a result of the limited possibilities for financing organizational expansion of the EU bureaucracy, and partially a function of the relative newness of some EU competencies. Such capacity has required development over decades, or even generations in the member states.

4.4 Forms of Participation

An important dimension of analysis emphasizes the forms of participation in EU governance. It concerns governance processes and institutional arrangements

[10] There are numerous examples of this phenomenon. See, for example, Andersen (1999) or Nylander (2000) pertaining to the energy sector, and Vogel's (1993) overview of the development of environmental policy. The case studies taken up in chapters 5-7 also provide examples.

[11] This role is not insignificant, however, and has frequently marked the initial stage of European competence in a given policy area.

which facilitate or hinder the participation of interested social groups in policymaking, and which distribute advantages across different groups. These issues are relevant to concerns about the "democratic deficit" and other questions of legitimacy, and are distinct from issues regarding the levels at which policy is made (whether local, regional, national, supranational, etc.). This dimension encompasses forms of political participation and engagement (see Held, 1997), the extent to which the EU's neo-corporatist or pluralist forms of interest intermediation (Burns and Carson, 2003; Falkner, 1997; Schmitter, 1996b) may help facilitate the representation of various groups in society.

Table 6.3. Public/private continuum for policymaking and regulation

Self-regulation	Regulation	"Organic" democracy	Conventional representative democracy
"Private" decisions	**Quasi-private policymaking**	**Public/collective policymaking**	**Public/collective policymaking**
This includes self-monitoring and management: compliance to norms and laws, market regulation, professions, community, health, education. In many instances, self-regulatory arrangements may be supported and sanction by state agents.	Public arenas used as neutral arena for reaching agreement between market actors on rules-of-the-game (e.g., property rights). Efforts to keep system "closed" and participation limited to economically interested parties, technical experts.	Participation of "stakeholders" through mix of corporatist intermediation and/or lobbying in administrative/ legislative systems. Extensive use of expertise from multiple sources.	Arrangements for public representation based on democratic principles of representation. Accountability via public scrutiny, free elections.
Development of social dimension			

Table 6.3 highlights four different composite categories to be used in assessing forms of participation in governance. The first is conventional parliamentary democracy (see Held, 1996). The second category is what has been referred to as "organic" democracy, (Burns, 1999; Andersen and Burns, 1996), which entails the participation of organized actors or stakeholders through lobbying, and through mobilizing a wide range of discursive and organizational resources, including specialized expertise. The third category, labeled as "regulation by invitation", is exemplified by the market actors seeking to make their environment more manageable and predictable by inviting public authorities to participate in defining property rights and rules of engagement for the marketplace (see Fligstein and Stone Sweet, 2002). This type of policymaking tends to operate as more of a closed system, limiting partici-

pation to actors with special technical expertise or with ownership ("stockholder") interest. The fourth category entails private decisions and voluntary or self-regulation (which may be undertaken in an effort to stave off public intervention).

Policymaking in the EU has entailed in many sectors systematic increases in the policymaking participation of NGOs, increased openness and transparency in policymaking (with accompanying demands for transparency in lobbying activities), greater influence of formally democratic institutions in areas of contention, and less reliance on self-regulation (Carson, 2004).

4.5 Levels of Governance

The key dimension of analysis engages elements of the long-standing theoretical tension and dialog in EU research between intergovernmentalism and neo-functionalism, and between Westphalian-style states and some form of European supranational or federal arrangement. "Sovereignty" and "subsidiarity" are the watchwords for this dimension. However, this is not solely a struggle between national and supranational bodies; struggles over where policy authority should be properly located extend both above and below these levels, extending from the local to the international level (as illustrated in Table 6.4).

John Peterson (2001:290-291), for example, notes that "in Europe more than elsewhere the international, supranational, transnational, national, regional, and subnational are inextricably linked". Beginning with the local level, each successive level is "nested" in a context influenced by the level above it, and which it in turn influences to varying degrees (Hollingsworth, 2002b). The lines of influence may sometimes bypass the level above or below, as when local or regional governments set up lobbying activities in Brussels. As issues within each of the policy sectors covered in the case studies illustrate, sovereignty is in practice spread across these successive levels, whether formally by virtue of legal agreements, or by default, through the ability of some economic actors to relocate elsewhere.

Assessments of at which level policy authority should rest have varied considerably with the policy sector and over time. On the weak end of the spectrum, a passive consensus would permit EU engagement in certain issues deemed important, whether via work programs, support of research initiatives, or staging conferences or meetings with the goal of identifying common problems and potential European level remedies, etc. A greater degree of competence might include acknowledgement in the Treaties of an issue area or sector as an EU concern, but one that grants only limited competence to pass legislation. Legal competence with the ability to pass legislation on the basis of a qualified majority vote represents a greater degree of institutionalized authority, as does establishing a particular set of concerns as a core goal of the EU. An important, but less obvious and visible type of competence is the coordinating role the Commission may sometimes Commission on behalf of EU countries in international forums, such as the 1995 Beijing Conference on Women. Most important here is the overall constellation of legal competencies and organizational capacities, rather than any particular type of competence or capacity.

Table 6.4. Levels of governance (adapted from Hollingsworth, 2002b)

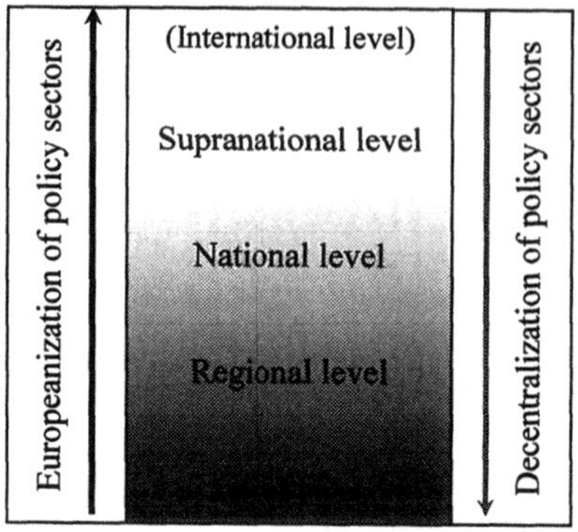

Attempting to "stack the deck" by influencing the rules by which policy disputes are decided is a well-worn strategy, so too is choosing the particular arena in which a given contest is decided (Nylander, 2000; Baumgartner and Jones, 1991). The importance of the contentiousness around the governance and integration dimensions is greatly magnified by the fluidness of institutional arrangements of the EU. The EU is very much a moving target.

As the EU's ability and mandate to pursue specific kinds of economic and social goals expands, one finds different kinds of relevant competence emerge at the supranational, EU level, as well as the development of new organizational structures and capacities to pursue them (such as with a series of work programs, or with the establishment of a new DG or department within an existing DG). The overall configuration of these competencies and capacities should make possible a wide range of activities, including the development over time of new constituencies to support EU action in the policy sector in question.

New Policy Paradigms and the EU Multi-level Problematique

Applying the PPP concept to an examination of EU policy developments poses a special problem. While a policy paradigm applied at the level of the nation-state speaks to questions of policy substance – what substantive principles should be prioritized and realized, examination of EU policymaking requires bringing a pair of other considerations under closer scrutiny. These are: a) questions of competence or jurisdiction – entailing the distinctions between levels, such as local, national, supranational, international, and b) questions of governance and process – by what procedures should public policy decisions be determined, who should participate and ultimately, whether it is a "public", EU issue at all. At the EU level, this means that in addition to feedback effects generated by the substance of actual policy, there is also an ongoing interplay between paradigmatic principles *defining the levels over which such decision making authority should be distributed and the governance procedures by which policy is created.* These considerations are not absent at the national level, but in the EU context they are unusually fluid, as we show in our case studies.

5. Theories of European Integration

Though much of the period of development of the European Union, two competing theoretical frameworks have tended to dominate. Structural-functionalist theories (Haas, 1992; Mitrany, 1948; Schmitter, 2004, among others) have typically been favored during periods in which expansion and integration were proceeding, while statist theories such as intergovernmentalism (Moravcsik, 1998) have done well in explaining periods of stagnation. While there remain several competing and sometimes conflicting theories and approaches in EU research, a significant consensus has emerged around the importance of institutions (Schmitter, 2004; Peterson, 2001; Stone-Sweet et al., 2001; Aspinwall and Schneider, 2000). Institutional analysis is particularly well suited to addressing a defining characteristic of EU policy: that developments in the principal policy-related spheres of activity are especially fluid and that they tend to move in conjunction with one another. These spheres include: (a) the substantive content of EU public policy, (b) the development of new policy authority[12] at the European level – whether by changing levels or by developing new areas of public authority (this is often referred to as "European integration"), and (c) the entry of new actors and development of new configurations and alliances of organized actors. One of the goals of the case studies included here is to identify ways in which these move in systematic relation to one another. The institutional complex defined by the combination of these factors represents a set of real-world compromises.

As will become clear in Part Three, analyses of EU policymaking bring to light important characteristics of policy processes that often remain hidden to analyses of national or local level policy processes. National policymaking systems tend to be more stable, while the policymaking apparatus of the European Union constitutes much more of a moving target and entails more frequent disputes regarding of "rules of the game" such as the location of policy authority for the policymaking process. Such rules of the game define not only what issues constitute problems that lie in the public arena, but also in which arena they should be decided, who should participate and on what basis, and what remedies are considered preferable (Burns and Flam 1987; Burns and Carson 2002).

[12] This is referred to as "competence" in EU terminology.

6. Concluding Remarks

Applying the paradigm concept in investigations of EU policy developments poses a special challenge. While a policy paradigm applied at the level of the nation-state speaks to questions of policy substance – what substantive principles should be prioritized and realized – examination of EU policymaking requires bringing a pair of other considerations into the scrutiny. These are: a) questions of competence or jurisdiction – entailing the distinctions between levels, such as local, national, supranational, international, and b) questions of governance and process – by what procedures should public policy decisions be determined, who should participate and ultimately, whether it is a "public", EU issue at all. At the EU level, this means that in addition to feedback effects generated by the substance of actual policy, there is also an ongoing interplay between paradigmatic principles *defining the levels over which such decision making authority should be distributed and the governance processes by which policy is created.* These considerations are not absent at the national level, but in the EU context they are unusually fluid, as we shall see in our case studies.

CHAPTER 7

Theoretical Framework and Methods for Conducting the EU Research on Paradigms and Paradigm Transformations

PART I: THEORETICAL FRAMEWORK

1. Introduction: Cognitive/Normative Frameworks

Public policy paradigms regulate social relationships and practices in relevant policy spheres or domains. By providing a cognitive/normative framework, such "mental maps" provide complexes of rules that are shared with others, providing potentialities for understanding, coordination, and shared identities. Surel (2000:500) (see Chapter 2 in this book) writes: "As in the cultural conception of ideology put forward by Geertz one of the principal "functions" of a cognitive and normative framework[1] shared by a number of actors is effectively to develop a "collective consciousness" in them; in other words, a subjective sense of belonging and producing a specific identity (Geertz, 1964). Cognitive and normative frame[work]s allow actors to make sense of their world, and to locate themselves and develop in a given community, by defining the field for exchange, by allowing meaning to be conferred on social events and dynamics, and by determining the possibilities of action. They thereby contribute to the construction of individuals or groups as social actors in a particular field."

Policy paradigms are simultaneously products and determinants of exchanges between individuals, groups, and the state (Surel, 2000:500). They facilitate and structure exchange processes by defining actor roles in terms of particular types of expertise and authority. Some actors in public policymaking have a privileged role in both producing and in diffusing cognitive and normative components. Sabatier, for example, refers to the policy-broker who is characterized by the capacity to make the link between one subsystem and another and to thereby facilitate the integration of subsystems of public policy in the public sphere. For Jobert and Muller, these mediators "hold a strategic decision-making position insofar as they construct the intellectual context in which negotiations and conflicts take place and alliances are created, which lead to the taking of decisions" (Jobert and Muller, 1994:50).

[1] We distinguish the "frame" concept and the complex framework represented by the paradigm conception (see Chapter 1 discussion on related concepts). Here we take the liberty of adjusting Geertz's statement to reflect this important distinction.

As has been demonstrated in earlier research (Hall, 1993; Sabatier and Jenkins-Smith, 1993; Carson, 2004) policy paradigms possess a varied topography in that some features are endowed with greater meaning and higher priority than others. This has practical meaning in that some elements are easier to change than others owing to their secondary status in defining roles, problem definitions and preferred remedies. It has analytical consequences in that a replacement or reordering of core dimensions defines a paradigm shift, while changes in the periphery do not – even though such peripheral changes may help set the stage for future paradigm shifts.

In addition to topography and the social regulation functions they perform, policy paradigms also possess a distinct architecture. Our EU case studies and other research have identified essential elements of the architecture of public policy paradigms. In the following section, we present that architecture in detail and its role as a blueprint for institutional design.

2. Paradigms as Idealized Rule Regimes

Paradigms are idealized rule regimes[2] consisting of a complex of norms, principles, and other rules, specifying social roles and relationships as well as ways of categorizing, thinking and analyzing questions in a given social setting or domain. By idealized, we mean that a paradigm serves as a model, or blueprint for institutional design, much as a theory or set of theories may serve as the basis of a research program (Carson, 2004). Policy paradigms are therefore neither utopian nor the work of philosophers; they are the product of actors engaged in real-world problem solving, claims-making, and governing – and negotiation and struggle. Nevertheless, a rule regime will differ from the paradigm that inspired it, sometimes significantly.

Hall's (1989) anthology examining the adoption of Keynesian economic policies in the US and Europe provides a textbook example of factors that contribute to differences between policy paradigm and rule regime. Even though they shared a common paradigmatic model, the US and European countries that adopted Keynesian policies did so in different ways and to very different degrees. The result was that the institutionalization of Keynesian policies in Europe much more closely resembled the Keynesian model than in the United States. These differences were the product of multiple factors. The process of constructing rule regimes is typically slow and often laborious, with major policy shifts often taking a decade or more (Sabatier, 1999). Adoption or institutionalization or a new rule regime proceeds though adjustment to path dependencies linked to external conditions, existing institutional structure, and power relations among influential actors. One result is that both policy paradigms and rule regimes are constructed over time through different processes that are asynchronous, and which produce inexact copies of the policy paradigm.

[2] These have been distinguished from "operationalized-" or "institutionalized policy paradigm" (Burns and Carson, 2002, 2005; Carson, 2004, 2008).

In spite of the differences between policy paradigms and the rule regimes they inspire, they share a common structure. They are composed of a common set of elements that define social problems and problem solving modes, organizational and actor relationships, and their relationships to one another. We conceptualize clusters of such elements in terms of distinct complexes of elements within the policy paradigm or rule regime. *One especially important point related to these differences is that a policy paradigm and its related rule regime are not one in the same thing. However, while there may remain significant differences between the policy paradigm and its rule regime in terms of content, they share a common architecture, or structure.*

2.1 The Architecture of an Idealized Rule Regime: Problem-solving Policy Complex and Organizational Complex

The policy paradigm is applied in a given policy domain in which designated policymakers – those agents in positions of appropriate responsibility and authority – make policy in pursuit of certain policy goals and the realization of appropriate or legitimate values in the policy space or domain, using putatively appropriate or legitimate means.

Our conceptualization of a public policy paradigm emphasizes its combination of cultural components and social structural components. These components consist of a) a cognitive-normative complex for problem-solving and policy choice to be used by the designated or key policymaking agents, and b) a social structural or organizational complex specifying the key roles and social relationships for the problem-solving and policy choice processes. In the course of seeking to establish a new paradigm or replace an established one, the change agents often initially lack a complete blueprint. They change some components, leaving other components unnoticed, or intending to change them at a later, more opportune moment.

The social structural complex of a paradigm specifies key social agents and their relations:

- who participates either as experts, as public authorities, or in some other capacity (also explicitly or implicitly, who is excluded);
- what collective decision-making procedures are to be followed;
- other norms, for instance relating to time and space.

The regime's problem-solving complex specifies components of the cognitive-normative framework for problem definition and solution:

- a sub-complex for defining problems or issues;
- a conceptualization or model of problems or issues including a causal model possibly specifying "evil" factors or agents;
- a value complex defining goals and priorities;
- a solution complex including technologies used in such solution efforts.

These elements that define in each of the complexes that comprise the policy paradigm architecture are summarized in Table 7.1 below.

Table 7.1. Elements Comprising Policy Paradigm Architecture

Cognitive-normative problem-solving complex:
- values, value orientations, goals
- model of the situation or issues: framing and conceptualization of "problem" or issue, its causes or mechanisms
- solution complex, the right and proper means to deal with the problem or issue

Social structural or organizational complex:
- appropriate agents: public authorities, experts, stakeholders
- their relationships (who does what in relation to whom)
- procedures for deliberating and deciding the nature of the problem and the right strategy or solution
- place
- time

Such policy regimes are not just discourses, or not just cognitive, although they are expressed or articulated in discourses, and they entail cognitive as well as normative factors. In addition, as pointed out above, there are particular organizational relations and activities as well as the performance of problem-solving activities (practices) and decision-making. Paradigms are "designed" in terms of the knowledge, perspective(s), and interests of those engaged in the paradigm formation and reformation process. They are, in short, social constructions.

The relationships between the two basic building blocks: social structure and cultural forms. The distinctions are analytical categories. There are more detailed subcategories within the problem-solving and organizational complexes, which are discussed later in this chapter. The important point to note regarding the different categories is that they exert different kinds of influences. The organizational complex exerts a relational pressure influencing and regulating overt behavior, while the influence that stems from the problem-solving policy complex is cognitive and conceptual and, of course, normative. In an instance where a policy paradigm is highly institutionalized, the two would be expected mirror one another to a very large extent. In instances where the level of institutionalization is much lower, such as in periods of transition or confrontation over paradigmatic elements, one would expect many gaps and inconsistencies, as a new policy paradigm is constructed over time and space.

The motivation to establish a new paradigm or replace an established one may be the result of policy failures or anomalies (for instance, serious unanticipated consequences of the established policy regime), pressures to reduce costs of implementation or operation, competition or conflict among key groups (experts, public authorities, political groups or parties), and pressures from external agents, among others. In chapters 14 and 15, after we have presented our case studies, we will specify and analyze the drivers of public policy paradigm shifts.

A paradigm shift may be piecemeal, e.g. entailing, on the one hand, only changes in the problem-solving sub-complex, or, on the other hand, only in the social organizational sub-complex. Change may be initiated in either or both sub-complexes, spinning off to other components in a complex or spill-over to the other sub-complex.

In the next section, we elaborate on the conceptualizations of two interrelated complexes of a policy paradigm: the social organization complex and a problem-solving complex (used by key policymaking agents).

2.2 Problem-Solving and Social Organizational Frameworks

As actors engage in judgment, planning, interpreting, innovating, and applying rules in a given institutional domain or field of interaction, institutional rule knowledge is combined with other types of knowledge. Such organization of rule knowledge and its applications is accomplished through a shared policy paradigm: the problem-solving, or *policy subcomplex and the social organizational complex* (see Figure 7.1).[3] The paradigm provides people with a set of organizing relationships and a cognitive-normative model with which to organize information, and to define and try to solve concrete problems of performance, production, and goal achievement in a given institutional domain. The problem-solving complex – associated with a particular policy space – is used by institutional actors in their concrete judgments and practices to define problems, problem-solving strategies, and solutions.[4] These complexes incorporate complexes of beliefs, classification schemes, normative ideas, and rules of thumb, which are used in conceptualizing and judging key institutional situations and processes, relevant problems, and possible solutions for dealing with key problems.

The organizing subcomplex and the problem-solving complex (making up the paradigm regime) are obviously intertwoven, but they are each affected in different ways in social change processes – particularly those driven by tangible problems. If, on the one hand, actors have a great investment in protecting the concrete organizational arrangements themselves – for reasons such as the desire to protect ideal and material interests, to preserve power or predictability – rules are tightened, enforcement mechanisms are deployed, and may even be strengthened (as in the case

[3] This is a usage which differs substantially from Kuhn's (1970) notion of "scientific paradigm" which refers to a theoretical model or framework for representing and explaining empirical phenomena, the theoretical and methodological rules to be followed, the instruments to be used, the problems to be investigated, and the standards by which research is to be judged. There are, of course, a number of parallels with our conceptualization of a public policy paradigm, a matter which we shall take up in a later article (see also footnote 4 in Chapter 1).

[4] The paradigm is a "rough" or "fuzzy" rule complex. Levels of knowledge of it vary among participants (Burns and Roszkowska, 2004). Also, it is "distributed knowledge" with variants among different individuals and groups.

of Michels's Iron Law of Oligarchy (1962)). There is an emphasis on protecting ideas and principles that are already materialized, and sometimes this is done at great cost and to the detriment of the long-term functioning of the institutional arrangements. If, on the other hand, actors have – or would like to make – a much greater investment in effectively solving problem(s) than possible under the earlier established arrangements, the actions taken will be quite different. Rules are consciously broken in spite of possible or likely sanctions, supporters are rallied around possibilities rather than certainties, and short-term, material interests may be set aside in favor of imagined or envisioned long-term opportunities. There is a substantial shift in risk-taking orientations and in the readiness to transform conditions.

A PPP, as a collectively produced and maintained entity, is often changed with reluctance – since collective identities and interests, including material interests, are often closely associated with it. This contributes to making changes difficult as participants judge negatively alteration in key elements that give them and their concrete institutional practices their identity, status, and power. A paradigm whose core principles, values, and normative practices are deeply embodied in concrete institutional and identity-giving practices will tend to be durable and resilient, even in the face of contradictory evidence and/or political pressure.

2.3 Key Components of the Policy Paradigm Architecture Expressed in Discourses

Discourses conceptually define and anchor a paradigm in a number of different ways. Discourses are written or oral expressions which are shaped and regulated according to particular rule complexes, codes. Typically, they are embedded in a particular institutional context, in which participants express orally and in writing accounts, explanations, etc. These are in the form of ordinary talk as well as other sources of text such as historical documents, diaries, reports, letters. Our approach combines deductive and inductive approaches. Institutional theory indicates appropriate forms and content. But also, through empirical studies, one discovers the emphases on giving and asking of accounts, normative assessments, interpretation and shaping and regulation of conceptions of social reality.

While Michel Foucault suggested a connection between the collectively representational and the interactional, arguing, among other things, that interpretative structures are embodied in discourse, we stress the embeddedness of discourses in institutions and institutional arrangements (see also Machado, 2000). Gubrium and Holstein (1997:117) point out: "Foucault focuses on the role discourse plays in constituting, configuring, and conveying knowledge. He contends that the way we understand and represent experience derives from, and is constrained by, sociohistorically anchored discourse structures. But these structures are not mere linguistic templates for expressing knowledge. Foucault argues that discourses are more than systems of signs or signifying elements that refer to the content or meanings of objects and actions. ... Instead, discourses are 'practices that systematically form the objects of which they speak. Of course, discourses are composed of signs; but what they do is more than use these signs to designate things'" "Foucault thus points directly to discourse, both its structures and articulations, as the essence of reality construction. The notion of practice provides the vehicle for linking substantive meaning to experience. ... It is much more like a complex and dynamic border engagement at the lived intersection of reality and intersection... Throughout his work, Foucault is skeptical of individual agency, tending to reject the active subject. Moving away from the interactional dynamics of reality construction, he engages in the archaeology and genealogy of knowledge."

Public policy paradigms may be expressed in discourses concerning "public problems", distribution of "expert authority", distribution of "policy authority and responsibility", and "appropriate solutions". Such institutionalized discourses refer to laws and written rules and other materials that define the location and other particulars of formal rule making authority, and set(s) of institutional practices or strategies for dealing with specific types of problems.[5] Discourses expressing a given paradigm can be analyzed in terms of the categories or complexes of definitions they contain (van Dijk, 1995; Sutton, 1998; Carson, 2004; Burns and Carson, 2005): 1) defining an issue/problem and its characteristics (issue/problem subcomplexes), 2) the form and range of acceptable solutions (solutions subcomplexes) 3) the goals and priorities that are to be achieved (goals subcomplex), 4) the location and types of sources considered to be valid authorities on the issue – therefore having legitimate information and/or facts to offer (expert authority subcomplexes), 5) the authorities who have formal or informal responsibility for addressing and/or resolving the issue/problem (policy responsibility and authority subcomplexes), and 6) (procedural subcomplexes).

(1) *Conceptualization/Problem-solving Sub-Complex.* Key issues or problems are defined and characterized within a cognitive-normative framework. Related questions concern how policymakers define crises, depending on their normative and cognitive presuppositions, or the degree to which policy ideas are blended with these presuppositions to initiate policy change in different policymaking contexts (Campbell, 2002:32). Here we find *causal narratives* – or narratives and statements that contain either implicit or explicit assumptions about the sources or causes of major problems as well as *narratives of threat* which indicate or describe who is affected and the likely consequences if the problems are not "solved". That is, the sub-complex includes characterizations of who is affected and how, and the broad categorizations of an issue or problem as social, moral, economic, political, etc.

---

[5] The state, markets, and civil society and their respective institutional structures include a range of institutional practices and strategies for addressing issues considered to be problems, and use a system of rules that establish formal authority for how and where to address various types of problems (Burns and Carson, 2002).

Discourses that define an issue or problem by defining and framing the nature, causes, or consequences of a problem fall within this category. Characterizations of who is affected and how, and the broad categorizations of an issue/problem as social, economic, political, etc., are a part of such definitions, as is the particular way in which a problem is dispersed, or subdivided into segments so as to make it more (or less) easy (apparently) to grasp and manage. Put in other words, these include: *causal narratives* – or narratives and statements that contain either implicit or explicit assumptions about the sources or causes of public issues and problems; narratives *of threat* – which help define the nature of a problem, describe who is affected and the likely consequences if it is not "solved", and classify the problem as social, economic, moral, etc.; *dispersion of the problem* – or the way in which the problem or issue is subdivided into more manageable pieces (Sutton, 1998).

(2) *Value sub-complex*: goals and priorities. Most public policy paradigms indicate the legitimate values and appropriate goals which policy should take into account and pursue. Policy processes are driven, in part, by the socially defined values and priorities. For instance, a policy paradigm may stress market or economic goals – or, conversely, social, health, or environmental goals. As we shall see, paradigm shifts may involve value re-orientation or re-prioritization, thus setting in motion a transformation of public policy.

(3) *Solution subcomplex* – specifies the form and range of acceptable solutions to institutional problems. Solution complexes include the particular way(s) in which the resolution of an issue or problem should be constructed, including the use of appropriate, available institutional practices, technologies, and strategies. Problems are often deliberately defined in ways that permit an issue to land in particular parts of an institutional apparatus (Nylander, 2000). This, in turn, dictates the range of both possible and likely responses (Baumgartner and Jones, 1991). Structures developed as the response to one set of circumstances are, not infrequently, adapted to new purposes.

(4) *Expert Authority Subcomplex* – the location and distribution of legitimate sources considered knowledgeable and authoritative on the issue or issues. It also defines who has the legitimacy to explain the causes and solutions of any particular relevant problem.[6] Who (or which) are the legitimate sources and authorities for informa-

[6] In some of the literature on public policy paradigm, the concept of an "epistemic community" is introduced. Such a community generates new ideas and disseminates them among policymakers as well as others in the community. They are networks of professionals and experts within an authoritative claim to policy-relevant knowledge, who share a set of normative beliefs, causal models, notions of empirical validity, and a common policy enterprise (Haas, 1992). Wittrock and others used to refer to "reform coalitions" that brought together intellectuals (social scientists, technicians) and political and administrative agents.

tion, facts and analysis regarding the problem? This includes the determination of who has the authority to produce information about an issue that is already the subject of discussion. Equally important, it also defines who has the legitimacy to define a particular problem into – or out of existence – or to redefine an issue or problem into another existence.

(5) *Authority and Responsibility Subcomplex* – defines who is the authority which has the formal or informal responsibility for addressing and/or resolving key issues and problems. On a more systemic level, it defines where the location and distribution of appropriate problem-solving responsibility and authority lies in the organization or institutional arrangement. This refers, among other things, to institutional authority with the responsibility for taking specific corrective action and and having legitimacy for making policy. This is related in part to expertise, as discussed below, but equally important, is grounded in the social roles and norms for determining who should be empowered to pass judgment, adopt new problem-solving strategies, or initiate necessary action on behalf of the institution or society as a whole.

(6) Procedures for making legitimate policy decisions. Typically, a developed public policy paradigm indicates procedures for making policy decisions, either in terms of designating persons with authority to make such decisions, or indicating those who should be involved in a collective process; for instance in the case of the EU, the engagement of the EP and the Council for co-legislation, following the preparations of the Commission for agricultural policy. Also, EU policymaking typically entails the engagement of multiple "stakeholders" – this being a powerful norm in the EU polity.

Figure 7.1 represents the structure and relationships between the complexes that define the paradigm – the shared cognitive-normative space. It illustrates the various flows that combine to produce the paradigm, and which the elements with which to produce conceptualizations of the "problems" to be addressed by policymakers, the roles of various actors in producing information, making decisions, establishing goals, and implementing appropriate solutions. The actions taken to implement solutions and the resulting outcomes stand outside the cognitive-normative model and feed back into it. To the extent they are visible, the range of actual of outcomes will tend to either reinforce or undermine the various elements defined by the paradigm. Of course, exogenous factors may also intervene to modify the outcomes that would otherwise be produced, although these interaction effects may not be obvious or clear cut. Persistent or significant failure to produce the desired outcomes (in this case, policy or market failures) will tend to undermine one or more elements of the paradigm, creating pressures for adjustment. Where this undermines core, defining elements, it may eventually lead to a paradigm shift.

Figure 7.1. Public Policy Paradigm

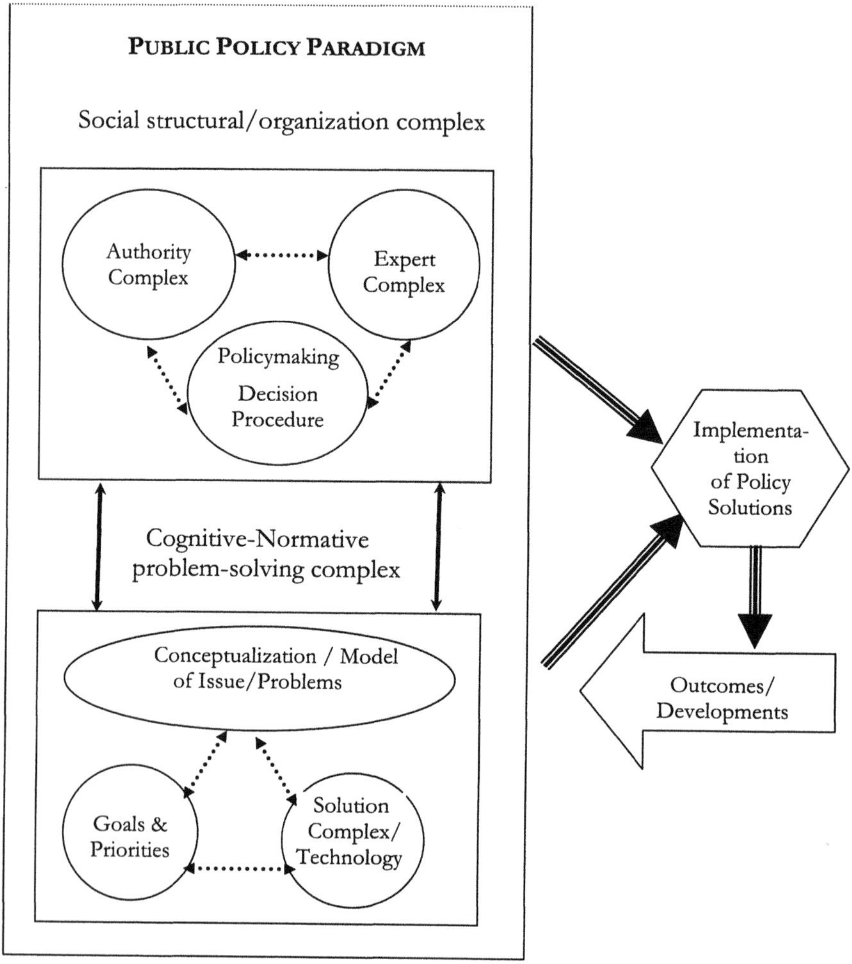

Which of the complexes or their components constitute the core or most favored part of the paradigm may vary from context to context; some of the components or dimensions of the public policy paradigm are likely to be considered more central than others. This is an important distinction when it comes to understanding and explaining which components are first changed – or where there is likely to be systematic resistance to changing particular components. In general, actors representing and bearing a paradigm – those whose identity is most closely associated with its *core* components or dimensions, their material and ideal interests, their sense of order are typically ready to resist significant change in these components. Peripheral components can generally be negotiated and adapted much more easily. They do not concern, for instance, powerful interests related to social power (such as property rights or political power) or to identity issues.

Each policy paradigm is grounded in a particular set of fundamental assumptions and beliefs about reality that a group of actors shares.[7] It forms the framework for organizing their perceptions, judgments, and action that determines which phenomena are included in the picture – and which are excluded (Kuhn, 1970; Lakoff and Johnson, 1980). It is also the basis for operationally assigning values to certain actions and conditions, and encouraging and pursuing certain activities (or discouraging or even prohibiting others)[8]. A paradigmatic rule regime is used in a policy context in the process of identifying, defining and classifying problems (and "non-problems"), potential solutions to such problems (including the use of appropriate and effective technologies and techniques), and source(s) of decision-making and expert authority in the institutional arrangement. These judgments play a key role in the giving and asking of accounts and in justifying or legitimizing actions.

The rule regime as a universal institutional framework specifies key actors, their roles and relationships, that is who should be involved and in what capacities (also explicitly or implicitly who is excluded), procedures and other tools for managing interactions and decisions; it also specifies goals and priorities, defines problems, solutions, tools of analysis (models, statistics, etc.). These are historically articulated and evolve over time.

In its character as an operative rule regime (Burns & Flam, 1987), an institutionalized public policy paradigm constrains and regulates conditions and processes in a given policy domain.

- it consists of a model of the situation to be regulated, the source of problems, the policy variables to be manipulated. It also may model the regulator and its interaction with the regulatees;
- It identifies the instruments used in regulation whether through legal constraints, taxes, subsidies, other incentive structures;
- It identifies the actors who will lead and manage;
- It also identifies the actors and processes/interactions who will be subject to regulation, making assumptions about their interests, behavioral tendencies;
- It identifies the actors who provide the expertise, special knowledge for operation of the system;

---

[7] A shared paradigm must be simplified for purposes of communication. At the same time it has definitional power – the power to define, interpret, and prescribe action for dealing with reality.

[8] In this respect, it relates to the notion of "master frame" used in the social movements literature (Nylander, 2000), or that of "meta narrative", within which individual issues or policy questions can be contextualized and "framed" (Gottweis, 1998:30-33).

- It specifies the relations among these actors including power and influence relations;
- In short, it is a socially constructed and maintained control system.

Typically, associated with a rule regime are supporting arguments, interpretations, applications. Institutional arrangements are designed to teach, realize, implement, protect or defend the norms and values of the regime. Agents other than key or core ones may be specified in a paradigm regime such as "subjects", "participants", extraordinary and informal advisors, allies, potential allies also "opponents", "enemies". In general, there are "external" agents who affect – or try to affect – the regime and its implementation, its maintenance or change.

With respect to the EU, the structure of the above-described definitions manifests itself in a number of ways. For example, during the evolution of the EU, some categorizations of issues/problems have been defined as lying within the competence of the EU (market related issues), while others fall primarily outside (more typically, non-market social issues). If the perceived cause or effect of a problem falls outside of EU competence, it tends to be invisible to its policymaking structure. New areas of competence emerge, in part, where market integration or development results in new social problems, as in the case of equal pay provisions, where there was concern that social costs might create market "distortions" and unfair competition. Where EU policy or institutional arrangements such as the single market might be (or might be seen as) the source of these new problems, the incentives to action are likely to be particularly strong. In our EU asbestos policy case study, Canada (especially the Province of Ontario) was active in trying to block a change in EU asbestos policy. Concerning Gender, the UN, many NGOs. In chemicals, NGO, CEFIC and the chemical industry, the US government, US Chamber of Commerce, etc. In the case of EU climate change policy, NGOs and the USA (and diverse agents) were key external influences.

2.4 Anomalies as Change Catalysts: Gaps, Flaws, and Competence

We have identified three distinct areas in which anomalies or issues of competence may provide the basis for a policy paradigm or rule regime to be challenged. Once source of potential problems lies within the paradigm itself, in inevitable gaps and flaws that may not initially be apparent or important. In such cases, the policy regime may fail to properly manage a potential problem due either to lack of knowledge of how best to proceed – or as a result of the faithful application of a flawed model. A second source of problem lies in the consistency between the policy paradigm and the rule regime that represents its institutionalization. As inevitable as failures of logic or incompleteness, inconsistencies between model and regime will emerge in the process of institutionalization as products of compromise, negotiation, and misunderstanding. The third problem lies in issues of competence, as realized in organizational and human failures that obstruct the effective application of the rule regime. These might include, for example, failure to use the agreed upon decision making procedures or ineffectively carrying out prescribed activities, or implementing the model as conceptualized.

Much of the day-to-day work of actors in a given institutional context has the effect of cementing and normalizing the institutionalized paradigm in a sense similar to what Kuhn (1970) characterized as "normal science," and we refer to as conditions of *normality*. Problems appear manageable, there is a high degree of consensus, and there is no sense of crisis or bold challenge. Because a paradigm necessarily focuses attention on certain phenomena while obscuring others – it is used to select and also restructure data so that they fit within the framework of its basic assumptions, categories, and rules[9]. Because of paradigm selectivity, its biased rules of interpretation, and its inherent limitations, the actors utilizing a given paradigm will experience difficulties in understanding, explaining, or knowing how to manage some types of situation or problem. Some of these problems arise in connection with – or as a by-product of, actions guided by the paradigm itself. That is, meaningful action – viewed from the perspective of the paradigm – generates anomalies and failures that some participants define as special or exceptional "problems" (Spector and Kitsuse, 1987). Such problems are not only cognitive; they are also practical. They fail to be adequately addressed, and goals are not achieved. The stage is set for entrepreneurial actors to suggest new approaches and solutions.

Anomalies, in the form of gaps, flaws, and competence issues may become visible and thereby provide occasion to undermine the policy paradigm or its rule regime. A typical response to such anomalies might entail filling in the gap through further paradigm development or characterizing the problem as an exceptional case. Overt flaws in paradigmatic logic may prove more disruptive where real-world developments in a given policy sector expose failed logic or faulty assumptions. The most damaging situation occurs in instances where the policy paradigm is understood not to merely have missed important factors or misunderstood them, but to be the cause of problems that emerge. Some power shifts are catalyzed by policy failure that is interpreted not as paradigm failure, but as incompetence in implementing a paradigm that continues to enjoy widespread support.

2.5 Change in a Policy Paradigm

One institutional paradigm can be distinguished from another in that it entails a distinctly different, and often incommensurable, way of framing, conceptualizing, judging, and acting in relation to particular classes of "problems" and "issues." Incommensurability refers to core paradigmatic elements rather than routine adjustments and corrections (and can be likened to the cognitive switching that occurs with figure-ground images). The properties of two distinct phenomena are present, but focusing on one involves making the other a secondary property – or obscures it altogether. This becomes particularly important when actors guided by alternative

[9] This phenomenon is expressed in its more extreme form in the saying "if your only tool is a hammer, then every problem is a nail".

paradigms compete with one another or each tries to impose her respective paradigm in a given institutional domain. Two competing institutional paradigms – each with its reality-defining features and discourses – may embrace competing organizational modes or decision-making principles, for instance, "bureaucratic hierarchy" versus "democratic procedure," or "market problem-solving" versus "welfare" or "re-distributive" problem-solving" (see later).[10] While these may coexist within a single institution, conditions under which each is applied and one or the other is generally accorded primacy during conditions of stability. As we discuss below, conditions of instability are characterized by figure-ground switching in core paradigmatic elements and can be identified through the specific discourses that express these competing orientations.

The architecture of the PPP rule regime indicates the dimensions of potential change (see figure above):

Social organizational complex:

- adding to or substracting agents (or categories of agents) in the complex, or changing the definitions or conceptions of agents;
- changes in the relationships among the agents; for instance, power relationships are changed, or roles and role relationships are reformed. Agent configurations are altered.
- changes in the procedures to make decisions;
- changes in time, place, context.

Problem-solving complex:

- changes in key values or goals;
- change in the model of representation of the situation, causality, possible policy variables;
- changes in the issue-problem complex, the "conceptualization of the problem";
- changes in the solution complex.

Changes in a paradigm may involve one or more of these dimensioins. Radical change would entail significant changes in multiple dimensions. Some changes are relatively modest. But even if only a few dimensions are changed initially, some changes much greater secondary consequences than others, for example:

- Shift from public agency responsibility to private (the laws, incentive structures, etc. differ substantially).
- Shift from covering one population (the middle classes) to another (lower classes or marginal groups), or both.
- Shift from narrow scope of policy to comprehensive scope which will affect many more populations and involve a much greater array of methods, types of knowledge and expertise

---

[10] Such inconsistencies can be conceptualized as a source of cultural/institutional dissonance, a sociological version of the cognitive dissonance experienced by individuals and described by Leon Festinger's theory (Festinger, 1957; Machado, 1998; Machado & Burns, 1998).

- Shifts in types of experts also may lead to new conceptualization of the problem and possible solutions, the application of new methods to deal with the problem(s).

Changes may be made in the problem-solving complex (II) but not in the social organizational complex (I). Or, changes in the organizational complex (I) need not necessarily follow immediately in the problem-solving complex, for instances changes in the agents and their relationships might entail operating with the same problem-solving complex. Changes in the types of experts engaged, however, are likely to lead to changes in the problem-solving complex II. Also, changes in values and changes in the model of reality are likely to impact on "problem definitions" and potential "solutions" as well as the experts recognized as appropriate.

Changes in paradigms – their cognitive-normative frameworks as well as their social organizational properties – are brought about by agents, either within an institutional arrangement or outside of it operating on the components and relationships – this type of power is referred to as meta-power (McGinty et al, 2009). The processes are typically multi-level in that some of the actors who are part of the policy system may, under certain conditions, operate on the system changing it, although they are part and parcel of it.

There may also be external drivers, exercising influence over paradigm stability or change, For instance, (1) External agents try to exercise influence over public polices (Canada in the case of asbestos, discussed later in the book; NGOs and UN Beijing influencing EU gender policies), EU chemicals policy subject to influence attempts by multiple NGOs, foreign states such as the USA, member-states with special interests in chemicals (Germany, UK, France); EU climate change policy was influenced by the US government through international interactions. (2) External or socio-economic material resource crisis may challenge or call into question one or more components of an established public policy paradigm.

PART II: METHODS OF INVESTIGATING PPPs AND THEIR TRANSFORMATIONS

Multiple methods are essential for investigating and analyzing paradigms and paradigm shifts. Some methods, such as those of discourse analysis, are used to investigate and analyze the architecture of paradigms, or the restructuring of such architectures in paradigm shifts. Investigating and analyzing the statements or discourses in documents and interviews is one effective type of method. A second complex of methods are used in analyzing paradigm shifts, in particular investigating the "political processes" whereby restructuring or transformation of paradigms takes place: the agents and networks involved, the strategies and counter-strategies, the mobilization and exercise of power, the processes of struggle and negotiation, and the resulting outcomes and developments.

3. Investigating PPPs and Their Transformation

3.1 The Case Studies of Jenson, Hall, Coleman et al. as well as Others

The early developers and investigators of the public policy paradigm concept, several of whose work is republished here (Part II) studied "public policy entrepreneurs" (Woodward et al.) who innovated by bringing about a shift of paradigms or introducing a paradigm in an area previously not covered or covered by an entirely different paradigm. One made use of documents, archival material and/or interviews. All worked with case study approaches (Ragin, 1987; Yin, 2003).

(a) Jenson drew upon a wide range of materials including law cases, mass media, government documents. She followed shifts in the discourses (in the larger societal context) and investigated the concrete changes in policies in France and USA – and drew comparative conclusions.

(b) Hall used existing literature – also like Jenson in an historical approach – to investigate paradigms and paradigm shifts. Hall refers to a large literature on the series of alterations made to the system of monetary policy and control in the U.K.

(c) Coleman et al. (1996) (see Chapter 5) make use of government documents, reports, and secondary literature as well as interviews with officials and other interests involved. Coleman et al. (1997) investigated and analyzed the proposals and counter-proposals in the negotiation process as well as the eventual agreement(s) which entailed then a new policy.

In all of these studies, the investigators looked at the arguments and counter-arguments presented in written and oral statements, followed by changes in actual policy, in particular changes in policy goals and policy strategy.

3.2 The EU Investigations

In our own work on EU policy paradigms and their transformation, we have frequently used comparative case study analysis (Ragin, 1987; Yin, 2003), the results of which are presented in Chapter 14. The particular case studies were selected because they entailed major shifts in policy, under different conditions and through diverse processes. The investigations examined these shifts to see more precisely what was (and was not) changed as well as to analyze and explain the drivers of the shifts.

A number of relevant actors in each policy area were interviewed – typically, there was considerable convergence in their "stories". We also made use of documents, including other accounts of the change from a variety of sources, and in a number of cases, we could draw on materials from other related studies to cross-check our data and interpretations of it.

Choice of Cases

The complexity of the EU policymaking system presents a special challenge for generalizing from one or a few cases. Case studies of individual policy sectors cannot be taken as examples of the EU in miniature in the anthropological sense (Andersen, 1999). Accordingly, our goal here has been to use the patterns of similarities and differences in the individual case studies to make theoretically informed generalizations about the types of conditions and processes that have contributed to certain EU policy developments. These have been investigated in terms of both conceptual and institutional change. We have sought to manage the problem of comparability of case studies pointed out by Bennett and George (1997) by using a comparison between six differing configurations of "similar" and "least similar" cases within the context of the EU's policy contexts. Europeanization and integration, with particular attention to social, health, and environmental issues (gender, food, asbestos, chemicals, and climate change). The case policy is a more purely Europeanization (and anti-national monopoly case). The "dependent" variables are the processes by which the concerns in question com to be prioritized as the subject of EU policymaking, and by which issues defined in terms of their social and environmental dimensions come to be prioritized over the economic and market aspects. Gas (and also electricity) as well as climate change concerned European market integration; climate change, however, had also environmental and health aspects.

This sets the stage for struggle over fundamental issue and problem definitions, over authority and responsibility for addressing those problems, and over the specific types of public policy responses generated. The six cases represent different paths to "Europeanization" as a movement of the particular policy sector to the supranational level; four of the cases moved on the continuum from a primarily market conception to primarily "social" principles, while two (gas and climate change) embraced the European market conception (but with a strong environmental consideration in the case of the establishment of the European Trading System (ETS) for dealing with GHG emissions). The cases also represent quite different stages along their respective paths, as well as different stages in the process of conceptualization and institutionalization as policy questions. These differences are particularly relevant for comparative purposes and policy paradigm theoretical development.

Among the case studies, food policy has been the subject of a great deal of EU policymaking activity, driven at least in part by numerous crises. Asbestos and chemicals policy offered an area in which similar issues of health risk were grappled with – and similar problems encountered. While the issues are equally contentious, the change processes in the chemicals area were not significantly driven or fueled by EU-level crises, and thus represent a different path to conceptual and institutional change. Nor has the new chemicals policy progressed as far as the new food safety policy.

Gender as a European issue combined important elements of health & gender equality, but it is also interesting because economic arguments were posited – even though the issue represented no real direct challenge to the market paradigm. Its main linkage to market issues is through the origins of EU gender equality policy in equal treatment in pay. Unlike the first two cases, its social aspects are not seen as challenged or constrained by economic considerations. It emerges as an EU issue via another path, and for that reason serves as an important illustration.

National gas regimes and emerging national ETS systems were both incompatible with one of the primary cornerstones of the EU, namely market integration. The policy change initiatives aimed at the form of an integrated market, and hence a further step toward Europeanization.

Methods of Investigation

In general, the research reported here makes use of qualitative approaches with relatively thick historical description and process tracing; these studies use detailed analyses of sources such as participants or participant observers, policy documents, and related studies to determine how the policymakers and other influentials defined problems, crises, and proposals for change depending on their normative and cognitive presuppositions (see Campbell, 2002:32).

How have we empirically investigated paradigms, for example identifying them, characterizing them, following their development. Related questions concern the identification and measurement of paradigm shift as well as of the conditions under which such shifts do or do not take place.

One makes use primarily of verbal communications, written as well as spoken materials or statements (that is, documents,[11] pronouncements and speeches, associated with policy preparations, policy formulations, programs which are directed by policy. Also, one conducts interviews with informants as well as key actors who are carriers and users of a paradigm, asking about the core categories. One tries to map the policy conceptions and preferences of policymakers and then determine how they have interpreted and assessed the consequences of policy-relevant events, for example, the EU food crises.

One difficulty in analyzing such discourses is distinguishing between the "talk" that has weight and that which does not. One general method makes the distinction by tracing discourses that have been (1) adopted by important actors and expressed in their own discourses and actions, and (2) reflected at the institutional level in public statements, operating principles, and/or organizational procedures, programs, and structures. Patterns of change are apparent where these discourses, their

---

[11] In the case of the EU research, for example, the written materials included EU official documents such as Treaties, Directives, Memoranda, reports, minutes and journals; organizational publications and formal comments offered by business, labor, and public interest organizations (NGOs) in response to perceived problems and specific EU proposals; news coverage published by mainstream newspapers and trade journals. Also, use can be made of secondary literature identifying and analyzing underlying assumptions, concepts, and values embraced by actors in the policymaking process and the broader society.

assumptions, preferences, and arguments differ in principle and content from previous ones.

There may be gaps between the statements and the practices, between the rhetorical policy paradigm and the operative paradigm. This also can be extended to studies of political hypocracy. All of this may be considered a part of the Public Policy paradigm research program.

Public policy or problem-solving discourses can be investigated systematically making use of *the categories or complexes of defining rules they contain* (Burns and Carson, 2002, 2005; Carson, 2001; Sutton, 1998), the "problem-solving rules" and the rules of "social organization"[12] (see section below).

Data Collection

Our analytical strategy has been to get at the policy effects of how various actors conceptualize the content of public policy, the various arenas in which struggle over policymaking takes place, and the roles of key actors in the process (as well as that of the institutions of governance, and of their allies and competitors). We have sought to identify these conceptual elements primarily in verbal communications, both in spoken and written materials, including interviews with informants on the EU level and the use of a variety of formal and informal documents. These written materials include: EU official documents such as Treaties, Directives, Communications, reports, minutes, and journals; organizational publications and formal comments offered by business, labor, and public interest organizations (NGOs) in response to perceived problems and specific EU proposals; news coverage published by mainstream newspapers and trade journals. We have also drawn heavily on the secondary literature, when available. This has facilitated the identification of underlying assumptions, concepts, and values embraced by actors in the policymaking process and the broader society (Bash, 1995). One difficulty in discourse analysis is distinguishing between the "talk" that has weight and that which does not. The general method employed in this analysis makes this distinction by tracing discourses that have been 1) adopted by influential actors, commanding attention and people as well as resources and manifested in their own discourses and actions, and 2) reflected at the institutional level in public statements, operating principles,

[12] Elsewhere (Burns and Carson, 2005) we have distinguished the dominant discourses characteristic of particular types of issue situations: (A) Discourses of normality contrasted with discourses associated with three types of crisis conditions: (B) Uncertainty and potential discovery discourses articulated under conditions of Social Integration; (C) Oppositional normative discourses (under conditions of a social cleavage or lack of integration but apparent systemic order; (D) Chaos and transformative discourses associated with chaos, deep societal crisis, characterized by profound cleavages in the situation and lack of systemic knowledge and order. One of the common responses is to call for a dictator to establish an order (the Hobbesian solution). There may be related discourses about returning to a "Golden Age" or establishing a "New Age", based on a new paradigm constructed around an alternative complex of core principles and assumptions.

and/or organizational structure. Patterns of change are apparent where these discourses differ in principle and content from previous ones and institutional arrangements also differ from earlier arrangements on key dimensions.

Documentary Materials and Research Issues

The complexity of the EU apparatus, the pace at which it is changing, and the incredible volume of EU materials available present a number of significant challenges. One of these challenges is the need to filter through an enormous volume of primary documents to identify the most important and relevant. Access to a considerable volume of materials was gained via Internet, which provided quick and convenient access to an extraordinary volume of information. This approach also had its limits; one notices a definite reduction in the volume of virtually all materials available as one probes further back in relatively recent history, particularly around 1995. For the most part, use of primary source materials from prior to 1995 was limited to documents that other researchers or actors had deemed important enough to reference. In such cases, materials were hunted down using more traditional means, although EU Directives and Treaty Language were a notable exception in their availability on the web.

While the Internet and the EU's new policy of transparency have provided access to information, they have exacerbated the problem of sifting through large volumes of material. Interviews with informants were the most important key to identifying key issues and events, and tracking down many of the most relevant and important documents.

Interviews

The interview materials used for this research consist of interviews with more than 40 different informants on a number of separate research trips to Brussels. Follow up contacts were also made with some of these informants via phone, email, or in person. Carson conducted his interviews during the periods of June 13-16, 2000; February 17-20, 2001; April 17-20, 2001, and March 1-5, 2004; Calvo conducted interviews in the Spring, 2008; Burns conducted interviews via telephone, internet, and also face to face in the spring and summer of 2008. Svein Andersen conducted more than 20 interviews in his research over several years after 2000. Interviewees consisted of a number of different actors representing a variety of different interests and roles, including European Commission (EC) officials, Member State (MS) officials, and representatives of various business and trade groups, labor organizations, and other NGOs[13].

---

[13] NGOs are for the purposes of this work defined as public interest organizations that are organized along not for profit principles. The addition of designations such as "health," "social," or environment is descriptive. Although business interest organizations are also technically "non-governmental" organizations, they are distinguished from the broader category of NGOs based on their distinct economic interests and relatively high control of economic resources. Labor

Most interviews were recorded on tape (or electronically), when acceptable to the interview person and supplemented with handwritten notes. Formal statements and positions of IPs were frequently available in print form from the relevant individual and organizational actors, including EU institutions. The approach to interviews was semi-structured, focusing broadly on the issue area, but leaving it to the interviewee to identify the particulars that he/she saw as important. This approach was guided by a desire to reduce interviewer influence on the way in the informants presented the issues, struggles, and characterizations about the policy developments in question and to get a sense of how various actors viewed the issues, their role in them, and the role of the EU and other actors. For example, Carson's early interviews regarding food safety and asbestos were more exploratory in nature – he did not yet know what specific questions he should be asking. As he became more familiar and knowledgeable in a particular area, he added more specific follow-up questions, and where possible, used the discussions to test his understanding of the various dimensions of a given issue, the surrounding conflicts, etc. He also had subsequent telephone or email contact with several of the people he met in the course of the initial interviews.[14]

The interviewers treated the interviewees in most cases as informants, with the interview materials viewed as background and explanatory information and not to be attributed without first gaining their permission. Identities were as a rule kept confidential, and in all but a very few instances, the interview information has been corroborated by other sources for accuracy. In cases where we have used information gained in interviews that is not corroborated by other sources, we have noted that the source is from an interview and the statement(s) uncertain in their reliability and/or validity...

The general strategies used to identify the most important discourses and the conceptual differences they contained included (1) looking for conflicts concerning the issues and policy areas in question, particularly conflicts based on fundamentally different ways of conceptualizing a given issue, and especially those conflicts that took place as critical discourses were expressed in new institutional arrangements; (2) identifying actors whose roles or positions were considered significant in a given policy area, (3) looking for different types of actors whose perspectives and/or po-

---

unions are also given a separate designation in view of their generally high degree level of institutionalization in the policymaking process, and their related special status together with business groups as "social partners".

[14] In general, whether or not written questions preceded the interview, Carson sought answers to such questions as the follow: "What is the position role of your organization in addressing this issue(s)?" Your position?; "How would you characterize the most important aspects of the issue(s) in policy area X?" What was the process by which the policy changes in question took place? What factors were most important in the policy developments that occurred? Who were your allies or opponents in these efforts, and who else played an important role? Other questions were directed to the specifics of the case study in question, or the role of the particular interviewee.

sitions differed; (4) examining journalistic accounts of policy development or issues in the areas in question (such accounts obviously influence the way the public sees the issue, but also tend to identify key actors; journalists must also translate the issue from technical or bureaucratic language to make it accessible to the readership); and (5) tracing the development of discourses over time – particularly as these discourses find concrete institutional form. These strategies were aided by the analytical distinctions in the architecture of policy paradigms discussed in Chapter 1 (also, see Chapter 15), in which discourses are examined for the ways in which they identify and define problems, recommend or exclude various categories of solutions, which actors/institutions are suitable for implementing those solutions, and who is to be trusted as a source of information and expertise. The actors that produce the discourses frequently identify areas of conflict, competing actors, acceptable sources of authority, competing views of a given set of circumstances or developments, etc. The process of following these "references" is not fundamentally different from the processes of tracing back references and controversies in the academic literature.

Another important question that arises is how to distinguish between "front stage" accounts and "back stage" accounts (Goffman, 1972), or between objective and subjective characterizations of "reality". While this concern is applicable to interviews, it is even more appropriate for the consideration of materials that may have been carefully structured and edited (Scott, 2000). Natural Resources Canada's "fact sheet" on asbestos is a prime example of such a carefully organized characterization of an issue. A number of strategies are useful here, although the goal in this instance is not to screen out and discard subjective accounts, since they are essential to understanding both calculated and unconscious discursive struggles for dominance over the conceptual terrain represented by competing paradigms. Comparisons made to identify patterns of similarity and difference are essential here. This includes identifying discontinuities and inconsistencies that develop over time or those that can be found between the advertised description of intention or purpose and observable actions, and tracing the evolution of ideas to institutional form. The process of gathering data has been guided by these considerations, and by the necessity of being able to make such comparisons.

In addition to the interviews, one of us (Carson) also benefited a great deal from discussions connected with participation at an OECD/EU sponsored Workshop (Bruge, Belgium, 26-28 June, 2000), and participation at the European Health Forum, sponsored by the European Commission, among others (Salzburg, Austria, 27-30 September, 2000). These gave an opportunity to follow formal presentations, and also provided the occasion for numerous informal conversations with EU and national officials, and with representatives of various NGOs. Carson made observations and drew conclusions regarding the same general and specific questions indicated earlier, and subsequent notes from these discussions and workshop materials became part of the case study material.

4. Analysis

4.1 Analysis of Paradigmatic Discourses

A PPP is communicated through discourses – both descriptive narratives and conceptual forms – and through social action and interaction. These discourses and actions define social problems and potential solution complexes, and suggest, for instance, the assignment of authority and responsibility in a given or appropriate area of activity. Through their characterizations of goals and purposes, and accounts of institutional performance – successes as well as failures – actors in a given institution express or reveal their common paradigm. It is the means by which they perceive and judge the world, and organize, understand, and regulate their activities in a given policy space or domain.

Particular policy discourses, serving as a means of describing, interpreting, and dealing with real problems and issues, are inspired and organized – directed and purposeful – on the basis of the PPP. The discourses indicate, among other things, parameters of appropriate problems, leaders, solutions to problems, and performances. For instance, they may concern whether the current performance or status of current policy and its institutional context represents improvement or deterioration over earlier performance or status. In general, a PPP encompasses a range of institutional practices and strategies for addressing issues considered to be problems, and for defining or establishing authority for how to address various types of problems.

Paradigms are articulated, in part, through discourses concerning institutionally defined "problems," or "threats" and "crisis", the expressed distribution of institutional "authority and responsibility", the distribution of "expert authority", and "appropriate solutions" to deal with defined problems. The discourses refer to written rules and laws, and basic socio-cognitive principles that define the location and other aspects of authority, and set(s) of institutional strategies and practices for dealing with specific types of problems and issues (concerning public policy areas, see Sutton, 1998; Carson, 2001). The methodological approach outlined here analyzes the ways in which discourses, on the one hand, express and articulate a public policy paradigm and, on the other hand, frame and define reality (see, for example, Spector and Kitsuse, 1987; Hardy and Phillips, 1999; Kemeny, 1983).

Discourses provide evidence with which to identify socio-cognitive models (Dryzek, 1996a; van Dijk, 1995; Lakoff and Johnson, 1980) such as paradigms, and the processes by which they change (see earlier discussion). Defined here as primarily written and verbal communications, public policy discourses frame and articulate a given view of reality (see Kemeny, 2002; Bacchi, 1999; Hardy and Phillips, 1999; Spector and Kitsuse, 1987, among others). These can be analyzed as expressions or reflections of one or more paradigms through which actors perceive the world – a means of organizing, understanding, interpreting, and giving meaning their experience (Dryzek, 1996). Discourses may serve to either legitimize or challenge the existing order, and may be institutionalized – formalized and codified into rules, policies, and laws. These formulations, like rule systems, intersect and conflict with – or reinforce each other – to shape the environment within which policymaking takes place. These also tend to either reinforce or undermine the various underlying assumptions and values that form the foundations of a paradigm.

In general, these discourses may take either metaphoric or descriptive forms. Metaphors simplify. They serve to more easily convey complex concepts by communicating them in condensed, simplified terms, and to impart meaning by presenting one set of concepts in terms of another set, the meaning of which is already established (Lakoff, 1996; Lakoff and Johnson, 1980). Thus, opponents of genetically modified materials in foods have dubbed such products "Frankenstein foods," or, global women's networks have succeeded to a significant extent in defining women's rights as human rights. Descriptive narratives, on the other hand, serve to elaborate and specify the detail of the concepts being communicated or expressed. These are more often expressed in the language of the rational, systematic work of experts, particularly scientific experts, in what Potter (1996) refers to as the "empiricist discourse". Public policy discourses are communicated using both. Each of these delineates paradigmatic elements in its own particular way: problem definitions, approaches for quantifying and evaluating, appropriate agents and authorities, interpretations of events and occurrences and attributions of cause.

4.2 Limitations of Paradigm Discourses

There are numerous challenges to assessing the weight, influence, and importance of a particular set of discourses, a pair of which we take up here. The first challenge is the fact that "talk" is subject to conscious construction, manipulation, and misrepresentation, as captured in sayings such as "talk is cheap". Simply put, there is frequently inconsistency between what is claimed and what can be empirically verified – or between what actors say claim to be working for and what is indicated by the policies they pursue or by their actual behavior. However, given the contested nature of public policy paradigms, deliberate efforts to construct and frame arguments in more salient, persuasive terms to influence others are relevant and important. This is in part because they are part of a process of establishing relevance and meaning for policy arguments to make them seem more relevant and/or persuasive than might otherwise be the case. A simple example of this is the "Right to Work" effort in the USA, which focuses not on a basic right to employment, as the label might imply, but on an employee's right to choose not to join and pay membership dues to a union when he or she already has a job. The movement is employer-sponsored and generally anti-union. In the EU, pharmaceutical companies have argued that they might be forced for economic reasons to move production from EU countries whose health systems use their bargaining power to negotiate relatively low prices for their products (Nylander, 2000). Even though the connection between prices paid for pharmaceuticals in any given country and the location of production facilities could be considered dubious, the threat of plant closings may contribute to making national health authorities conscious of possible undesirable side effects connected with driving a hard bargain. In this particular instance, even the implicit threat of plant closings is framed in the softer and more politically acceptable terms of companies potentially being "forced" to relocate by circumstances not of their own choosing[15].

Part of the remedy for sorting out the underlying paradigm from instrumental representations is to seek to identify the more global consistencies and conceptual patterns revealed in a given policy discourse, and to trace their coherence and consistency with actors' associated efforts to defend or modify institutional rules. Of course, coherence and consistency often appear to be in short supply, given the often-intense competition between agents who are promoting their own particular paradigm, discourses can be quite intertwined and confused. The fact that even competing paradigms may share many common elements only further contributes to such confusion (Carson, 2001).

A second problem is that even in the absence of the sort of external static and interference described above, not all paradigms are equally coherent – and all paradigms (like all theories) contain inherent gaps, inconsistencies, and incompatibilities. These can be rooted in actor interests, in the natural limitations of human rationality in building up a conceptual model, in attempts to maintain incompatible elements within a given paradigm, and, as with the scientific paradigm, in a particular paradigm simply being inaccurate in significant ways in its underlying assumptions – a less than adequate match with reality. More basic inconsistencies result in a less compelling paradigm when attention is drawn to them. In addition, there are often multiple variations of a given paradigm. What distinguishes between different paradigms on the one hand, and variations on a theme, on the other, is the differences in underlying assumptions and the complex of core principles.

4.3 Different Paths to European Integration: Comparative Analysis of Case Studies

Many of the important developments in European integration over the past decades have emerged from the "low politics" of sector-specific developments in the ongoing policymaking activity of the EU (Fligstein, 2001a; Peterson, 2001; Cram, 1997). While sector-specific policymaking takes place within the larger institutional context defined by the Treaties, empirical research demonstrates that there is an ongoing two-way interaction between sectoral policymaking and eventual Treaty revisions (Helfferich and Kolb, 2001; Nylander, 2000; Vogel, 1995). There is a similar two-way interplay across policy sectors[16], in which policy innovations in one sec-

[15] See Jonathan Potter (1996:150-175) for an excellent discussion of how actors use "externalizing devices" to rhetorically position themselves in relation to the data and arguments they employ.

[16] This "spillover" was seen by neo-functionalists (see Schmitter, 2004; Holland, 1994; Haas, 1948) as an important driver of European integration.

tor are subsequently emulated in others. This is in part because entrepreneurial actors are able to anchor new concepts, claims, and arguments into a common complex of overarching discourses, norms, and rules. Examining these processes in the work within individual policy sectors can therefore be expected to reveal useful patterns in how the nature of policymaking in the EU evolves over time.

Following this approach, revisions in the series of Treaties that form the quasi-constitutional basis of EU law are less defining moments than they are notable events in the larger process of institutionalizing specific policy ideas, goals, and priorities. In Simon Bulmer's (1997) words, they are but "the tip of the iceberg". Treaty-defined competencies are obviously important, but the historical record of the EU's evolution makes it clear that both the Commission and the Council of Ministers have frequently chosen not to wait for new competencies to be established in the treaties before forging into new territory; such excursions have often helped set the stage for future Treaty revision (Cram, 1997; Vogel, 1995; Addison and Siebert, 1991). The emergence of new problems and stretching of old limits establishes the context within which the treaty-negotiating intergovernmental conferences take place. An important goal of the case studies in this research is therefore to better understand some of the ways in which day-to-day policy processes contribute to European integration on a grand scale; it sees the intergovernmental bargaining that produces the new Treaty revisions as part of a larger process of institution building.

Case Comparisons

Our general approach, while grounded in a theoretical perspective, is descriptive and comparative, meaning we compare the patterns of policy development over time and across the six cases. The individual case studies we have included here examine the processes by which policy concerns emerge to be taken up at the European level, and eventually take precedence over national priorities and/or market priorities. The case comparisons are intended to identify commonalities, differences, and spillover effects, and in general, how the cases may be related to one another. This also requires clarifying some assumptions, since in the case of the EU, substantive content and the level of governance at which policy is taken up may vary in conjunction with one another. Conventional comparative approaches to analyzing policy and policymaking processes in the EU have had to finesse certain assumptions related to the conventional state and its authority to make policy (Peterson, 2001). Vogel (2000; 1997), for example, proceeds under an implicit assumption that the EU functions as a federal state analogous to the USA in his comparative examination of chemicals policy in Europe and the US. This assumption depends on differences in governance structures not being a significant source of the policy differences. Leibfried and Pierson (1995a) make this assumption explicit, pointing to the strongly federal characteristics of the EU/member state relationships, and the fact that it is no longer possible to understand what was once considered domestic policy in European states without also taking into account the "emergent multi-tiered system of governance" that is the EU. Working from such assumptions is clearly legitimate, although it is not without its limits. While there is a perpetual tension between state and federal authority in US policymaking, this is vastly different from the comparative fluidness and sometimes indeterminate quality of policymaking authority in the EU. For example, getting an issue on the political agenda in the EU may require skillful framing of problems not only to make them relevant and salient, but also to define them as matters which the EU possesses the legal competence to take up. Alternatively, the rules that define whether a particular issue or policy can be addressed at the EU level sometimes change in conjunction with the substantive policy measures being contemplated. Taking both into account tells us something about the process of Europeanization of a policy sector.

We have approached the case studies in a manner similar to Burawoy's (1991b) extended case method[17], which is characterized by an ongoing dialog between theoretical concepts and empirical data. Burawoy (1991b:11) points out that "to be sure, knowledge of the literature is not the contaminating influence that Glaser and Strauss attribute to it, but neither is it a sine qua non of research". Indeed, numerous scholars (including Glaser and Strauss, 1967) have noted that our observations are quite dependent on the concepts through which we view the world (Sabatier, 1999; Sayer, 1999; Becker, 1998; Kuhn, 1970), even if those concepts are not consciously organized and formalized as theory. Central to Burawoy's (1991b:9) argument is that "what is interesting in the field emerges from our theory"; this remains the case even where the empirical data requires theory to be revised. Burawoy's approach seeks out anomalies that are revealed by situating the empirical phenomena in their historical and cultural context, enabling the further development and refinement of theoretical constructs.

The method for organizing the case studies is consistent with the logic recommended by Bennett and George (1997), which urges "structured" comparisons – a process of posing the same theoretically derived, categorical questions to each of the cases. Cases are chosen based on there being present important developments relevant to the categories/questions of theoretical interest or relevance. Given a focus on identifying cases with comparative value, Bennett and George point out that they should be comparable on the basis of a carefully defined "class" of events or developments" (1997: 2). In this instance, the "developments" can be briefly summarized as a reordering of core policy assumptions, priorities, and goals as well as organizational arrangements that constitute the paradigm guiding policymaking – a reordering which constitutes a conceptual, or paradigmatic shift. Such a shift in-

[17] It should be noted that important evidence was gathered via interviews with informants rather than participant observation. However, our understanding of the interviews was supplemented by previous experience connected with policy making and interest organizations as well as the very considerable research on EU policymaking.

cludes a redefinition of the actors considered to have a legitimate interest in decision making regarding issues in that policy sector – typically an expansion in the cases under examination – and either a de-facto or a formal recognition of that legitimacy via the adoption of new procedures that facilitate their participation. In addition, it entails an institutionalization of new areas of policymaking competence at the European level.

As with Burawoy's (1991b) approach, this model counsels that cases should be chosen which involve developments relevant to the theoretical framework used. The common developments in each and all of the cases concern the conceptual and organizational shift to greater EU governance and regulation, that is, the emergence of new policymaking power and competence at the EU level, what is partly covered by the notion of "Europeanization". Also, four of our studies (gender, chemicals, asbestos, and food) illustrate a shift from more purely market considerations to social, health, and environmental priorities along with the expansion of participation in the policy process. The development of the EU Emission Trading Scheme (ETS) also was driven by environmental concerns but exploited market mechanisms to pursue these goals. What differs between the cases is the set of factors that drive the policy change, the nature of actor constellations that fuel the change, and the extent of institutionalization of the new policy paradigm. Comparison of these developments should provide insight into the processes by which the kinds of concerns in question come to be prioritized as the subject of EU policymaking, those by which the "social" aspect of these issues comes to be prioritized over the economic, and the resulting ways in which costs, benefits, and risks are defined and regulated by public policy.

We have approached the research questions posed earlier through individual case studies that trace important policy developments in several EU policy sectors: food, chemicals and asbestos, climate change, energy and gender equality. The food case examines the dramatic changes in EU food policy that were influenced by the crisis surrounding Bovine Spongioform Encephalopathy (i.e., "mad cow disease") in British beef, and the subsequent dioxin contamination of Belgian poultry. One of the chemicals cases examines the processes that culminated in a European ban on the commercial product asbestos. The principles on which the asbestos case turned were adopted in a subsequent broad revision of the principles governing EU chemicals policy. The gender equality case examines the evolution of EU initiatives to pursue gender equality goals, from its beginnings in the Treaty of Rome's equal pay article, to its liberation from the bounds of labor market and work issues in pursuing non-economic goals such as human rights. As part of this, domestic violence against women was made an EU issue.

The policy sectors dealing with food, chemicals, and gender equality are difficult policy cases to compare. Several important factors recommend these as good comparative cases. First, within each there are fundamental tensions between market and social goals that extend beyond the policy sector itself to influence the further development of the EU. Food and chemicals are among the most important products in Europe's common market. Many of the issues that arise under gender equality are evident in some of the tensions between employers and workers, and more broadly, questions about which kinds of issues are appropriately regulated by public bodies and which are best left in the private sphere. Second, the groups affected in the three policy sectors constitute important political constituencies that may align themselves either for or against European integration – either narrowly, within a given policy sector, or more generally, linked to integration overall. Moreover, each has contributed to cross cutting cleavages among organized actors that are generally in agreement at the national level[18]. Third, social concerns connected with each of these cases have followed a similar patterns of institutionalization in the Treaties – from first being mentioned as an issue that required attention, to being included within the general competence of EU institutions, to being "mainstreamed" – although both the ways and the degree to which each has been institutionalized varies significantly.

There are also important and potentially instructive differences. First, the nature of the social/market tensions differs. In the food and chemicals cases, important conflicts revolve around where the burden of proof of lies in managing known hazards and potential risks. This affects what types of potential social and economic costs can be externalized across time and social groups, and which must be borne by the producers who are the clearest short-term beneficiaries. The nature of actor constellations is also different. The changes in food policy were precipitated to a significant extent by the concerted, but non-coordinated action of European citizens refusing to purchase British beef. Consumer and public health NGOs played an important supporting role, but were not the driving force. In the case of banning asbestos, the gradual unraveling of the coalition opposed to its ban was a central factor, while organized groups in key member states pressed for the ban. In the gender equality case, the painstaking work of women's organizations at the every level of governance from local to national to international eventually put the issue of combating domestic violence on the European agenda. The nature of the factors driving change also differs. Although there are incremental, evolutionary developments that contribute to change in each of the sectors over time, the food case is much more crisis driven at the European level, while developments in policy on gender equality have been incremental and steady by comparison.

5. Concluding Remarks

There are a number of methodological issues in collecting documents and interviews, analyzing them, and drawing conclusions as we do in our case studies. Our

[18] This phenomena was evident the vote on monetary union in Sweden in the fall of 2003. Each of the major political parties had significant factions on both sides of the issue, and the respective reasons for supporting or opposing EMU differed a great deal within the coalitions on each side.

analysis is guided by our conceptions of paradigms as cognitive and normative systems orienting and guiding actors sharing a given paradigm, distinguishing states of the world, problems, identifying solutions, organization form, etc. Also, of importance in our research has been the basic question: when can one say that a shift has taken place: (i) the phenomological approach would conclude that a shift has taken place when participants say a shift has occurred; (ii) another approach close to the one we use is to investigate whether or not significant changes have taken place in one or more of the dimensions that make up a policy paradigms; conclusions are more secure when several changes have been brought about in paradigm architecture.

But problems remain, among others:

- The changes in a paradigm may be small and incremental but over time add up to a major change.
- There may be momentary success in establishing a new paradigm but no long-term endurance. A reversal or collapse of the new paradigm takes places after a shorter or longer period of time, even if some institutionalization has been accomplished.

CHAPTER 8

Mad Cows, Polluted Poultry, and The Transformation of EU Food Policy

Marcus Carson

The Temporary Committee to follow up the recommendations on BSE...expects that in the future the Commission will follow a policy in which higher priority is given to the principles of health and consumer protection than to other key principles of the internal market...

- European Parliament's Temporary Committee concerning follow up on BSE (1997/11/14)

1. Introduction: Emerging Health Dimensions

The start of the new millennium was marked by a quite remarkable process of change in the food policy of the EU – one in which the policy orientation appears to have shifted past a tipping point – both conceptually and institutionally – from an emphasis on the commodity and market aspects of food, to placing first priority on food-related public health and consumer concerns. As was the case with the coming of the new millennium, this shift in EU food policy had been underway for some time. It was also accompanied – and in this case facilitated – by the concerns of a variety of interests, a series of important events and developments, and ongoing preparations and activities. The policy shift was a reflection of significant changes in the way in which food policy is understood and conceptualized. This in turn, influenced which types of food-related problems were considered appropriate and important for EU-level policymaking. At the same time, this policy shift was institutionalized in a variety of different ways within European Union institutions: reordered priorities, organizational restructuring, and the writing of new rules-of-the-game at the European level.

Early EU food policy issues were seen as largely agricultural in nature, with an emphasis on the security of the food supply and the economic viability of farms, and these initial problems were gradually addressed. But the initial problems were eventually replaced by new ones that were an outgrowth of earlier policies – in particular, the need for new markets and the desire in many quarters for lower commodity prices. This new focus fit quite well with the broader push for the Single Market, and resulted in the European policymaking apparatus being brought to bear upon the various obstacles to open trade in agricultural products and foodstuffs within Europe. Another new set of problems emerged with the development of the single market in the early 1990s. These problems were manifested in the form of a series of food-related crises that once again shifted attention, reshaping the way in which the EU's responsibility for food policy is understood and conceptualized. Food safety, public health, and consumer choice became the issues to which the newly emerging food policy was addressed – and around which new institutional structures were organized.

The European Food Safety Authority (EFSA), the regulatory agency now being set up in Parma, Italy, and the reorganized DG Health and Consumer Protection (the former DG–XXIV), had a markedly different mission than the component parts transferred in from DG Industry (DG–III) or DG Agriculture (DG–VI). This in itself represented a major departure from the EU's sometimes single-mindedly single market mission of the late 1980s and much of the 1990s – even if knowledgeable observers have argued that at least in its early stages, the establishment of the EFSA represents more of a reconfiguration than the creation of any structure or capacity[1]. At the same time, the raison d'être of the EFSA points both forward as well as backwards; in addition to its newly explicit priority of protecting consumer interests and the public health. The policy changes embodied in the EFSA can be seen as an important step toward protecting many of the achievements materialized in the creation of the European Single Market – and the marketability of European agricultural products on a world market. With the internal market largely in place, any lack of attention to the new problems generated could potentially have contributed to its undoing, as the struggles around food safety have illustrated. Remarkably, the two short paragraphs in the Amsterdam Treaty (Articles 152 and 153) calling for a high level of consumer and public health protection in the development and implementation of *all* EU policies may prove not only to be an unexpectedly potent protection against the excesses of poorly or insufficiently regulated markets – they may also serve as powerful leverage for DG Health and Consumer Protection with the other DGs during internal negotiations to craft Commission proposals. While these developments appeared almost certain to contribute to the further "Europeanization" of new areas of public policy, they were by no means certain; they might easily have taken a very different path.

One likely alternate path could well have been a de-facto return to the regulation and management of food safety issues by individual member states. As of November of 1999, the bans imposed on British meat exports by both the French and the German governments were still in place, with the Commission initiating infringement proceedings against France (IP/99/850). This was three years after the connection between "mad cow disease" and human health first jolted public consciousness – and it is only one among several examples of the ongoing tensions between national and supranational policymaking in the food arena. And in spite of the ongoing public concern and controversy regarding BSE (Bovine Spongiform Encephalopathy, i.e., "mad cow disease"), the EU continued to experience difficul-

[1] This observation was repeated in interviews with Commission staff and NGO representatives.

ty persuading many member states to implement regulations designed to tighten up on the agricultural practices that contributed to the spread of BSE.

One interpretation of the changes currently underway might be that the Commission seized the proverbial bull by the horns, taking steps to set in place the structures necessary to protect both the single market and the public health by prioritizing European citizens' health and consumer interests. A plausible alternative explanation is that a shift in priorities – from that of fostering less regulated and less encumbered markets to ensuring food safety and public health – had already taken place in other quarters, i.e., among a substantial segment of European populations, within the European Parliament, and within some member states. It was up to the Commission to decide whether to attempt to ensure that this reordering of priorities in food policy would be decisively reflected in coordinated action at the European level – or to watch it unfold on its own within the member states. The pattern of developments that led to the transformation of food policy suggests some combination of these forces.

EU Food Fights

Food has long been among the more difficult and often contentious policy arenas in the EU. From the beginning of efforts to create the Single Market in the 1980s, a complex, often-difficult dynamic has characterized this arena. Evidence of this contentiousness has been apparent in actions such as farmers from nearby member states converging on Brussels with demands for policies to protect them from the changes being embraced and promoted by the EU in the pursuit of the single market. The rapid growth of interest group presence and lobbying in Brussels during the 1990s serves as a different kind of evidence – an approach to influencing EU policymaking on behalf of particular interests (Andersen and Burns, 1996; Andersen and Eliassen, 1996a; van Schendelen, 1993; Andersen and Eliassen, 1991). This growth includes organizations oriented toward a variety of commercial interests (farm, processor, and distributor) as well as public interests (consumer, public health, and environment) related to food and food production. However, comparatively speaking, the public interest groups are meagerly-financed and vastly outnumbered (Nylander, 2000). Given the political and economic stakes connected to food and agricultural production, it is no surprise that Member States themselves have played an important, albeit often inconsistent role in shaping developments in EU food policy. Actors external to the EU such as the World Trade Organization (WTO), the World Health Organization (WHO), and external trading partners such as the USA have also exerted a powerful influence. Of course, the EU is not merely an arena in which these and other interests compete for dominance; many of the EU's various institutions are important actors in their own right (Nylander, 2000; Cram, 1997).

A series of high profile, food-related crises and conflicts played a central and continuing role in the most recent transformation of EU food policy. These include crises of public confidence resulting from the unintentional or careless introduction of dangerous substances into the food supply. The crises surrounding BSE-infected British beef or dioxin-tainted Belgian poultry are two of the most important examples of such incidents, although they are hardly the only ones. Significant conflicts generated by the deliberate introduction of certain substances into the food chain in pursuit of greater agricultural productivity have also been quite important. These include the struggles over the use of hormones or antibiotics in meat production, or the conflicts regarding the introduction of genetically modified organisms (GMOs). Less high profile issues such as chemical or pesticide residues or other contaminants in crops are also subjects of conflict.

2. The Evolution of EU Action on Food Policy

The food crises of the late 1990s took place in the context of an ongoing evolution of EU food policy. EU policy had institutionalized different ways of conceptualizing food over time, reflected both in institutional structure and concrete policy priorities. These can be traced, for example, through the successive DGs that have been invested with the primary responsibility for EU food policy (specifically, from the DGs responsible for Agriculture, to Industry, to Public Health and Consumer Affairs), as well as through the broad policy priorities established by the member states and the Commission. These should be seen as distinct and separate from, though intimately related to the events and crises and conflicts mentioned above (and which are described in greater detail in the next section).

2.1 Back on the Farm

The role of the farmer has been a complex one, since in addition to representing the starting point on the "food chain" and economically very important to member states, farmers have been both a culturally significant and politically powerful force to be reckoned with. This importance was recognized with the negotiation of a Common Agricultural Policy (CAP) in the waning years of the 1950s, and its implementation in 1962 (EC: DG Agriculture, no. 2). The CAP was originally developed to help achieve self-sufficiency in food production by stabilizing agricultural markets. Farmers were intended as the principal beneficiaries (EC: DG Agriculture, no. 3) of a wide range of policies set forth in the CAP, including price supports and subsidies. As self-sufficiency was achieved and European food exports grew, these policies came under attack from a variety of sources as unfair trade practices that created undesirable market distortions. The antagonists included supranational organizations such as the WTO and large farm exporters outside of the EU such as the USA (Buckwell Report, 1997). From within the EU, pressures came in the form of the drive toward a European Single Market.

Partially in response to these pressures, the CAP was modified in the late 1980s, changing the configuration of subsidies and bringing in a "social dimension" – in this case, rural development – into the picture. Another sign of institutional adjustment to the changing perceptions was the leakage of some areas of relevant policy from DG Agriculture to DG Industry; in relation to the latter, processors and distributors of agricultural goods in particular, found a more compatible and sympathetic orientation. This was probably further facilitated by an erosion of consensus among farmers themselves as to the value of the CAP, based at least in part on the seemingly unanticipated ways in which it benefited or disadvantaged particular subgroups among them (Buckwell Report, 1997). Overall, the CAP can be seen as having been forced into its first modifications and revisions by two sets of influences. Externally, the movement toward the Europeanization and internationalization of agricultural markets has been unsympathetic, even hostile toward farm subsidies and price supports that made up an important element of the CAP. International organizations such as the WTO have exerted pressure to reduce or remove both production supports and inhibitions to trade. Internally, the complexity of the system and the perception of an uneven and inequitable distribution of benefits had already eroded support among farmers, while other food business interests, and some consumer organizations, such as BEUC (the European Consumers' Organization) argued the need for increased competition to bring greater choice at reduced prices.

More recently, the CAP has been seen as an important contributor to both environmental and food safety problems, and the series of food scares and crises beginning with the BSE crisis served to cement such concerns (Buckwell, 1997). The CAP was seen in these instances as contributing to unhealthy production practices that led to the crises by essentially eclipsing food safety and environmental concerns. The CAP went through a major revision as a part of Agenda 2000, a package of proposals addressing a wide range of future challenges faced by the EU. Farm support mechanisms continue to be restructured and price supports reduced, environmental considerations increasingly taken into account, and public health concerns such as food safety prioritized (EPHA, 1999:2-3). These changes represent an ongoing formalization of new institutional arrangements consistent with the new paradigm oriented toward public health aspects of food.

2.2 From the Farm to the Single Market

Agricultural products – animal feeds, raw materials, and consumer products – were from the beginning a central element of the drive toward a European Single Market. The creation of a single market in foodstuffs and other agricultural products, however, required significant deregulation and reorganization of existing national laws pertaining to food. Sweden, for example, was required to accept lower standards for the presence of a variety of food additives and pesticides (Joffe and De Broe, 1998). Of course, Sweden is by no means the only country to trade away certain of its public health standards and practices for membership in the EU. Neither should this be taken to mean that harmonization of standards invariably meant a drop to the lowest common denominator, although the most stringent standards were generally reduced, while the lowest were generally forced upward (De Winter, 1998).

Much of the EU's economic growth in the production and consumption of food and drink products since the mid-1980s has been in the "added value" sector – processed foods (COM(97)176: 4). This growing demand for processed food products and the subsidies and price supports (for the raw materials) contained in the CAP suggest that it was the middle actors in the food chain, food processors and distributors, who stood to gain most from deregulation and opening markets. On one end of the supply line, competition between more and different sources for raw agricultural products offers a greater number of choices in balancing price, quality, and other specific characteristics of concern to food processors. On the other end, the benefit of more markets in which products can be sold is self-explanatory. The loosening of national regulatory structures was a key element in pursuing the twin goals of cheaper supplies and increased sales, and consistent with the broader, supportive attitude toward deregulation that existed. Majone (1996) has characterized the pattern of deregulation/re-regulation at the member state/EU level as the substitution of member state regulation with regulation at the European level. And while it is quite true that the EU market mission entailed far more than the dismantling of significant elements of nation-based regulatory structure, it is also true that the basic nature of the early EU regulations in the food sector was quite different than the national-level regulations they replaced. Until relatively recently, EU food legislation was ridiculed, at least by consumer and public health groups, as being largely concerned with standardization for better market compatibility – i.e. the size and shape of tomatoes, fruit, etc. – rather than food quality or safety (De Winter, 1998). This derived in large part from efforts to further enhance cross-border trade in agricultural products by addressing technical questions.

Barriers to the "free movement of foodstuffs" within the EU were approached from two directions: harmonization and mutual recognition. Harmonization has been a top-down approach in which legislation adopted at the EU level must be implemented in member states within established parameters. Mutual recognition[2] is a horizontal approach that applies where there is no specific EU law. This is a bilateral, negotiated approach, based on member states' general acceptance of products from other EU countries unless there is proof of a specific problem. Under mutual recognition, the burden of proof has in practice rested with the member state wishing to exclude the products of another member state. It is the failure of this negotiated approach in specific instances that has been the source of much of recent EU food law (De Winter, 1998; COM(97)176).

---

[2] As noted in Chapter 4, mutual recognition was ushered in with the European Court of Justice's decision in the 1979 Cassis de Dijon case, then modified and formalized in the Single European Act (1987).

The majority of the EU's food regulation was set in place between 1985 and 1992 (COM(97)176), and aimed toward achieving the single market in foodstuffs. It primarily addressed the problem of barriers to trade, and also dealt with specific problems and conflicts that arose in that process. Standards were, therefore, directed more at promoting trade and resolving disputes than at assuring food safety. While barriers to the free movement of foodstuffs were seen as one sort of problem, new problems with the quality or safety of food products were quite another. The achievement of the single market in food products helped produce some of these problems, and turned some problems that would have otherwise largely been contained within individual member states into "European" problems. The BSE and dioxin crises are good examples of these. With less open markets, the actual safety problems would have been more confined to the countries of origin, while action to block the products at the borders of receiving countries would have been a great deal more straightforward. In the context of a higher authority, however, both the safety issues and the related political problems became truly European in character.

Many of these new problems could be seen as the direct result of the "Europeanization" of food markets and the accompanying deregulation at the national and EU levels. Pressures for increased productivity were intensified by the opening of markets, forcing significant changes in agricultural production methods. Other of these issues can be seen more as long-standing conditions which became "problems" as a result of changing standards and expectations. These derived in part from technological developments that have vastly increased the capacity for managing and assuring food safety. Still others have arisen from increasing public awareness sparked by repeated crises. What began with problems with food safety quickly evolved into a crisis of confidence in the responsible European institutions, which were already viewed with a healthy measure of distrust by significant segments of European populations. That this intensified the need for a decisive response is clear from the subsequent repeated references in EU documents to food policy. But such decisive action did not (and perhaps could not) take place until after a reordering of priorities that took place in the wake of the crisis triggered by mad cow disease.

2.3 Reordering Priorities: A New Balancing Act

The Commission's food policy "Green Paper"[3], which set forth new food safety principles (COM(97)176), can be seen as representing the most recent turning point in the orientation of EU food policy. It represents an extraordinarily delicate balance between competing policy agendas – looking simultaneously backward and forward – while framing the fate of the goals of divergent public policy agendas in a single recommended course of action. And while it was undertaken in 1993 in DG Industry and developed as a consensus document in collaboration with the

[3] Referred to as the "Green Paper" in the remainder of this chapter.

DG responsible for Agriculture, it clearly set out the conceptual framework that guided later actions. It is this framework that was subsequently institutionalized and placed within DG Health and Consumer Protection. Interestingly, it was bottled up in DG Industry the careful balance it struck. It was only after the BSE crisis erupted, undermining public confidence in both EU institutions and the single market, that it was updated and released[4].

The Green Paper leads with an overall assessment establishing the context for the detail to come: that "the majority of national food law has been harmonized at the Community level" and that "recent studies...have shown that the Community's legislative programme in the foodstuffs sector has had a generally positive impact" (COM(97)176:1). It goes on to point to two criticisms that will form the basis of the broad principles that inform its recommendations, that: "some criticisms have been expressed of overly detailed legislation, fragmentation...and problems in the day-to-day functioning of the internal market", and that "in the light of certain recent events, in particular, BSE, others have raised doubts about the capacity of the legislation to entirely fulfill its objectives *to ensure a high level of protection of public health and consumer protection*" (COM(97)176: 1, emphasis mine). These statements can be interpreted as saying "we're doing pretty well, but a few problems remain and it is important that we attend to them". The problems pointed to are framed as a product of circumstances; in no way is the finger of blame directed toward guiding principles or individual actors. The language, however, also belies the depth of the EU political crisis triggered by the BSE connection to human health and food safety.

The document continues with a discussion of each key policy area connected to food (and in the process, each key area of interest group activity) (COM(97)176:4-11). Rather than pointing to problems arising from policy developed in the respective sectors, however, it validates each of these areas with respect to food policy: the importance of the food sector to European economies, the CAP, the internal market, industrial policy, and the consumer dimensions of food safety and public health. This has the effect of indicating to each relevant category of interest that their goals and concerns are considered to be legitimate and important, and will be carefully taken into account as the Commission charts its new course. It then proceeds to set forth a set of principles that makes it possible to link the fate of the goals of each distinct area of food policy to the success of the others. The ever-present tension between national and supranational competence and authority was not overlooked; these principles would be realized at the European level, with respect for and the participation of the individual member states.

Overall, it appears that the Green Paper succeeded in facilitating three key developments. First, as a consensus document, it captured the most pressing concerns and problems faced by staff and officials within the Commission, and par-

[4] This was confirmed in an interview with a Commission official who was involved in the process.

ticularly within DG Agriculture. In doing so, it seems quite likely that the process itself produced somewhat of a re-alignment of thinking within the Commission's staff and officials (Nylander, 2000). That the document was bottled up for some time before a serious external crisis prompted its release suggests that political concerns were the source of the delay. However, the fact that events in the BSE crisis unfolded according to patterns already identified in earlier drafts of the paper may well have contributed after the crisis to the overall credibility of its approach. It also suggests that the kinds of problems and conflicts that led to the BSE crisis were already quite familiar to Commission staff involved in coping with the day-to-day questions regarding food safety.

At the same time the Green Paper provided a picture of the sort of consensus that could be mustered within the Commission, its release also served as the Commission's "finger in the wind" for assessing the reactions of actors external to the Commission, including likely political reactions. But in presenting to both Commission and external actors a document to which to respond, it also offered a coherent response to a growing set of problems – and one that was more appealing than the apparent alternative of staying the course. The first major test for the approach came with the dioxin crisis, in which the Commission's actions (and the way in which they were received) stood in stark contrast to those taken early on in response to the emergence of BSE. That the concrete plans set forth in the subsequent White Paper on Food Safety follow the Green Paper quite closely can be seen as evidence of the persuasiveness, and perhaps the necessity of its approach (for a variety of philosophical and practical reasons), as judged by actors external to the Commission.

A third, and perhaps the most important policy effect of the document is that it initiated a re-prioritization of core operating principles in food policy, explicitly placing public health and food safety concerns ahead of other goals, including goals guided by a neo-liberal inspired orientation toward minimalist regulation. One clear extension of this reordering of priorities was the extension of the Precautionary Principle from environmental matters to food policy, shifting the burden of proof in food safety matters from public to private interests. Perhaps key to the eventual success of this shift is that it cast the achievement and maintenance of market goals as being dependent on the protection of public health in general, and food safety in particular. And while the social and economic aftermath of two major food safety crises suggests this to be a perfectly accurate assessment of European reality with regard to food, it seems highly unlikely that the possible political implications of this structuring of the problem were not well understood (at least by some key actors).

2.4 Institutionalizing New Priorities: The European Food Authority

The first EU food legislation was passed in 1962 (regulating the use of food colorings). However, most of the subsequent food regulation (as opposed to single market legislation that has required *deregulation* at the member state level) has been passed since the 1992 implementation of the single market. The bulk of this legislation was in response to specific new problems arising from opening markets to food import/export, and from market deregulation in general (De Winter, 1998). The reactive nature of much of EU food legislation prior to the release of the Green Paper (COM(97)176) resulted in a patchwork of new regulations that possessed neither the regulatory coherence nor the institutional structure necessary to prevent – or effectively respond to – breakdowns in food safety such as those that occurred prompting the BSE and dioxin crises. It is precisely these two problems to which the White Paper on Food Safety[5] (COM(1999) 719) is addressed in setting forth the formal principles and intended organizational framework for the Commission's new food policy. Thus, the White Paper included an action plan (COM(99) 719:Annex, pgs. 37-52) that outlines 84 individual steps, with a time frame, for (a) building a coherent, systematic set of policies for ensuring food safety, and (b) establishing the institutional structure at the European level for implementing and managing this new system of regulation.

While the White Paper could be perhaps most simply understood as a blueprint for future Commission actions on food policy, it was clearly also a political document. Like the Green Paper, it anchors the proposed action in the context of both the economic and social aspects of food (including environmental concerns), taking a significant step toward institutionalizing food safety and public health as the principal priority:

> *The European Union's food policy must be built around high food safety standards, which serve to protect, and promote, the health of the consumer. The production and consumption of food is central to any society, and has economic, social, and in many cases, environmental consequences. Although health protection must always take priority, these issues must also be taken into account in the development of food policy. In addition, the state and quality of the environment, in particular the ecosystems, may affect different stages of the food chain. Environment policy therefore plays an important role in ensuring safe food for the consumer. (COM(1999)719: 6).*

Two steps already taken gave extra weight to this shift in guiding principles. First, the "Precautionary Principle" outlined in the White Paper had already been applied with respect to food products being imported from outside the EU, for example, in the case of GMOs or hormone treated meat. The Precautionary Principle effectively shifts the burden of proof of the safety of food products from governments or consumers to the producers and distributors of those products, and represents a fundamentally different approach from raising or lowering the standard of proof required for opposing sides to prevail. The principle also represented a dramatic reversal of policy from that of avoiding regulation in order to permit market forces to correct problems without the intervention of public authorities, to, the adoption of regulation to assure the protection of public health and consumer safety.

---

[5] Hereafter referred to as the "White Paper".

A second significant step was the relocation of the organizational structures dealing with food safety to the DG responsible for health and consumer protection (then DG-XXIV). This step gave concrete institutional form to Articles 151 and 152 of the Amsterdam Treaty, which, as noted earlier, *requires* a high level of protection of the public health, and of consumers' health, safety, and economic interests in all policies of the European Union (Amsterdam Treaty, 1999). The treaty article these replaced, Article 129 of the Maastricht Treaty, required that health and consumer questions be *taken into consideration* in the development of the single market, a mandate that fell far short of the new treaty language. These new Articles appear to have provided unexpectedly powerful leverage – legal trump cards woven into the Amsterdam Treaty – that permit particular social concerns to be prioritized over the market mission outlined in Article 2 of the Amsterdam and Maastricht Treaties. DG Health and Consumer Protection was created as recently as 1995, and even in 1998 was considered to be one of the weaker of the DGs (Sutton, 1999). In view of the priorities articulated by then-President Prodi (SPEECH/00/41), it would seem that both DG Health and Consumer Protection and the portfolio for which it was responsible had quickly become rising stars within the EU – and increasingly important to its future.

At the time, several observers regarded this reorganization with concern and skepticism, because many of the civil servants being relocated to staff the food safety work within DG Health and Consumer Protection came from DG-Enterprise (formerly DG-III – DG Industry) and DG-Agriculture (formerly DG-VI). These DGs are known to operate with quite different missions – on quite different core principles[6] – than those articulated for DG Health and Consumer Protection. One might expect these concerns to be well-founded, based on the different organizational missions of the respective DGs. The quite different ways of identifying, defining, and addressing problems represented by these organizational principles and priorities might easily contribute to internal conflict and organizational ineffectiveness, even a subtle undermining of the institutional mechanisms envisioned in the White Paper. An interpretation more encouraging to the advocates of the changes outlined in the White Paper is that these staffers had long since made the necessary conceptual transition. Having already had to wrestle with the problems to which the actions outlined in the White Paper are a response, the staffers in question had arguably already become intensely aware of the problems created and the need for a shift of perspectives to address them. To the extent that these changes were being facilitated by entrepreneurs within the Commission, one might say that they engineered their own move, with those who remain unconvinced staying behind.

[6] DG Industry (DG-III Commissioner Martin Bangeman made no secret of his understanding of his organization's mission as protecting and promoting the interests of Europe's business interests (Nylander, 2000).

The White Paper also envisioned the creation of an independent system of scientific evidence for the Commission, housed within the EFSA. The goal, first and foremost, was to give the EU the expertise and capacity to produce its own data on food safety risks independent of other interested parties and organized around principles compatible with the EU's stated food safety policy priorities. This too, was the response to a specific problem. The Commission was inhibited from taking earlier action regarding BSE-related risks by its own lack of sufficient awareness of the possible risks. Some of the scientific opinion downplaying the possible risks of BSE appeared to have been heavily influenced by former British Agricultural Ministry officials sitting on the key committee within DG Agriculture. Among other things, this made clear the need for more credible and disinterested sources of scientific information. In addition to providing the Commission with better scientific information, this step also helps to avoid conflicting accounts within the EU, making the EFSA a prime "interpreter" of relevant events and developments.

3. Mad Cows, Carcinogenic Chickens – EU Responses to Food Safety Crises

The struggles and conflicts over food safety during the middle and late 1990s created a serious crisis for the EU. The case examples briefly sketched out in the following pages describe these key events and conflicts to which EU institutions, and the Commission in particular, were required to respond. These events have helped shape the evolution of new EU food policy, at the same time that existing EU food, commercial, and agricultural policy has helped shape its responses to these crises and conflicts. They are by no means a complete account of events, actor's roles or other developments. Nevertheless, taken together, they illustrate an important part of the environment within which EU institutions operated and to which they sought to respond – particularly during the latter half of the 1990s and beyond – with their various policy initiatives on public health and consumer food issues. The cases begin with what appears to be widely regarded as the single most important set of developments in the shaping of EU food policy – the BSE crisis. The BSE crisis is the case most often referred to in descriptions and discussions of consumer issues generally, and food safety in particular, and is frequently described as a pivotal point in EU food policy (Collins, 1999) Accordingly, it is presented with the greatest level of detail. The next significant food scare – the contamination of Belgian poultry products with cancer-causing dioxins – is also presented at some length. Other cases that have become significant public and political controversies, including conflicts over hormone-treated meat, the use of antibiotics in animal feed, or GMOs in food, are briefly mentioned, but not presented in any detail.

3.1 Mad Cows and Tainted Food: The BSE Crises

When the European Commission issued its directive banning the export of most British beef products on March 27, 1996 (Decision 96/239/EC), it was seen as a dramatic move to control a rapidly developing food safety crisis. This extraordinary step followed by only one week the announcement of British Secretary of State for Health Stephen Dorrel of a possible link between BSE and a new variant of invariably fatal Creutzfeld-Jacobs Disease (CJD). Nevertheless, these events came more than ten years after the first identification of BSE in British cattle, and came as the ninth in a string of formal measures dating back to 1989 which had been taken by the Commission in efforts to deal with the various potential hazards posed by BSE. Two months after the Commission's ban on British beef exports was issued, the British government retaliated with a decision to obstruct the working of European institutions in an effort to force a lifting of the ban, and on June 11 of 1996, a plan for the gradual lifting of the ban based on meeting strict criteria was adopted (BSE Vademecum, 1998). The prohibition, however, was not the first action by the Commission pertaining to banning British beef products. In 1990 it had supported both its single market mission and the British Government by demanding and obtained the lifting of BSE-related bans of British beef products set in place by the German and French governments in exchange for promises to beef up its own health measures.

These decisions took place in a context of incomplete and often conflicting information regarding the nature and level of risk. The science regarding BSE was painfully incomplete, leaving policymakers to deal with the problem with limited information. Even the various sources of scientific and other information available could be seen as suspect – tied to particular interests in these struggles and therefore to be viewed with suspicion[7]. This uncertainty and suspicion served to fuel political fights both between member states and between member states and the EU, particularly the Commission. As the source of the problems came to be better understood, it also focused public attention on methods of animal production, in this case the recycling of animal by-products for animal feed (Consumer Voice, No 1, 2000: 7), and on the export of potentially tainted beef products across one possible line of defense – national borders.

This effect is likely to have been unusually powerful in view of significant news coverage of "mad cow disease" over the course of a decade. News of the spread of the disease outside Britain[8] and the destruction of literally tens of thousands of in-

---

[7] Some of the officials working for DG Agriculture on veterinary matters had been previously employed by national veterinary services linked to the governments involved and were implicated in some of the mishandling of the BSE affair (Bulletin EU 1/2-1997).

[8] The first cases of BSE were identified in the UK (1985), Ireland (1989), Portugal (1990), and France (1991), with the epidemic in the UK peaking in 1992 with 37,280 cases officially recorded (BSE Vademecum, 1998). As of October of 1996, a total of 163,071 cattle at 33,657 farms had

fected cattle would have been hard for most people to miss. The Lancet put forth a theory of possible transmission to humans as early as 1990 (BSE Vademecum, 1998). When the possible connection of BSE to the death of 19-year old Stephen Churchill and several others from a previously unknown variant of CJD[9] was made explicit and public by the British health secretary, it triggered "an unprecedented crisis of confidence among European consumers with regard to beef and bovine products" (GIS-BSE (96)7.5: 3), confirming their worst fears. People across Europe were immediately aware of a vaguely-defined, potentially deadly hazard that could be as close as the nearest butcher shop or grocery store – or their own table. Beef consumption across Europe plummeted, regardless of product origin (GIS-BSE (96)7.5), spreading the economic effects of BSE far more rapidly than the health hazard itself, whether bovine or human. The inquiry initiated by the European Parliament (EP) on 17 July 1996 into the Commission's handling of BSE related matters, as well as subsequent Commission policy decisions, suggest that the above-mentioned crisis of confidence referred not only to beef products, but also applied to the EU itself, particularly the Commission.

The Commission came under pressure – or more accurately, under attack – on a number of fronts. When the political appeals by British officials including Prime Minister John Major (Bull. EU 1/2-1997) to remove the ban failed, the UK turned to the European Court of Justice seeking an immediate suspension of the decision implementing the ban, as well as an annulment of the decision (Case C-180/97). Among other things, the UK argued that the both BSE and CJD had been known to exist long before the decision, that the Commission had acted in disregard for the Treaty principles of the free movement of goods and the establishment of the internal market, and that in any case, it had overstepped its legal authority (Case C-180/97: 8,9). In this instance, the Commission was backed by the court – and by public opinion – on every count. However, the Commission did not emerge unscathed; it had its own previous course of action to answer for.

The European Parliament's (EP's) Temporary Committee of Inquiry into BSE was backed up with the threat of a motion of censure – the EP's legal trump card which would have forced a resignation of the Commission (A4-0362/97) The Parliamentary Committee submitted a scathing report on 7 February 1997 (A4-0020/97), which in its findings presented evidence of what it considered to be considerable negligence and mal-administration on the part of both the Commission

---

been reported in the UK. Some 450 cases had been recorded in other European countries, with the majority of these found in Switzerland (233) (GIS-BSE (96)7.5).

[9] While the link between BSE and the new variant of CJD (designated V-CJD) remained speculative, statements released by the WHO in April 1996 and a study published in the 24 October 1996 issue of *Nature* seemed to confirm the probable connection. As of October 1996, 15 cases of V-CJD had been identified, with 14 cases in the UK and one in France (GIS-BSE (96)7.5). By November 1998, 30 fatalities from V-CJD had been identified, 29 in the UK and 1 in France (COM (97) 509 final: 58).

and the UK Government. It found that the UK Government consistently put producer interests above public health and safety interests within its own internal handling of BSE in the early stages, and that perhaps based on this more general orientation, it had also failed to consistently follow either its own agreements with the Commission and to implement the Commission Directives aimed at containing the spread of the disease. The Commission was found to have failed to sufficiently monitor and enforce UK compliance with its BSE-related Directives, up to and including the March 27th ban. Perhaps more serious was the apparent influence of the UK's Chief Veterinary Officer, M.K. Meldrum, on the actions taken by DG Agriculture. This influence was "obviously increased by the preponderance of British experts and Ministry of Agriculture officials on the BSE Subgroup of the Scientific and Veterinary Committee" (A4-0020/97:8). One effect of such influence was to reduce interest in further research and to greatly reduce the flow of needed scientific information regarding BSE. In addition, a temporary Commission official who was entrusted with the day-to-day management of the BSE affair was a former official of the British Ministry of Agriculture. Finally, the available evidence suggested that lobbying by agricultural processors helped to reinforce the wait-and-see approach being taken. The general argument used was that there was *insufficient justification for taking measures that might cause concerns among consumers.*

The EP's report included in its official findings that 1) the Commission had given priority to management of the market and the "huge economic interests at stake in the meat, feeding stuff and animal residue processing industries" (A4-0020/97:34) rather than to possible human health risks; 2) the Commission followed an overall policy of downplaying the problem; 3) that DG Employment, Industrial Relations, and Social Affairs had failed to act to prevent risks to human health presented by BSE; 4) that the workings of the Scientific Veterinary Committee could be characterized at best as lacking transparency, and in less diplomatic terms, that important information may have been intentionally withheld; 5) and that the Commission's response to the investigation could generally be characterized one of obstruction. The Committee's recommendations for the future included in the report were preceded by a clear message about the stakes involved: "The appropriate sanctions available to the Parliament under the Treaty with a view to calling the Commission politically to account are a motion of no confidence, pursuant to Article 144 of the Treaty, or the initiation of proceedings for failure to act/a breach of the Treaty, pursuant to Article 175" (A4-0020/97:36).

It was the connection to food safety and human health that distinguished the perception of – and handling of – the BSE crisis prior to the March 26th, 1996 announcement, from the actions taken in its wake. The BSE affair can be seen as the source of several distinctly different, yet related crises. Prior to 1996, it was largely understood – and certainly handled by the Commission – as an agricultural and economic crisis – and a possible threat to speedy progress toward the single market. This pitted farmers and processors faced with the costs of lost or blocked sales resulting from the epidemic, against farmers, processors, and member states who were as yet apparently free from the disease. Public health was a concern expressed by European public interest organizations such as the European Consumers' Organization (BEUC) and the European Public Health Alliance (EPHA) and some scientists, and echoed by some within the European Parliament and later by the World Health Organization (WHO). But these concerns took a back seat, with the burden of proof that a hazard existed resting with those expressing concerns for public health and consumer safety. Following the announcement of a possible BSE/V-CJD link, the dimensions of the crisis were transformed. While the economic and market considerations remained, they were effectively eclipsed by the crisis in consumer confidence in food safety, a potential public health crisis, and the political crises generated by questions about actions taken and why so little had been done to cope with these potential problems much earlier. These crises helped to set in motion a significant array of changes based at least in part on the need to restore some measure of consumer confidence in food safety – and in the political accountability of the Commission and the EU itself.

As was previously pointed out, the BSE crisis has been repeatedly referred to in Commission documents as a clear turning point in EU food and consumer policy. The changes underway since then proceeded not only under continued political pressure from the European Parliament, but also under the continued pressure and awareness generated by a series of similar crises and conflicts regarding consumer and food safety, and public health. But these other crises and conflicts took place in a context already broadly shaped by the events connected with the BSE affair.

3.2 Carcinogenic Chickens: The Dioxin Crisis

As if to prove to European citizens and EU institutions that the food safety crisis generated by the dubious handling of BSE was no fluke, the next public crisis unfolded virtually under the collective noses of EU officials in Belgium. Late in the afternoon of Friday 27 May 1999, EU officials and the Belgian public were notified that Belgian chicken, eggs, and possibly other products had been heavily contaminated with the carcinogen dioxin. Indications of the emerging crisis became more visible as poultry products began disappearing from grocery store shelves the next day on the orders of Belgian Public Health Minister Marcel Colla (BG-b, 1999). But even as store shelves were being emptied, stories of the crisis began to flood the news – including stories of possible scandal and allegations of cover-up, and that the Belgian Government had known of the problem as early as February. By Monday, May 30th media coverage had exploded (Lok and Powell, 2000).

Other governments did not wait long to respond. The European Commission adopted emergency protective measures on June 3, after consultation with the Standing Veterinary Committee, banning the export of the potentially contaminated Belgian food products and calling for their removal and destruction across EU Member states (Decision 99/788/EC). The measures were amended to include pigs and bovine animals a day later upon the receipt of new information from the Belgian authorities. The EU announcement included critical remarks about the timeliness of notification by Belgian authorities and also mentioned the possibility of legal procedures directed against Belgium for failure to comply with EU food safety notification requirements (PR-1, 99-06-02; James, 1999). Other nations both within and outside of the EU responded with similar speed: countries across the EU followed with their own actions, while the US Food and Drug Administration issued a decision to ban all imports from the European union of products containing chicken or pork (FSIS, 99-06-03)[10].

The contamination was uncovered largely by accident, when the De Brabander farm experienced serious problems with its hens, prompting them to contact their insurer. The expert engaged by the insurer, also an official with the West Flanders veterinary inspectorate, traced the problem to fat in the animal feed and sent a sample off for testing. The Belgian Ministry of Agriculture was notified of the problem on March 19th. The problem, which was determined to be dioxin contamination of the feed, was first traced to the Verkest company, which had processed the animal fat used by the feed company, then to another firm, Fogra, which had sold animal fat to Verkest. Whether by accident or through negligence, the Verkest-rendered animal fat had been stored in an inadequately cleaned container that had previously contained some form of dioxin-containing industrial oils. The contaminated animal fat had been sold to eight Belgian animal foodstuffs manufacturers, along with one French and one Dutch company, in the last half of January 1999. Fogra was later found to have exported some of its product to Spain where it was used to produce cooking oil. The contaminated feed was subsequently sold to an estimated 417 poultry producing companies, mostly in Belgium (BG-a; BG-b).

The Belgian Agriculture and Health Ministries officially confirmed the presence of extremely high levels of dioxin in the animal feed and chicken fat on April 24th, 1999. But although they then officially notified the French and Dutch authorities, it was not until over a month later, on May 27, that the Commission was notified, after further tests and more investigatory work revealed the breadth of the problem (BG-b; Lok and Powell, 2000).

The Belgian government was harshly criticized by the Commission for its failure to inform it much sooner of the problem, but it was likely the firestorm in the news media that did the most damage. News stories referenced past threats to food safety, including the 'mad cow' scare. The Belgian government was accused in various

[10] The ban on all EU-produced poultry and pig products should be seen in the context of an ongoing trade dispute at the WTO between the US and the EU regarding the EU's refusal to permit the import of hormone-treated meat from the US. The US argued that the EU was using the ban to protect against competition from US beef producers. The EU, on the other hand, had banned the use of growth hormones and several antibiotics in animal feed based on public health concerns. It is not clear to what extent the dioxin crisis may have provided legitimacy for retaliatory action by the US related to the hormone case.

reports of "serving the economic interests of farmers' unions and the meat industry", and of trying to protect themselves in preparation for the general elections on 13 June, instead of protecting public health. Belgian newspapers were especially harsh, calling the incident 'total havoc' and 'a human and economic catastrophe" (Lok and Powell, 2000:9). The speculation arising from the many details that remained unclear only served to intensify the frenzy. On June 2, the Ministers of Public Health and of Agriculture offered their resignations, joining as victims of the crisis more than 400 poultry farms and tens of thousands of chickens (James, 1999). Belgian voters completed the rout two weeks later, denying what had appeared to be a near-certain re-election to the center-left governing coalition.

Although the Belgian government was harshly criticized for its handling of the affair, the Commission appeared to have learned from previous experience, stepping in decisively in order to "protect public health." Lok and Powell (2000) suggest that the Commission was overly aggressive and confrontational in its response in general, and with the Belgian government in particular, and that this stance further complicated the process of coping with the crisis. To the extent this was the case, several factors can be identified that may have influenced such an approach. First, there was a likely need for the Commission to demonstrate to the broader public that it had indeed recognized its previous errors, and that it had indeed adopted a "food policy which gives pride of place to consumer protection and consumer health" (Bulletin EU 1/2-1997:5). Second, given that the Belgian government exacerbated the crisis by delaying notification of the Commission, it seems clear there was an important message to be sent to other member states regarding their conduct in the event of similar developments. Third, the Commission had already covered considerable ground in its reorganization and reprioritization in the wake of the BSE crisis. A major policy document on food, the Green Paper on food safety, had been revised and issued in 1997. Two important follow-up documents, a clarification of the application of the Precautionary Principle (COM(2000) 1) and a White Paper (COM(99) 719) containing the Commission's proposals for implementing its food safety priorities, were also well underway. So while the dioxin crisis served as a dramatic reminder of the weaknesses in Europe's regulatory systems for food safety, it also served as a test case for the EU's transformed institutional conceptualization of food – and for its new and improved approach to protecting consumers and the public health.

4. Paradigm Shift, Institutional Shift & the Transformation of EU Food Policy

The overall evolution of EU food policy appears to be following the path of food itself – a stepwise progression from farm to market to consumer and public health[11]. As is also the case with food in its movement from farm to market to table, each of these steps in the transformation of a policy sector entails processes that are themselves quite complex – and without which the transformation from one phase to the next is unlikely to take place. EU food policy must remain fixed at the intersection of agriculture, market, and public health and consumer policy. A transformation took place in the form of a reordering of core, priority principles around which food policy is organized, and in the way in which related EU institutions are organized to reflect those priorities and principles.

There are several ways to trace the story of the evolution of EU food policy. The shift of core principles and priorities from market orientation to public health/consumer orientation and their institutionalization has already been highlighted as a central theme. Another related story is the Europeanization of the public health and consumer safety issues connected with food policy. These narratives represent paradigmatic and institutional shifts in the food sector in the guiding principles of governance. A third related story is how policy entrepreneurs, particularly within the Commission, enlist opportunities created by external crises to recast particular issues according to a particular new policy paradigm. In this sense, both public interest groups and the advocates of greater European integration made important gains.

4.1 Paradigm shift

The evidence strongly suggests that the paradigmatic shift in EU food safety policy staved off a return to national level regulation. While substantial adjustments to the policy dictated by the market paradigm might have addressed many of the actual public health and safety issues, the demands created by the public confidence and related political crisis forced more revolutionary action. The Green Paper on food safety (COM(97) 176) has been singled out earlier in this chapter as the official turning point in EU food policy because it represents the formal announcement of the change in hierarchy of core principals guiding EU food policy: from taking health and safety into consideration, to ensuring a high level of protection of consumers' health, safety and economic interests. Because there had been disagreement within the Commission about the content of the paper, its release became possible only after the crisis, and in direct response to it.

An important step toward the institutionalization of the principles outlined in the Green Paper was realized in the EU constitutional framework in the form of the legal mandate provided by the treaties. Articles 152 and 153 (Amsterdam Treaty, 1999), which, radically although subtly, strengthened the place of public health and consumer interests in EU policymaking, and emerged at least in part, from responses to the handling of the BSE crisis. This was noted as part of the background

[11] This can be rephrased as a progression from an emphasis on producer interests to market interests to public interest. At the beginning of the 1990s, the CAP balance was tipping from producer interests toward market interests (Daugbjerg, 2003).

to the evolution of EU food policy, but, is worth pointing to again as a reminder that it was not only an important part of the context within which policy evolution took place. It represents a deeper institutionalization of the paradigm shift with respect to public health and consumer safety issues – the formal acknowledgement by member states of the new paradigmatic order in these policy sectors. It was also intertwined with, and was yet another reflection of, the changing perceptions regarding the kinds of issues that can be considered European versus national or local.

4.2 DG Hopping

The shift in perspective was also institutionalized at a more mundane level. The movement of the high priority responsibilities for EU food policy within EU institutions – from DG Agriculture to DG Industry to DG Health and Consumer Protection – was more than symbolic. This is especially true, given that DG Health and Consumer Protection was only created in 1995, and as recently as 1998 was generally seen as quite weak in comparison with the other two DGs (Sutton, 1999). The different missions of the respective DGs offer a hint of which competing principles for food policy were likely to dominate the framing of policy and action.

DG Agriculture indicated as its mission that it was "responsible for the European Union's policies on agriculture and rural development" (DG Agriculture, 2000). Information found on the DG Agriculture home page explicitly downplayed the earlier focus on agricultural markets: "the focus of the CAP has shifted somewhat from the previous dominance of market measures" and directs attention elsewhere, "including the important social role of agriculture in the EU…" (DG Agriculture, 2000).

The stated mission of DG Industry was until late 1999 "to promote the competitiveness of European industry" and to "improve the functioning of markets, in particular the Internal market, in order to provide a stable, coherent and predictable environment for business"(DG Industry, 1999). The previous Commissioner, Martin Bangeman, was known for being equally unequivocal in communicating his sense of mission (Nylander, 2000). This was a comparatively direct and unapologetic statement of purpose from a DG considered to have been among the most influential of the DGs, and with a powerful pro-business constituency. Interestingly, the DG did make a gesture toward more socially-oriented goals, but did so by describing competitiveness as "the ability of industry to generate rising standards of living for the population as a whole…" (DG Industry, 1999). When the new Commission came into place in late 1999, the name of DG Industry was changed to DG Enterprise and the mission language softened to say that the "mission of the Enterprise Directorate General is to address the entire business environment to enable enterprises to strengthen their competitiveness, grow and develop in a way that is compatible *with the overall EU goal of sustainable development*" (DG Enterprise, 2000, emphasis added). While the extent to which such changes in language represent fundamental changes in mission remains to be seen, the consistency of the language with other developments in the EU suggest something more than a simple facelift. Even so, the bulk of responsibility for food policy was shifted to DG Health and Consumer Protection.

The statement of mission for DG Health and Consumer Protection was as explicitly consumer oriented as the statement of DG Industry was business oriented: "to ensure a high level of protection of consumers' health, safety and economic interests as well as of public health at the level of the European union" (DG Health and Consumer Protection, 2000). The statement was given greater force by the fact that it was drawn almost directly from the relevant articles of the 1999 Treaty (Amsterdam Treaty, 1999, Articles 152, 153.).

It would be naive, of course, to take such statements of purpose strictly at face value, ignoring the political and symbolic character of both the statements and the institutions whose purposes they reflected. It is possible to compare statements presented to different audiences or in different forums, and it is even more helpful to compare claims with actions. But even taking the most cynical perspective possible – that such statements are no more than political rhetoric and represent no substantive change – they do create important pressures. Political legitimacy and trust require at least a measure of consistency to be maintained between what is said and what is done. In fact, the shift in prioritization of guiding principles did appear to be increasingly reflected in public statements (i.e., in relevant DG mission statements and in numerous speeches, see SPEECH/00/41) and in new actions being taken by the Commission (i.e., Commission actions taken to block Belgian poultry exports – or to block the import of U.S. beef containing potentially dangerous growth hormones), and in the further institutionalization of these principles in the organizational structure of the EU (i.e., in the new Food Safety Authority).

Several inferences can be drawn from the presentation, or framing, of the guiding principles of DG Agriculture. Prior to the late 1980s, the role of DG-Agriculture was clearly defined as supporting and administering the CAP and its earlier policy focus, and later, even supporting the need for market reforms. Second, the newer, more "social" focus suggests a changing set of policy priorities for the DG, since it characterizes agricultural policy through the framework of social concerns – concerns that are only indirectly agricultural. While such statements may be influenced by a perceived need to present the DG's goals in terms of a newly popular and legitimized set of priorities, other evidence also points to deeper institutional adjustment. If, as the evaluation of the CAP for the Commission stated, the "legitimacy of the CAP is in danger" (Buckwell Report, 1997: 5:1), then the legitimacy and authority of the DG responsible for its substance and implementation were also in danger. The qualification of the mission of DG Enterprise points in a similar direction. And while this hardly meant that DG Enterprise would be competing with DG Health and Consumer Protection to champion citizens' and consumers' health, safety, and rights, it does suggest that the goals and purposes of the respective DGs are inherently and inevitably different in a way that requires some clear set of principles and rules for establishing priority, or "pride of place" in the many areas where conflicts exist.

This is, of course, only the tip of the iceberg, as the changes reflected in legal documents establishing both legal competence and operating principles demonstrate. In the context of events that have unfolded over the past decade, Articles 152 and 153 of the Amsterdam Treaty have taken on a level of priority that was probably quite unexpected when they were agreed upon.

5. Public Policy Paradigm: Defining the Nature of the Problem and the Structure of the Institutions that Address Them

The broad conceptualization of the problems to be solved has consistently driven the EU discussion – and policymaking – regarding food. From the 1950s until the 1980s, the pair of dominant problems were seen to be adequate food supply and maintaining a "healthy" enough agricultural system to sustain both producers (farmers) and consumers (European citizens). The political power and economic resources of the EU were directed toward achieving these goals. When the push for the single market materialized, the main problem of adequate food supply seemed to have been addressed, but new problems had already emerged as a result of CAP. The new problems were largely seen in terms of market-inspired goals: they were high cost and low productivity, and to a lesser extent, a lack of consumer choice. Achievement of these goals meant dismantling at least part of the previous system, including economic supports and regulatory mechanisms, to achieve a common market in agriculture. The fact that some of the regulatory mechanisms that inhibited agricultural trade had public health benefits seemed not to be a consideration – the problem was defined differently, as the need for a stronger, united market, necessitating the removal of obstacles to trade. This would, in turn, increase choice, lower prices, and achieve greater agricultural efficiency. The fact that enormous economic interests were at stake only served to propel developments further and faster.

European food policy has now taken yet another major turn – toward considerations of public health and consumer safety as the principal priority. This turn too, has been triggered by the emergence of new problems. When Commission President Jacques Santer observed before the European Parliament back in 1997 (Bulletin EU 1/2-1997: 4) that the food crisis that threatened his presidency was a direct result of then-dominant principles guiding EU food policy, he echoed what at some level many European citizens already understood to be true. The transformation of EU food policy has evolved since the mid-1990s, following from that understanding of responsibility and the demand for effective measures. It began with the paradigmatic shift announced in the Green Paper on food safety, and has been institutionalized in the rule changes and organizational restructuring that have and are continuing to take place.

These contentions and conclusions regarding the transformation in EU food policy might be taken as encouraging news by critics of the market ideology that has guided important EU developments since the 1980s – and by those with concerns more narrowly directed to public health. We would all do well, however, not to rest too comfortably – the new principles are not yet deeply institutionalized, although the current changes appear to be having an effect. However, this process is ongoing, and unanticipated events and resourceful actors could easily combine to shift both attention and directions once again. One food producers' organization, for example, highlights its concerns about food safety by redirecting attention to practices in the kitchen – covering stored food, proper cooking, not leaving food out, etc. While these are certainly legitimate concerns, they are not only of a quite different nature – they also shift the attention and sense of responsibility for food safety from producer to consumer.

Public interest groups are clearly aware of this potential for subtle redirection. In their comments on the 2000 paper clarifying the use of the Precautionary Principle (COM(2000) 1), the EPHA points out that the principle is essentially political in nature, and that the scientific evidence to which the Commission communication refers is itself based on its own underlying assumptions which can be influenced by other interests (EPHA, 2000). This was precisely the problem in the early stages of the BSE epidemic, when the possibility of transmission to humans was first raised. The BEUC made similarly keen observations earlier regarding consumer policy and the provisions in the Amsterdam Treaty (BEUC/300/98). The definition of issues as either fundamentally technical, or political in nature, moves policy questions into very different decision processes, as Nylander (2000:112-146) observed in the struggle over the law on biotechnology patents in the EU.

While there is great demand for consultation with consumer and public health organizations at the moment, there are also problems. They continue to lack the practical resources that make effective participation possible on a rapidly increasing scale. This threatens to reduce their ability to focus sufficiently on important issues, while at the same time it risks creating the impression that they are not as concerned as they have claimed. Their ability to be heard has in part depended upon the severity and of, and the level of public awareness of, the problems to which they address themselves. Nor have these obstacles gone unnoticed by commercial interests, which in some cases have established what might be cynically referred to as front groups – consumer-led, industry-financed organizations to enhance their own credibility and position of issues of interest (see Nylander, 2000:112-146).

In spite of such ongoing questions, there are also parallel forces at work that reinforce the transformation in EU food policy. At the international level, the World Trade Organization (WTO) issued its decision in 1999 prioritizing public health concerns over trade interests[12] – one of the few times free trade rules have been overruled by public health concerns. Within the EU, social concerns are being reflected in a range of other policy decisions – some of which are taken up in subsequent chapters. Even within food policy, discussions have extended beyond strict questions of food safety (defined as the absence of harmful foreign substances) to the health impacts of normal components of food products such as fat and other nutritional content. These discussions are likely to reinforce more fundamental safety concerns, as well as continue to contribute to the further Europeanization of food policy as new regulations, and monitoring and enforcement mechanisms are deployed.

6. Concluding Remarks

The principal phases or components of this policy transformation process can be described in terms of: a) paradigm shift – the shift in core guiding principles and conceptualizations, b) action and interaction – with discourses and activities that reflect the challenging paradigm's re-ordering of priorities, and c) institutional change (system shift) – the institutionalization of new organizing principles in the reorganization of European policymaking and administrative structures, and allocation of resources (in relation to food issues). These phases can be seen as separate, although interconnected and contemporaneous, with one setting the stage for the other. The details of the transformation – how extensive the change is that takes place, how dramatic or disruptive that change is, and how quickly change takes place – are influenced by the particular confluence of three factors: policy paradigm, actors and their relationships, and institutional structure. External events and developments – in this case, the byproducts of food policy guided by the market paradigm – provide the real-world problems and issues to which the elements are addressed.

This interplay can be traced in the empirical evidence in a) the nature of the problems identified and prioritized, and the context in which they are seen; b) in the different ways in which particular actors have been able to successfully define and frame concrete problems, and how they have been able to exercise power and authority in dealing with them; and c) the institutional changes that took place within the EU, including treaty language, internal guiding principles and policy priorities, and the particular institutional actors granted power and responsibility with respect to food policy. Finally, this evolution can be seen as the response to events and other developments, including crises, or "anomalies", that developed, at least in part, as a direct result of the particular configuration at an earlier point in time, of conceptual orientation, interested actors, and institutional structure. Several general

[12] The WTO decided in favor of France (citing public health concerns) in its refusal to import Canadian asbestos, a known cancer-causing agent (Olson, 2000-06-16).

conclusions can be drawn from the empirical evidence relating to PPP Theory, and are presented below.

(1) Problematic anomalies are the catalyst – and often an essential feature – of processes of paradigm shifts[13]. They generate pressure for response and adjustment of the dominant paradigm. Actors guided by a competing paradigm may take advantage of such problems to promote an alternative set of explanations for, and solutions to, pressing problems, but they do not create them. Neither do demands for change find much purchase in the absence of a perceived problem. Public interest groups raised numerous concerns and cautions about food safety and public health issues in the years prior to the BSE crisis. Actors within the Commission had clearly come to understand and recognize the validity of these concerns, given that *much of the Green Paper on Food Safety (COM(97) 176) was drafted before the crisis exploded.* Even while the core principles of the market paradigm suggested that competitive forces would successfully weed out such problems, the Commission had taken some regulatory action to protect food safety – but generally *within* the restrictions of the market paradigm.

(2) The effect that an anomaly has on its related policy paradigm is related to how the source of the problem is understood. To the extent that the problem is seen to be either unexplained or unaccounted for by the paradigm, there will be pressures to modify or adapt the paradigm to address the problem. This would typically entail adjustment in the more peripheral areas of the paradigm – first in methods and approaches as reflected in specific policy measures. The Commission's pre-BSE responses to food safety concerns, articulated in numerous issue-specific safety directives and actions, can be seen as just such an adjustment response. While certain actors (in particular, European public interest organizations) saw the emerging problems as more deeply rooted, their number or severity had not reached a level that could be referred to as a "critical mass". The Commission demonstrated this by pressing for the removal of national bans on British beef products in response to the first signs of a problem, actions that clearly suggest that the problem was understood as a trade and agricultural problem and to be dealt with within those frameworks. Emerging problems that were more clearly related to public health and food safety were addressed with adjustments in practices and rules within the single market framework.

---

[13] There distinction between anomalies and problems is an important one. As it is used here, an anomaly is a development or condition that is either inadequately accounted for by the explanations and attributions contained within a given paradigm, or even produced by the implementation of the paradigm. Problems are usefully described by Spector and Kitsuse (1987:74) as "the activities of those who assert the existence of conditions and define them as problems". In the strictest sense, therefore, an anomaly may or may not be defined as a problem – it is the claims-making activity of social actors that produces this result. There are many phenomena that are poorly, if at all accounted for, by any given institutionalized public policy paradigm. It is the problem-causing anomaly that is of interest here.

(3) The nature of a problem and its threat to a given policy paradigm changes radically, however, to the extent that the paradigm itself is seen as a source of the problem –whether as directly caused by policies guided by that paradigm or a side effect. The BSE crisis provides the textbook case. By the time of the BSE crisis, the EU's CAP had already been under siege for some time. In addition to being seen as the cause of undesirable market distortions, it was being blamed for environmental problems and even undermining the quality of European food products. While the single market programme sought to address the various market distortions created by state-level regulation and earlier EU food policy, it was not addressed to food quality or safety except as an expected side effect of unleashing competitive forces. Public interest groups, including environmental, public health, and consumer groups, continued to sound alarms about potential problems. Meanwhile, the implementation of the single market was accompanied by concerns over the weakening or dismantling of existing regulatory structures for food safety, and more generally, the EU's increasing intrusion on what until recently been considered a national, rather than supranational policymaking arena. When the announcement of a connection between BSE and an invariably fatal human disease sent shock waves across Europe, the stage for a crisis encompassing numerous paradigms was already set: 1) mad cow disease had already been in the news for years – long enough for its source to have been traced to animal feed and agricultural practices generated by the intensification of competition in agricultural production. There had long been speculation regarding the possibility of BSE spreading from cows to humans, and concerns expressed that economic interests were being prioritized over public health and safety; 2) the widespread economic downturn experienced over much of Europe during the 1990s contributed to intensified debate about the requirements placed upon member states' policies by a supranational authority, and its role in prioritizing economic interests over broader public concerns; 3) specific actions taken by the EU in support of the British government with respect to BSE, including the apparent British role in downplaying any response by the Commission, made the EU appear as an accomplice, if not the primary cause of the crisis. This generated crises on three fronts: 1) a food safety crisis – pertaining to actual risk of contracting a fatal disease from eating beef products; 2) a crisis of public confidence – relating to a more general undermining of public confidence in the safety of food and the institutions for its assurance; 3) a political crisis – a crisis of confidence in European institutions, the Commission in particular. Inevitably, the dominant paradigm by which the Commission and the European Union were understood – the market paradigm and the actors most clearly associated with it – were seen as the source of developments that had become difficult to deny as a serious problem and threat. That the British government continued to deny any real food safety problem only served to undermine what credibility that may have remained. The actions eventually taken contributed to not only holding the regulation of agricultural and foodstuffs markets at the EU level, but by effectively drawing food

safety much more firmly into the European arena. A failure to do this would likely have resulted in many more member states asserting public health concerns through their erection of new national barriers to trade in agricultural and food products. This would have obviously implied a failure of the idea of a European single market.

(4) A paradigm shift can be said to have taken place when one set of core paradigmatic principals is replaced by another, with institutional and practical consequences. This is likely to entail a reordering of the priority order of these core principals rather than the complete rejection of all or part of that core. The reordering, however, must dictate a course of action that would not be possible under – or would be incommensurable with – the ordering it replaces. It might therefore be asserted that it is the particular structuring and prioritizing of fundamental principals that represents the core of the paradigm. Thus, establishing the single market while taking into account public health concerns dictates a radically different direction over time for policy decisions and organizational structures than *assuring* a high level of public health and consumer safety in *all* European Union policy. The adaptation of the Precautionary Principle from environmental policy to food policy and shifting the burden of proof connected with potential food safety problems provides a clear example. The rapid and public response of the Commission to dioxin contamination of Belgian poultry products not only greatly reduced the ongoing, actual danger to public health, it also sent a clear message about in whose favor such decisions might be resolved in the future. The clumsiness of the Belgian government in the episode provided the Commission an unwitting "villain" against which to play hero (making a much more interesting, intrigue-filled, and newsworthy story). While the EU ban on several Belgian products undoubtedly harmed many innocent farmers whose products had not been contaminated, the demonstration of the direction in which uncertainty would be addressed undoubtedly reduced unnecessary exposure to dioxins, while doing much to rebuild public confidence in a European role in assuring food safety.

(5) Tipping point – Changes in the peripheral or secondary elements of a policy paradigm may serve to reinforce and more deeply embed a currently dominant institutionalized paradigm – or they may serve to weaken and undermine it, paving the way for the replacement of the paradigm by a challenger. This effect depends in part on the extent to which the changes influence factors in three categories: 1) their effect on the legitimacy or effectiveness of claims-making activities that define social problems (while changes in rules or the practices that characterize their implementation may, for example, ameliorate or eliminate a problem, the responses themselves may also serve to legitimize such problems as relevant issues); 2) their effect on how the material interests of powerful actors are played out; and 3) their tendency to increase or decrease the overall coherence, or internal consistency, of the paradigm.

The UK and the Commission took numerous steps to address the BSE epidemic from the time of its initial discovery. The most public of these was to slaughter tens of thousands of British cows – at enormous cost. They also took steps to remove from the food chain the suspected sources of the infection, which derived from recycling animal by-products into animal feed. This was a quite invasive set of steps in the context of a paradigm that promotes minimal regulation or other governmental intervention. It was undoubtedly made possible by the fact that economic interests – including both agricultural and food processing industries – were also being severely hurt by the problem. Action was needed, since British farmers were not voluntarily slaughtering their potentially infected herds, and the subsequent cheating on related regulations suggested that some farmers and producers would not, even with government intervention, voluntarily place public health concerns above their own economic interest. The governmental intervention in commercial agricultural activities clearly legitimized and publicized the problem, as it would be almost inconceivable to order the destruction of so many animals in the absence of a major threat. The need for intervention by public authorities in market matters was also legitimized, since agricultural markets did not appear to be self-correcting. This undermined the market paradigm and reinforced the challenging perspective – a paradigm that called for vigorous public intervention in the market. The fact that the problem was not only a public health concern, but also threatened influential market actors across Europe, changed the stakes; the BSE issue expanded food safety questions beyond public health and into the capacity of the market to function properly. The convergence of "claims-making" activities across the interests (and re-alignment of interests), combined with the gradual legitimizing of decisive intervention by public authorities in market matters, and the subsequent undermining of the market paradigm with respect to food concerns, crystallized with the announcement of the possible connection between BSE and human health. A hidden villain became the public threat, while some kind of action by public authorities became the solution, transforming the perception of at least some forms of government intervention from "problem" to "solution". Only the British government held fast to the problem-causing paradigm, as if to prove people's worst fears about the type of food policy it could produce.

Since the release of the Green Paper on food safety (COM(97)176), actions taken by the EU have tended to flesh out and reinforce the new paradigm. In addition to deeper formalization in the treaties (Amsterdam Treaty, 1999) these actions are reflected in the paradigmatic principles, such as those expressed in the formalization and clarification of the Precautionary Principle. They are also reflected in the more peripheral areas of practice, including the implementation of policy decisions on food safety, for example, the EU actions in response to the dioxin crisis. The most important theoretical generalization that can be drawn here is that the effects of changes in paradigmatic elements are likely to be cumulative and context dependent – rather than sequential and ordered according to their place in any hierarchy.

Finally, such paradigmatic changes are increasingly reflected in institutional reorganization – representing the system shift following the paradigm shift. This reorganization is having the effect of making the institutional structure of the EU – particularly the Commission and its DGs – more coherent and compatible with the new policy paradigm.

CHAPTER 9

From Freely Traded to Product-non-grata: Banning Asbestos in the European Union

Marcus Carson

1. Introduction

While most if not all paradigm shifts proceed via incremental processes, the most obvious are typically catalyzed by crises that also makes the shift more apparent. Even so, a paradigmatic shift may be almost entirely the product of developments that appear minor and therefore largely escape notice. Such incrementalism is likely to be the case, for example, when the accumulation of new knowledge is gradual and where the configurations of powerful interested actors remains relatively stable. Incremental adjustments (what Hall refers to as first level changes) are generally made to policies as part of ongoing processes of managing emerging problems that do not fit the model or were not anticipated by it. Such developments typically require that effective claims be made in order to be addressed in policy. But even where policy adjustments may resolve apparent problems, they may also serve to legitimize critique of the established paradigm – both by giving credence to claims that the model is flawed, and by introducing new inconsistencies into the institutionalized model. Such adjustments may accumulate sufficiently over time to contribute to a significant challenge. The appearance of stability may be supported by influential actors who are invested in the institutionalized paradigm and able either to explain away emerging anomalies or to otherwise suppress potential challenges. Even when they occur unfold via incremental processes, paradigmatic and system shift still entail social conflict. However, overt conflict may be dampened by the defection over time of key actors whose interests change or who may "see the writing on the wall" (Burns and Carson, 2005).

This chapter examines the developments that culminated with the EU banishing a successful commercial product from its internal market in 2005 – an example in which both paradigm change and institutional change proceed largely incrementally. It was precisely the sort of incremental process described above by which the EU shifted over time from its initial steps to require the gathering of information about the asbestos exposure of workers to what eventually became a virtually complete ban on asbestos-containing products within the Single European Market. The asbestos case provides an excellent example not only of how minor conceptual change can accumulate over time to generate a paradigmatic shift, but also how such a shift may be resisted by powerful interested actors seeking to preserve the benefits derived from established ideas and assumptions. It also shows how incremental changes in institutionalized rule arrangements may result from conceptual changes, and how these system changes may in turn also serve to further legitimize claims supporting much broader reforms. In concrete terms, the asbestos case illustrates how the fight over institutional changes – the regulation and eventual banning of a product – was first and foremost a battle over issue conceptualization and fundamental guiding principles – in this instance, whether to assign priority to market goals, or to protecting public health. These principles defined in turn how the related issues of burden of proof and the nature of the standards by which that charge could be met.

The general perception of asbestos has been transformed from that of "miracle mineral" to "deadly dust" over the course of the past century. The incorporation of this conceptual shift into EU regulation of asbestos took place over the shorter span of three decades, but nonetheless followed a similar progression. What began with initial recommendations for worker safety and protection from exposure was subsequently expanded to include increasingly strict regulations on exposure, uses, and varieties of asbestos. These restrictions were eventually transformed into an outright ban on the import and use of asbestos in European markets[1].

This successively stringent regulation was pursued with what was appears to have been a trio of purposes which have at different times conflicted with or complemented one another. On the one hand, EU officials sought to develop and maintain a common body of regulations for chemicals and asbestos at the EU level, and to avoid increased national-level regulation – with both in support of the overarching goal of greater market integration. On the other hand, EU officials and public interest organizations sought to regulate a commercially important product to safeguard workers and protect public health – goals it was eventually concluded were incompatible with the continued presence of the product on the market. Finally, there is the interest in expanding EU authority to broaden and deepen its reach in diverse policy sectors as part of the larger project of European integration. As the course of events demonstrates, developments moved with most certainty toward greater EU competence where these three purposes have been seen as compatible with and tended to reinforce one another.

The asbestos case was described by one European Commission official at DG Environment as a "classic example" of how the EU policymaking proceeds incrementally with the regulation of health and environmental hazards through negotiation and consensus building. In this respect, it offers insights into how the regulation of other hazardous substances that present public health risks in the workplace and the environment are likely to be approached within the European Union.

[1] With limited exceptions, including some industrial gaskets. The ban went into effect January 1, 2005.

Another Commission official characterized the asbestos case as a poor indicator of the course of future action in the EU, or at the WTO level. Indeed, some of the most important lessons to be found in the asbestos case were made possible by the ways in which asbestos differs from other potential health hazards, such as the use of antibiotics or growth hormones in meat production, the release of genetically modified organisms into the environment and the food chain, or the chemicals in various products and production processes.

As a public policy problem, asbestos shares important characteristics in common with chemical pollutants and other threats to health and environment that entail externalized costs with severe negative consequences. "Externalized costs" (anticipated or unanticipated) refer to those costs left out of the original economic transaction that have been "commonized" or left to be paid by actors who were not part of that transaction. They may include not only the direct economic costs associated with cleanup of substances discovered to be hazardous, but also future environmental and health harms. This type of externalization may occur, for example, where benefits of a product are comparatively direct and immediate, while the harms generated by its use are time-delayed and diffused across the population. As with many products, the benefits of asbestos once seemed broadly distributed. Fire resistance protected life and property while the large business enterprises that mined and manufactured asbestos products provided employment and earned healthy profits. But although this distribution of benefits has proven to be tragically one sided, establishing that truth as fact and incorporating it into public policy has proven a long and difficult process. Even if the lengthy time lapse between exposure and the development of asbestos-caused illnesses did not prevented epidemiologists from establishing definitive linkages between exposure and illness, this lag-time provided opportunities for delaying tactics, cover-ups, and even manipulation of scientific research that have in turn exposed more people to serious harm (Castleman and Lehman, 1998). Once established as a useful and profitable product, asbestos has proven exceedingly difficult to eliminate from the market.

The hazard and risk properties of asbestos rather closely parallel those of chemicals and are therefore dealt with in the EU under chemicals policy. These products often entail the difficult-to-trace and identify hazards of substances that are bio-accumulative, carcinogenic, or otherwise result in long-term environmental damage, health problems, or death. Moreover, the political history of asbestos regulation is strikingly similar to that of polychlorinated biphenyls (PCBs) (Koppe and Keys, 2001) and of benzene (Infante, 2001), for example, suggesting that while some of the intrinsic properties of the substances may differ, the politics of markets and regulation of such substances have been quite similar. Following this pattern, the increasingly restrictive regulation of asbestos developed in concert with the broader EU chemicals policy.

Important differences in inherent properties do distinguish asbestos from most chemical substances, just as important differences distinguish different classes of chemical substances from one another, the benefits they offer, and the nature of the hazards they present. In contrast to many chemicals, asbestos presents relatively little environmental concern per se. The major issues are occupational health and safety and public health. Its widespread use goes back more than a century, as does at least a portion of the data on the health hazards it presents. The configuration of interests is also somewhat different. Given that asbestos is a naturally occurring mineral fiber and is mined rather than synthesized, production is geographically bound in ways that distinguishes it from chemicals manufacturing.

EU Chemicals Policy has itself been influenced in critical ways by health hazards, regulatory problems, and political conflicts similar to those encountered in the asbestos case. We argue here that the revised principles for chemicals regulation presented in the White Paper and subsequent regulatory measures (including REACH) are in significant ways a reflection of the struggles over asbestos. These struggles included disputes over the core principles guiding regulation, the interpretation of scientific evidence, the political power of economic interests, and the Commission's various interests in furthering European integration.

Although the progressively restrictive regulation of asbestos was not crisis-driven at the EU level, it did entail considerable conflict. The attrition over time of numerous powerful asbestos supporters within the EU effectively reduced the internal opposition to adopting a ban. Outside of the EU, however, major asbestos producers, including the Canadian government, continued to press their case. They directed their forceful combination of political hardball and skillful persuasion at targets including national governments and supranational governance, and even international organizations concerned with science. Their lobbying efforts sought to challenge the interpretation of relevant scientific data and methodology and how that data framed issues of asbestos hazards for public policy. An important aspect of this contention was how remaining scientific uncertainties, particularly the few aspects of hazard and risk left unresolved by science, were understood and interpreted by policymakers and the general public.

2. Asbestos: comercial, public health and policy history

Asbestos was long considered a public health and commercial miracle. A naturally occurring mineral fiber, its several beneficial properties – durability, tensile strength, and heat and fire resistance – made it very valuable at a time when fire ranked among the most serious public health hazards. Beginning in the early 1880s, English and French textile industries produced fireproof fabrics woven from asbestos fibers. The products filled a market niche and asbestos use was quickly expanded to other areas. Its most important applications included not only construction materials such as asbestos cement board and pipe, but also products such as brake linings and heat resistant seals. Asbestos insulation applied through spray techniques enjoyed a brief, though extensive popularity (Vogel, 1999; AI, 1996). It is still common in building materials in workplaces and public spaces, in the form of asbestos cement, ceiling tiles and insulating products.

Ironically, it is the very properties that make asbestos useful that make it deadly. Its fire resistance resulted in its promotion to reduce fire hazards, only to create another far less visible and immediate, but equally lethal. The long microscopic fibers are extremely durable, but because the human body cannot break down and remove the fibers from the lungs once inhaled, they remain there and cause irritation. Over time, that irritation often results in a variety of serious respiratory ailments and forms of cancer. The substance has now become synonymous with the incurable, often-deadly lung diseases it causes. The "signature diseases" associated with asbestos exposure are asbestosis, an irreversible lung fibrosis that impedes the lungs' capacity to take up oxygen, and an otherwise rare form of cancer, mesothelioma (Gee and Greenberg, 2001).[2] The relatively long latency periods of asbestos-induced respiratory illnesses – roughly 15 years for asbestosis and 20-40 years for mesothelioma – complicated the process of establishing the linkages between asbestos and the deadly illnesses it produces.

The health hazards of asbestos are by no means a recent discovery; deadly side effects were apparent early on among workers who were most exposed to the airborne fibers. In 1906, deaths among workers at a French asbestos spinning and weaving factory were linked to asbestos by factory inspector Denis Auribault. British Dr. Montague Murray reported asbestosis among British textile workers the same year (Brodeur, 1985). The potent carcinogenic properties of asbestos were recognized by German researchers by the late 1930s, and beginning in the late 1940s, British cancer statistics began to provide an epidemiological dimension to the picture. The hazards of asbestos were already well documented by the 1950s (Tweedale, 2000). During the 1960s and 70s, Dr. Irving Selikoff and his associates led the pioneering work in the United States on asbestos and its health effects.

People working in environments with high concentrations of asbestos dust were most exposed to the hazards – "canaries in the coal mine". Workers with high exposure developed asbestosis, then other lung problems including mesothelioma and other cancers. They also brought home the dust on their clothes, inadvertently exposing their families. Moreover, asbestos products eventually deteriorate, releasing the fibers. Insulation and ceiling tiles are especially prone to deterioration and subsequent release of asbestos fibers. Large public buildings such as offices, hospitals, and schools have been built and insulated with asbestos containing materials. Asbestos cement and brake linings, while clearly more stable, also deteriorate with normal use. What had first come to be seen as a health hazard for a relatively circumscribed class of workers was in reality an indiscriminate threat to office or hospital workers, teachers, and children – even public officials.

---

[2] Asbestos exposure is the only known cause of mesothelioma, and can result from even extremely small exposure.

In spite of the alarm raised by a growing body of research, the accumulating evidence of asbestos-related health problems was for decades deemed inconclusive – in any case, not sufficient to remove a successful and profitable product from the market. The burden of proof for banning asbestos rested with academic researchers, public health professionals and victims' groups. In practice, the standards required to meet it have meant that even very minor scientific uncertainties or disagreements have provided support for a "wait and see" approach (Carson, 2004). These factors stacked the deck in favor of continued use.

At least a portion of what appeared to be scientific uncertainty was manufactured. It has been repeatedly revealed, often in the "discovery" process in U.S. legal proceedings in which internal company documents were forced out of corporate files by class-action lawsuits, that results from industry-funded studies were routinely kept confidential and company lawyers and managers exercised editorial rights (Castleman, 2001). These activities have been likened to those of the tobacco industry, which actively sought to manipulate the scientific discussion on the effects of tobacco and helped sympathetic scientists gain positions where their views could influence public policy (Lancet, 2000). Castleman (2007), for example, has identified numerous instances of corporate defendants in asbestos litigation financing the publication of articles in the scientific literature as part of their defense strategy.

The first significant regulatory breakthroughs were made in the early 1970s in occupational health and safety. An initial wave of governmental regulations of asbestos in North America and Western Europe began systematically replacing voluntary measures that had proven to be ineffective. These pertained primarily to workplace exposure. The 1970 U.S. Occupational Safety and Health Act (OSHA) included asbestos regulation as part of a larger package of worker protection measures. Denmark initiated its ban in 1972, prohibiting spray application of asbestos insulation, and banning the import of crocidolite asbestos. Sweden followed soon after, banning crocidolite in 1975 and prohibiting asbestos cement products in 1976. The Netherlands and France adopted measures regulating asbestos in 1977 (DG-III DEN). In the USA, the Environmental Protection Agency (EPA) finalized regulations in 1989 to phase out most uses of asbestos under the 1976 Toxic Substances Control Act. However, responding to an asbestos industry court challenge, the conservative 5th Circuit Court of Appeals in New Orleans overturned the regulations on the grounds that the EPA had overstepped its authority[3].

The European Union was not far behind the US in its efforts to reduce the hazards of asbestos exposure. As the EPA was finalizing its regulations, the EU was setting in place its own restrictions and in 1991 made the preliminary announce-

[3] Asbestos remains legal in the United States, although banning legislation proposed by US Senator Patty Murray of Washington is believed to stand a good chance of passage. The U.S. Geological Survey estimates the some 26 million pounds of asbestos was imported into the US as recently as 2001 in roofing materials, brake linings, and other products (USGS, 2007).

ment that it would pursue a European ban. That announcement proved overly optimistic. With several asbestos-producing EU member states remaining opposed to a ban, the EU lacked the unanimity necessary to implement a Directive protecting public health. But an abrupt French turnaround shifted the center of gravity among EU member states, reviving the stalled EU effort to implement a near-total ban on asbestos – one which then proceeded with striking speed. France's announcement on July 3, 1996, that it would prohibit "the production, import, and sale of asbestos containing products, notably asbestos cement" (c.f. AI, 1996:1) beginning January 1 of the following year, therefore carried far-reaching repercussions. France had long been among the staunchest supporters of the asbestos industry's arguments that Chrysotile asbestos, considered the least dangerous of six types of asbestos, could be used and managed safely. The EU ban on virtually all types and uses of asbestos was adopted in 1999 and went into effect on January 1, 2005. But it was not without a fight.

3. Leading Actors

The news of France's asbestos ban was received disapprovingly by asbestos producers and in Canada, then the world's third largest exporter of Chrysotile asbestos (Perron, 1999; Morel-àl'Huissier, 1995). Since France's policy reversal would clear the way for the European Commission's proposed asbestos ban, they faced the unhappy prospect of losing their few remaining European export markets (then accounting for roughly 7-8% of Canada's asbestos exports). Moreover, the controversy could have global consequences, since actions in Europe could further erode the credibility of asbestos producers and exporters, risking reductions in the exports to developing countries that had become their bread and butter.

In spite of the central roles of the EU and France on one side, and Canada on the other, European policy developments pertaining to asbestos cannot be explained in terms of a clash of titans or a struggle between nation-states. A diverse array of organized actors helped shape EU policy developments connected with asbestos and developments within key member states. Member states were being lobbied by internal constituencies that included commercial and public health interests in varying mixes. A network of labor, public interest, and victim's organizations pressed for ever-tighter restrictions and advocated a complete ban. The asbestos industry and businesses using asbestos products argued for the continuation of a "safe use" policy. National governments served as proxies for some of these interests, but in addition, pursued their own particular nationalistic concerns. International organizations that deal with health and workplace health and safety standards – the World Health Organization (WHO), the International Labor Organization (ILO), and the joint WHO/ILO sponsored International Program on Chemical Safety (IPCS) played a subtle, yet significant role through making various pronouncements and judgments regarding the scientific evidence on the hazards asbestos poses.

The European Trade Union Confederation, the UK-based transnational network International Ban Asbestos Secretariat (IBAS), and other NGOs such as the ANDEVA, a French NGO working on behalf of asbestos victims, provided a mobilized and focused European constituency to which the European Commission and Parliament felt a need to respond and which at the same time helped to legitimize EU action. They helped make the available scientific evidence relevant and understandable in human terms, enlisted the support of the European Parliament to press the Commission into renewed action, and emphasized how future health costs could undermine Europe's economic health. Victims' organizations in France and the UK mobilized to press for bans in their respective countries, then extended their activities to Brussels to lobby the European Commission and Parliament.

On the other side of the equation, the Canadian government acted as global coordinator for an array of sophisticated lobbying and public relations efforts aimed at protecting international asbestos markets. Canada also supports with its political clout, credibility, and financing, the Asbestos Institute (NRC, AI, 2001), which organizes activities directed toward "promoting the safe use of asbestos". Canada had more at stake than keeping open international markets. While only about 2,500 jobs were directly connected with asbestos exports, virtually all of its asbestos mining and production industry lies within the politically sensitive province of Quebec. Where Canada might have otherwise found it more expedient to obscure or downplay its many lobbying activities on the world stage, it had an essential interest in advertising those activities to the people of Quebec. Consequently, Canada's efforts were remarkably transparent: lobbying activities that might ordinarily be documented only as internal memos and progress reports were publicized as speeches, press releases, and other revealing information. Canada's arguments are representative of the most important arguments made on behalf of the "safe use" of asbestos, mirroring the arguments of commercial interests – particularly asbestos producers.

The European Commission also grappled with a complex array of concerns. Commission documents note that regulatory differences arising from "renegade" actions of member states to regulate or ban asbestos "form a barrier to trade and have a direct impact on the establishment and operation of the common market" (Directive 85/610/EEC). Adding to regulatory inconsistency, Sweden, Finland, and Austria entered the EU in 1995 with bans in place. Challenging their asbestos bans to support market integration would likely have exacerbated the Commission's problems with public legitimacy or perceived "democratic deficit". But while political legitimacy and harmonized market regulation were important goals, the Commission was also clearly motivated by growing public health concerns. Even before 1990, Commission officials were persuaded that the risks posed by asbestos were unacceptable (DG-III – DEN: 3). One might also expect an enhanced sensitivity to the hazards of asbestos on the part of long-time Commission staff – the Berlaymont Building, the Commission's headquarters and a symbol of the European Union, was hurriedly abandoned in December of 1991 after deteriorating asbestos building materials were discovered to be contaminating the Commission's very workspace.

4. EU Regulation of Asbestos Hazards

The EU first regulated the use of asbestos in 1983, marking what would be the initial steps toward a formal EU re-conceptualization of asbestos from that of commercial product with life-saving fire-retardant and other useful properties, to that of a significant health hazard for workers – and eventually for others as well. The action came toward the end of a first international wave of legislation that sought to ameliorate the most obvious asbestos hazards. It sought to reduce exposure to asbestos in the workplace by limiting the emissions of asbestos in the work environment and took steps to restrict the use of certain specific types of asbestos.

This EU-level regulation consisted of two separate Directives. The first (83/477/ECC) sought to establish initial European-level standards for occupational health and safety pertaining specifically to asbestos – seeking to protect workers against asbestos exposure. In this case, the principle of singling out certain "chemical, physical, and biological agents at work" (including asbestos) for extra attention had already been established under the earlier Directive (80/1107/EEC). This directive had two important consequences. First, it helped further anchor a growing European consensus that defined asbestos use as a serious problem in the form of a demonstrated health hazard – in this instance, primarily in its more focused form as an occupational health and safety issue. It was also the area in which the scientific evidence on the issue was most advanced and clear cut. Second, it established a foothold for the EU as an actor with a legitimate role to play in addressing the problems posed by asbestos. This legitimacy was helped by earlier precedent that had already confirmed the EU's general competence to intervene in workplace health and safety issues given that they fell within the scope established in the Treaties.

The language of this first occupational safety and health directive clearly stated that it was not to be seen as a maximum standard that would limit "the right of Member States to apply or introduce laws, regulations or administrative provisions ensuring greater protections for workers" (80/1107/EEC, Article 7), but neither did it establish any real floor. Article 3.2 clarified the optional nature of the Directive, noting that "Member States shall determine the extent, *if any*, to which each of the measures provided...is to apply..." (emphasis added). The Directive did establish the first legal basis for collecting comparable data on the extent to which asbestos dust might be present in workplaces. Employers were required to report on asbestos use in detail, to assess the risk to workers of exposure, to measure such exposure using comparable methods, and to report such information to the responsible authority of the Member State. Exposure limits were specified, with employers required to take steps to both stay within those limits and make additional efforts to minimize overall exposure, and set standards for medical surveillance and procedures for workers who had been exposed. Finally, employers were required to consult with workers and their unions regarding all asbestos-related information and practices. The Directive also took the significant step of prohibiting application by spraying – probably the most clearly dangerous occupational contact with the fiber. But as already indicated, these "requirements" were essentially up to the member states to accept or reject. It is arguable that the most important long-term effect of the legislation was to transform asbestos in EU law from a vague, diffused health threat that might be present to one that was much more clearly specified as to location and volume. Volume was comparable to independent standards and from one location to the next. What might have previously been identified only as the general presence of asbestos contamination could now be evaluated from established points of reference – for example, as being 2, 3, or 50 times the levels considered allowable[4].

The second 1983 directive (Directive 83/478/ECC) introduced the first Community-wide restrictions on the marketing and use of products containing asbestos. This measure also built on the precedent set by the earlier EU directive restricting the sale and use of substances considered to present a particularly serious danger to health or environment (Directive 76/769/EEC). Anchoring itself in the legitimacy established by the earlier legislation, the marketing directive (83/478/EEC) extended to asbestos both the regulatory uniformity and tighter restrictions of the earlier measure, phasing in a ban (with exceptions) on the marketing and use of crocidolite asbestos, the most demonstrably hazardous variety, and requiring warning labels on all products containing asbestos. Two years later, in 1985, a follow-up directive (85/610/EEC) extended that ban to include six specified uses of all other types of asbestos. Included among these newly restricted uses were toys, materials applied by spraying, and retail products in powered form.

The above measures extended into public health, an area in which EU competence was not yet established. However, the rationale that was provided located the actions within the framework of the EU's competence to establish the single market. Part of the argument presented in the Directive for adopting such restrictions was the fact that member states had already enacted a variety of different regulations governing hazardous substances (including arsenic, benzene, mercury, lead, and other materials), and that "*these differences constitute an obstacle to trade and directly affect the establishment and functioning of the common market*" (85/610/EEC, emphasis added). What cannot be determined from that language is the extent to which EU-level asbestos regulation was driven by the desire to protect and enhance uniform regulation within the single market on the one hand, and the extent to which arguing in terms of the market served as both legal basis and legitimating cover for

[4] This would be characterized by Beck (1995) as meaningless – simply reinforcing the status quo. It has another effect, however, and that is to begin to challenge and erode the paradigm that conflates more technology with "progress" by giving level of threat needed form and tangibility.

very real health and environmental concerns, on the other. What is clear is that the market arguments provided the only clear legal basis for action, given that the first EU competence in public health did not come into force until the Maastricht Treaty (1993-Article 129)[5]. It was also significant that a 1987 Directive (87/217/EEC) to reduce and prevent environmental pollution by asbestos explicitly stated that "A Member State may, in order to protect health and the environment, introduce provisions which are more stringent than those of this Directive, in compliance with the conditions laid down by the Treaty" (87/217/EEC, Article 9). Nor can it be considered a coincidence that this "environmental" measure followed the first formal EU competence to address environmental issues.

The pattern of asbestos regulation stands in contrast to environmental policy being developed during the same period, which Vogel (1993) has characterized as seeking to set both floor and ceiling for member state environmental regulation – an approach more consistent with the goal of regulatory harmonization. Given that several member states had already banned asbestos, it is easy to understand how some member states would have wanted to assure that the Directive served only as a floor, and not as a ceiling. Moreover, including such language could be read as a clear invitation to enact more stringent regulations, rather than serving to reduce the kinds of differences that constituted an "obstacle" to the proper functioning of the common market.

The absence of obvious struggle around these early EU-level restrictions suggest that major disagreements had already been resolved in other arenas, both national and international. In fact, initial EU regulations essentially codified what had become a reasonably broad base-level consensus; the need for at least some level of formal legal controls had already been established by science, by experience, and by precedent elsewhere. Roughly similar standards for asbestos use were, for example, adopted by the General Conference of the International Labor Organization (ILO) as the Asbestos Convention in June of 1986. The rules of the Convention paralleled the EU Directives, though they were somewhat weaker: the principle of substitution was introduced, crocidolite asbestos was prohibited, and the spraying of all forms of asbestos was prohibited (ILO, 1986 – C162 Asbestos Convention). The legal force of the Asbestos Convention, however, was contingent upon its ratification by ILO members. The Convention was based in part on a report developed by a committee of scientific experts working with the International Program on Chemical Safety (IPCS)[6], which emphasized that the recognized risks of asbestos could be minimized and managed with adequate controls (Castleman & Lemen, 1998).

[5] It was granted some rudimentary, but formal authority one year later under Article 100a(3) of the Single European Act (1986), which urged the Commission to seek a high level of protection in such matters as related to the single market.

[6] The IPCS is jointly sponsored by the WHO, the ILO, and the UNEP.

The Directives represented concrete steps toward reducing the hazards of asbestos use based on public health concerns, although even then, public interest groups already considered them utterly insufficient to protect public health. Stricter regulations at the national, international, and EU levels served to further legitimize the health hazard claims about asbestos being made by unions, public interest NGOs, and public health officials. But commercial interests also benefited; given the number and variety of asbestos regulations materializing across Europe, the prospect of greater consistency, uniformity and predictability undoubtedly made EU action more appealing to many businesses. The extensive documentation produced by legal battles in the United States and Europe (mostly in the UK), and the general pattern of controls being imposed on both continents (sometimes including the banning of the most hazardous uses and types of asbestos) also suggests that the question of whether or not asbestos should be considered a matter for public regulation had already been conceded in favor of more defensible territory – embracing regulation as a pre-emptive strategy for avoiding just the sort of ban that the EU eventually concluded was necessary. This approach has been characterized as "safe use" by asbestos producers ("controlled use" by sympathetic governments), although the global pattern of asbestos exports and monitoring of use supports the contention that producers were far more interested in the "use" element of the slogan and less concerned about "safe" or "controlled" in practice[7]. In any case, conversion to substitutes in Europe had not yet progressed very far, so among other barriers, opposition from companies that either produced or used asbestos products still presented a formidable obstacle to going further at the time. In addition, the tougher restrictions could be seen as improving the longer-term prospects for asbestos use by better controlling the risks and actual measurable harm connected with its use.

4.1 Restructuring Policy Priorities: Small Changes, Large Consequences

A second round of EU legislation further tightened EU restrictions on asbestos use in 1991. As previously, the new Directives were taken up in the context of new 'market disturbances' – as additional member states implemented increasingly restrictive asbestos regulation at the national level. Labor unions and public interest groups were making demands similar to those lodged earlier, but external conditions had also changed somewhat. Changed conditions contributed to permitting a further tightening of the limits for occupational exposure under Directive 91/382/EEC (amending the earlier Directive 83/477/EEC). EU background doc-

[7] The vast majority of asbestos exports and product use is now in developing countries. While part of the eventual EU and WTO arguments focused on whether the "safe use" of asbestos is practically possible in industrialized countries with a great deal of experience of regulation and monitoring – such regulations are routinely violated in the U.S. (Infante, WTO proceedings, 2001-03-12). According to advocacy groups, effective regulation and monitoring is woefully inadequate – or even non-existent – in many developing countries (ETUC/TUTB; IBAS).

uments suggest that "more scientific evidence about the dangers of asbestos had emerged and safer substitutes had been developed to replace asbestos in many uses" (DG-III, Detailed Explanatory Note: 2). Of these two factors, the development of substitutes is believed by public interest groups to have been most significant[8]. It helped reduce and undermine the network of opposition to a ban, leaving asbestos producers with an eroding base of business allies within the EU. The issue of "more scientific evidence" is discussed further in the next section.

The paradigmatic shift in the EU policy for dealing with asbestos was not announced with the release of a new EU policy paper. Nor was it announced in a news conference hastily put together in response to some political or environmental crisis. Instead, it emerged as a change in emphasis that was subtle in its immediate effect, but which had large long-term consequences. Two steps in particular broke new ground. *All* types of asbestos were classified as Category I carcinogens (defined as substances known to cause cancer in humans) under Directive 67/548/EEC (amended to include asbestos in 1991). This brought asbestos under an established body of regulation pertaining to substances known to cause cancer in humans (this list includes, polychlorinated biphenyl (PCB) and vinyl chloride, and dioxins, among other substances). The second, more radical step was to introduce a complete ban on the marketing and manufacture involving all types of asbestos fibers *with exceptions*. Chrysotile, although still permitted, was prohibited (Directive 91/659/EEC) for an extended list of 14 specified categories of products (including, in addition to the earlier list, roofing felt, low density insulating or soundproofing materials, and most textiles). Products containing chrysotile asbestos that were not listed in the restrictions (including asbestos cement products) were not barred, so although the scope of the chrysotile restrictions had widened a great deal, it remained.

This was not intended to be the end of the line. "Even in 1991, the Commission realised that more needed to be done to restrict the marketing and use of Chrysotile asbestos" (DG-III -DEN:3). The "Detailed Explanatory Note" (DEN) produced by experts within DG Enterprise and Industry in 1996 set the stage for subsequent efforts to close the final loopholes permitting asbestos use. It characterized the asbestos-related policy of the European Community in the early 1990s as one of "controlled use". But it also noted that during the 1990s, an increasing number of Member States considered the Community's policy to be insufficient to protect public health. Commission officials announced their intention with the passage of the 1991 asbestos ban Directive to complete the reversal of its approach from regulating to banning asbestos. It would shift the balance of its policy on asbestos, including chrysotile, from banning particular types of asbestos for specified uses, to

[8] According to one trade union official interviewed, the availability of workable substitutes has been an important element in the erosion of the numbers of commercial enterprises with an interest in continued use of asbestos.

imposing a Community-wide ban on all forms of asbestos while permitting only certain specified exceptions (DG-III. DEN).

The significance of this shift in orientation is that it effectively transferred the burden of proof from public interest groups, unions, and public health officials, to the remaining asbestos producers and manufacturers. Rather than requiring those with health concerns to demonstrate in each individual case and with scientific certainty that a particular type of asbestos or specific application was sufficiently dangerous to prohibit, the producers and manufacturers would have to prove that there were overriding reasons to permit the hazard, and that the hazard could be acceptably managed. The announcement proved premature, however. Plans to complete the transition and phase out asbestos use foundered on the lack of the necessary qualified majority. Later Commission documents make this point diplomatically: "At the adoption of Directive 91/659/EEC, the Commission announced its intention to propose a community-wide ban with exceptions. In 1993, the Commission's services drew up a draft proposal for such a ban. However, after 7 meetings with the Member States it became clear that there were a wide variety of views and that the required qualified majority could not be reached without further background information" (DG-III – DEN: 3).

4.2 Asbestos and "Political Science"

Six years later, the stalemate finally broke. Several factors had changed to permit the movement to ban asbestos to proceed. One element that appears not to have significantly changed is the science underlying the ban proposals. Overall, the scientific evidence on which the arguments were based remained largely the same as before. Nevertheless, Commission documents published in preparation for revisiting the ban referred to new scientific developments in advocating the need for taking a more restrictive approach to asbestos regulation (DG-III – DEN). However, that was probably deemed necessary for reasons of sensitivity to the positions held by certain EU member states (both past and future) and in view of the WTO challenge promised by Canada.

This interpretation was supported by adversaries on both sides of the asbestos debate. Both the European Trade Union Confederation (ETUC) and the International Ban Asbestos Secretariat (IBAS) pointed out that the science has been well established since the 1970s or earlier, and that the "new developments" largely added detail to what was already well-understood about asbestos hazards (ETUC/TUTB; IBAS). Even as early as 1983, official EU documents had pointed out that "current scientific knowledge is not such that a level can be established below which risks to health cease to exist…" (83/487/EEC). (Infante, 2000). Among asbestos supporters, a Canadian Government spokesperson complained that scientific knowledge was not the deciding factor: "We believe the ban in France, and the one proposed by the EU, is not based on sound science and was taken on strictly political grounds" (Benjelloun, 2000:4; AI, 1997). The sentiment was echoed in detail by the Canadian-based Asbestos Institute (AI, 2001). This "political" interpretation might suggest that these policy changes were the fruits of decades of hard work on the part of the public health, labor, environmental, and victims' organizations that have long sought to ban asbestos outright (AI, 1996). But while such organizations played an essential role in raising awareness of the hazards and by demanding reforms, little evidence supports the contention that the EU ban was "political" in the sense that the Asbestos Institute sought to portray – that grassroots organizations intimidated governments into approving more restrictive regulation. Notwithstanding the arguments about scientific progress made in Commission documents, it was indeed the politics that had changed. The political constellation around the asbestos issue had changed dramatically. Equally important was the changed conceptual framework with which the scientific evidence was to be judged.

The network of actors with a stake in supporting the continued use of asbestos had seriously eroded. European commercial enterprises, for example, had increasingly switched to substitutes. This changeover was likely driven in part by a desire to use safer materials, but it also appears that many businesses expected a ban eventually to be adopted and sought to make the transition on their own schedule rather than waiting to be forced. An example of one such company was ETERNIT, a Belgian-based company and large producer of building materials including fiber cement and board products. Their conversion to substitutes, while it did not occur until after the regulatory actions of the early 1990s, permitted the company to phase out their manufacturing of asbestos products before the ban took place and thus escape economic consequences of delaying the changeover until forced. Their work expanded to include business connected to the handling and removal of asbestos. ETERNIT's position shifted from that of being harmed by a ban to being positioned to benefit. Ironically, at least some of their current work entails the removal of products that they themselves manufactured and/or installed. The policy effect of such developments, however, was that such defections substantially undermined the network of political support available within Europe for the asbestos producers to draw on.

Another factor with clearly political consequences was that several member states chose not to wait for "further background information", to act on their own concerns that existing regulation was insufficient to protect public health. At the EU level, that same public health reasoning pressed for once again taking up the issue of closing Europe's borders to the import of new asbestos or asbestos-containing products. But increasingly stringent national regulation carried an added incentive: as member states took matters into their own hands, they "successively imposed further national restrictions on products not covered by harmonization, *creating disunity in the Internal Market*" (DG-III, DGN:3 emphasis added). This was a problem that could leak over into other areas of EU trade policy, raising the question of whether the product in question was worth the precedent-setting that takes place with members taking regulation regarding market matters into their own hands. The EU faced a trade-off between intervening in market affairs to ban a particular product or accepting increased inconsistency in internal market regulations as member states independently decided to prioritize public health principles. With fewer European allies available for the asbestos industry to enlist, the balance on this question shifted toward supporting market intervention to ban asbestos.

Of all the "political" factors influencing EU action on asbestos in the 1990s, the head count among member states was arguably the most important. When in 1997 the Commission once again took up the question of banning asbestos, it was this time armed with the necessary qualified majority. Austria, Sweden, and Finland had joined the EU in 1995 with asbestos bans already in place. By the time the Commission revisited an across the board ban on asbestos products, Belgium had followed France's lead in adopting its own ban in 1998, and three other member states (the UK, Ireland, and Luxembourg) had also indicated their support. The three remaining holdouts, Spain, Portugal, and Greece, continued to oppose to any regulatory change "for scientific and technical reasons and because the economic effects it would have on their asbestos-cement industries" (DG-III, DEN: 3).

The UK and France, struggling with the domestic political and health consequences of asbestos, were key to reviving the European Commission's stalled efforts to institute a complete ban. A European-level ban became important enough to the British government that it was at one point considered a top priority of the British Presidency of the EU, also making the UK a primary target of Canada in its bid to deflect such efforts. Tony Blair and his Labour Party had made unequivocal promises during 1996 elections that they intended to ban further asbestos use. After their election success, indications were that the new Labour government would quickly implement a ban. But equivocation and backpedaling by the Health and Safety Executive (HSW) soon raised doubts about the government's resolve. In fact, Canada had launched its lobbying effort with all the force it could muster, sending delegations of trade union members, public officials, and scientists to the UK to argue against the ban. British journalists were treated to expense-paid study visits to Canada to be educated about Canada's "safe use" principle, which included visits to the affected communities and tours of the mines. According to an interview with a British EU official within DG Enterprise and Industry, Canada's lobbying efforts "went all the way up the Prime Minister level." Canada's efforts appear to have had a significant affect, though not in the end result. The British ban was delayed, but eventually passed as a formality under the protection of the EU ban on asbestos.

The French turnabout on asbestos was part of a broader shift in French public policy regarding the management of risk, linked to a domestic policy crisis generated by the mid-1980s contamination of France's blood supply with the AIDS virus[9]. But the French government response was also pushed along by asbestos related scandals on the home front. As with the UK, Canada attempted to intervene to forestall the ban, hoping to take advantage of cultural and linguistic ties with France. However, in all probability, the Canadians underestimated the sense of vulnerability felt by many French officials. Nothing that Canada could offer – or threaten – could quite compare to the potential legal and political consequences at home of failing to act responsibly. France's reversal helped make an EU ban feasible, but once France had made its decision, it also needed help. Canada had made clear its intention to challenge the French decision at the WTO. A Europe-wide ban would lend important legitimacy and crucial support to the French ban.

4.3 Institutionalizing the New Paradigm: Closing European Borders

Important political, economic, and social considerations remained. One was the continued opposition of three member states, including Greece, Spain, and Portugal, and the likely consequences in terms of unemployment and other economic effects. They argued that the EU ban presented no problem to nations that had already implemented a ban, and that they had been able to adopt their bans on their own terms in order to minimize the disruptive effects. Another problem was the certainty of a WTO challenge by Canada, which if successful, could force the EU to withdraw its ban. These factors required the ban to be approached with sensitivity to the hardships likely to be faced by the three dissenting member states and people in the affected industries. They also required the "proof" – the scientific data upon which the ban was to be based – to be assembled with Canadian arguments in mind.

The internal political, economic, and social considerations of implementing a complete ban were taken up in the process of meetings and deliberations through which the final Directive was developed. Officials from DG Enterprise and Industry made visits to mines and factories where owners and employees who would be adversely affected in member states could express their disagreement. On one visit, workers (under the watchful eye of their employers) requested the delegation members and the EU to let them make their own choices and take their own risks[10] – unemployment with few other options would be the likely consequence of a ban. This is an obvious problems, and the prospect of taking out of workers' hands decisions about the their occupational risks and effectively putting people out of work

[9] More than 4000 people were infected, and over 1000 of them had died as of the time of the trial and conviction of four senior French health officials deemed responsible for failing to take appropriate action based on available knowledge (ETC-1999/02/09, see also Guardian-1999/02/06). Former Prime Minister Laurent Fabius and two cabinet members were charged and acquitted amid much controversy, but the impression the case made on public officials was nevertheless quite powerful.

[10] This account was provided by an observer present at the meeting.

so deliberately, provided a sympathetic portrait of the disadvantages of the decision being prepared. However, such requests overlooked the obvious lack of choice offered to people exposed "downstream" and often without their knowledge – a group that has often included the very families the workers are laboring to support.

In practice, these human and economic concerns were addressed by including a five-year phase-in period to permit more time for adaptation and conversion to substitutes in Greece, Portugal, & Spain. This phase-in period was based in part on a study commissioned by DG Enterprise and Industry to examine the economic impact on the countries in question. The study determined that there would be no substantial additional benefits from a longer phase-in period (DG III-DEN).

The Commission's handling of the scientific issues connected with the ban was directed to both the internal and external concerns. Strong evidence was clearly necessary to justify imposing additional economic hardships on people in member states who were perhaps least prepared to manage them. Given Canada's promised WTO challenge, however, it was clear that the scientific evidence would eventually be judged against the standards and obligations established under international agreements, including the GATT and the WTO.

In view of the importance of the scientific data to buttress the eventual political decisions regarding the management of risk, the Commission services, in this instance, DG Enterprise and Industry (formerly DG III), began the process of marshalling the scientific facts behind the ban. It began with the report by INSERM, (the French scientific agency that had been responsible for evaluating the risks of asbestos) a report the Canadian-based trade group the Asbestos Institute had already labeled as both "flawed" and "political". The Commission services also ordered a review of all the existing literature on the epidemiology and risks of asbestos. This represented no new research, both because of the time and expense that would have been required for the Commission to establish its own research program. Neither was it necessary in the view of the Commission and others – the level of certainty about the risks of asbestos was already considered quite sufficient to justify the ban being proposed.

The report was then referred to the Commission's own Scientific Committee on Toxicity, Ecotoxicity and the Environment (CSTEE)[11] for review and an opinion regarding the conclusions of the ERM report. Canada's lobbying efforts were successful in redirecting the committee's attention. A lengthy submission by Canadian scientists succeeded in reframing the context of the questions posed by the Commission – away from the uncertainties inherent in public policy decisions and toward the remaining areas of scientific uncertainty. The CSTEE conclusion was that "the ERM Report provides no new evidence which indicates that a change in the risk assessment for Chrysotile is appropriate" (CSTEE opinion of 2/9/98). In fact,

[11] The CSTEE operates under the supervision of DG SANCO – Public Health and Consumer Protection.

this conclusion was largely irrelevant to the course of action being contemplated by the Commission for two reasons: first, it ignored the question of whether there were less hazardous substitutes available. Second, it was not so much any change in risk that was motivating the proposed ban, but rather a different approach to dealing with the level of risk that had already been established. Nevertheless, this result put the Commission in the awkward position of choosing between accepting further delays, or appearing to ignore the conclusions of its own scientific committee and thereby weakening an important basis of its arguments. Given the circumstances, accepting delay appeared to be the wiser course.

Commission officials responded creatively, by making a second and much more specific request for an opinion from the Committee – this time for an analysis of the safety/hazard of substitute products relative to the hazards of asbestos. The request for the follow up opinion read: "on the basis of the available data, do any of the following substitute fibres pose an equal or greater risk to human health than chrysotile asbestos? Cellulose fibres? PVA fibres? P-aramid fibres?" (CSTEE Minutes, 1999/01/18). Given a much less open-ended remit, the conclusion of the second CSTEE opinion read quite differently than the first: "A major concern with fibres is their carcinogenic potential. There is sufficient evidence that all forms of asbestos, including Chrysotile, are carcinogenic to man. No evidence of fibre-caused cancer occurrence in man is available for any of the three candidate substitutes…" (CSTEE, 1998/09/15).

4.4 Defending Public Health Priorities at the WTO

While the WTO challenge was formally directed at France's ban (and not that enacted by the EU), the decisions would still have clear consequences for the EU ban; the bans were similar and based on the same scientific evidence and reasoning. In essence, the EU was defending its own ban by proxy.

The fundamental assumptions that guide the WTO complaint procedures are precisely those that had to be overcome in order to first regulate asbestos, then prohibit it. The starting assumption is that such actions represent a barrier to trade unless proven otherwise. The burden of proof lies with the party that wishes to prioritize some non-market benefit over free trade, while the official standard remains that of scientific certainty. This is seen as a serious problem by observers who argue that trade regulations must be balanced by attention to other competing priorities, particularly needs for improved health and environmental protection (Castleman, 2002, 1999b).

The final decision that upheld the prioritization of public health concerns came in spite of the deck being stacked against such a finding. A variety of related factors conspired to make this possible. The WTO panel itself faced contradictory choices regarding the rules under which to take up the case. Not surprisingly given the criticism that has been directed at the trade body, the appellate body was also concerned about the consequences of the case for WTO. Even so, the favorable decision hinged at least in part on the unanimity of experts (a first, and probably a mistake on the part of Canada – it was in the selection of experts that the case was won (by the EU) and lost (by Canada). It is also significant that the Precautionary Principle was *not* a factor in the legal case – lawyers representing the EU wanted to present the French/European decision to implement an asbestos ban as entailing no scientific uncertainty (even though the Precautionary Principle was relevant to the EU legislation – the asbestos case contributed to its concrete development and articulation, and the principle was applied in approaching the remaining uncertainties)[12]. In the end, the WTO declined to uphold the Canadian complaint, although the decision itself was not an unequivocal victory for supporters of the ban. The EU asbestos ban became effective on January 1, 2005.

5. Evolution and Revolution in Asbestos Regulation

The EU asbestos regulation case offers practical lessons about the EU and its policy processes, as well as theoretical insights. The steps from first legislative mention of asbestos in 1980 to the initial decision to pursue an asbestos ban in 1991 can be considered part of a larger policy learning process in which the EU systematically redefined asbestos as a threat to workers and the general public, established its legitimacy and authority to act on the problem, and then shifted its regulatory presumptions from general acceptance with exceptions to prohibition of products containing asbestos with exceptions. In the early stages, it was a largely negotiated process in which EU regulation represented the institutionalization of what largely had become consensus at the national level and within international organizations. Here, the EU echoed the policy examples set in the U.S., in EU member states, or international bodies such as the ILO. Although much of the early action on asbestos was facilitated by the influence of changes taking place elsewhere, Commission officials and staff learned important lessons from their experience. This was particularly true as negotiations broke down in 1991, giving way to conflict and stalemate. In grappling with the various public health, economic, and political problems posed by asbestos use, the Commission encountered obstacles to bringing European policy in line with its own redefinition of asbestos as a serious health threat, and which by its very nature could not be managed with "safe use" strategies that applied at best only to a small portion of the product life-cycle. These factors became part of a distinctively EU story when the Commission broke fresh ground in 1991, announcing its intention to completely ban the import and use of asbestos within European borders, following a similar ban by the U.S. Environmental Protection Agency (although as noted above, the US ban was overturned by the courts). The EU stepped into a position of global leadership on the issue as it even-

[12] The preparations and strategies for the WTO defense were described in an interview with a high-level member of the EU's legal team.

tually enacted the ban and subsequently took up the defense of the French ban (and indirectly, its own) at the WTO.

The EU effort to ban asbestos not only generated new conflicts between Canada and its European trade partners, it brought the new goals pursued by European officials into direct conflict with the institutionalized core assumptions, goals and rules of the policy paradigm that has guided the broader EU chemicals policy in which it is embedded. That paradigm has emphasized market integration, economic development, and the corrective capacity of market mechanisms. It was structured by taken-for-granted assumptions about how uncertainty and possible hazards are to be dealt with, where the balance of benefits and risks are distributed by policymaking activities, which actors must shoulder the respective burdens of proof, and that scientific unanimity constitutes the standard that must be met to deliver proof. The influence of market interests tended to encourage obscuring or misrepresenting asbestos hazards. Self-interested actors chose to withhold or downplay relevant knowledge, leading to severe economic and public health consequences. Political pressures to maintain the status quo both internally and externally were also important. In order to move forward with its ban, the EU was forced, in effect, to reorder the policy priorities it applied to asbestos and reverse its own operating assumptions, then defend that reversal.

The striking paradox in the asbestos case is that it is an instance in which regulators found themselves seeking to protect the single European market for a specific category of products by eliminating one of those products. The challenge became one of how to justify a ban in the larger context of the formal rules governing EU policymaking. What are the various rule-defined conditions that must be met in order to legitimately remove a product from the market? A policy paradigm that emphasizes the commercial characteristics of market products, and the self-correcting capacity of markets to resolve problems, sets a high hurdle to clear before adopting regulatory measures.

An asbestos ban was logically inconsistent with the institutionalized, broadly market-oriented paradigmatic framework for producing regulations in the EU, but is consistent with the revised principles announced in the Chemicals White Paper. Legislating a ban on a commercial product for public health reasons proved difficult. First, it had to be framed as an exceptional case within the broader chemicals policy – and as a threat to the single market project. This enabled the ban to be pursued via the qualified majority voting procedure rather than the unanimity required for non-market measures. Had the Commission's effort to implement a ban in the early 1990s been successful, the matter might have ended there. However, given that the EU and its member states are party to an international-level set of agreements about policy principles embodied in the WTO, the EU was forced to approach its ban more systematically by addressing the fundamental principles under which the policy was passed and defended at the WTO in order to have a reasonable chance to define the measures not as a barrier to trade, but as necessary steps to ensure the protection of public health.

5.1 Paradigm shifts and Institutional Change

Three prominent themes are apparent in the emergence and transformation of EU policy on asbestos. The first is the process of paradigm shift in the form of a reframing and reconceptualization of asbestos from durable and inexpensive fireproof building material, to a health hazard for unprotected workers, to a widespread public health hazard and confirmed killer. The second thread is the process of institutionalization and legitimization of that reconceptualization via institutional changes (in the form of EU regulations) that first seek to mitigate the unwanted side effects of asbestos, but eventually bar its use altogether. The third is the process of organized interests aligning themselves for and against the use of asbestos, the ways in which each deployed different types of knowledge about asbestos to promote their respective positions, and the eventual erosion of the interests that benefit economically from its use. One salient element of this story is the way in which these three themes are linked through social struggle over which characteristics of asbestos are emphasized and acted upon, and over the ways in which it was given expression in EU law. Powerful interests engaged to establish or undermine various claims of hazard and risk on the one hand, and to mobilize the forms of institutional power to which they had access on the other. One obvious problem in this case was that the very same physical properties that made asbestos useful proved to be a serious longer-term hazard.

As we argue here, the EU paradigm shift regarding asbestos entailed not only a reframing and reconceptualization of what asbestos represented, but also of how to deal with it. This remained an incremental process even as the critical reversal of principles took place in the form of a shift from a starting assumption that asbestos was an acceptable product (albeit with increasing restrictions) to an assumption that was not (except under specific limited circumstances). This shift also entailed a reversal of the burden of proof, shifting the responsibility for providing evidence for making exceptions from actors concerned with worker and public health to those interested in marketing or using the product. In terms of the more broadly applicable set of principles being applied, this shift also entailed relocating the asbestos question from the sphere of issues dealing primarily with market competition to a sphere primarily focused on human health. In effect, the logic of how to deal with and regulate asbestos fundamentally changed.

The second theme, regarding the process of institutionalization, is that it can be distinguished as a separate process that interacted with the paradigm change process. We argue this separation based on a straightforward logic. Not only was the EU asbestos ban adopted many years after the announcement that the Commission would seek agreement among member states on such a ban. The supermajority of member states required to adopt the ban meant that a conceptual change that had already been embraced by a majority of interested parties (and arguably the vast majority Europeans) had to wait to be formally adopted. This of course raises the question of which actors must embrace a revised set of guiding principles for one to constitute that a paradigm shift has taken place. Here we leave the more subtle nuances of that question for later exploration and point to the fact that the institutional embodiment of the paradigmatic shift was delayed for a significant period of time by a small minority. Arguing that paradigmatic and systemic shift are analytically separate is not to say that they do not influence one another. As we have already noted, there are important feedback effects. The institutional changes leading up to adoption of fundamentally different guiding principles several times served to legitimize the contention that the evidence was inconsistent with asbestos supporters "safe use" arguments. This supported the claims made by public health interests that there were far too many anomalies in asbestos industry efforts to account for or explain away evidence of asbestos related disease and disability.

The third theoretical theme focuses on the role of actors, particularly organized and resource rich actors, in both the above processes. We see that paradigmatic and institutional change are by no means a natural byproduct of scientific discoveries – or even what could be reasonably characterized as widespread scientific consensus. The scientific evidence and its interpretation – its relevance to policy areas outside of science, and the meaning of the measure of scientific uncertainty and doubt that must always remain – all are potential areas of contention between societal actors. In this instance, the nature of organized actors clearly spanned the multi-level spectrum, ranging from local to international, and included not only states, but also social movement-type organizations, international organizations, and the EU's particular form of supra-national governance. In part due to the diversity of organized actors engaged in this struggle, all three of these possible areas of contention involving scientific knowledge were drawn in. Finally, the role of logical inconsistency in undermining a paradigmatic model clearly varies based on which actors succeed in defining the aspects of an issue or phenomenon that receives attention – especially if one concurs with Baumgartner and Jones (2005) that public and policymaker attention are an arguably scarce resource. A focus on remaining uncertainty versus certainty tends to emphasize very different problems. Similarly, promoting "safe use" drew attention to mining and manufacturing safety while actively ignoring exposures resulting from the limited life-span of asbestos products or from unknowing misuse by end-users misuse. Inconsistency presents little problem where it is not the focus of attention (Neuman and Tabak, 2003). The asbestos case demonstrates how paradigm politics entails a struggle among interested actors to define by directing and redirecting attention.

6. Concluding Remarks

The asbestos case illustrates the evolutionary, punctuated disequilibrium that has contributed to a major reorientation of EU policy pertaining to risk regulation and environment – developments also illustrated in other cases examined in this volume. The struggles over asbestos were part of a broader long-term process that included disputes over the interpretation of scientific evidence, the power of economic interests, and the Commission's interests in furthering European integration. Among the more interesting factors was the confluence of interests that put the EU in the position of protecting the integrity of its single market regulatory framework by prioritizing and protecting public health. The very weakness of the EU in terms of public legitimacy and "democratic deficits" helped reinforce that path rather than removing regulations protecting public health. In legal terms, framing of the issue as protecting the regulatory consistency of the internal market permitted the ban to be passed using a qualified majority rather than having to clear the higher – and in this case impossible – threshold of unanimity. These changes would have been interesting even if they had they simply represented isolated changes. However, they have been part of a broader, highly significant policy reorientation of EU risk regulation impelled by developments including the BSE crisis (Carson, 2004), and by a long-term evolution of EU environmental policy and chemicals regulation.

The development of EU asbestos regulation has shadowed the development of the larger body of chemicals regulation of which it is a part. As a rule, it has been subject to the same policy assumptions and standards of proof, the same policy authority as defined in the successive Treaties. Changes in both of these areas have been hotly contested. As was the case with asbestos, the vast majority of the chemical products and substances in use today were placed on the market under an assumption of acceptability: that the various benefits of a new product outweighed the risks of its use in the absence of definitive evidence to the contrary. That assumption has been supported and reinforced by the general lack of comprehensive and publicly available information regarding the hazard and risk properties of the substances. It is reinforced by the fact that many of the harmful effects are long term in nature, generated by overall bioaccumulation or by the fact that these substances can escape over time from the products containing them.

Such developments would seem to argue against conclusions such as Beck's (1995) that incremental changes are meaningless, or at best, of little value. His point that such changes may only support the established order is well taken. However, the way in which the EU asbestos case unfolded over time argues that incremental changes may either support the established order or may serve to legitimize critiques, and that these effects may differ at different points in time. Moreover, the nature of the effect is influenced by the degree to which organized actors who are system critics mobilize and how they construct their strategies. It is arguably a complex chess game in which the kinds of paradigmatic and system shift embodied in the EU asbestos case are influenced by how skillfully the involved actors play out their respective strategies.

CHAPTER 10

The "REACH" Saga: A Revolution in Regulating Chemicals[1]

Tom R. Burns, Dolores Calvo, and Marcus Carson

1. Introduction

The comprehensive EU chemical regulation policy – REACH[2] – in effect since June, 2007 was one of the most radical and contentious policy initiatives of the EU, involving almost 10 years of debate, mobilization, struggle, and negotiations between industry, the Council of the European Union, the Parliament, and the Commission, labor unions as well as industry, environmental, consumer and animal rights NGOs, among others. Arguably never has a public policy process in the EU involved so many players with such intensity. Why so much energy and contentiousness? Chemicals, which permeate all aspects of our lives, went from being thousands of more or less presumably "neutral" substances to being the objects of intense inquiry – a systematic "inquisition of chemicals" in Europe (which includes imports). After some 200 years of laissez faire, what some would call a "totalitarian regime" was imposed to identify, register, assess hazards and risks, authorize and judge safe or not so safe, unsafe, or possibly subject to banning a chemical from EU markets.

We should bear in mind the pervasiveness of chemicals in our lives.[3] And most of up to 99% of the chemicals produced and sold in Europe as well as imported have never been tested for their impact on human health and the environment. Thousands of untested chemicals are used in a vast array of everyday consumer products. Numerous chemicals are introduced in food and drink chains. Some of the substances are strongly suspected of causing health problems including cancer, reproductive and genetic disruptions. In addition, many pollute the environment

---

[1] In writing this overview, we have drawn heavily on the excellent book by Gunnar Lind (2004). Also important has been the valuable woork of Chapman (2007) as well as Hansen and Blainey (2006).

[2] REACH is an acronym for "registration, evaluation, authorization and restriction of chemicals."

[3] They cover agricultural chemicals including fertilisers, biocides, food additives, insecticides, pesticides, herbicides, etc; biotechnologies, chlorine, bromines, fluorides (and other halogens), colorants (for food, textiles, plastics, dyes, among others); detergents, oleochemicals (fatty acids, glycerines, alcohols, fatty nitrites and their derivatives; paints, coatings and adhesives, petrochemistry (main suppliers of raw materials and intermediaries to most of the chemical industry; plastics; lead oxide, photographic chemicals; munitions; chemical weapons (see Lind, 2004:20).

and damage wild life. The few that have been tested and regulated depend on the initiative of regulators. The latter must prove toxic, carciogenic, reproductive impacts if the chemicals are to be regulated at all.

At the same time, the chemicals industry is central to the European economy, GDP, economic growth and jobs (this explains also some of the politics, which we will discuss later). Europe is the world's largest producer of chemicals, making up approximately 35 percent of global sales (most exports go to the USA and Asia). The industry is the largest industrial sector in Europe. It employs somewhat less than 2 million people but up to 3 million jobs are dependent on it (Lind, 2004).[4]

In the context of almost 10 years of concern and struggle to regulate the EU chemical industry, the EU could announce at the end of 2006 (December 18) that (see Appendix 2 for complete document):[5]

> *After three years of negotiations, the Council adopted today by unanimity REACH (registration, evaluation, authorisation and restriction of chemicals) legislation, the cornerstone of the new European chemicals policy which replaces around 40 legislative instruments currently in force. In the framework of the co-decision procedure, negotiations between the Council and the European Parliament took place over the last three months in order to reach an agreement …that … could enter into force on 1 June 2007.*

The *compromise package* was agreed upon in the informal trilogue on 30 November 2006 and was adopted by the Plenary of the European Parliament on 13 December 2006.

The EU chemicals policy shift was partly quantitative (comprehensiveness), partly qualitative (changes in responsibilities, relationships, methods). As the Commission's document Reach in brief points out, the REACH system represents a significant policy shift in a number of respects (European Commission 2007:3-5): REACH reallocates responsibilities from public authorities to companies when it comes to making available information about substances and risk assessments. Manufacturers and importers have to provide critical information about substances they place on the market. The new system establishes a single set of rules for both existing and new chemical substances. REACH also includes downstream users/producers in the exchange of information, this being a key innovation). The paradigmatic shift consisted basically in the transformation of several key principles and priorities. Prior to REACH it was assumed that products which were already on the market were safe unless proven otherwise – and the burden of proof was on consumers, government authorities, and NGOs.

---

[4] The major EU chemical producing nations are Germany, France, Italy and Britain. The two largests chemical companies in the world are German (BASF and Bayer) followed by a number of US companies (Dow Chemical, DuPont, ExxonMobil). In addition to its multi-nationals (not only Germany but British and Dutch companies such as British Petroleum and Shell and French (Atofina, 6th in size in the world)), Europe has around 25,000 small and medium-sized companies with less than 500 employees.

[5] REACH involved Regulation (EC) No 1907/2006; Directive 2006/121/EC. The new system came into force on June 1st, 2007 (DG Environment 2008a), replacing Directive 67/548/EEC and all its amendments (DG Environment 2008b; European Commission 2007: 17-18).

REACH calls for the reporting and eventual regulation of tens of thousands of chemicals (the official announcement refers up to 30,000). They will be required to be registered, tested (if they have not already been so) and authorized in the case that the chemicals are produced and sold in substantial quantities. Hazards must be identified and analyzed. Among the hazards are "pathological, carcogenic, reproductive and/or genetic dangers." In general, chemicals which are considered hazards to human health or to the environment must be managed in special ways, or possibly even be banned.

REACH's radicality has been pointed up, in part, by the extreme reactions of the industry and several heads of state including the US Government and key EU member states. This chapter examines the background, the contentious process which led up to the REACH legislation, and the dimensions which distinguish pre-REACH policy from REACH and explains this unique accomplishment, against all odds.

2. Pre-REACH Chemical Policy

In 2001 when the White Paper "Strategy for a future Chemicals Policy" (COM(2001) 88 final) was presented, EU chemical regulation was based on a hodgepodge of different Directives and Regulations (European Commission, 2007). The main EU legal instruments were: the Directive 67/548/EEC on the *classification, packaging and labelling of dangerous substances*; Directive 88/379/EEC on the *classification, packaging and labelling of dangerous preparations*;[6] Regulation (EEC) 793/93 on the *evaluation and control of the risks of existing substances*; and Directive 76/769/EEC on the *restrictions on the marketing and use of certain dangerous substances and preparations*.[7]

The 6th amendment in 1979 (Directive 79/831/EEC) introduced the principle of "the protection of the environment from the dangerous effects of substances". It also established a notification procedure for *new substances* and required all "existing" substances to be listed in the European Inventory of Existing Commercial Chemical Substances (EINECS). This inventory would list all substances on the market from before September 18th, 1981.[8]

---

[6] "Preparations" consist of mixtures of substances.

[7] The Council Directive 67/548/EEC of June 27th, 1967 on the approximation of laws, regulations and administrative provisions relating to the classification, packaging and labelling of dangerous substances aimed at the approximation of laws, regulations and administrative provisions of Member States to secure the functioning of the common market and the protection of health and safety (specially for workers in contact with dangerous substances) (67/548/EEC). This first EU Directive on chemicals was several times amended.

[8] All chemical substances reported as marketed before this threshold date of 1981 were defined as "existing" substances (perhaps as many as 100.000 different substances by 1981), while substances introduced in the market after the date (more than 3800) were denominated "new" and added to the European List of Notified Chemical Substances (ELINCS) (DG Environment 2008b; European Commission 2007: 3).

In 1992 the 7th amendment of the Directive (92/32/EEC) set the requirement of "risk assessment" in the case of new substances. Until then no assessment of risks was required (Chapman 2007: 64). A system of risk assessment for existing substances was introduced afterwards by the 1993 Regulation (793/93). In both cases, regulators were in charge of risk assessment. Regulation 793/93 required producers and importers to obtain information about the substances; however, in case of lack of data, they were not obliged to conduct further tests or to obtain and present required information (Chapman 2007: 64-65).

"Existing substances" were produced, imported and marketed even if there was little or no information about their hazards. Absence of data about an existing substance was not a sufficient reason for restrictions on production and import of this substance (Chapman 2007: 65). The marketing of a substance could be restricted only if an assessment of risk had been conducted by regulators. And before a risk assessment could be carried out, there had to be information suggesting that the substance *might* cause harm and to place it on a priority list for testing.

A series of White Papers signalled the beginning of the end of this patchwork of different Directives and Regulations. The White Paper "Strategy for a future Chemicals Policy" (COM(2001) 88 final), the White Paper on Environmental Liability (COM(2000) 66 final), and the Communication from the Commission on the Precautionary Principle (COM(2000) 1) were setting the stage for a new EU approach to regulation of chemical substances (Carson 2004). In a certain sense, these papers and the socio-political pressures driving them were the cognitive-normative beginnings of a major policy paradigm shift.

3. The Context of the REACH Initiative: Growing International Attention and Regulatory Efforts

From the 1970s there was rapidly increasing global awareness and concern about damage to the environment – the UN Stockholm Conference on the Human Environment (UNCHE) in 1972 is symbolic. In 1972 the "Stockholm Declaration" was formulated. For the first time long-term chemical pollution was officially addressed internationally – it was recognised as an issue of global concern. At the conference, a number of guiding principles for the protection of the environment were adopted. These have been critical in the successive development of other instruments (Lind, 2004: 39).[9] In 1973 (elaborated 1978) there was global agreement on regulation of the pollution from ships (MARPOL). Also, the Convention on the Protection of the Marine Environment of the Baltic Sea Area (HELCOM) was signed in Helsinki in 1974 by all the Baltic coastal states. There were other major internatioinal agreements as well as national developments. Private initiatives also

[9] Another important outcome of this conference was the agreement to create a new programme for global environmental protection under the United Nations: UNEP.

were launched. The International Council of Chemical Associations (ICCA) established "Responsible Care" in 1985.[10]

Diagram 10.1: Time Trends of International Multilateral Environmental Agreements by Agreement Type (1879-2002).

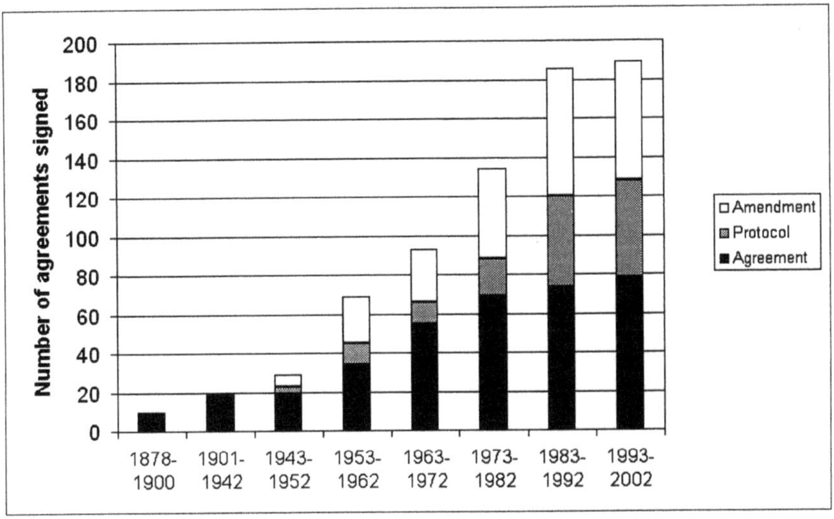

Diagram source: Ronald B. Mitchell. 2002-2009. International Environmental Agreements Database Project (Version 2007.1). Available at: http://iea.uoregon.edu/. Date accessed: 7 August 2009

In the 1990s, a period of intensive international and national activity relating to chemicals emerged. Already in 1990 the OECD deveoped its "High Production Volume Programme" concerning large-volume chemical products. It stressed that the effects of many of these chemicals were little known, and that this ignorance should be addressed. The Rio Declaration and Agenda 21 were published in 1992. The aims were to reduce unsustainable consumption patterns and to establish precautionary principles. Agenda 21, when it concerned chemicals, was to deal with, among other problems, chemical hazards to human health, the atmosphere, agricul-

[10] These and other private, voluntary initiatives did not lead very far, however (although arguably they contributed to the growing attention to and concern about chemicals). For instance, in 1997, the International Federation of Chemical, Energy, Mine and General Workers' Union (ICEM) presented a survey showing that Responsible Care "had no impact on most of the world's chemical workers;" ICEM concluded that "the voluntary nature of the Responsible Care programme may mean that it is more a public relations exercise" (cited in Lind, 2004:47). Industry initiatives such as "Stakeholder Dialogues" of 1999 and 2000 gave no results either. The extraordinary developments under the UN as well as the EU (in particular, the formation of REACH) simply crowded out or overwhelmed these weak industry initiatives.

ture, and water as well as other areas such as hazard waste. Passage of the OSPAR Convention (1992)[11] also took place in this period – it determined to eliminate the pollution of the North-East Atlantic. Another important development was the launching of negotiations in the mid-1990s to eliminate releases of persistent organic pollutants (POP). The negotiations focused on the 12 most hazardous substances – the "Dirty Dozen". In a historic agreement (the Stockholm Convention or the POPs Treaty) in Stockholm in May 2001, the nations of the world for the first time agreed to eliminate *all releases of particular chemical substances* (Lind, 2004: 40).[12] Earlier at Kyoto, 1997, 3 of the greenhouse gases that were agreed to be regulated are man-made chemicals: HFCs, PFCs, and SF6.[13]

Following several major efforts in the 1970s, one can trace a cascade of initiatives and accomplishments from the 1980s through the 1990s, which set the stage for major policy initiatives such as the directives indicated below as well as the REACH initiative taking place in the 2000s (this is a limited selection, for suggestive purposes only).

1988: OECD. Chemical Accidents Programme (addresses prevention, preparedness and response related to accidents involving hazardous chemical substances.
1990: OECD. High Production Volume (HPV) and SIDS Programme. Voluntary programme to look at chemicals introduce in more than 1000 tonnes (about 5000 estimated) while little is known about the toxicity for some 75-85% of them.
1992: Contracting parties at UNCED agree to address the threat from chemicals.
1992: OSPAR Convention (see text).
1993: OECD: Pollutant Release and Transfer Registers (in close cooperation with WHO, UNEP, IPCS, UNITAR).
1994: OECD Pesticides and Biocides Programme.
1995: Esjberg Declaration. Baltic countries agree to phase out releases of hazardous substances in the North Sea within one generation (25 years).
1998: Founding moments of REACH idea.
2001: Stockholm Convention on POPs (see text).
2001: Commission presents "White Paper on a Strategy for Future Chemicals Policy".

In addition to REACH, there were a number of other major EU initiatives and developments which were part of a context of critical assessment and movement to establish systematic regulation of chemicals, for instance:

The EU Cosmetics Directive (applying to one of the major industries in Europe). In January 2003, the European Union amended its cosmetics directive

[11] The OSPAR Convention, adopted in 1992, concerned the Protection of the Marine Environment of the North-East Atlantic (from Gilbraltar to northern Norway and Russia.

[12] Lind (2004:40) hopes and expects that eventually other POPs are likely to be added to the list to be banned globally.

[13] Hydrofluorocarbons (HFCs) are composed entirely of carbon, hydrogen, and fluorine; perfluorocarbons (PFCs) are man-made compounds containing of fluorine and carbon; sulphurhexafluoride (SF6) is another man-made heavy gas consisting of suphur and fluoride.

from 1976 (76/768/EEC) to ban from cosmetics the use of chemicals that are known or strongly suspected of causing cancer, mutation or birth defects. The amendment went into force in September 2004. Companies were required to remove these chemicals from cosmetic and personal care products sold in the EU.

Waste in Electrical and Electronic Equipment (WEEE) (2005). This directive required that electronic producers take responsibility for the products they have sold when they no longer have a functioning life. They are to be recovered and recycled.

Restriction on Hazardous Substances in Electrical and Electronic Equipment. This directive prohibited the use of cadmium, lead, mercury and a number of other toxic materials in electronics and equipment produced or imported into the EU (it had a major impact not only on EU computer and other electronic production but on USA production (in the latter case, because of resulting import restrictions).

In sum, from the 1970s on, it became increasingly apparent to many policymakers that established regulatory systems for chemicals were inadequate or defunct. These systems were not able to fully protect human health and the environment. The impact on human health and the environment of tens of thousands of chemicals, as the OECD had stressed for a long time, were really quite unknown. This emerging view set the stage in the late 1990s for the REACH initiative.

4. The First Steps Toward a Radically New EU Chemicals Policy

In March, 1998, an informal meeting took place in Chester, U.K., among some members of the environmental council with representatives from Austria, Denmark, Finland, Netherlands, and Sweden (Austria, Finland, and Sweden had become new EU members in 1995).[14] They felt something major needed to be done about the regulation of chemicals. January-June 1998 was also the period of the UK's EU Presidency of the Council of Ministers, and it had selected "chemicals in the environment" as one of its Presidency themes). There was a huge backlog of un-investigated chemicals and a very limited number of risk assessments for existing substances. Substantial data about the potential of commercial chemicals to cause harm to human health and the environment were simply not available. In particular, there was an obvious lack of progress with the 110 priority substances, which the OECD had indicated as calling for systematic investigation; concern was also expressed about the 30,000 or so existing substances in production with potentials to cause damage to the environment and humans, for instance through endocrine disruption. The risk assessment method – a key technique – in established

[14] Already in 1997, the Swedish government called for an overhaul of EU chemical policies in the pursuit of a "non-toxic environment" (ENDS, 1997).

regulatory regimes had been applied to only a very small fraction of the total of existing substances on the EU market (Lind, 2004:51).[15]

The Chester group prepared a joint position paper which would be taken up for discussion at an informal Council meeting in April (Lind, 2004:55). The paper stressed "operational problems" with current regulation and already articulated key policy components that provided part of the skeleton for the later full fledged REACH proposal, for instance:

- there should be operative goals (reference was made to the Esbjerg Declaration);[16]
- burden of proof should be shifted to the producers; the producers or suppliers of chemical products should be required to inform consumers of the possible impact of chemicals in the products on human health and the environment;
- guidelines should be formulated on precaution, substitution, and safe management of chemicals;
- product substances that have irreversible toxic effects or are persistent and bio-accumulative should be banned;
- costs for research on hazards and risk assessment should be the responsibility of industry rather than government.

A major general problem, it was stated, was the lack of a comprehensive chemicals policy. These considerations were presented at the informal meeting in April. It was agreed that EU chemicals policies be reviewed and, among other things, its gaps and weaknesses identified. It was proposed that the concept of a framework directive be eventually considered (Lind, 2004:56). The EU Commision was asked to report back on its findings by the end of 1998.

In November 1998, the Commission Review of existing chemical regulation reported numerous weaknesses. More than 20 issues were raised, some of them those very same principles identified by the small EU countries (Austria, Denmark, Finland, Netherlands, and Sweden) that brought up the call for a review in March/April (Lind, 2004:59). Besides reversing the burden of proof that chemicals were safe, costs of testing would be borne by the industry. Also, there was a drive to:

---

[15] Risk assessment entailed not only hazard identification, but the assessment of dose-response linkages and likely degree of damage. Only after this could one characterise the degree of risk and develop a risk management regime. The process is slow and resource demanding. Chemicals were consider "innocent" until harm has been proved; typically, governments, including the EU had the responsibility for identifying risky chemicals and conducting risk assessments (Lind, 2004:51).

[16] North Sea Ministers adopted a declaration in 1995 which voiced concerning regarding the state of the North Sea and defined an operational objective (for the first time): All releases of hazardous substances to the Baltic marine environment must cease within one generation (before the year 2020); the only acceptable level of hazardous substances are background levels (Lind, 2004:45).

- make hazard identification a pillar of any new regime
- create a clear strategy for assessing the harmful effects of existing substances – not only new ones
- require the substitution of safer alternatives for hazardous chemicals

The stage was being set for launching a new policy paradigm. The Commission report came at the end of 1998 and supported the idea of preparing a regulatory instrument for chemistry. In December 1998, the Council of the EU (and, in particular, the Environment Council) supported the work of the Commission in its proposal to prepare a new law.

During the Autumn of 1998, there were other movements as well. In October, 1998 the European Parliament (EP) called for efforts to deal with endocrine disruption, and set in motion its own initiative. About the same time, sensing the quickly developing public policy mood, the chemical industry (ICCA and the European Chemical Industry Council (CEFIC)) launched several new programs, among them, the Long-Range Initiative (LRI) to support relevant research in areas of public concern[17] and the HPV programme concerned with high production volume chemicals.[18]

In February, 1999, the Commission organized a stakeholder Brainstorming Conference (Lind, 2004:59). Most major stakeholders were represented. The European Chemical Industry Council (CEFIC) made a number of promises including one to substantially increase its funding for LRI research. By June, 1999, the Council was ready to launch its move toward a new chemicals policy. It adopted "Conclusions for a Future Strategy", requesting that the Commission propose a new chemicals strategy for regulation by the end of 2000. There were several key features stressed, among others: The idea of a need for a new integrated and coherent policy to protect humans and the environment; principles of sustainability and pre-

---

[17] In October 1998, ICCA also launched the Long-range Research Initiative (LRI), financed by chemicals industries in the USA, EU and Japan. It provides support for research to focus on scientific understanding of the mechanisms via which chemicals have impact on human health and the environment. Subjects targeted are endocrine disrupters, exposure assessment, carcinogenesis, respiratory toxicity, immunotoxicity and allergies.

[18] *The HPV Initiative*. In October 1998, ICCA announced a global industrial initiative to speed up the process of data collection and hazard assessment of existing chemicals. According to the plans, the initiative would establish a priority list of 1,000 High Production Volume (HPV) chemicals. These substances would then be screened for potential effects on human health and the environment according to the same procedure that was already used by the OECD in the Screening Information Datasets (SIDS). The screening was intended as a first indicator of potential effects and "should not be mistaken for a risk assessment." The screening of the 1,000 HPVs was intended to provide an improved basis for risk assessment in existing programmes, and to be completed by the end of 2004. The HPV Initiative was financed through industry which also stated that the results of the screenings be made available to authorities and to the general public. The industry only published summaries, however, of what it was willing to release.

caution would be central to the new regime;[19] a shift of the burden of proof from government or consumers to industry; industry information and data about the properties of chemicals would be made available to users and the public; dangerous chemicals would be substituted with less dangerous ones.

In June 2000 the EU Commissioner of Environment, Margot Wallström informed the Environment Council of progress on the White Paper.[20] It would be ready before the end of 2000. However, already by October 2000 DG Industry and DG Enterprise began to raise questions and formulate criticisms: "besides looking at the consequences such as protection of human health and the environment, [the policy] needs to consider the importance of a favorable regulatory climate for the competitiveness of the European chemicals industry" (Lind, 2004:62).

In the late 1990s, as mentioned earlier, the Chemical Industry had taken a number of initiatives, fully aware of the movement taking place within the EU. CEFIC stressed the idea that there was a need for a regulatory framework that would promote innovation. In June, 1999 the industry increased its efforts to establish public confidence. CEFIC made a commitment to "responsible risk management of chemicals." It called for dialogue with Green Groups, Consumer Groups, the Commission, and national governments. In December, 1999, CEFIC launched stakeholder dialogue meetings (a later one was organized in December, 2000) but no results came out of these meetings, and there were no additional meetings after 2000. In April 2000 the industry and "academia" called for partnership with government, expressed through the ALLCHEM-E Alliance. At the WHO meeting at this time, CEFIC promised to increase contributions to its Long-range Initiative (LRI) from 4.5 million € to 20 million €.

Toward the end of 2000, industry appears to have switched its strategy. While initially (late 1990s) it had reacted to the threat of REACH by highlighting voluntary programmes, by the end of 2000-early 2001, industry began to oppose the EU regulatory proposal openly and forcefully, using the arguments of "competitiveness", "economic losses", "loss of jobs," which were stressed also by several governments, as we report below.

The Commission adopted in February 27, 2001 the "White Paper on a Strategy for Future Chemicals Policy." The White Paper proposed a new system for the Registration, Evaluation and Authorisation of Chemicals (REACH) produced and marketed within the EU (COM(2001) 88 final).[21] The Paper proposed to take pre-

---

[19] In April, 1999 the Council called for the introduction of the Precautionary Principle – this was the first step toward institutionalizing the principle in EU policymaking. By February 2000 the EU communicates the Precautionary Principle as a cornerstone of EU regulation.

[20] A further "Swedish connection" (see German critique of the Swedish influence in matters of chemicals) was the involvement of the Swedish Chemicals Inspectorate, KemI, in the preparations of the White Paper.

[21] The revised principles of chemical regulation put forward by the White Paper of 2001 mirrored emblematic struggles that had taken place over asbestos. Those struggles "included disputes over

cautionary measures to protect citizens from hazardous chemicals and to make industry responsible for providing safety information about its chemicals. Under REACH, chemicals were to be subjected to regulation not only on the basis of their toxicity but on the basis of particular intrinsic properties such as persistence, bioaccumulation and toxicity, or if they were very persistent and very bioaccumulative (vPvB) (or persistent, bioaccumulative and toxic properties (PBT)). That is, *proven toxicity itself would not be necessary for regulatory action to be taken.*

The Commission stated that substitution of the most hazardous chemicals should be an important aim of the reform. A number of other objectives were explicitly laid out (Lind, 2004:62). In addition to protection of human health and the environment, and the principles indicated earlier, the White Paper emphasized the importance of

- increased transparency,
- integration with international efforts,
- promotion of non-animal testing,
- conformity with EU international obligations under the WTO,
- prevention of fragmentation of the internal market,
- maintenance and enhancement of the competitiveness of the EU chemicals industry.

The idea of REACH was taking political form and would arguably lead into one of the most contentious legislative processes in EU history.

Reactions to the Commission proposal from the EP and the Council were generally positive. They not only supported the White Paper but stressed the importance of developing it further. In June 2001 the Council called for the Commission to present a proposal for a regulatory framework – and to do this by the end of 2001. There were also arguments for more stringency in the proposal (Lind, 2004: 72). The Environment Committee at the European Parliament as well as the Council suggested some tightening up of the regulatory regime. They wanted, among other things, a more proactive, preventive approach and a full implementation of the substitution principle as a key aim of REACH. Many NGOs, following developments since 1998, supported the White Paper but had reservations (see views presented below).

In April 2001 Commissioners Margot Wallström (DG Environment) and Erkki Liikanen (DG Enterprise) launched a conference (with two workshops) engaging key stakeholders to discuss REACH. The first workshop addressed the REACH process and how best to implement the new policy in a cost-effective way. The second workshop concentrated on major stakeholder contributions.

During the Spring of 2001 many stakeholders initiated lobbying campaigns and communicated their views through the media. CEFIC along with trade unions as

---

the core principles guiding regulation, the interpretation of scientific evidence, the political power of economic interests, and the Commission's various interests in furthering European integration" (Carson 2004: 145-146).

well as political, environmental, consumer and animal protection groups reacted supported (but also some opposed) REACH. Eventually, even government officials and Heads of State from major industrial (chemical) countries engaged in the debate and struggle (see below). Much of the feedback response to the REACH proposal took place, interestingly, through the Internet.

During the Summer and part of the Autumn of 2001, DG Environment worked to prepare the legislative proposal, taking into account feedback and suggestions from the Council, EP, stakeholder meetings, and reports from eight Technical Working Groups with experts providing advice in specific areas. (The REACH proposal had headings ("Blocks") similar to the working groups).

The reactions of industry and trade unions, and environment NGOs were of course different and opposing on a number of critical issues (Lind, 2004: 78-79). Industry felt that the Commission was catering to the environmental movement, at the same time that the environmental NGOs felt that the Commission was catering to industry![22] Earlier in the year, CEFIC expressed support for the objectives of REACH, but insisted at the same time that REACH as formulated would not work. In September, 2001 CEFIC presented its own version of REACH. In addition to CEFIC's ongoing critique, there came intensive criticism from the US Government and key EU Heads of State (Blair, Jospin, and Schroeder) (see below).

Unfortunately, in November an early draft of the "authorisation block" leaked out fom the Commission. The draft revealed that there was considerable *disagreement* between DG Environment and DG Enterprise on many issues, e.g., regarding which substances would be banned and which would require authorization to be able to continue production. DG Environment insisted that PBT and vPvB substances be subject specific regulatory action. The Commision's proposal was accepted November 15, 2001. In general, there was a strengthening of REACH on some points and a weakening on others.

With backing of the Environment Council to increase the protection of human health and the environment, DG Environment had the initiative (and advantage)

---

[22] The anti-REACH lobby, especially in Germany, took on the character of a vendetta against "the Swedes." It was pointed out that many of the key EU persons engaged in the issue were women from Sweden: Commissioner Margot Wallström, Inger Schörling, Chair of the Environment Committee at the EP and Eva Hellsten, Head of DG Environment Chemicals Unit. They were portrayed as a trio trying to demolish the chemicals industry and were even referred to in Germany as "The Swedish Witches". It was pointed out that Sweden did not have a chemicals industry of any real significance. The rhetorical question was raised, "What do Swedes know about the importance of chemicals industry?" (Lind, 2004:112) There was a history of contention from early on in Sweden's EU membership. As ENDS (2001) reports, "Sweden's strict approach to chemicals has been a bone of contention with the EU since its accession. In many cases it has had to compromise, though in one recent clash a European Court advisor endorsed its regulatory style." The persistent push for much stricter EU regulation of chemicals was expected to cause powerful reactions from some EU member states not ready for robust policies, as did become the case (see later).

through the initial stages of drafting REACH. However, as criticism against REACH emerged from the chemical industry and powerful industrial countries (particularly, Germany, U.K., and France as well as the USA), DG Enterprise took more initiative in 2002 and the following years, increasingly trying to turn the framing of the policy toward "competitiveness" as well as issues of costs, jobs, and income particularly. The vested interests and power of the chemical industry were mobilized within the Commission and in the Council (Heads of State, especially Germany, France, and the U.K.) but also externally through the mass media. At the end of 2002, the German Industry Federation (BDI) called in the consultancy firm Arthur D. Little to make an estimate of the economic impact of REACH. The consultants' conclusion was dire. According to their report, REACH would cause millions of job losses in Germany and would have a disastrous impact on the German economy as a whole. (Six months later (July 2003), the leading German economic institutes unanimously criticized the Arthur D. Little study as methodologically weak and based on flawed assumptions. But damage had already been done).

During the long course of the debate and the formation of positions, the Commission itself became divided between interests of health and the environment – represented by DG Environment – and interests of the chemicals industry represented by DG Enterprise. Later, other industry-friendly parts of the EU become centrally involved, in particular, the ("super") Competitivity Council (see below).[23]

During the first period of revision, most of the proposals of the motion remained, although some points were taken out or rephrased, while some additional points were inserted. In the end, the European Parliament voted on the Resolution calling for a strengthening of REACH on several points.

Environmental NGOs also played a central role (as is typical of much EU policymaking) (Lind, 2004:86-87; see Andersen and Burns, 1996). The four largest environmental NGOs – the European Environment Bureau, Friends of the Earth, Greenpeace and WWF – submitted a joint document in the consultation. The groups supported the spirit of REACH and wrote that the Draft Regulation went part of the way towards phasing out the production and use of hazardous substances. The NGOs particularly welcomed the fact that PBT and vPvB substances as well as EDCs would be covered by the scope of the authorisation stage and that substances would not be allowed to be marketed if there were insufficient data about them. However, they also identified a number of crucial flaws in the Draft Regulation (similar in several instances to those identified by the EP).[24] Consumers'

[23] It needs to be emphasized again that the EU is not a single agent but a configuration of competing and conflict agents, especially when a contentious policy area like chemicals becomes an issue (see Chapter 6).

[24] During this period there was a major U.K. Royal Commission report on chemicals (Lind, 2004: 94). The U.K. Commission thought that the new EU chemicals strategy REACH was insufficient in that the phase-out of persistent and bio-accumulating substances would take too long. It be-

Organizations as well supported the introduction of more protective regulation on chemicals, especially concerning chemicals used as constituents of articles (the regulatory name for consumer products in the draft). The two largest consumer NGOs – The European Consumers Organisation (BEUC) and Euro-Coop – strongly backed up the REACH draft but remained critical of some key aspects.

Industry, and CEFIC in particular, opposed the required authorization of, for instance, endocrine disruptors and potentially carcinogenic substances. Besides its critique that the system was not workable, it claimed that it would put the industry at a disadvantage compared to its main compeitors in the USA and Japan. Costs would destroy the industry and millions of jobs would be lost. While the White Paper had estimated that the costs would be €2.1 billion over 11 years, industry studies indicated much more substantial effects. As pointed out earlier, a German industry commissioned study claimed that 1.8 million jobs would be lost in Germany alone. A French study concluded that for France the loss of GDP growth would be up to €88 billion as well as a loss of up to 670,000 jobs.

In addition to CEFIC's critique (as well as that from other industries inside and outside the EU),[25] there also came intensive critique from the USA. Key USA private and public agents became intensively involved. The U.S. chemicals industry, the U.S. Chamber of Commerce, and the George W. Bush Administration. Secretary of State Colin Powell sent several cables to U.S. embassies in Europe calling for them to act against REACH. *Lobbying efforts should be focused particularly on national governments*, arguing that they would be "much more sensitive to impacts on EU competitiveness, employment and other implications than Commission bureaucrats" (Corporate Europe Observatory, 2005:8; Lind, 2004:128).[26] US lobbying was so extreme that it prompted a letter of protest from 68 medical, healthcare, aca-

---

lieved such substances should be substituted for safer substances within one decade. An important tool in this work would be the precautionary principle.

[25] A study of industry's argumentation was made by The Stockholm Environment Institute in 1999 showing that among the arguments that are typically raised by industry in opposition to new environmental regulation: (i) The proposed policy may be counterproductive, adding to costs as well as failing to yield environmental benefits, that is, a lose-lose situation. (ii) The environmental goal may be valid, but the proposed instrument is inefficient in that it imposes unnecessary costs. (iii) The proposed instrument may lead to changes in competitive conditions that may disadvantage important sections of industry or place industry at a disadvantage compared to those in other countries or regions. (iv) Economic and technical constraints may limit the achievement of higher environmental standards.

[26] US lobbying stressed that the Draft Regulatory Proposal among other things: (i) would probably be unworkable; (ii) departs from ongoing international regulatory cooperation; (iii) imposes substantial costs while providing uncertain benefits; moreover, the REACH apparatus lacks "a realistic cost-benefit analysis"; (iv) it would adversely impact small and medium sized companies; (v) it would disrupt global trade, and in particular transatlantic trade; (vi) it would adversely impact on innovation and development; (vii) it would create market uncertainty; (viii) it is unclear regarding administrative coordination and consistency; (ix) it raise concerns regarding consortia and data sharing; (x) it might unfairly treat U.S. companies and products (Lind, 2004:128).

demic, scientific and environment NGOs in the USA (Lind, 2004:84). The U.S. government pressured the EU Commission to, among other things: 1) Reduce the scope of the regulation to better focus EU resources on substances that are likely to pose the highest risks; 2) Develop an EU approach which supplements – and does not supplant – ongoing international cooperative efforts to effectively address the risks posed by existing chemicals; 3) Clarify and simplify the process by which regulatory decisions will be made; and 4) Ensure that the impacts of the EU regulation – both positive and negative – are fully and transparently assessed. The Commission should also ensure that its final proposal is fully consistent with the EU's international obligations (especially with respect to WTO and related regimes).

As Greg Lebedev (President and CEO of the American Chemical Council) expressed it in May, 2004, the mobilization on the other side of the Atlantic was a major accomplishment. REACH was, in his view, "the most serious risk to our industry in a generation… we knew the cards the EU authorities were holding and we called their hand. Because 21st century advocacy is global in nature, we teamed with our sister organization in Europe, CEFIC, whose job it is confront this massive EU initiative. CEFIC took the lead, but the ACC put its shoulder to the EU wheel and it paid off… We arranged for multiple elements of our government – the Department of Commerce, the U.S. Trade Representative, the Environmental Protection Agency, and the Department of State – all to express the understandable reservations about this proposed rule and its trans-Atlantic implications" (Corporate Europe Observatory, 2005:8).

In May, 2003, the Commission published its draft proposal. The chemicals industry urged the Commission to delay the adoption of the REACH proposal in order to launch a broad internet consultation on the draft legislation. The Commission accepted the delay – ostensibly for what appeared to be the good cause of democracy – it meant, however, that the European Parliament would not be able to vote on REACH until *after* the enlargement of the EU. Industry lobbyists had hoped that politicians from the new Member States would be more likely to support the chemical industry's position rather than the REACH position. In May through July the Commission conducted an internet consultation on REACH. Industry associations and chemicals companies deluged the Commission with comments criticising the draft proposal.

Consultations taking place from May to July 2003 resulted in 6500 responses, many from the chemicals industry, its employees and associated organizations, but also from a diverse group of stakeholders (see Lind (2004:83) for some of the diverse perspectives). A joint declaration in favour of a stricter REACH directive was signed by 429 NGOs and over 22,000 individuals, as a comment in the consultation to the Draft Regulation (Lind, 2004:62). The signatories represented environmental, consumer and health interests. Specifically, the declaration stated: "We, the undersigned, 429 organisations and 22,464 citizens around the world, from Australia to Zaire, wish to ensure that our health and that of the environment will be properly protected from hazardous chemicals. We therefore ask the European Commission to ensure that the new chemicals legislation enforces: An obligation to phase out chemicals that accumulate in wildlife, in humans or in the environment, and those that disrupt hormones. Restricted uses of such chemicals should only be permitted temporarily, if safer alternatives are not available, and their use is essential to society; there should be a full right to know, for both consumers and businesses, including what chemicals are present in products; and a requirement that products imported into the EU have to conform to the same safety standards as those made in the EU. The draft legislation does not implement these three points. We consider that the new system will not be workable, and will not effectively protect future generations, unless these measures are taken. Please take this declaration as our submission to the Commission's consultation on the workability of the chemicals legislation" (Lind, 2004:91-92).

Industry and its spokespersons also stressed "workability", as well as, of course, the purely economic aspects. In June, 2003 in Hamburg, the German Chancellor Schröder gave a supportive speech at the CEFIC General Assembly emphasizing that… "other viewpoints are dominating industrial issues, which cannot and should not be the case." He had praise for DG Enterprise…And he pleaded, "Please EU Commission review the draft regulation in the interest of innovation and employment in Europe" (Lind, 2004: 86). The governments of the UK, France and Germany submitted comments on the Draft Regulation. The comments voiced concern regarding the same issues as the chemicals industry and the US Government had already brought up: bureaucratic impediments, lack of workability, loss of competitiveness for the EU, trade-loss effects, loss of jobs, etc.

On 20 September 2003, as the Commission was busy redrafting the regulation after the comments from the internet consultation, the Heads of States of France, Germany, and the U.K. went one step further – in trying to influence the policy outcome. In a joint letter to Romano Prodi, the President of the Commission, Prime Minister Tony Blair, President Jaques Chirac and Chancellor Gerhard Schröder reiterated their concerns about REACH (see Appendix 1).[27] They pointed out that in March 2003, the European Council had sent a clear signal for strengthening the competitiveness of the industries in the EU and to reduce bureaucracy facing chemical companies, thus facilitating the achievement of economic growth and compliance with the "Lisbon Strategy." They expressed forcefully that "a future EU chemicals policy must be designed in such a way as to ensure environmental, health and consumer protection *without endangering the international competitiveness of the European chemicals industry*." The concerns of the three Heads of State could be summarised as follows (much along the lines of CEFIC and the U.S. Government):

[27] Corporate European Observatory (2005:8) reports that "According to Julian Scola, European communications officer at WWF, the intervention of the three heavyweight politicians was unprecedented. 'Departmental ministers are usually unaware [of legislation], so to have heads of states getting involved even before the directive is published is extraordinary.'"

(i) the Draft Regulation is too bureaucratic; (ii) it may be unworkable; (iii) it does not prioritise the substances of most concern, and (iv) it may have a negative impact on competitiveness, jobs and the economy.

The letter itself, the context in which it was written, and its specific demands were clearly a very forceful statement from three key EU countries, encompassing major chemical producers in the EU. The implicit message was that economy must be prioritized and that protection of the environment, health and consumers are not compatible with international competitiveness (see letter in Appendix 1).

In sum, the October 2003 proposal for REACH, which the Commission reported in (COM(2003) 644 final), met fierce opposition from the industry, especially aimed at the requirements of registration, evaluation and authorisation of all chemicals of more than 1 ton on the market and meeting defined deadlines in doing so. Several of the clauses of the REACH proposal became "political footballs", as we shall see.

According to the proposal, enterprises that manufacture or import more than one ton of a chemical substance per year would be required to register it in a central database. The explicit aims of the proposed Regulation were, on the one hand, to improve the protection of human health and the environment. At the same time it was claimed that the Commission wanted to maintain the competitiveness and enhance the innovative capability of the EU chemicals industry. REACH would give much greater responsibility to industry to manage the risks from chemicals and to provide safety information on the substances. This information would be passed down the chain of production and use. The Commission intended its proposal to be a streamlined and cost-effective system. The proposal was drafted in close consultation with many of the interested parties, but the opposition – especially from industry – had been and remained substantial. Nevertheless, the draft Proposal reflected a number of the demands of the chemicals industry. It contained few of the improvements requested by the Council and Parliament as well as the many suggestions of NGOs and individuals. The Director General of the UK Chemical Industries *Judith Hackitt* stated in 2005: "Our greatest achievement in terms of cost and business impact reduction occurred in 2003, when we succeeded in getting the Commission to adopt a proposal with a more realistic scope." Lind (2004:124) judged the Draft Regulation as a severly "watered down version of the White Paper." There were, according to Lind, 2004: 83, two particularly severe cutbacks from the earlier formulation:

- the requirement of substitution of hazardous substances with less hazardous substances – was removed. The ready availability of safer alternatives was explicitly ruled out as reason enough to decline authorization of a hazardous substance.
- There was a shift from a requirement that producers or importers of products that *can* lead to significant harmful exposure of human and environment

be replaced by the statement that "substances released in volumes above one tonne and that are *likely* to cause harm..."[28]

Nonetheless, the draft proposal continued to redefine the duties of producers, importers and users, above all emphasizing the public's right to know and to be protected. The burden of proof would still be on industry, not on consumers, government, or NGOs. It would forbid production or import and use of a chemical if obligatory information is not provided in a given time frame – as Greenpeace put it, "no data – no market."

At this point, the REACH proposal was to be considered by the European Parliament and the EU's Council of Ministers for adoption under the so-called "co-decision procedure."[29]

During the late Autumn, 2003 and early Winter, 2004, reactions to the proposal came from environment and consumer NGOs, most of whom were furious at what they perceived as the "watered down version" of REACH. Their influence was greatest in the EP. So the struggle of major societal actors becomes increasingly focused on the interplay between the EP and the Council. But there were also power shifts inside the Commission at the time (see below). In general, lines of battle were drawn within the EU's institutional setup. And in this context of struggle, those supporting the public health and environment causes were to lose several more battles, but in a certain sense they were on the way to winning a major war.

5. Power Games and Tactial Retreat on REACH

In October 2003 DG Environment Commissioner Margot Wallström and the DG Enterprise Commissioner Erkki Liikanen presented the Commission's Final Proposal for the new REACH system for regulating chemical substances produced within or imported to the EU (COM(2003)644final). Ironically, the competence and authority to deal with REACH within the Comission had been removed two weeks earlier (October 16-17 2003) from DG Environment and given to the Competitivity Council (CC). CC at the Council of the EU was to assume the "leadership" role for REACH in the future (see below).[30]

From almost the beginning of the REACH conception, the EU Council of Environment, the Commission's DG Environment and EP's Committee on Envi-

---

[28] The EU Parliament (especially with a united Conservative block) rejected a registry/registration of substances below 1 ton. Of course, this meant that thousands of chemicals, some of them toxic to human health and the environment would be kept below the radar screen. But the final formulation of REACH states, many of these chemicals can be reviewed in the future.

[29] The Eu "co-decision procedure" means the joint adoption of legislation by the Council of the European Union and the European Parliament. The two agents must agree on an identical text before any proposal can become law.

[30] Lind (2004:124) observes that the entire Commission did not officially stand behind the document as a Commission proposal. Instead it was a document from DG Environment and DG Enterprise. This was arguably a strong signal that there were internal conflicts over the proposal.

ronment had driven the REACH policy proposal. But in the context of the larger struggle for control of chemical policy, the idea was formed in early Autumn, 2005, by the Council – upon initiative of the Italian EU Presidency (led by Silvio Berlusconi) – to shift the competence and authority for REACH from the Council of Environment and DG Environment to CC (as Blair et al.'s letter intimated (see Appendix 1)). The Council grounded this on the so-called Lisbon Strategy...[31] The CC consisted mainly of the Ministers of Industry and Economy and Energy in the EU. Such a shift had been one of the persistent demands of the Chemical Industry.

Through this political-administrative move, CC was to be involved centrally in the continuation of the REACH legislative process. This, of course, was an effort at "reframing" and, potentially, re-structuring radically the REACH proposal. *Arguably, the move came too late. A law – and not just any law but a highly complex, very technical law – had more or less been formulated – and any changes would have to be negotiated relative to the already "established" formulation. And the negotiations would be extremely difficult and uncertain in the face of the very substantial complexity and technical character of the law as well as the widespread support for a radical change.* Also, the Council where key opposition countries such as U.K., France, and Germany weighed heavy and where USA influence was greatest was, however, *only one side in the EU co-decision process.* The European Parliament (with its ties to many key environmental and social NGOs) was the other. Ultimately, revisions in REACH was a matter for the Council and the European Parliament to work out – differences between them which would have to be ironed out, typically in the spirit of hard bargaining as well as a readiness to compromise.

As in the shift of responsibility for REACH from DG Environment to the CC, there were parallel efforts at a "coup d'etat" in the European Parliament. Conservative members of the Committees on Industry and on Legal Affairs attempted a takeover of the REACH legislative process in the EP, arguing the appropriateness of their "leadership,"[32] particularly since CC had taken over REACH from DG Environment. Through a decision of the Parliament's Conference of presidents[33] in February, 2004, the Environment Committee successfully retained its leading role in the REACH legislative process. However, Conservative Members of the Indus-

[31] At the Lisbon summit in March 2000, European Union leaders set out a new strategy, based on a consensus among Member States, to modernize Europe. This became known as the Lisbon Strategy.

[32] REACH had been handled by the EP Committee on Environment since the White Paper was presented in 2001. In December 2003 the REACH Proposal was officially allocated to the Committee on Environment by the President of the Parliament, Pat Cox. However, the Committee on Industry and the Committee on Legal Affairs each claimed they should have the lead competency since the competency had been taken from DG Environment and given to the Competetivity Council. Nevertheless, the Committee on Environment defended its lead on the issue in letters to the President (Lind, 2004: 127-128).

[33] The Conference of Presidents consists of the President of Parliament and the chairmen of the various political groupings in the EP (who may arrange to be represented by a member of their group).

try and Legal Affairs Committees did manage to delay the legislative progress by disputing the responsibility of the Environment Committee for REACH. This made it impossible for the European Parliament to have a "first reading vote"[34] before the EU enlargement in May, 2004, and the elections of a new Parliament in June 2004.

The REACH process was substantially delayed. The Proposal had been communicated to the European Parliament and the Council in November 2003. Because of the necessity of waiting until after the Parliamentary elections in June 2004 – and the establishment of a new Parliament, the "first reading vote" would not be accomplished until November, 2005. However, already in the Autumn of 2004, the debate over REACH heated up in anticipation of the key decisions that were expected eventually in the Autumn of 2005 and Spring of 2006. Industry and environmental NGOs pressured individuals and party groups. The EP's rapporteur for REACH, Guido Sacconi, referred to the "unbelievable pressure" that big business as well as business associations brought to bear on the Parliament and the "hardline campaign of disinformation" they conducted in the run-up to the vote (ENDS Europe, November, 2005).

Throughout the process of the first reading of the European Parliament in Autumn, 2005, several key EP Committees were involved. Besides the Committees of the Environment and Public Health and Food Safety, the Committee for Internal Market and Consumer Protection and the Committee for Industry, Research and Energy were involved in the deliberations (European Commission 2006: 18). Seven other parliamentary committees tabled amendments – there were 160 or more amendments considered by the EP! Several of the most important amendments concerned the substitution principle, requiring producers and users of chemical substances to substitute less hazardous alternatives for dangerous substances or processes.

---

[34] The Commission prepares a legislative proposal, which is submitted to the EU Parliament and to the Council. The procedure then consists of several (2 or more) readings. Initially, the EP President refers the proposal to the committee responsible. The latter may add amendments. Eventually, it is submitted to a plenary session of the EP where debate, amendment-making, and a vote takes place. The proposal then goes to Council for its "first reading", which is handled by a working group in dialogue with the EP and, in particular, the relevant parliamentary committee. The Council takes a vote, adopting the act or taking a common problem. It is returned to the EP where it is referred again to committee, which recommends for a 2nd reading. In a plenary session, there is voting by a qualified majority and is approved, rejected or amended. Again, it returns to Council where a working group considers it, before the Council takes a vote on it. If there are negative opinions about EP amendments, then Council unanimity is required. Otherwise, EP amendments are accepted by default. The act is adopted by the Council. In the case that not all amendments are accepted, then a "Concilliatory Committee" is convened. There are a number of complex procedures which may ultimately lead to a Third Reading and acceptance, or failure to adopt.

The European Parliament in its "first reading vote" on November 17, 2005, backed the (re)introduction into REACH of the 'substitution principle': that is, the mandatory substitution of very hazardous chemicals when safer alternatives are available. To the regret of some, the Parliament also approved exemption of thousands of chemicals from the requirement to provide health and safety information. This was, of course, a typical outcome of complex struggle, negotiation and voting processes.

In the Council (in connection with its first reading in December, 2005), several Member States only partially accepted the substitution principle supported by the Parliament, and at the same time voted to allow a number of very hazardous types of chemicals to remain on the market, even when safer alternatives were available. The Council of Ministers also drastically reduced the requirement for safety data on thousands of chemicals which would stay on the market, despite the lack of any health or safety provisions.[35] On December 13th, 2005, after the Parliament's first reading, the Council reached a political agreement on a common text for REACH, what is referred to as a "common position". The UK presidency proposed as part of the Council debate on REACH a number of changes, but did not respond favorably to industry requests for reducing data requirements on many chemicals. The Common Position text became the formal, agreed position of all EU member state governments and was the version of REACH considered by the EP in its "second reading."

The EU Commission aimed to complete a second reading by the end of 2006 (A "second reading" is usually a faster process than the first reading, as only differences between Parliament and Council positions should be discussed, and various issues are time-limited). Second Readings would take place in Autumn, 2006.

In the meantime, the lobbying efforts of big business and industry NGOs such as CEFIC continued during the Spring and summer of 2006. Environmental, consumer, and animal welfare groups also struggled with industry and others (e.g., groups of conservatives, some media like the *Economist,* laissez-faire political parties) opposed to intensive regulation. The struggles concerned the architecture as well as details of the final REACH text ("Common Position"). During the Summer, the Finnish EU Presidency and the EU Commission pleaded with the EP membership to accept the shape of the REACH formulation agreed by the EU governments in December (and articulated in the common position document).

But the struggles went on unabated. The EP Environment Committee took a firm stance at its second-reading vote on 10 October 2006. Basically following the recommendations of its rapporteur Guido Sacconi, it voted, by a large majority, to reinstate most of its amendments from the first reading which had not been accepted by the Member States. Apart from the substitution of the most hazardous

[35] REACH accounting system required material safety data sheets for all chemicals classified as hazardous, for instance information on tests, etc. there will be independent peer review processes organized by the EU regulatory agency.

substances, the amendments related to operators' "duty of care", a compulsory chemical safety report for chemicals in amounts of less than 10 tonnes and the promotion of alternatives to animal testing.

Substitution, in particular, remained a contentious issue, with Sacconi asking for more clarity as to how carcinogens and other highly toxic substances could ever be authorized, when there are alternatives. "Substitution must be obligatory," he insisted. But the Council stuck to its position that such substances should be permitted if they are "adequately controlled." Sacconi insisted on some institutional mechanism that would guarantee that such substances eventually be replaced, for instance through "an R&D plan." Opposition to this position came from Germany, the UK, Malta, and Poland. Those supporting stricter substitution rules included France, the Benelux countries, Denmark, Hungary, Sweden and environmental and health NGOs. Another issue concerned appointments to the new Agency of chemical regulation. Sacconi insisted that Parliament appoint two people to the agency's management board, but the Council refused to accept this.

Attempts to bridge the differences with the Council through formal mechanisms had thus far failed, and the prognosis for passage of REACH in the near future looked dim. The "second vote" of the Plenary Session of the EP had to be deferred from November to December. EP Rapporteur for REACH, Guido Sacconi, was pessimistic about getting an agreement. However, at the end of November an informal trilogue was organized, where the three key EU institutions (the Council, the EP, and the Commission) agreed to a final text compromise. (Apparently, the Finnish Presidency (for the 2nd half of 2006) played a key role in mediating the compromise agreement (Fasey, 2008:2-3). The EP had its 2nd Reading vote on December 13. The vote was 529 for to 98 against and 24 abstentions and was supported by major political groups. On December 18, the Council unanimously adopted the REACH Programme at its 2nd Reading.

After the years of multi-lateral negotiations over the Commission's REACH Proposal of October 2003, the REACH Regulation was finally adopted by the European Parliament and the Council of Ministers in December 2006 (see Appendix 1).[36] The new system came into force on June 1st, 2007. The REACH documentation consisted of preambles and principles, 14 major Parts with organizing chapters, around 130 subsections, 17 annexes with lists, detailed requirements, methods, appendices – in total more than 800 pages. The law replaced around 40 legislative instruments in force at the time.

6. Discussion: The Multiple Issues and Complex Accomplishments

REACH has been established through a long process of multi-agent discussion, debate and negotiation in the context of the European Commission, Member State

[36] Regulation (EC) No 1907/2006; Directive 2006/121/EC.

Governments and the European Parliament as well as civil society (see Chapter 6 about the EU structure and its institutions). The entire process, from the formulation of the initial idea to its implementation as a piece of legislation took almost 10 years. It involved a wide variety of major European agents. Beside DG Environment, DG Enterprise & Industry, the Council, the EU Parliament and Member States; the struggle over REACH involved at the EU level other principal actors: the European Chemical Industry Council (CEFIC), the Confederation of European Business (former UNICE, BusinessEurope since January 2007) and, from civil society, the European Environmental Bureau (EEB) which coordinates the work of different environmental NGOs. Green Peace and the WWF (through its DetoX Campaign) also played important roles. Many industry NGOs and NGOs of environment, consumer issues, and animal welfare were heavily engaged in the REACH processes.

Table 10.1. REACH: Proponents and Opponents

Oppose REACH – Support Low Regulation and Voluntary Measures (e.g. revision of pre-reach arrangements)	**Ambiguous Agents**	**Support REACH – Tighter,Comprehensive Regulatory Regime**
The Chemicals Industry (CEFIC, ICCA) Some Member State Governments (especially U.K., France, and Germany) Industrial Federations The US Government	DG Enterprise Competitivity Council The Council Animal Rights Organizations	Environment Council (consisting of EU Ministers of Environment) The Commission, especially DG Environment The European Parliament (in large part) Some Member State Governments (especially, Austria, Denmark, Finland, Sweden, the Netherlands) European Workers' Unions Some Industries Environment NGOs Consumer NGOs

Table 10.1 gives too neat a picture of the configurations of actors. The struggle was not simply black and white, "bad guys" and "good guys". Some of those supporting REACH were internal critics. Some such as "animal rights organizations" which were opposed to some aspects of REACH, were usually regarded as belonging to the "environmental camp" (however, they were opposed to the level of animal testing that REACH would require, an issue which industry managed to exploit during the drawn-out struggle over REACH.

Among the most contentious and debated issues in the REACH process were the registration requirements and the authorization procedures (Chapman 2007: 70). Regarding registration, there were issues about the specific tonnage threshold (that is, the level of production which would require registration), the amount of data required, the question of a single registration for each substance, and the extent of the 'right to know'.[37]

For different reasons, the chemical industry and animal protection organizations had similar positions at the beginning of the debate about registration requirements (Chapman 2007: 70). The animal rights organizations opposed animal testing, which would have to increase if more data were required from companies, while the chemical industry wanted to minimize its cost figures for animal testing by limiting requirements for information in the registration process, especially for substances in low quantities. The views opposed to experiments on animals were to some extent successful, influencing in particular Article 13 of the REACH Regulation[38] (Chapman, 2007: 71).

The substances incorporated in articles in quantities above 1 tonne per year have to be registered following normal rules (including tonnage deadlines and specified information requirements) if they are to be released as articles (European Commission 2007: 9). The threshold is different if the substances included in articles are of 'very high concern' listed in Annex XIV as prescribed by the REACH regulation (Annex XIV of the REACH Regulation (Regulation (EC) No 1907/2006) lists the substances subject to authorization, while Annex XIII refers to the criteria for the identification of Persistent, Bioaccumulative and Toxic substances (PBT), and very Persistent and very Bioaccumulative substances (vPvB)), i.e. substances that are potentially carcinogenic, mutagenic or toxic to reproduction (CMR category 1 or 2)[39] PBT substances; vPvB substances; and substances of

[37] Also, REACH cost estimates differed very substantially, with industry estimates 10 times more than those obtained from the EU Commission. In April 2005, a further study on the socio-economic impacts of REACH was published confirming the Commission's initial assessment that REACH would not lead to a devastating financial impact on the European chemical industry (EurActiv 2008). This did not settle, however, many of the most contentious issues under debate.[37]

[38] Article 13.1 states, for instance, "[i]n particular for human toxicity, information shall be generated whenever possible by means other than vertebrate animal tests, through the use of alternative methods, for example, in vitro methods or qualitative or quantitative structure-activity relationship models or from information from structurally related substances (grouping or read-across)" (Regulation (EC) No 1907/2006). The promotion of alternatives to the animal testing of chemicals, an issue that has been of primary concern to many MEPs, became included among the goals of REACH. To avoid duplication of tests already performed on animals, interested parties would have 45 days to state their views prior any new project involving animal tests. Alternative methods must be validated by the Commission, once recognised by the agency, or international institutions. The Commission must submit a report every three years on the use of alternative tests and, if necessary, make fresh legislative proposals.

[39] CMR is defined as a substance of very high concern which is carcinogenic (causes cancer), mutagenic (causes damage to genes) or reproductively-toxic (causes either a decrease in fertility or problems with development of the foetus). CMRs category 1 and 2 are subject to authorization under REACH.

‘equivalent concern’ such as endocrine disrupters that are identified from scientific evidence and on a case-by-case basis as likely to be harmful to humans or the environment (The majority of the endocrine disrupting chemicals would have to undergo authorization in the REACH system. Serious human health effects which have so far been associated with endocrine disrupting chemicals are testicular cancer, breast cancer, prostate cancer, decrease in sperm concentration and semen volume, cryptorchidism, hypospadia and impaired development of the immune system and the nervous system. All these effects would qualify a substance either to be classified as carcinogenic or as toxic for reproduction and so would trigger its necessary submission to authorisation. Furthermore, adverse effects on the endocrine system of wildlife species have been causally linked to certain POPs, which would be subject to authorisation as much as CMR, PBT and vPvB (ibid: 10). The ECHA has to be informed in cases of substances of very high concern included in articles above a concentration limit of 0.1% weight by weight and present above 1 tonne per year, unless humans and environment are not to be exposed in normal conditions of use and disposal (ibid; Chapman 2007: 68). Additionally, the ECHA keeps the right to demand the registration of a substance in an article if risks to human health or the environment are suspected to occur with its release from the article (European Commission 2007: 10).

A major point of contention about registration had to do with the problem of tonnage thresholds – that is, whether the information requirements for registration should be based on the quantity of the substance used or produced per company per year. The chemical industry opposed tonnage thresholds, *the argument being that testing should be demanded according to possible risks of a substance, rather than the quantities in which a substance is being used or produced* (Chapman 2007: 71). Resistance to industry pressures were successful, and the debate turned more to *how much* testing was necessary for registration. Industry gained some terrain on this point, since already the 2003 proposal demanded much less data for substances produced or imported in quantities below 10 tonnes per year per company than previous proposals. Later, these data requirements were increased again for substances with dispersive uses, those incorporated into articles, and substances for which evidence exists that they might entail risks to human health or the environment (Chapman 2007: 71; see also: European Environmental Bureau 2003: 4).

The issue of joint registrations was also a highly contentious question. One registration per substance carried the benefits of reduced costs and testing, but it also closely affected the sensitive question of “commercial confidentiality”, with companies having to share information on the chemicals they use (Chapman 2007: 72; WWF 2004: 62). The ‘one substance, one registration’ position eventually won (Chapman 2007: 72). At least in part, since despite the provision of joint presentation of dossiers (optional in the case of chemical safety reports), producers and importers could indeed avoid this joint submission of registration dossiers under certain circumstances (European Commission 2007: 8).

The early REACH proposal of October 2003 (COM(2003) 644 final) did not consider the 'right to know' of the chemical ingredients of imported or EU-made articles. These provisions were added later. This right to know was resisted by companies but demanded by environmental NGOs (Chapman 2007: 72; European Environmental Bureau 2003: 5-6). Industry argued that this right to know might compromise commercial confidentiality. Indeed, REACH considers certain information provided in registration dossiers to be "commercially sensitive" and thus not "publicly available"[40] (European Commission 2007: 15). Given this provision, registrants can always argue that any particular information must be handled as confidential (Chapman 2007: 72). In the case of substances contained in articles, which are of very high concern, consumers presumably would have the right to know. However, consumers may have to act proactively for information about a product when they wish to know its components (Chapman 2007: 72-73; European Commission 2007: 5, 15; European Environmental Bureau 2003: 5).

The evaluation component comprises dossier evaluation and substance evaluation. Dossier evaluation is performed by the ECHA and includes checking both the compliance of registration dossiers and testing proposals to avoid unnecessary animal testing (Chapman 2007: 68; European Union 2007: 11-12). Substance evaluation is carried out by the ECHA in coordination with competent authorities in the Member States. The ECHA and Member State's authorities may request extra information on substances from the industry to further elucidate if a substance may present a risk to humans or the environment (European Union 2007: 12). The evaluation process may lead the authorities to either restrict the use of the substance or recommend its authorisation (EU 2007:12).

Authorisation is required for substances of "very high concern" (European Commission 2007: 12). The ECHA is to publish a list of very high concern substances which are candidates to be included in Annex XIV (ibid: 13). An authorization is approved if the applicant demonstrates that risks from a substance are "adequately controlled", or that the socio-economic benefits of its use outweigh the risks and suitable alternative substances or processes are not available. Downstream users can either apply for their own authorisations or use authorised substances obtained directly from a company to whom an authorisation has been granted. Downstream users still have to inform the ECHA that they are using the given substance (ibid: 13).

[40] As the Commission summarises "[n]on-confidential information on chemicals, for example to allow those exposed to chemicals to make decisions on the acceptability of the related risks, will be made available. This is done in such a way that the interests of the public's 'right to know' is balanced with the need to keep certain information confidential. Some information will be published on the Agency's web site, some information will generally be always kept confidential, and some may be made available on request in accordance with the Commission's normal rules on access to information" (European Commission 2007: 15).

The authorisation procedure set by REACH changes the burden of proof of regulation (Chapman 2007: 69). The burden of proof has now been placed on producers and downstream users of chemicals. Those who intend to produce or use a certain substance (subject to authorization) are required to prove that risks are controlled, or that the socio-economic benefits are more important than the risks involved, taking into consideration also alternative substances or processes. Previously, it was the regulator who had to demonstrate the risks of a substance (Chapman, 2007:69-71).[41]

For the most dangerous substances, producers are required to submit a substitution plan to replace them with safer alternatives. Where no alternative exists, producers have to present a research and development plan aimed at finding alternatives. Endocrine disruptors must be subject to adequate control. However, a review clause says that their inclusion in a list of substances that require express authorisation may be considered, six years after the regulation takes effect, on the basis of the latest scientific data and in the light of an analysis of their socio-economic costs and benefits

Another related major issue among the contentious struggles and debates concerned the 'substitution principle'. The issue here was whether a hazardous substance should be authorised if an alternative is available. Environmental NGOs and the Greens in the European Parliament demanded that authorities require producers and users of chemical substances to substitute dangerous substances or processes for the least hazardous alternatives and argued for this substitution principle to be part of the authorisation process (Chapman 2007: 73; European Environmental Bureau 2003: 3). The demand found limited success. An authorization is granted if the applicant demonstrates that risks from a substance are 'adequately controlled', or that the socio-economic benefits outweigh the risks and suitable alternative substances or processes are not available (European Commission 2007:13). However, if there are alternatives, a substitution plan has to be submitted together with the application for authorisation (Chapman 2007: 73). Of course, the applicants can argue that there are no alternatives available, if that is more conve-

[41] The debate about *authorisation* revolved around several different issues. One of the questions had to do with the scope of substances subject to authorisation under REACH. According to the REACH proposal, only substances of very high concern (CMR category 1 or 2, PBT substances, vPvB substances, and substances of equivalent concern) would be subject to authorisation (COM(2003) 644 final: 15-16). WWF, for instance, argued that the criteria for substances of equivalent concern be more flexible (WWF 2004: 66); it defined as a "very high burden of evidence" (WWF 2004: 69) the requirement that substances of equivalent concern be "identified as causing serious and irreversible effects to humans or the environment" in order to be classified as subject to authorization (COM(2003) 644 final: Article 54.f). On the other end of the debate, the industry asked for a more restricted scope for authorisation limited to CMRs, leaving out PBTs, vPvBs, and substances of equivalent concern (see, for instance, summary of the stakeholder debate on REACH: Lowell Center for Sustainable Production 2008). In the REACH regulation only substances of very high concern are subject to authorisation. (Chapman 2007: 73).

nient for them. And more importantly, the viability of an alternative applies just to the applicant who presents the substitution plan, it is not for the utilisation of the chemical in general (Chapman 2007: 73).

Finally, through the restrictions procedure, Member States or the ECHA may propose restrictions on the use or manufacture of substances (or regulate the conditions for their production and use) if there exists "an unacceptable risk" to human health or the environment (European Commission 2007: 13). REACH also incorporates existing restrictions set in Directive 76/769/EEC – for instance, the ban on asbestos (ibid: 14) (see Chapter 9).

7. The Paradigm Shift: Key Dimensions

The EU chemicals policy paradigm shift was partly quantitative (number and range of chemicals covered), partly qualitative (changes in responsibilities, relationships, methods). Its radicalness is pointed up, in part, by the extreme reactions of the chemical industry and several heads of state including key EU member states and the US Government. This chapter has reported on some of the struggles, negotiations, and final resolutions leading up to the REACH legislation in 2006.

As Table 10.2 indicates, REACH is not only much more comprehensive than any previous chemical policy. It aims to be much more discriminatory and selective. Particular dimensions differentiating regulatory systems before-REACH and after-REACH are, among others:

(1) Earlier, chemicals which were known to be problematic – toxic or carciogenic – were attended to if they appeared on the "radar screen," so to speak. REACH introduced a system of trying to identify early most of the important chemicals which might be a problem. All significant chemicals (defined by weight of input into society) must be registered and eventually shown to be "safe enough." The key principle makes volume a basis of data requirements (importance of a substance in terms of its weight). The system is tiered. More weight, more information required.[42]

(2) There is a reversal of the burden of proof from government and consumers to producers, importers and downstream users of substances. Before it was the regulator who had to show hazards and prove risks. Now a producer must show that chemicals are either not hazardous or, if hazardous, are necessary (that is, there

[42] While there are data requirements starting at 1 ton or more, that is, they must register (without registration, the substance cannot be manufactured or imported). Data demands begin at 10 tons (all available in vitro data, in vivo data, historical data, data from valid (Q)SARS ((quantitative) structure activity relationship) and data from structurally related substances shall be assessed first. Chemical safety assessment (CSA) is required for 10 ton or more: there should be assessments of human health hazards, physico-chemical hazards, environmental hazards, and PBT and vPVb. If the CSA determines that the substance should be classified as dangerous or as a PBT or vPvB, the CSA must include, in addition, a chemical safety report (CSR): This communicates hazard and risk information; all identified uses of a substance.

are no substitutes available) and adequately controlled. This is the basic architecture of EU authorization of chemicals with hazardous properties. Even chemicals which entail considerable risks may be still authoritized when the risks involved are judged to be outweighted by socio-economic benefits (and there is no possibility of effective substitution).

(3) In general, the legislation mandates greater information flow, and the sharing and access to greater information. The responsibility for providing data is shifted from public authorities to the industries producing, utilizing, and distributing substances. Transparency and openness, in particular the provision of data and information by producers, are keystones of the new system. Industry is to make available information and data on hazards, risks, safety requirements to down-stream companies as well as to regulators, consumers and the public. Downstream producers are also required to provide data on the chemicals they make use of. A new legal framework for liability in case of future harms caused by the use of chemical products provides a more visible connection between benefits and potential harms (Lind, 2002:144).

(4) There are several powerful sanctions and these are not necessarily applicable only to hazardous chemicals. Failure to provide relevant information about chemicals produced will be sanctioned: "no data (registration), no market" (Green Peace's formulation of the principle). Chemicals which are judged to be far too hazardous – especially if their benefits to society are not considered to offset their hazards are likely to be banned. This would eliminate their market.

(5) At the foundations of REACH are the precautionary and sustainability principles (which in themselves represent major cognitive-normative paradigm shifts). Regulators no longer need to provide proof of hazard in order to restrict or regulate a chemical heavily.

(6) REACH provides a clear strategy and well-defined procedures for assessing hazards and harmful effects of new substances as well as all existing substances. There is no "grandfather clause." Given the number of chemicals in question, sampling of dousier reviews is to be introduced – all of this can assure ultimately that hazardous chemicals which are not presently on the "radar screen" will sooner or later be brought into view. The system does not concern merely the mass producers of chemicals. As indicated earlier, those who introduce chemicals into the substances they sell are also covered. Those chemicals which are covered by the REACH controls and appear in articles with more than .1% of the content require registration of the articles.

(7) The EP and many NGOs supporting REACH insisted on the "duty of care" principle, namely that the manufacture, import and placing on the market of substances must be carried out "with such responsibility and care as may be required to ensure that, under reasonably foreseeable conditions, human health and the environment are not adversely affected". Along these lines, a clause was added to REACH by EP on the duty to inform the public about dangerous substances con-

tained in products. The distribution chain, including consumers who request it, must be informed of the presence of any chemical in an amount greater than 0.1% of the total product weight.

Industrial users of chemicals ("downstream users") are also required to provide information about substances they use under REACH (downstream users were not included in the previous legislative framework for chemical substances). By using information provided by their suppliers (manufacturers and importers), they are expected to employ safety and risk management measures (European Union 2007: 11).

Table 10.2. Chemical Policy Paradigm Shift

	PRIOR TO REACH	REACH REGIME
Problems or issues	Control of chemicals which are known to be harmful to human health or environment	Control of chemicals including tens of thousands whose impact on human health and the environment are unknown
Model of chemicals and their risk to human health and environment	Most chemicals are neutral. Only a few are hazardous	Many unregulated chemicals entail unknown hazards. They permeate our everyday life in ways largely unknown (systemic unintended effects)
Model of socio-economic causality and regulation	Industry, technically knowledgeable and trustworthy	Industry's knowledge limited, particularly regarding hazards to human health and environment. Also, industry not complete trustworthy
Goals to regulate chemicals	Regulate chemicals on the radar screen, that is those which have been identified and "scientifically proven" to be dangerous or highly risky	All significant chemicals (above a weight of input into the system) must be registered and their safety specified (no risks, acceptable risk, and unacceptable risk). A hazardous or risky substance is one that is toxic, can cause cancer or mutation, or is harmful to reproduction.
Responsible Agents for solving problems and regulating	A number of particular regulatory agencies	Comprehensive Regulatory Agency, ECHA and producers, importers, and downstream users/producers, that is all of those involved in putting chemicals into the socio-economic system. Peer review system of controls of hazard assessments or material data safety reports

Methods to manage hazards; solution complex	Diverse and limited laws. Major stress on voluntary methods. Most existing substances not regulated. Risk assessment of any recognized hazardous (or presumed hazardous substances). No administrative or political decisions without scientific certainty. Core of the EU "risk management" process	Stress on legal requirements for registration which is comprehensive, covering tens of thousands of chemicals. Complex machinery of requiring reporting, registration, also authorisation, and possible banning of chemicals. Precautionary principle[43] applies more than scientific certainty. Action can be taken prior to risk assessment. Banning assures effective hazard management in the cases of chemicals that may entail high risks but continue to be used
Actors most directly affected	Chemical companies	Chemical companies including down stream companies as well.
Expertise and Knowledge Requirements	Engineers, chemists; pathologists	Chemists, engineers, pathologists.
Key discourses	Responsibility of regulators. Risk determination or assessment, "solid science," "risk management", "competitivity" "compliance with Lisbon Strategy"	"non-toxic environment", "responsibility and accountability shifted to industry." Substitution. Precautionary principle. Transparency. Extensive sharing of information.

8. Concluding Remarks

The REACH process entailed long, complex, and contentious negotiations, beginning in 1998 and ending late in 2006. Not only were their major divisions between industry, supported by, on the one side, political parties and other agents (including media such as The Economist that tend to be opposed to most government regulation); and, on the other side, environmental ministries and political parties as well as environmental, consumer and animal rights organizations particularly concerned about the impact of chemicals on human health and the environment.

There were also cleavages and tensions within the EU: between Parliament and the Council and also within EU institutions: in Parliament (between, for instance, the Committee on Environment and Committees on Industry and Legal Affairs); in

[43] This principle and its dissemination was associatged by some neo-conservative and anti-regulatory groups with Swedes. Right-wing and anti-regulation think-tanks attacked the precautionary principle (one of the foundations of REACH), and described it as a "good idea" that had been taken too far by "the Swedes." For example, in an outrageous article under the headline "How Swedish it is" in TechCentralStation, a free-market writer, Roger Bate, described the Swedish focus on environmental and health protection as being dangerous to innovation, jobs and progress: "Unless the Swedish folly with misuse of science and precaution is exposed, other countries may follow down its path." (Lind, 2004:112).

the Commission (between DG Environment and DG Enterprise), and in the Council itself between the countries fighting to defend the old paradigm of a priviledged position for the chemical industry and limited regulation and those states pushing for a new tougher regime of regulation (for instance, Sweden, Austria, Finland, and Denmark).

In short, there were divisions and conflicts among EU institutions, member-states, political parties, NGOs, and expert groups. For example, the EP found it difficult to agree on a position because of competing differences among political and national interests (Fasey, 2008:2). Several individual member-states played powerful roles: chemistry states (UK, France, and Germany) and environmental states (in particular, Austria, Sweden, Denmark, and Finland), industry NGOs and environmental, health, and animal welfare NGOs.

At the same time, that all the EU member states had agreed in December, 2005, on a "Common Position" for REACH, there were substantial differences among them, which made it difficult when they had to re-negotiate a modification or compromise with the EP and the Commission (Fasey, 2008:2). This points up a classic problem with the complex EU arrangements: there is built in inertia and rigidity around an established negotiated equilibrium – given the vast number of actors involved in, and the complexity of, deliberations and negotiations.

REACH is arguably, the most comprehensive regulation of chemicals attempted under capitalist conditions in modern times: systematical monitoring and regulating of tens of thousands of chemicals – of course, many chemicals are not yet covered. They were excluded in the course of the negotiations and compromises reached. At the same time, the "handwriting is on the wall." There will be within ten years a review, even of chemicals which are not known to definitely affect health and environment, e.g. chemicals characterized as "very persistent and very bio-accumulative", VPvB.

REACH entailed the further institutionalization of several major principles and rules.

New Principles:

- Shift from preoccupation with economic bottom-line to a stress on health and the environment over economic interests and power.
- Shift of burden of responsibility from consumers and regulators to producers, importers and downstream users/producers. Producers must provide evidence that products are not hazardous, or if hazardous, necessary (no available substitutes) and adequately controlled. Along the same line, producers become responsible for multiple "spinoffs and spillovers" ("collateral damage") of their production processes and products.
- Principle of transparency, in particular extensive sharing of information among stakeholders, thus a new conception of "public" to encompass "private."

- Substitution principle: producers are expected to search for and/or develop substitutes for hazardous chemicals.
- Further institutionalization of the precautionary principle when it comes to hazardous or potentially hazardous materials and production processes.

The REACH approach will have, of course, to be modified: inefficiencies ironed out, routine procedures developed, and the arrangements streamlined (see Hansson and Rudén (2005) and Rudén and Hansson (2006), among others). Yet, it is a milestone. This type of approach is applicable to the regulation and development of automobiles, electronic equipment and devices, airplanes, bio-technologies, nano-materials, etc.

The REACH development like that of food safety and gender mainstreaming and other similar reforms point to a reversal of laissez-faire thinking and practice, which has allowed for too long potentially hazardous goods like asbestos and foods with dioxin to be put on markets – and spread in society – without adequate controls. This progress is one more step toward *sustainable capitalism – where considerations of health, welfare and environment are no longer neglected or slighted in the name of economic gain and development driven by economic and particular technological interests.* This entails as well a shift from laissez-faire to stakeholder responsibility and engagement.

The entire REACH process involving thousands of actors (see section 4) is an extraordinary demonstration of organic, post-parliamentary democracy (Andersen and Burns, 1996; Burns, 1999; Burns et al, 2000). Such a process enabled taking into account a substantial range of concerns and issues (and agents engaged in or representing these). At the same time, however, such super-participatory arrangements slow down and complicates the decision process (above all, in the reaching of agreements). This style of multi-lateral negotiation may mitigate some of the "collateral damage" ("externalities") of any major reform which is likely to impact on diverse aspects of the economy(employment, development of a major industry like chemistry), administration, health of the population, state of the environment, etc. In this sense, also, REACH is a major lesson in new forms of participation and deliberation, negotiation, compromise, multilateral agreements.

Appendix 1

Berlin, 20 September 2003

Dear President,

On our initiative on 21 March 2003, the European Council sent out a clear signal for strengthening the industrial competitiveness of the EU. We agreed that we had to reduce the bureaucracy that European companies encounter and decisively improve the regulatory framework within which our companies, faced with strong competition, must manoeuvre.

To achieve this, we must ensure we do not place unnecessary burdens on industry. We continue to call on the Commission to conduct an analysis of current market and competitive conditions. *We will therefore suggest to our partners that the Commission present a report to the European Council at its December meeting containing suggestions for the optimization of industrial framework conditions in order to avoid risks of de-industrialisation.*

It is also essential to comprehensively assess all important Community projects with respect to their potential effects on industrial competitiveness. The review of EU chemicals policy provides the first concrete opportunity to apply the described principles in a manner that could serve as an example for other areas of industry.

A future EU chemicals policy must be designed in such a way as to ensure environmental, health and consumer protection without endangering the international competitiveness of the European chemical industry. We would also want the new regulatory system to keep animal testing to an absolute minimum.

The Consultation Document published by the Commission in May 2003 contains certain positive elements in this regard. However, the ideas currently being considered give us cause for concern. In particular, we consider the envisaged registration procedure to be too bureaucratic and unnecessarily complicated. We are concerned in addition that the proposed regulatory system does not prioritise sufficiently between the handling of substances, that it will as a result not be workable in practice and that it will be difficult to convince stakeholders that we have created an effective system for targeting and handling those substances which present real safety or environmental concerns. It is still a long way from being the fast, simple and cost-efficient procedure that was promised.

For this reason, France, Germany and the United Kingdom have brought forward comments on the workability and impact of proposals made in the consultation document. We made suggestions for substantial changes to the proposals so that they can be an effective approach for sustainable development.

We are also concerned about the potential impact of the new requirements on the competitiveness of EU businesses exporting to Third Country Markets, and about the position of EU businesses competing in the EU with Third Country suppliers able to avoid these requirements when sending products to our markets.

We must ensure that the proposals do not disadvantage legitimate EU business interests in the global market by imposing requirements which are not pertinent to protecting health and environment. With this in mind, the Commission should carry out a full evaluation of the concrete effects of the planned regulations on the European chemicals industry, as well as on the economy, taking account of the effects throughout the supply chain. The proposals presented to the European Parliament and the Council should create an effective framework which allows EU business to continue to thrive.

To this end, the Commission must work with the Presidency of the Council to ensure that the Competitiveness Council – in accordance with the European Council decision – plays an effective role in the handling of this legislation. We would be grateful if you could take up these proposals and help contribute to making the planned new regulation of the chemicals regime a successful example of our joint efforts to strengthen the industrial competitiveness of the EU.

Yours sincerely

Tony Blair
Jacques Chirac
Gerhard Schröder

Appendix 2: Communication of the EU on December 18, 2006

After three years of negotiations, the Council adopted today by unanimity the REACH Regulation (registration, evaluation, authorisation and restriction of chemicals), the cornerstone of the new European chemicals policy **which replaces around 40 legislative instruments currently in force.** In the framework of the codecision procedure, negotiations between the Council and the European Parliament took place over the last three months in order to reach an agreement ...that ... could enter into force on 1 June 2007.

The *compromise package* was agreed upon in the informal trilogue on 30 November 2006 and was adopted by the Plenary of the European Parliament on 13 December 2006 (See item 3).

(1) [The] **objectives of the new EU chemicals legislation**

The Community chemicals policy aims at avoiding chemical contamination of air, water, soil and the human environment in order to preserve biodiversity and to safeguard workers' and citizens' health and safety. This policy seeks to balance health and environmental benefits with the need to sustain a competitive, innovative and job-creating European industry and the proper functioning of the internal market.

In this context, the main objectives of the new REACH system are:

- To establish a coherent registration system designed to provide basic hazard and risk information on new and *existing chemical substances manufactured in or imported into the* EU;
- *To reverse the burden of proof*, moving it away from Member States' authorities to producing and importing companies, who will be responsible for demonstrating that substances can be used safely;
- *To introduce responsibility for downstream users to provide information on uses and associated risk management measures relating to substances*;
- To maintain the existing restriction system and *to introduce an authorisation procedure for the most hazardous substances as a new instrument*;
- To ensure greater transparency and openness for the public *by providing easier access to relevant information on chemicals*;
- To establish a European central entity (the Agency) to facilitate the administration of REACH and ensure that the system is applied in a harmonised way across the EU.

(2) **Main features of REACH**

REACH will apply to all substances and for substances manufactured or imported in quantities over 1 tonne per year. Special registration and evaluation requirements will be introduced. This Regulation is expected to be applied to *approximatively 30.000 substances.* The REACH system is based on the following:

- a initial phase of pre-registration which will take around 18 months and during which the Agency will inform companies of the REACH provisions.
- the registration of phase-in substances ("existing substances") will start three and a half years from the entry into force of REACH and in this first phase [this involves] substances of high concern or substances manufactured or imported over 1000 tonnes. Registration of phase-in substances manufactured or imported between 10-1000 tonnes will take place six years after the entry into force of this new Regulation. A period of 11 years is foreseen before starting the registration of low-volume substances (1-10 tonnes).
- the regulation also includes rules on the role of distributors and downstream users in the supply chain, especially as regards how manufacturers, importers or downstream users should react to information on identified uses provided by distributors and/or downstream users. The text also clarifies that downstream users can participate in a Substance Information Forum and specifies the cases in which downstream users should conduct a Chemical Safety Assessment and prepare a Chemical Safety Report.

- the Agency, placed in Helsinki, will play a central coordinating role in the evaluation of substances carried out by Member States' authorities which have the required expertise in this field.
- the aim of the authorisation scheme is to assuring that *substances of high concern are properly controlled and to replace progressively such substances by less dangerous substances. Authorisations will be granted where an applicant can demonstrate that a substance can be adequately controlled or if this is not the case if the applicant is able to show that the socio-economic benefits outweigh the risks to human health or the environment arising from the use of substances.*

(3) **Main key features of the EP-Council agreement.** The negotiations between the Council and the European Parliament have been mainly focussed on the following topics: duty of care, communication of information, animal welfare, comitology, registration and data-sharing, the Agency and the authorisation including substitution.

- On registration, the compromise law provides that seven years after the entry into force of REACH, the Commission shall review whether or not carcinogenic, mutagenic or toxic for reproduction substances (CMR substances) in the 1-10 tonnes band should be covered by a Chemical Safety Assessment. As far as testing methods for reproductive toxicity are concerned, the text in the common position was retained but the Commission will review these testing requirements twelve years after the entry into force of REACH.
- On the Agency, the agreement reached stipulates on one hand that the European Parliament will appoint two representatives [to] the Managing Board. On other hand, the candidate selected by the Commission will be invited to make a statement to the European Parliament prior to his or her appointment as Executive Director.
- On authorisation/substitution, the compromise includes the following modifications of the Council's common position:
- persistent, bioaccumulative and toxic properties (PBT) or very persistent and very bioaccumulative properties (vPvB) substances identified under Article 56(f) have been excluded from the "adequate control route". *Six years after the entry into force of REACH, the Commission will review whether or not to extend this to substances with such endocrine disrupting properties;*[44]
- *When suitable alternatives are available taking into account the risk posed by the uses of the substance, a substitution plan shall be a mandatory part of an application for both the "adequate control route" and for the "socio-economic route".*

---

[44] Endocrine disrupters have been an issue for a long time in Europe. They were initially in, then out, and finally out, but with the possibility that the regulatory agency after a number of years has the authority to introduce them. Initially, the idea was that the majority of the endocrine disrupting chemicals would have to undergo authorisation in the REACH system. Serious human health effects which have so far been associated with endocrine disrupting chemicals are testicular cancer, breast cancer, prostate cancer, decrease in sperm concentration and semen volume, cryptorchidism, hypospadia and impaired development of the immune system and the nervous system. All these effects would qualify a substance either to be classified as carcinogenic or as toxic for reproduction and so would trigger its submission to authorisation. Furthermore, adverse effects on the endocrine system of wildlife species have been causally linked to certain POPs, which will, in any case, be subject to authorisation.

CHAPTER 11

The Emergence of an EU Energy Policy Paradigm

Svein S. Andersen

1. Introduction

The focus of this chapter is the development towards a common EU energy policy, with an emphasis on the *transformation* of EU natural gas policy and markets. Until the mid 1990s EU research was dominated by intergovernmental and neo-functional theory. These perspectives were used to explain integration in any area of EU-cooperation (Andersen and Sitter 2006). Later the institutional turn has opened up for a wider set of explanations to capture variations and nuances in different areas of EU-integration (Bulmer 1994, Pierson 1996, Olsen 2001, Aspinwall and Schneider 2001). This article employs an institutional perspective, using the concept of policy paradigm to explain the development of EU energy policy over the last 15 years. It emphasizes the role of abstract and universalistic paradigms as a source of normative and cognitive authority that play a key role in undermining, transforming or replacing specific and institutionalized policy paradigm on the national level that for a long time have proven very resistant to change.

Energy policy is in many ways a problematic case for the EU, but also characteristic of the general EU-development. Member state energy policies were for a long time strongly embedded in national policy paradigms with a statist orientation. Attempts to introduce a common liberal EU energy policy went through periods of stagnation and conflict – before the break-through during the late1990s. The new liberal policy paradigm remains incomplete, in that it has serious omissions and modifications. The transpositions of EU-directives and the impact of EU-policies on national regulation and industry organization over the last decade vary considerably. Omissions and modifications are due to political opposition in member states and in the industry. As a result, the emerging new energy paradigm in Europe reflects inconsistencies and contradictions (Andersen and Sitter 2006).

A public policy paradigm can be defined as a series of beliefs and ideas, shared by key policy makers and reflected in informal and formal rules and regulations. Policy paradigms have two important elements. One is the normative and ontological element, the fundamental values that are based on a specific worldview. It underlies individual and collective identities that, in turn, govern the definitions of meaningful problems and objectives to be pursued. Such beliefs about 'what should be done' represent a normative core. A second normative element is about 'how things should be done'. This element is also cognitive in nature. It rests on general causal theories underpinning a sector strategy, as well as the specific instruments that might be employed (Capano 2003). Public policy paradigms may vary across policy sectors and between national, EU and a wider international level.

One type of policy paradigms is specific and operational, reflecting institutional history in a particular, often national, setting. Such paradigms explain path dependencies in periods of stability. They channel and constrain policy makers and the dynamic of the policymaking process (Jenson 1989, Andersen 1993, Dobbin 1994, Hall 1993, Hall and Soskice 2001). Another type of paradigm is general and universalistic, like general theories and recipes that have to be adapted to particular settings. These may provide support for existing policy paradigms. For a long time there was a general belief in the Western world that key aspects of energy supplies and its role on industrial policy and welfare could not be realized by market arrangements. Often, however, general policy paradigms represent alternative frameworks that challenges and changes specific paradigms. They represent authoritative models of organization that may initiate or channel change. The growing international belief in the liberal markets during the 1980s and early 1990s put national energy policy in EU countries under pressure. For this reason national changes often can be viewed as variations over more general international trends (Hall 1989, Meyer et al 1997, Meyer 2001).

The relationship between specific policy paradigms and more general paradigms are often discussed as a relationship between the national and international level. The nature of the EU introduces an intervening level. An EU policy paradigm may be anchored in international policy frameworks, but they need to be more specific and to be formulated as legal rules. On the other hand, an EU paradigm must allow for national variation in the way rules are transposed and implemented. It is a policy paradigm in the sense that it defines a normative core and the general causal relationship to be relied on. However, political considerations makes it necessary to modify the scope of such a paradigm and to allow for national variations with respect to specific priorities and instruments. The institutionalization of an EU energy policy paradigm, therefore, is a complex institutional transformation.

With the exception of the UK, initiatives towards a common EU energy policy did not originate within national policy contexts of member states. EU initiatives reflected international trends as well as the growing weight of the EU as a supernational institution embracing a liberal market model as reflected in the Single market. The transformation of EU energy policy over the last 15 years can be regarded as the parallel re-institutionalization of policy-paradigms at the EU and at the national level. This transformation is not only a matter of sector change, but also part of a wider EU-integration process. It is a break-through for a liberal market perspective. New initiatives were strongly contested by large majority of national interests and the energy industry. The development of EU common policy is not only a matter of transferring authority from national to a supra-national level. It also involves a redefinition of issues in an abstract and universalistic language that can accommodate the many different interests and ambitions.

Present energy policies in the EU reflect that a new paradigm has emerged. However, the impact of the new paradigm varies in sectors and across countries. At the same time, the nature of EU-integration is changing. Recent EU-expansion, in term of new members and new policy areas, has introduced a heterogeneity that limits what can reasonably be expected in term of convergence. Still, it is clear that national policy paradigms have been challenged and transformed, and sometimes replaced, by a new EU paradigm. This development challenges the notion of EU as an intergovernmental institution, and also the proposition that policy paradigms always constrain or block radical changes (Dobbin 1994, Hall 1993, Hall and Soskice 2001). The story of EU energy policy is more in line with integration theory and institutional perspectives that emphasize the causal impact of abstract and universalistic cognitive and normative models. Such models emphasize diffusion (Meyer 2001) and the processes through which general and abstract models are translated into local contexts (Czarniawska and Sevon 1996). However, the paradigmatic aspects of such changes are not directly addressed.

The development in the energy sector is not unique, in the sense that similar tensions may be found in many policy areas. Still, the case of energy seems particularly suited to study such transformation processes. The article discusses two key questions: First, how and in what ways the transformation of EU energy policy represents a paradigm shift? Second, how can the transformation be explained, against initial resistance of most member states and industrial actors? Below we will first briefly summarize how energy policy has developed and the attempts to explain this development drawing upon institutional theories about EU-integration. Such perspectives pay little attention to the role of policy paradigms in EU-integration processes. We then present an alternative institutional perspective that will be the basis for a more detailed description and analysis of the emerging EU energy policy paradigms over the last 15 years.

2. Policy Failure and Transformation – Problems of Explanations

Various attempts have been made to explain Europeanization of energy policy, or the lack of it, within general theories about EU development.

Up to the 1980s EU energy policy was regarded as a spectacular failure (George 1985:100). It had been characterized by strong conflicts between a common policy, on the one hand, and divergent national policies, on the other. Despite its inclusion in the very first treaties on the European Community (European Coal and Steel Community treaty) energy was for a long time more or less unaffected by common market legislation, and few energy policy decisions were taken at the central EU-level (Schmitter 1996). A number of EU policies and regulation affected energy production, transportation, sales and consumption in many ways (general rules as well as more targeted ones, like taxes on mineral oil). Still, the EU remained far from a common energy policy. National policy paradigms were strong, emphasizing reasonable prices and security of supplies. Policy objectives were linked to industrial development and social welfare. Energy 'was too important to leave to the market'.

The development up to the 1980s is consistent with an intergovernmental model of EU-integration. This model explains the development towards more EU-integration (super-national authority) and common policy by pointing to the gradual emergence of common and overlapping interests among member states. This process is driven by rational actors that actively build coalitions (Morgenthau 1973, Waltz 1979). The lack of a common EU policy in the energy sector is consistent with a lack of overlapping interests between member countries (and state dominated energy sectors). From the late 1950s to the early 1970s inter-state co-operation did not seem necessary. During the 1970s national interests were too diverse, as reflected in the very different national reactions to the oil crises. However, failures and successes of EU energy policy pose asymmetric problems of explanations. It is easier to explain why diverse and conflicting self-interests prevent common policies than to explain how a common denominator emerges (Scharpf 1988). This became increasingly clear as new initiatives emerged in EU during the 1980s.

In the late 1980s and early 1990s number of important EU initiatives were taken to strengthen the super-national influence over particular energy sectors (Matlary 1991, 1997, Lyons 1992, 1994, Padgett 1992). Directives aiming at the liberalization of the natural gas market created particularly strong resistance from most countries and state-dominated industrial interests. Initiatives did not reflect a bottom-up process depicted by the intergovernmental model (Schmitter 1996, Matlary 1996). They were pushed by the Commission, which exploited institutional rules on the EU-level to take the initiative, and to redefine the energy sector in relation to the Single market. This was a policy area where super-national institutions had been assigned tasks that the neo-functionalists call inherently expansive (Cameron 1991: 25). Rather than Europeanization of energy policy driving EU-integration, it was the other way around (Andersen 2001).

Despite strong and widespread political opposition, the Commission continued to push for reforms. However, the political realities forced the Commission to re-think its strategy. First, some of the most provocative elements of the proposals were either taken out or reformulated in such a way that its content was open for negotiations. Second, rather than presenting the whole reform package, reforms were presented in steps. The expectation was that a gradual transformation would pave the way for further reforms as the new system started to take shape. This was particularly important in the European gas market. Gradually, the liberal perspective gained a foothold. A major gas directive was passed in 1998, and transposed into national law in most countries. Additional directives were passed in the following years. However, the speed and vigour with which national governments and the EU court have pursued this new legislation vary considerably. At the same time rapid expansion of the EU, in terms of member states and new policy areas, has changed the nature of EU-integration. There is increased heterogeneity and a relative lack of capacity in the Commission and the court system to pursue implementation of directives (Andersen and Sitter 2006).

The radical transformation that has taken place in the natural gas sector over the last decade is an example of an issue being redefined in terms of the internal market logic based on a general market paradigm. Results have been mixed, but in some areas EU-level policies and regulation are emerging. Such changes are in line with, but unique versions of, global trends towards liberalisation. In the EU they take place within a special institutional context that at the same time reinforces, elaborates and modifies such external influences. A key to an understanding of this development is how the EU – as an institutional framework and a set of central institutional actors – interact with underlying interests in the energy sector in the different stages of EU development. This interaction demonstrates the close link between EU decision-making and the problem of defining collective interests, on the one hand, and the dynamics of EU-integration, on the other hand.

Often decision-making within the EU is characterised by considerable political entrepreneurship exploiting the established EU institutional framework, leading to unexpected processes and outcomes. Such entrepreneurship is primarily exercised by the Commission, but other actors may engage in this (Nylander 2000). Studies of energy policy typically conclude that such entrepreneurship play a key role in explaining the successes of the 1990s (Andersen 1995, Schmidt 1997, Matlary 1997, Eldvik 1999, Nylander 2000). Neither decision-making nor outcomes are consistent with an intergovernmental model. Most member states are initially against initiatives. However, they do not dominate the policymaking process and preferences seem to be changing as part of the EU-level bargaining process (in contrast to exogenous driven domestic preference changes assumed by the intergovernmental model).

Many studies of energy policymaking conclude that there are integration forces at work and that the EU process and the Commission have an autonomous influence (Schmidt 1997, Matlary 1998). The source of this autonomy is existing EU law and obligations that serves as a context for legitimate political entrepreneurship. Schmidt (1997), comparing Europeanization electricity and telecommunication policies, argues that the mix of intergovernmental and supranational factors varies with the distribution of, and relationship between, mobilised interests. Lack of a positive shared sector interest may be overruled by more general member state commitments to the internal market and to the EU-integration process. Accepting Commission initiatives and adjusting to them may be seen as a learning process where preferences are adjusted, as side payments in nested or even secret games. Presumably, the costs of not accepting a certain sector policy, although not in one's interest, would be greater since it could harm a more general and long term interest. If the member states were really against it, they would revoke earlier commitments, the argument goes. Legal rules project state interests, and legitimacy of Commission entrepreneurship in the final analysis rests on a cost-benefit analysis.

This line of argument has some merit. From an empirical perspective, however, it raises the problem of how state interest may explain process and outcomes even when the expressed sector interests are the exact opposite, and when 'broader underlying' interests may be unobservable except as an *ex post* rationalisation. Theoretically, the explanatory value of given interests is problematic when they are changed by external pressures and the momentum of the EU process. Although assumptions about rationality are strict, almost all decision may be rationalised along such *ex post* lines. This kind of problem has been discussed by Pierson (1996) in his version of historical institutionalism. In addition, there is the problem of actors being unable to calculate future consequences in situations that are unclear. Interviews with key actors in the energy sector during the mid 1990s emphasized exactly that. They described their acceptance of a new liberal paradigm as a result of reflection and persuasion that led them to believe that the new model might be beneficial, or that it could at least be handled somehow.

The discussion so far points to the need for a more dynamic understanding of policy paradigms and an additional explanatory mechanism that allows for legitimacy and cognitive appeal as causal mechanisms. This way to think about policy paradigms has been introduced in sociological institutional theory. Below we will present this argument in more detail and link it to a broader understanding of EU-integration.

2.1 Sociological Institutionalism – an Alternative Perspective

For a long time the inter-governmental theory and integration theory were the two dominant theories used to explain EU-integration. For intergovernmentalists, integration is mainly based on an accommodation of national self-interests and this is reflected in changes on both the EU and national level. In integration theory, in contrast, the concept of spill-over (economic and politic) underlines the impact of the institutional context. There is a dynamic relationship between the level of EU-integration and national formulations of interests; the EU-elites play a key role in identifying positive gains and new collective formulations of policy. The efficiency of EU-level solutions undermines the sub-optimal nation-state arrangements. None of these theories include the concept of policy paradigms. The micro-dynamics of both theories rests on rational actors calculating on the basis of given self-interests. In integration theory interests are reformulated under pressure from prior commitments and competition.

From the alternative perspective of neo-institutional sociology, EU-integration may be viewed as part of a wider 'modernisation process'. The concept of institution is used here simply to refer to a location of meaning and identity outside the social system under examination (Meyer 2001:3). The argument is that certain forms of organisation and arguments spread from international models characterised by abstract and universalistic principles; norms and cognitive frames constitute paradigms that drives institutional standardisation in various areas. Such paradigms may be more or less developed, more or less contested. Increasingly, we find that they reflect international experiences, codified in scientific and legal language.

International organisations, like OECD and WTO in the economic area, play a key role in developing models that become authoritative frameworks or paradigms. These paradigms are part of an international culture that reflects values, cognitive models and general action recipes. Regional and local institution-building and change increasingly relate to and reflect such general paradigms. In this way they shape economic and political responses to challenges in the international environment. Arguments about efficiency and functionality will be embedded in a broader cultural context where legitimacy or appropriateness becomes an important element. When facing questions of institutional change involving different types of policy paradigms it is difficult to calculate and evaluate efficiency. Authoritative reasons outweigh means-end calculation.

Research within the perspective of a neo-institutional sociology has also produced a number of studies that emphasise the role of national policy paradigms in the Western world, as specific operationalizations of a general and rationalised values and worldviews. Such studies stress that local models represent socially constructed rationality, sometimes discussed as policy paradigms. National paradigms may adjust to changes, but their basic assumptions and structure seem surprisingly stable over long periods of time (Andersen 1993, Dobbin 1994). In such studies the internal legitimacy of these paradigms is the key factor that explain continuity. How such stable pattern is reproduced in the face of global pressures is not always clear. Presumably, the degree of perceived in-efficiency and the resonance between global and local models play a key role.

Dynamics is related to the relationship between abstract and universal paradigms, on the one hand, and local and particular paradigms, on the other hand. External legitimacy is not only linked to economic performance pressures, but institutional models heavily vested in cultural forms. Solutions are not local constructions, but variations over international trends and themes that facilitate and shape changes. The argument here is that the impact of these particular cultural forms helps account for two aspects of EU transformations. First, it bridges the gap between EU's transformational capacity and a weak organisational core. Second, it helps us understand why EU-level outcomes seem to reflect broader international trends, rather than just the overlapping perspectives and interests emerging from existing national paradigms.

In its standard formulation neo-institutional sociological theory has little to say about the role of the EU as an independent institution between the broad international trends and national adaptation. The mechanisms for change are assumed to work directly on the national level, so that the EU is explained as a variation over global modernisation processes where the nation state is the dominant actor. Here there is a parallel to the new intergovernmentalism that views the EU as primarily transnational in character, but where ordinary diplomacy can produce extraordinary results. In neo-institutional sociology the EU is regarded as an 'especially intense form of elaborating the global system' (Meyer 2001: 14). At most it would seem to synchronise national changes. This perspective is also reflected in attempts to introduce elements of such thinking in the international regime literature (Finnemore 1996). Collective international actors are only 'non-state' actors vested with cognitive and normative authority – 'otherhood' reflecting, focusing, elaborating and emitting authoritative 'globalised' institutional models.

Like nation states, the EU to a surprisingly high degree reflects broad international models and themes. However, the arguments presented here differ from the standard presentation of neo-institutional sociological theory in several ways.

First, the EU member countries represent historical traditions consistent with key elements in global rationalised culture and therefore have accumulated experience and competence in the form of embedded political, organisational and legal concepts and rules. Such characteristics make each country perceptive to, and able to, influence external change impulses. At the same time such elements may also serve as the common denominator that makes it possible to find collective solutions in situations characterised by diverse interests and policy paradigms.

Second, the EU is seen as a collective institution that, over time, has acquired characteristics, which tend to reinforce elements of abstract and rationalised international paradigms. The institutional set-up and political culture emphasise such arguments even more than in other international organisations like WTO. At the same time co-operation is comprehensive and codified in an accumulated set of legally binding rules. This creates a context of legitimate discourse where legitimacy often becomes a question of legality.

Changes in EU energy policy – and the increasing integration of this policy area in the EU-system – reflect that new international paradigms of economic organisation have emerged. Such emerging frameworks affect both the EU and the individual countries directly. The general hypothesis is that, all things being equal, the external global models will spread more easily in situations where there is high degree of resonance with regional and national policy paradigms. However, when looking at particular cases, this hypothesis must be modified by a several other factors. Developed Western countries are more likely to be able to uphold their fairly successful models. This is more likely for large, powerful countries – or influential groups of countries – than for smaller countries. Such factors may influence the willingness of member countries to engage in reform processes.

In the area of energy, successes reflect the 'pull' of increased EU-integration despite diverse and conflicting interests, to be exploited by political entrepreneurs, primarily the Commission (Nylander 2000). These changes involve three stages that are closely linked. First, the introduction and legitimisation of an alternative EU-level model or framework, where arguments about appropriate organisational principles and form play a key role. Second, the gradual specification of the content of this framework, towards the formulation of an EU-level policy paradigm where implications of alternative organisational forms are debated and negotiated. Third, the national implementation and modification that further gives substance to the new EU-level paradigm. The relationship between such processes may very; in terms of being sequential or parallel, and with respect to the type of interaction that takes place between them.

Fligstein (1996) discusses the creation of the internal market programme as the construction of a market. He argues that the concept of the internal market served a 'concept of control', bringing together a number of ideas and proposals in a way which creates commitment to the wider EU-integration project. However, he says little about how this general framework is translated into specific sector legislation. This is the focus here, and we will pursue this though the example of EU natural gas policy.

3. Natural Gas – the Emergence of a New EU Energy Policy Paradigm

For a long time energy sectors in the Western world was influenced by strong state regulation and hierarchy. Sometime during the 1980s this dominant international model became contested. This led to far-reaching changes in the US, but also in other countries, most notable the UK. In both the US and in the UK, energy had been heavily regulated for decades (Tugwell 1988), and liberalisation of the energy sectors followed a political break-through for 'market ideology'. The sources of this change are outside the scope of this chapter (but see Hall 1989, Haas 1992). However, as a result, an international model of energy policy has emerged emphasising a more active use of markets, with less political interference. In the following discussion we will focus on the EU policy initiatives in the natural gas market, which were introduced from 1990. In 1992 the Commission launched a formal *Proposal for a Council directive concerning common rules for the internal market in natural gas*. This became the focus for the prolonged conflict that eventually led to the passing of the modified *Gas directive* in 1998.

The external pressures motivating the Commission's preparatory work on a gas market proposal were not related to competitive pressures undermining existing national energy sector arrangements. The initiative must be viewed in the context of the Single market, and the content of the proposal primarily reflected the growing support for international institutional models emphasising market organisation of the energy sectors. The model for a reorganised gas market was inspired by an emerging international paradigm which served as a normative model. This model was most clearly expressed in the US system with its emphasis on an active competition authority. In other words, the Commission initiative did not reflect local performance problems, but the normative appeal of a general model emphasising market functionality and a strong competition authority.

The change towards a new international economic policy paradigm for energy reflected the general political climate, but also changes in the international supply situation that had been 'normalised' after more than a decade of turbulence. The change in the dominant political-economic perspective on energy was partly formalised by the Energy Charter Treaty during the early 1990s (Dore and Debauw 1995). This Treaty brought together the former Soviet and its satellites and the OECD countries. In the EU the liberalization of the energy sector was first carried out in the UK during the mid 1980s. These reforms, most importantly privatisations, were primarily motivated and legitimated by a revival of liberal ideology in economic policy (so-called 'Thatcherism') (Andersen 1993). At the EU-level, pressures for change were picked up and reinforced by the Commission and the British government, as part of the Single market programme.

There were, however, some special characteristics of the energy sectors in EU countries that complicated the process. Such characteristics represented historical experiences and perceptions of market failures as well as political objectives. There were real reasons why the energy sector had been organised with clear elements of state control and hierarchy. Major energy resources were concentrated in a few countries outside the EU (for instance, the Middle East) and this had led to concern for supply and price stability. Also, there was a strong tendency in European countries to view the energy sector as more than just an economic sector. State interests were heavily biased by the fact that energy sectors were dominated by monopolistic companies (often state owned) and regulatory authorities, which could articulate clear and strong interests within established national paradigms. The preceding decade of turbulence in the oil market has reinforced this. Although linked by supply pipelines, the European gas market consisted of separate national markets (Arentsen 2004).

The natural gas sector was relatively new, expanding during the 1980s, almost as a 'counter culture' to the Single market programme. It was characterised by high degree of state regulation and an oligopolistic sector organisation. In its report The internal market on energy the Commission (1988:57) stated that "Natural or regional monopolies or virtual monopolies dominate the natural gas transmission and distribution industry in Europe ... The biggest barriers to free movement of natural gas in Europe are government controls on natural gas imports and exports and undertakings holding a monopoly or dominant position enabling them to block the movements of natural gas"'. The energy sector was deliberately kept out of the first round of the internal market 'package'. However, it was never the Commission's intention to make a permanent exception. That would violate the general pattern of economic reform.

Estrada et al (1988) provided an authoritative overview over the West-European gas market by the late 1980s. Their conclusion was that the impressive 'existing structure... is well founded in a complex network of economic and political interests' (p. 254). Discussing the potential for transformation in the 1990s they conclude that: 'It does take a lot of imagination to foresee the present structure being undermined' (i.e. liberalised). Political 'undercurrents have to grow to a wave of political determination and a forceful coalition of economic interests to become a serious challenge for the status quo' (p. 259). For such, and other, reasons it would take some time before EU's Single market philosophy could be transformed into an operational energy policy paradigm at the EU-level.

The introduction of a new EU policy paradigm, as a directive proposal concerning the liberalisation of EU natural gas markets, challenged key elements in the existing system. The transmission companies, linking major sellers and buyers had an especially strong position. They would use their monopoly to serve as an intermediary, buying from a few producers and selling to national monopolies, with high profits. As a consequence, there was no gas-to-gas competition. Natural gas was priced according to competing energy sources, most often oil. The benefit of the system was that long-term contracts made it possible to secure the financing of gas field and transportation development, and thereby security of supplies. However, the Commission's general argument that increased EU-wide competition would improve global competitiveness was assumed to hold also for energy. When energy policy initiatives were introduced a few years later it was thought that it would be possible to achieve success despite strong national resistance, precisely because of the momentum of the Single market and international trends.

The gas directive proposal (1992) led to intense conflicts

The gas directive proposal was part of a package. Other directives concerned price transparency for electricity and gas contracts and transit rights for electricity and gas. The gas directive proposal aimed at liberalising the gas market by attacking the present structure. The proposal covered four major areas.

One major issue concerned market opening; i.e. how much of the gas market should be opened for competition, and who should have the right to send gas through transmission lines. The latter had so far been the exclusive right of the pipeline owners. The proposal introduced the concept of regulated third party access with an EU-level regulatory authority[1]. This became the major source of controversy in the years to come. The second major issue concerned the impact of liberalisation on long-term contracts (take-or pay) that traditionally had been a key instrument to secure investments and long term supplies. The third issue was whether it was possible to impose special obligations (equal price, supply security, environmental protection etc.) on suppliers all over Europe. The fourth issue concerned the need to establish separate markets around various functions in the gas market, which had before been 'bundled' by monopolies.

[1] Third party access (TPA) means that gas should not only be transported between two parties (usually the producer and the merchant pipeline) but also for a third party (usually the customer in the end of the pipeline), thus providing a direct link between producer and consumer.

The Commission proposal reflected a strategy for deregulation *and* liberalisation. However, with the exception of the UK, no EU member countries had any clear recognition of the crucial role to be played by EU regulatory authorities in the implementation and policing of competition and liberalisation (Stern 1998: xxii). The introduction of the directive proposal led to strong confrontation and polarisation, where a clear majority (11 of 12 member states at that time) rejected the Commission initiative, and so did industry. The Commission's attempt to involve the industry through committees, to achieve dialogue and find common ground, broke down. Why was the initiative not dropped? Part of the answer was that the existing national industrial models in the majority of member countries did not have the appropriate form in the new international and EU context where market models were on the offensive. Representatives of traditional models were used to argue that 'energy was too important to leave to the market', they were unprepared for the new discourses focusing mainly on market functionality.

The degree of resonance and conflict between the emerging EU policy paradigm and pre-existing national paradigms varied. The national paradigms reflected traditions of state – economy relations in various countries, and the countries' position with respect to natural gas resources, affecting interests related to an emerging European market. Most countries were only, or primarily, consumers and heavily dependent on import. For this reason the Commission initiatives found it politically feasible to start its reform effort with an up stream focus (production and transmission). The expectation was that consumer prices would be lower in a (more) deregulated market. This would also lead to expansion of local market, pushing out other types of energy that were seen as a threat to the environment (coal, nuclear). However, a major concern for most consumer countries was related to security of supplies, traditionally dealt with through diversification of supply countries and long term contracts.

Countries with producer and/or exporter interests were most directly affected, but also here interests differed. British gas production was primarily for domestic consumption. The UK was the first to privatise its state gas monopoly. The country pushed for the EU reform, but knew that it would take time. In the meantime the national market could be protected and developed. In the wider picture the active British position in this area could balance some of the blame for its scepticism towards EU-integration in other areas. The Netherlands, the other major EU producer and exporter, had a production and sales monopoly based on a partnership between the government and private international companies. It had played a key role in developing the European gas industry as major exporter; there was initially no interest in reforms.

The EU gas directive was motivated by a wish to increase gas-to-gas competition and to lower prices. It would also make it difficult to keep up member states' traditional statist structures (strong regulation, direct ownership and state companies) and national (state-dominated) sales monopolies. This was a particular challenge for Norway as the major Western country supplying the EU with natural gas. As an EEA member (which brings it under EU directives), Norway would be affected by the new directive. In addition to the opposition of some member states, the European gas industry was strongly against the reform initiatives. The national gas industries, serving national markets, were not experiencing problems in terms of technical efficiency or earnings. They had vested interests in national infrastructure – for example pipelines – that the Commission wanted to open up for competitive use. The only industrial interests that supported the Commission were large industrial customers (like the chemical industry) that hoped for lower prices.

The first years after the introduction of the Commission proposal for a directive were characterised by strong opposition, periodic stalemate and uncertainty about the feasibility of the project. '...(M)any of the established actors in European gas industries ...regarded the introduction of liberalization as the equivalent of the end of civilization' (Stern 1998: 91). The opposition in the natural gas sector was to a certain extent legitimised by the general scepticism towards further EU-integration, symbolised by reactions to the Maastricht treaty. Despite strong and intense opposing discussion on the natural gas directive, the idea was kept alive, mainly due to the Commission. The legitimacy of Commission actions rested on formal mandates and earlier state-commitments. Such earlier state-commitments were weighed against the costs of accepting new sector arrangements. However, the proposed policy paradigm also reflected a new appropriate form for organising any economic activity. In the face of this member states found it hard to come up with legitimate reasons for preserving the existing national sector arrangements. Although opposition to parts of the proposal was still strong, it gradually became clear that natural gas issues had to be addressed in terms of new concepts and perspectives.

However, up to the mid-1990s, the fate of the natural gas reform in the EU remained quite uncertain. In 1994 the original Commission proposal was formally rejected. Over the next few years the EU Commission worked on an alternative, some would say a watered down version of the original directive. Key concepts and formulations were altered, but the general perspective and normative orientation remained the same. The observed development contradicts an intergovernmentalist model of explanation, as pointed out by several students of EU energy policy (Matlary 1997, Eldevik 1999). Member states were not the privileged actors; changes involved not only interests, but also new perspectives and models. And such changes could not realistically be seen as autonomous domestic processes. The EU was not just an arena for given interests (Eldevik 1999:82-83).

4. Paradigm Elaboration and Strategic Re-orientation

From the mid-1990s the nature of discussions over the gas market reform changed in several ways. A key element in the Commission's formulation of the new paradigm had been to develop implications of market theory, emphasising market functionality with political considerations related to security of supply and public service obligations. This had made it possible to rethink a number of issues. Another key element was that the legitimacy of existing national energy paradigms had been undermined along the way. This was not primarily due to failure of performance, but the general de-legitimation of statist models of economic organization in the EU. In addition, there was the direct impact of market ideology in individual countries, sometimes pushed by privatisation schemes (in part, to finance public deficits).

Gradually we find changes in the arguments and the nature of confrontation over the EU gas market reform. This happened partly in political negotiations, partly through long drawn out expert-driven arguments. Along the way we find a more active role of EU court decisions, and also new strategic initiatives from parts of industry. This trend reflected that the new policy paradigm was becoming legitimized as a framework. Arguments were more about appropriateness than specific consequences. More and more it appeared that traditional member state and industry views could not be sustained over time. The implementation of the electricity directive served as a model, both in term of providing legitimacy and in clarifying the strategic implications of a new perspective. The new general EU-dynamics, related to the Amsterdam Treaty and the introduction of the Euro reinforced such processes. Increasingly the question was not if a new gas market directive was to be passed, but when and with what provisions. Increasingly arguments involved specific calculations of future gains and strategic opportunities.

Stern (1992:ix), a major authority on the EU gas market, was one of the first to argue that the debate on the liberalisation of the natural gas sector put far too much stress on the European Commission initiatives and too little on the actions of powerful market players. His book *Third party access in European gas industries* (1992) has the subtitle 'Regulation driven or market led'? This book does not, however, challenge the role of the Commission as the promoter of an alternative new framework for European natural gas policy. The argument is, rather, that the *content* of major provisions, like third party access, most likely will materialise as a result of actions taken by major players. The alternative would be the imposition of more clear-cut EU regulations by a powerful EU-level regulatory authority. In later work Stern (1998) also describes how market strategies as well as a more active court system has been instrumental in bringing about changes. His analysis provides a good account of how a contested new framework is specified in political processes that runs parallel to processes in the court and market system.

In the period up to the passing of a modified gas directive in 1998, important changes were made in controversial areas referred to above.

The original proposal for an EU-level framework regulating third party access to pipelines was inspired by a so-called common carrier concept from the US, but this was effectively blocked. A key controversy throughout the 1990s was how to secure so-called voluntary or negotiated third party access to pipelines that controlled the flow of natural gas. Related to this was the question of how much of the traded volume should be covered by such arrangements. Another key controversy concerned the problems of securing long-term investment, and thereby supplies, in a system that undermined traditional long-term contracts. Gradually a new concept of security developed, emphasising the mutual interdependence between exporters and importers and the reduced operational risk in an integrated European system. The controversy over the nature and level of public obligations to be met by companies was resolved, partly through the anticipated use of the court system. The controversy over unbundling of commercial functions led to a general acceptance of the principle, in line with competition law[2].

Compared to other member countries, Britain represented a mature market and British companies needed access to existing pipeline networks to take advantage of this. Consequently, Britain wanted to achieve explicit rules for third party access and a high degree of market opening as soon as possible. The proposed 28 per cent minimum of third party access that became the result was considered too low. Also, Britain would like to see regulated access, where companies' access to pipelines was regulated through a tariff. On the other hand, most other countries still had reservations about even the modified liberalisation directive, but a few countries had changed their positions. For some time the Netherlands was working against reform. As it turned out, it became possible for the Dutch interests to reposition themselves under a new regime, to see advantages that might outweigh costs. After resisting the new regime for several years, the Dutch were among the first to change their strategy (1995). Also, Spain was characterised by a pronounced change in attitude to the new directive. In both countries governments decided to move towards opening up the market more quickly than dictated by the directive.

Other countries remained reluctant throughout the whole process. In France, part of the defence for the national model was pursued through the court systems. The objective was to limit the role of competition to preserve the public service obligation. In Germany the dominant position of Ruhrgas prevented rapid political changes. However, as will be discussed below, important changes were introduced through the market. Norway, as one of three major exporters to the EU (together with Russia and Algeria) waged a lobbying campaign against the new natural gas directive. Under the old regime the three major exporters were involved in a strategic game with a few European buyers. In Norway natural gas was produced by several companies and production had to be regulated through one central negotiating authority (GFU). This strengthened Norway's position in the market, but an important part of this arrangement was also to coordinate production in such a way that it improved the exploitation of resources. The challenge was to find a way to preserve a legitimate form of such regulation.

Part of the change in national positions was due to pressures from the EU Commission. It threatened both France and other countries with court cases for

---

[2] Unbundling refers to the separation of different commercial functions, such as pipeline transport and local distribution, where the objective is to achieve transparency and competition between specialised companies.

violating competition law. In the context of growing support for the emerging new paradigm, and with reorientations going on in other countries, Commission pressures created incentives for reform under domestic control. In some countries changes were motivated by new company initiatives. The announcement by the German gas company Wintershall to build new pipelines in 1989 (to further the consumer interests of the parent company BASF) and in 1990 (in partnership with the Russian Gazprom) introduced competition vis-a-vis the dominant Ruhrgas.

4.1 The Reformulated Gas Directive

The first directive on the liberalization of the EU gas market was passed in 1998. It was a weak compromise full of unsolved issues (Hanscher 2003). On the one hand, it opened up an alternative to the pre-existing monopoly system. On the other hand, the direct and immediate requirements of the directive were limited. The directive required that a minimum of 28 per cent of traded volume be opened for competition when implemented (fall 2000). This number was to be increased over time, but even in 2008, member countries could refuse small customers the choice of supplier as long as 43 per cent was covered by the liberalised system. Systems for regulating third party access to pipelines were to be developed on the national level. In addition, companies could apply for exception from the third party access article if serious economic and financial problems should arise as a consequence. The so-called public service obligations allowed for national protection of vulnerable customers, protection of final customers' rights, social and economic cohesion, environmental protection, and security of supply[3].

The directive contained very few super-national regulations, and the member countries had preserved considerable freedom to regulate national markets in the future (Arentsen 2004). Two of the most important battles, determination of tariff methodologies and regulatory provisions for enforcing competition and third party access at the EU-level, were defeated already before the first attempts of finding an agreement (in 1994). In the words of Stern (1998:xviii):

> *The value of the directive, therefore, lies not so much in its specific provisions, which are likely to be rapidly overtaken by events, but rather in the fact that it established both the principle of access to (pipeline) networks, and the assurance that opponents of competition and liberalisation cannot indefinitely procrastinate in the opening up of their gas markets.*

Increasingly national regulatory efforts and new market strategies became important in providing the content and pace of market liberalisation. However, the emerging EU-level policy paradigm would not have seemed possible without the persistent role of the Commission in pushing for an alternative framework. The legitimacy of the framework was a precondition for the dynamics to be observed over later years. In this process there was ample room for the interests and strategies of member states, industry interests and courts. Still, the legitimacy of an alter-

[3] Specified in the Commission's amendment of the initial directive. COM (2001/125) Commission communication: Completing the internal energy market.

native normative framework is preceding and facilitating such strategies, rather than emerging from them.

Member states were committed to bring into force the laws, regulations and administrative provisions necessary to comply with the gas directive no later than in 2000. However, by mid-2002 some countries like France and Germany had only partially transposed the directive into national law. Because of the emerging status of their gas industry, Portugal and Greece had a 10-years derogation from most of the directive's obligations. Other countries, like Italy and Spain had gone further than required. The UK was going further than everyone else. However, the overall picture was mixed, reflecting different national considerations.

Compared to the original draft, the 1998 directive was rather modest, but crucial in changing the basic rules of the game. On the other hand, the directive did not go very far in specifying how liberalisation should be achieved in practice. As Stern (1998:viii) puts it: "Not only are the most crucial commitments and provisions defined in rather general terms, but the options to adopt 'negotiated access' (rather than 'regulated access') could give many transmission companies an ideal opportunity to indulge in protracted and inconclusive 'negotiations'."

A further clarification of what was meant by different concepts and provisions in the directive was left to the implementation process. The emphasis on subsidiarity, as a political necessity, opened up for different national approaches with respect to how various provisions should be secured at the national level. This meant that the further elaboration of the new policy paradigm shifted from the EU-level to member state level. To ensure that implementation took place in time, and in accordance with the directive, the Commission created two follow-up committees. One consisted of country representatives (including EEA countries), the other of industry representatives. These Committees partly reflect the Commission's responsibility to secure implementation, but they are based on voluntary co-operation.

The implementation process faced the challenge of balancing three important aspects: (1) To clarify the implications of the directive in relation to various national settings, allowing for a certain degree of flexibility with respect to the speed of reform and specific organisational solutions, and at the same time making sure that solutions were consistent with the directive and general EU competition law. In other words, the problems was to secure convergence around one common paradigm for a liberalized gas market, while at the same time allowing for a certain degree of divergence with respect to how this model is operationalized in diverse national contexts, even over a longer time period.

(2) Concerning third party access to pipe lines, one of the key issues, countries could choose either negotiated access (based on publications of the main commercial conditions applicable) or (nationally) regulated access based on published tariffs, or a combination of these two systems. Eight countries went for regulated third party access, and two countries for a combination of the two models. Only

three countries chose negotiated access, but in a restricted form. The directive required countries to achieve a minimum level of market opening, 20 per cent by August 2000 and 33 per cent by 2008. However, at this time (Spring, 2008) most countries have wanted to go further and faster than this. This was also the case for the required expansion of eligible customers, and so-called unbundling of commercial functions.

(3) According to article 21 of the directive member states should designate a 'competent authority, independent of the parties, to settle expeditiously disputes'. Member states should also (article 22) 'create appropriate and efficient mechanisms for regulation, control and transparency so as to avoid abuse of a dominant position'. Member states chose different regulatory approaches. Few member states planned to establish independent regulators for gas and few wanted sector regulators for natural gas as such. The majority wanted to leave regulatory responsibilities in the hands of the general energy or common gas/ electricity regulators. In some countries, the ministry responsible for energy matters was to play a key role in the regulatory system.

Similar patterns can be found with respect to other articles of the directive. The point here is that national solutions may vary considerable and still be within the general model laid down in the directive. An important aspect of the implementation process is to ensure that various solutions are consistent with the demands of equal treatment and general provisions of EU competition law. This also means that legitimacy of national structures depends on consistency with the underlying model, and that this legitimacy in many ways becomes equivalent to the *legality* of particular arrangements.

By August 2002 all member states (except Portugal) had adopted some form of third party access to the transmission network. Even Gas de France had adopted a hybrid of negotiated and regulated access in the absence of a national gas law. However, the meeting of European Gas Regulatory Forum in 2003 considered that the 1998 directive did not go far enough to create a truly internal EU market. For instance, the negotiated third party access enabled the gas transmission companies, which was usually national or regional monopolies, to negotiate individual gas transportation terms and argue for higher tariffs (Farnejad 2004). A new gas directive in 2003 was passed to address the shortcomings of the liberalization process in the gas market. This directive made it compulsory to adopt a 'regulated' access tariff, and to establish an independent regulator for the gas industry. In addition, a non-discriminatory third party access was to be developed through legal unbundling of gas transport from trading services.

It should be no great surprise that also the transposition and implementation of the new directive demonstrated considerable differences among member states. The heterogeneity in the EU gas market increased considerably with the enlargement in 2004. Many of the new member countries lacked the necessary capacity and competence. However, the enlargement not only affected the situation in the gas market, it changed what could reasonably be expected in terms of common EU-integration. The EU has become a colourful and heterogeneous family of states. The scope of the EU has been broadened to cover new policy areas. However, not all member states are equally eager, let alone able, to participate in all aspects of integration. The ways states transpose, implement and pursue EU rules have changed. Common EU rules go hand in hand with differentiation and re-politicisation of Single Market regulation at the national level (Andersen and Sitter 2006).

Table 11.1. Paradigm Emergence for the EU natural gas market

	Prior to 1998/2000	1998/2000-Present
Problem issue	Prior to 1990, no real issue for the EU. Between 1990-1998 attempts to introduce a radical reform, based on market principles and American experiences meets resistance from member-states and companies and needs to be modified.	Establish an EU internal market. Break-up national monopolies and oligopolies. Liberalization, but need to overcome variations and imperfections in market arrangements and national regulatory forms.
Goals	Prior to 1990, no goals. Realistic reform goals emerge during the 1990s are articulated in the new directive proposal at the end of decade.	Privatization, increased competition and lower prices. Specialized competition through 'unbundling.' Uniform national regulation through the EU policy
Agents responsible	Member states, their gas companies, other private interests. During the 1990s, the Commission assumes primary responsibility for establishing an internal market	EU, active Commission, EU court, national governments, regulators
Models of socio-economic causality	Gas production and distribution run by national monopolies serving national interests, lack of particular competition and transparency. During the 1990s, the Commission lead intense discussions about how EU authority and market principles should be applied to transform the gas industry.	National agents form monopolies and oligopolistic structures to advance their interests. EU Power must be mobilized to break down these structures and to establish the structures of an internal market. Market forces will reinforce change.

Methods/strategies to deal with problem	Prior to 1990, no need for EU methods/strategies (there was no issue). During the 1990s, the EU Commission with support from some member countries acts to break up national monopolies and develops a negotiated model for an internal EU market.	Stress integrated market mechanism. Use of legislation and regulation to break up old system. Push countries, companies to accept principles of internal market; use competence of EU-law and the court system as well as political pressure, bench-marking, and continuous piecemeal legislation regulating the gas market.
Actors most affected	Prior to 1990, the EU had no policy or strategy and only indirect impact on national governments and gas companies, which were the primary agents. During the 1990s, the EU, in developing its strategy of liberalization, threatens national governments and gas companies.	National Governments, gas companies, other energy companies, big industrial consumers, limited involvement of private individuals
Expertise, knowledge requirements	Experts on national law, national administrators and distribution systems	Experts on market theory, EU law, EU regulation, experts on market strategy, mergers and acquisitions

The tendency towards differentiated integration is also reflected in the way gas and energy companies are allowed to use market rules to consolidate and strengthen dominant market positions in regional and national markets. Important countries like Germany, France, Italy and Spain support their national champions. Only a few major companies will be able to operate on a pan-European level. There is a tendency towards Europeanization of the industry structure; the trend towards a fully open pan-European market has been weakened. The EU directives in the gas market aimed at unbundling between the different vertical functions of the industry. While this is happening to some degree, there is a trend towards horizontal integration across different types of energy industries, like gas and electricity. This has happened first in Germany, later in other countries like Belgium and France.

To summarize: when the EU gas market reform reached the implementation stage, the dynamics of EU gas market liberalisation was moved from the EU-level to the national level. In the following years the elaboration of the EU model rested heavily on national processes, but also industry strategies and court decisions. These processes were important in providing the new EU policy paradigm its specific content. However, the gas directive has changed the basic logic and unleashed dynamic forces of liberalisation. An important part of this is the increased weight of the market in relation to politics. If companies go to court with complaints that certain arrangements do not function properly, there will be pressures for change. In the coming years we are probably going to see a further structural transformation of the market, with the introduction of new technology, new companies, new types of actors (traders) and price formation increasingly realized through the spot market[4].

5. Understanding Complex Transformation

Changes in EU energy policy are indirectly driven by international economic competition (for instance, the goal of lower energy prices), but the formulations of new policies reflect a general paradigmatic shift in the role of markets. This shift is reinforced by the institutionalization of the EU Single market and changes in energy market reforms in countries like the US and UK. The construction of a new EU energy policy paradigm is not, however, simply an application of a general liberal model or a copying of the US and UK. The new EU paradigm emerges as a result of a radical and complex transformation process reflecting political realities as well as arguments about market functionality and market failure. The consistent pressures for reform in the face of widespread and intense opposition rests on the EU's increased supranational authority vested in law, decision-making procedures, as well as a normative model of EU-integration. The principle of subsidiarity opens up 'flexible' implementation under EU competition law.

The major gas directives passed in 1998 and 2003 were watered down versions of the original proposal. Still, they represented a fundamental challenge to national policy paradigms. The normative core of a liberal paradigm is active regulation to increase market functionality, and not to modify or replace the market mechanism. The 'what to do' in the energy sector was defined more narrowly, in terms of sector efficiency. The cognitive core, the 'how to do it' emphasized private ownership and the market mechanisms, rather than state ownership and intervention. With the exception of the UK, the new policy paradigm represented a break with strong national institutional traditions. The proposed policy reform was in line with the universal and proper form of 'modern' economic organization. Opposition was formulated in terms of particularistic concerns and statist language that had little legitimacy in the context of the Single Market. When it became clear that the liberal paradigm would be a new framework for policy making, states and industry actors looked for ways to accommodate specific interests and to gain time to learn, adapt and develop new strategies.

Because of the tensions and conflicts between the EU and national level, the implementation should take place under the principle of subsidiarity. The directive entailed a new policy paradigm, which in principle represented a new normative model that every country, as well as industry, accepted. On the other hand, there

[4] As a centrally located informant put it: 'We don't know exactly what is going to happen, but we have confidence in the future'.

were 'grey areas' as to what some elements of the directive actually implied. The principle of subsidiarity is an instrument to handle this, but the problem remained how to make sure that country specific interpretations did not violate common competition law, linking legitimacy and legality. For this reason two implementation committees were established to handle implementation under subsidiarity – one for the national regulator and one for the industry. Such committees are voluntary, but also linked to the Commission's mandate to monitor implementation.

The transformation of the EU energy policy paradigm weakened the role of the national governments, and strengthened the role of law and the energy companies. This was a movement towards a 'minimalist' type of regulation, often seen as a characteristic of the EU. However, the preceding transformation involves considerable state-like EU authority and capability for keeping initiatives on track, securing an outcome, and implementing decisions – while preserving the general direction of reform. This ability to carry out radical reforms, which transform 'almost unchangeable' national policy paradigms seems to contradict the image of the EU as an organisationally weak system, with a weak core, unclear institutional boundaries (Kohler-Koch and Eising, 1999) and with a high degree of freedom for political entrepreneurship and open access for a wide variety of actors (Andersen and Eliassen, 2001).

The institutionalisations of new policy paradigms are reflexive processes where actors change perceptions about interests (energy as commodity as opposed to being a part of economic/social policy), about the proper way to organise and control activities ('some sort of market' which will unleash new dynamics), and even about self-image and identities (what is the meaning of sovereignty). This does not in any way imply a romantic notion of conflicts being transcended in a collective heaven of EU co-operation. Conflicts persist, but they are framed in other ways, and as in all political processes some gain more than others do, and some lose.

The persistence of interests and conflicts is an important reason why some have suggested that complex transformation and learning should be explained in terms of rational actors influenced by the reinforcement of the 'stick and 'carrot'. Such a model seems to make more sense when actors face non-paradigmatic changes which facilitate 'single loop' learning, or when powerful actors may shape or control the process. In situations of radical and complex transformation, the ability to calculate interests in a future state is limited, and reinforcement often has to rely on arguments about appropriate form. The process around the natural gas directive illustrates the latter.

How are good and authoritative arguments constructed? What makes old arguments lose their power? This study suggests a process where the authorisation of arguments in relation to a wider paradigmatic framework plays a key role as a source of legitimacy, but arguments are not developed from scratch. Concepts and ideas are downloaded from various institutional settings, often from international experience codified in scientific knowledge or legal concepts and rules (OECD,

WTO). This is the case also from the wider EU context, as, for instance, established competition law. As integration proceeds, the available repertoire of embedded concepts and rules for defining issues will increase. It will be easier to find elements to build upon in the institutionalisation of new areas. This also means that certain elements become de-legitimated, because they do not have the proper form or cannot be relabelled within a new frame.

On the other hand, the EU member states represent historical traditions that also represent stores of accumulated insight, embedded and operational knowledge. This is reflected in the discourses over the EU directives and in the search for authoritative and legitimate arguments on the national level. The long drawn-out process of confrontation, stalemate and compromise was characterised by the parallel de-legitimisation of traditional statist models, on the one hand, and the legitimisation of a new market oriented model. This process took place at the central EU level as well as at the national level; and the relative weight of central policy, court decisions and industrial initiatives varied over time.

This chapter did not allow for a detailed confrontation between theoretical ideas and data; a reconstruction of how and through what mechanisms changes have taken place in the EU energy policy. Broad social changes of this nature take place in many ways, at many levels and sometimes in rather diffuse ways. Various aspect of this change may be analysed differently. However, the discussion suggests that the transformation of the EU energy sector illustrates some general point within a neo-institutional sociological perspective:

First, EU energy reforms have been part of a broader, global change strengthening the legitimacy of market models. However, Europeanization of policy is not only a copying process, it also represents modifications that feedback on the wider change process.

Second, The EU system has demonstrated a surprising capability to carry out radical reforms – even against the will of a majority of states – despite an apparently weak organisational core. This suggests that the legitimacy of the general paradigms vested in this loose structure plays a key role in keeping such processes on track and provides direction. The legitimisation of a new operational paradigm, over time, opens up for calculation of strategic opportunities and efficiencies, and not the other way around.

Third, the Europeanization of the nation state does not imply uniformity of structure. National structures may reflect the general European model to different degrees, not only as a matter of transition. However, the legitimacy of national forms increasingly becomes a question of legality. This means that national arrangements may be preserved to the extent that they can be defended or relabelled in proper legal terms.

A final comment concerns the dynamics of the process leading to the institutionalization of a new public policy paradigm in the area of EU energy policy. To some extent actors are borrowing from international frames supported by international organizations like the WTO. Early US reforms in the gas market had an important influence on the early stage, as did the British experience later on. To some extent such influences can be viewed as diffusion processes, where principles and models are translated into new EU and national contexts. However, the EU gas market reform also highlights the importance of learning and persuasion and the highly political and distinct nature of such processes. The resulting paradigms shift is not simply a matter of adopting something different, but a process of active construction of a market.

CHAPTER 12

The Irony of EU Climate Policy: A Crooked Path to a Paradigm Shift[1]

Tom R. Burns

1. Introduction

The processes leading up to and involving the EU in mediating and adopting the Kyoto Protocol reveal how rapidly political positions and images can change – often in unexpected ways. Briefly, it is fair to say that the United States laid the intellectual and international political grounds the market-oriented components of the Kyoto Protocol at the same time that the European Union was for a long time unsympathetic to what became a key part of the treaty, namely the "emission trading scheme and related economic mechanisms". Ironically, the EU now appears as if it was the founder of the Kyoto Protocol's emission trading scheme (ETS) at the same time that the USA became the global climate "outsider" if not "villain" during the Bush years.[2]

In what sense can one claim that a public policy paradigm shift took place with the EU adoption and implementation of the ETS. We suggest below that the properties of the ETS (and related mechanisms) were very different from earlier EU climate change public policy initiatives and programs; in general, earlier efforts were command-and-control and taxation types of regime as opposed to more purely market-oriented regimes (although the different institutional arrangements may all be based to a greater or lesser extent on "economic motivations)." The ETS development represents in our view a paradigm shift for EU climate change policymaking, in particular by not only adopting "market mechanisms" but by moving these mechanisms to an EU central level ("Europeanization"). We shall also map out the complicated socio-political process whereby this shift came about, a shift full of twists and ironies. There also seems to be important lessons to draw from this. One concerns the importance of signing an agreement and thereby establishing a governance structure, which in itself creates a new setting for shifts in agent positions and further institutional adaptation and innovation.

[1] We are grateful to Bo Kjellen, Stephen Schneider, and Matti Vainio for their comments and suggestions on an earlier draft of this article and to Mikael Roman who was initially involved in the research for this chapter.

[2] A great deal has been happening in the USA since 2000, much of it, however, on the level of states (California) and regions (New England area) (Roman and Carson, 2009).

2. The Crooked Path Leading to the Kyoto Protocol

One should bear in mind that the EU was intensively involved in climate change issues for a substantial period of time prior to Kyoto, for instance, already in the early 1980s and at the Rio Summit (1992). As Beuermann (2002: 18) stresses, "The EU has consistently been the largest political grouping emphasing the urgency of the issue and pressing for stronger policy responses, and has played a key role throughout the policy process. However, it has historically fallen far short of its potential and ambitions. Its effectiveness was disputed and external judgments have been very mixed."

In general, the EU favored central measures such as the coordination of member-state policies including harmonization of energy taxes across the EU (to eliminate competitive advantages based on differences in such taxes among EU countries), adoption of energy efficiency measures, establishment of speed limits on motor vehicle traffic and improvements in transport management (Wettestad, 2000:27ff).[3] In the 1980s, EU plans for an EU-wide carbon or energy tax was vehemently opposed by some industries (transport, agriculture, petroleum, and chemicals) and several member-states, particularly the U.K. and Ireland, vehemently and effectively opposed this initiative. Consequently, it faced a serious barrier according to EU "constitutional rules", the introduction of an EU tax would require unanimous support of the member states.[4]

2.1 The USA versus EU in Climate Change Initiatives

Differences in EU and USA positions with regards to the climate issue were laid already with the negotiations of the Climate Convention in 1992. That same year at the Rio Summit, then US President George H.W. Bush was heavily criticized for being reluctant to sign the proposed Convention under the argument that 'it could seriously damage the US economy'. Basically, his argument was that any policy

[3] Carbon Taxes Carbon taxes are simply direct payments to government (collection body), based on the carbon content of the fuel being consumed; given that the primary objective of the abatement policy is to lower carbon dioxide emissions, carbon taxes make sense economically and environmentally because they tax the externality (carbon) directly. Since coal generates the greatest amount of carbon emissions, it is therefore taxed in greater proportion than oil and natural gas, which have lower carbon concentrations (Coal contains .03 tons of carbon per million Btu of energy, while oil and natural gas contain only .024 and .016 tons, respectively) (Baumert, 1998).

[4] MacKenzie (2009: 16-17) emphasizes, "The unanimity requirement was too demanding for a Europe-wide carbon tax to be feasible politically: 'We learned our lesson in that respect', said an interviewee involved in the tax proposal… The initial proposal for a harmonized European carbon tax was, as one policymaker interviewee put it, 'killed basically by the U.K.', which was concerned to keep jurisdiction over tax at the national level, although other member states were potential opponents as well, and 'if one member state, even a very tiny member state, said no' to a tax measure, 'it was no.' As another interviewee said, 'taxation is always fraught with obstacles, and if it isn't one member state who is objecting it's another. And it [the objection] might rotate around the member states because they all have their electoral cycles'."

measures to reduce emissions needed thoughtful revision, presumably combining various market incentives in order to guarantee continued economic growth. The USA prior to Kyoto (e.g. Berlin, 1995 (see later)) was very much against the setting of quotas, stressing voluntary and market-type mechanisms and insisting that any regime cover all countries including poorer countries.

In a number of areas, the EU was highly active and innovative at the same time that in any comparison of CO_2 emissions, the EU appeared – and continues to appear – relatively successful in limiting its share of global emissions (see Table 12.1).

Table 12.1. Total GHG Emissions (CO_2, CH_4, N_2O, PFCs, HFCs, SF_6) in 2000 (CAIT, 2009)

Country/Region	Share of global emissions (percent)	Tons per capita	Avg. Annual Growth 1990-2005	Total Growth 1990-2005
United States	20.6	24.5	-0.1	-1.9
EU-27	14.82	10.2	-0.7	-10.0
Japan	3.96	10.3	0.6	10.0
Sweden	0.21	7.9	-0.7	-9.8
China	14.52	3.8	3.8	74.8
India	4.80	1.6	1.8	30.3
Brazil	2.84	5.4	1.1	17.6
Russia	5.74	13.0	-2.4	-31.0

2.2 After Roll-back a Process of Groping Ahead

The backdrop to the EU paradigm shift was first, the so-called "roll-back" in the period after 1992 (Zapfel and Vainio, 2002). The tax effort was dropped in 1994 as a result of strong opposition from some industries (transport, agriculture, petroleum and chemicals), from EU Directorates other than Environment (and Energy) and from some member states, above all the U.K. but also from some of those receiving structural funds (e.g., Ireland, Spain, and Portugal).

After the collapse of the carbon tax initiative prior to Kyoto, the EU focused on determining climate change goals within the EU – both collectively and by individual member states. The EU devoted considerable effort to establish binding 'common and coordinated' polices and measures (PAMs) – despite early indications that few EU members shared this enthusiasm (some aspiring to EU membership were sympathetic but never fully endorsed the EU proposals). Part of the EU's motivation apparently rested on the hope that the USA might eventually agree also to binding PAMs.

The EU had obvious political will and a powerful rhetoric about dealing with climate change but was weak when it came to action and implementation. Some industrialized countries and NGOs pointed to the "credibility gap" between the EU's political goals and rhetoric, on the one hand, and the lack of a coherent, implementation strategy, on the other hand (especially after the collapse of the carbon tax initiative).

The EU (up to and during Kyoto) gave much of its attention to ways to distribute emissioin-reduction targets within the EU zone and ways to accomplish a Kyoto Treaty. While calling for PAM proposals, it never came up with concrete mechanisms for reducing emissions (Yamin, 2000: 59). But it managed to establish target-sharing agreements for the EU zone, and this can be seen as a major achievement (Wettestad, 2000:36) (see Table 12.2). And, as we shall see, it played a key mediating role in bringing about the Kyoto accomplishment itself. All in all, major accomplishments, but in the context of great expectations, somewhat disappointing for many.

2.3 Kyoto Process

By the time of Kyoto meetings (December, 1997) the EU had little to show for its efforts over two decades at trying to achieve major emission reductions in the EU area despite headway of some individual countries. The EU Commission (DG Environment?) worked hard to get the EU members to agree to country specific emission reductions, and made considerable progress at this – although there was no EU-wide mechanism. Apparently, the EU hoped that other countries, particularly the developed countries (Annex I countries in UN terminology) and, above all, the USA would agree to substantial reductions and support binding policies and mechanisms.

However, the USA was reluctant to establish goals for emissions and was determined that the agreement should include an array of flexible, market-based approaches for reducing emissions (MacKenzie, 2008). Already in Berlin (Spring, 1995) and afterwards, the USA had market type mechanism(s) to propose and had the expertise and experience to promote them. In order to "involve" the USA as a major player, the EU supported the American mechanisms without particularly wanting (or knowing precisely how) to buy into them. But one must keep in mind to what extent the EU found itself struggling rather fruitlessly for the climate change cause. The USA (and the alliance JUSCANNZ[5] along with OPEC) were arguing that there was no scientific consensus about anthrogeneric climate change and, in any case the developing countries should not be made exceptions (while the latter opposed this vigorously, claiming that this was a "post-colonial strategy" to keep them from fully developing).

The context was a challenging one. In the view of some, the USA had a *de facto* veto (Buermann, 2002:17). MacKenzie (2009:12) reports, "The Clinton administration entered the Kyoto negotiations determined that 'the agreement should include an array of flexible, market-based approaches for reducing emissions'; it was con-

[5] This grouping, which was a counter-point to the EU and the Group-77 of developing countries consisted of Japan, the US, Canada, Australia, New Zealand, and Norway (we have found no reports about how comfortable Norway felt with these "fellow-travellers".

vinced that those approaches would keep the net costs 'relatively modest'.[6] In pushing for the use of emissions trading in curbing global warming, the Clinton administration faced opposition both from the European Union (which preferred mandatory measures) and from third-world countries, many of which saw the argument that greenhouse-gas emissions could more cheaply be curbed among themselves as 'carbon colonialism'. The US negotiators, however, possessed energy, professionalism, the clout of the world's sole superpower, and strong conviction of the correctness of what one observer of the negotiations called 'economic ideology ... dominated by general equilibrium concepts that focus upon economic efficiency and imply that flexibility achieves the same environmental benefits at lower costs: hence, the more flexibility the better'" (Grubb, 1999: 99, 112). At the same time, before leaving for Kyoto, Clinton received a clear message from the U.S. Senate, through the so-called Byrd-Hagel resolution (1997), not to sign any treaty that would affect the performance of the US economy and did not include the participation of developing countries.[7]

At the start of the Kyoto process, the USA negotiators were apparently "rigid" and unsupportive of other proposals but loosened up after the first week and made agreement at Kyoto possible subsequently (reported to us by one of our interviewees involved in the Kyoto process).[8]

The USA, EU, and Group 77.[9] They had their well-known positions as the negotiations of the Kyoto Protocol started in 1997. The Clinton administration had already made some of this clear in Berlin 1995 ("Berlin Mandate").[10] In Berlin and again prior to and during Kyoto the US representation declared its skepticism toward fixed and absolute reductions of greenhouse gases (GHG) and emphasized, instead, its market-oriented mechanisms that would, it argued, facilitate effective

[6] Detailed economic modelling conducted for the U.S. administration suggested that unrestricted international trading could reduce the costs to the US to a fifth of what they would be if the necessary reductions had to be achieved domestically alone. The resultant cost, the administration claimed, would be a mere $7 bn a year, 0.07 per cent of anticipated 2010 gross domestic product (MacKenzie, 2009:12).

[7] The Byrd-Hagel Resolution (1997) came with a vote of 95-0 that it would not ratify any treaty that had these or similar implications.

[8] Concerning hostility to the USA, one should bear in mind that in these UN fora, there has often been considerable hostility directed at the USA, as in Rio de Janeiro, 1992).

[9] Group 77 was formed by developing countries in 1964 from the geographical regions of Africa, Asia, and Latin America. There were 77 countries at the time, in contrast to the 135 countries today.

[10] The Mandate required Parties (to these UN engagements) to elaborate a protocol or other legal instrument to strengthen the commitments of developed countries (Annex I), but there were many unresolved issues, as at Kyoto and later (and still confronting the world community). The EU played a key role in Berlin, as at Kyoto, in making these international meetings relatively successful (Yamin, 2000).

GHG mitigation. Among other things it proposed a "cap-and-trade system."[11] Also, the USA insisted on the full participation of developing countries, that is the Kyoto impositions would apply to all developing countries as well as developed countries. This was opposed by the Group 77; the EU, on the other hand, could accept this Group 77 position. There was considerable opposition to the USA position, reflecting very much skepticism about the intentions of the USA administration. Clearly, the issue had moral connotations and the introduction of market-oriented instruments did not find much genuine support. Krämer (2006:289-290) claims that "It [the EU] went to the negotiations on the Kyoto Protocol with the intention to resist attempts by the US to introduce emission trading systems. Confronted by the US with the alternative to either not have a Kyoto agreement or to accept a trading system, the EU accepted the introduction of flexible market instruments into the Kyoto Protocol. It then tried to make the best of it, anticipating the entry into effect of a global emission trading system and also adoption of legislation to establish other flexible mechanisms under the Kyoto Protocol."

Prior to and through the Kyoto processs, the EU played a mediating role with respect to the USA, increasing the likelihood (but no guarantee) that the USA would sign on. It also, mediated with developing countries, in particular Group-77 (minus the OPEC countries). The Group-77 led by India, Brazil, and China (China was not formally a member of Group-77) represented the interests of developing countries and opposed (successfully) a number of US demands (see later discussion).

The USA was a "tough bargainer" at Kyoto, particularly concerning its market-oriented proposals. In order to keep the USA in the bargaining process, the EU went along with accepting some of the USA's demands on ETS market mechanisms, to which it was largely indifferent if not opposed. The UK supported the U.S. idea, while Sweden, for example, saw it mainly as a way to engage the corporate sector. Many environmental NGOs and some EU countries were uninterested or opposed; for instance, Denmark, Austria, and Germany felt such measures would detract from more substantial actions and also would provide loopholes for doing a minimum about GHG emissions. But all in all, Kyoto largely reflected U.S. thinking (Bodansky, 2002:2).

The USA succeeded in gaining not only the inclusion in the Kyoto protocol of market mechanisms (art. 3(10), article 3(11) and article 17) along with a more comprehensive basket approach: 6 gases instead of 3. The key to the USA agreement to ambitious GHG targets was a concurrent agreement that a system of emissions trading among industrialized countries be established, by which nations with binding limits could buy and sell among themselves the right to release greenhouse gases. The Protocol also authorized the Clean Development Mechanism (CDM), by

[11] In a "cap and trade system", allowances to emit are designated by the government, that is, a certain quantity is allowed to be emitted during the year. Any amount over that allowance must be purchased on the emissions market, or, otherwise, a fine must be paid.

which industrialized countries (Annex I countries in UN terminology) could meet part of their obligations for reducing their emission levels by investing in projects that reduce carbon emissions in developing countries (non-Annex I countries) and receive appropriate emission credits. That is, through the CDM, countries can meet their domestic emission reduction targets by *buying greenhouse gas reduction units from projects in* non-Annex I (mostly developing countries) to the Kyoto protocol. In this way countries can lower the costs of complying with their Kyoto targets by investing in greenhouse gas reductions in a non-Annex I country where reductions are cheaper, and then applying the credit for those reductions towards their commitment goal.

Another parallel arrangement was the *Joint Implementation* (JI), a mechanism to enable Annex I countries (i.e. countries with explicit commitments) to meet their Kyoto targets by participating in projects with Annex I countries to generate emissions credits, known as Emission Reduction Units (ERU). These could be used by Annex I countries to comply with their targets or to sell on the international emissions trading market. The basic idea is that Emission Reduction Units (ERUs) in Annex I countries could be purchased by entities in Annex I countries and used to meet ETS obligations. In other words, through the Joint Implementation, any Annex I country can invest in emission reduction projects (referred to as "Joint Implementation Projects") in any other Annex I country as an alternative to reducing emissions domestically.

A JI project might involve, for example, replacing a coal-fired power plant with a more efficient combined heat and power plant. Most JI projects are expected to take place in so-called "economies in transition," noted in Annex B of the Kyoto Protocol. Currently Russia and Ukraine are slated to host the greatest number of JI projects. Unlike the case of the Clean Development Mechanism, the JI has caused less concern of spurious emission reductions, as the JI, unlike the CDM, takes place in countries which have an emission reduction requirement.[12]

What happened at Kyoto is instructive. Basically, several core US proposals concerning emissions trading were included in the final Protocol. However, the Clinton administration had to accept the exceptionism of developing countries in the first commitment period – otherwise the latter would have refused to sign.[13] Thus, the G-77 countries were left outside of the agreement except that they could participate in the special exchange mechanisms (CDM as indicated above) with developed countries (Annex I countries) in supporting appropriate emission projects in developing countries. The developed countries had to accept fixed commitments

[12] The process of receiving credit for JI projects is somewhat complex. Emission reductions are awarded credits called *Emission Reduction Units* (ERUs), where one ERU represents an emission reduction equaling one tonne of CO_2 equivalent.

[13] The USA even pushed for a provision that would have allowed developing countries to voluntarily "opt in" to binding commitments, but China and India, among others, blocked this measure (Leonie Haimson, "A History of Climate Change Negotiations").

to reduce GHG gases in a fixed time schedule at given levels, varying for different countries and regions (see Table 12.2). These conditions predictably made it highly improbable that the Kyoto Protocol would be ratified in the US Senate (as all USA treaties must), since the Byrd-Hagel Senate Resolution (1997) had made this very clear prior to Kyote. Not surprisingly, the Clinton administration never even attempted to bring the Protocol up for ratification in the Senate after Kyoto.

Table 12.2. Target Commitments for the Reduction of the GHG Emissions in the Kyoto Protocol (Gupta and Grubb, 2000:8)[14]

Country	Target Commitment (percentage below 1990 levels for the period 2008-2012)
European Union (15 member-states)	-8
USA	-7
Australia	+8
Canada	-6
Japan	-6
Russia (1990 base year)	0
Ukraine	0
Czech Republic, Hungary, Poland (base years:1988-1990)	-6-8

At the conclusion of the Kyoto meeting (COP-3), December 11, 1997, more than 150 nations of the world adopted the Protocol. This extraordinary agreement committeed industrialized nations to make legally binding reductions in emissions of six greenhouse gases – carbon dioxide, methane, nitrous oxide, hydrofluorocarbons (HFCs), perfluorocarbons (PFCs) and sulfur hexafluoride (SF6). The reductions required varied from country to country, but would cut emissions an average of about 5 percent below 1990s levels by the period 2008-2012. The U.S. delegation agreed to reductions of 7 percent, Japan to reductions of 6 percent, and the members of the European Union to joint reductions of 8 percent.[15] Table 12.2 shows quantified emissions targets to limit GHG emissions during the first commitment period from 2008-2012.[16]

While the USA's flexibility and support for the final Kyoto Agreement helped make Kyoto an international success, the US delegation's acceptance of clauses which the U.S. Senate had forbidden effectively assured that the USA in the future could never be a part of Kyoto in formal, real terms. The final Kyoto agreement broke with two major U.S. Senate demands which constitutionally has the respon-

---

[14] The levels presented in the table were the result of intense negotiations, where, for instance, the USA went from a "Target commitment" of 0% to 7% and the EU went from 15% to 8%.

[15] The period under the Kyoto Protocol during which Annex I Parties' GHG emissions, averaged for the period, must be within their emission targets from January 1, 2008 to December 31, 2012.

[16] The target is referred to as the "assigned amount" of emissions and measured in tons of CO_2.

sibility and power to approve US treaties like Kyoto). In the case of the USA, the Kyoto protocol was predictably doomed.

3. The Aftermath of Kyoto

After Kyoto, and a period of some initial lethargy and passivity, the EU established a bold ETS – arguably the most important ETS for CO_2 on a global level.[17] But this development was not immediate.

The Immediate Years after Kyoto: 1997-2000

Prior to and following Kyoto, the ETS was generally viewed with skepticism in the EU. In the months immediately following Kyoto, the EU was relatively passive toward the emission mechanism, in part because some member-states were positive, others indifferent or opposed.

The ETS was generally viewed at the EU with sceptecism ("the new kid on the block" as Zapfel and Vainio (2002:5-6) put it).[18] A common discourse in Brussels was, "well, this is being done to involve Russia and Ukraine." At the Commission – and generally in the EU – there were only a few specialists who knew about and understood the USA's emission trading schemes (based on its experience with sulfur dioxide and other emission controls). EU bureaucrats and NGOs as well as politicians with a concern about climate change felt more comfortable with established policy instruments such as a general tax or a directive setting constraints on polluting behavior.[19] As pointed out earlier, the EU and several key member-states like the U.K. supported the concept of emission trading, hoping to get the USA to buy into the protocol. This concept became the famous article 17 of the Kyoto Protocol (on emission trading).

At the grassroots level in Europe, however, several initiatives were launched (Zapfel and Vainio, 2002:8ff). A major private driver, British Petroleum (BP), established in 1998 an ET pilot scheme for a limited number of its business units (eventually 150 were involved) with an ambition to cut its emissions by 10% by 2010 from their level in 1990 (a goal comparable in magnitude to salient Kyoto targets (Zapfel and Vainio, 2002; MacKenzie, 2009:13). This initiative was partly the result of the US pressure group Environmental Defense Fund (EDF), the most

---

[17] We should bear in mind that ETS schemes have been established or are being established in Japan, Australia, and on the East and West Coasts of the USA, among other places (see Sterk et al, 2006 for an overview).

[18] Peter Zapfel and Matti Vainio of the Environment Directorate-General (Zapfel and Vainio 2002:1) write that at the time of the 1997 Kyoto Protocol 'the concept of emissions trading was known [in Europe] only in narrow scientific circles encompassing professors and students of European environmental economics and to a very limited audience of environmental policymakers and administrators in environmental agencies'.

[19] Baumert (1998:3) stresses, "In Kyoto, the EU was against emissions trading but was unable to overcome U.S. support for trading." Of course, eventually EU issues were re-channeled into developing effective rules and guidelines for a trading system.

active supporter for many years of emissions trading on the environmental side in the USA (Zapfel and Vainio, 2002:9).[20] On the public side, the Danish initiated legislation in May, 1998 and set up the first Member State emission trading scheme for the Danish power sector. More attention-getting was the establishment of the UK Emission Trading Group (ETG) in June 1999[21] (and the parallel publication of "A Greenhouse Gas Emissions Trading Scheme for the United Kingdom" by the UK Department for the Environment, Transport and the Regions in November 2000).[22]

This general trend was crowned at the end of 2000 when the German Federal Environment and Economics Ministries established a national stakeholder group to investigate domestic emissions trading. These developments brought wider recognition of such trading as a realistic policy alternative. In addition, some small EU Member States such as Austria, Finland and Ireland acknowledged that trading in GHG permits was something that they would like to pursue, but believed that their own trading volumes would be relatively small and their domestic markets quite narrow. National trading schemes would not make sense for them (although this did not stop Denmark!) (Zapfel and Vainio, 2002:9).

Kyoto takes Flight in Europe

At the grassroots levels in Europe, ETS initiatives were being launched; investigations and learning processes were taking place. In the face of a number of grassroots initiatives, the EU became concerned about fragmentation of European emission markets and the need, therefore, to establish some "European coherence." No small matter was the clear opportunity for the EU Commission to play an entrepreneurial role in this matter (Andersen and Burns, 1996; Carson, 2004). The EU took several initiatives in 2000 and 2001. A Green paper on "Greenhouse gas emissions trading within the European Union" (European Commission, 2000)

[20] The Environmental Defense Fund (EDF) viewed emissions trading as a way to end the polarity between business and environmental groups over the climate change issue. EDF forged a partnership with BP which in 1997, under its new chief executive John Browne, broke ranks with the other major oil companies, announcing that it accepted that global warming was a major threat and that action was needed. EDF's President, Fred Krupp, 'lobbied John Browne to adopt a cap and trade system' (Mackenzie, 2008: 13; Victor and House 2006: 2102).

[21] The Blair government, which came to political leadership in 1997, was particularly enthusiastic for emissions trading – it seemed a way to create a new market mechanism to achieve a goal that unfettered markets could not achieve on their own and that traditional governmental regulatory modes would achieve only at great expense – a conception consistent with many "New Labour" policies (MacKenzie, 2008).

[22] Two other U.K. schemes involving an element of trading were the Renewables Obligation, under which electricity suppliers must buy increasing proportions of their electricity from certified renewable sources, and the Energy Efficiency Commitment, under which gas and electricity suppliers had obligations to deliver energy savings, with a particular focus on low-income customers. Both schemes were administered by the government's Office of Gas and Electricity Markets. For more on these schemes, see Sorrell (2003).

was brought out in March 2000. The Paper highlighted a "bottoms-up pathway" to an emission trading scheme. The EU established a multi-stakeholder working group in the European Climate Change Programme, meeting 10 times between July 2000 and May 2001.[23] Group discussion focused on the "bottoms up" approach (already taking place) and a middle level approach stressing EU coordination and harmonisation of design features. Already, the EU was on the road which would lead to a commitment and to establish the first major world trading system in GHGs. European Commission staff members Zapfel and Vainio (2002:11) report:

> *"In May 2001 the [EU] stakeholder group concluded its work with the clear recommendation that European trading in GHG permits should be established "as soon as practicable". Astonishingly, the group – bringing together diverse interests with about 30 representatives from several Member States, industry, and environmental pressure groups – achieved a high degree of consensus and failed to adopt a consensual recommendation on only a few issues.*[24] *These were highlighted as areas of diverging opinions in the final report" (see European Commission 2001 Final Report).*

---

[23] According to Zapfel and Vainio (2002:7,9), an important factor in the EU development was the active involvement of experts from the US in the European debate, as the country not only with the biggest interest, but also with the broadest experience in applying the instrument. The US was eager to promote emissions trading to its strategic partners. "Immediately after the Kyoto conference US actors with an interest, but also real-life experience, in emissions trading (EPA staff, the environmental pressure group Environmental Defense, the think tank Center for Clean Air Policy, researchers at the Massachusetts Institute of Technology and other academics etc.) invested a lot of time and resources in participating in the European debate and discussions – with the EU Commission studying the SO2 experience in the USA" (MacKenzie, 2008:21). However, over time, the general lessons that they could transfer from existing and evolving trading schemes in the air quality realm (EPA Sulphur Allowance Trading, North-Eastern state-level Nox schemes, and the Californian RECLAIM programme) were more and more limited. Increasingly, the particularities of developing a trading programme aimed at GHGs in the European context dominated.

[24] MacKenzie (2008:17) observes, "There was certainly opposition to the compulsory Europe-wide trading scheme that eventually emerged. Environmental campaigners were (and often still are) sceptical of emissions markets that allow polluters the capacity to pay to keep polluting: a standard analogy is buying indulgences for sins. The European Commission team, however, took care to engage with leading, mainstream environmental NGOs, and the latter generally came to support the new market, albeit critically. Industry opposition was generally muted, with some sectors welcoming trading (certainly preferring it to a tax), though much of German industry was opposed, feeling it had already taken on onerous commitments under 'voluntary agreements' with the German government. The U.K. was again a potential obstacle: interviewees reported that it wanted the European market to be similar in its design to the U.K. scheme described above. But even if Germany and the U.K. had united in opposition, they would have fallen short of the votes required to form a blocking minority (Christiansen and Wettestad 2003:13). By the autumn of 2001, there were '[i]ndications that a qualified majority' in the premier decision-making body, the Council of the European Union (the 'Council of Ministers', as it used to be called) would indeed back emissions trading, and support in the European Parliament, whose agreement was also needed, was strong" (Christiansen and Wettestad 2003:7).

The European Commission advanced the issue to a new level in October, 2001, by adopting the proposal for a directive on EU-wide trading in GHG permits. The proposal foresaw the mandatory introduction of trading in GHG permits in all EU Member States by 2005. It proposed to apply consistently across Europe actions in particular sectors (power and heat generation, iron and steel, oil refining, pulp and paper, cement and other building materials) but would focus in the first step on CO_2 emissions only. The details of the initial allocation decisions would be largely left to Member States, according to the proposal (Zapfel and Vainio, 2002:11).

External events played a role in the aftermath of Kyoto by focusing increasing attention on the EU – thus maintaining the momentum of Kyoto. First, the Conference of the UN Parties at the Hague failed in November 2000 to adopt the rules for trading under Article 17, and a few months later, the USA pulled out of Kyoto altogether[25]. The US had already cut itself out informally (from 1998) and formalized this in early 2001 when George W. Bush only a few weeks (March 13) after taking office (January, 2001) declared that his administration would not ratify the Kyoto Protocol. He was essentially responding to the official position of the US Senate and many interests in US industry. This action evoked outrage in Europe and other parts of the world, where the newly elected President soon was viewed as the 'global climate change rogue'. Since then George Bush confirmed in several ways this image. Still, this should not detract from the larger democratic point that Bush actually responded to a valid position in the U.S. political system, i.e. the declared (negative) view of the Senate whose support is ultimately required to ratify international treaties. The one who actually broke with the U.S. political ethos was ironically the Clinton administration that acted against the instructions of the Senate, by going along with Kyoto (although clearly without a mandate), but never-

[25] Almost immediately after Kyoto there were significant setbacks. COP-4 convened in November, 1998 in Buenos Aires, Argentina. The aim of this meeting was to agree upon a plan to negotiate rules for key elements of the Kyoto Protocol including emissions trading and the CDM. Argentina and Kazakhstan indicated that they would adopt voluntary commitments to limit their emissions, seeing potential environmental and financial advantages in opting into an international emissions trading system (Haimson, 2004). These steps were opposed, however, by several powerful members of the developing country block (Group 77) which considered it the moral duty of industrialized nations to begin by reducing their emissions at home rather than engaging in international emissions trading and pushing for limits on developing countries. The USA continued to be a player and indicated its readiness to sign the Kyoto Protocol (although in fact this was very unlikely given the climate of the Republican dominated Senate). On the last night of the meeting, a group of developing countries – China, India, Saudi Arabia, Kuwait, Venezuela, and Nigeria –formed a "rejectionist" bloc and walked out of the negotiations at 3:00am. They were met outside the door by delegates from the small island states which have the most to lose from rising sea levels caused by climate change. There were also members from Argentina and a few other developing nations which recognized that the entire framework of the climate change treaty was in danger of collapsing. These delegates forced rejectionists back inside by threatening to take their place at the bargaining table. In this way, negotiations were forced to continue, and a November 2000 deadline to establish rules for emissions trading was set (Haimson, 2004).

theless helped make Kyoto an eventual reality. The outright USA rejection (early 2001) arguably also played a role in the EU mobilization and commitment to establishing a world trading system in GHGs.

In meetings organized by the Swedish EU Presidency, it was stated that the Kyoto Protocol was not dead, and that the EU should press ahead (on the other hand, Condoleeza Rice as National Security Advisor for the Bush Administration stressed that the Protocol was dead ("it was dead upon arrival of this administration" (cited in Kjellen, 2008:97)). Zapfel and Vainio (2002:12) argue: "These events united Europe and triggered further interest in the establishment of an EU-wide market in GHG permits and other measures to rebuild momentum in international climate mitigation efforts."[26] Once the USA was out of the picture, the EU and some NGOs solidified their commitment to the ETS paradigm and improved its contacts and discussions with Group 77.[27] MacKenzie (2009:18) stresses: ... "with a significant current of opinion amongst European policy-makers galvanized, momentum built up behind the project of building an European-wide trading scheme."[28] The EU persistently underlined that Kyoto "was the only shop in town" (Kjellen, 2008:98). By December, 2002, the design of the European scheme was agreed and completed (Engels, 2005). Less than a year later (October 2003), the

[26] Other factors that played a role related to concerns of business and their fears of taxes and direct regulation. There was also a misconception of emissions trading as "the cheap buy-out." This perception induced some business associations and companies to develop a strategic interest to continue the dialogue about the widely unknown and misunderstood instrument. And there were many market intermediaries and other potential service providers (auditing companies, consultants, lawyers, academics, commercial conference organizers) who saw a potential market arising and were more than willing to invest some resources under the header of business development (Kjellen, 2008; Zapfel and Vainio, 2002).

[27] According to MacKenzie (2008:17-18): The initial belief in Europe had been that a system of international emissions trading, based around the United Nations but led by the U.S., was on its way. As it became clear that this was not so, it was replaced by a sense that 'we have to make it happen at home first' (Zapfel and Vainio 2002:8). Indeed, the withdrawal of the U.S. seems to have reduced opposition in Europe to carbon trading, perhaps because that trading was no longer something the U.S. was trying to impose on reluctant partners. (Although I know of no direct evidence on the point, another factor in reducing opposition may have been that the withdrawal of the U.S., potentially a huge purchaser of credits such as Clean Development Mechanism certified emission reductions (CERs), reduced the costs to others of meeting Kyoto commitments.) America's new unilateralism – on climate, and on much else – provoked hostility. The tortuous diplomatic process of adding flesh to Kyoto's skeleton market may, paradoxically, have been facilitated by the withdrawal of the .US.: 'In a single stroke, the United States managed to focus the entire planet on a ... convoluted piece of diplomatic literature' (Benedick 2001). Four years after the Kyoto Protocol was signed, the 2001 Marrakesh Accords finally set out the detailed rules governing the international schemes – the Clean Development Mechanism and Joint Implementation – with which a European market could be linked.

[28] At the heart of emission market construction – an *in vivo* economic experiment – was a small team of officials of the European Commission, led by economist Jos Delbeke of the Commission's DG Environment (MacKenzie, 2008:16).

directive establishing the EU ETS was published (Directive 2003/87/EC of the European Parliament and the Council). It was followed in October, 2004 by the "linking directive" which allows countries of the EU to invest in projects that reduce emissions in developing countries as an alternative to reducing emissions (typically more expensive) in their own countries.[29] In January, 2005, Europe's carbon trading began operations.

Up to and following Kyoto, the EU reached an agreement on the allocation of targets for the individual member-states (see Table 12.3). The factors taken into account in the negotiations had to do with a country's economic and industrial strength, energy use profiles, achievements already accomplished, and plans for future reductions. The countries with the largest planned reductions were also among those most environmentally ambitious: Austria, Denmark, Germany, and the Netherlands. Sweden had already overfulfilled in achieving energy efficiency and relatively low emission levels. France and Finland both had low levels of CO_2 emissions. Several of the most polluting countries in the EU (Greece, Portugal, and Spain) were allowed to increase their emissions in order for them to catch up economically to the richer countries.

In sum, from the time it decided to back the USA proposals in order to keep the USA involved in the Kyoto process until around 2000, the EU was not well prepared – and relatively uninterested in or ambivalent toward ETS. It was neither an innovator nor an alert potential proponent who tries to find out what has been bought and how it might be used effectively. But the bottom-up process in the EU area gave a kick to the EU Commission and provided conditions for an unlikely, unholy alliance (industry, NGOs, EU bureaucrats, and some countries like the UK which favored such market mechanisms). The EU came to represent a system (or complex of mechanisms) to which early gut reaction was opposition and which, in any case, was not well understood very well and, in a certain sense, had little intention of doing so, at least at the time of Kyoto and shortly thereafter.

In a certain sense, the EU stumbled into a role of global leadership of emission trading. The EU became the great promoter of Kyoto mechanisms, setting up the first large-scale international ETS system for greenhouse gases (2005). The EU's behavior today might give the impression that it is the true parent of this regime. However, most of the intellectual and ideological bases of the regime came from US experience, competence, and forceful proposals. Moreover, the EU ended up adopting systems that were very different from anything they had advocated or knew about earlier. It was not until much later that the EU gained basic knowledge and expertise about the market-based mechanisms embodied in the Kyoto Protocol.

---

[29] European Commission 2004 Directive 2004/101/EC of the European Parliament and of the Council of 27 October 2004 amending Directive 3003/87/EC establishing a scheme for greenhouse gas emissions allowance trading within the Community, in respect of the Kyoto Protocol's project mechanisms. Official Journal of the European Union, L338/18, 13.11.2004.

Table 12.3. Greenhouse gas (CO_2+CH_4+N_2O) emissions, Burden Sharing Agreement, and Number of Installations in the EU-15 by country

Country	Share of EU emissions in 1990	Burden sharing target (BSA) (percent)30	Number of Installations covered (2005)31
Austria	1.7	-13.0	199
Belgium	3.2	-7.5	322
Denmark	1.7	-21.0	388
Finland	1.7	0.0	606
France	14.7	0.0	1,091
Germany	27.7	-21.0	1,866
Greece	2.4	25.0	152
Ireland	1.3	13.0	117
Italy	12.5	-6.5	1,005
Luxembourg	0.3	-28.0	15
Netherlands	4.8	-6.0	212
Portugal	1.6	27.0	255
Spain	7.0	15.0	1,021
Sweden	1.6	4.0	736
U.K.	17.9	-12.5	797
EU 15	100.0	-8.0	8,782

4. The EU's Climate Change Paradigm[32]

The ETS system is mandatory for and implemented only among private firms or government agencies as well as other organizations – not individual consumers (see the number of installations in each country, shown in Table 12.3). Member states are allotted an amount, which then must be allocated among business and government units and other organizations in each state. Thousands of installations will be assigned emission allowances, and their emission levels determined along with excesses and deficits, as the case may be. Also, over time the EU will "ratchet down" over time the emission allowances.

[30] Emission targets (reductions in most cases) for each Member State with the intent to ensure that the EU meets its overall 8% reduction commitment under the Protocol (see Table 2). The targets are expressd in terms of percentages by which Member States must reduce, or in come cases may maintain or increase, their emissions compared with the base year level (1990). Source: Annex 1 of the EU Commission (1999) 230 final of 19.05.1999.

[31] Source: Öko-Institut, CITL (5, July 2007), EEA 2007.

[32] European Union decision-making on environmental matters, however, falls into the terrain not of unanimity but of 'qualified majority voting'. No single country can stop an environmental measure: doing so takes a coalition of countries sufficiently populous (since voting weights roughly follow population) to form a 'blocking minority'.

The ETS is targeted at large energy-using installations in defined sectors: energy production, metals, construction, materials such as cement and paper. Under an emissions trading system, the quantity of emissions is fixed (often called a "cap") and the right to emit becomes a tradable commodity; the cap (say 10,000 tons of carbon) is divided into transferable units (10,000 permits of 1 ton of carbon each). Permits are often referred to as "GHG units," "quotas" or "allowances"[33].

The ETS system would require agents participating in the system to hold a number of permits greater or equal to their actual emissions level, otherwise fines would be imposed. Each EU country develops a national allocation plan (NAP), allocating its total number of emissions allowances (free of charge) to the individual installations covered by the scheme. At the end of each year, each and every installation must show sufficient allowances to cover its actual CO_2 emissions for the year.[34] An installation can meet its target by reducing CO_2 emissions or by buying surplus allowances from other firms operating in the ETS. Installations may also obtain emission credits in exchange projects through the JI and CDM mechanisms with non-Annex I and Annex I countries, respectively (the EU "Linking Directive", 2004); that is, EU countries can invest in these other countries to obtain reduction units which can be applied to their own emission targets (see page 6).[35]

Once permits are allocated (by auction, sale or free allocation) to the agents participating in the system, they are then tradable. This enables actors on the market to seek emissions reductions where they are least costly (Baumert, 1998). ETS market agents are free to chose their own compliance strategy – including how much to emit and how many allowances to trade.[36] While "economic incentives" were central in the earlier EU initiatives such as the carbon tax, the particular institutional mechanisms and actors are very different in the ETS. This market system would

---

[33] MacKenzie (2008:7) points out that "the question of whether an allowance is a property right was a crucial issue". The protection of property rights would make subsequent changes to a trading programme difficult; for the Kyoto Protocol there is a clause that the protocol does "not create or bestow any right, title or entitlement to emissions".

[34] There is an elaborate accounting system keeping track of the emission limits in relation to actual emissions (calculated on the basis of fuel use).

[35] As indicated earlier, there are Kyoto mechanisms (for instance, Joint Implementation and Clean Development Mechanism which enabled Annex I countries to obtain emission credits through "Emission Reduction Units" generated by Joint Implementation projects and "Certified Emission Reductions" generated by Clean Development Mechanism projects in developing countries (and producing Certified Emission Reductions (CERs)). Also, countries can increase the absorption of carbon in forests, agricultural soils, and other ecosystems ("carbon sinks") on their territory. Finally, the Protocol allows the generation of Removal Units for certain human-induced sink activities undertaken since 1990, which can also be counted toward a country's emission target (Sterk et al, 2006).

[36] Kruger and Egenhofer (2006:2) point out the difference in the regulator's role, "Consequently, the regulator's role is 'no longer that of grandly deciding what is best for firms and individuals, entertaining equitable appeals, and enforcing the results.' Rather the regulator acts more like an accountant or a bank's credit department."

generate a price for the GHGs in units such as tons – and thus transform GHGs from externalities into "costs" in the economy and market contexts. The ETS is referred to as a "market mechanism" rather than an administrative or regulatory mechanism (i.e., "bureaucratic") but requires a large apparatus to operate.[37]

Sanctions for exceeding allowances were set at 40€ per excess ton for the period 2005-2007 (and 100€ in the period 2008-2012) plus surrendering a corresponding amount of allowance in the next calendar year. Emission penalties are non-discretionary and automatic.[38] The names of non-compliant operators were to be published.[39]

MacKenzie (2008:1) illustrates the arrangement for an installation, in this case his University of Edinburgh as a "large combustion installation" with rated thermal outputs greater than 20 MW. "Even the university plant in the area in which hu-

---

[37] A large apparatus is being established to make this market possible. Each installation covered by the ETS – and there are thousands – must apply for a GHG emission permit; there must also be monitoring and reporting of emissions. And any results must be verified (as in business economic accounting). (The following remarks draws on Kruger and Egenhofer (2006)). Each installation develops a monitoring methodology based on their interpretation of the EU guidelines (The EU provides "Monitoring and Reporting Guidelines" (MRG)), which must be approved by the competent authority (CA) in each member state and which becomes also a permit. These methodologies are based largely on a combination of measurements of emissions factors, fuel use and production data.

Each installation must report their emissions according to the methodology specified in its permit and an independent third party must verify all self-reported emissions. Typically, the third party is a non-governmental independent entity, which has been accredited (this entails, of course, another whole apparatus). Accredited verifiers in principle have the final word on an installation report. It is the responsibility of the CA to assure that those accredited as verifiers are qualified and supervised through regular inspections and sample controls. A verifier's area of expertise includes a technical background, e.g., engineers who are familiar with the technical issues of emissions measurement.

The system provides for tracking and the publication of tracking results. Reported emissions data is collected in a registry that can be used to measure compliance by comparing the verified emissions of an installation with the number of allowances the installation holds (both those allocated and those possibly purchased through emission trading). Each year, on May 15th, the EU Central Administrator and each member state registry will display on their public website the verified emissions figure for each installation as well as the allowances surrendered for that installation and whether or not that installation is in compliance with its obligations.

[38] This is highly complex since the EU has no authority in this area, all administrative and criminal penalties are entirely the responsibility of member states; the European Court of Justice asserted in 2005 that the EU has the power to require member states to lay down criminal penalities for the purpose of protecting the environment (Kruger and Egenhofer, 2006:8).

[39] Kruger and Egenhofer (2006:9) stress the common interest of regulatees, investors, and regulators in achieving a high level of compliance: "Cheating or even the perception of cheating can risk devaluing allowances, thereby reducing or eliminating the economic incentive to cut emissions… Consistent and fraud-proof monitoring and verification procedures therefore have moved to the centre of emissions trading schemes."

manities and social sciences are taught totals 20.5 MW and thus must obtain permits to emit carbon dioxide. If it emits more CO_2 than it has allowances, it must buy further allowances on the market, or else it will be fined. If it emits less than its allowances, it may sell its excess allowances. Of course, many members of the university community will be largely oblivious (and if aware, not particularly interested) in this system – at least until the screws are eventually tightened ("the ratchet effect") and they are forced to think about ways to reduce their energy use and emissions."

5. Dimensions of the Climate Change Policy Paradigm Shift

As indicated in Part Two of this book, public policy paradigms are systematically distinguished on several key dimensions: what is the nature of the policy problem, who is to deal with it, that is should assume responsibility (public, private, mixed, and which "sectors"), what are goals and standards in relation to the policy problem, what methods are to be used in dealing with or managing the problem(s), and what are the necessary types of experts/knowledge, etc. Typically, there are also substantial institutional and role shifts, as in the case investigated here. The key dimensions of public policy paradigm theory enable us to identify patterns in the shift from the pre-Kyoto regime to a post-Kyoto form of EU climate change policy, as indicated in Table 12.4.

There was no fundamental change in the natural science and societal models of the causality of climate change nor in the perceived need and goals to substantially reduce humanly produced emissions. The major dimensions of paradigm shift were in the ways such reductions could be accomplished, in particular, the shift to a largely private market mechanism (except for the governmental imposition of "caps" and application of fines) and the Europenization of the ETS.[40]

In the ETS development, we can speak of a public policy paradigm shift in that substantial changes were made in the methods to deal with the challenge of reducing climate change through emission reductions. There were also shifts in the actors involved, particularly in the societal actors most directly regulated and affected as well as in the constellation of regulatory agents. Finally, there were shifts in the kinds of knowledge and expertise required, although economists and technicians are important in both systems – substantial numbers of technicians are necessary for the ETS.

[40] MacKenzie (2008:17) reports another issue: "The European Commission sought legal advice on whether a cap-and-trade market 'would fall under the environment chapter of the Treaty [of Rome]', and, as an interviewee reported, 'got the confirmation' that it did: a CO_2 cap was an environmental matter, and thus would not require unanimity. While the political structure of the European Union meant it was not feasible to give carbon a substantial, harmonized price via a tax, it potentially could be given a price via a cap-and-trade scheme. Emissions trading, which had previously seemed in Europe to be, in an interviewee's words, 'an academic idea which ... was seen as too far ... away from reality', could in fact be made real more easily than a tax could."

In sum, this paradigm shift was not single-dimensional. The table below indicates the properties of the ETS (and related mechanisms) differing from earlier EU climate change public policy initiatives and actions. It entailed a Europeanization of climate change policy in the form of the the EU's own ETS, but it also entailed the commodification of a substantial proportion of GHG emissions – in other words, a marketization of a significant part of climate change policy. As pointed out below in the concluding remarks there are, of course, other policy developments in the EU relating to climate change and energy, which are *not* particularly market oriented.

Table 12.4. EU Climate Change Policy Paradigm Shift

	PRIOR TO KYOTO	FOLLOWING KYOTO (AFTER 2003)
Problem issue	Climate Change due to GHGs	Climate Change due to GHGs
Goals with respect to reducing emissions of GHGs	Substantial reduction in GHG levels, CO_2 in particular	Substantial reduction in GHG levels, CO_2 in particular
Agents Responsible for dealing with problem	EU Government	EU, also regional actors (member-states), and market agents
Models of physical causality of a major part of GHGs	Emission of GHGs causes climate change	Emission of GHGs causes climate change
Models of Socio-economic causality	Anthropogenic	Anthropogenic
Methods/strategies to deal with the problem	Command and Control Mechanisms. Control of behavior of societal agents (individuals, households, companies, and government agencies) through administrative regulation and taxation[41].	"Cap and Trade" model provides market incentives and sanctions to control anthropogenic emissions. Imposition of mandatory absolute targets, CAPs (backed by economic sanctions) combined with trading opportunities (including speculative opportunities). Market agents are free to chose their own compliance strategy – including how much to emit and how many

[41] Carbon taxes, and all environmental taxes, are "price-based" policy instruments. Taxes increase the prices of certain goods and services, and thereby decrease the quantity demanded – the so-called "price effect." Emissions trading of permits or allowances is considered a "quantity-based" environmental policy instrument. *Although both policy approaches are "market-based," they are very different institutional arrangements and operate differently* – carbon taxes fix the marginal cost for carbon emissions and allow quantities emitted to adjust, while tradable permits *fix the total amount of carbon emitted* and allow price levels to fluctuate according to market forces (Baumert, 1998).

		allowances to trade, or how much fine to pay.[42]
Societal actors most directly affected	All energy/carbon consumers: companies, government agencies, everyday citizens and consumers in their places of residence, in their transport, etc.	Countries, governments, companies, energy-consuming installations with a capacity greater than 20MW in sectors that emit GHGs in their operations[43]
Responsible Agents	EU central agents that assure coordination and setting of constraints. The carbon/energy tax would be administered through the member states to all "consumers" of carbon including gasoline-driven vehicles, home heating, oil and aviation fuels.	Responsible actors: the EU in founding the market system and in legislating the "caps". Once set up, however, the argument is that "the market" would largely carry on its own (see footnote 37, however).
Expertise and Knowledge requirements	Technicians (determining the appropriate taxation for different carbon users and administrators, that is, for determining carbon or energy consumption levels and appropriate tax/carbon rates. Also, economists and other social scientists estimating impacts including inequity features.	Technicians (determining the emission levels of diverse facilities or emitting units); administrators to determine CAPs and to monitor actual emissions and follow the accounts of organizations – and to carry out checks and controls to determine actual compliance.
Key Discourse Defining and articulating	Administrative Constraint/ Regulation	"Market solves the problem", "flexibility", "discretion"
"Saints" and "villains" in the discourses	Regulators; bureaucrats, profligates, over-consumers, tax evaders	"Entrepreneurs", "False reporters" "counterfeiters" (of certificates)

6. Discussion: Quasi-Powers and Institutionalization Process

Public paradigm shifts are typically associated with the exercise of power, either the replacement of one leadership or elite with another (Chapter 7; see also, Chapter 4), or a piecemeal negotiation of a new paradigm between powerful actors

[42] It is worth noting that an ETS system is socio-politically defined as "market" and non-bureaucratic, whereas command-and-control systems and taxation are defined as "bureaucratic". In fact, the operation of an ETS requires a massive apparatus for the EU (and jobs for many, many people with technical backgrounds), costing billions of €s. See note 37.

[43] Emissions are counted from energy production installations (with an installed capacity greater than 20 MW, refining of mineral oil, coke production, production and processing of iron and steel, including roasting and sintering of iron ore, and production of cement, limie, glass, glass fibre and ceramic products. EU allowances are measured in metric tons of CO_2.

representing different interests (see Chapter 5), or the mobilization of power to introduce and impose a new paradigm (as in the establishment of REACH (Chapter 10). The case of the ETS shows power at play but operating in unexpected and ironic ways. The USA used its vast economic and strategic powers to get its way with its market proposals. It was reluctantly supported in its efforts by the EU which had little or no intrinsic or ideological interest in, or knowledge about such schemes. The EU played a mediating role in introducing the USA proposals into Kyoto.[44] Once institutionalized, however, they took on a life of their own. "Grassroots agents" including several EU member states (in particular, U.K., Denmark, Austria, and Germany) became interested in the mechanisms on their own. Their interest forced the hand of the EU to provide guidance and EU coherence, and it responded entrepreneurially to the new opportunity setting. Other factors were the failure of the follow-up Kyoto meetings (COPs) and, above all, the position of the USA (Bush Administration) pulling itself out completely and formally in the Spring of 2001. These developments point up the ironic story that trading in GHG permits (Article 17 of the Kyoto Protocol on emission trading), first inserted into the 1997 Kyoto Protocol at the insistance of the USA (and against the will of several EU Member states) turned out years later to be developed and implemented by the EU without participation of the USA (Zapfel and Vainio 2002:12).

---

[44] In the EU climate change policy process, we have reported substantially differences *within* the EU, between, for instance, those prepared to support a carbon or energy tax (e.g., Sweden) and those (U.K., Ireland) opposed (see also the analysis in Chapter 10 on chemicals).

We have also witnessed the EU acting effectively in an international context. The tensions and conflicts in the Kyoto process not only concerned the EU and the USA. Developing countries represented by Group 77 and led by India, Brazil and China (although China is not a member but still plays a key role among developing countries) played a major part.

As we have reported, the USA insisted on market mechanisms for Kyoto. It was also strongly opposed to binding targets and timetables for emission reduction (this US position of "flexibility" and non-commitment to targets was strongly supported by industry NGOs and OPEC). At the same time, the EU could accept binding targets and fixed timetables – a position particularly advocated by the Alliance of Small Island States (AOSIS). The EU also went along with "differentiated responsibilities" advocated by developing countries, whereas the US position was to reject this principle. That is, the EU was prepared to accept such a regime where different rules of emission control apply to developed and developing countries (Annex I and Annex II, respectively). Consequently, the EU and Group 77 agreed that the developed countries should take the lead in dealing with climate change and its adverse affects. There was an OECD proposal (led by the USA) to the effect that if Annex I countries fulfilled their commitment in the first phase of Kyoto, Annex II countries should be ready to accept quantified commitments in a subsequent phase. This was vigorously and effectively opposed by the Group 77. Most of the developing countries, particularly the industrializing leaders (Brazil, China, and India) insist on their sovereignty – in particular, their right to develop economically (Bodansky, 2002), and that developed countries created the problem and have much greater capacity to respond to the climate change problematique – the EU has supported this position over the opposition of the USA.

US as well as EU constitutional structures constrained the policy development relating to emissions control. The US President needs the support of the U.S. Senate (and was not able to gain that support) and in the EU, tax measures, which was the policy of first choice (see earlier) require unanimity among the member-states; a single dissenting country can block the decision. Plans in the early 1990s to levy such taxes across Europe met with fierce industry opposition and were dropped (see earlier) (MacKenzie (2009:16).

The pathway of the EU in relation to ETS shows us one of the peculiar ways that a paradigm shift may take place. It led from an initial EU lack of interest and even basic opposition to the conception, on the one hand, to eventually embracing the core market mechanisms of Kyoto. This was not only because of pressures from dynamic and assertive European interests (including that of the Commission to expand its domain of authority) but also the genuine commitment of the EU to do something concrete and effective and to become the global leader of climate change policy, in this case through ETS (which was not popular, however, with many environmental NGOs). The EU had already failed in its earlier major effort, namely a carbon tax. It had little to show in the 1990s and in the years immediately leading up to Kyoto. It felt the need and pressure to show results.

The EU's role in helping to bring about Kyoto must be considered its major accomplishment of this period. It realized two of its major aims: to establish concrete targets for emission reduction and to unite industrialized and developing countries. But this accomplishment, as it turned out, was paralleled by the dropout within a couple of years of the world's key player, namely the USA. The "US market mechanisms" introduced in order to keep the USA into the Kyoto process took on a life of their own – in part through "European bottom-up" initiatives: these developments evoked a EU response by 2000. But several external events also played a role because they put the EU in the limelight (rather than leaving it offstage as the stand-in for the major player). Responsibility was forced on it, at least if the momentum of Kyoto was to be maintained. First, the Conference of the Parties failed at the Hague in November 2000 to adopt the rules for trading under Article 17 (the ETS mechanism) and a few months later, the new Bush Administration pulled out of Kyoto altogether. Suddenly the EU was center-stage and was more or less compelled to play a central role it never anticipated. With the USA more or less completely out of the picture, the EU more easily assumed a European unequivocal adoption and leadership of the development of an ETS. The ETS became the EU's crowning achievement[45]. Within 5 years there was an EU ETS, which has had its growing pains (see below), but from which others, for instance, those backing the California plan are drawing invaluable lessons.

---

[45] And bear in mind that the EU arrived at this point having lacked much previous knowledge and commitment (as well as experience) with respect to such means.

In a balanced assessment, one must arguably conclude that the EU has accomplished a great deal – but far short of its initial great ambitions and expectations. Many states and NGOs had expected the EU would manage much more than the ETS (toward which many remain suspicious).

Concluding Remarks

A significant public policy paradigm shift took place with the EU adoption and implementation of the ETS. We have suggested that the properties of the ETS (and related mechanisms such as JI and CDM) were very different from earlier EU climate change public policy initiatives and actions. The policy shift entailed, on the one hand, a Europeanization of climate change policy in the form of ETS, and, on the other hand, a "marketization" of a significant part of EU climate change policy. There are, of course, other policy developments in the EU relating to climate change and energy, which are not particularly market oriented (see below).

Going back at least to the 1980s, the EU was oriented to centralized policies and measures relating to coordination and command and control mechanisms.[46] The most characteristic of these was the idea of introducing a carbon/energy tax for the entire EU; which ended in failure (there remains even today, however, interest and potentiality in such taxation schemes (see below)). But other considerations, which have in part been realized, was to harmonize energy taxes across the EU (to eliminate any comparative advantages or competitivity based on differences in such taxes among EU countries). Still, other considerations were fiscal and economic instruments, energy efficiency measures, speed limits on motor vehicle traffic, improved transport management.

The ETS is not the entire EU climate change policy profile.[47] Decisions beginning in 2003 led to the establishment of a comprehensive initiative, "Intelligent Energy Europe," including such programmes as:[48] (1) energy saving (SAVE); (2) new and renewable energy sources (ALTENER); (3) energy aspects of transport (STEER); and (4) renewable energy sources and energy efficiency in developing countries (COOPENER). The EU has adopted a number of other measures that

---

[46] Baumert (1998:3) stresses, "The European Union has traditionally been in favor of strong coordinated policies and measures, such as energy/carbon taxes, among countries. Because the EU is already relatively energy efficient (improvements have been made steadily since the late 1980s, through energy deregulation, taxes and agreements with industrial sectors), carbon taxes would be less of a burden than in the U.S."

[47] Among a range of EU initiatives, we find promotion of electricity from renewable energy sources ("green electricity"), renewable energy in EU's overall composition from less than 7% today to 20% by 2020, the promotion of co-generation (CHP), the promotion of energy performance of buildings (all new buildings as well as large existing buildings undergoing innovation), energy labelling of domestic appliances, landfill directive, research funding for energy (saving; new and alternative energy sources), energy certification prior to sale, transport and climate; support of energy crops, voluntary agreements with auto companies to cut CO_2 emissions.

[48] Intelligent Energy Europe http://ec.europa.eu/energy/intelligent/projects/index_en.htm.

(directly or indirectly) affect the emission of greenhouse gases, such as a directive on landfills (1999) that tries through better monitoring of landfills and the reduction of land filling of biodegradable waste to reduce methane gas generation; a directive (2002) on the promotion of electricity from renewable energy sources; a directive (2003) on the promotion of the use of bio-fuels or other renewable fuels for transport; a directive (2004) establishing a system to monitor the emission of greenhouse gases and for implementing the Kyoto Protocol; and other measures, in particular in the areas of transport, energy, and agriculture policy (Kramer, 2006). There have also been numerous EU voluntary agreements with auto producers relating to CO_2 emissions from cars, and with producers of electronic equipment concerning energy efficiency. And there is still a possibility – with the changes in public opinion – that the EU will reconsider a carbon or energy tax. If such a system of EU taxation were established, then two contrasting paradigms of regulation (taxation and cap and trade) would be operative at the same time, but with some potential for conflicting interactions and unintended consequences.

All in all, in spite of the setbacks since the 1990s, the EU climate change achievements are substantial. As Krämer (2006:290) points out: "There does not seem to be any developed State which has, with the same political determination, invented a climate change policy and put it into operation." As Bodansky (who served as the climate change coordinator at the US Department of State and played a central role in formulating and negotiating U.S. climate change policy, including Kyoto) stresses (2002:1-2) that "Whatever its flaws, [Kyoto] represents a serious effort to address a serious problem. Given the enormity of the climate change issue, that is no small achievement. If Kyoto were to fail, we have no assurance that a replacement would emerge in a reasonable time."

Epilogue

The ETS, after an initial great success with the price of a ton of carbon emission reaching 31€/ton, its market collapsed in the Spring 2006, and the price plummeted to 0.10€/ton. The major reason for this was that The Czech Republic, the Netherlands, Estonia, the Walloon region of Belgium, and France reported to the European Commission 2005 emissions of CO_2 that were significantly lower than the number of allowances issued to their industries. With allowances far exceeding actual emissions, there was no need to purchase emission certificates to cover deficiencies.

Excessive allowances is apparently a common problem with this type of market regulatory mechanism (MacKenzie, 2009:26). This suggests the importance of governmental and technical advisors in guiding the EU government to set limits and allocating allowances.

MacKenzie (2009:26) argues that the "politics of allocation" show tendencies to over-allocation: Measurements of existing levels of emissions are often far more uncertain than one might imagine, the potential straightforwardly and cheaply to achieve abatement is often grossly underestimated, and – crucially – the political exigencies of getting markets established may make stringency infeasible.

The emissions market scheme must be viewed as "an experiment" (MacKenzie, 2009:24). The first year of the ETS demonstrated in what sense this was very true. One learns by doing (see similar conclusions about REACH in Chapter 10). Since the collapse of the carbon market, there have been systematic efforts to tighten up the system, which has led to better functioning (the current market price of a ton of CO_2 is between 10 and 30 Euros (Spring and Summer, 2009).

MacKenzie (2009) also stresses the substantial techno-political features of the ETS such as the ratchet and the formula[49] used to determine national allocation plans (NAP).[50] He suggests the importance of mobilizing expertise for such a system. We would add that a further institutional strategy worth consideration would be to "depoliticize" the ratchet and NAP formula, perhaps, through the functional equivalent of the autonomous "Central Bank" to technically determine allocations as well as grade of ratcheting.

However, the point here is not so much the effective functioning of ETS as a socio-technical or socio-economic system (see MacKenzie, 2009 about these) – extremely interesting matters in themselves – but the role of political ideas impacting, and shifts in political ideas and positions making substantial and particular differences in policymaking.

[49] Using a formula would presumably reduce the zone of negotiation and make for equilibria. For instance, the formula that the EU uses at present calculates a country's needed annual average allocation of allowances on the basis of 2005 emissions x GDP growth x carbon intensity improvement (MacKenzie, 2008: 29). But apparently there has been much contention around each of the factors of the eequation, and, in a number of cases, member-states have gone to the European Court to press their issues (MacKenzie, 2008:29).

[50] Also, critical here is an economic model to simulate a market equilibrium solution for energy supply and demand in the EU member states (according to MacKenzie (2008) such a model has been established).

CHAPTER 13

Toward a New Social Order? Mainstreaming Gender Equality in EU Policymaking

Dolores Calvo, Tom R. Burns, and Marcus Carson

1. Gender Equality Policy in the European Union

European Union (EU) gender equality policy emerged from its comparatively mundane beginnings as a necessary accommodation in the Treaty of Rome to becoming a standard-setter for EU social policy (Gelb, 1999). Many women activists and scholars consider the policies of the EU to have contributed significantly overall to promoting equality between women and men (Rossilli, 2000b; Gelb, 1999; Walby, 1999a, 1999c). EU gender equality legislation has often forced member states to do better than they otherwise would have done without the leverage EU law provides (Walby, 1999a; Rees, 1998; Hoskyns, 1996).

Nevertheless, the most striking quality of the assessments of EU performance on gender equality goals is their strong ambivalence. Many observers have noted, for example, that progress on gender equality goals has also come with significant tradeoffs. EU gender equality policy has come as part of a larger package of market integration that has weakened many national-level social protections considered important to women (Rosilli, 2000; Hoskyns, 1996, Ostner & Lewis, 1995). This sentiment echoes earlier cautions by Hoskyns (1996) and by Kenis (1991) that the EU social dimension may be largely an adjunct to its market making goals. Young (2000:94) captures the more skeptical view in her argument that there is nothing in EU gender equality policy that does not benefit a neo-liberal model of capitalism at least as much as it benefits women.

To be sure, there are significant flaws in both performance and policy that leave EU gender equality policy open to earned criticism. The EU has thus far fallen short of its promise to forcefully confront gender inequalities and other forms of discrimination, while its supranational nature imposes difficult burdens[1] on grassroots efforts to mobilize (Elman, 2001). There is much evidence to support these arguments. And although the EU's gender equality goals are quite broad, all of the EU Directives pertaining to gender equality are connected with women's workforce

[1] It should be noted, however, that it also opens new opportunities in connection with the EU need to strengthen its legitimacy and with its reliance on the kinds of expertise that the women's movement has proven adept at developing.

participation (Hobson, 2003a, 2000b). The limited scope of Article 119 in the Treaty of Rome (the equal pay article) virtually guaranteed this, as has the generally limited authority granted the EU in subsequent Treaties. The EU's authority to pursue non-market gender equality goals therefore has been, and remains, limited to soft-law approaches such as Action Programs (Joachim, 2002).

There is no straightforward policy response to these criticisms. As already noted, the EU's lack of a more substantial social policy generally is a result of a variety of factors (Rossilli, 2000a). The subsidiarity principle's inclusion in the Maastricht Treaty was in large part a response to frequent initiatives of the Commission, with member states seeking protection of their sovereignty on matters of social policy (Ostner, 2000). Such resistance and increasing alertness to encroachment on the part of member states may require more indirect strategies for promoting social goals generally, and gender equality specifically, at the European level.

1.1 Early Development of Gender Equality in the EU

The development of EU gender equality policy over time generally follows a trio of themes, which can be characterized as equal treatment, positive action, and mainstreaming[2]. The first two are bound directly or indirectly to women's workforce participation, which is where their legal basis in the EU Treaties is anchored. Equal treatment can be characterized as a demand based on the realization that rules were being applied differently based on gender, and that such differences frequently worked to women's disadvantage. The positive action theme stems from the realization that equal application of laws and other rules does not remedy structural disadvantages that women face, and that corrective measures must be taken that are based on a principle of difference.

"Mainstreaming" and the "soft law" approach of defining European problems and facilitating member state consensus and cooperation on those problems are two important examples of indirect and "soft" approaches to expanding competence and to making policy (Burns and Carson, 2002 Carson, 2004). Geyer (2000: 122), for example, characterizes gender mainstreaming as "a way of making policy without making policy", although it might be more accurate to characterize it as a way of gaining the legal authority to take up all manner of gender equality issues without the problems associated with specifying exactly which ones in always delicate Treaty negotiations. Gender mainstreaming represents an effort to reconcile the earlier two principles of equal treatment and positive action by subordinating them to the guiding principle that all EU policies should contribute to the goal of greater equality between women and men (Rees, 1998). Mainstreaming also represents a broadening of gender equality goals that transcends the boundaries of the work, although this expansion comes at a price. The nature of the breakthrough represented by gender mainstreaming is that EU gender equality policy has been

---

[2] Theresa Rees (1998) refers to these themes as "tinkering", "tailoring", and "transforming", based on the degree to which she sees them as capable of producing policy change.

freed from its connection to work. The important trade-off made in gaining that freedom is a loss of the focus and specificity that has facilitated policymaking to improve gender equality, and the mobilization necessary to motivate or support it (Shaw, 2000). The gender mainstreaming provisions included in the Treaty of Amsterdam (1999) are seen by some as a major breakthrough in EU competence (Rees, 1998). The institutionalization of that competence will take time, however, and has thus far been uneven (Pollack and Hafner-Burton, 2000). As is the case with EU gender equality policy overall, the views on mainstreaming are thoroughly ambivalent (Shaw, 2002; Helfferich and Kolb, 2001; Hoskyns, 2000; Pollack and Hafner-Burton, 2000), reflecting the still significant gap between the promises and possibilities it offers and the actual results that have so far been delivered.

1.2 Equality Through Equal Treatment

Quite apart from its origins and at least some of the Member State's underlying intentions, Article 119 provided a clear statement of policy principle at the constitutional level. However, it was a principle with neither clear legal definition nor the organizational capacity necessary to realize it in practice; it lacked institutional priority, administrative apparatus, and the engagement of European-level actors necessary to make it an effective instrument[3]. While this probably eased the difficult process of getting the EEC Treaty negotiated and ratified, these deficiencies presented a substantial challenge for implementation – one that was taken up by key women in the second wave of women's mobilization in the late 1960s and early 1970s.

The broad social context set the stage for a pair of key developments. During the mid-to-late 1960s, the established order was being called into questioned on multiple fronts. Militancy was strong among unions, students were organizing, and women were engaging at new levels; all were challenging the conventional assumptions of the day. Particularly important were the engagement of strong leaders among female labor activists in Germany and France, and the eye-opening effects of the Herstal Equal Pay strike in Belgium[4] – which became in many ways the embodiment of the problem of unequal (and unfair) treatment of women workers. The Herstal strike, which involved as many as 3000 women and caused some 4,500 other workers to be laid off between February 15th and May 9th, 1956, challenged in particular the different rules applied to setting women's and men's pay levels. The principle of equal pay had been raised and discussed, but little had so far been done. In the Herstal case, the Belgian arms factory in Herstal was intransigent, but

---

[3] This was also true of the Treaty provisions more generally. There was a high degree of uncertainty regarding the strength of the various Articles, and the extent to which they superceded national law, although this changed over time as the European Court of Justice issued its early rulings (Weiler, 1991).

[4] The Herstal pay strike is considered a watershed event in women's organizing and mobilization. See Hoskyns (1996:60-61), for additional detail.

neither did the principle unions involved at the plant(s), the socialist Fédération Générale du Travail de Belgique (FGTB) and the Catholic Confédération des Syndicats Chrétiens (CSC), manage their responsibilities to their women members well. The women's struggle and eventual victory generated shock waves that reached far beyond their particular effort.

Among those inspired by the breakthrough embodied in the strike was Elaine Vogel-Polsky, a Belgian attorney who specialized in social and labor law cases[5]. Vogel-Polsky saw an opportunity to push the ECJ to give meaning to Article 119, by challenging it to apply the Article in a manner consistent with other Treaty provisions. At the core of Vogel-Polsky's argument was that the equal pay Article should have equal legal standing and provide for the same right of direct applicability as Treaty provisions considered essential to the building of the common market. In essence, she was arguing that the Article should be considered directly applicable to the terms of employer/employee relationships. After a great deal of effort searching for the appropriate test case (including unsuccessful attempts to engage the major labor unions), she was put in touch with Gabrielle Defrenne. Defrenne, an "air hostess" (as they were referred to at the time) with 17 years of work with Sabena Airlines, had in accordance with company policy been forced to resign her job upon turning forty (as had others before her). The direct result was the loss of a job, but the indirect result was the loss of future earnings and future retirement benefits, among other things. Defrenne agreed to provide the test case, but was apparently reticent about playing any other significant private or public role in the case[6].

The Defrenne cases[7] went to an activist court whose member judges were described as having "shared the formative experience of the second world war", and as having "been united in their determination to give reality to the process of European integration…" (Hoskyns, 1996:71). Even so, they exercised caution in their judgments, while responding with the logical consistency that Vogel-Polsky's framing of the issue demanded. In their 1976 Decision, they spoke to the fundamental question of consistency across policy spheres posed by Vogel-Polsky: if an Article (in this case, Article 95 of the Rome Treaty) pertaining to discriminatory acts within

[5] For the authoritative account of the development of EU gender equality policy and the role of some of the individual women policy entrepreneurs in these early developments, see Catherine Hoskyns (1996: 60-94). The description of events here summarizes Hoskyns's research.

[6] Cichowski (2001: 113-114) seeks to identify basic mechanisms of institutional evolution on the issue of sex equality, describing the Defrenne case as an instance of a process by which "self-interested private litigants and lawyers are able to activate the EU legal system". However, it seems clear from the particulars of the case that adherence to broader policy principles, and not self-interest in the normal sense of the term, was the motivation for bringing this particular case. It also appears to have played an important role in the ECJ decision.

[7] The Defrenne challenge came in the form of two separate cases under different aspects of law, and arrived at the ECJ via separate legal paths. The first of the cases ruled on was the second case filed. The original case was the standard setter (Hoskyns, 1996:67-74).

the context of the common market superceded national law and gave individuals direct access to the courts so seek redress (which meant in effect that the provision would have the direct force of law without the need to be transposed into national law), should this not also be the case for the equal pay provision embodied in Article 119? The affirmative answer to this question provided by the ECJ anchored (and further institutionalized) a single important principle of gender equality at a level comparable to that of the principles by which the common market was being established. Nevertheless, the lack of existing organizational capacity at the time, both within the European Institutions and women's organizations (and would take many years to develop), meant that building on this victory would necessarily be a gradual and painstaking process.

Concurrent Developments

Even while the Defrenne Cases were working their way toward an ECJ decision, the realization of the principle of gender equality through equal treatment was being pursued via another route. It was developed through the enactment of a 1975 Directive requiring the harmonization of member state laws (Directive 75/117/EEC)[8]. Member states were required to provide legal remedies, including job protections for women bringing discrimination charges, and the Directive defined what was meant by equal pay for equal work, calling for the elimination of "all discrimination on grounds of sex with regard to all aspects and conditions of remuneration" (Directive 75/117/EEC: Article 1). The Directive continued the pattern of characterizing the principle of equal treatment as an economic issue, describing the goal of equal pay as "an integral part of the establishment and functioning of the common market", although whether this language represented the necessary political framing of the issue or its underlying conceptualization is open to debate.

Rather than putting the issue to rest, the new directive highlighted other forms of unequal treatment and raised yet further questions regarding the economic dimensions of gender inequality. If equal treatment in paycheck matters could be considered "integral", then what about the economic consequences of other discrimination on the part of employers, as well as education and social protection systems? Two additional Directives targeting employment-related discrimination against women followed, the first of these in 1976 on implementing the principle of equal treatment regarding access to employment, vocational training and promotion, and working conditions (Directive 76/207/EEC), and the second in 1979 requiring the progressive implementation of equal treatment in connection with social security (Directive 79/7/EEC). The EU adopted these early legislative instruments during a period in which new territory was being staked out for equality between the sexes. In addition, state intervention in markets, whether on behalf of

[8] This cannot have escaped the attention of the European Court of Justice's judges, and probably made the practical step embodied in their eventual Decision a smaller, more manageable one.

workers and for ensuring the public welfare, was still seen as necessary and appropriate. Keynesian economic policy was still widely accepted (Hall, 1993) and welfare state institutions were still being expanded and consolidated across Europe (Baldwin, 1990).

The 1970s was also a period of slipping momentum in the development of the European Community, which fostered additional openness to new policies and reaching out to new constituencies. All three Directives approached the principle of equality through seeking to legally limit market/employment violations of the principle of equal treatment. But as with many of the other initial forays into social legislation, these efforts were quite preliminary, circumscribing only the most obvious violations of the principle of equality.

Notwithstanding the neo-liberal flavor of much of the 1980s, efforts to pursue the development of EU social policy continued. The 1980s and early 1990s can be characterized as a period of consolidation of gains made, with an expansion of women's formal and informal roles within the Commission, a further mapping out by the ECJ of the meaning of Article 119 and the major directives issued under its authority, and an expansion of activity pertaining to women's concerns within Directorate-General (DG) V (now referred to as DG Employment, Social Affairs and Equal Opportunities) and within the framework of a succession of Action Programs (Rees, 1998; Geyer, 2000). It included an expansion of women's formal role within the Commission, and development of the Commission's organizational capacity (much of it in DG-V) to address gender equality issues. It also included a regrouping and reorganizing of the array of transnational, European women's organizations. For example, an Advisory Committee on Equal Opportunities for Women and Men was established at the end of 1982 (82/43/EEC) to create a structure for regular consultation and evaluation of EU gender equality policies. NGO activity at the EU level was also promoted and supported. The European Women's Lobby (EWL) was founded in 1990 with funding from the Commission. Its goal was to function as an EU level NGO for fostering coordination among women's organizations and communication with the Commission.

The European Court of Justice continued to flesh out EU gender equality through case law, although not without limits. While the ECJ demonstrated a willingness to intervene in the "private" domain of employers, it also continued to recognize certain boundaries. In the Hoffmann case (Case 184/83) it ruled that the Equal Treatment Directive was "not designed to settle questions concerned with the organization of the family, or to alter the division of responsibility between parents". Viewing the decision in the case as a significant setback, Scheiwe (1994) argued: "a rigid separating line between the two spheres, the market and the family, has been erected in case law and used by the Court to justify a narrow interpretation of the equal treatment Directives. The ECJ argues that the equal treatment directives are not designed to alter the division of labour of couples in private households or to take into account family obligations of employees (Scheiwe, 1994: 261, c.f. Beveridge and Nott, 1996: 385).

1.3 Positive Action

Progress also began to emerge on new fronts, in the form of new measures based on similar goals, but a different underlying principle – the principle of difference. In the process, key new Directives began reaching in new and different ways into the sphere adherents of a neo-liberal paradigm might generally consider to be the "private" area of "contractual relationship" between employer and employee. One intervention in this sense was a 1997 Framework Directive dealing with part-time work (Directive 97/81/EC). Based on the consultation between the Social Partners (the peak industry and trade union associations at the EU level – UNICE, CEEP, ETUC), this Directive targeted structural discrimination against part-time workers, the majority of whom are women, in terms of benefits and working conditions. Other, earlier legislation along these lines included Directive 92/85/EEC, to protect the safety & health of pregnant workers or those breast-feeding. However, this directive was passed not as an equality measure, but as a health and safety measure in order to enable its passage by qualified majority rather than unanimous vote (Beveridge and Nott, 1996:389). In addition, a Framework Agreement on parental leave was negotiated by the Social Partners, which later became Directive 96/34/EEC. Both these Directives were aimed at helping to address problems faced by women in their efforts to combine work and family, but the policies also addressed another pair of pressing problems linked to EU market concerns. First, was the more general demographic shift toward an older population driven by lower birth rates; the second was the related challenge to draw women over time into the workforce in greater numbers. Both these economic goals were served by reducing the conflict and disadvantage women in the workforce face as a result of contradictions in the realms of work and family; the expected benefits were seized on to strengthen arguments for supporting the Directives[9]. These Directives imposed new rules and costs on market actors, many of whom would likely have been unwilling to take on such costs voluntarily. Moreover, such costs were not imposed by international competitors such as the USA[10]. There was a clear precedent for this sort of multi-purpose social policy. Sweden and Hungary, for example, implemented women-friendly policies dealing with work/family issues including child care and parental leave, and did this during periods of labor shortage (Asztalos Morell, 1999; Florin and Nilsson, 1999). It is important to note, however, that these developments were not merely driven by functional needs. Rather, the labor short-

[9] See also the discussion in section "Mainstreaming Practice: Reconciliation between work and private life" below.

[10] Although the US did pass legislation providing for up to twelve weeks of *unpaid* family and medical leave in 1993. It does not apply to employers with fewer than 50 employees (see US Department of Labor, 1993).

ages opened up opportunities for skilled actors inside and outside state bureaucracies who were interested in strengthening gender equality (Hobson, 2003b).

2. Mainstreaming and Policy Development within the EU

The mainstreaming of gender equality cleared the way for the EU to engage in a number of issues ranging from domestic violence to women in science and women in decision-making roles. The Commission and member states went to the Fourth World Conference on Women in Beijing (1995) to promote the idea of mainstreaming gender equality and returned with a larger package that included, among other challenges, that of combating domestic violence.

Gender equality was not the only policy sector "mainstreamed" in the Amsterdam Treaty – language assigning responsibility for the EU to ensure a "high level of public health" in all policies was also included (Articles 152, 153). In both cases there was considerable pressure for deeper EU involvement that was generated on the one hand by women's groups and EU officials seeking to expand gender equality beyond the boundaries of the workplace, and in the case of public health, driven by a food safety crisis that deeply shook the EU (see Chapter 8). Both of these followed the mainstreaming of environmental concerns, a set of problems understood to be transnational significantly earlier.

The Treaties that have provided the legal basis of the EU have served in practice as a sort of constitutional framework. Especially in the area of constructing the internal market, the Treaties have provided a legal structure around which to build concerted action, rather than legally defined boxes within which to house it. But this authority has been lacking in several non-economic areas, essentially barring the EU from taking action in some areas or requiring difficult to reach unanimity among the member states. The "mainstreaming" of gender – and of environmental and public health concerns – subtly changed this, although far less subtly than most imagined, by providing an open-ended, if more modest, mandate. It represented a deeper institutionalization of the paradigm shift with respect to public health and consumer safety issues – the formal acknowledgement by member states of the new paradigmatic order in these policy sectors. It is also intertwined with, and is yet another reflection of, the changing perceptions regarding the kinds of issues that can be considered European versus national or local.

2.1 The unfolding of gender mainstreaming

As early as 1990, the Third Community Action Programme on Equal Opportunities for Women and Men (1991–1995) introduced the idea of gender mainstreaming within the EU (Stratigaki 2005: 170; see also Hantrais 2000b: 122-123), recognising that "existing policies were failing to have any impact on the majority of women's lives and lacked coherence" (Booth & Bennett 2002: 439).

However, it was the 1995 Platform for Action of the Fourth World Conference on Women in Beijing what represented the entry of gender mainstreaming into the core of international public policy. The Platform defined the term of gender mainstreaming and secured the commitment of governments and United Nations institutions to incorporate a gender perspective in all policy-making areas (Pollack and Hafter-Burton 2000: 435; Booth & Bennett 2002: 438; Stratigaki 2005: 172-173; Carson 2004: 200-210).

The EU delegation in Beijing played a leading role in putting forward the principle of mainstreaming in the context of the Fourth World Conference on Women and returned from Beijing with a renovated and even more extended gender agenda. In 1996 the European Commission (EC) officially adopted the gender mainstreaming approach (Hantrais 2000b: 124). While the 1995 Platform for Action of the Fourth World Conference on Women in Beijing provided the general frame able to legitimise the introduction of gender mainstreaming into public policy at the international level, the major shift in the dominant gender approach at EU level was reflected in the 1996 communication from the Commission of European Communities, and was later formalised by the Treaty of Amsterdam.

The 1996 communication from the Commission of European Communities referred to the challenge of building "a new partnership between men and women" and the necessity of incorporating a gender mainstreaming approach in order to achieve this "new partnership". In the document, gender mainstreaming was defined as involving:

> *"[N]ot restricting efforts to promote equality to the implementation of specific measures to help women, but mobilising all general policies and measures specifically for the purpose of achieving equality by actively and openly taking into account at the planning stage their possible effects on the respective situation of men and women (gender perspective). This means systematically examining measures and policies and taking into account such possible effects when defining and implementing them." (European Commission 1996b: 2, underlined in the original)*

The Fourth Action Programme on Equal Opportunities for Women and Men (1996–2000), proposed by the Commission and adopted by the Council, presented mainstreaming as its most important component, together with previous specific actions such as equal treatment legislation and positive action policies (Pollack and Hafter-Burton 2000: 436; see also Hantrais 2000b: 123; Stratigaki 2005: 177). As Hoskyns (2000: 53) says, the Fourth Action Programme introduced three general themes. The first was mainstreaming as an "organising principle", implying that gender issues should go beyond the boundaries of the then DG Employment and Social Affairs (current DG Employment, Social Affairs and Equal Opportunities) by being introduced into *all* Community policies. The second theme in the Programme was "subsidiarity"[11], here the concern was to identify the specific roles that

[11] The "subsidiarity" principle included in the Treaty of Maastricht stipulates that "[i]n areas which do not fall within its exclusive competence, the Community shall take action [...] only if and in so far as the objectives of the proposed action cannot be sufficiently achieved by the Member States and can therefore, by reason of the scale or effects of the proposed action, be better achieved by the Community" (Article 3b, Treaty on European Union 1992).

Member States and EU institutions should play in the making of gender equality policy (Hoskyns 2000: 53). It was proposed that Member States should develop methods in order to integrate a gender perspective into all policy areas (Booth & Bennett 2002: 439). The third concern was to promote the reconciliation of work and family responsibilities for both men and women. The limits of the workplace were – to some extent – trespassed, as the focus moved also to the boundary between paid and unpaid work and the (traditional) roles of women and men (Hoskyns 2000: 54).

The 1997 Treaty of Amsterdam (effective in 1999) had provisions reflecting the EU's new approach to equal opportunities and the deeper development of its competence in this area. Article 141 replaced Article 119 of the Treaty of Rome strengthening the original language on equal pay and the legal basis for gender equality. Yet the most important and advanced of the provisions in the new Treaty were the amendments to Articles 2 and 3 (Lewis 2006; Pollack and Hafter-Burton 2000). The reformulated articles made the promotion of equal opportunities for women and men *throughout all Community areas* – instead of just equal pay and equal treatment in the work place – a central goal of the EU, formalising the commitment to gender mainstreaming (Booth & Bennett 2002: 443; Lewis 2006: 426; Pollack and Hafter-Burton 2000: 437)[12].

Later on, the Fifth Community Action Programme on Equal Opportunities (2001-2006) presented as its main objectives the coordination, support and financing of different transnational projects as part of the implementation of the "Community's global framework strategy on gender equality" that had been adopted by the Commission in June 2000 (Booth & Bennett 2002: 431-432; Mazey 2002: 234-235)[13].

As currently defined by the Commission, EU gender equality policy:

"[T]akes a comprehensive approach which includes legislation, mainstreaming and positive actions. Financial support is also available via an action programme. The key objective is to eliminate inequalities and promote gender equality throughout the European Community in accordance with Articles 2 and 3 of the EC Treaty (gender mainstreaming) as well as Article 141 (equality between women and men in matters of employment and occupation) and Article 13 (sex discrimination within and outside the work place)."[14]

---

[12] Article 2 of the Treaty of Amsterdam states: "[t]he Community shall have as its task [...] to promote throughout the Community a harmonious, balanced and sustainable development of economic activities, a high level of employment and of social protection, equality between men and women..." (Treaty of Amsterdam 1997: 22). Article 3 of the Treaty states that in all its activities the Community "shall aim to eliminate inequalities, and to promote equality, between men and women" (Treaty of Amsterdam 1997: 23).

[13] See also http://ec.europa.eu/employment_social/gender_equality/actions/index_en.html, Accessed on February 2007.

[14] Available at http://ec.europa.eu/employment_social/gender_equality/index_en.html, Acceded on January 2007.

2.2 The practice of mainstreaming

Within the EU, the DG that formally deals, in general, with much of the gender equality agenda is the DG Employment, Social Affairs and Equal Opportunities (DG-ESAEO hereafter). It does so, on the one hand, by formulating and overseeing legislation as well as implementing specific programmes aiming at improving equal opportunities and, on the other hand, by "ensuring that the gender issue is taken into account in all fields of Community action"[15].

Within the DG-ESAEO, two units deal with gender equality issues: the "Equality between Women and Men" Unit and the "Equality, Action against discrimination: legal questions" Unit, both at the Directorate G "Equality between Men and Women, Action against discrimination, Civil Society". Through its Equality between Women and Men Unit and assisted by the Advisory Committee on Equal Opportunities for Women and Men, the High Level Group on Gender Mainstreaming, and the Commission's Inter-Service Group on Gender Equality, the DG-ESAEO coordinates the gender mainstreaming strategy and assists other DGs and services of the Commission to gender-mainstream their policies. It also formulates the action programmes providing financing in order to achieve three main objectives: awareness raising, analysis and evaluation, and capacity building[16].

Key policy areas which have been identified by DG-ESAEO are: Employment and labour market (which is the oldest), Gender pay gap, education and training, gender balance in decision-making, women and science, reconciliation between work and private life, gender budgeting, social inclusion and social protection, development cooperation, structural funds, gender equality at international level, migrant women, men's role in promoting gender equality, and gender based violence and trafficking in women.

EU's current strategy is to focus on a relatively few areas, which are expressed in the "Roadmap for equality for women and men 2006-2010"[17] (adopted by the EC in March 2006 and coordinated by the Equality between Women and Men Unit). The six priority areas for EU action are:

- eradication of all forms of gender based violence (section 3 below),
- promotion of gender equality in external and development policies – i.e. beyond the frontiers of the EU (European Commission 2006a: 2) (section 4.1 below).
- reconciliation of private and professional life (section 4.2 below)
- equal representation in decision-making (section 4.4 below),
- elimination of gender stereotypes,

[15] Available at http://ec.europa.eu/dgs/employment_social/index_en.htm, Acceded on February 2007.

[16] Available at http://ec.europa.eu/employment_social/gender_equality/index_en.html, Acceded on February 2007.

[17] The Roadmap is the successor of the Community Action Programmes on Equal Opportunities for Women and Men.

- economic independence for women and men (employment, social security, etc.).

The first four are briefly examined below along with three areas, two in which the Commission has been highly active and innovative, "structural funds" (section 4.3) and "women in science" (section 4.5), and a third "migrant women" (section 4.6), which is a marginalized area in two senses.

Table 13.1. Selection of Mainstreaming Sectors Discussed Below

Policy areas	Responsible EU entities
Domestic Violence	DG for Justice, Freedom and Security
Development cooperation	DG Development, DG Europe AID
Reconciliation between work and private life	DG Employment, Social Affairs, and Equal Opportunity
Women in Science	DG Research
Women in Societal Decision-making	DG Employment, Social Affairs, and Equal Opportunity
Migrant Women	DG for Justice, Freedom and Security

The expansion of the gender equality agenda has taken place within a broader context of policy developments characterised by a growing concern on social issues within the EU. With a recurrent reference to the 'European social model' in EU documents – many times presented as an alternative to the 'US model', social policy in general has "achieved a higher profile at EU level" (Lewis 2006: 424).

3. The Case of Domestic Violence as an EU Issue

3.1 Introduction

The issue of men's violence against women is one mainstreaming development that many considered far beyond EU competency and, in general, public policy. But the EU once again found support – and a special niche – where many national governments had failed or were ignoring the issue.

The efforts towards addressing violence against women as an EU issue were to a great extent symbolic, since EU insiders understood that there were structural limitations (as in constraints on EU competence) on what measures could be undertaken in practice. Still, those insiders (including Barbara Helferich, the former head of the European Women's Lobby (EWL)) were interested in pressing and extending those limits. Some may have been motivated substantially by a belief in the EU idea, others were mostly interested in any possible leverage that could be won on the issue of domestic violence, and were willing to work together with the "Europeans". Women's activist groups, including the Women's lobby, pushed very hard on the domestic violence issue. so to the extent that EU action on domestic violence was symbolic, there was an engaged audience who cared a great deal about it.

The mainstreaming of gender equality cleared the way for the EU to engage in the issue of domestic violence, but the progress made through international work to redefine accepted norms and establish violence against women as a legitimate international issue made it a relatively safe issue for the EU to take up.

The kickoff of the Commission's *Campaign against Domestic Violence* in January of 1999 marked an important milestone in the effort to establish "domestic" violence as a truly European problem. It was also symbolic of the expansion of the European Union's authority to pursue its stated goal of equality between women and men, and more broadly, to develop the EU "social dimension". It would be an overstatement, however, to characterize the Campaign as a decisive step in EU policy regarding domestic violence against women. The Campaign was not considered especially effective – some of the women's groups active on the issue were not even aware it was underway (EWL, 2000) (although one could point out that the possibility of EU action on domestic violence had not yet entered their thoughts). Nor did it mark any new EU legislative competence. The EU remains barred for the most part from directly legislating on such matters – which is one indicator of the "Europeanization" of a public policy question. Its legal authority remains largely limited to a "coordination and facilitation" role. Neither did the Campaign generate any revolution in public policy within member states – although the progress report produced for the Finnish EU Presidency at the end of the Campaign suggested that existing efforts had been supported and some new action had been initiated (CESIS, 2000).

Nevertheless, both the European Campaign against Domestic Violence and the developments that contributed to its realization have served to strengthen the legitimacy of European institutions to engage in a sphere of social life frequently considered properly off-limits from the intervention of even national or local governments. They also lent additional force and credibility to long-standing claims made by women's movement activists and organizations regarding the nature and pervasiveness of the such violence against women, its underlying causes, and its detrimental effects on women, children, and men – and on society as a whole.

3.2 A European Problem?

The basic questions is then how and why did domestic violence emerge as a matter of public policy concern at the EU level, and what is its connection to EU policies for promoting equality between women and men, including "gender mainstreaming"? Given both the historically economic emphasis of the EU and the limitations of the Treaties that have served as a de facto constitution since its inception, that domestic violence has been taken up at the EU level at all is a matter worth noting. Non-economic gender equality issues such as domestic violence are nowhere to be seen in a world viewed from the perspective of a market paradigm that emphasizes economic relationships, integration through the lowering of regulatory barriers to trade, and the construction of the single market. In such a framework, domestic violence is a non-problem – it simply fails to come into view.

Given the difficulty in getting domestic violence on the policy agenda at the national level (Kelly, 1999; Walby, 1999a), getting the issue on the EU agenda seems doubly unlikely. At the national level where social policy has received much attention, violence against women has been often swept under the rug and explicitly marked as off-limits – as a "private", family matter. The report produced for the Finnish EU Presidency in 2000 highlighted the stubborn persistence of the sentiment that *domestic violence is not a matter for public policymaking*. It pointed out, for example, "in the UK, the perception even by some official bodies is that domestic violence is not a serious problem (except in extreme cases) and that *it is a private, family matter where State bodies should not interfere*" (emphasis added) (CESIS Study, April 2000:27).

The upshot of these two factors, whether paradigmatic blindness or studied indifference, is that domestic violence has tended to be not seen as a problem, and therefore *not* a matter of public policy. The persistence of such sentiments would suggest that the arrival of domestic violence on the EU agenda is indeed a noteworthy development – even if it is a development that marks a particular type of progress, and not a resolution of the problem.

Nor did the fledgling European institutions possess more than a rudimentary organizational capacity of any sort that could enable them to take action even in those areas in which their constitutional mandate was clearly set forth[18]. So while the principle of gender equality showed up remarkably early on the EU agenda, domestic violence remained as invisible in Brussels as almost everywhere else up until the 1990s. When domestic violence finally was put on the EU policy agenda, it was on a foundation that was straining the confines of an EU gender equality policy bound to women's role in the workforce. It was also built on the progress made in a critical mass of EU member states and at the international level. It emerged as an EU concern in the area of overlap between gender equality, human rights, public health and a broader social dimension; this has been reinforced by a deepening understanding of domestic violence and by developments in other areas of public policy.

Domestic violence was made an EU issue in the confluence of two separate currents of policy development. One current entailed transforming domestic violence from a private into a public issue – first on the national, and then on the

---

[18] The equal pay provision in the Treaty of Rome (Article 19) languished without action for well over a decade. This was in due to numerous factors, and the EU lacked any organized infrastructure developed around the principle of gender equality.

international agenda through wide-ranging grassroots advocacy work and the engagement of new expertise (Joachim, 2002). These efforts eventually intersected with the development of EU gender equality policy, which had evolved along a very different path over the decades since Article 119 was written into the Treaty of Rome (1958).

Putting domestic violence on the EU agenda required skillful organizing and mobilization along these parallel tracks and across multiple levels of governance (local and national, supranational, and international).[19] At the national level, the issue was drawn out of *the "private" domain considered properly off limits to the reach of public institutions and establishing it as a legitimate public policy concern.* In individual countries, the demand was for equal application of the law to the private family sphere, that is to define and treat domestic violence as a crime like any other form of battery.

At the EU level, bringing domestic violence onto the agenda required an expansion of EU policy competence beyond workplace concerns to include non-economic issues of equality between men and women. In the European Union, domestic violence was increasingly defined as an obstacle to the goal of equality between women and men, and the achievement of a "high level of public health", and even to the achievement of prosperity that is to be provided by economic integration – each of these being core goals of the EU based in the Treaties and therefore within the EU competence of engagement.

Overcoming the obstacles at these respective levels entailed a process of navigating a variety of conceptual and institutional hurdles. It required establishing and institutionalizing new paradigmatic ideas and norms through a formulation of discourses that defined the phenomenon as a serious problem, and redefined the understanding of its causes and perpetrators, and which authorities should be responsible for implementing the appropriate remedies. The effects of successful efforts at the national and international levels then set the stage for a convergence at the EU level that opened the political space for domestic violence to be taken up as an EU issue. In each case, these arguments possess some of the same core concerns that permit women's organizations to unite across a diversity of life experiences and geography.

3.4. From "Silent Epidemic" to "Social Problem"

Violence against women takes numerous forms, reaching into many areas and institutions of social life. Domestic violence, or battering – the violence that takes place

[19] At the international level, domestic violence was established through a series of stages as a transnational problem, thereby removing it from the exclusive jurisdiction of individual states. Here, establishing domestic violence as an issue was part of the larger package of advances at the international level and the UN, connected with promoting equality by defining women's rights as human rights (West, 1999). Domestic violence has been defined as a violation of agreed-upon human rights norms and conventions to which states have a responsibility to respond – failing to do so is to be complicit in violation of women's human rights.

in the context of family or intimate relationships – has proven to be among the most sensitive and complex among these. Even the terms used are often an area of contention; domestic or family violence are fundamentally acts of violence committed by men. Yet, such labels have sometimes been used to suggest gender neutrality and shared responsibility, minimizing the typically one-way nature of the violence (Dobash and Dobash, 1992; Kurz, 1989). The all too common perception of the problem was captured in the language of a North Carolina Court decision from the 1980s:

> *If no permanent injury has been inflicted, no malice, cruelty nor dangerous violence shown by the husband, it is better to draw the curtain, shut out the public gaze, and leave the parties to forgive and forget (Browne, 1987, c.f. Kurz, 1989:496).*

Liz Kelly (1999) observes that knowledge and awareness of gendered violence were quite limited as recently as the early 1970s. This and a lack of concrete, systematic data contributed to the problem remaining a largely indistinct, seemingly invisible phenomenon until the 1990s, and it was therefore largely absent from the public agenda. Kelly (1999:125) summarizes one of the conceptual hurdles, pointing out that "for men the threat of basic security primarily concerns the public sphere, whereas for women and children the home (the private) is one of the most likely settings in which violence occurs".

One clear consequence of the lack of clear conceptualization of the issue and corresponding absence of formal knowledge was that there existed, in effect, *no clearly defined social problem to which public policy might address, in part because the pervasiveness of the problem was not widely understood.* Yet, when women began establishing battered women's shelters in the mid to late 1970s in the U.S. and the UK, they often rapidly filled up and were even forced to turn away women seeking safety (Schechter, 1982). The seemingly anecdotal evidence provided by overfull shelters and periodic coverage in the news media has been repeatedly substantiated by subsequent research, pointing to a long-standing and shockingly widespread phenomenon that nevertheless was difficult to establish as a public concern.

The "anecdotal" evidence offered by news coverage of hardship and tragedy has been a crucial factor in making a previously "invisible" problem real and tangible – in providing images and metaphors that capture the phenomena, and incrementally building a public consciousness of domestic violence as a problem to be addressed. It provided easily grasped evidence of the ways in which the institutionalized discourses failed to see or account for the problem. Nancy Fraser (1989:174) highlights the discursive/conceptual change:

> *Until about fifteen years ago, the term 'wife battering' did not exist. When spoken of publicly at all, this phenomenon was called 'wife beating' and was often treated comically, as in "Have you stopped beating your wife?" Linguistically, it was classed with the disciplining of children and servants as a 'domestic' – as opposed to a public (and 'political') – matter. Then, feminist activists renamed the practice with a term drawn from criminal law and created a new kind of public discourse. They claimed that battery was not a personal, domestic problem, but a systemic, political one; its etiology was not to be traced to individual*

women's or men's emotional problems but, rather, to the ways these problems refracted pervasive social relations of male dominance and female subordination.

The conceptual shift Fraser points to was realized to an important extent in research as well as in policymaking. Both activists and researchers further fleshed out the problem with sharpened concepts, empirical data, and causal explanations[20] that have tended to discredit both earlier institutional arrangements that made such violence invisible and the various discourses that have been used to explain or defend them. Demie Kurz points to the overall effect in noting how "researchers, by providing statistical evidence documenting the extent of wife abuse, have played a critical role in making it a social issue" (Kurz, 1989:489). Kurz also explains this process in terms of the replacement of one conceptual model applied to understanding such violence, the "family violence" model, with another – "men's violence against women". Although the models are similar in a number of respects, they are fundamentally different in their core assumptions (which are only made explicit in the feminist, "men's violence" model). The result is that the kind of data gathered is substantively different than before, as are the kinds of policy recommendations that emanate from the research. Taken together, these have had important consequences for establishing domestic violence as a recognized social problem, which public policy should address. In this respect, Kurz remarks on the progress made in reconceptualizing the problem: "'wife abuse' has been transformed from a private, largely invisible matter, to one viewed as a social problem for which appropriate remedies should be sought" (Kurz, 1989:489). The 1990s brought continual changes as women's organizations mobilized and built on earlier gains, as new data was collected, analyzed, and distributed, and as the increasing prominence of closely related social issues offered new anchor points for dealing with battering. The private-becoming-public status of domestic violence is captured in some of the slogans employed by efforts to establish the issue of domestic violence as a public problem, such as "Breaking the Silence" used in the European Campaign Against Domestic Violence, or "the silent epidemic", used in Swedish materials targeting violence against women. Nevertheless, the issue of men's domestic violence against women remains a highly sensitive area for public policy.[21]

This change in conceptualization – represented here as a paradigmatic shift – continues to diffuse and be institutionalized in small increments among industrialized and even developing nations. The gains, however, remain tentative and preliminary; they have been only partially and unevenly institutionalized.

---

[20] See Judith Innes (1994) for an especially clear and insightful discussion of the importance of scientific data and concepts and the social indicators based on them, in the formulation of problems and public policy.

[21] Even in Sweden, considered by many to have made greater progress toward gender equality than most countries, characterized battering descriptively as "men's violence against women" rather than more generically as "family violence" or "domestic violence" and drew uncomfortable reactions (Mattsson, 2001; Eduards, 1997; Elman, 1996).

3.4. Convergence: Domestic Violence, Human Rights, and Multi-Level Advocacy

Remarkably, the documents that mark the shift to expand the EU's broader policy paradigm to include domestic violence were formalized not in Brussels, but in Beijing[22]. The Platform for Action that emerged from the Beijing Conference (1995) defined domestic violence and other violence against women as a violation of human rights requiring "immediate and direct attention". The implicit and explicit argument of these UN documents (and others) was that these are "public issues," and therefore legitimate questions for governing institutions to take up and address. The agreements struck in Beijing go beyond legitimating as a public issue all forms of violence against women. Since they define it as a violation of women's human rights, seeking to address such violence becomes an acknowledged responsibility of the state.

The consensus building process in Beijing was facilitated by Commission officials, although not directly, and not without some difficulty. The EU is not a member of the UN, but an observer. Spain, which held the EU Presidency at the time, formally represented EU member states, while the Commission acted as a coordinator and provided support for the Spanish Presidency. Commission officials participated in a supporting role in the planning of the conference as well as the process of the conference itself; its most important goal was helping the member states "to agree on a common position for the European Union" (EC, 2000:3). Consultation with European women's NGOs was largely pro forma – at least initially.

"Europe gained an incredible weight in the negotiations, because it spoke with one voice", and it was able to significantly influence the eventual consensus.[23] The final document, the Beijing Platform for Action (UN, 1995), added linkages between long-standing and widely accepted principles of human rights, currently influential discourses supporting equality between women and men, and a conception of violence against women that defines the expected policy responses based on the nature of the violence, and not on the particular sphere of social life (i.e. family) in which it takes place. The imperative to combat violence became the priority, superseding both state sovereignty and family privacy.[24]

---

[22] This "convergence" occurred at the international level, with the Commission and EU member states participating in the process. One result is that instead of an EU Green Paper outlining EU principles, goals, and a general plan of action, the "Beijing Platform for Action" became the EU working document.

[23] Interview with former NGO activist, March 2004.

[24] These linkages are clear in the language of the Platform: *The advancement of women and the achievement of equality between women and men are a matter of human rights and a condition for social justice and should not be seen in isolation as a women's issue. They are the only way to build a sustainable, just and developed society. Empowerment of women and equality between women and men are prerequisites for achieving political, social, economic, cultural and environmental security among all peoples* (Beijing Platform for Action, 1995: paragraph 41).

In approving the Platform, representatives of individual governments embraced a feminist definition of the problem, as well as the causal linkages it elaborated. Lack of equality between the sexes is a structural obstacle to achieving a shared goal – security on all levels, while violence against women is an important source of inequality (in addition to the other problems it poses). The implicit and explicit argument of these UN documents (and others) is that these are public issues, and therefore not only legitimate questions for democratic institutions to take up and address – it is imperative they do so.

Implementation is often primarily the responsibility of Governments, but is also dependent on a wide range of institutions in the public, private, and non-governmental sectors of the community, national, subregional/regional and international levels (UN: Beijing Declaration: Art. 286).[25]

Furthermore, providing remedies is defined as a matter of governmental responsibility at all levels, from local to transnational – a statement that directly contravenes the sentiment that sees such problems as a private matter and stresses their universalistic character:

The human rights of women and of the girl-child are an inalienable, integral and indivisible part of universal human rights. The full and equal participation of women in political, civil, economic, social and cultural life, at the national, regional and international levels, and the eradication of all forms of discrimination on grounds of sex are priority objectives of the international community... Gender-based violence and all forms of sexual harassment and exploitation, including those resulting from cultural prejudice and in-

---

Violence against women is one of the crucial social mechanisms by which women are forced into a subordinate position compared with men. In many cases, violence against women and girls occurs in the family or within the home, where it is often tolerated (Beijing Platform for Action, 1995: paragraph 117).

[25] While Beijing clearly represented a major summit for women, the evidence suggests that at least in the past, such international conferences have probably been taken less seriously by individual states and other actors (including potential opponents as states and within states). This made it possible to make commitments under conditions in which the "stakes" were seemingly lower, especially given the "soft-law" status of a "Platform" or "Declaration", in contrast with a treaty, convention, or other form of legally binding legislation. In addition, in accepting responsibility for implementing the appropriate measures, governments retain control of the issue, and in so doing, avoid ceding authority. Nevertheless, the endorsement was by representatives of UN member states, and that endorsement entails some measure of moral obligation that can be leveraged into more substantive obligations, just as the norms that apply to human rights have been increasingly solidified and institutionalized (Gelb, 1999; Risse and Sikkink, 1999; Gelb, 1989). States therefore embraced the logic and causal relationships identified in the Platform statements, but without having to swallow all at once all that it might come to mean. This prepared the way in the EU to begin thinking about domestic violence in new terms.

The breakthroughs of the Beijing Conference were in fact the culmination of many years of painstaking work with the UN and elsewhere by the transnational network of women's organizations. In a process that proceeded through several steps beginning with the 1976 International Tribunal on Crimes Against Women in Brussels, Domestic violence was formally included in the UN's definition of gender-based discrimination in 1992, and was fully embraced by the UN as a human rights issue at the UN's Vienna World Conference on Human Rights in July of 1993 (UN:A/CONF.157.23).

ternational trafficking, are incompatible with the dignity and worth of the human person, and must be eliminated (UN:A/CONF.157.23, Article 18).

Incorporating women's rights as "inalienable, integral and indivisible part of universal human rights" was no small accomplishment. Despite the obvious commonalities between specific women's rights and human rights more generally, human rights advocates were skittish about defining domestic violence as a violation of human rights for fear of weakening or confusing their own claims. While human rights violations were committed by the state or in the name of the state, the state's role in domestic violence has generally been seen as more removed (A notable exception to this view is Walby (2002), who argues that the state, with its monopoly on the use of violence, has essentially continued to sanction domestic violence by choosing to look the other way).[26]

In arguing for a new set of institutionalized arrangements, the 1993 Vienna Declaration and Programme of Action carefully references and anchors itself in a vast web of earlier law, declarations, documents, commitments, and action. It echoed the principles and positions of the previous half century of work – a period during much of which domestic violence was a non-issue. Nevertheless, a decidedly new spin was achieved – and presumably, a new result over time – by applying established principles to new issues or problems. The Beijing Conference itself represented both the culmination of this and other earlier work, and the launching point for new activity.[27]

[26] The immediate follow-up to the Vienna Conference was the 1994 Session of the UN Commission on Human Rights, which approved several resolutions dealing with gender equality and women's human rights, building on and reinforcing the language of the Vienna Declaration. John Crook (1994:813) suggests that the resolutions, especially the one dealing with violence against women, represented a "modest reconceptualization of human rights... seemingly at odds with long-standing paradigms of human rights in the UN system". Crook characterizes the old paradigm as one concerned with relationships between the state and individuals, with the essential obligations falling to the state. Among the notable acts of the 1994 meeting was a "landmark resolution" creating a special Rapporteur on the global problem of violence against women (Crook, 1994:813). In Crook's words, "the new special rapporteur's mandate extends to forms of domestic violence and traditional practices that may have been seen previously as cultural matters outside the sphere of international human rights protection".

[27] It also provided the added credibility of an official, internationally-sanctioned voice on the specific transnational problem of men's violence against women. Each of these incremental steps can be seen as part of the much larger process of institutionalization of a new policy paradigm – one that redefines the relationship between women and men, and redefines the role of states as having legitimacy and responsibility to take the actions necessary to further that process. In the European Union context, this would first require a reconceptualization of gender equality – which had long been confined to a market context – to include all EU policies. However, this was only a precondition to accepting domestic violence as an EU issue. Taking that additional step to would require accepting the EU as competent to intervene in the context in which domestic violence occurs – the private sphere of the family. This would require a very different view of EU competence than that expressed by the European Court of Justice in its ruling in the

3.5 Domestic Violence Becomes an EU Concern

The European Parliament's (EP) Committee on Women's Rights and Equal Opportunities first pushed the issue of domestic violence into view on the EU radar screen with a 1986 resolution calling for the EU member states to organize campaigns to "awaken public awareness to the existence and extent of violence against women" (EP, 1986: paragraph 2), and calling attention to the problem of "violence in the private sphere". The resolution's authors took their inspiration from the work of the 1985 UN World Conference on Women in Nairobi, Kenya, at which violence against women was named as a major obstacle to achieving equality between women and men. They also sought to establish legitimacy for the EP to speak out through reference to international declarations and agreements. The resolution referenced documents that included the UN Universal Declaration of Human Rights (1948), the UN Convention on the Elimination of all forms of Discrimination Against Women (CEDAW, 1979), and Articles 100 and 235 in the Treaty of Rome (1958). Nevertheless, the message of the resolution fell largely on deaf ears within EU institutions. If the assumed "private" nature of domestic violence made it a challenge to put on national policy agendas, it was an issue that was doubly private in the EU context, given that non-economic issues of gender equality were still seen to lie in the "private" sphere and beyond the EU's legal mandate.

In September of 1990, the Europeans' Women Lobby (EWL) was established with encouragement from the European Parliament and through encouragement and financial support from the European Commission. Hoskyns (1996:185-191) notes that it might have been organized and supported earlier, but differences in philosophy and priority delayed the process. While the founding of the EWL did not put these issues to rest (minority and feminist women's groups were said to be marginalized in the process), it did provide a systematic channel through which numerous demands were channeled to the Commission. The independent voice of the EWL was conditioned, of course, by its dependence upon the Commission for a large portion of its budget, but at the same time, it was dependent upon affiliate groups throughout the EU for its legitimacy[28]. This endowed it with both advantages and liabilities in its role as an intermediary between the Commission and the diverse array of women's organizations across Europe – a situation of which the EWL leadership was quite aware.

As it became clear in the mid-1990s that a new Intergovernmental Conference (IGC) would be making revisions to the Maastricht Treaty, the EWL and other

Hoffmann case (Case 184/83), in which it confirmed "family" matters as being outside the scope of EU law.

[28] Hoskyns (1996) highlights some of the tensions present in the formation and the developmental stages of the EWL. She identifies a general bias toward professional and well-educated women and .at least partial marginalization of important constituencies within the women's movement, particularly feminists, women of color, and migrant women.

groups began preparing an ambitious agenda to unlock EU gender equality policy that had by then reached its limits in the context of the workplace. In the 1995 to 1997 time frame, both gender mainstreaming and domestic violence would be put on the EU agenda.

When domestic violence did finally begin to find an official place on the EU agenda, it was on the coattails of the established goals and priorities connected with gender equality, and part of a larger package concerning violence against women more generally. The first mention of violence against women in EU official documents post-Beijing was made a concern in the 1996 communication on "Trafficking in Women" (COM (1996) 567). The problem, causes, and consequences of violence were characterized in terms that clearly drew on the expressions of the Beijing Platform.

One year later, in July of 1997, the EP, led by Rapporteur MEP Marianne Eriksson (Sweden) and others, revived its call for a Europe-wide campaign to counter violence against women. As before, the report anchored itself in the legitimacy of earlier agreements and actions adopted by European and international institutions, though updated to reflect recent progress in Vienna and Beijing, as well as a 1990 resolution on combating private violence adopted by the Council of Europe (CoE, R(90)2). Echoing the Beijing Platform in many respects, it pointed to the myth that domestic violence is a "private matter". It also recommended appropriate measures to be taken, suggesting the need for detailed assessment of the significant hidden social and economic costs associated with the various forms of violence against women (along the lines of research already being carried out in the Netherlands), and noting that although "it would be neither desirable nor possible to harmonise Member State's legislation on violence against women... Member States that lag behind should be urged to reform their legislation" (EP-A4-0250/97). On the one hand, this sort of statement recognized concerns about subsidiarity, on the other, it recognized that legislative changes are only a part of the solution. The culture that supports such violence must also be changed (Galtung, 1990)

At the same time, the EWL was establishing a forum for women's NGOs to better pressure policymakers to take responsibility for dealing with violence against women in the EU. Part of this activity entailed the creation of an Observatory on Violence against Women, which consisted of an expert group of women with special expertise on the problem of violence against women, with representation from each of the EU member states.

Also in 1997, the Daphne Initiative was launched with €3 million in funding, a pilot project which included financial support for specific projects targeting domestic violence. The budgeted amount was miniscule in proportion to other EU expenditures. But this meager allotment can be better understood in the overall resource context, since it easily dwarfed the resources available to many grassroots organizations.

Moreover, where such expenditures have been recurring in subsequent years, they represented a concrete investment in building the organizational capacity of the respective national or transnational women's organizations. The Women Against Violence in Europe (WAVE) network was initially organized, following the Beijing Conference and based in Vienna, Austria, received its initial funding from this EU initiative, as has the EWL's Policy Action Center.

The Commission launched their European Campaign against Domestic Violence in 1999 following prompting from the European Parliament, with support and leadership from five successive EU presidencies. In the process, the commission adopted the language and reasoning used by the women's movement and formalized in UN documents. In 2000, after a 3 year trial run, the Commission relaunched Daphne as a 4-year program, allocating €20 million to support NGO activities combating domestic violence and men's violence against women more generally[29].

It was not solely EU participation in Beijing that opened the door to placing domestic violence to the EU agenda. Following the experience in Beijing, the EWL and other European women's NGOs organized to make the 1996 Intergovernmental Conference (which eventually produced the Amsterdam Treaty) their focal point for seeking to expand beyond the workplace EU competence on gender equality policy. Article 6 of the Amsterdam Treaty (1999) echoed Beijing in its emphasis on the importance of "respect for human rights and fundamental freedoms and the rule of law". Other changes the EWL and women's NGOs were successful in getting adopted in the Amsterdam Treaty (1999) made equal opportunities for both women and men a core objective of the EU. The Directorate for Justice and Home Affairs (current DG for Justice, Freedom and Security), where the Daphne Program is based, was created earlier, following the addition of a new pillar of the Union in the Maastricht Treaty (1992) (Joachim, 2002). Swedish Commissioner of Justice and Home Affairs Anita Gradin is credited with making the Daphne Program a reality through a combination of administrative skill and legal creativity.

In spite of this general broadening of EU competence on issues of gender equality, however, the legal basis of the Daphne Program lies not in the equal opportunities article, but in the Article 152 of the Amsterdam Treaty (1999), which requires ensuring a high level of public health in all Community policies. Officials at Justice and Home Affairs argue that establishing equal opportunities between women and men as a core value of the EU does not provide sufficient legal basis for initiating new stand-alone policy – even if it requires assuring equal opportunities in all policies the EU does initiate. This is illustrative of one of the dangers of mainstreaming (see later discussion). Member states continue to be extremely sensitive to EU intrusion in their criminal law.

[29] The Daphne II Program was approved in early 2004, with an allocation of €50 million over 5 years. Although this figure represents an increase in funding for the Daphne Program, it will now be distributed across 25 member states rather than 15.

3.6 Discourse, Anomaly, and Policy Paradigms

One of the more striking qualities of the discourses cited and adopted at the EU level condemning domestic violence is the way in which domestic violence is made relevant – and an obstacle – to reaching many of the other core purposes of the EU. It is, as established in Beijing, a fundamental violation of women's human rights. *But it is also presented as an economic problem in that it undermines economic development and workforce participation and increases health costs. It is also considered a pervasive public health problem that weakens EU goals in that area and contributes to pushing up health costs, and it is a problem that undermines democracy and participation, etc.* Examining the problem from a Swedish perspective, Maud Eduards and Gunnel Gustafsson (1997) express legitimate concern about this kind of discursive development[30], pointing out that it becomes not a matter of ending domestic violence for women's sake, but rather for the sake of democracy, of the economy, of society, etc. This is significant, since, as this book argues more generally, the way in which an issue is conceptualized has important consequences for how it is dealt with in public policy, by whom, and for what purposes. Defining the problem in terms other than women's human rights runs the risk of weakening the problem definitions that the women's movement has worked so diligently to establish.

4. The Diversity of Context Dependence of Gender Mainstreaming

Below we consider several of the areas where "mainstreaming" has been implemented to varying degrees: Development cooperation, reconciliation between work and private life, and migrant women as well as the issues of women's participation in societal decision-making, science, and structural funds.. They show differences in the patterns of development and levels of success in response to the introduction of the mainstreaming principle.

4.1 Mainstreaming Practice: Development cooperation

The DG for Development deals with the formulation and implementation of the Community's cooperation policy with respect to developing countries. The EU is one of the world's largest providers of official development aid (Pollack and Hafter-Burton 2000: 445), and its development mission is "to help to reduce and ultimately to eradicate poverty in the developing countries through the promotion of sustainable development, democracy, peace and security"[31]. The DG Development together with the DG EuropeAid has been working on the introduction of the mainstreaming strategy within development cooperation, with the DG-ESAEO as coordinator. Several Council and Parliament regulations and communications

[30] Although Eduards and Gustafsson's concerns were expressed in connection to developments in Sweden, the general principle applies to EU discourses as well.

[31] Available at http://ec.europa.eu/development/About/Mission_en.cfm, Acceded on March 2007.

have been formulated in order to mainstream gender in development cooperation, for example, the Council Regulation (EC) No 2836/98 of December 1998 on integrating gender issues in development cooperation, the Regulation of the European Parliament and of the Council on promoting gender equality in development cooperation (EC) 806/2004 of April 2004, and the Communication from the Commission to the Council and the European Parliament – Programme of Action for the mainstreaming of gender equality in Community Development Cooperation adopted in June 2001[32].

The EC defines the promotion of gender equality as a high priority of its development cooperation policy (Council of the European Union 2005; DG Development 2006). According to the Commission, by mainstreaming gender equality in development policy, the EU would be able to a) "promote equality worldwide", b) reduce poverty, since women are particularly affected by poverty, and c) help to accomplish the United Nations Millennium Development Goals[33].

Within this area, the EC policy is defined by the Platform for Action of the Fourth World Conference on Women in Beijing (1995) and also by different EC policy documents such as the Council Resolution on Integrating Gender Issues in Development Cooperation (12874/95), the EC Regulation 2836/98, and the Regulation (806/2004) on 'Promoting gender equality in development cooperation' implemented during 2004-2006 (DG Development 2006: 1).

In practice, the strategy of mainstreaming has included training on gender issues, use of gender disaggregated data, gender analysis in policies and programmes, and circulation of best practices relating to gender issues[34].

According to Ole Elgström (2000), the first Communication from the Commission dealing with gender issues in the area of development cooperation launched in 1995 (European Commission 1995) was the result of norm negotiations within an advocacy network providing input to the EU gender officials who were to produce the communication (463-466).

At the beginnings of the 1990s, gender issues had already been introduced into aid policies of some northern Member States – as well as future members such as Sweden (Elgström 2000: 463). Within the Development Assistance Committee (DAC) of the Organisation for Economic Co-operation and Development (OECD) existed an "advocacy network", a network of gender experts from different Member States that promoted women's issues within the field of foreign assistance and aid, exchanging information and expertise (ibid).

---

[32] Available at http://ec.europa.eu/employment_social/gender_equality/gender_mainstreaming/devel/development_cooperation_en.html, Acceded on March 2007.

[33] Available at http://ec.europa.eu/employment_social/gender_equality/gender_mainstreaming-/devel/development_cooperation_en.html, Acceded on March 2007.

[34] Available at http://ec.europa.eu/employment_social/gender_equality/gender_mainstreaming-/devel/development_cooperation_en.html, Acceded on March 2007.

At EU level, the proposal to produce a "gender resolution" in relation to EU development cooperation policies was partly due to pressures from NGOs and some Member States such as Denmark (Elgström 2000: 463). However, Elgström suggests that "even more important probably was the emerging perception among high-level DG officials that the Union had to have a gender policy to present at the forthcoming (1995) Women's Conference in Beijing" (ibid). The author argues that "all relevant decision-makers agreed that the formulation of some kind of women-oriented document was necessary to provide the EU with a platform for the conference" (ibid). In May 1993, the Council officially resolve to produce a gender policy document (ibid: 464). The decision coincided with the renaming of the small gender desk of the DG Development: "women in development" (WID) was renamed "gender and development" (GAD). According to Elgström, this organisational change indicated "an ideological shift from 'women projects' to a broader emphasis on the roles of women and men in development (the GAD approach)" (ibid: 464; see also Poulsen 2006).

In October 1994, the gender expert group first met to work towards the formulation of the EU gender policy document (Elgström 2000: 464). Different possible formulations of a Council Communication were discussed and "three conceptual pillars" were proposed: equity, empowerment and efficiency (ibid: 464-465). Finally, in September 1995 with the advice of the expert group, the EU gender officials presented the Commission Communication on Integrating Gender Issues in Development Cooperation (ibid: 466). Also in September 1995, the Conference on Women in Beijing with its emphasis on gender mainstreaming provided further support and inspiration for women advocates and gender experts within the EU (ibid: 464).

While the Beijing Conference on Women in 1995 offered new opportunities for mainstreaming gender equality within the EU development policy area, there are still several obstacles to the success of mainstreaming in this area (Pollack and Hafter-Burton 2000: 446). Nevertheless, development cooperation is an area where mainstreaming has been pioneered and has had substantial impact (Mazey 2002: 236).

In sum, the mainstreaming strategy appears to have been easier to introduce into the policy area development cooperation because of the favourable conditions given by prior experience in gender issues, institutional arrangements and policy instruments, as well as the availability of gender expertise and "change agents" pushing the new conceptions of gender and gender equality (Mazey 2002).

4.2 Reconciliation between Work and Private Life

Within the policy area reconciliation between work and private life, the main goal has been to increase women's participation in the labour market by addressing the home and family responsibilities of women and men. In practice, the strategy has been reduced to recommendations that Member States should secure the provision of childcare services, care for dependents other than children, parental leave, and the promotion of flexible working patterns[35]. Even though the EU has also advised Member States to initiate awareness raising activities in order to encourage men to share responsibilities for care of children[36], the actions taken have remained by far in the realm of the workplace. And women are still the main carers of children and other dependants (European Commission 2006a).

Hantrais points out that the 1990s directives did not imply a break point with the employment-basis of equality policy. Despite the directives' apparent shifted focus towards non-labour market factors such as the reconciliation of employment with family life, equality policy remained based on employment as the central element (2000b: 121).

The Commission proposal for a Council Directive on parental leave and leave for family reasons issued in 1983 and amended in 1984[37] was not adopted for more than ten years (Hantrais 2000b: 119). However, in 1992 the Council recommendation 'on child care' was adopted, though it was less binding, stipulating special leave for parents taking care of their own children, together with measures to promote shared responsibility on childcare and education within the family (Hantrais 2000b: 119-220). The Council Directive of 1996 made provision for parental leave of a minimum of three months to be used up to the time when the child is eight years old. Payment under the leave period was not defined as mandatory, and the leave was granted to both parents and could not be transferred from one to the other. Member States were free to regulate the conditions in which the directive should be implemented. The directive was only binding concerning the results to be achieved (Hantrais 2000b: 121).

---

[35] "The Directive 92/85/EEC deals with the protection of health and safety of pregnant workers and workers who have recently given birth or are breastfeeding. It also addresses maternity leave and discrimination in the work place. Discrimination on grounds of pregnancy is also covered by the legislation on equal treatment in employment and occupation. Directive 96/34 sets out minimum requirements on parental leave for male and female workers, and related employment protection." (Available at http://ec.europa.eu/employment_social/gender_equality/legislation/-pregnant_en.html, Acceded on March 2007). In 2002, during the European Council in Barcelona, EU leaders set specific targets for "the provision of childcare facilities under the broader agenda for economic growth and jobs – with the aim of raising employment rates for women and men. Member States should provide childcare facilities for 90% of children between three years old and mandatory school age, and for 33% of children under three years old, by 2010. Childcare facilities must be affordable, accessible and of a good quality, in order to allow everyone, and in particular women to enter and remain on the labour market." (Available at http://ec.europa.eu/employment_social/gender_equality/gender_mainstreaming/familylife/family_life_reconciliation_en.html, Acceded on March 2007).

[36] Available at http://ec.europa.eu/employment_social/gender_equality/gender_mainstreaming-/familylife/family_life_reconciliation_en.html, Acceded on March 2007.

[37] It refers to the Commission proposal for a Council Directive on parental leave and leave for family reasons (COM(83) 686 final, 22 November 1983). Amended proposal (COM(84) 631 final, 9 November 1984).

What is more, most of the reconciliation policies such as parental leave and part-time work arrangements are much more used by women than men and therefore a gender imbalance is produced which negatively influences women's job careers, pension level and their economic independence (European Commission 2006a: 5). Thus, despite several resolutions, recommendations, directives, reports, and studies produced, the concept of mainstreaming seems to be somehow lost within this policy area, as the focus is very much on facilitating women's incorporation into the labour market – without taking into consideration the gender impact that the very reconciliation policies may have, rather than challenging the 'gender contract' and the reproduction of gender stereotypes[38].

In fact, when it comes to reconciliation between work and private life in general, Lewis suggests that the logic behind the policy trajectory in this area is limited to enhance the participation of women in the labour market. The author points out that "work/family reconciliation policies moved away from their clear association with equal opportunities policies in the early and mid-1990s, to a much more unequivocal, instrumental link to employment policies" with a more exclusive focus on securing the provision of childcare services in order to enable higher rates of female labour participation (2006: 432-433).

In a similar vein, Stratigaki (2004) argues that during the 1990s, the concept of 'reconciliation of working and family life', which had been introduced to encourage gender equality in the labour market, shifted from an emphasis in its feminist meaning, i.e. 'sharing family responsibilities between women and men', to a meaning defined by a market-oriented logic, that is 'encouraging flexible forms of employment'.

Overall, this area shows a trajectory of difficult introduction of the mainstreaming principle. Even if there are gender knowledge and policy instruments, the dominant policy logic and policy goals are too much tied to the economic sphere and the labour market rationale (Lewis 2006, Stratigaki 2004), which has more to do with the equal treatment and positive action paradigms than with any definition of gender inequality in terms of structural inequality. However, notwithstanding the actual shortcomings, reconciliation between work and private life is a policy area that potentially challenges the public-private divide and the reproduction of gender stereotypes.

4.3 Women in Science

As in the case of women in societal decision-making (see below), women are considerably underrepresented in academic environments, and are subject to vertical and horizontal segregation. This is indicated by women being less paid, receiving fewer research grants, being more excluded from power networks, i.e. generally absent from higher academic positions than their male counterparts. Also female researchers who want career advancement often have significant childcare and/or domestic

[38] Even though the Commission recognises this flaw (see e.g. European Commission 2008).

responsibilities to bear while faced with expectations and engagement in work according to the "male model" (ETAN Report, 2000).[39] Some of the conclusions of the ETAN report are clear in this regard (see also Rees, 2001):

- The higher the position in the scientific hierarchy, the lower the percentage of women;
- Women now constitute about 50% of first degree students in many countries while the percentage of full women professors is very low, circa 12% compare with male professors circa 88%;
- Men are appointed to academic posts in numbers disproportionate to those in the recruitment pool at each grade.

The European Commission took a number of initiatives to address issues of women in science, in particular the launching of an action plan for women in science that led to the establishment of the Helsinki Group beginning in 1999 and still continuing with representatives of all member states and a mandate to promote women in science (Dewandre, 2002). The ETAN study (2000) analyzed some of the causes of the large under-representation of women in scientific research, as well as a series of gender impact studies and conferences on research and gender. Another institutional initiative, "The Gender Watch System", monitors policy developments and tries to ensure that gender dimensions are systematically taken into account.

In October 2006, the European Commission established an expert group of independent experts, known as Women in Research Decision-Making (WIRDEM).

The task of WIRDEM (DG Research, 2008) has been:

- to review procedures for evaluating and promoting research personnel and to identify examples of good practice at institutional and national levels.
- to identify and review positive actions and gender equality measures in place to promote women into senior positions in public research at institutional (including universities, research institutions and research councils) as well as national levels.
- to identify which measures have proven successful and which are not, and the reasons for this, and to determine whether transparent and fair evaluation and promotion procedures alone are sufficient to improve gender balance in research – decision-making positions.
- to produce a report of in-depth best practice examples (case studies), including recommendations to facilitate the design of a framework for better targeted actions at European level.

Using the 7th Framework Programme of Research and Technological Development (FP7), DG Research established the European Platform of Women Scientists (EPWS). The objectives of this network have been:

[39] Note: "Often demands for total dedication to work are not really necessary for the proper functioning of scientific institutions and the positive outcome of research but has more of a symbolic value" (ETAN:2000:77).

- to build a structural link between female scientists and research policy makers;
- to establish itself as a key actor into the research policy debate
- to empower women scientists helping them to participate in the policy debate and to enhance their professional and career advancement.

Finally, the European Commission set up an expert advisory group with the purpose of "giving recommendations to the European Commission itself, adapted to different national realities, on the improvement of transparency and accountability of procedures used in selection committees for grants and fellowship awards, and access to research funding in general". The expert group has produced a report "The gender challenge in research funding – Assessing the European national scenes" (2009) finding clear differences among EU member states in application procedures and results.

These initiatives have raises consciousness about the "glass roof" of science and have provided a platform for women NGOs and networks to pressure the policy-makers. Indeed, since 1999, the Commission has tried to systematically increase women's role in research and research institutions. At the start of FP5 (1998-2002), a *40% target* was set for Marie Curie scholarships, advisory groups, assessment panels and monitoring panels as well as programme committees.[40]

There has been a steady increase in women's roles in the EU science institutional arrangements since the 1990s. The percentage of women on monitoring panels – whose function is to focus and comment on the progress achieved in implementing the programme's thematic priorities – rose from 4% in FP4 to 35% in FP5 and to 50% in FP6. There was 34% women representation on evaluation committees in 2006 – highest on the panel for "Science and Society" (51%), lowest for the panel on Euroatom (9%).

Since 1999, the rate of approval for research applications headed by women is more or less on a par with the levels for men. That is, the "success rates" have been similar for FP6 (2002-2006) and FP7 (2006-2013). However, men come in with 4-5 times as many proposals as do women. And men are much more likely to be a scientific coordinator for a proposal and or a scientist in charge (of partner participatory teams).[41]

---

[40] In 7th Framework Programme's Ethics Reviews and the reviewers, it is stated that the ethics review is intended, among other things, to promote gender balance in the review process. The explicit aim is to prevent EU funding being used "for research activities" that could contravene fundamental rights.

[41] The relatively newly established European Research Council (ERC) has had two programmes, the programme for younger researchers (3-8 years after the Ph.D.) StG and the AdG programme for advanced researchers with "demonstrated excellence" over the previous 10 years. There were more than 9000 applications for the younger researcher grants with an acceptance rate of about 3% (this overview comes from Antonoyiannakis et al (2009:809). For the advanced grants there were more than 2000 applications with an acceptance rate of about 3%. For the younger grants in 2007, women researchers share of submissions and awards was 30% and 26.7%, respectively.

In general, women in science has been a highly visible and relatively rapid developing sector for mainstreaming. Women are being rapidly integrated into the EU research institutions as well as research funding developments.

4.4 Women in Societal Decision-making

Gender equality is a basic value of the EU, a fundamental right. Equal participation of women and men in decision-making is viewed as symbolizing the level of political advancement of societies. As in the case of "women in science," monitoring and reporting is one of the major EU devices, to influence public opinion and pressures for policy. For instance, the report, *Women and Men in Decision-making 2007 – Analysis of the Situation and Trends* and related data bases are intended to help promote equal participation of women and men in decision-making by raising awareness and stimulating initiatives by government and non-government bodies as well as the business sector to address gender gaps and inequities. In general, the report shows that, although progress is being made, women are still under-represented in all spheres of power in most Member States and in the EU Institutions. The Commission supports EU as well as Member State action in mainstreaming through collecting, analyzing and disseminating comparable data on the persistent gender gaps.

The report shows (Commission, 2008:52-53):

In the area of politics, the proportion of women members of parliament has risen from 16% in 1997 to 24% in 2007, but ranges from 9% in Hungary to 48% in Sweden. Eight of the 20 countries that have achieved the level of 30% are within the EU – Sweden, Finland, the Netherlands, Denmark, Spain, Belgium, Germany, and Austria.[42] The European Parliament has 31% women. On the other hand seven EU countries have levels under 15% – the Czech Republic, Cyprus, Ireland, Slovenia, Hungary, Romania, and Malta.

In national governments, men outnumber women in the cabinets of EU governments by about three to one – since Beijing, EU-15 has risen from 16% to 27%. The report points out that although a commitment to balanced representation is evident in some countries – Spain (41% women), Sweden (46%), Finland (60%) –

There was more or less equal success for men and women in the physical sciences and engineering, a higher rate for men in the biological sciences and higher rates for women in the social sciences and humanities. For the advanced grants, women were responsible for 14.1% of the applications and 11.6% of the awards. These levels for women correspond, according to the authors, to the demographics of professorships in European universities where women make up about 30% of assistant and associate professorships and 15% of full (Grade A) professors. Also as Antonoviannakis et al (2009:809) point out that there are some indications of a degree of bias. But a key factor, as suggested in the text, is women's lower rates of project submission.

[42] The report singles out Belgium as a country which achieved the greatest improvement in gender balance over the 10 year period (from 12% to 35%). This result was accomplished through legislation enforcing parity among candidates and equal visibility on ballot papers.

the cabinets of Slovakia, Greece and Turkey include just one woman each and that of Romania has no women members at all.[43]

In the area of economy: No central bank head in the 27 EU Member States is a woman. Only 1 in 6 women are part of the highest decision-making bodies. In the EU institutions, the pattern is similar: the three financial institutions (European Central Bank, European Investment Bank, and the European Investment Fund) are led by men, and there is an average of just below 16% women in positions of influence.

Although women account for 44% of all workers, they comprise only 32% of those considered as heads of businesses (chief executives, directors, and managers of small businesses). They are particularly unrepresented (10% only) on the boards of leading companies.

In the area of Public administration: Among the EU member states women currently fill nearly 33% of the top two levels of administration. Within EU institutions there has been some improvement in the top two levels of administration – from 14% to just under 20% in the period 1999 to 2007. The Commission itself has a ratio of 37% women, but only 19% in the Committee for the Regions and 23% in the European Economic and Social Committee.

In general, these figures indicate improvements in relation to data from previous years.[44]

Given these gaps and persistent shortcomings in gender equality, the Commission has vigorously promoted networking and the exchange of experiences and good practices at the European level. The European Community Network of Women in Decision-making" in politics and the economy, was launched in June 2008. Its aim has been to promote women in decision-making positions in politics and the economy in Europe, exchanging and disseminating information about good practices and successful strategies.[45] The Commission also established the European Institute for Gender Equality in 2007 in Vilnius, Lithuania to work for the promotion of gender equality, gender mainstreaming in all Community and resulting national policies and against discrimination based on sex.[46] Another important initiative was PROGRESS, the EU's employment and social solidarity programme. PROGRESS was launched also in 2007 and will run until 2013. It gives financial support to actions against discrimination and social exclusion, and acting to create equal opportunities for men and women with respect to employment and social integration.[47]

---

[43] See European commission: employment, Social Affairs and Equal Opportunities database http://ec.europa.eu/employment_social/women_men_stats/measures_in4_en.htm.

[44] See http://ec.europa.eu/employment_social/women_men_stats/index_en.htm.

[45] See http://ec.europa.eu/social/main.jsp?langId=en&catId=418&newsId=133&furtherNews=yes.

[46] See http://ec.europa.eu/social/main.jsp?catId=732&langId=en.

[47] See http://ec.europa.eu/social/main.jsp?catId=327&langId=en.

4.5 Structural Funds

Structural funds are major EU instrument for supporting poorer regions within the community and in financing the integration of European infrastructure. Member-states such as Greece, Ireland, Portugal, and Spain and now the new member-states from Eastern Europe have gained considerable support through such funds. Even richer countries such as Germany and Sweden have regions which received EU structural support.

Already in 1996, the Council adopted a resolution on mainstreaming equal opportunities for men and women into the European Structural Funds (Council, 1996). Measures taken illustrate some of the ways in which the EU uses diverse conventional and unconventional means to realize policy goals, in this case gender equality.

- Selection criteria for Structural Fund project were to include *additional points* to projects which contribute to gender equality, that is balanced participation
- Member state applicants (especially those states known to emphasize mainstreaming should identify clearly, on the one hand, general funding allocated to specific gender equality actions and, on the other hand, programmes and projects contributing to equality in the member-state. These contextual efforts would be viewed positively in consideration of applications from the member-state.
- For assessing the impact of gender equality, one should establish clear qualitative and quantitative indicators and gender-disaggregated statistics for monitoring and evaluating results.
- One makes use of gender equality expertise in the managing authorities for structural funds in member-states, monitoring committees, local programme and project management; and to ensure the presence of representatives of equality bodies and relevant research institutes within Structural Fund Monitoring Committees.
- One tries to spread information about best practices and effective strategies (institutionalization of mimicking mechanisms) in structural fund financing.

4.6 Mainstreaming Practice: Migrant Women

With the Treaty of Amsterdam, the EU gained competence in the field of immigration (Hantrais 2000b:208-209). Immigration became an area of concern for the Council of Ministers. The Treaty of Amsterdam stated that the EU must be an area of "freedom, security and justice", where the free movement of persons should be assured together with proper measures with regard to external border controls, asylum, immigration, and the prevention and combating of crime[48]. Needless to say, freedom of movement does not apply to non-European nationals (Hantrais 2000b:207). The necessity of a Community policy on immigration has been on the

[48] The DG that currently deals with matters of immigration is the DG for Justice, Freedom and Security.

agenda since the mid-1980s (ibid: 207). In July 1985 a Council Resolution on guidelines for a Community policy on migration was issued, identifying immigration and associated issues as problems to be addressed by the Community (ibid: 207). Also in 1985 the Schengen Agreement on asylum and visas was signed. By 1994 it had been ratified by all Member States except for Denmark, Ireland and the United Kingdom. According to Hantrais, "the intention of the signatories was to harmonise frontier controls and procedures over asylum-seekers, and abolish internal borders controls" (ibid: 208).

In October 1999, heads of EU Member States set up the basis for a common EU immigration policy. In November 2004, the Hague Programme determined the objectives to be implemented "with a view to establishing a common immigration and asylum policy for the period 2005-2010". In May 2005, the Commission presented an action plan to implement the programme approved in The Hague (European Women's Lobby 2006:6)[49].

When immigration policy is discussed, the emphasis is placed on the 'economic' migrants (see European Commission 2005a). And the 'women variable' is taking into account almost exclusively when related to employment performance (see European Commission 2004). This emphasis on the economic dimension of migration depicts a particular context for the introduction of mainstreaming into this policy area. Even if the 'efficiency rhetoric' is used across all issue areas to give reasons for the introduction of mainstreaming, within this area this rhetoric with statements about the necessity of utilising women's skills to achieve economic growth is even more openly presented and, eventually, may limit the scope of the mainstreaming strategy.

Hence, when it comes to the promotion of gender equality and mainstreaming, the DG-ESAEO emphasise that migrant women are worse off than their male counterparts, lagging behind in labour market integration. The DG stresses that even though migrant women and men have similar unemployment rates, there is a striking exception for the high skilled labour force segment where women tend to be unemployed more than men. Migrant women are concentrated in low paid industries and occupations[50].

The DG-ESAEO also recognises that a gender perspective is to a large extent lacking in integration policies. From the DG's perspective, this gap impedes the full utilisation the potentialities of migrant women in the labour market. And the effective integration of immigrants in the labour market as well as in society is one of

---

[49] See also http://ec.europa.eu/justice_home/fsj/immigration/fsj_immigration_intro_en.htm#part_1 and http://ec.europa.eu/justice_home/fsj/intro/fsj_intro_en.htm, Acceded on March 2007.

[50] Available at http://ec.europa.eu/employment_social/gender_equality/gender_mainstreaming/migrant/migrant_en.html, Acceded on March 2007. See also European Commission (2005b: 5).

the key factors for success in reaching the Lisbon targets[51]. Thus, the DG argues, the EU must incorporate a gender perspective in immigration and integration policies[52]. However, until now concrete measures have been not taken[53].

In its 2004 "First Annual Report on Migration and Integration", the Commission acknowledged that "[a] systematic mainstreaming of *gender considerations* seems to be lacking in most Member States when dealing with immigration, both in terms of policy and data" (European Commission 2004: 6, bold in the original). Since then, not much progress has been done and women continue being invisible in immigration policies.

According to the EWL, one of the reasons for the "invisibility" of migrant women in the European framework on immigration and integration is "the *absence of a policy at European level covering gender and ethnic background*, as issues related to gender and to ethnic minorities tend to be covered by separate and compartmentalised policies rather than an integrated approach" (European Women's Lobby 2006: 10, bold in the original).

In the "Roadmap for equality for women and men 2006-2010" of March 2006, the Commission tackled the issue of 'multiple discrimination' that immigrant and ethnic minorities suffer and committed itself to promoting "gender equality in migration and integration policies in order to ensure women's rights and civic participation, to fully use their employment potential and to improve their access to education and lifelong learning" (European Commission 2006a:4).

Despite the commitments and acknowledges, mainstreaming gender equality in the policy area migrant women has not showed much progress so far. Kofman and Sales suggest that EU policy towards migrant women in general has been traditionally "gender blind", albeit its effects are gendered because they generally suppose the women's dependence on a male (2000: 195, 203). This blindness constitutes an important obstacle to the introduction of the gender mainstreaming mandate.

All in all, the policy area migrant women seems to have the poorer performance when it comes to mainstreaming gender equality. The lack of favourable conditions for the advance of gender mainstreaming in this area could be related to both, on the one hand, a lack of institutional arrangements, policy instruments, gender expertise, and the absence of "change agents" able to introduce and concretise the mainstreaming paradigm and, on the other hand, the predominance of the economic dimension of migration within the general discussion about EU immigration

[51] It refers to the targets determined for the Lisbon Strategy. The strategy was agreed at the EU Lisbon Summit of March 2000 and it aims at making the EU economy the most competitive and dynamic knowledge-based economy in the world by 2010.

[52] Available at http://ec.europa.eu/employment_social/gender_equality/gender_mainstreaming-/migrant/migrant_en.html, Acceded on March 2007. See also European Commission (2005b: 5).

[53] It seems ironic that there is a stress on "developing countries" (and especially women) at the same time that immigrant women and their particular problems are largely ignored.

policy which favours a definition of the problem of gender inequality in terms of, and limited to the question of, labour market participation.

Summing up:

The mainstreaming paradigm developed the argument that gender equality is a fundamental right within the European Union and, as such, it must be integrated in all relevant policy and legislative processes. In areas where the EU lacks legal authority (or competence), it has developed a number of special policy strategies, illustrated in the selection of mainstreaming initiatives pointed out above:

(1) drive policy relevant research, revealing patterns of gender exclusion and discrimination
(2) promote knowledge of "best practices" for gender advancement on the EU and member-state levels.
(3) use EU funds to leverage promotion of gender equality, for instance, through structural and research funds.
(4) support networking and the formation of NGOs concerning with gender issues.

5. Discussion

5.1 The EU's Different Approaches to Gender Equality

Within the European Union, we have found three phases of gender policy, each phase entailing a somewhat different approach to equality (see Table 13.1): equal treatment (1957-1980),[54] positive action (1981-1990) and mainstreaming (1991-present)[55] (Rees 1998, 2000, 2002). There is a developmental logic that links these three approaches with each successive logic emerging on the foundation (and shortcomings) of its predecessor. It would be extremely unlikely for them to have unfolded in an alternate order. Nevertheless, as discussed later, the three approaches should be understood as complementary rather than competing (see Daly 2005:438; Squires 2005:370; Walby 2005:329; Council of Europe 1998). Also, there is overlap in the phases.

---

[54] However, it was not until the 70s that the Article 119 of the Treaty of Rome was followed up by a series of Directives (Rees 1998:52).

[55] As said, the 1996 Communication from the Commission (COM(96) 67 final) constituted a turning point in the dominant gender approach at EU level. However, the process of introduction of mainstreaming started some years before with the 1990 Third Community Action Programme on Equal Opportunities for Women and Men and, also, with the preparation for Beijing where the EU delegation had a leading role in pushing the mainstreaming principle into the Platform. And then, Beijing gave a new impulse to the introduction of mainstreaming at EU level, so when back from Beijing it was just a question of writing the Communication. The 1996 Communication was written basically at DG-ESAEO, some drafts circulated before Beijing from this DG to other services (interview with a Commission functionary who participated in the process, May 2008).

As we have seen, *equal treatment* is based on the idea that women and men should be treated the same (Rees 2002). *Positive action* aims to secure *equality of outcome* by equalising the starting positions, instead of focusing on securing the equality of access (Rees 1998:34). *Mainstreaming* is the systematic integration of gender equality into all systems and structures, policies, programmes, processes and projects (Rees 2002:2; also 1998:40-42, 188-200).

In the 1970's, gender equality policies implemented by EU countries were mainly oriented to equal treatment. In the decade that followed, the focus shifted to *positive action*. It was in the 1990s when the *mainstreaming approach* gained importance (Rees 2002: 2-3).

The origin of the equal treatment approach can be traced back to the Article 119 of the Treaty of Rome on equal pay for men and women (Treaty of Rome 1957; Carson 2004:103; Hantrais 2000b:115; Hoskyns 2000:2; Lewis 2006:420; Stratigaki 2005:169-170). The introduction of this article became the foundation for one of the European community's main commitments to social policy in general (Lewis 2006:420).

Even if equal treatment is based on the idea that women and men should be treated the same, it often implied that men's conditions were taken as the norm (Rees 2002:2). Treating women and men the same does not necessarily mean treating them equally (Rees 2002: 2). Moreover, by focusing on equal treatment of men and women as workers, the European law on equal opportunities has not dealt with the causes of inequality that lie – more broadly – in the "gender contract"[56] (Rees 1998:32).

As Rees (1998) explains, equal treatment legislation does not cope with the causes of inequality but just attempts to moderate its symptoms. Since it does not analyse the causes of inequality, equal treatment fails to produce equal outcomes. It does not problematise, for instance, the implications of social hierarchies. This gap in the analysis limits equal treatment actual achievements. Equal treatment proposes that all individuals should be equally treated as such. It does not acknowledge that individuals are part of particular groups and hold positions in bigger structures and the significance of this in cultural reproduction (Rees, 1998). Positive action and positive discrimination measures have in many occasions been introduced to balance the shortcomings of equal treatment (Rees, 1998:32, 34).

Given women's unequal position in society, positive action measures intend to create conditions to overcome the resulting disadvantaged starting point. The positive action approach recognises that men and women are different. It recognises 'sameness' and 'difference'. That is, it is rooted in the idea that even if there are similarities between women and men, there are also significant differences. Positive

[56] The concept of gender contract refers to a social contract that specifies what women and men should do and think. It informs "expectation about the domestic division of labour and power relation which, in turn, shape systems and structures than reinforce those expectations" (Rees 1998: 32, see also 194-199).

action, then, attempts to reduce the gap for these differences which are interpreted as a deficit in women (Rees 2002:2). However, "positive action measures do not challenge the culture and practice of the mainstream: they simply assist women to fit in. This is where gender mainstreaming comes in" (Rees 2000:3).

Mainstreaming, unlike equal treatment and its focus on individuals' rights to equality and unlike positive action and its focus on group disadvantage, looks into the institutions and structures that constitute the root of individual and group disadvantage (Rees 2000:4). Mainstreaming aims at transforming the gender hierarchy by identifying the hidden and unrecognised ways in which all systems and structures are "male-centred", i.e. biased in favour of men, and seeks to redress the balance (Rees 1998:189; 2002:2; Lewis 2006:426). As such, mainstreaming also represents an effort to expand the application of gender equality principles beyond the sphere of work and economy. Hence, there should be both a) the opportunity for transformation – addressing root causes rather than symptoms, and b) extension beyond the economic sphere. Yet, as Mazey points out, gender mainstreaming is not intended to replace positive action measures and equal treatment legislation, but rather to complement them (2002:231). The three approaches to gender equality in fact coexist in the EU's programmes (Walby 2005:329; see also Daly 2005: 437-439).

Rees suggests that although mainstreaming has long-term goals and relies on the law and positive action concrete measures, it is probably the only strategy with the capability to produce real transformations on gender equality issues (Rees 2000:4). As an approach that seeks to transform institutions, the adoption of gender mainstreaming represents a breakthrough in the ways of thinking about and dealing with gender equality issues within the EU (Rees 1998, 2000, 2002)[57].

From equal treatment to positive action to mainstreaming, problem definitions, proposed solutions, and the attributions of responsibilities have changed substantially. The major breakthrough thus lies in the change in conception of what gender inequality means, what should be done about it, and who is supposed to do it.

The conception of gender inequality lies neither in the fact that the law is different for men and women to the detriment of the later nor in the fact of group disadvantage, but rather it lies in inherent structural and systemic inequality. What should be done?[58] For gender inequality to be tackled, those male-centred structures and systems have to be transformed. It is not a question of changing one or more laws or of implementing specific positive discrimination measures (although these are important) but of transforming structures by reorganising policy processes and systems. Who is to do it? The authorities for addressing the problem are

[57] Several scholars have noted that there are considerable risks in this shift to mainstreaming. See the discussion about risks and shortcomings of mainstreaming below.

[58] This question is inspired by Carol Lee Bacchi's approach called "What's the Problem represented to be?" (1999).

not just legislators or gender experts but "all actors routinely involved in policy-making" (Verloo 2004: 8), that is, a wide range of stakeholders.

5.2 Gender Mainstreaming under Debate

Mainstreaming reflects the kind of ambition that we have seen driving other policy transformations in the EU, for instance, chemicals or energy. There is a developmental logic in the culmination of gender policy in the mainstreaming approach, in its comprehensiveness and efforts to overcome the shortcomings of its predecessors.

Nonetheless, the assessments of mainstreaming among scholars can be characterised as ambivalent and sometimes conflicting (Bennett & Booth 2002; Daly 2005; Hantrais 2000a, 2000b; Lewis 2006; Lombardo 2005; Lombardo & Meier 2006; Mazey 2000, 2002; Pollack and Hafter-Burton 2000, 2002; Rees 1998, 2000, 2002; Shaw 2002; Squires 2005; Stratigaki 2005; Verloo 2004, 2005; Walby 2004, 2005). The reasons for the lack of consensus may have to do with the fact that while it is a "potentially radical strategy" (Mazey 2000: 342), the concrete impacts of gender mainstreaming have been highly uneven. Even the very content of mainstreaming is under dispute. However, most agree that the concept of gender mainstreaming challenges to a greater or lesser extent patriarchal structures and the "gender contract" (Rees 1998; Stratigaki 2005, among others) even though gender mainstreaming as a strategy is weakly institutionalised and much about it remains uncertain and unpredictable (Pollack and Hafter-Burton 2000; Mazey 2002).

The expansion of EU gender equality policy that mainstreaming entails moving equality between women and men beyond the workplace to become a EU core goal is considered by some commentators as a loss of specificity with regards to what exactly gender equality means. As Mazey mentions, one of the risks that the adoption of mainstreaming strategy entails is that "gender equality becomes everybody's – and nobody's – responsibility" (2002: 228). Hoskyns suggests that contrary to the single focus on labour market legislations that characterised the early days of gender equality policy, the current increased scope of gender policy, which has reached areas such as trafficking in women and violence against women, has a much lower level of legal enforcement (2002: 1). The author says that "the EU has gone from a 'narrow but deep' policy on women's rights to one which at first glance at least appears 'broad but shallow'" (ibid). Moreover, even if in principle mainstreaming represents an effort to expand the application of gender equality principles beyond the sphere of work and economy, Bennett and Booth suggest that the policy development of mainstreaming has been limited by the all-too-narrow economic focus of the EC (2002: 443).

According to Rees, gender mainstreaming represents a "paradigm shift in thinking about gender equality", though "misappropriated and misunderstood" (2002: 11). Lombardo and Meier regard gender mainstreaming definition as an "open signifier that can be filled with both feminist and non-feminist meanings" (2006: 161).

Stratigaki argues that mainstreaming has become an "abstract 'principle'" and "empty rhetoric" (2005: 174-175). More generally, the author points out: "EU policy discourse may evolve rhetoric devoid of substance" (Stratigaki 2005: 180)[59]. This concern about the content of mainstreaming is shared also by Bennett and Booth (2002: 433) who suggest that since mainstreaming "remains a 'fuzzy' concept", the practice of mainstreaming is still chaotic and that "mainstreaming gender equality has been interpreted as merely a new set of methods" (Bennett and Booth, 2002: 442). Similarly, Rees (1998: 191-194) refers to the dangers of paying too much attention to the technical aspects of mainstreaming instead of its content. Pollack and Hafner-Burton (2000: 434) stress that, while gender mainstreaming is a "potentially revolutionary concept" that aims at including a gender dimension in all EU policies, it demands that all central actors in the policy process adopt a gender perspective; certainly one of the main problems in this regard is that some of these actors have little experience, knowledge or interest in gender issues. Stratigaki (2005: 169) points out that, in principle, gender mainstreaming questions the whole policy cycle by considering the gender perspective in all phases, unlike positive action which only considers the policy delivery phase. However, in practice, policy measures and strategies are still produced within gender hierarchies, and the result in many cases is still the reproduction of inequalities. Therefore, for gender mainstreaming to be effective, both gender specific policies, legislations and strategies against accumulated inequalities are required.

The gender mainstreaming strategy appears to have been inspired by both economic concerns and social justice goals (Hantrais 2000b: 124; Pollack and Hafter-Burton 2000; Rees 1998, 2000, 2002). Most scholars argue that what dominates gender equality policy is an efficiency rhetoric where statements about the necessity of using women's skills – or not wasting the human capital women have to offer – to achieve economic growth abound (Pollack and Hafter-Burton 2000; Lewis 2006; Lombardo & Meier 2006). Lewis points out that, historically, gender equality has appeared pursuing both market-making and social justice objectives (2006: 421). Even after the transformations and important shifts in the 1990s, gender equality still is an instrument of a wider agenda on employment and economic growth within the EU (Lewis 2006: 432-433). Stratigaki (2005: 180) argues that it has been more feasible to include equality priorities in the agenda when they were in line with broader economic goals. In this process, gender equality has been coopted by economic priorities and its meaning and purpose adapted accordingly.

In fact, the DGs' different attitudes towards the Commission's gender mainstreaming approach can be explained by the fact that the DGs are differently positioned, on the one hand, with respect to a "neo-liberal" frame that insist on the importance of the building of free markets and, on the other hand, with respect to

[59] The author's argument goes even further concluding that gender mainstreaming implementation "was manipulated so that it served to counteract the emerging demand of women for binding positive action measures in decision-making bodies" (2005: 181).

an "interventionist" frame with a stronger emphasis on social concerns (Pollack and Hafter-Burton 2000: 435). Accordingly, the DGs of the EC differ considerably when it comes to political opportunities they can offer to women's advocates and the dominant policy frames that define their purpose and objectives (Pollack and Hafter-Burton 2000: 439)[60]. Pollack and Hafter-Burton examine why and how the EU adopted a policy of gender mainstreaming in the first place, and how it has been implemented in practice. Drawing on concepts of social movement theory such as political opportunities, mobilising structures, and strategic framing, they suggest that when it comes to political opportunities, the EU's institutions provide a variety of "access points" for women's advocates and élite allies within the policy process. Moreover, the authors (2000: 434) argue that with the adoption of the Maastricht Treaty in 1993 and *the incorporation in 1995 of three new Member States with a well established commitment to gender equality (Austria, Finland and Sweden), the political opportunity structure of the EU turned out to be systematically more favourable to gender issues.* Regarding mobilising structures, there are specific supranational actors at the EU level, especially the Equal Opportunities Unit of the Commission and the Women's Rights Committee of the European Parliament, that constitute the core of a transnational network of experts and activists in the field of equal opportunities, and they have been successful in "placing on the agenda a wide range of issues previously beyond the scope of EU policy-making" (Pollack and Hafter-Burton, 2000: 434-435). And when it comes to the role of framing processes, they argue that the acceptance and implementation of gender mainstreaming "depends on the resonance between the proposed policy frame and the dominant frame(s) of the EU institutions" (Pollack and Hafter-Burton, 2000: 435).

Pollack and Hafter-Burton (2000: 453) affirm that there is some evidence showing that a gender perspective has been gradually introduced into existing policies[61] with the likely consequence of transforming EU discourses and policy procedures and even national policies, albeit a radical change of the EU agenda from a gender perspective has hardly occurred. Mazey (2002: 228, 236, 238) also considers that while not fully institutionalised, gender mainstreaming has offered European feminists, particularly the EWL, new opportunities to engender EU policies and debates, even within policy areas that had been traditionally "gender blind". According to Pollack and Hafter-Burton (2000: 440, 450), advocates of gender mainstreaming have strategically framed the issue to "fit" the dominant frame of a given DG by underlying the "efficiency" dimension of mainstreaming, that is, how much can be achieved in terms of economic growth and competition if gender is included

[60] As different DGs work based on differing conceptual models, different Commissions have also been guided by differing priorities and overarching ideologies. The progress and/or stagnation of the gender mainstreaming strategy, therefore, can be also attributed to the particular characteristics of the different Commissions.

[61] Pollack and Hafter-Burton examine five issue areas: Development, Structural Funds, Employment and Social Affairs, Competition, and Science, Research and Development.

in the policy process; nevertheless, the advance of gender mainstreaming has been uneven within the different DGs examined by the authors.

Lombardo and Meier (2006: 158) point out that this "strategic framing" that defines the necessity of gender equality in terms of being a mean to achieve higher efficiency may eventually de-gender the issue, "since the goal is efficiency rather than gender equality" (see also Verloo 2005). In this regard, Lewis (2006: 427) argues that mainstreaming runs the risk of "being used instrumentally to serve the dominant policy frame" and of being reduced to a "tick-box"[62] within the policy-making process. In a similar vein, Shaw (2002: 221) suggests the dangers of mainstreaming because its "apparent inclusiveness" can lead either to include or to exclude radical standpoints, and again this inclusiveness can reduce mainstreaming to an additional box in a checklist without having any concrete consequence on real people's life.

Even Pollack and Hafter-Burton (2002: 351, 364) later argue that this strategic framing has watered down mainstreaming. Instead of as an overt challenge to the ends sought by EU policymakers, women's advocates have "sold" mainstreaming as a "means" to those ends. As a result, mainstreaming has become an "integrationist" rather than an "agenda-setting" approach, integrating gender issues into particular policies – without challenging the dominant policy paradigm – instead of rethinking the core purposes of the EU from a gender perspective (see also Squires 2005: 373-374)[63].

In this regard, Mieke Verloo (2005) poses the questions: "What happens in processes of strategical framing? Why would it be that integration rather than transformation is the inevitable result of strategical framing processes?" and she argues that strategical framing entails a process of establishing a connection between a feminist goal – e.g. gender equality – and some major goal of a given organisation, which should engage or is engaging in gender mainstreaming, thus gaining the commitment of this organisation to gender mainstreaming. The strategies link the two goals by "stretching" the gender equality goal, without challenging the mainstream goals of policymakers. The gender equality goal is adapted to fit the mainstream goal/s. This "dual agenda", Verloo (2005) says, is presented as if a "win-win situation" were possible. In these conceptualisations, power is "put into brackets" and gender mainstreaming is depicted as a "harmonious process". However, she argues, "if gender inequality is about power and privileges, then gender mainstreaming should be about abolishing privileges". Thus, the question is: why is a process of abolishing privileges conceptualised as harmony? And, as possible an-

---

[62] Gender mainstreaming as an item in a list of tasks that should be performed. If a mark is put in the tick-box, it shows that something has been already done. To say that mainstreaming might be reduced to a tick-box in policymaking processes is a way of saying that there is a risk that nothing more is needed but just to tick the box.

[63] Pollack and Hafter-Burton follow Jahan (1995) while identifying these two different approaches to mainstreaming.

swer, the author suggests that this conceptualisation "helps in organising acceptance of gender mainstreaming, by making it less threatening". Verloo (2005: 357-360) also suggests that radical feminist voices are excluded as a consequence of the prevention of struggle and that the conceptualisation of mainstreaming gender equality as harmony, which is meant to facilitate the process of change, is eventually counterproductive.

Several different aspects or dimensions of the problem seem to structure part of the current debate on mainstreaming so far. There is agreement that mainstreaming is a potentially transformative strategy that is however still weakly institutionalised and not fully implemented. The gap between mainstreaming rhetoric and actual outcomes seems to be still considerable. This gap between what mainstreaming promises and what it fulfils raises the question of whether mainstreaming means the incorporation of a 'gender perspective' into all policies and therefore the possibility of transforming gender biased structures or it represents just political rhetoric to avoid real structural changes. Yet more importantly, it is worth underlying that the most interesting aspect of mainstreaming is that it supposes a change in assumptions about the causes of gender inequality. As said, mainstreaming supposes a quite different definition of the problem of gender inequality, the solution to it, and the attribution of responsibility. In this sense, gender mainstreaming represents a paradigmatic shift in the way of thinking on and dealing with gender equality within the EU. Nonetheless, the question remains to what extent this process of paradigmatic shift has taken place, or put it differently, to what extent the general mainstreaming paradigm has been adapted or concretised to work into different policy areas.

5.3 Gender Mainstreaming: A Paradigm Shift

The EU approach to equal opportunities has evolved during the past three decades. It shifted from an approach focused on equal pay and equal treatment in the workplace to a progressive introduction of positive action measures, and finally to an EU commitment to mainstream gender equality in all EU policy areas (Pollack and Hafter-Burton 2000: 432). Indeed, this new agenda comprises a "dual-track approach" or "dual strategy" that combines gender mainstreaming and specific actions to promote gender equality (Mazey 2002: 234; Hantrais 2000b: 124; Pollack and Hafter-Burton 2000: 432, 450; see also Stratigaki 2005: 178; Walby 2005: 329).

Table 13.2 indicates in what sense a paradigm shift has taken place. Initially (in the first phase, 1957-1980) gender policy meant women at work. Gradually but surely during the 1980s the scope of gender policy was extended beyond the workplace into women's family conditions, rights to maternity leave, and other related developments. In the third phase (1991-present) we find a substantial shift to women in society and a focus on and a systematic attempt to deal with institutions and structures that operate in ways biased in favor of men (i.e., structural discrimination).

Table 13.2. Gender Policy Paradigm Shift

	Early Phase Equal Treatment (1957 – Treaty of Rome – 1980)	Transition Phase: Positive Discrimination/ Compensatory (1981-1990)	Mainstreaming (1991-present)
Problem Definition	Inequality in workplaces and labor market laws Women and men are not treated the same but are differently represented in and protected by law, leaving women worse off.	Unequal starting positions for women and men. Women are disadvantaged as a group, because they are women, have families and children.	Gender inequality in all areas of society that is the result of institutions and structures that operate in ways biased to individual and group disadvantage (in favor of men)
Models of the problem	Identification/specification of certain types of legal inequalities. Individual disadvantage	Identification of certain types of inequality and compensatory possibilities. Complementing workplace/labor market area with family model	Identification of structural and hidden sources of inequality. Different models in different areas
Key discourses	Inequality & equal treatment/equal opportunity	Inequality, positive discrimination, compensatory action	Structural discrimination "Patriarchal society" Transformation of gender hierarchy
Key goals in gender policy	Reduce or eliminate unequal treatment/unequal opportunity	Compensate and introduce positive discrimination	Transformation of gender hierarchy + specific gender goals in each policy sector
Methods to deal with (solution complex)	Strategies for insuring equal treatment/equal opportunity, e.g. changing laws to secure formal equal rights for women and men.	Strategies of Compensation, and positive discrimination to offset specific problems caused by disadvantageous starting positions. Extending policy coverage to women in their family roles and the relationship between work and family	See to it that gender issue is taken into account in all areas of community action; incorporate gender perspective in all systems and structures, policies, programs, processes and projects. Develop strategies to address the structural and hidden sources of gender inequality in each policy sector
Responsible Public Agents	DG ESAEO (Commission), EP, the Council, and ECJ	Expanded DG ESAEO, EP, and The Council	Expanded DG ESAEO[64] plus all actors routinely involved in policymaking at the Commission, EP, and the Council
Experts/ knowledge	Lawyers, economists and labor market sociologists	Economists, family and gender experts, sociologists and other social scientists (social work), gender equality units and agencies, NGOs	All social sciences, including criminologists, gender equality units and agencies, NGOs

[64] It could be said that DG-ESAEO has the coordination and monitoring role, and also a sort of "vigilant" role.

The key factors in the paradigm shift are (1) the much greater comprehensiveness of gender policy (there are parallels in the new chemicals policy – an ambition to cover everything). This is because the problem definition has changed. The major breakthrough lies in this change. A change in conceptions of "what gender inequality means." That is a key factor in the paradigm shift and one of the consequences of this change is the radical extension of public policy to cover all domains, to mainstream gender all policy areas. This extends the range of issues, policy contexts, and measures taken. One of the reasons this major shift seems to be so difficult to implement or actually introduce is because it demands that all actors involved in policy making see and understand the very structures where they are situated as male-centered and the consequences of this.

(2) A variety of new models of problems and new methods characterize the development. That is, there are such a number and variety of areas ranging from violence to participation in decision-making, women in science, etc that understanding the problems in any given area requires particular knowledge and models (even if in back of it all is a patriarchal structure, the mechanisms are very different in science, or in politics, or in the market). The policy measures/methods will also differ substantially, since the measures should be adjusted to the institutional conditions and mechanism(s) where they are applied.

(3) New discourses where gender equality has taken on new meanings and implications. Structural (often hidden forms of) inequality – or sources of inequality – have become more often articulated.

(4) Responsible authorities and the experts/knowledge (new epistemic communities) have also shifted. Networks of experts from the academic field have had an important role in the specification of concepts and strategies. Also, there is the aim to include the civil society through, for instance, the funding of NGOs actions and campaigns.

6. Concluding Remarks

The EU made gender equality a core goal. In doing this, the EU evolved from, on the one hand, its previous approach that limited the issue to only the labour market to, on the other hand, an extensive approach that looks into gender relations in a much broader perspective (Hoskyns 2000: 3).

Throughout the important developments during the 1990s, the emergence of a new public policy paradigm in EU policy-making became apparent. The driving forces in many policy-making areas were based on social priorities. Contrary to a common belief that EU policy was following the neo-liberal trends of deregulation, the EU imposed regulation that mainly served social purposes on market actors. Examples of such regulations are the protection of public health, preservation of the environment and gender equality.

As the studies in this book show, actual developments in social policy – in policy sectors such as food, chemicals and gender equality – go well beyond the symbolic or minor accommodations that might be deemed necessary to further market goals.

The important shifts in these policy sectors have occurred within the broader context of the contending opinions about the purpose of the EU itself, where views on the EU as a "Common Market" contrast with views on the EU as a "European Social Model" built on democratic participation and a high level of social welfare. It becomes evident as well that while this broader context has an influence on any policy sector, the achievements or failures within policy sectors – as well as market developments – also have an influence on the broader context of the tension between the two competing models.

Thus, the introduction of mainstreaming into policy areas such as health, environment and gender and the advance of gender equality as EU's core goal can be understood as part of this trend towards a more "social" Europe – as both a "window of opportunity" from which to pursue social goals and as an expression of a growing attention to and concern about social issues. But key figures in the women's movement have expressed considerable ambivalence about "mainstreaming", since on the one hand, it risked watering down the push for gender equality within the employment sphere and the implementation of specific focused actions, while at the same time it expanded the areas where gender considerations could be taken up legitimately.

The "parallel tracks" phenomenon suggests that the evolution of EU gender equality policy has been driven from "below" and "above", in particular at the European level. National and international women activists and organizations have nudged EU policy along through periods of relative inactivity or painfully slow progress punctuated by occasional surges forward – a process of fits and starts that resembles the evolution of the EU itself. At the same time, it has been facilitated by contemporaneous developments within individual member states and at the international level it has also been driven in large part by women's activism. Perhaps not surprisingly, efforts to strengthen the EU role in promoting gender equality have often been supported and facilitated by individual member states and by international organizations once they themselves have adopted new policies, and by EU institutions as they have developed the competence and capacity to promote new initiatives. These levels are linked in that the process of institutionalizing a new policy paradigm follows a similar path, although in each case it must be adapted to institution-specific norms and rules and made relevant to their broader purposes. Thus, different discourses and arguments have been emphasized in the process of anchoring domestic violence as a policy concern at the local and national, supranational (EU), and international levels (i.e., UN) as compared to women's participation in public decision-making or in science.

As the above descriptions suggest, progress in addressing the problems of any particular policy sector is closely linked to broader issues of gender equality in women's mobilization, EU discourses, and EU policymaking. Gender equality has a range of meanings in the EU, as elsewhere. In the framework of the treaties, gender equality goals have been expressed in concepts ranging from "equal treatment" to "mainstreaming". What is clear is that the local, national, and transnational networks of women activists and their NGOs have played a central role in the process of defining these meanings (Keck and Sikkink, 1998; Hoskyns, 1996; Lovenduski, 1986). These developments were also nurtured and driven forward by an array of EU-level actors: women's organizations and other sympathetic NGOs, officials within the European Commission, members of the European Parliament, and civil servants and officials within several Member States. Moreover, international organizations such as the United Nations (UN), the International Labor Organization (ILO) and the World Health Organization (WHO) have been important sources of influence.

This constellation of actors has labored in a socio-political and cultural environment that more often than not made invisible many of the problems connected with women's situation including the issue of violence against women. The national policy and political environment has generally not been encouraging; even where the general reluctance of individual states to pass legislation and take action has been overcome, there remain large gaps between formal laws, actual enforcement, and day-to-day practice – even among the EU countries considered relatively "advanced" on issues related to gender equality. In spite of frequent criticisms regarding the EU's "democratic deficit", the EU gender developments have emerged in a relatively open and participatory polity through effective activism, often specific to each cause, e.g., violence against women, and against a backdrop of more general EU-level and transnational activism seeking to improve equality between the sexes.

CHAPTER 14

Paradigm Shift and Regime Change: Case Comparisons and Analysis

1. Introduction

The case studies presented in the preceding chapters share a number of common characteristics. Each case entails a paradigmatic shift, with subsequent changes in a policy paradigm entailing steps in an extended process of development and institutionalization of the new paradigm. The paradigm shift is defined in the reconfiguration of core or constitutional principles that guide policy; such a reconfiguration can be identified in specific actions intended to codify those new principles. Nevertheless, a paradigm shift is always defined from a particular reference point – an issue we return to in the final chapter. In our case studies, development and institutionalization of the new paradigm involves rule changes that redefine policymaking competencies and procedures, and in the creation of new regulations and organizational structures at the European level (although not necessarily in that order). In each instance, these processes have been driven by or accompanied by the engagement of new actors and changes in authority, conceptions of expertise, and procedures.

To be sure, the developments in each of these cases come with specific limitations and qualifications, which were highlighted in the respective chapters. The most straightforward limitation is that the process of institutionalization of the new competence has had a relatively short time to unfold, and there is no guarantee that the mobilization required to support a continuation of the new policy paradigm will be sustained.

The energy case provides an instance in which developments followed a broader and already established trend of liberalizing markets and redefining their boundaries as European rather than national; in this case, Europeanization entailed setting aside previous concerns about national security and control over pricing in favor of a new competitive integrated energy market. Following a counter trend, four of our six individual cases are illustrative of the ways in which particular social or environmental concerns gained a fundamentally different level of influence in EU policymaking over the course of the past two decades. As a whole, the shifts in food policy, chemicals (and asbestos) policy, and gender equality policy have been characterized as a replacement of the "free market paradigm" with a "social Europe" paradigm (Carson, 2004), but also involves the expansion of EU authority and scope, that is, Europeanization. The climate change case can be seen as mixed, since it entails prioritizing social-ecological concerns but also creates a new European-level market in the ETS.

The results presented in this chapter highlight commonalities and differences across the cases and examine the processes by which fundamental shifts have taken place in each of the sectors investigated. It concludes by drawing on the case studies to offer a number of theoretical observations that we go on to develop further in Chapter 15. The developments traced in the case studies have progressed in varying degrees in each of the policy sectors – in part a function of the different institutional and historical context in which each has unfolded. Previous, long-standing concerns and goals were not simply replaced by the new ones. Rather, the policy orientation in each sector was qualitatively changed through a reordering of guiding principles and underlying assumptions on which those principles are based. In each instance, the new paradigm is also presented as a means for protecting the achieved goals of the earlier paradigm and policy regime. Taken together, these cases exhibit important similarities in their patterns of development that illustrate the various processes, mechanisms and dynamics involved in paradigm shift and institutionalization.

2. Patterns of Change: Paradigm Shift across Six Cases

The liberalization of the European gas market provides what might be considered a typical example of Europeanization in its extension of the market liberal paradigm (as applied to the European Single Market) to cover the liberalization of the national level natural gas sector. Within the rational context of policy paradigm A in the national energy sector, gas was conceptualized as a potential source of energy vulnerability. Core goals were defined in terms of ensuring supply at an acceptable price. Markets were not considered sufficiently reliable to be trusted with the provision of such an essential good as energy, and the means of assuring affordable supplies of gas entailed monopoly regulated by the state.

One particularly interesting element of the gas case is the fact that there were no policy failures at the national level driving a search for different kinds of remedies. Instead, as the kinds of security concerns in which the monopoly model was rooted faded, the monopoly system was itself defined as an issue by Commission entrepreneurs in that its logic was at odds with the constitutional principles defined by the European Single Market. A new paradigm for the gas sector (gas paradigm B) was articulated by the Commission in 1992 with its "Proposal for a Council directive concerning common rules for the internal market in natural gas". Although the proposal generated considerable conflict, a directive was drafted and eventually adopted in 1998 in considerably weaker form, marking the shift in to market logic. Individual actors – including both sectoral actors and individual member states – shifted their own positions from opposition to acceptance at different points during this six year period, often based on a belief that the policy shift was inevitable and that it would be preferable to try to steer the change. The core principles of the newly defined paradigm were designed to be logically consistent with the general paradigm guiding the Single Market conception, including regulation via competitive market principles, and with the market defined at the European rather than national level.

In contrast, the EU paradigm guiding gender equality was introduced during a much earlier period. Moreover, rather than a more general paradigm being applied to a specific sector, a sector-specific paradigm was expanded to apply more generally across sectors.

The principle of equality between the sexes and the related goal of ensuring equal treatment of women and men in the workplace was established as a basic principle of the EU already in the 1970s with the Defrenne case, and subsequently with equal treatment Directives that were also adopted during the 1970s (gender policy paradigm A). More than two decades later, Articles 2 and 3 of the Amsterdam Treaty (1999) codified an expansion of this principle into other arenas as "constitutional" principles of the EU, establishing not only that "the promotion of equality between men and women is a task of the European Community", but also that "in all its activities the Community shall aim to eliminate inequalities and to promote equality between men and women". The paradigm shift in EU gender equality policy lies in its substantial expansion via "mainstreaming" into other policy sectors combined with the fundamental change in the means for pursuing those goals (gender paradigm B). The policy orientation of EU gender equality goals was thereby dramatically expanded beyond equality issues rooted in women's workforce participation, where it had been largely locked in place since the founding of the union. One early example of the effects of that expansion is how the issue of domestic violence – a problem long considered off limits even to national governments – found space on the European agenda (Carson, 2004). As with the gas case, the shift entailed newly defined authority at the European level, and the application of a fundamentally revised core of principles to existing policy areas.

Similarly, both environment and public health were "mainstreamed", with the treaty requirement for achieving "a high level of protection" in health and environment (the EU had previously been granted treaty-based authority in the Maastricht Treaty (1992) to "consider" these issues in its activities). Although these fairly general statements of principle were subtle and not the subject of great controversy at the time they were adopted, far reaching new bodies of rules have been constructed to realize these principles in the face of health and environmental challenges. In the process, significant new EU level constraints on the activities considered acceptable for market actors have been established. As applied to each of the policy sectors examined, these new constitutional principles fundamentally alter the "asymmetry" highlighted by Scharpf (2002). Market integration remains a core mission of the EU, but that integration is now to be pursued within the broader frameworks of improving gender equality, achieving a high level of public health, and ensuring a high level of environmental protection. Moreover, the integrated market activities already in place are being tempered to reduce specific types of risks and harms as identified in the sustainability discourse. Asymmetry does remain in terms of the number of votes required to adopt policies pertaining to the different sectors so that directives aimed at gender equality, protection of public health, and environmental preservation still require supermajorities, while market integration can proceed via "nondecision" or simple majority vote.

As summarized in Tables 14.1 and 14.2, the *paradigm shift* in each of the cases entailed a reconceptualization of the issues and problems to which the EU needed to respond, and included a corresponding reorientation of the guiding principles and policy goals guiding policymaking in the sector. As a general rule, such reconceptualization also has required new areas of EU policymaking authority to be defined. Each of our cases has also entailed a "Europeanization" of the policy sector, or a shift of the level of governance at which the policies in question were to be decided. Separate from the shift of authority from national to supranational levels, our research identifies such shifts in the clear expression of a revised complex of constitutional principles coupled with actions that initiate the implementation of the new model.

The paradigm shift in EU food policy took place when the central priority of EU food policy was wrenched by crisis from its market-making orientation to an overriding concern with food safety and public health. Under food policy paradigm A, the commercial product characteristics of food were prioritized. Conflicts between food safety and market principles were resolved in favor of keeping markets open and protecting economic actors. For example, at the onset of the BSE crisis, the European Commission challenged member states that sought to block the import of British beef, arguing such efforts constituted a violation of internal market rules. The Green and White Papers on food safety, issued following the BSE crisis, outlined fundamental revisions of those principles in considerable detail (see Chapter 8). Carson (2004) makes the case that the publication of the White Paper on Food Safety constitutes the paradigmatic shift in food policy in that it outlined a systematic reorientation of core principles for guiding EU food policy and included concrete proposals for realizing those reordered principles and policy goals. By the definition of paradigm shift we propose in this book, the food safety White Paper would mark the beginning of the paradigm shift phase that stretches to the adoption of the Directive establishing the European Food Safety Authority, that is, the implementation of the social organizational components. However, concrete action began prior to the adoption of the FSA. Even as the White Paper was being published, the European Commission carried out an internal reorganization of responsibility for food safety.

Table 14.1. Conditions, Change Agents, and Mechanisms of Paradigm Shifts

	FOOD SAFETY	ASBESTOS BAN	CHEMICALS /REACH	NATURAL GAS	CLIMATE MITIGATION	GENDER EQUALITY
Emerging issue or problem which threatens health, environment, sensibilities of key groups or their constituencies	BSE & dioxin threat not only to health but to the concept of the EU integrated market	Asbestos threat to health and to the consistency of the internal market (asbestos ban in some countries but not in others)	Chemical threats to human health and environment. Growing international concern, also in the EU, in particular new member-states such as Sweden and NGO movements (health, environment, animal rights)	Gas outside the EU domain a threat to the single market mandate – a normative gap	Climate change challenge, international pressures, NGO pressures, EU ambitions	Domestic violence & other gender gaps and normative issues ignored or neglected, nationally and internationally
AGENTS & INTERACTION PROCESSES						
Drivers of Change: Key actors responding to conditions with reform actions	DG Enterprise, Commission's public health administration.	DG Enterprise, public interest NGOs, Anti-asbestos victim groups, Labor unions (ILO)	DG Environment, EP, Particular member-states such as Sweden Environmental orgs (Euro, national, international levels) Public health groups.	Council of the European Union, ECJ	DG Environment Commission as a whole. Some business enterprises, environmental NGOs	EP, DG Employment and Social Affairs. EU and national women's organizations & networks. United Nations

Main Opposition	UK and Belgium governments, national Agriculture ministries	Canada asbestos industry. Industrial users of asbestos (potentially WTO)	Chemicals industry, EU member states (France, U.K., Germany) and USA	National monopolies, some member state governments	Several member states, some environmental NGOs	Employers; Some member states
Mode of change	Crisis driven – so relatively rapid response but part of a longer-term complex learning process. DG consumption. Commission entrepreneurship	Incremental reduction in scope of use. Increasingly restrictive. Entailed long-term complex learning process. Part of the chemical regulation revolution	Change in international context; movement driven, several member-states as public entrepreneurs	EU Use of constitutional and administrative powers to force a new system in accordance with market mandate	Constitutional constraint, Imitation, 2nd best strategy Diffusion of a model Emergence of new norms and values	Change in international context, UN and NGO agents pushing – diffusion of norms and values. Member-states as public entrepreneurs
OUTCOMES AND DEVELOPMENTS						
Paradigm shift From PARADIGM A ⇩ To PARADIGM B	Market: Food as market commodity ⇩ Public Health: Food as health & security issue	Market: Asbestos as commercial product ⇩ Asbestos as health hazard	Market-chemicals as commercial products ⇩ Public Health and Environment: Systematic control of chemicals as hazards	Gas as national issue, often Monopoly ⇩ European integrated Market	Climate change mitigation through taxation and administration; national and regional emission markets ⇩ Climate change Mitigation through an EU Emission Market	Market conception of gender: Equal pay for equal work; ⇩ Societal mainstreaming of gender equality as a core EU value

Organizational/ institutional changes (authority-responsibility complex)	Creation of EFA – Food authority. Creation of DG Health and Consumers as powerful commission agent	Asbestos (ban) is the EU responsibility and subject to its authority	Creation of ECHA	Development of EU gas market. Laws and regulations to establish the integrated gas market	Creation of the ETS	Creation of many organizations. Expanded responsibility-authority for DG Employment
Fundamental changes in EU authority?	Europenization. EU gains authority for food safety	Europenization. Asbestos subject to EU regulation	Extension of Europenization. Authority for monitoring and regulating all chemical	Europenization: market regulation at EU level	Europenization Shift from national ETSs	Europenization of multiple sectors in connection with gender mainstreaming

Table 14.2. Components of the New Paradigms (B)

	Food Safety	**Asbestos**	**Chemicals**	**Gas**	**Kyoto (ETS)**	**Gender**
Problem-solving framework						
Goals & Priorities	Health and food security goals	Total elimination of asbestos in EU zone, in buildings, offices, and homes	Effective control of chemicals identifying unknown or unacknowledged hazards, banning or limiting most high risk chemicals	EU integrated market for gas	Achieve reduction of GHG Emissions in the EU community	Gender equality as core EU value to be accomplished in all policy areas

Conceptualization/ Model of Problems	Problems of contamination & disease	Demonstrated high risk for human health	Many chemicals are risky for humans, other species, and the environment and must be regulated by EU public policy	National monopolies & barriers as problem and source of inefficiencies (e.g., high prices). Incompatibility of the national model with the vision of an EU integrated market	"Cap & Trade" is a 2nd best option to doing nothing or waiting until taxation becomes viable	Gender inequality & discrimination in all sectors of society
Solution Complex /Means	EU level monitoring & regulation	Banning asbestos in the EU area	Control of chemicals from manufacturers, importers, and downstream users, including powers to ban chemicals or to limit their applicability	Shift from national monopoly model to EU integrated market model	Establish ETS as well as other measures to reduce emissions	EU policy intervention necessary in all areas of public policy
Social Organizational Complex						
Authority & Responsibility Sub-complex	Level change. Creation of EFA for health and security goals	Level change. EU responsibility and authority for asbestos ban	Level Change. EU responsibility and authority, Creation of new agency, ECHA	Level change. EU responsibility and authority for an integrated market	Level Change; Creation of EU's ETS	Level change and multi-sectorial policy model
Expert Sub-complex	EU experts, EFA mobilization	EU & national experts (technicians & administrators)	EU experts, ECHA Mobilization of experts	EU & national experts	EU & national Experts on "cap and trade" mechanisms	Wide Spectrum of EU, national, and NGOs with sector specific expertise
Decision making Procedural Sub-complex	Multi-stakeholder Participation: multiple EU & national as well as NGO actors involved	EU administration with member-state implementation	Multi-stakeholder Participation: multiple EU & national as well as NGOs organizations	EU establishes procedures for transition, for third-party participation in gas transmission. Involvement of ECJ.	EU, member states negotiate caps and impose sanctions for non-compliance	Multi-stakeholder participation, typically specialized in multiple sectors.

In what amounted to a test of the new paradigm (food paradigm B) as articulated in the food safety White Paper, a subsequent food crisis was resolved by EU officials forcefully acting to protect the safety of the food supply. The EU response to the handling of dioxin contamination by the Belgian government provided the earliest concrete indication that these new principles were actually being implemented.

Not unlike food policy, the policy paradigm that previously guided the regulation of asbestos and chemical products prioritized the commercial product characteristics of those substances. Many potential and anticipated costs were "externalized" by minimizing or even actively overlooking evidence of problems such as possible sources of exposure during later phases of the product life cycle, unanticipated uses, eventual disposal, etc. Problems that emerged with enough consequence to gain recognition were initially dealt with in an ad hoc manner. However, the ad hoc responses were eventually replaced with systematic efforts following a new, more coherent logic that prioritized health and environmental considerations over many commercial concerns.

Asbestos provides a somewhat simplified example, and as we argue, amounted to a dress rehearsal for the eventual struggle over chemicals. Under asbestos policy paradigm A, asbestos was permitted on the market in spite of evidence of problems dating to the early 1900s. As specific conditions or applications were demonstrated beyond a doubt to be unacceptably hazardous, restrictions were introduced and over time were expanded. Here again, occupational and public health concerns led to restrictions which temper the application of market principles, but they remained reactive – and therefore largely secondary. With the 1991 Directive (91/659/EEC), however, the logic changed. In a reversal of logic that can be characterized as a paradigm shift, occupational and especially public health were prioritized; specified uses of asbestos were permitted as exceptions to a general rule that asbestos should no longer be used. Under asbestos policy paradigm B, only existing applications believed to present minimal, and therefore acceptable risk, were permitted. As damning evidence mounted, exceptions were eventually narrowed and two years later, the European Commission recommended a complete ban. However, several more years would pass before it could be fully institutionalized. As Carson (2004) presents the case, the paradigm shift took place in a single act, with the adoption of the new logic contained in the 1991 Directive. However, it is also possible to interpret that point as part of a build-up (similar to the Food Safety Green Paper that identified a clear logic for addressing the problems that had emerged) and to take the Commission's proposal to adopt a complete ban of asbestos as the most clearly identifiable point marking the start of the paradigm shift phase. In this case, the paradigm shift phase is concluded in 1999 with the adoption of the ban, which is then institutionalized over subsequent years.

Similarly, chemicals policy paradigm A prioritized market goals, permitting chemical products to be developed and marketed with little knowledge of their short and long-term health and environmental effects. Problems were dealt with on a national level as they emerged and were made an issue by environmentalists (for example, Rachael Carson's "Silent Spring") or by citizens affected by contamination and health problems. The new logic was foreshadowed by the 1981 Directive that required the evaluation of all *new chemicals* to be introduced on the market. However, that Directive permitted products already on the market to remain, except where overwhelming evidence for their restriction was accepted. The logic remained clear however, as summarized by Vogel (1993:127) "while attempting to respond to growing public pressures for stricter environmental standards, [the EU] was equally determined to prevent environmental regulation from interfering with economic integration. When faced with a tension between the two, it chose the latter over the former…". This orientation was revisited in the late 1990s – in part through issues connected to food safety and asbestos, which invoked similar types of issues and revolved around the same basic set of fundamental principles. Beginning in 2000, a series of policy statements was used to announce the adoption of new guiding principles, including the White Paper on the Precautionary Principle (COM(2000) 1 final) and the White Paper on Environmental Liability (COM(2000) 6 final). In many ways, the White Paper outlining a Strategy for a Future Chemicals Policy (COM(2001) 88 final) represents the crown of this set of developments – again, in its articulation of a coherent set of revised principles and measures by which chemical products should be regulated. As with asbestos, chemicals policy under policy paradigm B (later defined as REACH) entailed a reversal of the underlying assumptions regarding product safety, burden of proof, and the treatment of risks that had previously been externalized. REACH now required the assessment of thousands of products already on the market, but for which there was currently insufficient publicly available data to properly assess safety.

The paradigm shift in EU climate policy follows a pattern roughly similar to the preceding cases. Under climate policy paradigm A, climate concerns and goals regarding GHG reductions were introduced as an important set of considerations that were to temper the application of EU principles guiding energy production and use, transport, and other GHG-producing economic activities. The subsidiarity of GHG reduction goals to free market principles was reflected in the nature of the remedies adopted: incentives for energy conservation and use of renewable energy sources and the like. The shift to paradigm B is indicated in the embrace of measures that might reasonably be expected to have at least a short-term detrimental effect on the EU priority of economic growth (the 1980s). This was first expressed in the willingness to pursue adoption of a European carbon tax, then followed up with the embrace of an EU level emissions trading system as a functional alternative. Where climate paradigm A is characterized by economic growth priorities with consideration for climate, paradigm B is characterized by the adoption of environmental protection principles as a more pressing priority, with consideration for the economic effects. As previously noted, this case is also interesting in that a new

European level market was created – partially in response to individual member states taking initiatives in the absence of meaningful EU action. The EU not only accepted a means of pricing carbon that it had earlier opposed, but also embraced the role of global advocate and leader for such means.

3. New Actors and Actor Configurations as Drivers and Institutional Agents

The conceptual and institutional changes identified above have been driven by or accompanied by actors who are new to EU level policymaking, or whose centrality in these processes has been significantly strengthened. New forms of expertise have been brought in to provide information, authority and responsibility for making decisions and taking action has been reassigned, new authorities have been established, and organized actors who were once peripheral to the process have taken on important roles. In some instances, this has come through a process of the EU seeking greater popular legitimacy through broadened participation and democratization, resulting in an increased presence and participation, for example, by NGOs representing broad public interests. It has also generated an expanded role for conventional democratic institutions within the EU, such as the European Parliament.

The shifts in configurations of influential actors were somewhat different in each of the cases, although in all five cases in which social or environmental principles gained importance, NGOs played an important role. The Commission played a central entrepreneurial role in all of the cases (although not without making some serious mistakes) and the European Parliament most often played an important role in support of a greater emphasis on social and environmental issues. It was perhaps the type of mobilization of actors within civil society that differed most.

Andersen's account of the transformation in gas policy notes how the shift was surprising precisely because of the lack of a constituency demanding or asking for such a shift. Entrepreneurs within the Commission provided the impetus from the beginning, but commercial actors and public authorities in the UK perceived advantages in being early movers, and were eventually followed by industry groups in the Netherlands and elsewhere. New authorities were established at both the national and EU level for seeing to it that the Directive's provisions were being implemented and for creating the new Europe-wide system.

In the climate change case, the shift from the EU Commission preferred carbon tax to an emissions trading system was the result of a combination of the structural requirements for adopting a tax (unanimity principle for issues of taxation) and opposition by key member states, as well as the side effects of an international negotiation process.

In the food case, the crisis and changes were driven to a great extent by the non-organized, concerted action of European citizens refusing to buy British beef – or any beef products at all for a period of time. This action was accompanied by a belief that responsibility for the risk of exposure to illness lay as much with the EU and its policies as with the British government and meat producers. It was this attribution that contributed so much to the sense of political crisis. Following the BSE crisis, the role of NGOs such as consumer and public health groups was greatly strengthened and their expertise taken much more seriously. Their concerns had proven to be very well founded, and the Commission needed the legitimacy provided by NGO participation in developing policy proposals. There was also a reallocation of authority within the European Commission apparatus. For example, DG Agriculture lost its coordinating role on food safety issues to DG Public Health and Consumer Protection. Finally, a new regulatory apparatus was created with the European Food Safety Authority, located in Parma, Italy.

In contrast, there was no mass mobilization in the asbestos case. In part, this was a result of many European states having already banned asbestos. The exception was victims' organizations in France and the UK, with the European Trade Union Confederation, public health and consumer organizations also supporting a ban. In the asbestos case, the Commission was again the principle entrepreneur. It took up the arguments made by NGOs and made use of data provided by experts associated with the ban asbestos movement. The Commission proposal to ban asbestos eventually gained the support of two key member states: France and the UK, as a result of domestic developments. As outlined earlier, the French shift in position change was crisis-driven by events tangentially related to asbestos, while the UK was seeking to transfer a problem elsewhere in order to avoid threatened retaliation by Canada. International organizations, particularly the WTO, played an influential role in the process. The EU was forced, in part, to rely on new forms of expertise to develop its evidence and reasoning for the ban, keeping a possible WTO challenge in mind.

The REACH and climate change cases were powerfully influenced through mobilization by environmental NGOs, the leadership of particular member states, and even the support of key actors within the business community. In each of these cases, the institutionalization process was highly influenced by the way in which the internal chess match was played by entrepreneurs within the Commission and the European Parliament.

The gender equality case is the one most clearly driven by transnational grassroots activism and mobilization. Changes in EU policy were initially driven by entrepreneurial actors using Article 119. By the beginning of the 1990s, the transnational network of women's NGOs had managed to gain a base both above, though work at a series of UN Conferences connected with human rights, and below, at the member state level, through shelter movements and other mobilization around equality issues. These activities converged at the EU level in the mid 1990s, when women's groups managed to take advantage of the historical development of equality policy to build new openings. The women's rights as human rights framework gained Commission and member state support at Vienna (1993), then Beijing (1995), and the Beijing documents were brought back to Brussels as rough work plan and tool for monitoring progress on equality goals. In this instance, an international organization, the UN, served as both a forum and a legitimating tool to support advances in the EU gender equality agenda.

Opposition in each of the cases was also important, with some previously powerful actors losing ground, disappearing from view, or changing sides. In the food case, a struggle between producers and other market actors over the CAP provided an opening for a new food safety regime as powerful actors to some extent negated one anothers influence. In the asbestos case, the coalition of business support for the asbestos industry eroded as manufacturers shifted to other products, and those who might resist the ban for ideological reasons quietly withdrew in hopes that the problem would go away. The greatest opposition came from asbestos producers outside the EU. In the chemicals sector, external opposition was also fundamentally important, with the Bush Administration and US chemical companies mounting an aggressive campaign to block REACH. Nor was there easy consensus within the EU. A collection of powerful organizations actively resisted many important elements of the proposed regulations. Especially interesting was the last minute bid to strip DG Environment of its ownership of the issue and shift it to the more market-sympathetic actor, the Competitivity Council. In the case of gender, there was little discernable opposition to seeking to eliminate domestic violence. Here, however, resistance took the form of national level opposition to EU "intrusion" in the area of member state criminal law, for example.

4. Institutionalizing New Policy Regimes

A *process of institutionalization* of the paradigm changes described above is also apparent in each of our cases, with significant variation in the pace and extent of institutionalization. As discussed in Chapters 7 and 15, this institutionalization process entails changes in the organizational arrangements corresponding to the logic and prescriptions of the new paradigm. Such changes include typical organizational reforms that include creation of new organizational structures, systematic reconfiguration of policy authority, reallocation of resources, new types of problem remedies, and inclusion of new agents and forms of expertise. With respect to the EU, these types of changes have been both case-specific and more general. For example, EU authority and organizational capacity to engage in the social and ecological dimensions of a wide range of policy sectors has been broadened overall, and on occasion, abruptly. In all but the gas case, social and/or ecological concerns were initially given a base in the treaties through the provisions that initially authorized "consideration", then were "mainstreamed" through mandating that they be addressed and prioritized.[1] These mainstreamed provisions fall short of providing a constitutional footing equal to that of completing the single market because the

[1] It is important to note, however, that the EU has frequently engaged in policy areas in which it lacked formal authority.

voting requirements are typically more stringent. Nevertheless, they have created new windows and structures of opportunity that did not exist previously; this is especially the case where social or ecological issues can be framed in terms of protecting the internal market, as they were in the food, asbestos, and chemicals cases. Moreover, in the institutionalization of new constitutional principles and priorities, the new paradigms define conditions under which social and environmental concerns trump market goals in the case the two come into conflict.

In the individual cases, rule changes have contributed to the institutionalization of the new paradigm in varying degrees in an ongoing process. Patterns of development across the cases are similar in terms of policy substance, the nature and forms of participation in the governance process that produced that policy, and in the ways in which different forms of authority were gained or granted at the EU level. These developments are highlighted in Tables 14.1 and 14.2.

The institutionalization phase of the new liberal gas paradigm began with the adoption of the 1998 Directive. Andersen notes that in spite of its characterization as a "weak compromise full of unresolved issues", it fundamentally changed the rules, also setting in motion a process of transposition of the EU Directive at the national level. The Directive established specific minimum goals of 28% of market opening by August 2000, and up to 33% by 2008. Highlighting the process nature of institutionalization, the subsequent gas Directive adopted in 2003 was addressed both to issues left out of the original Directive, and to new obstacles and problems that had emerged in the implementation process.

The institutionalization or regime change connected with EU gender equality policy paradigm B in lies in its extension via "mainstreaming" into other policy sectors combined with the fundamental change in the means for pursuing those goals. The issue of domestic violence was given as one early example. The institutionalization of the expansion of EU gender equality policy into the area of domestic violence can be seen in the Daphne program, which was renewed for another program period in 2004 (and will be renewed again in 2009), but the slightly increased funding (€50 million) had to stretch over five years and a greatly enlarged number of member states. Interestingly, the legal base of the Daphne program remains Article 153 (public health) rather than the Treaty articles dealing with gender equality or non-discrimination, suggesting that the treaty base remains weak. Nevertheless, these are not the kinds of developments that observers would have predicted in the 1980s, or even in the early 1990s.

The slow institutionalization of the new gender equality paradigm has only just begun to reach into other spheres of activity, including reconciliation of work and private life and the situation of migrant women. In this case, institutionalization has proceeded more via soft measures than Directives, with efforts directed at identifying and measuring specific problems, fostering goal setting and collaboration, and developing organizational capacity. In many of not most of these activities, gender equality linked to the labor market continues to constitute the home base from which other efforts have been launched. Hence, issues such as parental leave or migrant women's access to the labor market reach into new territory while remaining anchored in established territory.

In the area of food policy, the European Food Safety Authority was finally put in place nearly five years after it was recommended in the White Paper on Food Safety. Nevertheless, EU institutions such as DG Health and Consumer Protection were already intensively engaged in work to ensure and monitor the safety of foodstuffs in European markets. Primary responsibility for food safety was in fact moved from DG Agriculture to DG Health. Here we can argue that the regulatory measures required by the new paradigm and the organizational apparatus required develop and implement them are in a process of ongoing development. This is a process that can be expected to continue to unfold over the next decade and beyond.

Chemicals policy is similar to food safety policy in that the process of evaluating the safety and risk properties of thousands of already on the market chemicals under the REACH policy has only just begun, and it will take many years to make a sizeable dent in even the chemical substances that are already the subject of significant concern. Considerable organizational capacity is necessary to manage and carry out this work, and even if important tasks have been delegated to industry, there are monitoring and compliance responsibilities that will require ongoing development and specification. Here also, we can observe that the institutionalization of the new policy regime is underway, and that development will likely continue for the foreseeable future.

In the asbestos case, institutionalizing the new paradigm was easy by comparison; the ban included a phase in to permit adjustment in the few European asbestos-producing countries. There are also ongoing health and safety issues with the asbestos that is already present in buildings and elsewhere, including concerns for the safety of workers who might carry out the removal and disposal of the substance. However, even with ongoing health concerns and the monitoring for compliance a ban requires, it did not require the creation of a substantial new agency or organizational capacity.

Crossover Institutionalization

Several of the actions that contribute to the institutionalization of a new paradigm extended across sectors – particularly those pertaining to public health and environment. In February 2004, an agreement was reached between the Parliament and the European Council on a new Environmental Liability Directive based on the proposals put forth by the Commission in the related White Paper (COM(2000) 66 final). The Liability Directive is a codification of the polluter pays principle, which was originally outlined in the 1972 Stockholm Declaration that was developed at the United Nations Conference on the Human Environment (UN, 1972). The principle was included in the Environmental Section of the Maastricht Treaty

(1993, Article 174(2)). Environmental and public health NGOs have expressed concern that it leaves significant holes (EEB, 2004). Apart from what are clearly legitimate criticisms,[2] the Directive set in place a common framework for allocating costs for environmental damage to polluters, and reducing the externalized costs borne by taxpayers.

In chemicals, the burden of proof was initially shifted with a 1981 Directive (79/831/EEC – see chapter 10) requiring the registration and approval of new products before they could be placed on the market. This was expanded systematically by the Precautionary Principle (outlined in COM(2000) 1 final), and is being realized more concretely under the REACH directive.

It is not only in the area of product hazards that the burden of proof has been shifted. A 1997 Directive (Directive 97/80/EEC) dealing with gender discrimination shifted the burden of proof to market actors – employers – not only in cases of direct discrimination, but in instances of indirect discrimination, where meeting the proof requirements had proven exceedingly difficult for the plaintiff. This is an early indication of the interest in expanding the mandate for pursuing increased gender equality.

5. Multi-level Developments

Our case studies clearly illustrate the importance of a pair of effects linked to multiple levels. The first is that in addition to other (especially neighboring) policy sectors being a potential source of new principles or of well-developed paradigms, other levels also provide an important source. In both instances, both alternative models and practical experience with those models are available to adapt to any given policy sector. Important new guiding principles were often apparent across multiple policy sectors, although their application within a given policy sector has varied, as has the time frame under which it was introduced. For example, Andersen's account of the emergence of a new paradigm in EU gas policy notes how the adjacent electricity sector provided both a model and experience with developing and implementing a liberalized system in the energy sector. At the same time, the impetus for change was based in the liberal market paradigm guiding the Single Market project.

Yet at the close of the same decade (1990s), strong limitations on free-market principles were articulated in the series of White Papers released in the wake of the food scares, starting with the White Paper on Food Safety (COM(99) 719), and continuing with the White Paper on the Precautionary Principle (COM(2000) 1 final) and the White Paper on Environmental Liability (COM(2000) 6 final). The White Paper outlining a Strategy for a Future Chemicals Policy (COM(2001) 88

[2] One of the more serious criticisms is the lack of a mandatory insurance, which could mean a violator would enter bankruptcy before it was able to pay the cost of the damage (for a discussion of possible impact of the anticipated Directive, see UK, 2002).

final) was issued shortly after and followed a logic that was consistent with the earlier White Papers. Each of these documents articulated guiding principles that set limits on the neo-liberal model of markets and economics, enumerating priorities intended to supersede allowing markets to self-correct, and setting out concrete goals and policy proposals for realizing new core social, health, and environmental principles. In this way, emphasis on new values connected with public health and environment developed in parallel with one another, even to the extent that the paradigms for each of the sectors shared a set of core policy principle. Moreover, many of the principles, assumptions, and goals articulated in the relevant documents had already been in play in some form or another for some time. What was new was their systematic articulation and elevation as first-order guiding principles and goals of the Union.

6. Concluding Remarks

Our case studies point up parallel developments:

- The march of European integration. Of course, the cases are successful ones, to be contrasted possibly to the single currency initiative (which saw some countries like UK, Denmark and Sweden electing to stay out). The cases point up also the great complexity, flexibility and creativity in the European experiment (Burns and Carson, 2002).
- Four of our cases (Food, asbestos, chemicals, and gender) show a policy shift from economic and market emphasis to health and environmental emphases (see Tables 14.1 and 14.2). Climate change policy effectively entailed European Single Market arrangements as did gas (earlier it was electricity markets). The gas initiative was intended to bring about European wide competition and presumably reduced prices. The ETS initiative entailed, of course, the use of a market mechanism for environmental purposes.

Recent developments regarding the environment, climate change, the use of chemicals, and other sustainability-related questions, call for additional nuance in the characterization of our cases. We see the current processes in terms of what might be better termed the construction of "sustainable Europe". Here, the trio of dimensions captured by the sustainability concept – ecological, social, and market economic dimensions – will have to be managed and balanced both in each's own right and in relation to one another. In each of the cases except for gas, social and/or ecological considerations came to be prioritized during the late 1990s and 2000s over the market integration goals that had dominated EU policymaking for much of the earlier decades.

CHAPTER 15

Elaborating Public Policy Paradigm Theory

1. Introduction

Through our case studies (overview in Chapter 14), we have shown that the architecture of particular PPPs were transformed in definable ways in each of our case studies. Chapter 7 also indicated several of the key mechanisms for bringing about paradigm shift. In chapter 14, on the basis of our case studies and the earlier work of Jenson, Hall, Coleman et al, among others, we could begin to formulate a typology of paradigm change mechanisms. In this chapter, we go on to elaborate the change drivers and their consequences.

The theoretical framework presented and developed in this book posits that "paradigm shifts" entail fundamental conceptual and organizational changes which guide policy in a markedly different direction than previous paradigms. In this instance, such shifts are accomplished in the articulation and adoption of a new problem-solving model within a particular policy sector. Such shifts are identifiable in the reconfiguration of the core principles used in defining the nature of policy problems and in guiding political problem-solving activities. The patterns in our case studies suggest strongly that the term "paradigm shift" is best used to characterize what amounts to conceptual and organizational tipping points in an ongoing, often incremental process of adjustment that began long before the actual "shift" is said to occur – and is likely to continue for some time afterwards. In this sense, our definition of paradigm shift encompasses both the articulation of a new model and the initial concrete steps taken to realize that model in practice. Given the nature of the process, it is likely that the actions constituting paradigm shift cannot be pinned down to a single moment in time and that we should instead think in terms of it as a phase in a broader process of change.

Therefore, institutionalization of a paradigm is best understood as a process rather than a point in time, and entails changes in the institutional arrangements, a rule regime, that give effect to the reordering of guiding principles and the redefinition of policy problems through changes in regulatory, organizational, and relational structures. Given that the process of institutionalizing a new paradigm frequently stretches over an extended period of time, and that such institutionalization must frequently take place within a variety of existing organizational/institutional cultures, policies adopted subsequent to paradigm change may not be entirely consistent with the new paradigm (see later discussion on paradigm blueprint versus an instantiation of it as a operative paradigm).

An operative policy paradigm may not necessarily be contemporaneous with the conceptual framework that has guided it. Indeed, each of our cases illustrates time lags, some of them considerable. This asynchronicity between conceptual change and operative change argues for an analytical distinction between paradigm shift and the institutionalization of that change (Carson, 2001; 2004) – for much the same reasons that Margaret Archer (1990) argued for an analytical separation of "culture" and "structure". As we spelled out in Chapter 7, this is one of the areas where we seek to extend our predecessors' theoretical efforts. Our cases illustrate both the typically punctuated incrementalism of the processes though which paradigm reconceptions take place, but they also demonstrate that such paradigm change is not tantamount to operative change. The basis of our argument is that different mechanisms drive and constrain changes in these two realms – indeed, the institutionalization of a new paradigm may ultimately be weak or even fail.

A second important theoretical extension pertains to the internal architecture of the policy paradigm. Drawing on the institutional analysis of Burns and Flam (1987) and Burns and Carson (2004) and Carson's (2004:46-48) development of the paradigm concept, we identify problem solving and social organizational complexes constituted of specific elements. Our contention is that any of these several elements – or combinations of elements and their relation to one another – typically constitute the core elements which define or identify a particular paradigm. A key tenet of Kuhn's paradigm was that some elements are more central, more important, than others. This insight was expanded upon by our contributors, and taken furthest in Yves Surel's efforts at integrating Peter Hall's work with similarly important efforts by Paul Sabatier, and by Jobert and Muller. For reasons we have already articulated, we prefer the term "constitutional" over "metaphysical" to apply to taken-for-granted assumptions and principles. Apart from that minor point, we find Surel's hierarchy to be particularly useful for distinguishing between paradigmatic models.

Paradigms are complexes of ideas of how to conceptualize, analyze, and deal with public issues – including conceptualizing and analyzing why an issue should be dealt with publicly, what kinds of knowledge, forms of causality, ways of distributing responsibility and authority, and ways to organize and arrange participation (and exclusions).

Paradigm transformation therefore entails a fundamental restructuring of elements of such problem-solving and organizational complexes and the relations between them. This reconfiguration may or may not entail the introduction of new principles or goals per se. Indeed, the dominant pattern in our cases is one in which new principles are introduced and adopted incrementally as considerations that temper the application of the existing institutionalized paradigm. The paradigm shift can be identified in some form of the re-ordering of core principles. When competing goals come into conflict with one another, the new paradigm is distinguishable in terms of a different priority ordering of principles, and thus different kinds of problem definitions, preferred remedies, authorities and experts, and, ultimately, different outcomes.

2. Changes in a PPP Rule Regime

The architecture of the PPP rule regime indicates the dimensions of potential change (see figures 7.1 and 7.2 in Chapter 7 as well as Tables 14.1 and 14.2 in Chapter 14):

Social organizational complex:

- adding to or subtracting agents (or categories of agents) in the complex (authorities, experts)
- changes in the relationships among the agents, e.g., authority relationships
- changes in the procedures to make decisions
- changes in dimensions of time, place, context

Problem-solving complex:

- changes in key values or goals
- change in the model of representation of the situation, conceptions of causality, possible policy variables
- changes in the issue-problem complex, the "conceptualization of the problem"
- changes in the solution complex

Changes in a paradigm may involve one or more of these dimensions. Radical change would entail significant changes in a number of PPP dimensions. When dimensions are changed, some are likely to have much greater impact than others in a given cultural and institutional context, for example:

- shift from public agency responsibility to private responsibility, or vice versa (the laws, incentive structures, and the roles and authority of agents, etc. will differ substantially).
- Shift from covering one population (the middle classes) to another (lower classes or marginal groups), or both.
- Shift from narrow scope of policy to comprehensive scope which will affect many more populations and social groups and involve a much greater array of methods, types of knowledge and expertise as in gender mainstreaming.
- Shifts in types of experts is also likely so lead to new conceptualization of the problem and possible solutions, the application of new methodologies and strategies to deal with the policy issue(s).

Changes may be made in the problem-solving complex but not in the social organizational complex. Or, vice versa, for instances changes in the agents with responsibility and authority who might continue to operate with the same problem-solving complex. But changes in the type of experts are likely to lead to changes in the problem-solving complex. Also, changes in values and changes in the model of reality are likely to impact on "problem definitions" and potential "solutions".

In sum, the paradigm regime as a universal institutional framework specifies key actors, their roles and relationships, that is who should be involved and in what capacities (also explicitly or implicitly who is excluded), procedures and other tools for managing interactions and decisions; it also specifies goals and priorities, and in elaborated forms, defines problems, solutions, tools of analysis (models, statistics, etc.). These are historically articulated and evolve over time. There are typically supporting arguments, interpretations, and pragmatic rules of applications and adaptations. Institutions are designed to teach, realize, implement, protect or/and defend these values.

Other actors than the "principals" and their "expert agents" may be specified such as "subjects", "participants", extraordinary and informal "advisors", allies or potential allies also "opponents", "enemies". In general, there are "external" agents who affect – or try to affect – the regime and its implementation, its maintenance or change. In our EU asbestos policy case study, Canada (in particular, the Province of Ontario) was active in trying to block a change in EU asbestos policy. Concerning Gender, the UN and many women's NGOs played a role. In chemicals, the chemical industry NGOs such as CEFIC, the US government, US Chamber of Commerce as well as environmental NGOs, etc. played various roles over the long process of determining a new EU chemical policy and regulatory apparatus. In the case of EU climate change policy, several EU member states and a number of NGOs and the USA as well as diverse other agents, within and outside the EU play a role in the formation of the EU ETS.

3. The Crooked Path from Paradigm Blueprint to Operative Regime

We distinguish analytically between a public policy paradigm (PPP) as a blueprint and an operating policy system for problem-solving and organizing relevant policy processes. The blueprint as an ideal type may be changed or adapted in the course of implementation – in its social, economic, and social context.

Adaptation of a paradigm blueprint arises because of:

- practical problems of implementation, among other things, because of material constraints and resource scarcity
- local or "situational" power conditions or other sources of agential or structural constraints
- lack of understanding of the functioning of the policy sector, or lack of sufficient resources even if one has sufficient authority or power to "decide" policy and to direct others.

Operative paradigms are the result of blueprints being translated into practice. They are not simply ideas, but concrete social organization and conceptual practices, patterns of actual thinking, acting and interacting – and judgments relating to realizing, putting ideas or concepts into practice. Thus, *one investigates policy paradigms as ideas as well as concrete practices.*

The relationship between a PPP regime – as a blueprint – and its practical embodiment has a direct effect on the various possibilities and probabilities for change; it presents actors with distinct opportunities for (and obstacles to) action. The character of this relationship appears to follow regular patterns. Interests develop in association with the implementation of formal organizational structures and new institutional arrangements (Michels, 1962). This occurs in part because social structure distribute advantages of power and material resources in particular ways. This general pattern can be clearly identified in accounts of the development of ideas in the making of public policy over time, and in a variety of different areas of public policy (Åsard and Bennett, 1997; Fowler, 1994; Weir, 1992; Baldwin, 1990; Olsson, 1990; Hall, 1989).

If a central feature of social institutions is that they condition the ways in which social interaction and collective decision-making are to proceed in a given domain of social life (Burns and Flam, 1987), the policy paradigm as a blueprint or ideal-type represents the socially constructed, idealized, relatively coherent and conceptual model upon which concrete forms are built (Burns and Carson, 2004). But while the formulation of further rules and regulations may be guided by a given paradigm blueprint, these rules are constructed in practice through adaptation as well as negotiation and compromise among the key agents directly involved. Because of the process of institutionalization unfolds over time, rule changes may be made in a piecemeal fashion, and may even be developed and carried out under the influence of competing conceptions and paradigms – so that the internal consistency of an institutionalized paradigm may be weak or undercut in the process of its institutionalization over time.

The degree of a paradigm's conceptual elaboration is likely to vary substantially, related to the extent to which the kinds of policy measures it recommends have been adopted and implemented and to the extent that intellectual expertise is engaged in efforts to develop the paradigm as a conceptual model for action. Although intertwined, institutional arrangements and paradigmatic models influence action differently and are themselves affected differently in change processes, particularly those driven by tangible institutional problems.

A public policy paradigm operates as a *socio-cognitive form*, a shared conception among a group or population of social actors. It can be discerned from what actors do, both in terms of discourses they choose and in terms of the kinds of purposes for which they mobilize and act (van Dijk, 1995). That is, it is reflected in: a) characteristic discourses and logically coherent complexes of approaches to defining and dealing with social problems; b) the realization of the paradigm through the actions and interactions of individuals and organized interests; and c) reproduction through its institutionalization as the guiding policymaking model in a specific area or areas of public policy, in the development of performance indicators and the giving of accounts, and in programs of education and training. These processes are not necessarily sequential, but constantly interacting with and influencing one another.

The blueprint of a paradigm therefore constitutes an idealized model complex, while the operative paradigm regime represents a compromised version of this ideal, implemented in a social context and in a practical situation. However, they both define more or less the same categories of elements and relationships. In a certain sense, the public policy paradigm as a blueprint or design framework is to concrete governance and regulatory institutions what theory is to a research program.

4. Drivers and Mechanisms of Public Policy Paradigm Shifts

In periods of "normality" (and related stability), those acting on the basis of a given public policy paradigm tend to work within the boundaries (the scope of a "master-frame") of the paradigm. Under certain conditions, a critique of the paradigm or its "solutions" may emerge: that is, there is a growing awareness of collective failings from utilizing the paradigm), and possibly a growing realization that the earlier problems – or new problems – cannot be solved within the established paradigm. The critical process leads under certain conditions to attempts at restructuring of it. Consequently, political agents or others may develop a fundamentally new paradigm or adopt what they judge to be an alternative paradigm based on different assumptions, categories, beliefs, values, etc. The core theoretical framework for explaining paradigm shifts (or the failures, thereof) is sketched in Figure 15.1.

Our approach stresses processes and the non-linearity of many paradigm developments, for example:

- changes in ideas and values lead not only to new conceptions but ultimately to new beliefs about appropriate experts and decision-making procedures.
- a process of paradigm transformation can begin with changes in agential and institutional arrangements. New types of experts brought in redefine and reframe problems and their solutions.
- Institutional and cultural changes provide a climate for new ideas and norms to emerge and develop.

PPP theory explains paradigm shifts as a function of value or interest conditions, conceptual conditions, and power conditions and processes. Major types of potential interests and values are indicated in Table 15.1.

Figure 15.1. Simplified Model of Paradigm Shifts

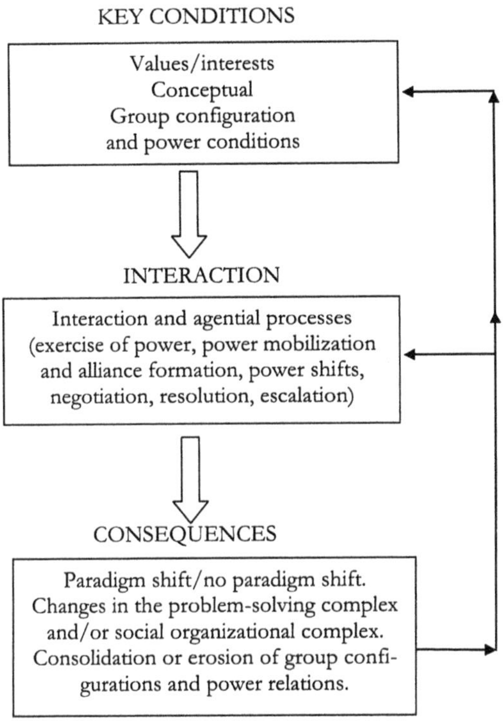

It is not enough that policies fail, or a substantial change in the value and normative context occurs, or even opportunities arise for power gains through advancing a new, competing paradigm. There must be actors or potential actors available who have power, or the capacity to mobilize power, to bring about a paradigm transformation. In our EU research, the policy situations investigated involved agents who had or acquired the power(s) – that is, they were able to mobilize sufficient power – to make a difference; at the same time that they were activated to respond to the problem or issue situations.

Table 15.1. Major Potential Drivers: Relevant Values and Interests Activating key groups and their constituencies in the studies presented here

MAJOR DRIVERS	CASES
Problem-solving crisis for responsible or concerned agents. Emergent problems or issues threaten values, interests; institutions; authority and status of key groups or their constituencies.	Food, asbestos, chemicals, climate change
Normative gap or failure. Established conditions and practices contradict in a clear-cut way established laws or societal norms, calling for corrective action (although strictly speaking there may be "no policy operating").	Gas, gender
Shift in the larger value and normative context which leads key groups to make changes in a paradigm.	Jensen, chemicals, gender
Power Interest. Opportunities for political, administrative, or economic gains by advancing a new or alternative paradigm.	EU entrepreneurship in all cases

As indicated below, there are several types of power factors related to paradigm shifts: domination structures involving agents who have learned or been persuaded about the need for an alternative paradigm; mobilization that bring about shifts in power; configurations of power relationships including concentrated power (autocracy), minimally dispersed power (oligarchy), or widely dispersed power (polyarchy). Power concerns in our studies here the capacities to restructure systems of thought, interaction, and social structure, namely what we refer to as meta-power (McGinty et al., 2009). One of the principal and general mechanisms occurs whenever a dominant agent is in a position of meta-power to initiate paradigm and related social transformations.[1]

Table 15.2. Power Structures in Paradigm Developments

Power Structures	Mechanisms	Cases
	ESTABLISHED POWER STRUCTURES	
Autocracy	A dominant agent enjoys a dominant position in the policy domain and uses her position to make substantial paradigm changes, to exercise meta-power.	EU Commission in the Food and gas cases

[1] Meta-power is linked to notions of restructuring and transformation, e.g. paradigm shift. The exercise of meta-power entails attempts to structure or re-structure the social and cultural matrix – within which interpersonal power activities and collective enterprises – are played out. This process we call meta-power, the capacity to construct the conditions, rules, and institutional formations under which individual and collective actors mobilize and apply resources to accomplish their intentions. Thus, the meta-power conceptualization breaks with past understandings of power and control by considering power over social structures across time and space.

Oligarchy	Multi-lateral negotiations and/or collective decision procedures (including voting) about paradigm shift	Coleman et al, EU REACH, and Gender mainstreaming cases. Many EU cases are of this character. Entrepreneurial agents push and struggle for a "necessary" new paradigm to deal with a complex of problems and anomalies, but must engage in multiple negotiations, bilateral as well as multilateral
Polyarchy	Multi-lateral negotiations and/or collective decision voting procedure (including voting arrangements).	Paradigm shift realized through following a legitimizing procedure, e.g., voting.
Exogenous power: structural and/or agential forces which directs or determines changes in paradigm components		For example, varieties of Neo-colonial processes
DYNAMICS OF POWER STRUCTURES		
Power Shift: a process (peaceful, possibly democratic, or violent such as a coup d'etait or revolution) which brings to power an agent or alliance with a substantially different paradigm conception or receptivity	A new agent comes to power with a new paradigm, or is receptive to the changing value/normative context and/or changes in the methodological /technological context or, possibly, organizing/management contest. The new power perceives opportunity to gain in power and status, by rejecting the established paradigm and replacing it with a new one.	Hall's study (the election that brought Thatcher to power). Also, the case of asbestos policy in the EU where Member States opposing a ban changed their position. There was sufficient support to tip EU policy toward effective banning of asbestos.
Power mobilization (this often is associated with a power shift) but need not result in such a shift. Here agents – possibly as the opposition in REACH – mobilize supporters and power resources to reinforce (or oppose) an existing policy or policy proposal	Mobilization may go on inside or outside the policy system, or both Mobilization results in a clear "tipping" from one position to a completely different one, as in the asbestos case. Or, in the case of REACH, the process ended initially in a stalemate. The Finnish EU president intervened in Autumn, 2006, and found a tipping point and REACH became law by consensus. The mobilization went on outside and inside of the EU – International government organizations (UN) and NGOs	REACH. Gender Mainstreaming

Power disintegrates or collapses	De-mobilization of power, for instance, the Center collapse, as in power shifts that favor decentralized entities. Or there is material (or economic) collapse to that the established paradigm framework cannot be maintained or reproduced.	For example, some failed states.
Polyarchy Dynamics	Diffusion through networks of more or less autonomous agents with no organized procedure (or a general refusal to activate or utilize). But the multiple micro-decisions have macro effects.	New ideas, techniques, technologies, management strategies spread among the more or less autonomous but interconnected agents.

4.1 Discussion

Conditions of Paradigm Shifts:

(1) **Policy failures, anomalies**. A "paradigm crisis" arises when policy failings occur and accumulate, or cognitive and control problems emerge (policies and programs lead to unacceptable or negative unintended consequences), and the status and authority of the original policy paradigm is undermined. The negative judgments may be those of key authorities or experts associated with the established paradigm – or, more often, challengers to the authority and expertise of the established groups.

(2) **Emergence of new ideological ideas**, a change in the normative context. Initiatives to change paradigm in such a way that a restructured paradigm is perceived or judged to fit better or to be more compatible with global values and norms. Those responsible and/or experts are driven to adopt these ideas and values – or are pressured by their constituencies or the general public. These generalized norms may concern gender equality, security, health, etc.

(3) **Power gain**. Power agents propose (or adopt) a new paradigm as a way of enhancing their power and/or undermining the power of those associated with the established paradigm. There may be no anomalies or performance failings of the established paradigm.

(4) **Competition**. Political or group competition may pressure a group to differentiate themselves from others. Interest in differentiating "them" from "us" results from agential processes in a group configuration or network.

(5) **Breaking of Solidarity**. A key shift in a paradigm, such as a transformation of dominant values (e.g. increased value placed on the environment or social welfare (or on the market) in conjunction with an economic crisis (and relative decrease in government revenues, or increases in the cost of fuel) may contribute to conflicts and the breakdown of an existing coalition, e.g. in an oligarchy or a majority within a polyarchy. For instance, this has happened in

the case of social welfare coalitions; or, environmental groups that were integrated earlier.[2]

(6) **Problematic change in practice**. Paradigm shifts result more from changes in institutional practices. The Marxian conception of the "contradiction" between institutional arrangements/cognitive-normative components ("the relations of production"), on the one hand, and new knowledge, new technologies, new practices ("the forces of production") sets the stage for "revolution" (of course, there are other possibilities, such as suppression of "forces of production").

(7) **Failure of Change Efforts**. The failure of mass mobilization to bring about a paradigm shift when structural conditions (problem situation or crisis) seem otherwise ripe may be accounted for by the absence of a resonant paradigm and/or insufficient power to overcome a dominant regime.

Below a few selected paradigm shift mechanisms are examined in more detail.

(I) **Autocracy with learning or imitation**. The agent in a position of substantial if not monopoly power able to initiate a new paradigm in order to deal with policy failures, problem-situations, anomalies, or threats to regime power.

Changes in the perspective of an authoritative agent, administrative or political, who, for instance, adopts a new paradigm in response to a crisis (food) or a normative gap according to EU principles (gas or asbestos). Of course there may be actors involved with some influence who "resist" or "countervail", the "exogenous" initiative as the long drawn-out (affecting) resistance within the EU to an asbestos ban.

Power, knowledge, interest, and values are key ingredients in institutional transformation. The power of elites to mobilize resources, such as wealth, legislative authority, and various – positive and negative – sanctions, to affect institutional arrangements, is of critical importance to their potential as institutional innovators. But emerging movements may also manage to mobilize sufficient power resources with which to challenge status quo-defending established elites, and to force or negotiate institutional change. The conflict between the establishment and challenging movements is the second most important factor in institutional dynamics. This conflict is fueled by actors' material and ideal interests, as well as a stake in a particular paradigm which they associate with "right and proper" institutional arrangements (for different patterns of agent-driven institutional innovation, see Burns and Carson, 2002; Burns and Dietz, 2001; Stinchcombe, 1968).

Prioritizing public health and consumer protection over market principles illustrates nicely one paradigm shift in the case of the EU food crisis (Chapter 8). Nu-

[2] The conditions and limits of change are of concern here. "Dissonance reduction mechanisms" plaz a role in overcoming anomalies, dissonance, and the like, thereby stabilizing a paradigm (as the professional paradigms investigated by Machado). There are also limits to such stabilizing mechanisms, as shown empirically by Machado (1998) and Machado and Burns (1998).

merous "risks" and "technical" problems emerged during the deregulation associated with the establishment of the internal market in food and agricultural products. These necessitated the development of a number of new regulations at the European level – ironically, under the guidance of the "free market" paradigm that calls for the removal of regulatory obstacles to trade. However, the new regulations remained ineffective and significant food-related crises developed – the best known among these being "mad cow disease" or BSE. As a result, the European Commission itself adopted a new paradigm – new by virtue of a reordering of guiding principles. It not only placed public health and consumer protection above free market deregulatory principles, but used this new principle to protect the hitherto progress in establishing the internal market in food. The new priorities/values have been steadily institutionalized in the subsequent regulatory actions with regard to food. The best example is the Commission's response to discovery of dioxin contamination of Belgian poultry, followed by an immediate ban on exports. This reaction contrasted with the early treatment of the BSE case in which the Commission sided initially with the British government. Strong movement is now visible toward the institutionalization of the new principles: the Commission has been re-organized, while primary responsibility/authority for dealing with food policy has been moved from the directorates dealing with agriculture and markets to a new directorate, Health and Consumer Protection. The proposed European Food Authority represents a further institutional expression of the new paradigm and its principles and values. Food policy in Europe is no longer seen only/primarily as a commodity or market issue.

(II) Power shift involving paradigm shift. Here one focuses on power shifts that bring to a position of meta-power an agent with a new or alternative paradigm (possibly entails exogenous actors or possibly an alliance of some insiders and outsiders). Replacing an earlier elite to institutionalize the new paradigm may occur relying on force, as in coup d'etat or violent revolution, through democratic process, such as elections or nominations, societal negotiation, or generational/cohort shift. A new group or coalition with a new paradigm or model of institutional arrangements appears on the scene and assumes a position of power, enabling it to bring about a substantial shift in the institutional paradigm and arrangements. This may be, but is not necessarily, preceded by a breakdown in consensus among established power elites about the appropriate paradigm or about reform of the existing paradigm. However, a breakdown in consensus facilitates a coalition between parts of the elites and the contender groups which refuse to defer to the established authority or to adhere to the established rule regime and its organizing principles and norms. Such new, emerging coalitions were apparent in the case of "peaceful" revolutions in, for example, Poland or Hungary, in 1989, which involved negotiated settlements and elections. In Poland the negotiated elections brought unexpected victory to groups advancing liberal market and political paradigms.

Coleman et al (Chapter 6) point out: "In Hall's trajectory, paradigm change is convulsive, involving national political conflict, often of a partisan sort, and drawing large parts of the population into the debate. In the second trajectory... fundamental change comes more slowly, conserves political stability and comes through the effective functioning of existing institutions. It also engages the whole citizenry less."

(III) Negotiated order as a paradigm shift. Under conditions of oligarchy or polyarchy agents may struggle among themselves not only for power but in the name of particular paradigms. Under regulated conditions, they engage in multilateral negotiation and, when successful, accomplish a "negotiated order", namely a new but compromised PPP. Our EU case of REACH serves as a good example of this. Coleman et a (1977:298) report about their research: "Following Risse-Kappen and Scharpf, we demonstrated that corporatist policy networks lend themselves to the cumulative, negotiated, problem-solving trajectory to paradigm change whereas state-directed or pressure group pluralist networks are more likely to be associated with crisis-driven changes... the corporatist network provided significant incentives to producers to channel their feedback through existing groups. In contrast, in Canada, the pluralist arrangements have left the field open to the creation of new ad hoc groups and provide fewer disincentives to direct political action by producers."

In general, the institutional context of policy processes is a major factor. Incremental, multi-lateral negotiated shifts versus change when one group simply replaces another. Or a dominant agent undergoes a profound change in beliefs and/or values ("political conversion"). Stinchcombe (1995) stressed the structural factors (the positions of actors in social structures) which enabled them to initiate development of new organizational arrangements within existing social structures.

(IV) Unintended, Piecemeal Development of a New Institutional Paradigm. Some paradigm shifts are un-intentional. That is, actors who introduce and develop a new paradigm often do not intend to do so, but instead drift into what turns into an unexpected and unintended paradigm shift. A new technology or technique, new institutional positions or member competencies/commitments which seem to lead to relatively minor changes in the institutional procedures and rules may in the long run actually cause problems which cannot be effectively analyzed and dealt with within the framework of the established paradigm – a reason to consider new rules and approaches. Failures and anomalies may continue to occur and to accumulate, forcing a growing awareness of the general problem and a critical judgment of the old paradigm. Receptivity to alternative paradigms – or, at least, to the abstract notion of a possible alternative – increases. On the basis of critical discussions and subsequent social learning, the stage is set for a paradigm shift – for innovation and transformation of the institutional arrangements.

More generally, cultural change, associated with an eventual paradigm shift, may occur in the most subtle and incremental ways. An institutional order may erode as a result of actors introducing in an ad hoc manner alien rules into the domain. For example, market concepts and conduct rules such as profit seeking may be applied to such domains as the family, community, or health care system, and result in the attenuation of the earlier organizing principles such as solidarity and justice – in turn leading to the disappearance of entire established patterns of activity and their replacement by new ones. These changes take place through diffusion of a norm, idea, technique or strategy. Power to introduce change is diffused or decentralized structures such as a market or network. There is no single agent or alliance.

Negative or Blocked Cases

PPP theory enables us to analyze and explain "negative cases," that is instances where there appear to be good reasons or opportunities to bring about a paradigm change, but no such change takes place.

Here we refer to on cases where attempts at a shift in paradigms fails or is blocked.

(1) Those in a position of autocratic power are committed to the established paradigm and oppose any initiatives at change. Moreover, there are no sufficiently powerful actors to challenge them. That is, monopoly of power is combined with commitment to the established paradigm and/or lack of any interest in an alternative paradigm. This would apply as well to oligarchic arrangements.

(2) An agent in a position of autocratic power has no interest or competence to make public policy more reflective or fitting in terms of a larger normative and value context. The encompassing context is viewed as irrelevant or as potentially a source of risky values or ideas that would threaten her domination.

(3) Or the dominant agent(s) have no perception or interest in making a paradigm shift in order to gain in power and status. This may be a result of risk aversion.

(4) An oligarchy with consensus is likely to operate like the autocrat, blocking efforts to launch a new paradigm.

(5) Power distributed in an oligarchy may enable a blocking of a paradigm shift – under conditions there is no effective procedure of mediation. REACH could possibly have ended up in this state, but the EU President (of Finland) intervened effectively to settle the differences and to produce a new paradigm.

(6) Limitations of unorganized, undirected networks in an extensive network of more or less autonomous agents – without a collective decision procedure. A paradigm requiring collective choice and/or collective implementation cannot be accomplished, thus effectively blocking the emergence of a collective operative paradigm. Of course, local solutions can be effectively pursued.

Stabilization of Paradigms

In our perspective, where conceptions, values, group and power configuration are potentially always in a state of flux, paradigm instability would be expected to be commonplace. However, a number of factors contribute to the stabilization of paradigms (and inertia in change). In the previous section, several power factors were identified which block change or erosion in an established paradigm: autocratic power, institutionalization of a paradigm, lack of alternative paradigms and/or powerful agents.

Thus, those conditions and processes which stabilize a paradigm, among other things, "protect" it from change initiatives. The general principles are:

- Institutionalization is a powerful stabilizing factor, particularly if its mechanisms of regulation and sanction minimize deviance (and, of course, innovation as a form of deviance).
- Autocratic power (or oligarchic power with consensus) can maintain and reproduce an established paradigm, even in the face of performance failings as long as the failings do not undermine the power of the autocrat (or the oligarchy).[3]
- There is no competing power and/or competing paradigm.
- There are minimal opportunities (or none at all) for power and status gains by switching paradigms or the dominant agent is risk adverse.
- More generally, the established paradigm is accepted and/or supported by powerful agents or alliances (under autocratic, oligarchic, even polyarchy with established voting procedures that provide majority rule). For instance, the established paradigm deals with key problem situations and issues (that is, the paradigm is a powerful one).
- Established policy orientation and organization fits larger power structures.
- No external power is available or interested.
- There is no effective power or movement for a power shift. Either there is indifference or acceptance of existing domination structures.
- Minimum level of paradigm coherence accomplished.

5. Stability and Change in the Paradigm World

5.1 Differentiating Between Paradigms: Incommensurability

The basic quality that differentiates competing public policy paradigms is their fundamentally different, incommensurable ways of seeing the world, and of identifying and ordering core principles upon which policy is formulated and decided. These include, for example, the relationship of individual to collective, how the "Us" and the "Them" of society are defined, and the consequent designation of appropriate roles and priority ordering of key institutions such as state, market, family, religion, and civil society. Because these core complexes are derived from divergent underlying assumptions about the nature of society, they are understood and evaluated in

[3] Even polyarchy with established voting procedure that provides majority rule can maintain a stable paradigm as long as the majority power is not eroded.

terms that are not completely translatable[4]. If it is the complex of core assumptions and priorities that defines a given paradigm, it is the "incommensurability" of the core complex with a competing paradigm that permits the two to be distinguished as qualitatively different from one another – as not mere variations on a theme, but fundamentally different themes.

These underlying assumptions are often taken for granted, and as a result, left largely invisible and unexamined. Charlesworth (1999) and Fraser (1989), for example, point to the kinds of taken-for-granted assumptions primarily related to gender roles, and these have often proven deeply enough embedded that they are exceedingly difficult to expose. Other examples of such presuppositions include the conception of human beings as 'rational self-interest maximizing individuals' or as basically "group-oriented creatures for whom rationality plays a limited role," or the belief that welfare is primarily an individual responsibility from one perspective, or a collective responsibility from another. Hall (1993:280) summarizes the consequences of this difference:

> *Paradigms are never fully commensurable in scientific or technical terms or social organizational terms. Because each paradigm contains its own account of how the world confronting policymakers operates and each account is different, it is often impossible for the advocates of different paradigms to agree on a common body of data against which a technical judgment in favor of one paradigm over another might be made, or on who should have responsibility and authority for policymaking, or which types of experts to engage in the policy preparations.*

Where dissimilar conceptions lead to the development of different kinds of data and indicators, the corresponding problem definitions, causal inferences, and assessments of success or failure will also tend to be dissimilar (Breslau, 1997; Innes, 1994). Even where the same data is used, the interpretation of the data is likely to be quite dissimilar – especially with regard to how to deal with gaps in knowledge[5], or which experts to use in analyzing and interpreting the data. These factors, in turn, tend to lead to dissimilar remedies for addressing a given set of social problems[6].

---

[4] There was a significant difference between the "hard" first version of Kuhn's conception of incommensurability and his "softer, gentler" later conceptualization he developed over time (Kuhn, 2000; Sankey, 1993). Where he appeared to initially suggest that one paradigm could not be grasped and comprehended from within another (Phillips, 1975), he modified his view over time to meaning that two paradigms could not be understood in the same terms: that one theory could not be translated into the other without the loss of essential elements.

[5] This is especially apparent in the case studies on food safety and asbestos regulation, and has also played an important role in establishing domestic violence as a problem at the national level.

[6] A good example of this the fight over health care reform in the United States during the early 1990s. Free market oriented actors argued that high prices were a result of the market distorting effects of government intervention and health insurance that "insulated" patients from the cost of care, advocating the development of individual medical savings accounts with which people in need of medical services could shop for the balance of cost and quality. Actors oriented toward health services as a fundamental right and human need argued that high prices for health services

In as much as different ways of seeing the world tend to emphasize or obscure different phenomena, *differing approaches to conceptually defining and responding to social problems will also emerge over time.* Differences in conceptualization focus attention on different qualities of an issue. They define different kinds of problems and legitimize different categories of actors to address them. The institutionalization of a paradigmatic shift entails differences in practice in fundamental areas, such as how decision-making power is organized, how and for what purposes markets are regulated, or how the public welfare is pursued; it also leads to a shifting of priority order among these areas. This may apply to competing paradigms operating within a given sphere of public policy where actors compete to prioritize the guiding principles of a particular institution in broader public policy. Such priority ordering of a common set of principles produces different outcomes over time, as with, for example, "free market" versus "social market" conceptions of how and for what purposes public policy regulating the economy should be structured.

There may be multiple paradigms that come into conflict where the actors within the institutions they guide compete for dominance and prioritization (as can be the case with for example, market, religion, and the state). Where such assumptions apply broadly to social institutions such as markets, governance, the state, religion, etc., they may represent oversimplifications, such as "political/state intervention in the market is bad" (or conversely, good), or may entail more nuanced and complex issues of balance between competing principles. It is this sort of prioritization and balancing act we are concerned with regarding EU policymaking both generally, and within the policy sectors being examined.

5.2 Different Paradigms: Motivating and Dividing Groups

There may be multiple policy paradigms addressed to a particular sphere of policy at any point in time, carried by groups of actors who may compete with one another in an effort to realize their particular ideals, values, interests, and goals. These actors possess relationships to power and relationships with one another. Moreover, a paradigm becomes "real" to the extent that the principles it contains are realized through the behavior of subscribing actors, and through the implementation of the kinds of policy measures it defines, the authorities it legitimizes, etc.

Based on these parameters, actors may choose to act (or not to act) on particular desires or wishes, and may choose to either follow or disregard particular rules or norms. Competition between actors contending for power rooted in paradigmatic ideals and ideas is played out through public discourses that carry with them

are instead a result of the incompatibility of health needs with price competition and free market transactions. They argued generally that prices and systemic capacity should be controlled in order that competition could take place around issues of quality, and recommended a system of national health insurance, rather than individual accounts, be implemented (Himmelstein and Woolhandler et al., 1989).

some need for internal, logical consistency[7]. Such discourses are typically aimed at focusing or redirecting attention, seeking to define certain problems into or out of existence, at offering a particular interpretation for the experience shared by members of various social groups, and at characterizing the various authorities and forms of institutional power as legitimate or not.

If, on the one hand, actors have a great investment in protecting the concrete institutional arrangements themselves, for reasons of power, security, predictability, and so on, rules are tightened, enforcement mechanisms are deployed, even strengthened (as in Michels' (1962) Iron Law of Oligarchy). The emphasis is on protecting ideas and principles that are already realized and institutionalized, and this may be done at considerable cost. If, on the other hand, actors have – or would like to make – a much greater investment in solving a problem(s) that the existing institutional arrangements and guiding paradigm have proven unable to manage, the actions taken are quite different. Rules are consciously broken in spite of possible or likely sanctions, supporters are rallied more around possibilities than certainties, and short-term, concrete interests may be set aside in favor of what are perceived to be long-term possibilities. There is a substantial shift in risk-taking orientations – or even what is defined as "risk".

5.3 Attracting a Following: Paradigms and Actors

It is not just any coherent system of ideas, beliefs, and definitions that attracts a significant following. The apparent potential to offer remedies to stubborn problems gives a paradigm relevance and salience to the important political/policy questions of the moment. In highlighting the sociological qualities of his concept, Kuhn fleshes out his characterizations of the scientific paradigm with the observation that it possesses two essential qualities: its conceptualization is "sufficiently unprecedented to attract an enduring group of adherents away from competing modes of scientific activity. Simultaneously, it was sufficiently open-ended to leave all sorts of problems for the redefined group of practitioners to resolve" (Kuhn, 1970:10). This, of course, is less a further elaboration of paradigmatic characteristics than it is a statement about what gives a paradigm weight and importance: believers. Notwithstanding the fundamental differences between science and policymaking, it suggests two vital qualities that draw actors to a particular policy paradigm. First, the conceptualization of how society should work and the courses of action it recommends (in a particular sphere, i.e., markets, welfare, governance, etc.) must be sufficiently plausible and compelling to attract adherents from other, competing paradigms. This requires at least some basis in empirical reality, although the standard for causal inferences in not that of science. Part of what makes it compelling is

[7] Neuman and Tabak (2003) point out that inconsistency is not a problem in itself, but may become a problem when attention is drawn to inconsistencies that are seen to have adverse consequences.

that it appears to more satisfactorily address urgent and currently irresolvable social problems.

Second, it must offer a *seemingly coherent approach* to the social phenomena to which it is addressed (designated as problems), rather than presenting a detailed prescription. This allows a certain "open-enderness", permitting the application of the paradigm to both a broad range of recognized social problems and those not yet defined. In a political context, a general approach instead of detailed prescription also makes it easier for actors who share core assumptions to join together around values and goals they support, and to overlook comparatively minor differences. Generality also presents a more diffuse target to opponents. A policy paradigm presents the possibility of an array of solutions to a variety of thorny problems, rather than being seen more narrowly as what could be argued as a specific solution to a specific problem.

What makes this open-endedness compelling is not certainty, but possibility and promise. In public policy, Keynesian style economic policies and market regulation were addressed to the failure of liberal market economies to self-regulate. The ascendancy of the neo-liberal, "free market" paradigm in North America and Europe in the 1980s and early 1990s gained its foothold in the stubborn economic and social problems that policies guided by the Keynesian model seemed unable to satisfactorily master (Hall, 1989). Within the EU, this general pattern was reflected in the development of the Single Market Program and a general shift toward deregulation. The general pattern is also apparent in historical terms specific to the EU. The dream of a federal Europe, or more generally, European integration, was conceptualized and presented as a general model for building relationships between states. It was believed that this web of relationships would preclude military conflict, in part by enhancing and regulating the economic exchange that was already expanding beyond the jurisdictional boundaries of individual nation-states.

Another important set of distinctions that can be made between scientific and public policy paradigms is in the nature of the contest between the agents who promote a particular paradigm, the means and standards by which a particular paradigm gains prominence, and the kinds of benefits that accrue to those whose paradigm prevails. These differences are particularly salient in the way in which resources are marshaled behind one or another paradigm, in claims-making activities, in efforts to establish or shore up legitimacy, and in the eventual fate of discarded paradigms. Nevertheless, struggles over scientific paradigms, ideas, and even facts have sometimes proven to be considerably less "scientific" than the front stage characterization would suggest. Collins (1999) makes this point in an examination of the debate regarding the existence of "gravity waves", which he demonstrates was won as much on the basis of rhetorical skill as the merits of scientific evidence. Potter (1996) emphasizes this phenomenon more generally in his discussion of "empiricist discourse", and the various ways in which scientists position themselves in relation to their arguments in order to establish the "facticity" of their scientific claims. Such struggles and tactics are quite apparent in the case studies presented in subsequent chapters.

While believers are important to the development and institutionalization of any paradigm, the process of institutionalization does not require all actors who press for the implementation of specific paradigmatic ideas to buy the whole package. Diverse actors may join together to press for particular policies while motivated by quite different goals or ideals (Sabatier and Jenkins-Smith, 1993). This may lead to unexpected coalitions or other configurations of actors – "strange bedfellows" – pressing for a given policy change, even while they continue to vehemently disagree in broader philosophical terms. Burns and Carson (2002), for example, note that paradigm replacement may be brought about via the replacement of elites with actors guided by ideals embodied in a new paradigm, or existing elites may adopt a new paradigm based on more instrumental motivations. They note that revolutionaries or reformers, once in power, may follow policies that are strikingly similar to those of their predecessors. In some of the former communist countries, a surprisingly stable group of elites presided over the transition to market economies. Risse and Sikkink (1999) arrive at similar conclusions in their examination of the leverage gained when human rights conventions are adopted. Some regimes, for example, have formally adopted human rights conventions in order to avoid international isolation. In seeking to give the appearance of complying, they may also set in motion a process of cognitive and institutional change that leads to substantively better compliance, even where that was not the initial intent. Carson et al (2001) has noted similar building of alliances in connection with EU policymaking in food and energy. One group may pursue a set of policies for instrumental reasons, while another may pursue the same policies in an effort to realize their ideal interests. These groups may or may not share the same long-term goals.

Such odd alliances are made possible in part by the fact that not all paradigmatic elements are equally important (Carson and Burns, 2002; Carson, 2001; Hall, 1993; Sabatier, 1993). Fellow travelers may follow a common path for a period even though they have very different or even contradictory "destinations" in mind – depending in part on their access to information, and their particular strategies, judgments, and misjudgments. Similarly, actors who share a particular destination in common may perceive entirely different paths in their respective efforts to get there.

5.4 The Process of a New Policy Paradigm Emerging, Gaining a Foothold, and Consolidating

The emergence of a new paradigm and its particular components can be traced over time using our standard regime categories or complexes. The discourses in these categories define concrete characteristics of the three dimensions elaborated above. Taken as a whole, these categories define a policy paradigm regime – a particular socio-cognitive order that when implemented, guides interaction and problem-solving activities (with respect to the case studies, this operates within the policy sector). A conceptual model of the problems that require attention and remedial action is constructed in the interplay between the ways in which the related issues/problems (problem/issue complex), legitimate authorities (responsibility/authority complex), and expertise (expert complex) are defined, and from which a general set of problem solving approaches (solution complex) and concrete policy goals can be developed. *Changes in the general and specific policy goals developed from this process are what Hall (1993) defines as constituting third order change.* But it is this overall "package" that constitutes the policy paradigm. These complexes are outlined in Table 15.3 below.

Table 15.3. Emergence/Institutionalization of a New Policy Paradigm

		Paradigm A: Time period 1	**Paradigm A/b: Time period 2**	**Paradigm B/a: Time period 3**
	Problem / issue complex	Type A problems/issues readily recognized and responded to by designated responsible actors. Type B problems/ issues are mostly "invisible" to the system, and not a "public" concern in the EU context.	Type B issues become visible in context of established EU goals and priorities. Partial conceptualization of Type B problems/issues, making them peripheral EU issue.	Type B problems/issues conceptualized as concerns fundamentally related to established EU goals and priorities, and possibly an obstacle to achieving them. Type B problems/issues defined as core EU concern and policy priority.
SOCIAL ORGANIZATIONAL COMPLEX	**Responsibility/authority Complex**	EU without authority (competence) or responsibility to take up Type B issues. Responsibility for managing B (to the extent it is recognized at all) lies elsewhere, perhaps at the national level, or may be "private" issue.	Partial responsibility for Type B issues because of relationship to EU integration goals and Type A goals, but formal authority absent or limited. Type B problems addressed by actors responsible for achieving Type A goals on ad hoc basis.	Solid EU authority and responsibility. Type B problems/issues addressed by actors charged with Type B responsibilities and goals. Pursuit of Type A goals limited to parameters established by Type B goals.

	Expert complex	Available experts well-versed in type A problems/issues Type B expertise outside EU and generally not available.	Recruitment of expertise to the EU through NGOs, through other affected or interested groups, or international bodies. Some expertise may exist within EU administration itself. Some engagement in identifying and defining type B concerns via "soft" approaches.	Agency or institute created at EU level to coordinate and develop Type B information and expertise, and to interpret its meaning with respect to established EU priorities. Scientific committees organized to develop or relay data and provide consultation.
	Conceptualization or model of issue	Elaborated Paradigm A. Causal patterns and relationships of Type A concerns to other EU goals clearly conceptualized and formulated. Little or no structured conceptualization of Type B concerns in terms of a model, or as EU issue, with consideration of Type B concerns largely absent.	Partial EU conceptualization of Type B causality patterns (with key elements provided by "third parties"), formulated mostly in relation to disturbance Type B problems cause for type A goals. Emerging conceptualization supported with evidence provided by "third party" actors who frame Type B issues in terms of concerns and goals derived from Paradigm A.	Elaborated conceptualization of Paradigm B, highlighting issues, problems, causality patterns and processes. Formulated in terms of Type B problems/issues as core focus. Type A model reformulated in terms of dependent relationships to type B processes. Experts engaged to further develop model of type B issues and relationships to type A goals and issues.
PROBLEM-SOLVING COMPLEX	Solution complex	EU solution neither necessary nor desirable because the phenomenon "invisible" from EU perspective, or because lack of EU competence means no EU solutions are available.	"Soft" solutions possible. "Hard" solutions may be situationally possible if there is unanimity, consensus. "Creative" interpretation of Type B problems may permit use of "hard" measures.	"Hard" solutions in the form of directives, establishment of regulatory agency (agencies) organized on logic of paradigm B, with clear goals and responsibilities, more systematic, comprehensive use of "soft" solutions.
Concrete policy goals & focus of attention		Type A goals clearly conceptualized and formulated. No EU goals related to problem/issue B.	Concrete goals defined by A pursued with some consideration for type B concerns.	Concrete Type B goals as priority focus, setting boundaries on Type A goals.

The discursive categories are intended to be generally applicable to policymaking, but the categorical descriptions in Table 15.3 are outlined with the EU policy process in mind. Also with EU policymaking and the sectors taken up in the case studies in mind, "Paradigm A" should be read as the institutionalized "market" paradigm, while "Paradigm B" should be read as representing the challenger, the "social" paradigm, in each of the cases. Paradigm A/b represents the market paradigm with social concerns managed as an adjunct within that paradigm, while Paradigm B/a represents the social paradigm, with market goals maintained, but placed in a position of serving social goals. In each of these competing paradigms, principles can be identified that tend to validate the claims and interests of one set of actors over another, that tend to legitimize the participation of certain groups more than others, and that tend to define certain kinds of problems as properly EU issues, and others as outside of its competence. These principles are systematically related to one another, and can be identified in the two distinct paradigms.

As noted earlier, a new paradigm does not emerge into open, uncontested conceptual or institutional terrain – actors must typically struggle for that space. When new issues first emerge into view, or are successfully brought into view by actors' formulation of claims, the initial responses are likely to include denial or refusal to acknowledge the issue as a "problem".

This is especially true if the claims-makers are "third parties" or "outsiders", external to the already institutionalized and recognized complex of responsible authorities or experts – although "insiders" may experience similar problems. The "issue" is more likely to be acknowledged as a problem to the extent that it can be seen to have undesirable consequences for the institutionalized order. Even if recognition grants some status to both claims-makers and the designation of the issue(s) as a "problem", *initial efforts to resolve or manage the problem are likely to be pursued from within the conceptual framework of the institutionalized paradigm*. Such approaches and strategies would fall within the middle column (Paradigm A/b). This may fail to produce satisfactory results, either because the nature of the problem is poorly understood within the framework of the institutionalized paradigm, or because causal processes connected with the issue are difficult to correctly conceptualize.

The key elements involved in the process of challenge and change are located in Paradigm A/b, Time Period 2. Some of the key developments in this process include the emergence of anomalies, or unanticipated issues that are successfully defined as problems. In an effort to manage them, authorities make adjustments to the institutionalized model in various places. If the problems connected with "Type B" issues appear to be resolved or under control, the adjustments may bring stability, and therefore not pose a fundamental challenge to the paradigmatic model. To the extent that the problem persists and creates disturbances, authorities may feel compelled to make other peripheral adjustments (in addition to acknowledging the issue as a problem). This may include accepting the expertise of outsiders as claims-makers (or policy entrepreneurs supporting their claims) as legitimate and engaging new kinds of expertise, assigning currently responsible actors with limited authority to manage the problem, and accepting or developing new kinds of indicators and knowledge in hopes of putting the issue to rest.

This is most likely to occur where ideal and material interests of members of the dominant group come into conflict, creating opportunities for observant, entrepreneurial actors to enter the discussion and tip the balance in one direction or another. In and of themselves, none of these adjustments constitutes fundamental change; rather, they represent the first or second order change referred to by Hall (1993). Taken together, however, they may eventually produce a profound reconceptualization of the problem/issue and associated patterns of causality that calls for a fundamentally different set of remedial approaches, strategies, and policy goals. One example of this is a situation where market intervention by public authorities appears necessary in order to prevent damaging effects of market failure from undermining the legitimacy of the paradigm and the elites who advocate it. However, the intervention itself, as a contravention of the model, tends to legitimize both further intervention and the actors who called for it. One typical way to seek to manage this problem is to characterize the problem as a "special case" or "aberration" – an exception to the rule that calls for unusual or unconventional measures[8]. Under certain circumstances, such processes may introduce greater incoherence into the paradigm, which in the face a crisis or persistent, unresolvable problems, may contribute to the replacement of the paradigm. Such replacement may come as governing elites embrace the new paradigm or – elites and paradigm may be replaced at the same time (Burns and Carson, 2002). This level of reconceptualization entails a reconfiguration of the core from which the solution complex and concrete policy goals are derived – the designation of new authorities, responsibilities, and expertise, but in a dominant, primary role rather than the secondary role through which they were first accepted into the social order.

The definition of new European level problems has generated opportunities for paradigm change supporting further European integration. This is especially true where problems are constructed in ways that present credible European-level solutions. Paradigm change is problem focused, with "problems" defined in terms of policy failures. These may be specified in terms of either policy failures or market failures – terms which tend to assign responsibility for the cause of the problem. In the end, they are simply different types of policy failure. Crisis can be considered a particularly acute type of policy failure that to a greater or lesser extent threatens the existing order (Fligstein, 2001a; Legro, 2000), opening greater possibilities for actors supporting an alternative paradigm to press for reforms. Crisis focuses attention on a specific issue – or represents widespread consensus that a specific issue is an important problem – although its source may continue to be a matter of intense dispute.

What has just been described here is a complex process of development that entails feedback loops between the complexes and at every level, suggesting that paradigm change may be the result of an untold number of incremental decisions, although some of these decisions may have large consequences. The difficulty that

[8] The case of asbestos, for example, was characterized as having little relation to chemicals or chemicals policy by industry representatives and others.

emerges is assessing just when it is possible to determine that the established paradigm has been replaced by its challenger. Hall's (1993) strategy to this problem is to identify a paradigmatic shift by mapping the institutional changes as they are implemented in accordance with the new model. He follows this pattern in his characterization of orders of change; the paradigm shift is apparent as the apparatus of governing institutions is redirected and brought to bear to achieve qualitatively different goals than previously. Following this logic, Hall (1993) traces the series of incremental policy adjustments that eventually culminated in a fundamental shift in British monetary policy, with the conclusion that the policy shift in Britain from a Keynesian approach to monetarism was goal driven on the part of some key actors (the Tories), and an unintended consequence of paradigmatic adjustments carried out by others (the British Labour Party). However, the conceptual shift is inferred primarily from the institutional shift, and therefore can be identified in only retrospects. This is the way in which the concept of paradigm shift has generally been employed.

The argument we make here, however, is that the paradigmatic blueprint and operational or institutional shifts are analytically distinct, and at least sometimes empirically distinct, meaning that the shift past the respective thresholds may occur at separate points in time, and that these separate turning points can often be identified in discourses. Paradigmatic and institutional change are likely to be empirically distinct where there is lag time between purely cognitive and/or normative change and organizational policy change. This is especially so where routines are deeply embedded and interests deeply entrenched, making the adoption of policies following the new logic an incremental process. It is likely to be more difficult to make a clear empirical distinction in cases where dramatic events or crises result in an immediate and radical reversal of policy[9]. However, even in such cases, it is likely that the some claims-makers' discourses can be found which suggest a prior recognition and understanding of what led to the crisis, but which in retrospect were given insufficient attention.

The elements outlined in Table 15.3 combine to define the separate dimensions of policy substance, forms of participation, and level of governance specified in section C. The authority complex, for example, defines the authorities responsible for dealing with a given issue/problem, including whether they operate at the local, national, or supranational level. The issue/problem complex may likewise be defined in terms that identify the nature of the problem and the level at which it is relevant (i.e. whether it is defined in terms of market or social concerns, and whether the issue should be considered "national" or "European").

Any of the dimensions of substance, forms of participation, or level of governance, can constitute the core of the paradigm, and therefore function as its center of gravity. Actors guided by a paradigm that primarily emphasizes policy substance

[9] Such as with the September 11, 2001 bombing of the World Trade Center.

over other considerations, for example, are more likely to seek out the level of governance and type of policymaking arena in which they believe they are most likely to prevail. A paradigm strongly defined by nationalism, on the other hand, would emphasize maintaining authority at the national level and seek to define and deal with most problems within national boundaries. Actors guided by a paradigm that stresses European integration as a core priority would tend to emphasize defining problems in European terms and seek to expand policymaking at that level. As noted earlier (by Hix, 1999a; Pollack, 1998a), the core complex is in practice likely to entail multiple priorities, with some elements comprising the core and tending to systematically take precedence over others. In addition, groups guided by different paradigms may press for a given policy for divergent reasons, such as the alliance (whether formal or informal) of neo-liberals and nationalists that Streek (1995) identifies as allies in seeking to Europeanize authority in the economic sphere while maintaining most authority for social policy at the national level.

New actor alliances may form around predominantly either ideal interests or predominantly material interests, or some combination of the two. Where such alliances shift the overall balance of power relationships connected to a particular sector or policy area, they may influence policy stability or change.

6. "Profound" Changes versus "Peripheral" Changes

6.1 Context Dependent Prioritization of Paradigm Components

As has been noted earlier, a vitally important aspect of the policy paradigm is that not all the rules and relationships defined by these complexes are equally important (Burns and Carson, 2002; Carson, 2001; Surel, 2000; Hall, 1993; Sabatier and Jenkins-Smith, 1993). A complex of fundamental assumptions, principles, values, and priorities distinguishes one public policy paradigm from another; it is the "incommensurability" (see Kuhn, 2000; 1970) of the complex of core elements that differentiates one paradigm from another (Burns & Carson, 2002; Carson, 2001). The practices, procedures, and forms of accounting or measurement they define constitute the secondary, or peripheral characteristics that distinguish variations of a given paradigm – and as Kuhn observed, *may even be shared with a competing paradigm*. But they are not necessarily innocuous, since secondary practices and characteristics that are incompatible with the core paradigmatic principles may generate tensions that raise questions about the paradigm's validity as a model of reality and its legitimacy for guiding policymaking. Where a neo-liberal free market paradigm, for example, defines markets as essentially self-regulating, government intervention in some area outside the accepted core area such as establishing property rights (see Campbell and Lindberg, 1990) or rules of exchange represents a diversion from the model. When obvious market failures prompt such intervention, the intervention may be characterized as an exceptional case in an effort to facilitate the disappearance from view of both the problem and the corrective response that, theoretically speaking, should not have been necessary. However, where a particular type of market failure occurs repeatedly, it opens opportunities to challenge the soundness of the paradigm itself, while the interventions that are undertaken to address the problem tend to legitimize challengers. Where such problems are persistent and therefore difficult to continue to characterize as exceptional, the question then becomes whether the (market or policy) failure itself is considered more problematic for maintaining the paradigm, or whether the de-legitimizing effects of the repeated corrective measure are. Actors who share a common core of assumptions and beliefs may differ in their assessment of how to best minimize the long-term harm to the policy paradigm they support.

Peter Hall's (1993) work explores these distinctions of core and secondary elements in terms of first, second, and third order change. It is here he draws his most direct parallels with Kuhn. Hall's three orders correspond with: 1) policy adjustments or calibrations, or the specific, often technical details of policy; 2) policy instruments, or the general types of laws and programs that are employed in efforts to address problems and meet goals; and 3) policy goals, or the broad purposes that a given class of policies is intended to serve. First order change is likely to be ongoing, incremental and often routine – "normal" policymaking. Second order change represents increasingly "strategic action" in developing policy, but does not directly challenge the fundamental goals of policy, and is therefore less likely to be conflict ridden. Third order change is quite the reverse: it is likely to entail different types of process, struggles for power, authority, and legitimacy, and marked changes in the discourses that describe what needs to be done. Hall summarizes what is at stake in third order change with what is perhaps his most profound insight:

> *The movement from one paradigm to another will ultimately entail a set of judgments that is more political in tone, and the outcome will depenbroader institutional framework… Faced with conflicting opinions from the experts, politicians will have to decide whom to regard as authoritative, especially on matters of technical complexity, and the policy community will engage in a contest for authority over the issues at hand (Hall, 1993:279).*

Hall's formulation is developed from his empirical observations of the evolutionary changes that led first to the gradual adoption, then to the erosion and eventual replacement of Keynesian regulation in economic policy (see Hall, 1989, 1992). Teresa Rees (1998) applies a similar set of distinctions in her examination of the development of gender equality policy in the European Union. Rees refers to the levels of change as "tinkering", "tailoring", and "transforming", reflecting her more descriptive than theoretical purposes. Rees (1998:26-48) examines three types of EU equal opportunities policies (anti-discrimination, positive action/positive discrimination, mainstreaming) based on the level at which they demand adjustment from the currently institutionalized arrangements. Anti-discrimination measures seek to remove specific barriers to women's participation within a larger set of institutional arrangements whose fundamental assumptions are taken for granted (and therefore remain unchallenged). Positive action measures, recognizing that "equal treatment" may simply freeze existing inequalities in place, seek to apply temporary measures to establish a new, more desirable equilibrium, but fundamental assumptions again remain unchallenged. Mainstreaming is seen as a strategy for systematically examining, challenging, and potentially transforming, the underlying assumptions and core goals of the particular institutional arrangements in question from a gendered perspective.

Paul Sabatier & Hank Jenkins-Smith (1993) also outline a set of distinctions between levels, but from a somewhat different perspective[10]. Rather than focus on the institutions that are targeted for reforms, they distinguish between fundamental and secondary elements of the belief systems that guide "advocacy coalitions". The most important aspect of this distinction in their analysis is that diverse organizational and individual actors may support specific policy measures for fundamentally different reasons. Examples of this are apparent in the way in which the British Labor government adopted Tory recommendations that contributed to the dismantling of Keynesian economic policies and their replacement with monetarist policies. Labor Party leaders were looking for a means to protect what they had built, while Conservatives were seeking to get their foot in the door and implement policies consistent with their more free market oriented policy views (Hall, 1992). Each of the case studies examining policy change in this dissertation include this "strange bedfellows" phenomenon in which some organized interests that generally disagree with one another may support a given policy proposal for reasons which at least superficially, seem incompatible. Thus public health NGOs might support strict regulations on asbestos to further their public goals, while free market oriented asbestos producers might support the same regulations as a way of mitigating problems that could precipitate more stringent regulations (such as a ban, for example). Examples of the reverse of these sorts of seemingly improbably alliances are also readily available, such as when organizational actors who share a common core set of beliefs split over disagreements about how best to realize those beliefs. This can be illustrated with Swedish political parties' positions during the referendum on the European Monetary Union (EMU). Social Democrats and Moderates often found themselves campaigning side by side *for* the proposal, even though their policy goals and reasons for supporting the EMU are substantively different overall. On the other hand, the Social Democrats (and other parties) were deeply split on the EMU issue, even while sharing a common set of core values and policy goals.

Surel (2000) notes the strong similarity between the paradigmatic orders identified by Hall (1993) and the levels of importance within the belief system model

[10] Sabatier and Jenkins-Smith develop a similar conceptual structure, but they discount institutions generally, relegating them to the status of "background conditions". This poses two significant problems for analysis of EU policymaking: First, there is form and structure to the "background conditions" that influences both how and where the efforts of actors pressing for change are most likely to bear fruit. Second, given that this governance structure has undergone periods of comparatively rapid change in the EU context, it cannot be taken as a constant.

outlined by Sabatier and Jenkins-Smith (1993). The levels do not correspond exactly, although each arrives at three different levels of importance. One reason they don't correspond precisely is Sabatier and Jenkins-Smith focus on the conceptual model, while Hall is analyzing the institutionalization of the new conceptual model as it takes place[11]. Burns and Carson (2002) make an analytical distinction between the policy paradigm, the model itself, the process of institutionalization, and its institutionalized form. The principles, goals and practices that constitute a paradigm can be mapped in terms of their transformation from the conceptual stage to being realized, and then institutionalized. Hall hints at this distinction in his discussion of competing models, one of which is replaced incrementally with the other, but for the most part, his focus lies in the transition, in the process of institutionalization itself.

The above distinctions – between defining and non-defining elements of a paradigm – come into play in the process of paradigmatic evolution/revolution and are important in three significant respects: 1) changes at the secondary, or more peripheral level tend to be less fraught with conflict and therefore more easily achieved, and 2) inconsistencies and incompatibilities between core and peripheral elements provide windows of opportunity for claims making activities, and 3) actors who fundamentally disagree at one level may support similar measures on the other (Sabatier and Jenkins-Smith, 1993). While the details of these particular groupings merit further exploration, it is the hierarchy of principles, or general core-periphery pattern, that is most relevant to the change processes investigated here. The process of institutionalization involves not only key events (staking out a new position or "anchoring" a new principle) but all the various forms of filling out that principle with supporting material – new laws and regulations, legal interpretations, compiling data, theorizing, mobilizing advocates and resources, and defending the reordered complex of core principles. "Tinkering and tailoring", while not directly challenging the fundamental assumptions and principles of the institutionalized model, may nevertheless serve to destabilize the existing institutionalized arrangements by generating incongruities and inconsistencies that highlight and legitimize new problems and shortcomings.

Hall would say a change in goals has major impact, more than a change in means. But we might argue rather that paradigm changes in experts considered appropriate have an enormous impact.

What changes would have less of an impact, e.g. the change in the agents of authority – for political reasons – who accept or follow the established paradigm typi-

[11] This distinction can be illustrated with Figure 15.1. Sabatier and Jenkins-Smith's "belief system" corresponds with the "paradigm" in the left upper portion of the diagram. Hall focuses on the point at which specific elements of the paradigm are formally adopted and institutionalized, becoming part of the "Institutional Rule System" in the upper right portion of the diagram. Since both are interested in significant policy change, it can be assumed that the paradigm is not the one upon which the currently institutionalized rule system is based.

cally would not lead to changes in the key components. But this is a highly contextualized characterization. A change in the political leadership does not necessarily lead to a major change in policy and institutional arrangements. The political leadership is dependent to a great extent on the administrative staff for articulating, organizing and implementing policy.

7. Concluding Remarks

Our theoretical work, which has been presented in this and earlier chapters, suggests several guiding principles and rules of thumb:

- Policy problem-solving shift and social organizational shift should be analytically distinguished, although they are typically closely interrelated.
- The problem-solving shift and the social organizational shift are part of an interactive, iterative process.
- Institutionalization of a policy problem-solving shift and/or a social organizational shift typically takes place over time. Even if a full complex of regime changes is adopted formalizing a new PP paradigm, real institutionalization requires further changes in organizational rules, reassignment and re-interpretation of key responsibilities, internalization of new standards, policy priorities, etc.

We have stressed the complex interplay between power and ideas. An autocratic actor or alliance may not only decides to transform (or, to the contrary, maintain) a policy paradigm – and may do so for a variety of reason(s). She might do this as a result of judging problem-solving (framing) and/or organizational failure in the policy sector. Or she experiences and adopts influencial changes in the larger value/normative context, that is the influence of the ideological and cultural context on policy thinking (as in Jenson's work). Finally, a dominant agent or a power mobilizing agent may judge opportunities to gain in power or status through rejecting the established paradigm and adopting a new one, although the established paradigm is relatively well-functioning.

The research has show some of the multiple paths and mechanisms whether paradigm shifts occur: (1) As autocratic actor or alliance decides to transform a policy paradigm for whatever reason(s); (2) There is a transformation of political conditions: power shifts (that brings to power carriers of a different paradigm); (3) New ideological and/causal ideas emerge which challenge key groups to reframe and restructure the established paradigm. (4) Power agents propose (or adopt) a new paradigm as a way of enhancing their power or legitimacy undermining the power of those associated with another paradigm, the established one or an alternative. That is, there may be no anomalies or failings of the established paradigm – and, indeed, it may be superior to the one peddled by the power seekers. (5) Paradigm change may be brought about by transformation of exogenous economic and other material conditions.

Further work on PPP theory will be necessary, among other questions:

- Where are the "tipping points" in each of the policy sectors we investigated? Our earlier argument is that we need to distinguish between conceptual or problem-solving tipping points that represent fundamental changes in understandings, definitions, and tools of analysis and organizational/structural tipping points, in which changed understandings are reinforced (or not) in formalized structures and decision-making procedures. These are inter-related, of course.
- PPPs are historic constructions, involving typically multiple agents and, therefore, **internal gaps, contradictions and incoherence are to be expected**. This explains the ineffectiveness and failure of many PPPs – although these faults may not be discovered for considerable periods of time. A type of "reality principle" eventually provides "tests" for the PPP. Our research on PPP shifts show changes in the complexes and components of the relevant rule regime, but not necessarily coherently or consistently. And the component or complex change may not be the most appropriate or effective one. Higher level commitments, interests, beliefs, and powers (meta-power) are key factors to be investigated.
- The "core" of the paradigm need not necessarily be the problem-solving model. For some actors or institutional settings, the defining core might be a particular type of legitimate source of expertise (i.e. science, the church, the DEMOS, etc), the type of actor that is suited to addressing problems in particular institutional settings (i.e., political versus market actors).
- Our approach to investigating and analyzing the architecture of paradigms through discourses should be and can be extended. Using narrative analysis (social semiotics), we differentiate not only the agents (heroes, the good guys) of problem-solving but the agents who are the sources of problems (the villains, the culprits, the "forces") or exploiters of the problems. Or, impersonal natural forces ("good or bad forces" (that is). And the solutions or strategies of the good guys, partly to neutralize or counter the villains or forces. Narratives have a beginning, middle, and eventual end.[12] There are different types of stories (a finite set of forms). (1) Heroic and epic narratives in which there are heroic or epic problems, but they are solvable or controllable by the hero(s) (he must deal with villains and negative forces). (2) Romantic narratives, which involve problems and crises but which end happily (but not so much through the actions of the hero(s) but through chance or through someone from the outside ("the good fairy") who solves everything. (3)

[12] One has intensional, non-dramatic narratives, e.g. science and mathematics articles.

Tragic narratives where there is hero(s) who have an epic struggle or question but fail.[13]

- As we have seen in several of our cases, the components in a PPP need not be consistent. Actors may set goals which are impossible to realize (or even unknown to what extent they are being or can be realized). Or the means used (the "solutions") may be inappropriate for the goals and problems undertaken. The conceptualization of the problem or the means designated or available need not fit or be appropriate for the goals and values to be realized, etc. Also, the types of solutions envisioned may not match the expertise that is indicated or available. Or available experts cannot deal with the problems or solutions. In other words, what is available in designated or appropriate expertise may not fit the types of problems and solutions that are specified in the PPP. Or the agent appropriate for responsibility and authority may not be able to cooperate – for ethnic, religious, or ideological reasons – with the experts considered appropriate for the situation.

Or, powerful agents inside or outside the institutional arrangements decide that the PPP is not legitimate, or not efficient, or effective and move to "reform" it. This relates to how theory of the drivers of shifts or transformations of PPPs.

---

[13] Nora Machado (2005), building on Goffman, stresses that humans in their "narratives" distinguish between "natural" settings (where there is neither human agency nor moral responsibility) and "social" settings (where there are agents with defined social responsibility and moral obligations).

CHAPTER 16

Conclusions

This book has presented and developed public policy paradigm theory as well as provided a number of applications of the theory in Parts II and III. The applications covered particular issue or problem contexts, configurations of actors, power conditions and dynamics, and policy developments. Earlier work of pioneers in public policy paradigm research were reproduced in Part II. This book is the first comprehensive theoretical and empirical treatment of public policy paradigms.[1] It considered theoretically, the architecture of paradigms, their role in framing and organizing action, and the ways in which paradigm transformations are brought about.[2] The theory construction drew upon three major developments in the social sciences: institutional theory, cognitive sociology, and social movements theory.

In the comparative investigations and analyses of selected EU policymaking processes, the authors were able to identify a few underlying dimensions. In particular, it was suggested that there were powerful forces and tendencies driving consideration of health, social and environmental aspects of policy situations. In a word, we claim that the EU is not only about markets. There occurred a partial "decommodification" (Esping-Andersen, 1985) of food, asbestos, and chemicals generally as well as gender. Gas remained a commodity but it went from a national commodity to an EU commodity. The exceptional and ironic case concerned GHGs – their commodification through the ETS market was developed in the interest of environmental considerations (after attempts at regulation by taxation failed to materialize).

There was level change in all cases – the Europeanization of policy typically involved new agents, authorities, and procedures at the EU level. That is, the EU policy initiatives in our cases not only dealt with concrete policy issues but entailed

[1] A book which we discovered a few months ago concerns economic paradigms and policymaking: Akira Iida's *Paradigm Theory and Policymaking: Reconfiguring the Future* (2004). Our book was too far advanced in the preparation for publication to engage with Professor Iida's work. It was apparently written in complete ignorance of the use the paradigm concept in policy studies, as discussed here.

[2] Besides those working in the area of public policy, we referred earlier (Chapter 1, note 4) to a group of researchers working in particularly Brazil and Italy who developed and applied the paradigm conceptualization in a non-Kuhnian way – it concerned industrial organization and the transformation of Ford/Taylor type production systems into new forms of industrial organization.

advances in EU power and status. The studies revealed also a variety of social organizational innovations and transformations as summarized in Chapter 14.

The EU Treaties served in practice as a type of constitutional framework, which was particularly strong in the area of the internal market – as witnessed by the gas and ETS case studies. Such fundamental authority has been lacking in many non-economic areas, thus barring the EU from taking action in some domains or requiring difficult-to-reach unanimity among member states. The "mainstreaming" of gender and of environmental and public health health concerns – subtly changed what appeared to be an all-too-market orientation, although far less subtly than many imagined, by providing an open-ended, if more modest, mandate. Our studies suggest the institutionalization of a more comprehensive paradigm shift with respect to public health and consumer safety issues as well as social and environmental issues – a development acknowledged by member states of a new paradigmatic order in these and other policy sectors (Carson, 2004). It is also intertwined with, and is yet another reflection of, the changing perceptions regarding the kinds of issues that can be considered "European" as opposed to national or local.

In each of the cases, the emergence of new, social, health, and environmentally focused policy principles and goals became part of a long-term development process in which market integration was initially the major thrust. In each of the EU cases reported here, the policy changes of the mid-to-late 1990s took place in the context of the long-term, ongoing development of new policy ideas and strategies. This dynamic is clearest in the area of gender equality policy as its history reaches most unambiguously and decisively back to the original Treaty of Rome (1957) – even if the first decisive steps were taken only in the 1970s. To the extent that occupational health and safety can be taken as a precursor to public health, then it too dates back to the original Treaties. Occupational health and safety gained qualified majority voting status with the Single European Act (1987), a development that is not completely consistent with what is often characterized as the neo-liberal character of the Act. Similarly, the environment awareness that informs chemicals policy emerged in the 1970s, but only gained formally legitimate status with the passage of the Single European Act.

Although policy developments in each of the sectors began at different points, they do appear to have gained substantial ground during the same general time period. Following a surge of social protest in the late 1960s and 1970s, significant gains were made in gender equality policy (both in new directives passed and in the ECJ), in chemicals policy pertained to health and safety regulations and in environmental protection (in particular, establishment of DG Environment and the implementation of the first of a series of action programs, as reported in Chapter 10).

The individual cases of food, asbestos and chemicals, gender equality, and climate policy each provide an interesting study in the emergence and gradual institutionalization of a new overarching paradigm conception. A comparison across the cases makes a strong case for a major secular trend. Notwithstanding the important differences in case characteristics and the overall timing of the developments, several of the parallels are striking. These developments can be traced, as outlined previously, through examining changes in: (1) policy substance; (2) policymaking participation and the processes by which policy is made; and (3) organizational capacity and competence at the EU level. In each instance, the underlying principles and policy goals that emerged placed a high priority on social and environmental concerns, setting boundaries on what kinds of market activity are considered desirable and acceptable. Participation on the part of NGOs, the European Parliament, and civil society increased in the process, and the general direction of new policy was more or less consistent with what these actors demanded. The "advocacy coalition" pressing for these changes included the Commission as a crucial actor, although its role has been at times ambiguous: reactive rather than initiating. Over the course of the 1990s, the formal competence and formal and informal capacity to engage in social, health, and environmental issues have been systematically expanded and developed at the EU level.

In sum, while market integration remains, in principle, a core mission of the EU, that integration must now be pursued in a manner consistent with improving gender equality and achieving a high level of public health and social and environmental protection. Moreover, the integrated market activities already in place have been and are being tempered, as suggested in the sustainability discourses, to reduce specific kinds of risks and hazards relating to human beings, other species, and the environment.

Bibliography

A4-0020/97. Report of Committee of Inquiry into BSE, 7 February, 1997. European Parliament.

A4-0050/99. Report on the mid-term report on the Community Programme concerning Safety, Hygiene and Health Protection at Work (1996-2000) Motion for a Resolution.

A4-0362/97. Report on the European Commission's follow up of the recommendations made by the Committee of Inquiry into BSE, 14 November, 1997, pp. 6, 9, 12, 16, 17, 43. EP.

Adams, Ian (1989). *The Logic of Political Belief: A Philosophical Analysis of Ideology*. New York: Harvester Wheatsheaf.

Addison, John T. and Stanley Siebert (1991). "The Social Charter of the European Community: Evolution and Controversies". *Industrial and Labor Relations Review*, 44(4): 597-625.

Agriculture and Agri-Food Canada (1994a). *Federal-Provincial Task Force on Orderly Marketing, Discussion Guide: Towards an action plan for the renewal of the dairy, poultry, and egg industries*, 28.01. 1994.

Agriculture and Agri-Food Canada (1994b). *Federal-Provincial Task Force on Orderly Marketing, Action plan towards the implementation of sustainable orderly marketing systems in the Canadian dairy, poultry, and egg industries*, March 23, 1994.

Agriculture and Agri-Food Canada (1995). *Agenda Jobs and Growth. Securing our future in agriculture and agri-food.* Ottawa: AAFC.

Agriculture Canada (1989). *Growing Together.* Ottawa: Agriculture Canada.

Ahrne, Göran (1994). *Social Organizations: Interaction Inside, Outside, and Between Organizations*. London: Sage.

AI (1996). "Background Information on the Ban of Asbestos Products in France". Asbestos Institute (dated July 22, 1996) http:/www.asbestosinstitute.ca/specialreports/-specialindex.html (Access Date: 2001/03/07).

AI (1997). "Politics, Not Science, Basis for France's Ban of Asbestos". *Asbestos Institute Newsletter.*

AI (2001). "About the Asbestos Institute: The Asbestos Institute Is Dedicated to Promoting the Safe Use of Asbestos in Canada and Throughout the World". Asbestos Institute http:/www.asbestos-institute.ca/asbinfo.html (Access Date: 2001/03/07).

Albertini, Mario (2002). "The Ventotene Manifesto – the Only Road to Follow" http://www.eurplace.org/diba/cultura/intralbe.html (Access Date: 2002/10/07).

Amsterdam Treaty (1999): (Treaty of European Communities) Available via Eur-Lex, http://europa.eu.int/eur-lex/.

Andersen, M.S. and D. Leifferink (eds.) (1997). *European Environmental Policy – The Pioneers*. Manchester: Manchester University Press.

Andersen, Svein S. (1993). *The Struggle over North Sea Oil and Gas*. Oslo: Scandinavian University Press.

——— (1995). *Europeisering av politikk. Indre marked, petroleum og miljø*. Oslo: Fagbokforlaget.

——— (1999). "European Integration and the Changing Paradigm of Energy Policy: The Case of Natural Gas Liberalization". ARENA Working Papers WP 99/12. http://www.arena.uio.no/publications/wp00_13.htm.

——— (2001). *Energy policy: interest interaction and supranational authority*, in Andersen, S.S. and K.A. Eliassen (eds.) *Making policy in Europe?* London: Sage.
Andersen, Svein S. and Tom R. Burns (1992). *Societal Decision-making: Democratic Challenges to State Democracy.* Dartmouth: Aldershot, USA.
——— (1996). "The European Union and the Erosion of Parliamentary Democracy: A Study of Post-Parliamentary Governance", *The European Union: How Democratic Is It?*, Svein S. Andersen and Kjell A. Eliassen (Eds.). London: Sage.
Andersen, Svein S. and Kjell A. Eliassen (Eds.) (1996b). *The European Union: How Democratic Is It?* London: Sage.
——— (2001). *Informal processes: lobbying, actor strategies, coalitions and dependencies*, in Andersen, S.S. and K.A. Eliassen (eds.): *Making policy in Europe?* London: Sage.
Andersen, S.S. and Sitter, N. (2006). 'Differentiated integration. What is it and how much can the EU accommodate? An organizational perspective'. *Journal of European Integration,* 28(4).
Antonoyiannakis, M., J. Hemmelskamp and F.C. Kafatos (2009). "The European Research Council Takes Flight." *Cell,* Vol. 136: 805-809.
Archer, Margaret S. (1996). *Culture and Agency: The Place of Culture in Social Theory.* Cambridge: Cambridge University Press.
Arditi, J. (2004). *Social Knowledge, Social ontology, and the Order of Things: Re-reading the Early Foucault.* Paper presented at the annual meeting of the American Sociological Association, Hilton San Francisco & Renaissance, CA, 2004-08-14, http://www.-allacademic.com/meta/p108336_index.html.
Arentsen, J. M. (2004). 'Politics and regulation of gas in Europe', in Finon, D. and Midttun, A. (eds.) *Reshaping European Gas and Electricity Industry: Regulation, Markets and Business Strategies.* London: Elsevier.
Åsard, Eric and Lance Bennett (1997). *Democracy and the Marketplace of Ideas: Communication and Government in Sweden and the United States.* Cambridge: Cambridge University Press.
Aspinwall, Mark D. and Gerald Schneider (2000). "Same Menu, Separate Tables: The Institutionalist Turn in Political Science and the Study of European Integration". *European Journal of Political Research,* 38: 1-36.
——— (Eds.) (2001). *The Rules of Integration: The Institutionalist Approach to European Studies,* Manchester, Manchester University Press.
Asztalos Morell, Ildikó (1999). *Emancipation's Dead-End Roads? Studies in the Formation and Development of the Hungarian Model for Agriculture and Gender (1956-1989).* Department of Sociology. Uppsala: Uppsala University, Acta Universitatis Upsaliensis.
Atkinson, M.M. and W.D. Coleman (1989). "Strong States and Weak States: Sectoral Policy Networks in Advanced Industrial Economies", *British Journal of Political Science*, 19, 1, 47-67.
Bacchi, Carol Lee (1999). *Women, Policy, and Politics: The Construction of Policy Problems.* London: Sage.
Baldwin, Peter (1990). *The Politics of Social Solidarity: Class Bases of the European Welfare State, 1875-1975.* New York: Cambridge University Press.
Baron, R., M. Bosi, A. Lanza & J. Pershing (1999). "A Preliminary Analysis of the EU Proposals on the Kyoto Mechanisms." *International Energy Agency*, Paris.
Bartolini, S. (1993). "On Time and Comparative Research", *J. of Theoretical Politics*, 5(2), 131-167.
Baumert, K. (1998). "Carbon Taxes vs. Emissions Trading: What's the Difference, and Which is Better?". http://env.chass.utoronto.ca/env200y/ESSAY2001/tax.htm.
Baumert, K.A., Herzog, T. and J. Pershing (2005). *Navigating the numbers: greenhouse gas data and international climate policy.* Washington, D.C.: World Resources Institute.

Baumgartner, Frank R. and Bryan D. Jones (1991). "Agenda Dynamics and Policy Subsystems." *Journal of Politics*, 53(4): 1044-1074.
——— (1993). *Agendas and Instability in American Politics*, Chicago, University of Chicago Press.
——— (Eds.) (2002). *Policy Dynamics*. Chicago, University of Chicago Press.
Beck, Ulrich (1995). Ecological Politics in an Age of Risk. Cambridge: Polity Press.
Becker, H. (1998). *Tricks of the trade: how to think about your research while you're doing it.* Chicago Ill.: Univ. of California Press.
Bellier, Irène (1997). "The Commission as an Actor: An Anthropologists View", in *Participation and Policy-Making in the European Union*, Helen Wallace and Alasdair R. Young (Eds.). Oxford: Clarendon Press.
Belzile, Andre (1994). "Uniformiser les programmes canadiens." *La Terre de Chez Nous*, 7-13 avril.
Benford, R.D. and D.A. Snow (2000). "Framing Processes and Social Movements: An Overview and Assessment". *Annual Review of Sociology*, 26: 611-639.
Benjelloun, Hind (2000). "The European Union's Ban on Asbestos". *The Synergist / American Industrial Hygene Association*, 11(8): available at: http://aiha.org.syn/aug00f.html (Access Date: 2001/2003/2017).
Bennett, Andrew and Alexander George (1997). "Research Design Tasks in Case Study Methods". Presented at the MacArthur Foundation Workshop on Case Study Methods, Belfer Center for Science and International Affairs (BCSIA), Harvard University, 17-19.10.1997.
Bennett, C. and Howlett, M. (1992). "The Lessons of Learning. Reconciling Theories of Policy Learning and Policy Change", *Policy Sciences*, 25(3), 275-294.
Bennett, Cinnamon and Christine Booth (2002). "Gender Mainstreaming in the European Union. Towards a New Conception and Practice of Equal Opportunities?". In *The European Journal of Women's Studies*, Vol. 9(4): 430–446. London: SAGE Publications.
Berger, Peter L. and Thomas Luckmann (1969). *The Social Construction of Reality: A Treatise in the Sociology of Knowledge*. London: Penguin Press.
BEUC/300/98 – "Consumer Policy and the Amsterdam Treaty" Bureau Européen des Unions de Consommateurs (BEUC), 1-10-1998.
Beuermann, C. (2002). "Climate Policy: Britain and Germany Compared." *Climate Policy: Toward an Agenda for Policy Learning between Britain and Germany.* London: Anglo-German Foundation for the Study of Industrial Society.
Beveridge, Fiona and Sue Nott (1996). "Gender Auditing – Making the Community Work for Women", in Sex Equality Law in the European Union, Tamara K. Hervy and David OKeeffe (Eds.). Chichester: John Wiley & Sons: 383-398.
Beveridge, William (1998 [1940]). "Peace by Federation?" in Altierro Spinelli and the British Federalists, John Pinder, (Ed.). London: Federal Trust: 19-43.
BG-a, (1999). "Dioxin Contamination: Brief Summary". Belgian Government, Brussels Belgium: http://dioxin.fgov.be/report/enbh01.htm (Access date: 2000/04/02).
BG-b, (1999). "Dioxin Contamination: Chronological order of the facts". Belgian Government, Brussels, Belgium: (http://dioxin.fgov.be/report/enbh02.htm) (Access date: 2000/04/02).
Bidmead, Harold S. (1948). "Uniting Europe: By Accident or by Design?" originally published June, 1948 in Political Comment Column of Petts Wood Observer http://www.eurocritic.demon.co.uk/eudesign.htm (Access Date: 2002/19/07).
Blumer, Herbert (1969). *Symbolic Interactionism*. Berkeley: Prentice-Hall.
Bodansky, D. (2004). "U.S. Climate Policy after Kyoto: Elements for Success." Washington, D.C.: Carnegie Endowment.

——— (2004). *International Climate Efforts Beyond 2012: A Survey of Approaches.* Arlington, Va.: Pew Center on Global Climate Change.

Booz-Allen and Hamilton (Australia) Ltd. (1995). *A report commissioned by the Grains Council of Australia's National Grain Marketing Strategic Planning Unit.* Canberra, January.

Bordieu, Pierre (1996). *The Rules of Art.* Stanford: Polity Press.

Boudon, R. (1996). "The 'Cognitivist Model'", *Rationality and Society.* Vol. 9:123-150.

Breslau, Daniel (1997). "The Political Power of Research Methods: Knowledge Regimes in U.S. Labor Market Policy". *Theory and Society,* 26: 869-902.

Brickman, R. S. Jasanoff, and T. Ilgen (1985). *Controlling Chemicals: The Politics of Regulation in Europe and the United States.* Ithaca, N.Y.: Cornell U. Press.

Brinton, M. and V. Nee (Eds.) (1998). *The New Institutionalism in Sociology,* New York: Russell Sage Foundation.

Brodeur, Paul (1985). *Outrageous Conduct: The Complete New Yorker Reports.* New York: Pantheon Books.

Brooks, Jonathan C. and Colin A. Carter (1994). *The Political Economy of US Agriculture.* Canberra: Commonwealth of Australia, ABARE Research Report 94, 8.

Browne, William P. (1988). *Private Interests, Public Policy and American Agriculture.* Lawrence, KS, University Press of Kansas.

Bruggeman, V. and B. Delvaux (2006). "EU energy policy and legislation under pressure since the UNFCCC and the Kyoto Protocol?" 223-239, in: Peeters and Deketelaere (eds.) *EU Climate Change Policy,* EE Publishing.

BSE Vademecum (1998). "Bovine Spongiform Encephalopathy (BSE), Information for consumers", 3rd.

Buckwell Report (1997). "Towards a Common Agricultural and Rural Policy for Europe", European Commission, DG Agriculture.

Bulletin EU 1/2-1997. "Speech by Jacques Santer, President of the European Commission, to Parliament on 18 February, 1997", European Parliament.

Bulmer, S. (1994). "The governance of the European Union: a new institutionalist approach", *Journal of Public Policy,* 13:351-80.

Bulmer, Simon J. (1997). "New Institutionalism, the Single Market, and EU Governance". ARENA Working Papers WP 97/25. http://www.arena.uio.no/publications/-wp97_25.htm (Access Date: 2002-6-10).

Burawoy, Michael (1991b). "Reconstructing Social Theories", in *Ethnography Unbound,* Michael Burawoy (Ed.), Berkeley: University of California Press: 8-27.

Burns, Tom R. and Dietz (2001). "Revolution: An evolutionary perspective". *International Sociology,* Vol. 16, No 4, pp. 531-555.

Burns, Tom R. and E. Roszkowska (2004). "Fuzzy Game and Equilibria: The Perspective of the General Theory of Games." In: S. K. Pal, L. Polkowski, and A. Skowron (eds.). *Rough-Neural Computing: Techniques for Computing with Words.* Springer Verlag, Berlin/London.

Burns, Tom R. (2008). "Rule System Theory: An Overview." *Rule System Theory: Applications and Explorations.* H. Flam and M. Carson. Berlin, Peter Lang.

——— (1999). "The Evolution of Parliaments and Societies in Europe: Challenges and Prospects". *European Journal of Social Theory,* 2(2): 167-194.

——— and Helena Flam (Eds.) (1987). *The Shaping of Social Organization: Social Rule System Theory with Applications.* London: Sage Publications.

Burns, Tom R. and Marcus Carson (2002). "Actors, Paradigms and Institutional Dynamics: The Theory of Social Rule Systems Applied to Radical Reforms", *Advancing Socio-Economics,* J. Rogers Hollingsworth (Ed.). Rowman & Littlefield: 109-145.

——— (2002). "European Union, neo-corporatist, and pluralist governance arrangements: lobbying and policy-making patterns in a comparative perspective." *International Journal of Regulation and Governance*, 2(2): 1-47.
——— (2003). "European Union, Neocorporatist and Pluralist Governance Arrangements: Lobbying and Policy-Making Patterns in Comparative Perspective". *Sociologia – Problemas e Praticas*, 42(May-Aug): 161-197.
——— (2005). "Social Order and Disorder: Institutions, Policy Paradigms and Discourses – an Interdisciplinary Approach", in *Critical Discourse Analysis: Theory and Interdisciplinarity*, Paul Chilton and Ruth Wodak (Eds.). Amsterdam/Philadelphia: John Benjamins Publishing Company.
——— and Johan Nylander (2001). "The European Union's Social Dimension: From Market to Welfare?", *International Journal of Regulation and Governance*, 1(2): 129-157.
BusinessEurope (The Confederation of European Business) (2008). www.businesseurope.eu.
Byrd-Hagel Resolution (1997). Recordings S8138, The Senate of the United States. Washington, D.C.:U.S. Printing Office.
CAIT (2009). CAIT.wri.org/figures.php.
Cameron, E. (1991). *The European Reformation.* Oxford: Clarendon Press.
Campbell, John L. (1998). "Institutional Analysis and the Role of Ideas in Political Economy". *Source Theory and Society*, 27(3): 377-409.
——— (2002). "Ideas, Politics, and Public Policy". *Annual Review of Sociology*, 28: 21-38.
——— and Leon N. Lindberg (1990). "Property Rights and the Organization of Economic Activity by the State". *American Sociological Review*, 5(5): 634-647.
Canada (1995). *Budget Plan.* Ottawa: February 27.
Canadian Dairy Commission (1995). *Annual Report*, 1994-1995.
——— (1996). *Bulletin*, July.
Capano, G. (2003). "Administrative traditions and policy change: when policy paradigms matter. The case of Italian administrative reform during the 1990s", *Public Administration*, 81(4), 781-801.
Carson, Marcus (2001). *From the People's Home to the Market: Paradigm Shift to System Shift in the Swedish Welfare State.* Bostadsforskningsinstitute/Institute for Housing and Urban Research. Gävle, Uppsala Universitet: Forskningsrapport/Research Report 1/01.
——— (2004). *From Common Market to Social Europe*? Department of Sociology. Stockholm, Stockholm University. PhD.
——— (2004). *From Common Market to Social Europe? Paradigm Shift and Institutional Change in European Union Policy on Food, Absestos and Chemicals, and Gender Equality.* Stockholm: Almqvist & Wiksell International.
——— (2008). "Of Mind and Matter: Policy Paradigms and Institutional Design". *Rule System Theory: Applications and Explorations.* H. Flam and M. Carson. Berlin, Peter Lang.
Case C-180/97. Judgement of the Court in United Kingdom of Great Britain and Northern Ireland versus the Commission of the European Communities. European Court of Justice.
Castleman, Barry (1999a). "Global Corporate Policies and International 'Double Standards' in Occupational and Environmental Health". *International Journal of Occupational and Environmental Health*, 5: 61-64.
——— (1999b). "The WTO Case: Health and Trade Implications". http://www.mnsi.net/~wohis/castleman.htm (Access Date: 2001/03/11).
——— (2001). Asbestos: Medical and Legal Aspects. New York: Aspen Law & Business.
——— (2002). "WTO Confidential: The Case of Asbestos". *International Journal of Health Services*, 32(3): 489-501.

——— and Richard Lemen (1998). "Corporate Junk Science in International Science Organizations". *Environment*, 19(1-2).

CESIS (2000). "Evaluation of the Campaign Against Domestic violence" carried out by Centro de Estudos para a Intervencão Social (CESIS) within the scope of the Portuguese 3 Presidency of the Union. Lisbon: April 2000.

Chalmers, A. (1987). *Qu'est-ce que la science?*, Paris, La Découverte.

Chapman, A. (2007). *Democratizing Technology. Risk, Responsibility and Regulation of Chemicals*. London: Earthscan.

Charlesworth, Hilary (1999). "Feminist Methods in International Law". *American Journal of International Law*, 93(2): 379-394.

Chilton, P. and R. Wodak (2005). *Critical Discourse Analysis: Theory and Interdisciplinarity*. Amsterdam/Philadelphia, John Benjamins Publishing Company.

Christiansen, A.C. and J. Wettestad (2003). "The EU as a Frontrunner on Green House Gas Emissions Trading." *Climate Policy* Vol. 3 (#1): 3-18.

Christiansen, Thomas, Knud Erik Jorgensen and Antje Wiener, (Eds.) (2001). The Social Construction of Europe. London: Sage Publications.

Christoforou, Theofanis (2000). "Settlement of Science-Based Trade Disputes in the WTO: A Critical Review of the Developing Case Law in the Face of Scientific Uncertainty". *Environmental Law Journal*, 8(3): 622-648.

Chryssochoou, Dimitris (1999). "Eurogovernance: Theories and Approaches to the EU", in Public Policy in the New Europe: Eurogovernance in Theory and Practice, Fergus Carr and Andrew Massey (Eds.). Cheltenham, UK: Edward Elgar: 3-26.

Churchill, W. 1946 Winston Churchill's Speech to the Academic Youth, Zurich, September 19, 1946. http://www.europa-web.de/europa/02wwswww/202histo/churchil.htm.

Cichowski, Rachel A. (2001). "Judicial Rulemaking and the Institutionalization of European Union Sex Equality Policy", *The Institutionalization of Europe*, Alec Stone Sweet, Wayne Sandholtz and Neil Fligstein (Eds.). Oxford: Oxford University Press: 113-136.

Cochrane, Willard W. and Mary E. Ryan (1976). *American Farm Policy, 1948-1973*. Minneapolis: University of Minnesota Press.

Coleman, W. (1998). "From protected development to market liberalism: paradigm change in agriculture." *J. of European Public Policy*, Vol. 5(4): 632-51.

Coleman, W.D. and Grace Skogstad (1990). *Policy Communities and Policy Networks: A Structural Approach*. In Coleman and Skogstad (eds.). *Policy Communities and Public Policy in Canada: A Structural Approach*. Toronto: Copp.

——— (1995). "Neo-Liberalism, Policy Networks, and Policy Change: Agricultural Policy Reform in Australia and Canada", *Australian Journal of Political Science*, 30: 242-263.

Coleman, William D., Grace D. Skogstad and Michael M. Atkinson (1996). "Paradigm Shifts and Policy Networks: Cumulative Change in Agriculture." *Journal of Public Policy*, 16(3): 273-301.

Collier, D. and Collier, R. (1991). *Shaping the Political Arena*, Princeton, Princeton University Press.

Collins, Harry M. (1999). "Tantalus and the Aliens: Publications, Audiences and the Search for Gravitational Waves". *Social Studies of Science*, 29(2): 163-197.

Colorni, Eugenio (1944). "Preface: The Italian Movement for European Federation" Rome, January 22, 1944. http://eurplace.org/diba/cultura/precolor.htm (Access Date: 2002/10/07).

COM(2000) 1 – (2000) "Communication from the Commission on the Precautionary Principle", 2nd February, 2000. European Commission.

COM(2000) 66 final. *White Paper on Environmental Liability*. Brussels, 9.2.2000.

COM(2001) 88 final – White Paper "Strategy for a Future Chemicals Policy", European Commission.
COM(2003) 644 final (2003). Proposal for a Regulation of the EP and of the Council concerning the Registration, Evaluation, Authorization and Restriction of Chemicals (REACH), establishing a ECA and amending Directive 1999/45/EC and Regulation (EC) {on Persistent Organic Pollutants} Proposal for a Directive of the EP and of the Council amending Council Directive 67/548/EEC in order to adapt it to Regulation (EC) of the EP and of the Council concerning the registration, evaluation, authorization and restriction of chemicals. Brussels, 29.10.2003.
COM(2007) 355 final (2007). Proposal for a Regulation of the European Parliament and of the Council on classification, labelling and packaging of substances and mixtures, and amending Directive 67/548/EEC and Regulation (EC) No 1907/2006.
COM(97) 176 – (1997). "The General Principles of Food law in the European Union", European Commission.
COM(99) 719 – (2000). "White Paper on Food Safety", European Commission.
Commission "Women and Science: Mobilising women to enrich European research", Communication of the Commission of the European Communities, 17 February. COM(1999) 76 (1999).
Commission of the European Communities (1997a). Proposal of a Council regulation (EC) on integrating gender issues in development co-operation. 9 June 1997. COM (97) 265 final.
——— (1997b). Commission staff working paper. Integrating gender issues in development co-operation. Progress report 1997. 3 November 1997. SEC (97) 2067.
Consultation Committee on the Future of the Dairy Industry (1992a). *Working Document.* Ottawa.
——— (1992b). *Report.* Ottawa.
Consumer Voice, No 1, 2000. Published by DG Sanco, European Commission.
Cormack, Mike (1992). *Ideology.* London: BT Batsford, Ltd.
Corporate Europe Observatory (2005). "Bulldozing REACH – the industry offensive to crush EU chemicals regulation." Briefing #2. Amsterdam: CEO.
Council Directive 67/548/EEC on the approximation of laws, regulations and administrative provisions relating to the classification, packaging and labeling of dangerous substances.
Council Directive 76/768. http://eur-lex.europa.eu/LexUriServ/LexUriServ.do?uri=-CONSLEG:1976L0768:20080424:EN:PDF.
Council Directive 76/769/EEC on the approximation of laws, regulations and administrative provisions of the Member States relating to restrictions on the marketing and use of certain dangerous substances and preparations.
Council Directive 79/831/EEC of 18 September 1979 amending for the sixth time Directive 67/548/EEC on the approximation of the laws, regulations and administrative provisions relating to the classification, packaging and labeling of dangerous substances. Effective September 1981.
Council Directive 80/1107/EEC of 27 November 1980 on the protection of workers from the risks related to exposure to chemical, physical, and biological agents at work.
Council Directive 83/477/EEC of 19 September 1983 on the protection of workers from the risks related to exposure to asbestos at work.
Council Directive 83/478/EEC of 19 September 1983 amending for the fifth time (asbestos) Directive 76/769/EEC on the approximation of laws, regulations and administrative provisions of the Member States relating to restrictions on the marketing and use of certain dangerous substances and preparations.

Council Directive 85/610/EEC of 20 December 1985 amending for the seventh time (asbestos) Directive 76/769/EEC on the approximation of laws, regulations and administrative provisions of the Member States relating to restrictions on the marketing and use of certain dangerous substances and preparations.

Council Directive 87/217/EEC of 19 March 1987 on the prevention and reduction of environmental pollution by asbestos.

Council Directive 91/382/EEC of 25 June 1991 amending Directive 83/477/EEC on the protection of workers from the risks related to exposure to asbestos at work.

Council Directive 91/659/EEC of 3 December 1991 adapting to technical progress Annex 1 to Council Directive 76/769/EEC on the approximation of laws, regulations and administrative provisions of the Member States relating to restrictions on the marketing and use of certain dangerous substances and preparations (asbestos).

Council Directive 92/32/EEC of 30 April 1992 amending for the seventh time Directive 67/548/EEC on the approximation of the laws, regulations and administrative provisions relating to the classification, packaging and labelling of dangerous substances. http://eur-lex.europa.eu/LexUriServ/LexUriServ.do?uri=CELEX:31992L0032:en:html.

Council Directive 97/80/EC of 15 December 1997 on the burden of proof in cases of discrimination based on sex.

Council Directive of 18/19 September 1979 amending for the sixth time Directive 67/548/EEC on the approximation of the laws, regulations and administrative provisions relating to the classification, packaging and labelling of dangerous substances (79/831/EEC).

Council Directive of 27 July 1976 on the approximation of the laws of the Member States relating to cosmetic products (76/768/EEC).

Council Directive of 27 June 1967 on the approximation of laws, regulations and administrative provisions relating to the classification, packaging and labelling of dangerous substances (67/548/EEC).

Council of Europe – Human Rights, Equality between Women and Men: http://www.coe.int/-T/e/human_rights/equality/.

Council of Europe (1998). 'Gender Mainstreaming, Conceptual Frameworks, Methodology and Presentation of Good Practices', Final Report of Activities of the Group of Specialists on Mainstreaming, Strasbourg, Council of Europe.

——— (2004). 'Gender Mainstreaming, Conceptual Frameworks, Methodology and Presentation of Good Practices', Final Report of Activities of the Group of Specialists on Mainstreaming, Strasbourg, Council of Europe, Directorate-General of Human Rights: Equality Division.

Council of the European Union (1995a). General secretariat. Draft resolution on integrating gender issues in development co-operation. 17, 21, 27 November, 6 December and suggested amendments of 5 December 1995. Doc. no. 238/1/95 REV (DEVGEN).

——— (1995b). Council resolution: Integrating gender issues in development co-operation. 20 December 1995. 12847/95 (Presse 374).

——— (2005). Joint Statement by the Council and the representatives of the Governments of the Member States meeting within the Council, the EP and the Commission on EU Development Policy: "The European Consensus". 14820/05. Brussels, 22.11.2005.

Cowles, M., J. Caporaso and T. Risse-Kappen (2001). *Transforming Europe: Europeanization and Domestic Change*. Ithaca, N.Y., Cornell University Press.

Cram, Laura (1994). "The European Commission as a Multi-Organization: Social Policy and It Policy in the EU". *Journal of European Public Policy*, 1(2): 195-217.

——— (1997). *Policy-Making in the European Union: Conceptual Lenses and the Integration Process.* London: Routledge.
——— (2001). "Whither the Commission? Reform, Renewal, and the Issue Attention Cycle". *Journal of European Public Policy,* 8(5): 770-786.
Crook, John R. (1994). "The Fiftieth Session of the UN Commission on Human Rights". American Journal of International Law, 88(4): 806-821.
CSTEE (1998/09/15). Committee on Toxicity, Ecotoxicity and the Environment. Opinion on Chrysotile asbestos and candidate substitutes expressed at the 5th CSTEE plenary meeting, Brussels 15 September 1998.
CSTEE (1999/01/18). Minutes of the 7th plenary meeting of the Scientific Committee on Toxicity, Ecotoxicity, and the Environment (CSTEE).
Culpepper, Pepper D. (1993). "Organisational Competition and the Neo-Corporatist Fallacy in French Agriculture", *West European Politics,* 16, 295-315.
Czarniawska, B. and Sevon, G. (1996). *Translating Organizational Change.* Berlin. Walter de Gruyter.
Dalton, R. J. and M. Kuechler, Eds. (1990). *Challenging the Political Order: New Social and Political Movements in Western Democracies.* Cambridge, UK, Polity Press.
Daly, Mary E. (2005). "Gender Mainstreaming in Theory and Practice". *Social Politics,* 12(3).
Daugbjerg, C. (2003). "Policy Feedback and Paradigm Shift in EU Agricultural Policy: The Effects of the Macsharry Reform on Future Reform". *Journal of European Public Policy,* 10(3): 421-437.
de Lara, P. (1997). "Un miracle sociologique. La 'construction sociale de la réalité'", *Le Débat,* 97, 114-129.
De Schoutheete, Philippe and Andrew Butler (Transl.) (2000). The Case for Europe: Unity, Diversity, and Democracy in the European Union. Boulder, CO: Lynne Rienner Publishers.
De Winter, Kees (1998). "Food and Health in the EU: Past Achievements and Future Challenges". *The Health Impact of European Single Market Legislation: Report of a Public Seminar.* European Public Health Alliance, Brussels, Belgium, 30 October 1998.
Decision 99/788/EC. "Decision of 3 December 1999 on protective measures with regard to contamination by dioxins…" Official Journal L310, 04/12/1999, p. 62–70.
Denzau, A. T. and D. C. North (1993). *Shared Mental Models: Ideologies and Institutions.* Economics Working Paper Archive at WUSTL.
Department for the Environment, Transport and the Regions (2000). "A Greenhouse Gas Emissions Trading Scheme for the United Kingdom." London: Department for the Environment, Transport and the Regions, United Kingdom. November 2000.
Dewandre, N. (2002). "Women In Science: European Strategies for Promoting Women in Science" *Science* January. 295(5553), 278–279.
DG Agriculture (2000). http://europa.eu.int/comm/dgs/agriculture/index_en.htm.
DG Development (2006). "Programming Document for 2005 and 2006: Promoting Gender Equality in Development Cooperation". European Commission. DG Development. Development Policy and Sectoral Issues Human and Social Development. Available at http://ec.europa.eu/europeaid/projects/gender/documents/programming_2005_2006_en.pdf, Acceded on Mars 2007.
DG Development. http://ec.europa.eu/dgs/development/index_en.htm.
DG Employment, Social Affairs & Equal Opportunities. Gender Equality: http://ec.europa.eu/employment_social/gender_equality/index_en.html.
DG Employment, Social Affairs & Equal Opportunities. Gender Mainstreaming: http://ec.europa.eu/employment_social/gender_equality/gender_mainstreaming/general_overview_en.html and http://ec.europa.eu/employment_social/equ_opp/gms_en.html

DG Employment, Social Affairs & Equal Opportunities: http://ec.europa.eu/dgs/-employment_social/index_en.htm.
DG Enterprise and Industry (2008). www.ec.europa.eu/environment/chemicals/reach/-reach_intro.htm.
DG for Employment Social Affairs and Equal Opportunities Unit G1 (2008). *Women and Men in Decision-making 2007*. Luxembourg: Official Publications of the European Commission.
DG for Justice, Freedom and Security: http://ec.europa.eu/justice_home/fsj/intro/fsj_intro-_en.htm.
DG for Research (2008). Communication "Mapping the maze: getting more women to the top in research" EUR 23311 (EN). European Commission. http://ec.europa.eu/-research/science-society/document_library/pdf_06/mapping-the-maze-getting-more-women-to-the-top-in-research_en.pdf.
DG for Research (2009). "The gender challenge in research funding – Assessing the European national scenes" http://bookshop.eu.int/eubookshop/download.action?fileName=-KINA23721ENC_002.pdf&eubphfUid=10129751&catalogNbr=KI-NA-23721-EN-C.
DG Health & Consumer Protection (2000) – (SG Sanco) (http://europa.eu.int/comm/-dgs/health_consumer/index_en.htm).
DG Industry (1999) Website: http://europa.eu.int/comm/dg03/mission_en.htm.
DG-IIII – DEN. – "Detailed Explanatory Note", DG Enterprise. http://europa.eu.int/comm/-dg03/directs/dg3c/asbdetainote.htm. (Access Date: 2001/02/22).
DiMaggio, Paul J. and Walter W. Powell (Eds.) (1991). *The new institutionalism in organizational analysis*. Chicago: University of Chicago Press.
Directive 2006/121/EC of the European Parliament and of the Council of 18 December 2006 amending Council Directive 67/548/EEC on the approximation of laws, regulations and administrative provisions relating to the classification, packaging and labeling of dangerous substances in order to adapt it to Regulation (EC) No 1907/2006 concerning the Registration, Evaluation, Authorization and Restriction of Chemicals (REACH) and establishing a European Chemicals Agency.
Directive 98/30/EC of the European Parliament and of the Council (1998). *Concerning Common Rules for the Internal Market for Natural Gas*. June 22. Brussels.
Dobash, R. Emerson and Russell P. Dobash (1992). *Women, Violence, & Social Change*. London: Routledge.
Dobbin, F. (1994). *Forging Industrial Policy. The United States, Britain and France in the Railway Age*. Cambridge: Cambridge University Press.
Dore, J. & R. De Bauw (1995). *The European Energy Charter. Origins, Aims and Prospects*. London: The Royal Institute of International Affairs.
Dosi, G. (1982). "Technological Paradigms and Technological Trajectories." *Research Policy*, Vol. II (3): 147-162.
——— (1984). *Technical Change and Industrial Transformation – The Theory and an Application to the Semiconductor Industry*. London: MacMillan Press.
Dryzek, John S. (1996a). *Democracy in Capitalist Times: Ideals, Limits, and Struggles*. New York: Oxford University Press.
Dudley, G. and Richardson, J. (1996). "Why Does Policy Change over Time? Adversarial Policy Communities, Alternative Policy Arenas, and British Trunk Roads Policy 1945-95", *Journal of European Public Policy*, 3, 1, 63-83.
Dunlap, R. (2008). "Promoting a Paradigm Change: Reflections on Early Contributions to Environmental Sociology." *Organization & Environment*. Vol. 21 (4):478-487.

———, F. Buttel, P. Dickens, and A. Gijswijt (2002). *Sociological Theory and the Environment: Classical Foundations, Contemporary Insights.* Lanham, Md.: Rowman & Littlefield.
Dunsire, A. (1978). *Implementation in a Bureaucracy*, Oxford, Martin Robertson.
Durkheim, E. (1964). *The Division of Labor in Society*, New York, The Free Press.
Earth Summit (1992). UN Conference on Environment and Development (UNCED), Rio de Janeiro, 3-14 June 1992.
Easton, D. (1965). *A Framework for Political Analysis.* Englewood Cliffs, N.J.: Prentice- Hall.
EC: DG–VI, no.2, 3. DG Agriculture Website information on the CAP.
Economic and Social Committee and the Committee of the Regions: 'A Roadmap for Equality between women and men 2006-2010', Impact Assessment" {COM(2006) 92 final}, Brussels, 1 March 2006.
EEA (European Environment Agency) (2007). *Annual European Community Greenhouse Gas Inventory 1990-2005 and Inventory Report 2007.* Submission to the UNFCCC Secretariat, EEA Technical Report No. 7/2007, European Environment Agency.
EEB (2001). EEB First Comments to the White Paper on the Future EU Chemicals Policy. Available at www.eeb.org/activities/chemicals/NR%201%20EEB%20comments-%20EU%20Chemicals%20Strategy%20.pdf, acceded on April 2008.
——— (2003). EEB Position on Commission proposal for a Regulation on REACH. Available at www.eeb.org/activities/chemicals/20031210-EEB-position-on-REACH.pdf, acceded on April 2008.
——— (2004). European Environmental Bureau press releases. http://www.eeb.org/press/-2004/press_2004.html.
——— (2008). www.eeb.org/activities/chemicals/Index.htm.
Eldevik, F. (1999). *Liberaliserng av gassmarkedet i Europa. EUs gassdirektiv av 1998.* ARENA Report 4/99. Oslo: ARENA.
Elgström, Ole (2000). "Norm Negotiations. The Construction of new norms regarding Gender and Development in EU Foreign Aid Policy". *Journal of European Public Policy*, Vol. 7, No. 3: 457–76.
Elman, R. Amy (2001). "Testing the Limits of European Citizenship: Ethnic Hatred and Male Violence". *NWSA Journal*, 13(3): 49-69.
ENDS Europe (1997). "Swedes call for clearer EU chemicals strategy." October, 1997.
——— (2001). "Sweden launches chemicals broadside at the EU". February 2, 2001.
——— (2005). "Reactions to REACH vote fly in thick and fast." Thursday, November 17, 2005.
EPHA (European Public Health Alliance) (1999). *Health Update #44.*
——— (2000). *Health Update* #49.
Estrada, J., H.O. Bergesen, A. More & A.K Sydnes (ed.) (1988). *Natural Gas In Europe.* London: Pinter Publishers.
ETAN Report on Women and Science. (ETAN – European Technology Assessment Network (2000). "Science policies in the European Union: Promoting excellence through mainstreaming gender equality" Luxembourg: Office for Official Publications of the European Communities, ftp://ftp.cordis.europa.eu/pub/etan/docs/women.pdf.
ETC (1999/02/09) "Fabius on Trial over Aids deaths" Issue 1355, Tuesday, 9 Feb. 1999. Electronic Telegraph Correspondent, http://www.telegraph.co.uk/.
ETUC/TUTB–European Trade Union Confederation/European Trade Union Technical Bureau for Health and Safety. http://www.etuc.org/tutb/uk/index.html
EU Commission (2002). "*Implementation of gender mainstreaming in the Structural Funds programming documents 2000-2006*" [COM(2002) 748 final].

EU Council Resolution (1996). "Resolution on mainstreaming equal opportunities for men and women into the European Structural Funds" [Official Journal C 386, 20.12.1996].
European Chemical Industry Council (2008). www.cefic.org.
European Chemicals Agency (ECHA) (2008). www.ec.europa.eu/echa.
European Commission (1995). "Communication from the Commission to the Council and the European Parliament on Integrating Gender Issues in Development Cooperation", COM(95) 423 final, Brussels, 18 September 1995.
——— (1996a). "Annual Report from the Commission: 'Equal Opportunities for Women and Men in the European Union'", COM(96) 650 final, Brussels.
——— (1996b). "Communication from the Commission: 'Incorporating Equal Opportunities for Women and Men into all Community Policies and Activities'", COM(96) 67 final, Brussels, 21.02.1996.
——— (1998). "Progress Report from the Commission on the Follow up of the Communication: 'Incorporating Equal Opportunities for Women and Men in All Commission Activities and Policies'", COM(98) 122 final, Brussels.
——— (2000). *The New Programming period 2000-2006: technical papers by theme: 'Mainstreaming Equal Opportunities for Women and Men in Structural Fund Programmes and Projects'*, Technical Paper 3, Brussels, March 2000.
——— (2001). Final Report: ECCP Working Group I "Flexible Mechanisms": http://europa.eu.int/comm./environment/climat/final_report.pdf, May.
——— (2001). *Proposal for a framework Directive for greenhouse gas emissions trading within the European Community* – COM(2001)581, October.
——— (2004). *Communication from the Commission to the Council, the European Parliament, the European Economic and Social Committee and the Committee of the Regions: First Annual Report on Migration and Integration*, COM(2004) 508 final, Brussels, 16.07.2004.
——— (2004). Directive 2004/101/EC of the European Parliament and of the Council of 27 October 2004 amending Directive 2003/87/EC establishing a scheme for greenhouse gas emissions allowance trading within the Community, in respect of the Kyoto Protocol's project mechanisms. *Official Journal of the European Union*, L338/18, 13.11.2004.
——— (2005a). *Green Paper: on an EU Approach to Managing Economic Migration (presented by the Commission)*, COM(2004) 811 final, Brussels, 11.01.2005.
——— (2005b). *Report from the Commission to the Council, the European Parliament, the European Economic and Social Committee and the Committee of the Regions: 'On equality between women and men 2005'*, COM(2005) 44 final, Brussels, 14.02.2005.
——— (2006a). *Communication from the Commission to the Council, the European Parliament, the European Economic and Social Committee and the Committee of the Regions: 'A Roadmap for equality between women and men 2006-2010'*, COM(2006) 92 final, Brussels, 1.03.2006.
——— (2006b). "Communication from the Commission to the Council, the European Parliament, the European Economic and Social Committee and the Committee of the Regions: 'On equality between women and men 2006'", COM(2006) 71 final, Brussels, 22.02.2006.
——— (2006c). *Report on equality between women and men 2006*, Directorate-General for Employment, Social Affairs and Equal Opportunities, Unit G.1, February 2006. (Document drawn up on the basis of COM(2006) 71 final).
——— (2007). Reach in Brief. Available at www.ec.europa.eu/environment/-chemicals/reach/pdf/2007_02_reach_in_brief.pdf, accessed on April 2008.
——— (2008). Report on Equality between women and men 2008. Directorate-General for Employment, Social Affairs and Equal Opportunities, Unit G.1, January 2008. (Document drawn up on the basis of COM(2008) 10 final).

European Union — Consolidated Versions of the Treaty on European Union and of the Treaty Establishing the European Community (consolidated text), Official Journal C 321E of 29 December 2006. Available at http://eur-lex.europa.eu/en/treaties/index.htm, Acceded on March 2007.
European Women's Lobby (2006). "EWL Public Seminar and Workshops: Equal rights, Equal Voices Migrant women in the EU. Resource Document", Brussels: 19-21 January 2006.
Eyerman, R. and A. Jamison (1991). *Social Movements. A Cognitive Approach.* Cambridge: Polity Press.
Falkner, Gerda (1997). "Corporatist Governance and Europeanization: No Future in the Multi-Level Game?" *European Integration online Papers (EIoP),* 1(11): http://eiop.or.at/eiop/texte/1997-011a.htm.
Farnejad, H. (2004). "EU gas directive and its impact on integrated European Companies", *Oil, Gas & Energy Law Intelligence* Vol. 2 – issue 5, December (1-13).
Fasey, A. (2008). "REACH is here; the politics are over, now the hard work starts." Lowell, Mass.: Lowell Center for Sustainable Production.
Faure, A., Pollet, G. and Warin, P. (eds.) (1995). *La construction du sens dans les politiques publiques,* Paris, L'Harmattan.
Finnemore, M. (1996). "Norms, culture and world politics: insights from sociology's institutionalism", *International Organization,* 50(2):325-47.
Fligstein, Neil (1996). "Markets as Politics: A Political-Cultural Approach to Market Institutions". *American Sociological Review,* 61: 656-673.
——— (2001a). "Institutional Entrepreneurs and Cultural Frames: The Case of the European Union's Single Market Program". *European Societies,* 3(3): 261-287.
——— (2001b). "Social Skill and the Theory of Fields". *Sociological Theory,* 19(2), July, *105-125.*
——— and Alec Stone Sweet (2002). "Constructing Polities and Markets: An Institutionalist Account of European Integration". *American Journal of Sociology,* 107(5).
Florin, Christina and Bengt Nilsson (1999). "Something in the Nature of a Bloodless Revolution... How New Gender Relations Became State Policy in Sweden in the 60s and 70s", in *State Policy and Gender System in the Two German States and Sweden 1945-1989,* Rolf Torstendahl (Ed.). Stockholm: Opuscula Historica Upsaliensis, no. 22.
Fowler, Carey (1994). *Unnatural Selection: Technology, Politics, and Plant Evolution.* Yverdon, Switzerland: Gordon and Breach.
Fransen, Frederic J. (2001). *The Supranational Politics of Jean Monnet: Ideas and Origins of the European Community.* Westport, Conn.: Greenwood Press.
Fraser, Nancy (1989). *Unruly Practices: Power, Discourse, and Gender in Contemporary Social Theory.* Minneapolis: University of Minnesota Press.
FSIS, 99-06-03 – US Food and Drug Administration release of information pertaining to ban of EU chicken and pork products due to possible dioxin contamination.
Galtung, Johan (1990). "Cultural Violence". *Journal of Peace Research,* 27(3): 291-305.
Gamson, W. A. (1992). *Talking Politics.* New York, Cambridge University Press.
Gardner, Bruce L. (1995). *Practical Policy Alternatives for the 1995 Farm Bill.* In Daniel A. Sumner (ed.) *Agricultural Policy Reform in the United States.* Washington, DC: The AEI Press. Grains Council of Australia (1993) Newsletter to all Wheatgrowers. Canberra: GCA.
Gee, David and Morris Greenberg (2001). "Asbestos: From 'Magic' to Malevolent Mineral", in *Late Lessons from Early Warnings: The Precautionary Principle 1896-2000,* Poul Harremoës et al (Eds.). Copenhagen: European Environmental Agency, Environmental Issue Report. No. 22: 52-63.

Geertz, C. (1964). "Ideology as a cultural system," in D. E. Apter (ed.) *Ideology and Discontent*, New York, The Free Press.

——— (1973). *The interpretation of cultures*. New York, N.Y., Basic Books.

Gelb, Joyce (1989). *Feminism and Politics: A Comparative Perspective*. Berkeley: University of California Press.

——— (1999). *Globalization and Feminism: The Impact of the New Transnationalisms*. Prepared for the Center for European and Germanic Studies. University of California, Berkeley.

George, S. (1985). *Politics and Policy in the European Community*. Oxford: Oxford University Press.

GIS-BSE (96) 7.5, "Bovine Spongiform Encephalopathy (BSE) Guide, Information for Consumers", Second Edition, 29.10.1996. European Commission.

Gitahy, L. (2000). *A new paradigm of industrial organization: the diffusion of technological and managerial innovations in the Brazilian industry*. Uppsala: Acta Universitatis Upsaliensis.

Glaser, B. and A. Strauss (1967). *The discovery of grounded theory: strategies for qualitative research*. New York: Aldine de Gruyter Publishers.

Goffman, E. (1972). *Frame Analysis*. New York, Harper and Row.

Gottweis, Herbert (1998). *Governing Molecules: The Discursive Politics of Genetic Engineering in Europe and the United States*. Cambridge, Mass.: MIT Press.

Griffiths, Richard T. (1995). "The European Integration Experience: 1945-58". *Orchestrating Europe: The Informal Politics of European Union 1973-1995*, Keith Middlemas, (Ed.). London: Fontana Press: 1-36.

Grubb, M., C. Vrolikj, and D. Brack (1999). *The Kyoto Protocol: A Guide and Assessment*. London: Royal Institute of International Affairs.

Gubrium J. and J. Holstein (1997). *The new language of qualitative method*. New York, N.Y.; Oxford: Oxford University Press.

Gupta, J. and M. Grubb (2000). *Climate Change and European Leadership: A Sustainable Role for Europe?* Dordrecht: Kluwer.

Gustafsson, Gunnel, Maud Eduards and Malin Rönnblom (1997). *Towards a New Democratic Order? Women's Organizing in Sweden in the 1990s*. Stockholm: Publica.

Haas, Ernst (1948). "The United States of Europe". *Political Science Quarterly*, 63(4): 528-550.

Haas, P. M. (1992). "Banning chlorofluorocarbons: epistemic community efforts to protect stratospheric ozone." *International Organizations*, 46(1): 187-224.

Haas, Peter (1992). "Introduction: epistemic communities and international policy co-ordination" in *International Organization*, 46:1-35.

Haimson, L. (2004). "A History of Climate Change Negotiations." http://climate-talks.net/2004-ENVRE130/PDF/20020731-Grist-History-of-Climate.pdf.

Hajer, M. A. (1995). *The Politics of Environmental Discourse*. Oxford, Clarendon Press.

Hall, Peter A. (1992). "The Movement from Keynesianism to Monetarism: Institutional Analysis and British Economic Policy in the 1970s", *Structuring Politics: Historical Institutionalism in Comparative Analysis*, Sven Steinmo, Kathleen Thelen and Frank Longstreth (Eds.). Cambridge: Cambridge University Press: 90-113.

——— (1997). "The Role of Interests, Institutions and Ideas in the Comparative Political Economy of the Industrialized Nations" in Lichbach, M. and Zuckerman, A. (eds.). *Comparative Politics*, Cambridge, Cambridge University Press.

——— (1998). "The Political Economy of Europe in an Era of Interdependence" in Kitschelt, H. et al (eds.). *Change and Continuity in Contemporary Capitalism*, New York, Cambridge University Press.

——— (ed.) (1989). *The Political Power of Economic Ideas: Keynesianism Across Nations*. New Jersey: Princeton University Press.

——— (1989b). "The Politics of Keynesian Ideas", *The Political Power of Economic Ideas*, Peter A. Hall (Ed.). Princeton: Princeton University Press: 361-391.

——— (1993). "Policy Paradigms, Social Learning and the State: The Case of Economic Policy-making in Britain", *Comparative Politics*, 25, 275-297.

Hall, Peter A. and Rosemary C. R. Taylor (1996). "Political Science and the Three New Institutionalisms". *Political Studies,* 44: 936-957.

Hall, Peter A. and Soskice, David. (2001). *Varieties of Capitalism: The Institutional Foundations of Comparative Advantage,* Oxford : Oxford University Press, 2001.

Hanscher, L. (1998). *EU Energy Policy*. Report 4/1998. BI: Senter for elektrisitetsstudier.

——— (2003). 'Harmonization of EU gas markets: The EU gas directive', in Arentsen, M.J. and Künneke, R.W. (eds.) *National Reforms in Natural Gas*. London: Elsevier

Hansen, B.G. and M. Blainey (2006). "REACH: A Step Change in the Management of Chemicals." RECIEL. 15(3): 270-280.

Hansson, S.O. and C. Rudén (2005). "Improving the Scientific Basis for Decisions in the REACH System." In: Claire Weill (ed.), *European Proposal for Chemicals Regulation: REACH and Beyond.* Paris: Les Actes IDDRI no 2: 46-51.

Hantrais, Linda (2000a). *Gendered policies in Europe: reconciling employment and family life*. Basingstoke: Macmillan.

——— (2000b). *Social policy in the European Union*. Basingstoke: Macmillan.

——— (2004). *Family policy matters: responding to family change in Europe*. Bristol: Policy.

Hardy, Cynthia and Nelson Phillips (1999). "No Joking Matter: Discursive Struggles in the Canadian Refugee System". *Organization Studies,* 20(1): 1-24.

Harremoës, Poul, David Gee, Malcolm MacGarvin, Andy Stirling, Jane Keys, Brian Wynne and Sofia Guedes Vaz (2001). *Late Lessons from Early Warnings: The Precautionary Principle 1896-2000*. Copenhagen: EEA, Environmental Issue Report. No. 22: 211 pgs.

Hassenteufel, P. (1997). *Les médecins face à l'État*, Paris, Presses de Sciences Po.

Hebert, Susannah (1999/02/10) "HIV Blood victims demand justice at minister's trial" Issue 1356, 10 February. Electronic Telegraph, http://www.telegraph.co.uk/.

Held, David (1997). *Models of Democracy*. Cambridge: Polity Press.

Helfferich, Barbara and Felix Kolb (2001). "Multi-Level Coordination in European Contentious Politics: The Case of the European Women's Lobby", *Contentious Europeans: Protest Politics in an Emerging Polity*, Doug Imig and Sidney Tarrow (Eds.). Lantham, Md: Rowman & Littlefield.

Henley, John (1999-02-06). "French Politicians on trial for mass AIDS infection". *Guardian.*

Héritier, Adrienne (2001). "Overt and Covert Institutionalization in Europe". *The Institutionalization of Europe*, Alec Stone Sweet, Wayne Sandholtz and Neil Fligstein (Eds.). Oxford: Oxford University Press: 56-70.

Himmelstein, David and Steffie Woolhandler et al. (1989). "A National Health Program for the United States: A Physicians' Proposal". *New England Journal of Medicine,* 320: 102-108.

Hix, Simon (1999b). *The Political System of the European Union*. London: MacMillan.

Hobson, Barbara (2000a). "Agency, Identities, and Institutions". *Social Politics,* 7(2): 238-243.

——— (2003a). "Some Reflections and Agendas for the Future". *Social Politics,* 10(2).

——— (Ed.) (2003b). *Recognition Struggles and Social Movements: Contested Identities, Power and Agency.* Cambridge: Cambridge University Press.

———, Jane Lewis and Birte Siim (2002). *Contested Concepts in Gender and Social Politics*. Cheltenham, UK; Northampton, MA: Edward Elgar.

Holland, Martin (1994). *European Integration: From Community to Union*. London: Pinter Publishers.

Hollingsworth, J. Rogers (2002a). "On Institutional Embeddedness". *Advancing Socio-Economics*, J. Rogers Hollingsworth, Karl H. Müller and Ellen Jane Hollingsworth (Eds.). New York: Rowman & Littlefield: 87-108.

——— (2002b). "On Multi-Level Analysis", in *Advancing Socio-Economics*, J. Rogers Hollingsworth, Karl H. Müller and Ellen Jane Hollingsworth (Eds.). New York: Rowman & Littlefield: 19-36.

———, Karl H. Müller and Ellen Jane Hollingsworth (2002). *Advancing Socio-Economics.* New York: Rowman & Littlefield.

Hooghe, Liesbet and Gary Marks (2001). "Types of Multi-Level Governance". European Integration online Papers (EIoP) 5(11), http://eiop.or.at/eiop/texte/2001-011a.htm (Access Date: 2001-10-01).

Hooke, Mitchell (1993). "The Australian Grains Industry: Planning for the Future", *Agricultural Science*, January.

Hoskyns, Catherine (1991). "The European Women's Lobby". In *Feminist Review*, No. 38: 67-70.

——— (2000). "A study of four Action Programmes on Equal Opportunities". In Hoskyns, Catherine (1996). Integrating Gender Women, Law and Politics in the European Union. London: Verso.

Hourcade, J.C., P. Courtois, and T. Lepesant (2000). "Socio-economics of policy formation and choices." In: Gupta and Grubb (eds.). *Climate Change and European Leadership: A Sustainable Role for Europe?* Dordrecht: Kluwer.

IBAS – (BAN) British Asbestos Newsletter – http://www.lkaz.demon.co.uk/.

ICOH (2000) International Commission on Occupational Health – Minutes of the Business Meeting of the Scientific Committee on Fibres of ICOH on the occasion of the 26th international Congress on Occupational Health in Singapore August 27 – September 2000.

ILO (1986) C162 – Convention Concerning Safety in the Use of Asbestos. International Labor Organization.

Immergut, Ellen I. (1992). "The Rules of the Game: The Logic of Health Policy-Making in France, Switzerland, and Sweden", in *Structuring Politics: Historical Institutionalism in Comparative Analysis*, Sven Steinmo, Kathleen Thelen and Frank Longstreth, (Eds.). Cambridge: Cambridge University Press: 57-89.

Infante, Peter F. (2000). Testimony – See "WTO (2001-03-12) Report of the Appellate Body, Annex VI." In section under Governmental Documents.

——— (2001). "Benzene, a Historical Perspective on the American and European Occupational Setting", in *Late Lessons from Early Warnings: The Precautionary Principle 1896-2000*, Poul Harremoës et al (Eds.). Copenhagen: European Environmental Agency, Environmental Issue Report. No. 22: 38-51.

Innes, Judith Eleanor (1994). *Knowledge and Public Policy: The Search for Meaningful Indicators.* New Brunswick & London: Transaction Publishers.

IP/99/572 – (1999/7/27) "The European Commission bans White Asbestos", News Release, European Commission.

IP/99/850 – (99/11/16). "Commission opens infringement proceedings against France for refusal to lift embargo on British beef", News release, European Commission.

IPCS (1999). International Programme on Chemical Safety.

Jachtenfuchs, Marcus (2002). "Deepening and Widening Integration Theory". *Journal of European Public Policy*, 9(4): 650-657.

Jacobsson, Kerstin (2001). "Employment and Social Policy Coordination. A New System of EU Governance". Scancor Workshop on "Transnational regulation and the regulation of states", Stanford, June 22-23, 2001.

——— (2002). *Soft Regulation and the Subtle Transformation of States: The Case of EU Employment Policy*. Score Rapportserie. Stockholm: SCORE.
Jahan, Rounaq (1995). The Elusive Agenda: Mainstreaming Women in Development. London: Zed Books.
James, B. (1999). "EU Weighs Export Ban on Belgian Poultry", *International Herald Tribune*, 1999-06-02 (http://iht.com/IHT/BJ/99/bj060299.html).
Jenkins-Smith, H. and Sabatier, P. (1993). "The Study of Public Policy Process" in Sabatier, P. and Jenkins-Smith, H. (eds.). *Policy Change and Learning*, Boulder, Westview Press, 1-9.
Jenson, Jane (1989). "Paradigms and political discourse: Protective legislation in France and the United States before 1914. *Canadian Journal of Political Science*, 22(2): 235-258.
Joachim, Jutta (2002). *Comparing the Influence of NGOs in Transnational Institutions: The UN, NGOs and the Case of Gender Violence*. Paper prepared for the 43rd Annual convention of the International Studies Association, New Orleans, LA USA, 24-27 March, 2002.
Jobert, Bruno (1992). "Représentations sociales, controverses et débats dans la conduite des politiques publiques", *Revue française de science politique*, 42, 2, 219-233.
——— (ed.) (1994). *Le tournant néo-libéral en Europe*, Paris, L'Harmattan.
——— and Pierre Muller (1987). *L'État en action*. Paris: PUF.
Joffe, M. and De Broe (1998). "Health Impact of European Single Market Legislation – Overview: Scope, Concepts, and Methods". The Health Impact of European Single Market Legislation: Report of a Public Seminar. European Public Health Alliance, Brussels, Belgium 30 October 1998: 1-9.
Johnston, H. (1995). "The Cultural Analysis of Social Movements". *Social Movements and Culture*. H. Johnston and B. Klandermans. Minneapolis, University of Minnesota Press: 3-24.
Johnston, Hank and Bert Klandermans (1995). *Social Movements and Culture*. Minneapolis: University of Minnesota Press.
Jones, B. D. and F. R. Baumgartner (2005). *The Politics of Attention: How Government Prioritizes Problems*. Chicago, University of Chicago Press.
Keck, Margaret E. and Kathryn Sikkink (1998). *Activists Beyond Borders*. Ithaca: Cornell University Press.
Keeler, John (1987). *The Politics of Neocorporatism in France*. Oxford, Oxford University Press.
——— (1993). "Opening the Window for Reform", *Comparative Political Studies*, 25(4), 433-486.
Kelly, Liz (1999). "Violence against Women: A Policy of Neglect or a Neglect of Policy?" in *New Agendas for Women*, Sylvia Walby (Ed.). London: Macmillan Press: 119-147.
Kemeny, Jim (1983). "Professional Ideologies and Organizational Structure: Tanks and the Military". *Archives Europeennes de Sociologie*, 24(2): 223-240.
——— (2002). "Society Versus the State: The Social Construction of Explanatory Narratives in Social Policy Research". *Housing, Theory and Society*, 19(3/4): 185-195.
Kenis, Patrick (1991). "Social Europe in the 1990s: Beyond an Adjunct to Achieving the Common Market?" *Futures* (September, 1991): 724-738.
Kingdon, J. (1984). *Agendas, Alternatives and Public Policies*, Boston, Little Brown.
Kingdon, J. W. (1995). *Agendas, Alternatives, and Public Policies*. New York, Addison-Wesley.
Kitschelt, H. P. (1986). "Political Opportunity Structure and Political Protest: Anti-Nuclear Movements in Four Democracies." *British Journal of Political Science* 16: 57-85.
Kjellén, B. (2008). *A New Diplomacy for Sustainable Development*. London-New York: Routledge.
Knoke, D., Pappi, F.U., Broadbent, J. and Y. Tsujinaka (1996). *Comparing Policy Networks: Labor politics in the U.S., Germany, and Japan*. Cambridge, Cambridge University Press.

Kofman, Eleonore and Rosemary Sales (2000). "The Implications of European Union Policies for Non-EU Migrant Women". In Rossilli, Mariagrazia (ed.), *Gender Policies in the European Union*. New York: Peter Lang Publishing.

Kohler, B. and R. Eising (1999). *The Transformation of Governance in the European Union*. London: Routledge.

Koppe, Janna G. and Jane Keys (2001). "Pcbs and the Precautionary Principle", in *Late Lessons from Early Warnings: The Precautionary Principle 1896-2000*, Poul Harremoës et al, (Eds.). Copenhagen: European Environmental Agency, Environmental Issue Report. No. 22: 64-75.

Krämer, L. (2006). "Some reflections on the EU mix of instruments on climate change." Pp. 279-296. In M. Peeters and K. Deketelaere (eds.). *EU Climate Change Policy: The Challenge of New Regulatory Initiatives*. Northampton, MA.: Edward Elgar.

Kruger, J. (2005). *Companies and Regulators in Emissions Trading Programs*. Discussion Paper 5-03. Washington, D.C. Resources for the Future.

——— and C. Egenhofer (2006). "Confidence through Compliance in Emissions Trading Markets." *Sustainable Development Law and Policy*. Vol. VI (#2):2-13.

Kuhn, T. S. (1962). *The Structure of Scientific Revolutions*, 1st. ed., Chicago: Univ. of Chicago Press.

Kuhn, Thomas S. (1970). *The Structure of Scientific Revolutions*. Chicago: University of Chicago Press.

——— (2000). "Commensurability, Comparability, Communicability", *The Road since Structure*, James Conant and John Haugeland (Eds.). Chicago: University of Chicago Press: 33-57.

Kuhn, T. S., J. Conant et al. (2000). *The road since structure: philosophical essays, 1970-1993, with an autobiographical interview*. Chicago, University of Chicago Press.

Kurz, Demie (1989). "Social Science Perspectives on Wife Abuse: Current Debates and Future Directions". *Gender and Society, Special Issue: Violence against Women*, 3(4): 489-505.

Lakoff, George (1996). *Moral Politics: What Conservatives Know That Liberals Don't*. Chicago: University of Chicago Press.

——— and Mark Johnson (1980). *Metaphors We Live By*. Chicago: University of Chicago Press.

Lancet (2000). "Resisting Smoke and Spin". *The Lancet*, 355(9211): 1197.

Lane, Jan-Erik and Svante Erisson (2002). *Culture and Politics: A Comparative Approach*. Aldershot: Ashgate.

Lasswell, H. (1951). "The Policy Orientation". *The Policy Sciences: Recent Developments in Scope and Methods*. D. Lerner and H. Lasswell. Stanford, CA, Stanford University Press.

Leca, J. (1997). *The Enduring Dialogue of Conflict and Order in a Changing World: Political Science at the Turn of the Century*, unpublished manuscript.

Legro, Jeffrey (2000). "The Transformation of Policy Ideas". *American Journal of Political Science*, 44(3): 419-432.

Lehmbruch, Gerhard (1984). *The Logic and Structural Conditions of Neo-Corporatist Concertation*, in John Goldthorpe (ed.) *Order and Conflict in Contemporary Capitalism*. Oxford: Oxford University Press.

Leibfried, Stephan and Paul Pierson (1995a). "Semisovereign Welfare States: Social Policy in a Multitiered Europe", in *European Social Policy: Between Fragmentation and Integration*, Stephan Leibfried and Paul Pierson (Eds.). Washington, D.C.: Brookings Institution: 43-77.

——— (Eds.) (1995b). *European Social Policy: Between Fragmentation and Integration*. Washington, D.C.: Brookings Institution.

Lewis, Jane (2006). "Work/family reconciliation, equal opportunities and social policies: the interpretation of policy trajectories at the EU level and the meaning of gender equality". *Journal of European Public Policy*, Vol. 13, No. 3: 420–437.

Lind, G. (2004). REACH: The Only Planet Guide to the Secrets of Chemicals Policy in the EU. What Happened and Why? Norrtälje, Sweden: Affärstryckeriet.

Lindblom, C. (1959). "The Science of Muddling-Through", *Public Administration Review*, 19, 79-83.
Lofstedt, Ragnar (2002). "The Precautionary Principle: Risk, Regulation, and Politics". Merton College, Oxford, 5-11 April 2002 http://www.21stcenturytrust.org/precprin.htm (Access Date: 2003/07/23).
Lok, C. and D. Powell (2000). "The Belgian Dioxin Crisis of the Summer of 1999: A Case Study in Crisis Communications and Management". Technical Report #13. Department of Food Science, University of Guelph, Ontario Canada.
Lombardo, Emanuela (2003). "EU Gender Policy. Trapped in the 'Wollstonecraft Dilemma'?". *The European Journal of Women's Studies*, 10(2): 159–180.
——— (2005). "Integrating or Setting the Agenda? Gender Mainstreaming in the European Constitution-Making Process". *Social Politics*, 12(3).
Lombardo, Emanuela and Petra Meier (2006). "Gender Mainstreaming in the EU. Incorporating a Feminist Reading?" *European Journal of Women's Studies*. London: SAGE Publications.
Lowell Center for Sustainable Production (University of Massachusetts Lowell) (2008). www.chemicalspolicy.org/reach.shtml.
Lutebacher, U. and D.F. Sprinz (1995). *International Relations and Global Climate Change*. Cambridge, Mass.: MIT Press.
Lyons, P. (1992). *EC Energy Policy. A Detailed Guide to the Community's Impact on the Energy Sector.* London: Financial Times Business Information.
——— (1994). *Energy Policies of the European Union*. London: EC Inform.
Maastricht Treaty (1993). (Treaty on European Union) Available via Eur-Lex, http://europa.eu.int/eur-lex/.
Machado, Nora (1998). *Using the bodies of the dead: Legal, ethical, and organizational dimensions of organ transplantation*. Dartmouth: Ashgate Publishers.
——— (2005), "Discretionary Death: Conditions, Dilemmas, and Normative Regulation". *Death Studies*, Volume 29, Issue 9, 791-809.
——— and Tom R. Burns (1998). "Complex Social Organizations: Multiple Organizing Modes, Structural Incongruence, and Mechanisms of Integration". *Public Administration*, 76: 335-385.
MacKenzie, D. (2007). "The Political Economy of Carbon Trading." *London Review of Books*, 29(7), dated 5 April 2007.
——— (2009). "Constructing Emissions Markets." *Material Markets: How Economic Agents are Constructed.* Oxford: Oxford University Press.
Majone, Giandomenico (1992). *Ideas, Interests and Policy Change*. EUI Working Paper SPS, No. 92/21. European University Institute.
——— (2002). "What Price Safety? The Precautionary Principle and Its Policy Implications". *Journal of Common Market Studies*, 40(1): 89-109.
——— (Ed.) (1996). *Regulating Europe*. London: Routledge.
March, J. (ed.) (1965). *Handbook of Organizations*. Chicago: Rand McNally.
March, James G. and Johan P. Olsen (1989). *Rediscovering Institutions. The Organizational Basis of Politics*. New York: Free Press.
Marin, Bernd (1985). *Austria: The Paradigm Case of Liberal Corporatism?* in Wyn Grant (ed.). *The Political Economy of Corporatism*. London, Macmillan, 89-125.
Marks, Gary, Fritz Scharpf, Philippe C. Schmitter and Wolfgang Streeck (Eds.) (1996). *Governance in the European Union*. London: Sage.
Marris, Claire (2000). "Swings and Roundabouts: French Public Policy on Agricultural Gmos 1996-1999". Centre d'Economie et d'Ethique pour l'Environnement et le Développment (C3ED).

Matlary J.H. (1991). *From the Internal Energy Market to a Community Energy Policy? An Analysis of Decision-making with Emphasis on Natural Gas.* FNI-Report 005. Lysaker: FNI.
——— (1996). *Internal Market Regime or New Polity Model: Whither the European Union?* ARENA Working Paper no. 26. Oslo: ARENA.
——— (1997). *Energy Policy in the European Union.* London: Macmillan Press.
Mazey, Sonia (2000). "Integrating gender – intellectual and 'real world' mainstreaming". *Journal of European Public Policy*, 7(3): 333–345.
——— (2001). *Gender mainstreaming in the EU: principles and practice.* London: Kogan Page.
——— (2002). "Gender Mainstreaming Strategies in the E.U.: Delivering on an Agenda?". *Feminist Legal Studies*, 10(3): 227–240.
McGinty, P., T. R.Burns, and P. Hall (2009). "Meta-Power", *Blackwell Encyclopedia of Sociology*, G. Ritzer (ed.). Oxford/NewYork: Blackwell.
McNamara, K. (1998). *The Currency of Ideas*, Ithaca and London, Cornell University Press.
Mériaux, O. (1995). "Référentiel, représentation(s) sociale(s) et idéologie" in Faure, A., Pollet, G. and Warin, P. (eds.). *La construction du sens dans les politiques publiques*, Paris, L'Harmattan, 49-68.
Meyer, J.W. (2001). "The European Union and globalisation of culture", in Andersen, S.S. (ed.) *Institutional Approaches to the Study of the European Union.* ARENA, University of Oslo, 3.
———, J. Boli, G.M. Thomas, and F.O. Ramirez (1997). 'World Society and the Nation-State'. *American Journal of Sociology*, 103(1).
Meyer, John W. and Brian Rowan (1977). "Institutionalized Organizations: Formal Structure as Myth and Ceremony". *American Journal of Sociology,* 83(2): 340-363.
Michels, Robert (1962). *Political Parties: A Sociological Study of the Oligarchical Tendencies of Modern Democracy.* New York: The Free Press.
Mitrany, David (1948). "The Functional Approach to World Organization". *International Affairs,* 24(3): 350-363.
Moravcsik, Andrew (1998). *The Choice for Europe: Social Purpose and State Power from Messina to Maastricht.* London: UCL Press.
——— (2002). "In Defense of the 'Democratic Deficit': Reassessing Legitimacy in the European Union". *Journal of Common Market Studies,* 40(4): 603-624.
Morel-ál'Huissier, Patrick (1995). "Chrysotile", in Canadian Minerals Yearbook: Natural Resources Canada: http://www.nrcan-rncan.gc.ca (Access Date: 2001/2003/2017).
Morgenthau, H.J. (1973). *Politics Among Nations: The Struggle for Power and Peace.* New York: Knopf.
Muller, P. (1994). *Les politiques publiques*, Paris, PUF.
——— and Surel, Y. (1996). "Crises de politiques et régulations cognitives: l'exemple des politiques du livre", *Pôle Sud*, 4, 92-106.
Nee, Victor (1998). "Sources of the New Institutionalism", *The New Institutionalism in Sociology,* Mary C. Brinton and Victor Nee (Eds.). New York: Russell Sage Foundation: 1-16.
Neuman, Yair and Iris Tabak (2003). "Inconsistency as an Interactional Problem: A Lesson from Political Rhetoric." *Journal of Psycholinguistic Research,* 32(3): 251-267.
New South Wales Farmers' Association (1993). *The Grain File.* Sydney: NSW Farmers Association.
Nicoll, William and Trevor C. Salmon (1994). *Understanding the New European Community.* London: Harvester Wheatsheaf.
North, Douglass C. (1981). *Structure and Change in Economic History.* New York: WW Norton and Company.
——— (1990). *Institutions, Institutional Change and Economic Performance.* Cambridge, Cambridge University Press.

NRC – Natural Resources Canada (http://www.nrcan.gc.ca).
NRC (2001). "Chrysotile Asbestos: Fact Sheet", Natural Resources Canada, http://www.nrcan.gc.ca/mms/pdf/chry_e.pdf (Access date: 2001/09/02).
Nugent, Neill (1995). *The Government and Politics of the European Union.* London: MacMillan Press.
Nylander, Johan (2000). "The Power of Framing: A New-Institutional Approach to Interest Group Participation in the European Union". *Doctoral Dissertation, Department of Sociology.* Uppsala: Uppsala University.
O'Riordan, T. and J. Jager (1996). *Politics of Climate Change in Europe: A European Perspective.* London: Routledge.
Ohlsson, S. (2000). "Falsification, Anomalies and the Naturalistic Approach to Cognitive Change." *Science & Education* 9: 1-2.
Oliver, P. E. and H. Johnston (2000). "What a Good Idea! Ideologies and Frames in Social Movement Research." *Mobilization,* 5(1): 37-54.
Olsen, J.P. (2001). *Organizing European institutions of government. A prelude to an institutional account of political integration.* in Andersen, S.S. (ed.) *Institutional Approaches to the Study of the European Union.* ARENA, University of Oslo, 3/2001.
Olson, Elizabeth (2000). "Health Tops Free Trade in WTO Ruling", *International Herald Tribune,* June 16, 2000. Pg. 16.
Olson, M. (1971). *The Logic of Collective Action: Public Goods and the Theory of Groups.* Cambridge, MA, Harvard University Press.
Olsson, Sven E. (1990). *Social Policy and the Welfare State in Sweden.* Lund: Archiv.
Ostner I. and Lewis J. (1995). "Gender and the Evolution of European Social Policies". In S. Leibfried and P. Pierson (eds.). *European Social Policy: Between Fragmentation and Integration.* Washington DC: Brookings Institution.
Ostner, Ilona (2000). "From Equal Pay to Equal Employability: Four Decades of European Gender Policies", *Gender Policies in the European Union,* Mariagrazia Rossilli (Ed.). New York, Peter Lang: 25-42.
Padgett, S. (1992). 'The Single European Market: the politics of realization", *Journal of Common Market Studies,* 1.
Paris Treaty (1952) (European coal and Steel community). Available via Eur-Lex, http://europa.eu.int/eur-lex/.
Parsons, Craig (2002). "Showing Ideas as Causes: The Origins of the European Union". *International Organization,* 56(1): 47-84.
Peeters, M. and K. Deketelaere (2006). *EU Climate Change Policy: The Challenge of New Regulatory Policy.* Northampton, MA.: Edward Elgar.
Perez, C. (1983). "Structural Change and Assimilation of New Technologies in the Economic and Social System." In: Freeman C. (ed.), *Design, Innovation and Long Cycles in Economic Development.* London: Design Research Publications.
——— (1985). "Microelectronics, Long Waves and World Structural Change: New Perspectives for Developing Countries." *World Development,* Vol. 13(3): 441-463.
Perron, Louis (1999). "Chrysotile", in Canadian Minerals Yearbook: http://www.nrcan-rncan.gc.ca (Access Date: 2001/03/17).
Perrow, Charles (1979). *Complex Organizations.* Glenview, IL, USA: Scott, Forseman & Company.
Peterson, John (1995). "Decision-Making in the European Union: Towards a Framework for Analysis". *Journal of European Public Policy,* 2(1): 69-93.
——— (2001). "The Choice for EU Theorists: Establishing a Common Framework for Analysis". *European Journal of Political Research,* 39(3): 289-318.

Pierson, Paul (1993). "When Effect Becomes Cause: Policy Feedback and Political Change", *World Politics*, 45, 595-628.
——— (1994). *Dismantling the Welfare State? Reagan, Thatcher and the Politics of Retrenchment.* New York, Cambridge University Press.
——— (1996). "The New Politics of the Welfare State". *World Politics*, 48, 143-179.
——— (1996). "The path to the European Integration – a historical institutionalist analysis". *Comparative Political Studies*, 29(2):123-163.
——— (1997). *Increasing Returns, Path Dependence and the Study of Politics*, EUI Florence, RSC Jean Monnet Chair Paper no 44.
——— (2001). *Big, Slow Moving... and Invisible: Macro Social Process in the Study of Comparative Politics.* http://www.people.fas.harvard.edu/~pierson/bigslow.pdf (Access Date: 2004/01/22).
Piggott, Roley (1990). *Agricultural Marketing*, in D.B. Williams (ed.). *Agriculture in the Australian Economy.* South Melbourne: Sydney University Press.
Pinder, John, (Ed.) (1998). *Altiero Spinelli and the British Federalists: Writings by Beveridge, Robbins, and Spinelli 1937-1943.* London: Federal Trust.
Pizer, W. A. (2006). "The Evolution of a Global Climate Change Agreement." *American Economic Review*, 96(2), 26-30.
Plantenga, Janneke and Chantal Remery (2005). "Reconciliation of work and private life. A comparative review of thirty European countries." European Commission, Directorate-General for Employment, Social Affairs and Equal Opportunities, EU Expert Group on Gender, Social Inclusion and Employment (EGGSIE). Luxembourg: Office for Official Publications of the European Communities.
Pollack, Mark A. (1998b). "The Engines of Integration? Supranational Autonomy and Influence in the European Union", in *European Integration and Supranational Governance*, Wayne Sandholtz and Alec Stone-Sweet, (Eds.). Oxford: Oxford University Press: 217-249.
——— and Emilie Hafner-Burton (2000). "Mainstreaming gender in the European Union". *Journal of European Public Policy*, 7(3): 432-56.
——— (2002). "Gender Mainstreaming and Global Governance". *Feminist Legal Studies*, 10(3): 285-298.
Potter, Jonathan (1996). *Representing Reality: Discourse, Rhetoric and Social Construction.* London; Thousand Oaks, CA: Sage.
Poulsen, Helle (2006). *The elusive gender. The International Labour Organization and the construction of gender equality.* PhD thesis. Department of Political Sciences. University of Copenhagen.
Powell, Walter W. and Paul DiMaggio (1991). *The New Institutionalism in Organizational Analysis.* Chicago: University of Chicago Press.
PR-1 (1999-06-02). "Commission decision on Dioxin contaminated poultry and poultry products". Press Release by the EC, DG Health and Consumer Protection.
Radaelli, C. (1995). "The Role of Knowledge in the Policy Process", *Journal of European Public Policy*, 2(2), 159-183.
——— (1998). *The Politics of Corporate Taxation in the European Union*, London, Routledge.
Ragin, Charles C. (1987). The comparative method: moving beyond qualitative and quantitative strategies. Berkeley: University of California Press.
REACH (2008). www.ecb.jrc.it/REACH Regulation (EC) No 1907/2006 of the European Parliament and of the Council of 18 December 2006 concerning the Registration, Evaluation, Authorisation and Restriction of Chemicals (REACH), establishing a European Chemicals Agency, amending Directive 1999/45/EC and repealing Council Regulation (EEC) No 793/93 and Commission Regulation (EC) No 1488/94 as well as Council Di-

rective 76/769/EEC and Commission Directives 91/155/EEC, 93/67/EEC, 93/105/EC and 2000/21/EC.
Rees, Teresa (1998). *Mainstreaming Equality in the European Union, Education, Training and Labour Market Policies.* London: Routledge.
——— (2000). "Mainstreaming Gender Equality in Science in the European Union: The 'ETAN Report'". Paper prepared for the Mainstreaming Gender in European Public Policy Workshop, University of Wisconsin-Madison.14-15th October 2000.
——— (2001). "Mainstreaming Gender Equality in Science in the European Union: the ETAN Report." *Gender and Education*, Vol. 13, Issue 3, 2001:243–260.
——— (2002). *Gender Mainstreaming: Misappropriated and Misunderstood?* Paper presented to the Department of Sociology University of Stockholm, February 21st 2002.
——— (2005). "Reflections on the Uneven Development of Gender Mainstreaming". *International Feminist Journal of Politics*, Vol. 7, No. 4.
Restivo, S. (1983). "The Myth of the Kuhnian Revolution." *Sociological Theory* 1: 293-305.
Risse, Thomas and Kathryn Sikkink (1999). "The Socialization of International Human Rights Norms into Domestic Practices: Introduction", *The Power of Human Rights: International Norms and Domestic Change*, Thomas Risse-Kappen, Stephen C. Ropp and Kathryn Sikkink (Eds.). Cambridge: Cambridge University Press: 1-38.
Risse-Kappen, Thomas (1996). "Exploring the Nature of the Beast: International Relations Theory and Comparative Policy Analysis Meet the European Union". *Journal of Common Market Studies*, 34, 53-80.
Ritzer, G. (1975). *Sociology: A Multi-Paradigm Science.* Boston: Allyn & Bacon.
ROHS (2006). http://www.rohs.eu/english/legislation/docs/launchers/launch-2006-692-EC.html.
Roman, M. and M. Carson (2009). *Sea Change: US Climate Policy Prospects under the Obama Administration.* Stockholm: The Commission on Sustainable Development.
Rosamond, Ben (2000). *Theories of European Integration.* Houndmills: Palgrave.
Rosenstock, M. (2006). "Energy taxation within the EU." Pp. 240-255. In Peeters and Deketelaere (eds.).
Rossilli, Mariagrazia (ed.) (2000). *Gender Policies in the European Union.* New York: Peter Lang Publishing.
Rudén, C. and S. O. Hansson (2006) "Improving REACH", *Regulatory Toxicology and Pharmacology* 44:33-42.
Sabatier, Paul A. (1993). "Policy Change over a Decade or More" in Sabatier, P. and Jenkins-Smith, H. (eds.) *Policy Change and Learning*, Boulder, Westview Press, 13-39.
——— (1998). "The Advocacy Coalition Framework: Revisions and Relevance for Europe", *Journal of European Public Policy*, 5, 1, 98-130.
——— (1999a). "The Need for Better Theories", *Theories of the Policy Process*, Paul Sabatier, and Hank Jenkins-Smith (Ed.). Boulder, CO: Westview Press: 3-18.
——— (2003). *Beliefs and Institutions in Water Resources Management: Advocacy Coalitions and Collaborative Governance.* Paper read at Symposium on Adaptive Governance and Florida's Water Conflicts, November 21-22, 2003, at Florida State University.
——— (Ed.) (1999b). *Theories of the Policy Process. Theoretical Lenses on Public Policy.* Boulder, CO, Westview Press.
——— and H. Jenkins-Smith (1999c). "The Advocacy Coalition Framework: An Assessment." In: P. Sabatier (Ed.). *Theories of the Policy Process. Theoretical Lenses on Public Policy.* Boulder, CO, Westview Press.

——— (Eds.) (1993). *Policy Change and Learning: An Advocacy Coalition Approach*. Boulder, CO: Westview Press.
Sandholtz, Wayne and Alec Stone-Sweet (Eds.) (1998). European Integration and Supranational Governance. Oxford: Oxford University Press.
Sankey, Howard (1993). "Kuhn's Changing Concept of Incommensurability". *The British Journal for the Philosophy of Science*, 44(4): 759-774.
Sayer, Andrew (1992). *Method in Social Science: A Realist Approach*. London: Routledge.
Scharpf, Fritz W. (1988). "The Joint Decision Trap: Lessons from German Federalism and European Integration". *Public Administration*, 66, 239-278.
——— (1989). "Decision Rules, Decision Styles and Policy Choices." *Journal of Theoretical Politics*, 1, 149-176.
——— (1997a). "Introduction: The Problem-Solving Capacity of Multi-Level Governance". *Journal of European Public Policy*, 4(4): 520-538.
——— (2001). "Notes toward a Theory of Multi-Level Governing in Europe". *Scandinavian Political Studies*, 24(1): 1-26.
——— (2002). "The European Social Model: Coping with the Challenges of Diversity". *Journal of Common Market Studies*, 40(4): 645-670.
Scheiwe, E. (1994). "EC Law's Unequal Treatment of the Family". *Social and Legal Studies*, 3: 243-265.
Scheuer, S. (2005). *EU Environmental Policy Handbook*. Brussels: European Environmental Bureau.
Schmidt, S. (1997). 'Sterile debates and dubious generalisations: European integration theory tested by Telecommunications and Electricity', *Journal of Public Policy* 16(3), 233-271.
Schmidt, Verena (2005). *Gender mainstreaming – an innovation in Europe?: the institutionalisation of gender mainstreaming in the European Commission*. Opladen: Budrich.
Schmitter, Philippe C. (1979). *Still the Century of Corporatism?* In Schmitter and Gerhard Lehmbruch (eds.). *Trends Toward Corporatist Intermediation*. London: Sage, 7-52.
——— (1996a). "Imagining the Future of the Euro-Polity with the Help of New Concepts", *Governance in the European Union*, Gary Marks, Fritz Scharpf, Philippe C. Schmitter and Wolfgang Streeck (Eds.). London: Sage: 121-150.
——— (1996b). "Examining the Present Euro-Polity with the Help of Past Theories", *Governance in the European Union*, Gary Marks, Fritz Scharpf, Philippe C. Schmitter and Wolfgang Streeck, (Eds.). London: Sage: 1-14.
——— (2004). "Neo-Neo-Functionalism: Déjá Vu, All over Again?" in *European Integration Theory*, Antje Wiener and Thomas Dietz (Eds.). Oxford: Oxford University Press: 45-74.
Schmitz, H. (1989). "Flexible Specialization – A New Paradigm of Small-Scale Industrialization." *Discussion Paper*, no. 261. Sussex: Institute of Development Studies, University of Sussex.
Schon, D. and Rein, M. (1994). *Frame Reflection: Resolving Intractable Policy Issues*, New York, Basic Books.
Schuker, Stephen A. (2000). "The European Union from Jean Monnet to the Euro: A Historical Overview," *The European Union: From Jean Monnet to the Euro*, Dean J. Kotlowski (Ed.). Athens, OH: Ohio University Press: 1-18.
Scott, John (2000). *A Matter of Record: Documentary Sources in Social Research*. Cambridge: Polity Press.
Scott, W. Richard (1987). "The Adolescence of Institutional Theory". *Administrative Science Quarterly*, 32(4): 493-511.
Shaw, Jo (2000). "Importing Gender: The Challenge of Feminism and the Analysis of the EU Legal Order". *Journal of European Public Policy*, 7(3): 406-431.

——— (2002). "The European Union and Gender Mainstreaming: Constitutionally Embedded or Comprehensively Marginalised?" *Feminist Legal Studies*, Vol. 10, No. 3: 213–226.
Single European Act (1987). Available via Eur-Lex, http://europa.eu.int/eur-lex/.
Skogstad, Grace (1987). *The Politics of Agricultural Policy-Making in Canada.* Toronto: University of Toronto Press.
——— (1990). "The Farm Policy Community and Public Policy in Ontario and Quebec", in Coleman and Skogstad (eds.). *Policy Communities and Public Policy in Canada: A Structural Approach.* Toronto: Copp Clark Pitman.
Snow, D.A. and R.D. Benford (1992). "Master Frames and Cycles of Protest", in *Frontiers in Social Movement Theory*, Aldon Morris and Carol McClurg Mueller (Eds.). New Haven: Yale University Press.
Snow, D.A., E.B. Rochford, Jr., S.K. Worden and R.D. Benford (1986). "Frame Alignment Processes, Micromobilization, and Movement Participation". *American Sociological Review,* 51: 464-481.
Sorrel, S. (2003). "Turning an early start into a false start: Implications of the EU emissions trading Directive for the UK Climate Change Levy and Climate Change Agreements" (CCNM/GF/SD/ENV(2003)7/FINAL). OECD Global Forum on sustainable Development: Emissions Trading. Concerted Action on Tradeable Emissions. 17-18 March, 2003 OECD Headquarters, Paris.
Spector, Malcolm and John I. Kitsuse (1987). *Constructing Social Problems.* New York: Aldine de Gruyter.
SPEECH/OO/41 – (2000). "2000–2005: Shaping the New Europe", Speech of Romano Prodi, President of the European Commission to European Parliament.
Spinelli, Altiero (1998 [1944]). "The United States of Europe and the Various Political Tendencies", *Altierro Spinelli and the British Federalists*, John Pinder (Ed.). London: Federal Trust: 73-85.
Spinelli, Altiero and Ernesto Rossi (1998 [1944]). "The Ventotene Manifesto", *Altiero Spinelli and the British Federalists: Writings by Beveridge, Robbins, and Spinelli 1937-1943*, John Pinder (Ed.). London: Federal Trust: 73-86.
Squires, Judith (2005). "Is Mainstreaming Transformative? Theorizing Mainstreaming in the Context of Diversity and Deliberation". *Social Politics*, 12(3).
Steinmo, S. (1989) "Political Institutions and Tax Policy in the United States, Sweden and Britain," *World Politics*, Vol. LXI, No. 4, pp. 500-535.
———, K. Thelen et al., Eds. (1992). *Structuring Politics: Historical Institutionalism in Comparative Analysis.* Cambridge, Cambridge University Press.
Stephens, J. (1973). "The Kuhnian Paradigm and Political Inquiry: An Appraisal." *American Journal of Political Science,* 17(3): 467-488.
Sterk, W., Braun, M., Haug, C., Korytarova, K., Scholten. A. (2006). "Ready to Link Up? Implications of Design Differences for Linking Domestic Emissions Trading Schemes." Wuppertal, Germany: Wuppertal Institut: JET-SET.
Stern, J.P. (1992). *Third Party Access in European Gas Industries: Regulation-driven or Market-led?* London: The Royal Institute of International Affairs.
——— (1998). *Competition and Liberalization in the European Gas Market. A Diversity Model.* London: The Royal Institute of International Affairs.
Stinchcombe, A. (1968). *Constructing social theories.* New York: Harcourt, Brace & World.
——— (1995). "Social Structure and Organizations." In J.G. March (ed.), *Handbook of Organizations*, 142-193. Chicago: Rand McNally.
Stone, D. (1988). *Policy Paradox and Political Reason*, Glenview, Scott, Foresman.

Stone-Sweet, Alec, Wayne Sandholtz and Neil Fligstein (2001). *The Institutionalization of Europe*. Oxford: Oxford University Press.
Stratigaki, Maria (2004). "The co-optation of gender concepts in EU policies: the case of 'reconciliation of work and family'". *Social Politics*, 11(1): 30–56.
——— (2005). "Gender Mainstreaming vs. Positive Action. An Ongoing Conflict in EU Gender Equality Policy". *European Journal of Women's Studies*. London: SAGE Publications.
Surel, Yves (1995). "Les politiques publiques comme paradigmes". In Faure, A., Pollet, G. and Warin, P. (eds.) *La construction du sens dans les politiques publiques*, Paris, L'Harmattan, 125-151.
——— (2000). "The Role of Cognitive and Normative Frames in Policy-Making". *Journal of European Public Policy*, 7(4): 495-512.
Sutton, Caroline (1998). *Swedish Alcohol Discourse: Constructions of a Social Problem*. Doctoral Dissertation, Department of Sociology, Uppsala University. Uppsala: Acta Universitatis Upsaliensis, Studia Sociologica Upsaliensia, 45.
Thelen, Kathleen and Sven Steinmo (1992). "Historical Institutionalism in Comparative Politics", in *Structuring Politics: Historical Institutionalism in Comparative Analysis*, Sven Steinmo, Kathleen Thelen and Frank Longstreth (Eds.). Cambridge: Cambridge University Press: 1-33.
Thompson, John B. (1990). *Ideology and Modern Culture*. Stanford: Stanford University Press.
Tilton, Tim (1990). *The Political Theory of Swedish Social Democracy*. Oxford: Clarendon Press.
Tower, Courtney (1994). *Opinions vary at safety net talks; little progress is made*. The Western Producer, April 14, 8.
Treaty of Amsterdam (1997). Treaty of Amsterdam amending the treaty on European Union, the treaties establishing the European communities and certain related acts. Amsterdam: 2 October 1997. Available at http://www.eurotreaties.com/amsterdamtreaty.pdf, Acceded on November 2006.
Treaty of Nice (2001). Official Journal C 80 of 10 March 2001. Available at http://eur-lex.europa.eu/en/treaties/index.htm, Acceded on March 2007.
Treaty of Rome (1957). Treaty establishing the European Economic Community. Available at http://eur-lex.europa.eu/en/treaties/treaties_founding.htm, Acceded on February 2007.
Treaty of Rome (1958): (Euratom) Available via Eur-Lex, http://europa.eu.int/eur-lex/.
Treaty of Rome (1958): (European Economic Community). Available via Eur-Lex, http://europa.eu.int/eur-lex/.
Treaty on European Union (1992). (Treaty of Maastricht signed in 1992). Official Journal C 191 of 29 July 1992. Available at http://eur-lex.europa.eu/en/treaties/dat/11992M/-htm/11992M.html#0001000001, Acceded on February 2007.
Trebeck, David (1990). *Farmer Organisations*, in D.B. Williams (ed.) *Agriculture in the Australian Economy*. South Melbourne: Sydney University Press.
Trubek, David M. and Louise G. Trubek (2003). "Hard and Soft Law in the Construction of Social Europe". SALTSA, OSE, UW Workshop on "Opening the Open Method of Coordination", European University Institute, Florence, Italy, July, 2003.
Tugwell, F. (1988). *The energy crisis and the American political economy. Politics and markets in the management of natural resources*. Stanford: Stanford University Press.
Tweedale, G. (2000) *Magic Mineral to Killer Dust: Turner & Newall and the Asbestos Hazard*. New York: Oxford University Press.
U.S. Department of Labor (1993). "Family and Medical Leave Act." Washington, D.C.: U.S. Government Publishing Office.
UN (1972). *Stockholm Declaration of the United Nations Conference on Human Environment*, 17 June 1972. A/CONF.48/14.

United Nations (1995). The Beijing Platform for Action. Fourth World Conference on Women, Division for the Advancement of Women, Department of Economics and Social Affairs. Available at http://www.un.org/womenwatch/daw/beijing/platform/, Acceded on January 2007.
United Nations 1993 Vienna Declaration and Programme of Action. UN:A/CONF. 157.23. http://www.unhchr.ch/huridocda/huridoca.nsf/(Symbol)/A.CONF.157.23.En.
United States General Accounting Office (1992). Canada and Australia Rely Heavily on Wheat Boards to Market Grain. Washington, D.C.: USGAO.
US Geological Survey (2007). *Mineral Commodities Summaries.* Washington, D.C.: U.S. Government Printing Office.
Usherwood, S. (1998). *Energy policy.* In Gløcker, Junius, Usherwood og Vassallo, *Guide to EU policies.* London: Blackstone Press.
van den Belt, Henk and Bart Gremmen (2002). "Between Precautionary Principle and 'Sound Science': Distributing the Burdens of Proof". *Journal of Agricultural and Environmental Ethics,* 15: 103-122.
van Dijk, Teun A. (1995). "Discourse Semantics and Ideology". *Discourse & Society,* 6(2): 243-289.
——— (1998). *Ideology: A Multidisciplinary Approach.* London, Sage.
van Waarden, Frans (1992). "Dimensions and types of policy networks". *European Journal of Political Research,* 21, 29-52.
Verloo, Mieke (2004). "Mainstreaming gender equality in Europe. A frame analysis approach", Conference of the Europeanists in Chicago, March 11-13, 2004.
Verloo, Mieke (2005). "Displacement and Empowerment: Reflections on the Concept and Practice of the Council of Europe Approach to Gender Mainstreaming and Gender Equality". *Social Politics,* 12(3): 344–65.
Victor, D. and J. House (2005). "BP's Emissions Trading Scheme." *Energy Policy* 34:2102.
Vogel, David (1993). "The Making of EC Environmental Policy", in *Making Policy in Europe: The Europeification of National Policy-Making,* Svein S. Andersen and Kjell A. Eliassen (Eds.). London: Sage: 115-132.
——— (1995). *Trading Up: Consumer and Environmental Regulation in a Global Economy.* Cambridge, Mass.: Harvard University Press.
——— (1997). "Trading up and Governing Across: Transnational Governance and Environmental Protection". *Journal of European Public Policy,* 4(4): 556-571.
——— (2003). "The Hare and the Tortoise Revisited: The New Politics of Consumer and Environmental Regulation in Europe." *British Journal of Political Science,* Vol. 33:557-580.
——— (2009). "Climate Change and EU Foreign Policy: The Negotiation of Burden Sharing." *International Politics.* Vol. 46 (#4): 469-490.
Vogel, Laurent (1999). "The WTO Asbestos Dispute: Workplace Health Dictated by Trade Rules?" *Lannee Sociale. Institute of Sociology, Brussels.*
Walby, Sylvia (2004). "The European Union and Gender Equality: Emergent Varieties of Gender Regime". *Social Politics,* Vol. 11, No. 1: 4–29.
——— (2005). "Gender Mainstreaming: Productive Tensions in Theory and Practice". *Social Politics,* 12(3).
Waltz, K. (1979). *Theory of International Politics.* New York: McGraw-Hill.
Weber, Max (1946). "From Max Weber: Essays in Sociology", in H. H. Gerth and C. Wright Mills (Eds.). New York: Oxford University Press.
WEEE (2005). Waste in Electrical and Electronic Equipment. Commission Decision 2005/618/EC of 18 August 2005 amending Directive 2002/95/EC of the European Parliament and of the Council for the purpose of establishing the maximum concentration

values for certain hazardous substances in electrical and electronic equipment (notified under document number C(2005) 3143).
WEEE (2005/2002). http://eur-lex.europa.eu/LexUriServ/LexUriServ.do?uri=CELEX:-32002L0096:EN:HTML.
Weir, Margaret (1992). "Ideas and the Politics of Bounded Innovation", *Structuring Politics: Historical Institutionalism in Comparative Analysis*, Sven Steinmo, Kathleen Thelen and Longstreth Frank (Eds.). Cambridge: Cambridge University Press: 188-216.
——— and Theda Skocpol (1985). *State Structures and the Possibilities for "Keynesian" Responses to the Great Depression in Sweden, Britain, and the United States*, in Peter B. Evans, Dietrich Rueschemeyer, and Skocpol (eds.) *Bringing the State Back In*. New York, Cambridge University Press.
Wendon, Bryan (1998). "The Commission as Image-Venue Entrepreneur in EU Social Policy". *Journal of European Public Policy*, 5(2): 339-353.
Wettestad, J. (2000). "The Complicated Development of EU Climate Policy: Lessons learnt." In J. Gupta and M. Grubb. *Climate Change and European Leadership: A Sustainable Role for Europe?* Dordrecht: Kluwer.
Williamson, Peter (1989). *Corporatism in Perspective*. London, Sage.
Wilson, Barry (1995a). "New national farm safety net 'teeters on the edge of a cliff'". *The Western Producer*, April 27, 5.
——— (1995b). "Safety net may have too many holes: CFA". *The Western Producer*, May 1, 1.
Wirth, David A. (2002). "European Communities – Measures Affecting Asbestos and Asbestos-Containing Products". *American Journal of International Law*, 96: 435-439.
Woodward, Alison E. (2001). "Gender Mainstreaming in European Policy: Innovation or Deception?" Discussion Paper FS I 01-103. Berlin: Wissenschaftszentrum Berlin für Sozialforschung.
WTO (2001-03-12) WT/DS135/R/Add.1 European Communities – Measures Affecting Asbestos and Asbestos-containing Products. Report of the Appellate Body, Annex VI. Meeting with Experts – 17 January 2000.
WWF (2004). The REACH files: A policy guide. Available at http://assets.panda.org/downloads/reachfilespolicyguide.pdf, accessed on April 2008.
WWF (2007). Navigating REACH. An activists' guide to using and improving the new EU chemicals legislation. Available at http://www.panda.org/about_wwf/where-_we_work/europe/what_we_do/epo/initiatives/chemicals/publications/index.cfm?uNewsID=115541, accessed on April 2008.
WWF (2008). www.panda.org/about_wwf/where_we_work/europe/what_we_do/epo/-initiatives/chemicals/index.cfm.
Yamin, F. (2000). "The role of the EU in climate negotiations." In Gupta and Grubb (eds.). *Climate Change and European Leadership: A Sustainable Role for Europe?* Dordrecht: Kluwer.
Yin, R. (2003). *Case study research: design and methods*. Thousand Oaks, Calif.: Sage Publications.
Young, Brigitte, Leon Lindberg, and J. Rogers Hollingsworth (1989). *The Governance of the American Dairy Industry: from regional dominance to regional cleavage*, in W.D. Coleman and H.J. Jacek (eds.). *Regionalism, Business Interests and Public Policy*. London, Sage.
Zald, M. and J. McCarthy (2003). *Social movements in an organizational society*. Transaction Publishers.
Zapfel, P. and M. Vainio (2002). "Pathways to European Greenhouse Gas Emissions Trading History and Misconceptions." Nota di Lavoro 85.2002 Fondazione Eni Enrico Mattei. http://www.feem.it/web/activ/_activ.html.
Zito, A. R. (2000). *Creating Environmental Policy in the European Union*. London: Macmillan.

Index

advocacy coalition..13, 29, 32, 35, 38, 404, 411
agency.......9, 22, 44, 45, 46, 103, 104, 109, 113, 147, 154, 172, 206, 218, 220, 239, 245, 246, 248, 250, 254, 259, 260, 366, 373, 379, 398, 408, 414, 422, 423, 424, 425, 427, 428, 430, 434
agents 5, 25, 46, 49, 71, 131, 136, 143, 144, 145, 148, 152, 154, 155, 164, 165, 209, 237, 238, 242, 247, 254, 255, 257, 279, 280, 300, 302, 303, 304, 305, 336, 345, 354, 363, 364, 369, 371, 379, 380, 381, 382, 383, 384, 385, 386, 389, 390, 391, 395, 406, 407, 408, 409, 419, 431
attention..12, 20, 22, 23, 27, 38, 41, 47, 53, 56, 59, 68, 70, 88, 94, 114, 153, 157, 159, 165, 169, 172, 183, 190, 193, 209, 218, 219, 223, 228, 229, 263, 288, 294, 296, 315, 324, 328, 331, 350, 356, 393, 394, 397, 398, 400, 401, 421, 429
belief system.13, 14, 16, 18, 21, 22, 30, 32, 38, 404, 405
bounded rationality.................................20
cognitive.5, 6, 7, 11, 12, 13, 17, 18, 19, 20, 21, 22, 23, 26, 27, 29, 30, 31, 32, 33, 34, 35, 36, 37, 39, 40, 41, 42, 43, 141, 143, 144, 145, 147, 149, 150, 153, 154, 155, 158, 170, 228, 253, 261, 262, 263, 266, 267, 268, 281, 386, 387, 396, 401, 409, 425, 433, 438
cognitive-normative 6, 17, 27, 143, 145, 147, 149, 155, 228, 253, 387
commission............112, 123, 333, 342, 365
conflict....20, 35, 36, 39, 47, 55, 57, 70, 87, 88, 101, 115, 118, 122, 131, 144, 162, 164, 174, 181, 201, 204, 220, 221, 237, 261, 269, 272, 317, 360, 372, 379, 387, 389, 393, 395, 400, 403, 405, 430, 438
Council of Ministers 124, 126, 131, 132, 133, 166, 231, 242, 245, 246, 295, 343
culture 12, 13, 14, 15, 22, 23, 25, 267, 268, 270, 332, 348, 378, 414, 425, 429, 430, 432, 438
discourse .. 7, 11, 16, 21, 29, 43, 45, 47, 48, 49, 50, 52, 54, 56, 57, 58, 59, 60, 61, 62, 63, 66, 73, 74, 81, 83, 85, 88, 89, 91, 94, 146, 155, 159, 164, 165, 268, 293, 304, 326, 334, 350, 362, 395, 417, 418, 425, 426, 429, 434, 438, 439
domestic violence 168, 169, 318, 322, 323, 324, 325, 326, 327, 328, 329, 330, 331, 332, 333, 334, 356, 361, 363, 371, 372, 392, 418
entrepreneurship.... 131, 265, 282, 364, 384
environmental dimension...................... 157
epistemic community..............26, 148, 426
equal treatment..... 158, 278, 312, 315, 316, 319, 320, 337, 338, 346, 347, 348, 353, 354, 357, 361, 404
equality....... 18, 47, 56, 57, 58, 64, 66, 158, 168, 169, 311, 312, 313, 314, 315, 316, 317, 318, 319, 320, 321, 323, 324, 325, 328, 329, 331, 335, 337, 342, 343, 344, 345, 346, 347, 348, 349, 350, 352, 353, 356, 357, 361, 362, 364, 370, 372, 415, 418, 420, 421, 423, 424, 435
EU institutions 161, 169, 178, 182, 186, 189, 190, 246, 255, 256, 320, 331, 342, 351, 356, 373
European Commission... 23, 131, 160, 162, 183, 186, 202, 207, 208, 216, 226, 227, 240, 244, 246, 248, 249, 250, 251, 252, 274, 294, 295, 296, 297, 298, 302, 308, 319, 321, 331, 335, 337, 338, 339, 340, 344, 345, 357, 362, 367, 370, 388, 413, 416, 418, 419, 420, 421, 422, 424, 426, 428, 434, 436, 437

European Court of Justice (ECJ)......9, 132, 133, 176, 184, 301, 313, 314, 315, 316, 330, 354, 363, 366, 410, 417
European integration....118, 121, 124, 126, 127, 132, 133, 139, 165, 166, 169, 189, 202, 204, 224, 235, 314, 375, 395, 400, 402, 436
European Parliament..9, 10, 119, 123, 131, 132, 149, 171, 173, 184, 185, 186, 192, 208, 226, 233, 235, 236, 237, 239, 242, 243, 244, 245, 246, 247, 251, 253, 256, 258, 259, 260, 295, 298, 331, 332, 333, 335, 341, 351, 354, 357, 363, 369, 370, 411, 413, 416, 419, 420, 422, 424, 434, 437, 439
European Union......7, 10, 18, 26, 117, 118, 120, 124, 126, 128, 130, 132, 134, 139, 171, 180, 181, 190, 196, 197, 201, 202, 206, 225, 230, 242, 243, 250, 254, 285, 289, 292, 294, 295, 298, 299, 302, 307, 311, 319, 323, 325, 328, 330, 335, 346, 403, 414, 415, 416, 417, 418, 419, 420, 421, 423, 424, 425, 426, 427, 428, 430, 431, 432, 433, 434, 435, 436, 437, 438, 439, 440
frames.7, 14, 15, 17, 20, 22, 23, 26, 29, 30, 31, 32, 33, 34, 35, 36, 37, 39, 40, 41, 42, 43, 267, 283, 351, 425, 433, 437, 438
framing...5, 14, 17, 26, 131, 148, 153, 167, 177, 190, 191, 224, 237, 314, 315, 351, 352, 406, 409, 415, 433
gender equality.8, 157, 168, 169, 311, 312, 314, 315, 316, 318, 320, 321, 322, 323, 324, 325, 327, 330, 331, 332, 333, 335, 336, 338, 339, 341, 342, 343, 344, 345, 346, 347, 348, 349, 350, 351, 352, 353, 354, 355, 356, 357, 359, 361, 363, 364, 365, 370, 372, 374, 386, 403, 410, 411, 417, 421, 423, 430, 434, 435, 438, 439
historical institutionalism.....19, 22, 23, 82, 266, 426, 428, 437, 438, 440
ideology..12, 14, 15, 16, 21, 22, 26, 33, 40, 55, 59, 64, 141, 193, 269, 270, 274, 289, 413, 419, 426, 438, 439
incommensurability....16, 17, 23, 153, 197, 391, 392, 402, 436
institutional paradigm.............25, 153, 388
institutionalism.......12, 21, 22, 23, 33, 266, 416, 422, 425, 432, 434, 438
institutionalization ... 12, 17, 19, 21, 22, 45, 47, 53, 65, 96, 125, 134, 142, 144, 152, 157, 161, 168, 169, 170, 189, 191, 194, 220, 222, 256, 257, 262, 281, 283, 304, 313, 318, 330, 343, 359, 360, 370, 371, 372, 373, 377, 378, 381, 388, 391, 393, 396, 397, 405, 406, 410, 418, 427, 438
Keynesian..... 13, 18, 27, 31, 32, 39, 68, 73, 74, 75, 80, 81, 82, 83, 84, 85, 86, 89, 90, 93, 142, 316, 395, 401, 403, 404, 427, 440
Kuhn... 5, 11, 12, 13, 30, 31, 32, 39, 42, 47, 74, 90, 145, 151, 153, 167, 378, 392, 394, 402, 403, 430, 436
leadership..... 25, 27, 34, 83, 101, 126, 220, 242, 243, 294, 298, 304, 306, 331, 333, 370, 406, 426, 428, 440
legislation. 7, 24, 27, 45, 49, 51, 52, 53, 57, 60, 62, 63, 64, 65, 73, 101, 112, 131, 133, 134, 137, 149, 176, 178, 179, 206, 209, 210, 212, 220, 226, 227, 239, 240, 242, 247, 252, 253, 258, 259, 263, 264, 269, 280, 290, 294, 311, 316, 317, 319, 320, 321, 329, 332, 337, 341, 347, 348, 357, 416, 421, 429, 435, 440
logic of appropriateness.........................20
mainstreaming.. 8, 257, 311, 312, 317, 318, 319, 320, 321, 322, 323, 332, 333, 334, 335, 336, 337, 338, 341, 342, 343, 344, 345, 346, 347, 348, 349, 350, 351, 352, 353, 354, 356, 357, 361, 364, 365, 372, 379, 385, 403, 410, 415, 420, 421, 423, 424, 429, 431, 432, 434, 435, 436, 437, 438, 439, 440
management. 17, 33, 35, 36, 75, 77, 82, 83, 87, 108, 109, 110, 111, 136, 172, 185, 216, 218, 232, 234, 246, 254, 255, 259, 286, 307, 343, 385, 386, 427, 431, 435, 438
market integration 128, 152, 157, 158, 202, 208, 221, 311, 344, 361, 375, 410, 411
master frame 14, 151
mechanisms.... 6, 12, 25, 30, 32, 33, 39, 41, 42, 43, 56, 86, 145, 168, 175, 181, 192, 194, 221, 233, 246, 266, 267, 278, 281, 283, 285, 287, 288, 289, 290, 291, 298, 300, 303, 305, 306, 307, 314, 329, 343, 355, 360, 363, 366, 377, 378, 382, 384, 387, 391, 394, 406, 414, 424, 431

meta-power....................155, 384, 388, 407
method..6, 45, 78, 110, 134, 135, 155, 158, 159, 167, 231, 426, 434, 436, 438
monetarism...27, 42, 79, 80, 81, 82, 83, 84, 85, 87, 89, 401, 426
negotiation......25, 142, 152, 155, 156, 174, 202, 245, 246, 257, 304, 309, 369, 381, 388, 389, 439
neo-liberalism...................................37, 40
non-government organization (NGO)....10, 152, 172, 208, 316, 328, 333, 363, 364, 366, 370
norm 40, 102, 149, 335, 347, 390, 423
paradigm shift.....12, 18, 25, 26, 27, 34, 37, 74, 75, 90, 93, 94, 95, 98, 99, 101, 106, 107, 108, 114, 117, 142, 145, 148, 149, 155, 156, 158, 189, 190, 194, 195, 197, 199, 201, 222, 223, 228, 252, 253, 263, 277, 285, 287, 302, 303, 304, 306, 318, 349, 353, 355, 359, 360, 361, 362, 364, 367, 368, 377, 378, 382, 384, 385, 387, 388, 389, 390, 401, 406, 410
paradigm transformation..5, 378, 382, 383, 409
path dependency................................19, 41
policy advocacy coalition..................23, 26
policy core..................................30, 31, 37
policy networks..22, 23, 88, 95, 96, 97, 99, 106, 114, 115, 131, 132, 134, 135, 389, 439
politics 5, 11, 12, 13, 19, 20, 38, 45, 46, 47, 48, 49, 54, 55, 56, 57, 59, 60, 61, 62, 64, 66, 67, 68, 69, 75, 77, 82, 84, 85, 86, 87, 88, 89, 92, 114, 115, 124, 127, 131, 165, 203, 215, 223, 226, 280, 308, 341, 342, 355, 413, 414, 415, 416, 417, 421, 425, 426, 427, 428, 429, 430, 431, 432, 433, 434, 435, 436, 437, 438, 439, 440
positive action 312, 319, 320, 338, 339, 346, 347, 348, 350, 353, 403
power..5, 11, 13, 14, 19, 22, 23, 24, 25, 27, 33, 34, 36, 37, 43, 45, 47, 48, 55, 56, 58, 59, 64, 68, 69, 70, 71, 73, 74, 75, 82, 83, 84, 87, 88, 89, 90, 92, 93, 94, 121, 122, 124, 125, 127, 131, 142, 145, 146, 151, 152, 153, 154, 155, 164, 168, 192, 194, 204, 222, 224, 235, 237, 242, 256, 279, 282, 291, 293, 294, 296, 301, 304, 338, 341, 347, 352, 380, 381, 382, 383, 384, 385, 386, 387, 388, 389, 390, 391, 393, 394, 396, 402, 403, 406, 409, 410, 416, 425, 426, 427, 432, 433, 435
precautionary principle 179, 180, 188, 193, 197, 198, 220, 228, 229, 234, 238, 255, 257, 364, 368, 374, 418, 425, 427, 428, 430, 431, 439
public policy paradigm (PPP) 5, 6, 7, 8, 11, 12, 17, 18, 22, 24, 25, 26, 27, 28, 38, 117, 138, 142, 143, 145, 146, 148, 149, 150, 151, 154, 155, 156, 163, 164, 192, 195, 261, 283, 285, 302, 307, 355, 377, 379, 380, 381, 382, 389, 390, 391, 395, 402, 407, 408, 409
public policy paradigm theory6, 8, 24, 302, 377, 409
regulation10, 46, 48, 49, 51, 54, 55, 59, 60, 62, 65, 73, 91, 103, 130, 135, 136, 137, 142, 146, 151, 168, 172, 176, 177, 179, 180, 189, 196, 198, 202, 203, 204, 206, 208, 209, 210, 211, 212, 213, 214, 215, 220, 223, 224, 225, 226, 227, 228, 230, 231, 232, 233, 234, 235, 236, 237, 238, 239, 240, 241, 245, 246, 247, 248, 251, 254, 255, 256, 257, 258, 259, 261, 263, 265, 269, 270, 272, 274, 275, 278, 279, 280, 281, 282, 297, 303, 304, 308, 335, 355, 361, 364, 365, 366, 367, 368, 391, 392, 395, 403, 409, 414, 416, 417, 418, 419, 422, 423, 427, 428, 429, 431, 434, 437, 439
rights 17, 56, 57, 58, 59, 60, 61, 65, 66, 104, 136, 151, 164, 168, 191, 206, 225, 247, 248, 255, 271, 276, 300, 324, 325, 328, 329, 330, 331, 333, 334, 340, 345, 348, 349, 351, 353, 354, 363, 370, 396, 402, 417, 420, 421, 425, 435
risk 146, 157, 183, 196, 203, 204, 209, 216, 218, 219, 222, 223, 224, 226, 228, 231, 232, 233, 234, 239, 250, 252, 254, 255, 259, 260, 275, 301, 334, 352, 365, 366, 367, 369, 373, 390, 391, 394, 415, 418, 431
rule regime..... 28, 142, 143, 151, 152, 153, 154, 377, 379, 388, 407
rule system.................................. 164, 405
schemata.. 14
self interest.. 19

social dimension ... 128, 136, 174, 311, 323, 324
social learning 68, 69, 70, 71, 72, 73, 76, 79, 85, 86, 88, 89, 92, 94, 95, 389
social movement 5, 14, 23, 48, 54, 151, 223, 351, 409, 440
societal paradigm 18, 32, 40, 42, 43, 45, 47, 48, 49, 50, 56, 57, 59, 60, 62, 63, 64, 65
socio-cognitive . 11, 12, 14, 18, 21, 22, 163, 381, 396
soft law 135, 312
state 7, 13, 19, 27, 29, 32, 34, 38, 39, 40, 41, 45, 48, 49, 50, 52, 53, 54, 57, 58, 59, 60, 61, 62, 63, 64, 65, 66, 67, 68, 69, 70, 71, 72, 76, 77, 79, 80, 81, 82, 84, 85, 86, 87, 88, 89, 90, 91, 92, 93, 94, 95, 96, 97, 98, 99, 100, 101, 102, 103, 104, 105, 106, 107, 108, 109, 110, 111, 112, 113, 114, 115, 119, 120, 121, 122, 129, 130, 133, 134, 136, 138, 140, 141, 147, 160, 166, 176, 180, 183, 196, 209, 211, 227, 232, 236, 237, 238, 239, 240, 245, 246, 247, 248, 250, 252, 257, 261, 264, 265, 266, 267, 269, 270, 272, 273, 274, 277, 281, 282, 283, 286, 294, 295, 299, 301, 308, 312, 313, 315, 318, 324, 328, 330, 332, 341, 343, 346, 360, 366, 370, 371, 389, 390, 391, 393, 414, 417, 425, 427, 429, 432, 433, 434, 435, 440
substitution 34, 42, 127, 176, 211, 232, 233, 235, 241, 244, 245, 246, 251, 253, 255, 257, 260, 364
theory ... 5, 6, 11, 13, 14, 15, 21, 26, 28, 45, 46, 58, 67, 68, 69, 70, 73, 76, 79, 80, 86, 89, 90, 142, 146, 154, 167, 184, 195, 261, 263, 266, 267, 268, 273, 280, 351, 382, 390, 392, 407, 408, 409, 414, 416, 417, 418, 421, 422, 423, 425, 426, 428, 429, 433, 435, 436, 437, 438, 439
treaties 23, 117, 119, 120, 127, 128, 131, 133, 135, 137, 158, 159, 165, 166, 169, 181, 189, 198, 209, 224, 263, 292, 293, 296, 312, 318, 323, 325, 357, 371, 410, 425, 438
values 11, 13, 14, 15, 19, 20, 23, 29, 30, 31, 32, 33, 35, 36, 40, 42, 43, 61, 97, 121, 122, 131, 143, 146, 148, 151, 152, 154, 155, 158, 159, 164, 261, 267, 364, 375, 379, 380, 382, 384, 386, 387, 388, 389, 390, 393, 395, 402, 405, 408, 440

www.ingramcontent.com/pod-product-compliance
Ingram Content Group UK Ltd.
Pitfield, Milton Keynes, MK11 3LW, UK
UKHW021843100926
8556IPUK00019B/1019

9 783631 579053